July 4–8, 2015
Vilnius, Lithuania

**Association for
Computing Machinery**

Advancing Computing as a Science & Profession

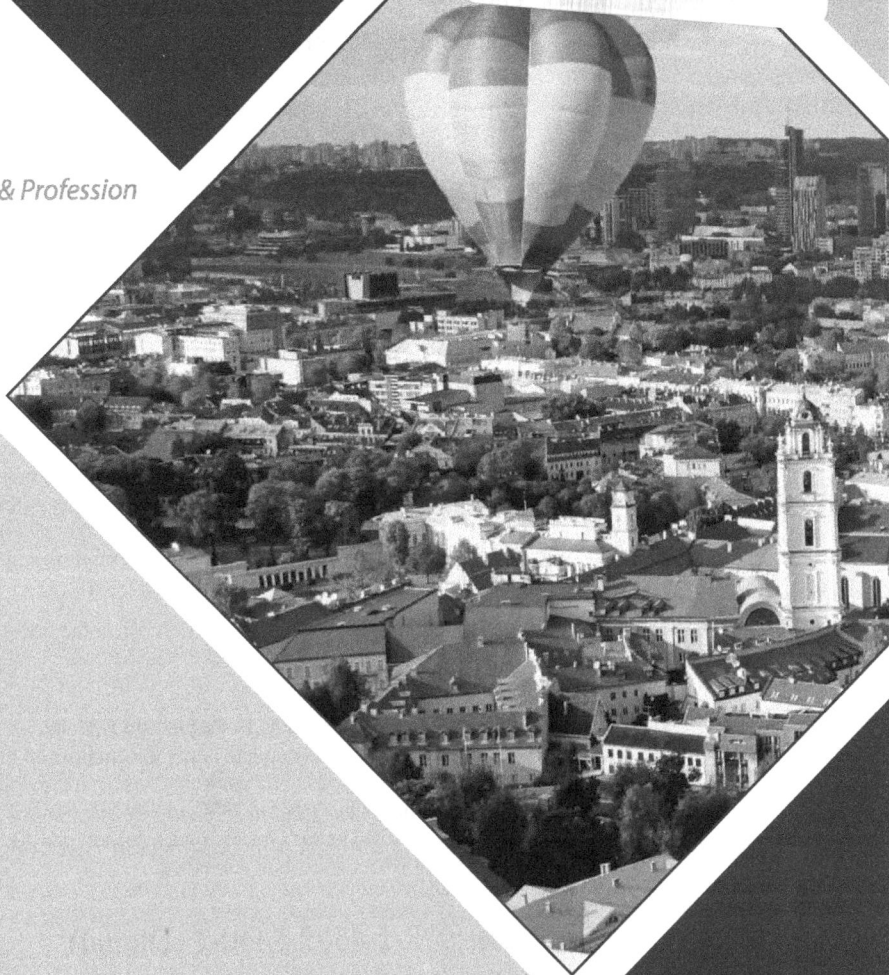

ITiCSE'15

Proceedings of the 2015 ACM Conference on
Innovation and Technology
in Computer Science Education

Sponsored by:
ACM SIGCSE

Supported by:
Vilnius University, Seimas of the Republic of Lithuania, and VU Institute of Mathematics and Informatics

**Association for
Computing Machinery**

Advancing Computing as a Science & Profession

The Association for Computing Machinery
2 Penn Plaza, Suite 701
New York, New York 10121-0701

Notice to Past Authors of ACM-Published Articles
ACM intends to create a complete electronic archive of all articles and/or other material previously published by ACM. If you have written a work that has been previously published by ACM in any journal or conference proceedings prior to 1978, or any SIG Newsletter at any time, and you do NOT want this work to appear in the ACM Digital Library, please inform permissions@acm.org, stating the title of the work, the author(s), and where and when published.

ISBN: 978-1-4503-3440-2 (Digital)

ISBN: 978-1-4503-3880-6 (Print)

Additional copies may be ordered prepaid from:

ACM Order Department
PO Box 30777
New York, NY 10087-0777, USA

Phone: 1-800-342-6626 (USA and Canada)
+1-212-626-0500 (Global)
Fax: +1-212-944-1318
E-mail: acmhelp@acm.org
Hours of Operation: 8:30 am – 4:30 pm ET

Printed in the USA

Foreword

Welcome to ITiCSE 2015 in Vilnius!

The ITiCSE conference celebrates its 20th anniversary in Vilnius, the capital of Lithuania and the geographical center of Europe, so declared in 1989 by scientists of the French National Institute of Geography.

ITiCSE will be held on July 6–8, starting on Lithuania's Statehood Day (July 6). This is an annual public holiday that commemorates the coronation in 1253 of Mindaugas as the first and only King of Lithuania. The conference venue is the Parliament buildings (Seimas) of the Republic of Lithuania, and the conference dinner is to served in the reconstructed Palace of the Grand Dukes of Lithuania, one of the most famous in Europe in the 15–17th centuries. ITiCSE 2015 is hosted by Vilnius University, one of the oldest and most famous establishments of higher education in Eastern and Central Europe, founded in 1579. The conference organizers represent the Lithuanian research group of Informatics and Informatics Engineering Didactics at the Institute of Mathematics and Informatics of Vilnius University.

This conference brings together delegates from all over the world to address pressing issues in computing education. In addition to invited lectures, papers, panels, posters, and tips, techniques & courseware sessions, the conference provides facilities and exposure for working groups and exhibitions.

The conference continues to be truly international with a total of 170 submissions from 40 countries on six continents, with authors from Africa (4), Asia (50), Europe (151), North America (119), Oceania (51), and South America (17). These submissions consisted of 124 research papers, 1 panel, 9 working group proposals, and 36 proposals for posters or for tips, techniques & courseware.

All research papers were double blind reviewed by at least four reviewers, though most papers received five or six reviews. A meta-review was conducted by the members of the conference committee to ensure the reliability of the reviews and to make recommendations to the chairs. A final selection phase was conducted by the program chairs who reviewed all reviews and meta-review recommendations before making their final decisions. As a result of this process, 54 research papers (43.5%) were selected for presentation and inclusion in the proceedings. The authors of the accepted papers come from 17 different countries on five continents.

All poster submissions were blind reviewed by two members of the conference committee, and tips, techniques & courseware submissions were blind reviewed by three members of the conference committee. Submissions in these categories were then reviewed by the conference chair before selection by the program chairs for final inclusion in the conference. Twenty-four were accepted, representing authors from 15 countries.

The two keynote speakers address the learning of programming and computational thinking. Professor Mordechai (Moti) Ben-Ari from the Weizmann Institute of Science, Israel, will give a talk titled *In Defense of Programming*, which defends the (perhaps controversial) position that programming is the fundamental activity of CS. In the other keynote talk Professor Maciej M. Syslo from Nicolaus Copernicus University and University of Wrocław, Poland, will address algorithmic and computational thinking as the way to computing for all students.

ITiCSE is famous for its working groups. Participating in a working group provides a unique opportunity to work with people from different countries who are interested and knowledgeable in the area of the working group. It is also one of the best ways to become part of the ITiCSE community. Seven working groups have been accepted over a broad spectrum of topics. The working groups range from general topics, such as computing education terminology, CS education in K-9 and K-12 schools, and designing an IT curriculum framework for graduates in 2025, to more specific topics such as developing a repository for high school CS questions, visual assessment tools and metadata annotations, and how students construct solutions to programming problems. The leaders of the accepted working groups come from over 13 countries.

Welcome to Vilnius and enjoy the vicennial ITiCSE conference and Lithuania's Statehood Day!

Valentina Dagienė
ITiCSE 2015 Conference Chair

Carsten Schulte, Tatjana Jevsikova
ITiCSE 2015 Co-Program Chairs

Table of Contents

Keynote Addresses

Session: Innovative Technologies for Learning I

Session: K-12 CS Challenges

Session: Assessment

Session: Computational Thinking

Tips, Techniques & Courseware I

Tips, Techniques & Courseware II

Posters I

Posters II

ITiCSE 2015 Conference Organization

Conference Chair: Valentina Dagienė *(Vilnius University, Lithuania)*

Program Co-Chairs: Carsten Schulte *(Berlin Freie University, Germany)*
Tatjana Jevsikova *(Vilnius University, Lithuania)*

Treasurer & Registration Chair: Cary Laxer *(Rose-Hulman Institute of Technology, USA)*

Working Groups: Päivi Kinnunen *(Aalto University, Finland)*
Noa Ragonis *(Beit Berl College and Technion, Israel)*

Panels: Elizabeth Adams *(James Madison University, USA)*

Tips, Techniques & Courseware: Michelle Craig *(University of Toronto, Canada)*
Ernesto Cuadros-Vargas *(San Pablo Catholic University, Peru)*

Proceedings: Michael Goldweber *(Xavier University, USA)*
Stan Kurkovsky *(Central Connecticut State University, USA)*

Posters: Jennifer Campbell *(University of Toronto, Canada)*
Alison Clear *(Eastern Institute of Technology, Auckland, New Zealand)*

Database Coordinator: John Dooley *(Knox College, USA)*

Evaluations: Ari Korhonen *(Aalto University, Finland)*

Student Volunteers: Simona Feiferytė *(Vilnius University)*
Eimantas Pėlikis *(Vilnius University)*
Elena Sutkutė *(Vilnius University)*

Website: Simon *(University of Newcastle, Australia)*

High School Liaison: Bruria Haberman *(Holon Institute of Technology and Weizmann Institute of Science, Israel)*
Bronius Skūpas *(Vilnius University, Lithuania)*

Local Committee: Vladimiras Dolgopolovas *(Vilnius University)*
Eglė Jasutė *(Vilnius University)*
Anita Juškevičienė *(Vilnius University)*
Gabrielė Stupurienė *(Vilnius University)*
Inga Žilinskienė *(Vilnius University)*

ITiCSE 2015 Reviewers

Raman Adaikkalavan (*Indiana University South Bend*)

Elizabeth S. Adams (*James Madison University*)

Rajeev Agrawal (*North Carolina A & T State University*)

Hend Al-Khalifa (*King Saud University*)

Barbara Anthony (*Southwestern University*)

Michal Armoni (*Weizmann Institute of Science*)

Doug Baldwin (*SUNY Geneseo*)

David Barnes (*University of Kent*)

Lewis Barnett (*University of Richmond*)

Tim Bell (*University of Canterbury*)

Mordechai Ben-Ari (*Weizmann Institute of Science*)

Jens Bennedsen (*Aarhus School of Engineering*)

Marie Bienkowski (*SRI International*)

Judith Bishop (*Microsoft Research*)

Dennis Brylow (*Marquette University*)

David Bunde (*Knox College*)

Barry Burd (*Drew University*)

Kevin Burger (*Arizona State University*)

Andre Paul Calitz (*Nelson Mandela Metropolitan University*)

Jennifer Campbell (*University of Toronto*)

Daniel Canas (*Wake Forest University*)

Jeffrey Carver (*University of Alabama*)

Steven Case (*University of West Florida*)

Lillian N. Cassel (*Villanova University*)

Tim Chamillard (*University of Colorado at Colorado Springs*)

Wei Kian Chen (*Champlain Cpllege*)

Peng-Wen Chen (*Oriental Institute of Technology*)

Li-hsiang Cheo (*William Paterson University of New Jersey*)

Jayan Kurian Chirayath (*Royal Melbourne Institute of Technology*)

David Chiu (*University of Puget Sound*)

Radhouane Chouchane (*Columbus State University*)

John Cigas (*Park University*)

Dawn Cizmar (*St. Edward's University*)

Peter Clarke (*Florida International University*)

Tony Clear (*Auckland University of Technology*)

Alison Clear (*Christchurch Polytechnic Institute of Technology*)

Joe Clifton (*University of Wisconsin, Platteville*)

Tim Comber (*Southern Cross University*)

Randy Connolly (*Mount Royal University*)

Stephen Cooper (*Stanford University*)

Michelle Craig (*University of Toronto*)

Joyce Blair Crowell (*Belmont University*)

Ernesto Cuadros-Vargas (*San Pablo Catholic University*)

Lawrence D'Antonio (*Ramapo College of New Jersey*)

Valentina Dagiene (*Vilnius University*)

Renzo Davoli (*University of Bologna*)

Adrienne Decker (*Rochester Institute of Technology*)

Katherine Deibel (*University of Washington-Seattle*)

Barbara Demo (*University Torino*)

Zachary Dodds (*Harvey Mudd College*)

Peter Drexel (*Plymouth State University*)

Joseph Ekstrom (*Brigham Young University*)

Stephanie Elzer (*Millersville University*)

Alec Engebretson (*Doane College*)

Henry Etlinger (*Rochester Institute of Technology*)

Sergio F. Lopes (*University of Minho*)

Alan Fekete (*University of Sydney*)

Maria Feldgen (*Universidad de Buenos Aires*)

Georgios Fesakis (*University of the Aegean*)

Samantha Foley (*University of Wisconsin-La Crosse*)

Alessio Gaspar (*University of South Florida Polytechnic*)

Rick Gee (*Okanagan College*)

Adrian German (*Indiana University*)

Paul Gestwicki (*Ball State University*)

Don Goelman (*Villanova University*)

Michael Goldweber (*Xavier University*)

Jean Goulet (*Universite de Sherbrooke*)

Mary Granger (*George Washington University*)

Simon Gray (*College of Wooster*)

John Hamer (*University of Glasgow*)

Brian Hanks (*BFH Educational Consulting*)

Stuart Hansen (*University of Wisconsin - Parkside*)

Orit Hazzan *(Technion – Israel Institute of Technology)*
Sarah Heckman *(North Carolina State University)*
Michael Helmick *(Google)*
Tyson Henry *(California State University, Chico)*
William Hooper *(Belmont University)*
Hoda Hosny *(The American University in Cairo)*
David Hovemeyer *(York College of Pennsylvania)*
Brian Howard *(DePauw University)*
James Huggins *(Kettering University)*
Janet Hughes *(University of Dundee)*
Petri Ihantola *(Tampere University of Technology)*
Matthew Jadud *(Berea College)*
Mark Jaeger *(Baker College)*
Tatjana Jevsikova *(Vilnius University)*
Mike Jipping *(Hope College)*
Colin Johnson *(University of Kent at Canterbury)*
Anthony Joseph *(Pace University)*
Mike Joy *(University of Warwick)*
Daniel Joyce *(Villanova University)*
Maria Jump *(King's College)*
Edward Jung *(Southern Polytechnic State University)*
Viggo Kann *(KTH)*
David Kauchak *(Middlebury College)*
Jennifer Kay *(Rowan University)*
David G. Kay *(University of California, Irvine)*
Petros Kefalas *(The University of Sheffield)*
Mark Kerstetter *(Western Michigan University)*
Nancy Kinnersley *(University of Kansas)*
Paivi Kinnunen *(Aalto Univeristy)*
Carsten Kleiner *(University of Applied Sciences & Arts Hannover)*
Ari Korhonen *(Aalto University)*
Joan Krone *(Denison University)*
Jan Kruger *(Unisa School for Business Leadership)*
Benjamin Kuperman *(Oberlin College)*
Stan Kurkovsky *(Central Connecticut State University)*
Zachary Kurmas *(Grand Valley State University)*
Clif Kussmaul *(Muhlenberg College)*
Joan Langdon *(Bowie State University)*
David Largent *(Ball State University)*
Eric Larson *(Seattle University)*

Alina Lazar *(Youngstown State University)*
Arthur Lee *(Claremont McKenna College)*
Gilliean Lee *(Lander University)*
Cynthia Lee *(Stanford University)*
Byong Lee *(Bennett College)*
Chi Un Lei *(University of Hong Kong)*
Andrew Luxton-Reilly *(The University of Auckland)*
Bonnie MacKellar *(St John's University)*
Dave Mason *(Ryerson University)*
Chris Mayfield *(James Madison University)*
Lester McCann *(The University of Arizona)*
O. William McClung *(Nebraska Wesleyan University)*
Jeffrey McConnell *(Canisius College)*
Sean McCulloch *(Ohio Wesleyan University)*
Roger McDermott *(Robert Gordon University)*
Chris McDonald *(The University of Western Australia)*
Hugh McGuire *(Grand Valley State University)*
Pedro Medeiros *(Universidade Nova de Lisboa)*
António Mendes *(Universidade de Coimbra)*
Susan Mengel *(Texas Tech University)*
Laurence Merkle *(Wright State University)*
Jose Carlos Metrolho *(Polytechnic Institute of Castelo Branco)*
Joe Miro *(Universitat de les Illes Balears)*
Patricia Morreale *(Kean University)*
Briana Morrison *(Southern Polytechnic State University)*
Srikanth Mudigonda *(Saint Louis University)*
Michael Murphy *(Concordia University Texas)*
Robert Noonan *(College of William and Mary)*
Keith O'Hara *(Bard College)*
Rainer Oechsle *(Trier University of Applied Sciences)*
Amos Olagunju *(St. Cloud State University)*
Lawrence Osborne *(Lamar University)*
Iraklis Paraskakis *(University of Sheffield)*
David Parker *(Salisbury University)*
James Paterson *(Glasgow Caledonian University)*
Eileen Peluso *(Lycoming College)*
Teresa Peterman *(Grand Valley State University)*
Andrew Petersen *(University of Toronto Mississauga)*
Chrisila C. Pettey *(Middle Tennessee State University)*
Nelishia Pillay *(University of KwaZulu-Natal)*

Wayne Pollock *(Hillsborough Community College)*
Sarah Monisha Pulimood *(The College of New Jersey)*
John Rager *(Amherst College)*
Noa Ragonis *(Beit Berl and Technion IIT)*
Samuel Rebelsky *(Grinnell College)*
Michael Redmond *(La Salle University)*
Charles Riedesel *(University of Nebraska - Lincoln)*
Suzanne Rivoire *(Sonoma State University)*
Christian Roberson *(Plymouth State University)*
Stefan Robila *(Montclair State University)*
Susan H. Rodger *(Duke University)*
Guido Rößling *(TU Darmstadt)*
Krishnendu Roy *(Valdosta State University)*
Martin Ruckert *(Munich University of Applied Sciences)*
Anthony Ruocco *(Roger Williams University)*
Rebecca Rutherfoord *(Southern Polytechnic State University)*
Roberta Evans Sabin *(Loyola College)*
Mehran Sahami *(Stanford University)*
Ian Sanders *(University of South Africa)*
André Santos *(ISCTE-IUL)*
Carsten Schulte *(Freie Universitaet Berlin)*
Otto Seppälä *(Aalto University)*
Amber Settle *(DePaul University)*
Cliff Shaffer *(Virginia Tech)*
Judy Sheard *(Monash University)*
Mark Sherriff *(University of Virginia)*
Yasuto Shirai *(Shizuoka University)*
Simon *(University of Newcastle)*
Bronius Skūpas *(Vilnius Lyceum, VU MII)*
Peter Smith *(California State University - Channel Islands)*

Raja Sooriamurthi *(Carnegie Mellon University)*
Jaime Spacco *(Knox College)*
Fred Strickland *(South University)*
Kazunari Sugiyama *(National University of Singapore)*
William Thacker *(Winthrop University)*
Megan Thomas *(California State University Stanislaus)*
Rebecca Thomas *(Bard College)*
William Turner *(Wabash College)*
Hakan Tuzun *(Hacettepe University)*
Ian Utting *(University of Kent at Canterbury)*
Jan Vahrenhold *(Westfälische Wilhelms-Universität Münster)*
Tammy VanDeGrift *(University of Portland)*
Brad Vander Zanden *(University of Tennessee)*
Yaakov Varol *(University of Nevada Reno)*
Jorge Vasconcelos *(Johns Hopkins University)*
Troy Vasiga *(University of Waterloo)*
Kam Vat *(University of Macau)*
Steven Vegdahl *(University of Portland)*
David Voorhees *(Le Moyne College)*
Sally Wahba *(Clemson University)*
Henry Walker *(Grinnell College)*
Xinli Wang *(Michigan Technological University)*
Thomas Way *(Villanova University)*
Linda Wilkens *(Providence College)*
Michael Wirth *(University of Guelph)*
Steven Wolfman *(University of British Columbia)*
Arthur Yanushka *(Christian Brothers University)*
Alan Zaring *(Ohio Wesleyan University)*
Daniel Zingaro *(University of Toronto)*

ITiCSE 2015 Working Groups

Working Group 1: Approaches to the Design and Conduct of Global Software Engineering Courses

Co-Leaders: Tony Clear *(Auckland University of Technology, New Zealand)*
Mats Daniels *(Uppsala University, Sweden)*
Sarah Beecham *(Lero – The Irish Software Engineering Centre, University of Limerick, Ireland)*

Participants: Roger McDermott *(Robert Gordon University, Scotland)*
Michael Oudshoorn *(Wentworth Institute of Technology, USA)*
John Barr *(Ithaca College, USA)*
Airina Savickaitė *(National Institute of Social Integration, Lithuania)*
John Noll *(Lero – The Irish Software Engineering Centre, University of Limerick, Ireland)*

Working Group 2: Educational Data Mining and Learning Analytics in How Students Construct Solutions to Programming Problems

Co-Leaders: Petri Ihantola *(Tampere University of Technology, Finland)*
Arto Vihavainen *(University of Helsinki, Finland)*

Participants: Alireza Ahadi *(University of Technology, Sydney, Australia)*
Matthew Butler *(Monash University, Australia)*
Jürgen Börstler *(Blekinge Institute of Technology, Sweden)*
Stephen Edwards *(Virginia Tech, USA)*
Essi Isohanni *(Tampere University of Technology, Finland)*
Ari Korhonen *(Aalto University, Finland)*
Andrew Petersen *(University of Toronto, Canada)*
Karen Petrie *(University of Dundee, Scotland)*
Kelly Rivers *(Carnegie Mellon University, USA)*
Miguel Ángel Rubio *(University of Granada, Spain)*
Judy Sheard *(Monash University, Australia)*
Jaime Spacco *(Knox College, USA)*
Claudia Szabo *(University of Adelaide, Australia)*
Daniel Toll *(Linnaeus University, Sweden)*

Working Group 3: Computer Science Education in K-12 Schools

Co-Leaders: Peter Hubwieser *(Technische Universität München, Germany)*
Michal Armoni *(Weizmann Institute of Science, Israel)*
Michail G. Giannakos *(Norwegian University of Science and Technology, Norway)*

Participants: Marc Berges *(Technische Universität München, Germany)*
Torsten Brinda *(Universität Duisburg-Essen, Germany)*
Ira Diethelm *(Carl von Ossietzky Universität Oldenburg, Germany)*
Egle Jasute *(Vilnius Jesuit High School, Lithuania)*
Jana Jackova *(Matej Bel University, Banska Bystrica, Slovakia)*
Johannes Magenheim *(University of Paderborn, Germany)*

Working Group 4: Key Concepts in K-9 Computer Science Education

Co-leaders: Erik Barendsen *(Radboud University Nijmegen, Netherlands)*
Linda Mannila *(Åbo Akademi University, Finland)*

Participants: Barbara Demo *(University of Turin, Italy)*
Natasa Grgurina *(University of Groningen, Netherlands)*
Cruz Izu *(The University of Adelaide, Australia)*
Claudio Mirolo *(University of Udine, Italy)*
Sue Sentence *(King's College London, UK)*
Amber Settle *(DePaul University, USA)*
Gabrielė Stupurienė *(Vilnius University, Lithuania)*

Working Group 5: A Repository for High School Computer Science Questions, Visual Assessment Tools and Metadata Annotations

Co-Leaders: Daniela Giordano *(University of Catania, Italy)*
Francesco Maiorana *(University of Catania, Italy)*
Ralph Morelli *(Trinity College Hartford, USA)*

Participants: Lina Cibulskaitė *(Vilnius University, Lithuania)*
Andrew Csizmadia *(Newman University, United Kingdom)*
Ene Koitla *(Estonian Information Technology Foundation for Education, Estonia)*
Simon Marsden *(University of Portsmouth, United Kingdom)*
Charles Riedesel *(University of Nebraska, United States of America)*
James Uhomoibhi *(Ulster University, United Kingdom)*

Working Group 6: Designing an Information Technology Curriculum Framework to Prepare Successful Graduates in 2025

Co-Leaders: Hala Alrumaih *(Al Imam Mohammad Ibn Saud Islamic University, Saudi Arabia)*
                 John Impagliazzo *(Hofstra University, USA)*
                 Barry Lunt *(Brigham Young University, USA)*
                 Mihaela Sabin *(University of New Hampshire, USA)*
                 Ming Zhang *(Peking University, China)*

Participants: Svetlana Peltsverger *(Kennesaw State University, USA)*
                 Cara Tang *(Portland Community College, USA)*
                 Barbara Viola *(VioTech Solutions, USA)*
                 Daina Gudoniene *(Vilnius University, Lithuania)*
                 Margaret Hamilton *(The University of Melbourne, Australia)*
                 Vsevolod Kotlyarov *(Peter the Great Saint-Petersburg State Polytechnic University, Russia)*
                 James McGuffee *(Northern Kentucky University, USA)*

Working Group 7: What's in a Name?: A Taxonomy of Computing Education Terminology

Co-leaders: Alison Clear *(Eastern Institute of Technology, New Zealand)*
                 Simon *(University of Newcastle, Australia)*

Participants: Janet Carter *(University of Kent, United Kingdom)*
                 Gerry Cross *(Mt Royal University, Canada)*
                 Dobrila Lopez *(Otago Polytechnic, New Zealand)*
                 Mike Lopez *(Otago Polytechnic, New Zealand)*
                 Atanas Radenski *(Chapman University, USA)*
                 Livia Tudor *(Petroleum-Gas University of Ploiesti, Romania)*

ITiCSE 2015 Sponsor & Supporters

Sponsor:

Supporters:

From Algorithmic to Computational Thinking: On the Way for Computing for all Students

Maciej M. Sysło
Nicolaus Copernicus University, University of Wrocław
Wrocław, Poland
syslo at mat.umk.pl

Abstract

Computational thinking, as coined by Jeannette Wing, is a fundamental skill for all to be able to live in today's world, a mode of thought that goes well beyond computing and provides a framework for reasoning about problems and methods of their solution. It has a long tradition as **algorithmic thinking** which within computer science is a competence to formulate a solution of a problem in the form of an algorithm and then to implement the algorithm as a computer program.

Computational thinking is not an adequate characterization of computer science as claimed by Peter Denning and he is right – it is a collection of key mental tools and practices originated in computing but addressed to all areas far beyond computer science. As an extension of algorithmic thinking, it includes thinking with many levels of abstraction as a problem solving approach inherently connected to computer science and addressed to all students to use computers and computing skills in solving problems in various school subjects coming from various scientific and applied areas. Computational thinking involves concepts, skills and competences that lie at the heart of computing, such as abstraction, decomposition, general-ization, approximation, heuristics, algorithm design, efficiency and complexity issues and therefore it is clear that basic computer science knowledge helps to systematically, correctly, and efficiently process information, perform tasks, and solve problems. Although coming from computer science, computational thinking is not only the study of computer science, though computers play an essential role in the design of problems' solutions. It is a very important and useful mode of thinking in almost all disciplines and school subjects as an insight into what can and cannot be computed.

In this talk we shall discuss a new computing curriculum addressed to ALL students in K-12 in Poland which motivates them to use computational thinking in solving problems in various school subjects. Moreover its goal is to encourage and prepare students from early school years to consider computing and related fields as disciplines of their future study and professional career. To this end, the curriculum allows teachers and schools to personalize learning and teaching according to students' interests, abilities, and needs.

The new computing curriculum benefits a lot from our experience in teaching informatics in our schools for almost 30 years – the first curriculum was approved by the ministry of education in 1985, 20 years after the first regular classes on informatics were held in two high schools in Wrocław and in Warsaw. Today, informatics is an obligatory subject in middle school (grades 7-9) and high school (grades 10-12) and it will replace computer lessons (mainly on ICT) in elementary schools (grades 1-6). The new curriculum is also addressed to vocational education.

Categories and Subject Descriptors: K.3.2 [**Computers and Education**]: Computer and Information Science Education – *Computer science education*

Keywords
Computational Thinking; Algorithmic Thinking; K-12 Computing Curriculum

Short Bio

Maciej M. Sysło is a mathematician and computer scientist, academic and school teacher, instructor at in-service courses for teachers, and one of the organizer of the Bebras Competition. He is also the author of informatics and ICT curricula, educational software, school textbooks and guidebooks for teachers. Sysło is a member of several national committees on education, and is the Polish representative to IFIP TC3.

He is the recipient of national and international awards and grants: Mombusho (Japan, 1974-1976), Humboldt (Germany, 1982-1984), Steinhaus (Poland, 1986), Car (Poland, 2010), Fulbright (USA, 1996-1997), Best Practices in Education Award (Informatics Europe, 2013), IFIP Outstanding Service Award (2014).

ITICSE'15, July 04–08, 2015, Vilnius, Lithuania.
ACM 978-1-4503-3440-2/15/07.
http://dx.doi.org/10.1145/2729094.2742582

In Defense of Programming

Mordechai (Moti) Ben-Ari
Weizmann Institute of Science
Rehovot, Israel
moti.ben-ari at weizmann.ac.il

Abstract

The activity of programming is often seen to be the epitome of all that is boring in computer science. The response of some educators is to attempt to show that programming is not the only and not even the primary activity of those engaged in CS. There is design, management, interaction with users, and so on. I would like to defend the (perhaps controversial) position that programming is the fundamental activity of CS and therefore shouldn't be swept under the rug. The position is based upon a broad view of what it means to program, so that whatever one's job title, almost everyone is programming, almost all the time. Furthermore, since the program is where "the rubber meets the road" (from a jingle used in ads for the Firestone tire company), any CS activity must be carried out with a primary focus on its contribution to the fitness of the end-product, the program. Finally, to carry out higher-level activities such as marketing and management, one must have extensive programming experience in order to successfully negotiate feasible specifications, deadlines and budgets for software development. The talk will conclude with the curricular consequences that can be drawn from this position.

Categories and Subject Descriptors: K.3.2 [**Computers and Education**]: Computer and Information Science Education – *Computer science education*

Keywords

Programming

Short Bio

Moti Ben-Ari is a professor in the Department of Science Teaching of the Weizmann Institute of Science, where he heads a group that develops courses in computer science for middle- and high-school students and carries out pedagogical research. He has a PhD degree in mathematics and computer science from Tel Aviv University. Ben-Ari's research interests include the use of visualization in teaching computer science, tools and techniques for learning concurrent and distributed computation, and teaching computer science to middle-school students, previously with Scratch and now with robotics activities. Ben-Ari is the author of a dozen textbooks on concurrent computation, programming languages, mathematical logic, and the nature of science. In 2004, he received the ACM/SIGCSE Award for Outstanding Contributions to Computer Science Education and in 2009 he was elected as a Distinguished Educator of the ACM.

ITICSE'15, July 04–08, 2015, Vilnius, Lithuania.
ACM 978-1-4503-3440-2/15/07.
http://dx.doi.org/10.1145/2729094.2742581

The JaeOS Project and the μARM Emulator

Marco Melletti
melletti.marco@gmail.com

Michael Goldweber
Xavier University
mikeyg@xavier.edu

Renzo Davoli
Universita' di Bologna
renzo@cs.unibo.it

ABSTRACT

As operating systems evolve, so must operating systems projects. Most operating systems courseware systems are based on the significantly out of date MIPS architecture, and only one of these supports multiprocessors. This paper introduces μARM, a pedagogically undergraduate-appropriate ARM7tdmi-based system emulator/architecture. Furthermore, we present JaeOS, a specification for a multi-layer OS supporting multiprocessing, VM, thread synchronization, external devices (disks, terminals, tape, printers, and network interfaces) and a file system.

Traditional OS projects like Nachos[5] or OS/161[10] provide students with a significant starting code base. Students then modify existing OS modules or add new ones. With μARM/JaeOS students undergo a pedagogically different experience of starting only with a hardware emulator and ending with a completely student written OS capable of running student written C programs.

Categories and Subject Descriptors

K.3.2 [**Computer and Information Science Education**]: Computer Science Education

General Terms

Design

Keywords

OS courseware, ARM Emulation, Accessibility

1. INTRODUCTION

While undergraduate computing curricula have evolved over the past thirty years or so, an operating systems course has remained a consistent fixture. This is in spite of the observation that the vast majority of our undergraduates will never be professionally engaged in the writing or maintenance of an operating system. What are the learning outcomes from an operating systems (OS) course that are so enduring?

Mastering topics such as the process/thread model and concurrency are central not only to operating systems, but to algorithmics in general, though one might find these topics in other courses. (e.g. Database Systems) One unique way the operating systems course stands out is that it affords students the opportunity to wrestle with and master complexity to a depth not otherwise available in the undergraduate computing curriculum. Theoretical explanations and small-to-medium size programming projects notwithstanding, they pale to the pedagogic value of having students read, understand and modify code from a large system, or better yet, write from scratch their own operating system. Given the desire for students to utilize software engineering practices (e.g. pair programming), layering, and abstraction in the service of creating a hugely complex artifact, it is difficult to name a better system choice than one that exposes how hardware interacts with software and furthermore demonstrates how both complexity and concurrency are actually dealt with; i.e. an operating system.[1]

As described, the lab activities for the OS course, not only reinforce fundamental OS concepts, but can also serve as a sort of programming capstone-like experience – a system sufficiently complex that students cannot remember, at the end of the semester, details of code written in the beginning of the semester (and must rely on their own documentation to refresh their memory). The choices for such "getting one's hands dirty" lab activities are many and can involve working either with real hardware or with emulated hardware, and with either a production quality operating system or with an education-oriented operating system.

Hence student activities can vary from working with complex, real operating systems, to educational, but still realistic ones, to studying/modifying existing software, to writing new creations from scratch. In spite of all the different possible choices, working with an education-oriented operating system in conjunction with emulated hardware is the most popular.

μARM is a new hardware emulator based on the ARM7tdmi architecture that presents a realistic, but not excessively complex architecture. μARM, a product of the Virtual Square Lab, is a cross between a real ARM7tdmi based system and

---

[1]The argument presented indicates that our goals could be met by a similarly complex project from some other undergraduate course. In the authors' experience, the only successful non-OS example of this is the now long defunct and no longer supported database project; Minibase.[19]

the typical machine architecture presented to students in operating systems textbooks.

JaeOS is the education-oriented operating system that students create to run on μARM. The pedagogic philosophy behind μARM/JaeOS is the same as that of μMPS2/Kaya[9, 8]; also a product of the Virtual Square Lab: The best way to learn about operating systems is to have students write a complete OS from scratch. JaeOS (and Kaya) is the design of an operating system: a semester long project where students write a complete OS, with no initially provided code, to run on "hardware" designed not for super fast instruction execution (i.e. a real ARM7), but to be both realistic and accessible to undergraduate students (μARM).

JaeOS is best described as simple, but complete. It supports a large variety of different peripheral device classes (printers, disks, terminals, etc.), process creation/termination, concurrency primitives, and up to eight potentially cooperating user processes, each running in their own virtual address space. μARM, as a separate ARM7 hardware emulator, is capable of running any compatible software, of which JaeOS is but one example.

Under μARM/JaeOS, students implement a very simple scheduler (Round Robin), a simple deadlock detection algorithm and a simple page replacement algorithm (FIFO). The complexity arises from how each part of the OS interacts with each other part. Furthermore, JaeOS interacts with the hardware in an authentic manner. If one were to build actual hardware to the μARMspecification, any student created JaeOS would run unaltered.

The rest of this paper is organized as follows. Section 2 presents a concise evaluation of related courseware systems. The μARM emulator is described in Section 3, while JaeOS is described in Section 4. Finally, the paper concludes with Section 5.

2. RELATED PROJECTS

As discussed above, the majority of OS courseware systems that have been proposed over the years deal with an education-oriented OS.

We group these systems into four categories.

- Systems that provide the code for a complete operating system. The best example of this is Minix[22], an open source operating system students can study both theoretically and practically by reading its source code and playing with the OS itself as it is meant to be run on real hardware. While students do not write significant amounts of code (any?), there is value in having students read and understand the code base for a large system.

- Systems that provide students with a functioning operating system which they must not only study but either enhance by writing replacement modules, and/or extend with new modules of their own. Examples of this include OSP2[12], PintOS[17] and BabyOS[13]. Again, there is value from studying a large code base. Students however miss out on understanding the complex module interactions when they simply upgrade a given existing module's algorithm. (e.g. Replace the Round Robin scheduler with a more sophisticated one.) Also some of these systems integrate the OS with the emulator blurring the hardware–software interface.

- Systems that provide a partially implemented kernel and require students to complete the kernel and extend it with additional modules. Examples include Topsy[7], OS/161[10], Awk-Linux[4] and GeekOS[11]. These systems are close to the μARM/JaeOS philosophy introduced above, but still provide some code for students to start with. How much code, and which modules are provided vary from system to system. We still see this pedagogically as a breadth versus depth question. The key learning outcomes for the OS lab experience are best served by an approach with the greatest breadth. Which brings us to the final category.

- Systems that provide the framework for students to build their own complete operating system. Examples of this include Nachos[5], μMPS2/Kaya[9, 8], and μARM/JaeOS. PortOS[2] is another example, but is outdated and seemingly no longer supported.

Nachos is an integrated OS simulator based on the MIPS architecture. A key characteristic of this simulator is the necessity to build the OS together with the simulator. Like OSP2 this introduces conceptual problems, making unclear the distinction between hardware and software. Hence, some hardware artifacts are presented as (class) objects. Finally, Nachos is sufficiently large such that many institutions provide code to the students, eliminating its "build the whole system" premise. In this case students, as in one of the above categories, are asked to replace existing modules, and/or extend the provided code with new modules of their own.

Since μARM/JaeOS is based on μMPS2/Kaya, a more indepth discussion of this system is provided.

2.1 Kaya and the μMPS2 Emulators

Kaya is an OS project that falls into the students build their own complete operating system category. In order for this task to be tractable by undergraduates over a 15 week semester, the following decisions were made:

- The OS project had to focus on completeness over complexity. All of the key components are present though implemented using unsophisticated algorithms. Complexity, and possibly deeper understanding, comes from implementing all of an OS's primary components and understanding the myriad of ways they interact. Given the choice of having students replace/update a module in an already existing system (e.g. update the scheduler from Round Robin to Multi-level Feedback Queues) or write a simple scheduler, but also write all the code modules that interact with the scheduler, we opted for the later. Updating a given module's algorithm does not force students to understand and manage the innate complexity of the system, while those that do have a deep understanding of the "gestalt" can easily understand the implications of a scheduler algorithm upgrade; even if they do not undertake the exercise.

This notion of completeness lies at the heart of our educational philosophy. It is relatively simple for students to learn OS-related techniques and algorithms as a myriad of unconnected topics. All OS instructors are familiar with students who can discuss the differences between page replacement algorithms, but who cannot see how paging-on-demand and seek-minimizing algorithms may interact. Or students who cannot see the difference between main memory and file system allocation but are nonetheless able to recite a list of allocation techniques for each. OS textbooks present each topic/chapter as a silo, while in reality these abstract concepts interoperate to create a complex integrated software artifact. Hence it is projects such as Kaya and JaeOS which can provide students with a view of the big picture that is so often missing. As all types of systems (not just OS's) grow in complexity, providing students with an educational experience where they are required to master the complexity of a significantly large "whole" will, in our opinion, only grow in importance.

- The target architecture had to be simple enough for undergraduates to be able to completely understand. If students are going to write a complete operating system, they would also need to fully understand the architecture.

  Real systems, both at the CPU/chip level and at the system level are very complicated artifacts. A primary engineering design goal for real systems is super fast execution, not student understanding. μMPS and its updated multicore variant μMPS2 are system emulators for an undergraduate appropriate target machine architecture.

  μMPS/2 are based on the MIPS R3000 chip and use the same instruction set architecture (ISA); integer instructions only. μMPS/2 however introduce some additional pedagogically appropriate features. (e.g. A VM on/off bit.) Furthermore, the emulated chip is embedded in a larger emulated system containing a system bus, and a host of connected peripheral devices which include both block and character devices. All of the peripheral devices use a simple direct memory mapped architecture with a uniform device register format. Finally, μMPS/2 implement a straight forward paged/segmented memory model along with a TLB that gets "refilled" via ROM code.[2]

The final component needed for student success is a sophisticated debugging environment. Hence the μMPS/2 emulators implement all expected debugging features. These include breakpoints, memory tracing, memory suspect breakpoints, in addition to special OS debugging features: break on interrupt, break on exception, and break on VM event. The emulator is executed via a GUI which was updated during the development of μMPS2.[3]

3. THE μARM EMULATOR

The μARM emulator is to an ARM7tdmi-based system as what the μMPS2 emulator is to a MIPS R3000-based

system; a pedagogically simplified CPU embedded in an easy to understand system architecture.

Given the widespread use of μMPS2/Kaya and the generally widely held opinion that the MIPS R3000 architecture is simpler than the ARM7 architecture, why develop the μARM emulator?

While the overall architecture structure remains plausibly realistic, the core element of μMPS2 the MIPS R3000 processor, is by this time largely out of use. The choice of the successor has been driven by four main aspects:

- Spreading of the technology: It is central to our philosophy to provide students with a constructive experience with a system based on a processor in widespread use. ARM architecture is widely diffused nowadays. Many portable devices, including tablets, smartphones and gaming consoles[18] mount this family of processors, along with embedded systems and experimental devices such as the Raspberry PI[21].

- ISA complexity: A processor with a small instruction set (RISC) is ideal to let the students understand assembled programs and BIOS code without getting lost in complex opcode tables, offering a readable and simple assembly language.

- Student Preparation: Though JaeOS is a C-based programming project, a course in Computer Architecture or Machine Organization, where students gain experience programming in an assembly language, is a prerequisite. At least one widely popular text to support this course[16] is migrating from the MIPS ISA to the ARM ISA.

- Adaptability to the present architecture: As proven by years of field experience, the μMPS/2 general architecture has been successful in its balance between simplicity and plausibility. Hence a processor that requires specific bus or memory interfaces would not be desired, as it would impose major modifications in its emulated specifications.

3.1 The processor

Given our pedagogic philosophy and their concomitant imposed restrictions, we settled on the ARM7tdmi[1] processor as the core element for μARM.

ARM7tdmi implements two well known RISC Instruction Sets (32-bit ARM-ISA and 16/32-bit Thumb-ISA) in a system architecture independent manner. This allows developers significant freedom with regard to coprocessor implementation and overall system structure. It is this freedom that permits μARM to emulate a 100% pure ARM7tdmi processor –integer instruction set only– in a system, along with coprocessors of our own pedagogically appropriate design.

Since the processor has been perfectly reproduced, one is free to use existing toolchains for JaeOS development. Hence, students can use available cross-compilers (e.g. emdebian[20], GCC ARM Embedded[14]) without the need for unusual interventions, or for the Virtual Square Lab to develop and support a dedicated cross compiler.

3.2 The Memory Subsystem

The physical memory subsystem implements a little endian random access memory of configurable size (up to 4 GB

---

[2]The ROM code, which extends CPU functionality by implementing full processor state context switches and a TLB refill algorithm is configurable and can be assigned as an advanced follow up project.

[3]Since μMPS2 completely subsumes μMPS –just run μMPS2 with a single core– and has a superior GUI, μMPS is no longer supported.

maximum), and a single 109 KB contiguous read only memory to be loaded with boot code and BIOS services code. An implementation of both is delivered with the emulator.

Virtual memory is implemented, as per ARM specification, via coprocessor 15. Our coprocessor 15 implements a simple TLB-based virtual memory subsystem very similar to that of the class tested μMPS2. This includes a paged, segmented environment supporting up to 128 unique address space ID's. (i.e. Coprocessor 15 and accompanying BIOS code recognize up to 128 segment tables.)

There are 3 segments: one for Kernel space (2 GB), and two 1 GB user space segments. Low addresses are reserved for the bus physical registers and reside in the Kernel segment.

3.3 General System Architecture

μARM emulates a central processor, coprocessor 15, a volatile memory subsystem along with a number of external devices, all connected to a system bus.

To offer the widest range of common and not-painful-to-program devices, μARM implements five device types; the first four being inherited from the MPS[15] emulator. μARM can support up to eight instances of each device type.

- Tape Devices: R/W sequential access block devices.

- Disk Devices: R/W random access, DMA supporting, block devices with realistic user configurable geometries and performance specifications.

- Printer Devices: Simple character devices that dump output to external files.

- Terminal Devices: Input/output interactive character devices.

- Network Devices: Ethernet devices implemented through VDE[6].

Each device type is provided with a hardware interrupt line to notify the CPU of device status changes. Each device instance is represented by a 4-words wide hardware register on the system bus used by the processor to send/receive information to/from each device and to implement full-handshake dialogues.

Finally, a TOD wall clock and an interval timer with a dedicated interrupt line are also connected to the system bus, allowing for timing functionalities (e.g. CPU scheduling).

3.4 The GUI

Interaction with μARM happens through its μMPS2 inspired, Qt toolkit implemented GUI. The interface is composed of several windows which let the user exercise the desired level of control over the simulation execution and output, while offering a series of high level debugging tools:

- Code and TLB modification breakpoints

- RAM inspector

- Processor and coprocessor registers matrix

- TLB contents inspector

The μARM GUI also takes advantage of the Qt toolkit's Accessibility layer, providing a somewhat exhaustive set of information compatible with the majority of screen readers for the visually impaired. Finally, a new emulation mode has been implemented which only updates the GUI when the simulation is paused (user request, system event or breakpoint) eliminating an oft-criticized screen flicker.

4. JaeOS

JaeOS is not an operating system one downloads to run on μARM. Instead it is the design of an operating system designed to be completed by undergraduate students during a traditional 15 week semester. The design is delivered via a set of documents to guide students in the realization of their project activities and to aid instructors in laying out in an easy and ordered way the assignments to be given to the class.

The curricular materials that come with μARM are composed of two reference documents: the hardware specification manual (The μARM Principles of Operation) and the JaeOS specification (Student Guide to the JaeOS Operating System Project).[4]

JaeOS is a multi-layer operating system, strongly based on the Kaya OS specification. Each layer serving both as a support level for the above layers and as a specific assignment phase, with increasing difficulty and abstraction. C is the suggested implementation language, but any programming language with a compiler capable of outputting ARM binaries could work as well.

JaeOS is structured as follows:

- Layer 0: This is the hardware layer composed of the various emulated hardware components (e.g. processor, coprocessor 15) in addition to the functionality provide by the boot and BIOS code.

- Layer/Phase 1: This first assignment is a simple data structures task designed to build student confidence with the emulator, the programming language and the debugging environment. Students write code managing all the data structures used by the kernel nucleus (Layer 2): Process control blocks (pcb) and semaphore queues. This phase is not strictly related to the course subject as semaphores and pcbs are only passive data structures at this point.

- Layer/Phase 2: The second layer/phase represents the kernel nucleus, providing low level system calls, a scheduling facility, exception, and interrupt handlers. Eight low level system calls provide services to the higher layers. These include process creation & termination, a semaphore blocking/unblocking service (i.e. P & V), an I/O synchronization service, and primitives to manage two different timing mechanisms. This phase takes advantage of the Layer 1 facilities to implement the "ready" queue, the semaphore blocked process queues, and I/O synchronization.

- Layer/Phase 3: This layer provides an environment for user processes to run, requiring students to implement both virtual memory, and the high level sys-

---

[4]JaeOS represents "Just Another Educational Operating System."

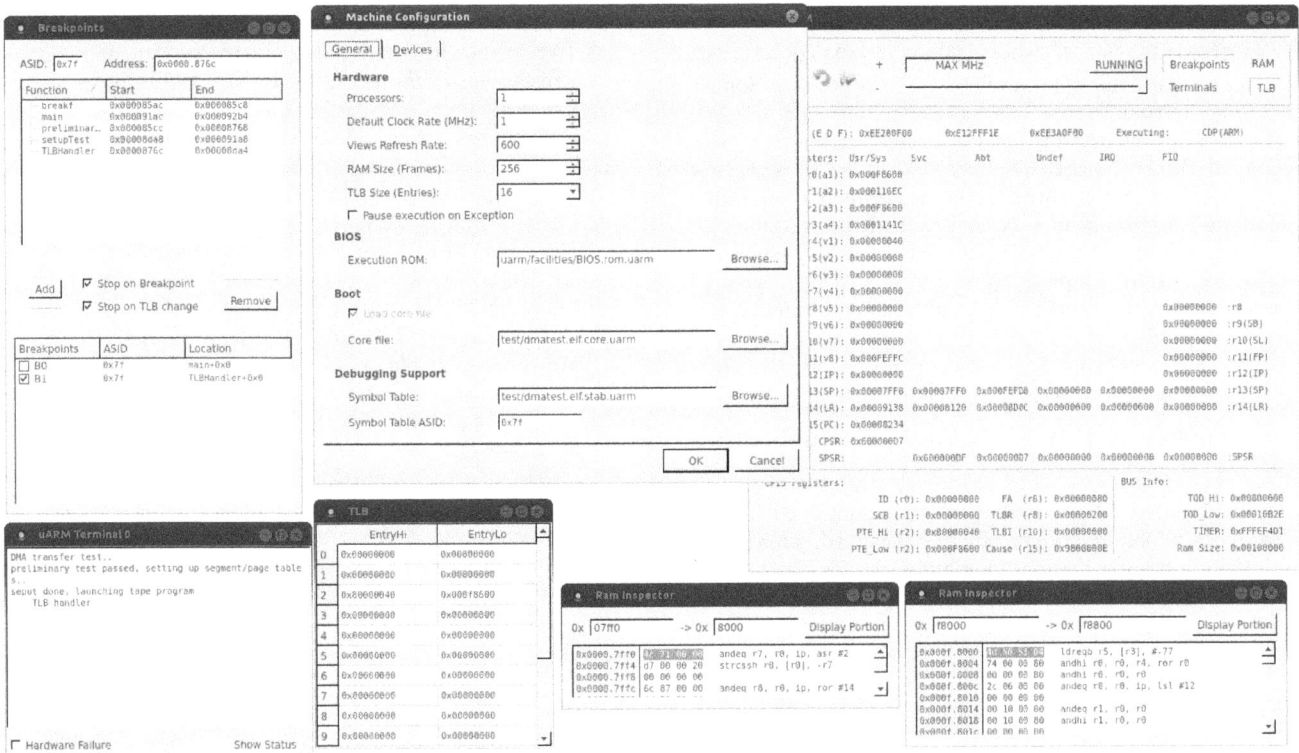

Figure 1: Main GUI components

tem calls to support user process access to the I/O devices. The virtual memory infrastructure allows user processes to each run in their own overlapping virtual memory space. There are two user space segments; segment 2 and segment 3. Segment 2 is for each user-level processes' private space, while segment 3 is a globally shared memory space to facilitate process cooperation. The recommend approach is to implement demand paging using a global FIFO page replacement algorithm. The I/O system calls provide user processes methods to access the available external devices. At this point JaeOS is capable of running multiple simultaneous user programs interacting with character and block oriented devices.

There are two *advanced* modules to this layer.

- A user-level semaphore service based on virtual addresses. (i.e. Addresses in the 1 GB shared virtual segment 3.) This synchronization service facilitates user process cooperation.

- A user-level process *delay* facility implemented using a daemon process and the Layer 2 timing mechanisms.

- Layer/Phase 4a: A simple file system. A simple flat file system is built using Layer 3's disk I/O primitives. Implemented system calls include file creation, deletion, renaming, open, close and write.

- Layer/Phase 4b: Support for the network interface. This phase is actually an alternative Layer/Phase 4a, since it is built on top of Layer 3, and makes no use of the Layer 4a file system. The objective of this layer

is building a network protocol stack in order to have multiple emulators communicating with each other. Moreover, since network devices are based on the Virtual Square Lab's Virtual Distributed Ethernet (VDE) tool[6], μARM network devices can communicate with any virtual or physical host equipped with VDE. Thus it is possible to test JaeOS network stacks in either real or emulated network environments.

- Layer/Phase 5: An interactive user "shell" program. This module is somewhat open-ended. Simple shell programs can simply interact with the Layer 4a file system. More sophisticated versions can extend to process creation and management.

Expectations for how many phases students might complete will vary from institution to institution. Experience with Kaya informs that institutions that deploy the project earlier rather than later typically complete through Phase 2. Institutions that deploy the project in students' final undergraduate year (i.e. as a programming-based capstone-like experience) typically complete through Phase 3; with about a 50-50 split with those that complete the advanced portions of Phase 3. Phases 4a, 4b, and 5 are rarely completed along with Phases 1-3 during the same semester, but are assigned as advanced projects in subsequent semesters.

It is important to observe that μARM is in no way tied to JaeOS. Hence, students, as well as other OS researchers, are free to develop other operating systems to run on μARM. While not necessarily appropriate for undergraduates, this represents the ultimate OS project; to not just implement an OS (e.g. JaeOS), but to design and implement a new operating system.

5. CONCLUSION

μARM is the latest offspring of a lineage of highly successful educational emulators developed by the Virtual Square Lab. The Virtual Square Lab has not undertaken any formal evaluation of μARM/JaeOS. There are, however, two anecdotal observations that inform our optimism regarding its utility. μMPS2 is currently in widespread use. Informal alumni surveys from a number of institutions that have been long time users of μMPS2/Kaya consistently name the Operating System course in general and the Kaya project in particular as their most impactful undergraduate experience.

μARM has benefitted from some key lessons learned from this evolutionary process. These include:

- The adoption of a well known and widely used instruction set architecture, ARM, and

- an updated GUI, based on a well maintained library and a widely adopted graphical standard, which provides a more consistent look-and-feel with other applications.

Furthermore, μARM is the Virtual Square's first emulator that is more usable for differently-abled students as it exploits the Qt Accessibility layer.

μARM inherits from its predecessors, along with some long running experience in educational operating system projects, a student accessible system architecture including a memory management unit and a set of realistic albeit simple to use I/O devices. This mix creates a unique testing facility which shields students from useless technical details of real hardware and system architecture, so they can implement a specially designed educational operating system; JaeOS. We believe that the key learning outcomes of mastering complexity (i.e. the myriad of interactions between modules and layers), understanding the hardware–software interface, and learning how both to implement and utilize concurrency are best accomplished by having students build an entire kernel.

Future developments of the project may include the support for multi-processor ARM architectures as well as a port of μARM to tablets or portable phones; a process made easier by the adoption of the Qt library.

6. ACKNOWLEDGMENTS

We would like to acknowledge the work of Ozalp Babaoglu and Fred Schneider, who over 30 years ago created the CHIP/HOCA system[3]. This system served as the inspiration for μMPS/Kaya and therefore also for μARM/JaeOS.

7. REFERENCES

[1] A. ARM. Technical reference manual, 2001.

[2] B. Atkin and E. G. Sirer. PortOS: an educational operating system for the post-pc environment. In *ACM SIGCSE Bulletin*, volume 34, pages 116–120. ACM, 2002.

[3] O. Babaoglu and F. B. Schneider. The HOCA operating system specifications. Technical report, Cornell University, 1983.

[4] Y.-P. Cheng and J.-C. Lin. Awk-Linux: A lightweight operating systems courseware. *Education, IEEE Transactions on*, 51(4):461–467, 2008.

[5] W. A. Christopher, S. J. Procter, and T. E. Anderson. The Nachos instructional operating system. In *Proceedings of the USENIX Winter 1993 Conference Proceedings on USENIX Winter 1993 Conference Proceedings*, pages 4–4. USENIX Association, 1993.

[6] R. Davoli. VDE: Virtual distributed ethernet. In *Proceedings of the First International Conference on Testbeds and Research Infrastructures for the Development of NeTworks and COMmunities*, TRIDENTCOM '05, pages 213–220, Washington, DC, USA, 2005. IEEE Computer Society.

[7] G. Fankhauser, C. Conrad, E. Zitzler, and B. Plattner. Topsy–a teachable operating system. *Computer Engineering and Networks Laboratory, ETH Zürich, Switzerland*, 2000.

[8] M. Goldweber, R. Davoli, and T. Jonjic. Supporting operating systems projects using the μMPS2 hardware simulator. In *Proceedings of the 17th ACM Annual Conference on Innovation and Technology in Computer Science Education*, ITiCSE '12, pages 63–68, New York, NY, USA, 2012. ACM.

[9] M. Goldweber, R. Davoli, and M. Morsiani. The Kaya OS project and the μMPS hardware emulator. In *ACM SIGCSE Bulletin*, volume 37, pages 49–53. ACM, 2005.

[10] D. A. Holland, A. T. Lim, and M. I. Seltzer. A new instructional operating system. In *ACM SIGCSE Bulletin*, volume 34, pages 111–115. ACM, 2002.

[11] D. Hovemeyer, J. K. Hollingsworth, and B. Bhattacharjee. Running on the bare metal with GeekOS. In *ACM SIGCSE Bulletin*, volume 36, pages 315–319. ACM, 2004.

[12] M. Kifer and S. Smolkaka. OSP 2.

[13] H. Liu, X. Chen, and Y. Gong. BabyOS: a fresh start. *ACM SIGCSE Bulletin*, 39(1):566–570, 2007.

[14] G. A. E. Maintainers. Gnu tools for arm embedded processors. *Adresse: https://launchpad. net/gcc-arm-embedded (besucht am 09.01. 2014)*.

[15] M. Morsiani and R. Davoli. Learning operating systems structure and implementation through the MPS computer system simulator. In *The Proceedings of the Thirtieth SIGCSE Technical Symposium on Computer Science Education*, SIGCSE '99, pages 63–67, New York, NY, USA, 1999. ACM.

[16] D. A. Patterson and J. L. Hennessy. *Computer Organization and Design: The Hardware/Software Interface*. Morgan Kaufmann, 5th edition, 2013.

[17] B. Pfaff, A. Romano, and G. Back. The PintOS instructional operating system kernel. In *ACM SIGCSE Bulletin*, volume 41, pages 453–457. ACM, 2009.

[18] W. Pheonix. Nintendo DS. *Japan: Capcom Games*, 2005.

[19] R. Ramakrishnan. The minibase database project.

[20] R. Stigge. Embedded linux development with debian for ARM. *Philosys GmbH, Oct*, 2007.

[21] E. Upton and G. Halfacree. *Raspberry Pi user guide*. John Wiley & Sons, 2013.

[22] A. S. Woodhull and A. S. Tanenbaum. Operating systems design and implementation, 1997.

A Teaching Assistant for Algorithm Construction

Patrice Frison
Université de Bretagne Sud
IRISA - Campus de Tohannic
56000 Vannes, France
Patrice.Frison@univ-ubs.fr

ABSTRACT

This paper describes a method and a tool that allows a teacher to interactively explain and construct basic algorithms to novice programmers by direct manipulations of variables, indexes and arrays. The method consists in gradually creating a program with the assistance of a tool that captures the teachers actions on the fly. The system offers possibilities for recording a sequence of actions and replaying them. Moreover it is able to take care of conditional statements, as well as loops and macro operations. The tool generates the corresponding program code. As a result, a complete algorithm can be designed and executed without writing a single line of code.

Categories and Subject Descriptors

D.1.7 [**Programming techniques**]: Visual Programming; D.2.2 [**Design Tools and Techniques**]: User interfaces; K.3. [**Computers and Education**]: Computer and Information Science Education

General Terms

Algorithms, Design, Languages, Human Factors

Keywords

Algorithm visualization, Direct manipulation, Novice programming environment, Programming by demonstration

1. INTRODUCTION

Understanding and writing algorithms is a difficult task for learners. As explained by Guzdial in [2] "The task of specializing programming environments for novices begins with the recognition that programming is a hard skill to learn". In the article entitled "Lowering the Barriers to Programming: A taxonomy of Programming Environments and Languages for Novice Programmers" [8], the authors show that a large number of systems have been proposed by researchers to help learners. The main goal of these systems

is to "make learning to program easier for novice programmers." All of these systems are dedicated to students and children. From our point of view, we believe that programming is also a hard skill "to teach". As opposed to many systems, our tool (called AlgoTouch) is designed with the goal of helping teachers by providing several useful features in a single tool.

We are concerned with teaching the design of array iterative algorithms (mainly searching and sorting). As noted by [4], even with specific environments, "novices have trouble constructing loops, and referencing array elements correctly within those loops through the use of array indices". Teachers can use AlgoTouch features to modify and dynamically test variables and arrays, to create loops, macros and programs and to animate them.

1.1 Teaching Algorithms

The general steps that the author uses to explain how to design an algorithm are what inspired the approach used by AlgoTouch:

1) *Explain the design principle.* Actually, every (basic) algorithm should be explained in natural language with simple words and verbs. This explanation allows the novice programmer to understand how the algorithm operates. For example, explaining the principle of a selection sort algorithm on an array is straightforward: find the maximum value in the array, exchange it with the first value, repeat the process starting at the second value, the third value, etc.

2) *Show how this algorithm works.* For example, with slides, or on a whiteboard, the teacher shows an array of perhaps a dozen values and simulates the algorithm. Variables are used to store temporary results, and indexes to address the array elements. The difficult part is to animate the algorithm. On a slide show, the task is very tedious and moreover, the teacher has to think of various cases. If a student asks for a special case, the slide show is useless. The teacher must use the whiteboard and draw the array, variables and indexes. Animating the algorithm in this way generally results in confusion as illustrated in figure 1.

3) *Translate the algorithm into a program.* This is the most difficult part. The teacher has to explain that a loop will be used – indicating: what must be initialized before entering the loop, under which conditions the loop must continue (while loop) and what are the statements of the body of the loop, including its evolution. Finally, the teacher shows the resulting program.

In this process, we can see that the teacher has two main difficulties: first showing "live" how the program operates and moreover, explaining how to gradually create the pro-

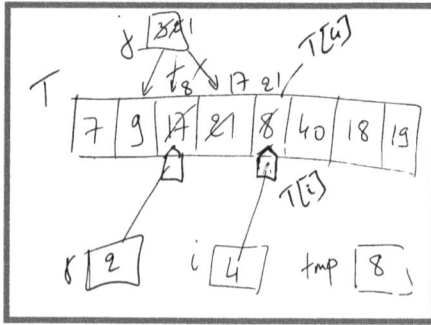

Figure 1: Whiteboard content after some simulations of an algorithm.

gram. AlgoTouch has been designed to help overcome these two problems. Many program visualization systems have been designed to animate such algorithms (see [11] for a recent survey). But most of them assume that the program has been written first. With our method, we want that the teacher generates the program on-the-fly, by demonstrating what to do. The animation is only the result of the method.

1.2 Teaching algorithms with AlgoTouch

Our proposed method concerns what we previously called "translate the algorithm into a program". When defining a single loop algorithm, the programmer must take care of four parts: the initialization of variables, the loop continuation, the loop itself (referred later as the body of the loop), and the loop termination. We defined a pseudo language the loop structure is inspired by the Eiffel language [9]:

```
From
    Statements
Until
    One or more exit conditions
Loop
    Statements
Terminate
    Statements
End
```

In the proposed method, we create these parts in the reverse order: the body (Loop part), the loop continuation (Until part) and finally the initialization (From part) and termination (Terminate part). The reason is to gradually define the algorithm from the general case to the details. At each stage, the tool will be used.

The main idea behind the method, is that the teacher executes operations of the body sequence with real elements of the algorithm (variables, arrays) on a typical case, then replays the sequence with different data to take care of conditional statements. At that stage, the body sequence can be executed several times to check that each step of the iteration operates properly.

When repeating the execution of the body, the teacher can show special cases where the loop must terminate. When this situation occurs, the teacher uses the tool to indicate that it is an exit condition, and the tool will generate the correct instructions.

When the algorithm is almost complete, the teacher has to define how to initialize the variables. It is simply done by executing the associated operations while the system records it. Then the teacher can verify that the algorithm operates

properly by running the loop. If initialization is not correct, it is necessary to re-record it, and run the program again.

In some algorithms, there may be statements that must be executed after exiting from the main loop. The teacher records these instructions (stored in the Terminate part).

In this paper we introduce the basic concepts of Algo-Touch. We then provide some details about the framework, followed by a detailed example of how to use the system. We conclude by explaining the future of the project in comparison with related work.

2. ALGOTOUCH BASIC CONCEPTS

AlgoTouch is based on very simple ideas: direct manipulation of programming objects (variables, indexes, arrays), recording a sequence of actions, replaying a recorded sequence, preparing loop construction and creating macro operations.

AlgoTouch is designed to be used mainly by teachers. Indeed it is a very simple tool to illustrate how algorithms operate. The teacher can show the "live" design of any simple algorithm on one or more arrays: creating the elements needed, manipulating them to show what happens, and finally, recording the different parts of the algorithm – mainly the iteration body of the algorithm. The whole process is very fast. If the algorithm does not operate properly, it is very easy to modify a step by re-recording it.

2.1 Direct Manipulation

The teacher must be able to manipulate the basic elements used by an algorithm using the whiteboard metaphor.

2.1.1 Variables, Constants, Arrays and Indexes

Variables are represented by a box with a name and a content (our prototype considers only integer variables). A variable is created by a single click on a button. The name, role and initial value of the variable are entered by the user. Then the name or value can be modified. Constants are also available.

Arrays are represented by a rectangular area containing the member elements of the array. Arrays of different size and content can be created. This allows the teacher to define an array adapted to the kind of algorithm under study, such as creating an array filled with increased integers starting from the value 1, or an array of decreasing values randomly chosen, etc. Moreover, at any time, the teacher can modify the content of the array. Note that when creating an array `A`, the constant `A.length` is automatically created.

Indexes are dedicated variables. An index is a variable attached to a specific array. AlgoTouch shows graphically what element of the array is actually pointed at by the index as shown in figure 2. The concept of index variable is similar to the one used in the Alvis Live! system [3].

2.1.2 Operations

The main operation used in any algorithm is assignment. The goal is to modify the content of a variable by the result of some expression. With direct manipulation, it is very easy to change the value of a variable `a` with the content of another variable `b`. The teacher drags the content of `b` and drops it on `a`. AlgoTouch shows that instruction `a = b` has been executed (C-like notation).

Simple arithmetic operators can be used, namely addition, subtraction, multiplication, division and remainder. The Al-

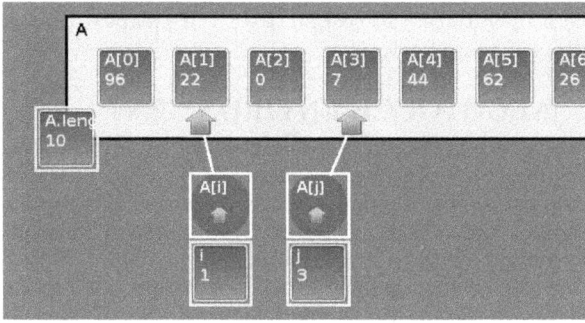

Figure 2: Indexes i, j and the associated array A. The icon above i is used to select A[i].

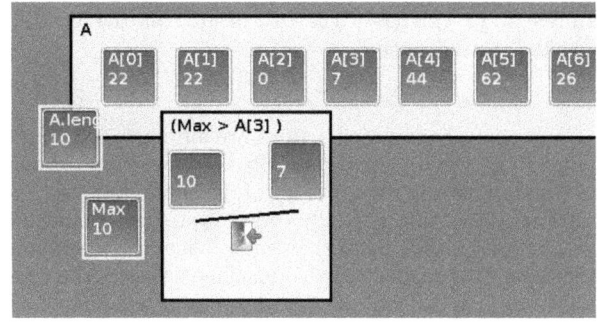

Figure 3: Comparing values with a scale.

goTouch prototype limits expressions to a single arithmetic operator. Actually, the goal of the system is to show how calculations can be done and therefore it is sufficient to use basic operators. To assign the result of an operation to a variable, the teacher first selects the result variable and the operator. The operator appears on the screen as a box with 3 rectangles, 2 for dropping the operands and one for calculating the result. The teacher places the content of each variable on the corresponding operand area, and activates the operation (by a double click). The result of the operation is shown on the result area. Finally, the result is moved to the assigned variable after validation.

For simplicity, increment and decrement operations of a variable content are available since these operations are frequently used. They consist in simple gestures: right (increment) or left (decrement) slide of the mouse over the variable.

All actions generate instructions in a C-like notation. Operations on arrays distinguish the access of a specific element (for instance A[1]) and the access of an indexed element A[i] where i is declared as an index. Figure 2 shows how AlgoTouch displays an array and index variables: an icon showing an arrow is used to associate i and A[i] (A[i] is written on the icon). The teacher can directly select the variable A[1], but he can also select the icon A[i]. The generated code takes care of it. For instance, if the user assigns A[1] to A[3] directly, the produced code is: A[3] = A[1] but if it assigns A[1] to A[3] through arrow icons A[i] and A[j] respectively, the generated code is: A[j] = A[i]. This will be useful to execute loops on array elements.

2.1.3 *Blind Mode and Need for Comparators*

With the previously defined elements and operations, we argue that both teachers and beginners can already "play" with algorithms. For the teacher, this mode is convenient to illustrate the concepts of variable, assignment, expression and indexed variables. It is possible to show how a machine can execute some task by moving things around. For instance the teacher can explain how to exchange the contents of two variables, or sort the content of an array into increasing order. This demonstration is purely manual, meaning that the teacher makes the decision how to rearrange the contents of an array by simply looking at the displayed values. For instance the teacher sorts the array by exchanging the first value with the maximum value, then by exchanging the second value with the next maximum value, and so on.

But this operation mode is not sufficient for writing real algorithms. Actually, when a program is running, the computer (not the teacher) has to decide what to do depending on the content of the data to deal with. In the direct manipulation mode, it is the teacher that makes decisions by "looking" at the variable values and therefore executing the right actions. To help students understand that the machine must make decisions, we have introduced the "blind mode" in which the content of all variables and arrays is not visible. The only way to have an idea of the content of two variables is to use a comparator.

A comparator looks like a scale, with the values to be compared placed on its pans. When the scale is activated by the teacher, the scale's pans move like a real scale (if the values are different). The teacher can continue the algorithm execution depending on the scale's result. For instance, when comparing the values of variables Max and A[3], the scale indicates that Max is greater than A[3], therefore the teacher executes operations corresponding to this case only. Figure 3 shows how a scale is drawn on the screen once it is activated. This mode is really useful for both the teacher and the students. The goal is to help students think about the problem without being influenced by the values of the example. This mode can be turned on and off as necessary. Note that the scale metaphor was introduced in ToonTalk [5].

2.2 Recording Mode

Once the teacher has done some preliminary manipulations to see how the algorithm may be designed, recording the body sequence of the algorithm iteration can be undertaken. It is necessary to first configure a typical state of the algorithm at a given step. For instance, one would initialize some variables, arrays, or indexes. Then after activating the Record mode the teacher executes the operations for this iteration, including those for the evolution of the loop. When the recording mode is turned off, the generated program reflects all actions that were executed.

2.2.1 *Conditional Statements*

What happens when the teacher activates a scale that compares two variables? As explained above the teacher will execute only the actions corresponding to the current state of the scale. For instance, when comparing variable a with b, if a is greater than b, the teacher will execute only the actions associated with this case. But what about the actions to do in the other case? We will explain later how the tool can take care of this problem in a very simple and intuitive way: this case will be executed on-the-fly while replaying the sequence.

2.2.2 Replay

The previously recorded actions are automatically transformed to program instructions. So, the teacher can show a real program produced as a result of its manipulations. This program is also automatically coded in a special machine-level code not visible by the students. When the teacher activates the `Play` mode, a virtual machine executes the code. At the end, the teacher can see the results (content of the variables and arrays) when examining the screen.

2.2.3 Recording While Executing

When executing the recorded program, the execution can be interrupted because some code is missing. This is typically the case when the teacher has used a comparator, for instance, by recording only the actions corresponding to one of the two possible outcomes (e.g., a is less than b). The code associated with the other condition is not available. In that case, the execution is stopped, a message is prompted to the teacher, explaining the problem and asking for recording actions of the missing case. Once the teacher has done it, the program is updated and ready to be executed again. This approach is similar to the one introduced by Pygmalion [10].

With this mechanism, the teacher must think of a specific test case when some part of the program has not been recorded. From a pedagogical point of view, this is interesting because a programmer must be rigorous in the design of a good program. Actually, AlgoTouch enforces testing activity in a continuous way.

2.3 Building a simple algorithm

Once the body of the iteration is built, the teacher can repeat its execution several times. But at some point, every loop must terminate. To do that, the teacher executes the recorded sequence several times until the loop must stop and then activates the `Exit case` mode. A scale is shown, and values associated with this exit case must be placed on the pans. For instance, if the loop must stop because the end of the array has been reached, the teacher places the index value on one side and the value of the array length on the other side. The scale indicates equality, meaning that the loop must stop if this occurs. AlgoTouch can record several exit cases since a loop may be stopped for different reasons. Once the exit cases have been defined, the algorithm is almost ready to run. After the teacher has specified the necessary initializations by recording the corresponding actions, finally, the teacher activates the `Execute Algorithm` mode. The tool will first execute the initialization sequence, then execute the loop by first checking the exit cases in sequence and running the iteration body if necessary. When one exit case is true, the algorithm stops after executing some termination code that the teacher has already recorded.

2.4 Building a full program with macros

Up to now, we have shown that the tool can create a single loop automatically. Actually, the system can save this loop as a macro operation with a name and a role. Then the teacher can create another loop structure and invoke the macro by its name as a single action. As a result, it is possible to create complex programs by creating different

macro operations. In section 4 we will create a program with two macro operations.

3. ALGOTOUCH ENVIRONMENT

The screen of the prototype consists of four areas as shown in figure 4: the design area where manipulation of the elements occur; the program area for displaying the generated program; the console area used by the system to display information for the user; and a toolbox area with buttons.

The design area is where variables, arrays, indexes and macros are shown. By simple touch gestures, the user can move these elements, drag and drop values into variables or arrays, and increase or decrease index values.

The console area displays the instructions produced when normal mode is activated. This can be useful for teachers when using the tools for the first time, explaining the basic instructions.

The program area (labeled "Instructions") contains the code produced by the user's manipulations, when the record mode is activated. The code is created as the user "plays" with the algorithm elements. Due to conditional statements, the code may contain some empty blocks corresponding to alternative cases. These blocks are easily identified since they contain a comment indicating that the block is not programmed yet (`TODO`), as illustrated in the example below.

The toolbox area contains buttons for commands – mainly for creating objects (a variable, an array of ten elements or an index) and for execution control (start recording, stop recording, replay the recorded sequence, record exit case, display a scale, execute the algorithm).

The system also offers a menu bar with some specific features concerning the project under design: saving, opening, creating and exporting the program.

4. FULL EXAMPLE

Let us examine a concrete example: selection sort. This algorithm has been chosen because it is a typical sorting algorithm but also to illustrate the main features of the system. As explained in a previous section, the teacher may give the following explanation: find the maximum value in the array, exchange it with the first value, repeat the process starting at the second value, the third value, etc. Now the teacher uses the tool to illustrate how to design the algorithm according to the previously explained method.

1) *Creating variables, indexes and array:*

```
Create array A of size 10 filled with random
   values. Let A be:
         [22, 96, 0, 7, 44, 62, ...].
   (constant A.length is set to 10)
Create indexes i and j associated with A.
```

2) *Demonstrating how the algorithm works:* index i is pointing to the first value of the array and index j is used to sequentially examine the values from i+1 to the end of the array. A[i] will contain the maximum value after completion of the algorithm. The teacher starts with j=i+1 and compares A[i] with A[j]. When A[j] is greater than A[i], the two values must be swapped. The teacher creates a new variable `tmp` needed to perform this operation. As it will take place several times, the teacher records the swap actions and stores them in a macro named Swap. Now when A[i] and A[j] must be swapped, the teacher activates the Swap macro. When j is equal to 10 (the length of the array),

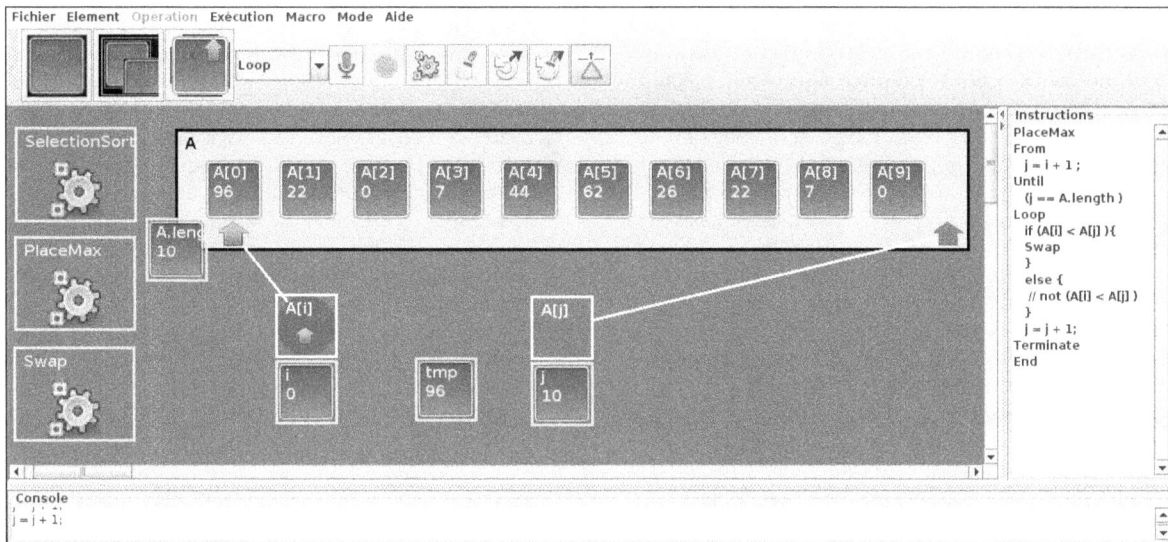

Figure 4: AlgoTouch Prototype.

the `A[j]` index turns red indicating that using `A[j]` is forbidden. The teacher knows that the maximum value of the array is now in `A[i]`. He must then redo the same processing starting with `i=2`, and `j=3` so now he decides to record the actions that he was doing manually in the previous stage.

3) *Finding automatically the maximum:* the teacher records the body of the loop as:

```
Display a scale
Drop values of A[i] and A[j]
  on the left and right pans respectively
Activate the scale
  (it shows that A[i] is smaller than A[j])
Activate the Swap macro
End scale
Increment j (for the next loop)
```

The following program is produced:

```
Loop
  if (A[i] < A[j] ){
  Swap
  } else {
  // not (A[i] < A[j] )
  // TODO 1
  }
  j = j + 1;
```

The teacher replays the loop several times to check if it operates correctly. At one time, the process is interrupted to record the `TODO` block. In this case, there is nothing to do, so the teacher stops the recording. Now the body of the loop is completed. The teacher replays the loop several times until the `j` index turns red. The teacher must then record the following exit case (a scale appears):

```
Drop j on one pan
Drop A.length on the other pan
Activate the scale
```

The system will produce instructions in the `Until` block to exit the loop if `i` equals `A.length`.

4) *Completing the loop and saving it as the PlaceMax macro:* at that stage a loop is programmed to place the maximum value in `A[i]` when `j` starts at `i+1`. The teacher must record this initialization by using the add operator.

Then the teacher can test the constructed algorithm by shuffling the values of the array and drop `0` into `i`. Running the algorithm will automatically place the maximum value in `A[0]`. By incrementing `i` and running the algorithm again, the second greatest value is placed in `A[1]`. The teacher decides to save this algorithm in a macro called `PlaceMax` whose program is shown in figure 4.

5) *Completing the selection sort algorithm:* when using `PlaceMax`, the teacher knows that the maximum value of `A` in the range `[i..A.length-1]` is placed in `A[i]`. He can record a loop to place the maximum value in `A[i]` and prepare the next loop by incrementing `i`:

```
Loop
  PlaceMax
  i = i + 1 ;
```

Starting at `i=0`, and executing this loop several times, he can show that the array is being sorted. When the `i` index reaches the last element of `A`, the loop must stop because the array is sorted. So the teacher records this exit case. The final program of the selection sort is the following:

```
Define SelectionSort
From
    i = 0 ;
Until
    (i == A.length )
Loop
    PlaceMax
    i = i + 1 ;
Terminate
End
```

Finally, the teacher can test several times the constructed algorithm by populating the array in different ways and running the program.

5. RELATED WORK

AlgoTouch is similar to Pygmalion [10] in its concept ("an electronic blackboard"): recording operations on real data, executing as soon as possible and completing code when conditional statements occur. It operates on typical computer elements like variables and arrays since its goal is to show

how to construct standard algorithms on arrays. A similar approach is used in ToonTalk [5], which replaces computational abstractions by concrete familiar objects and has been successfully used by thousands of children.

AlgoTouch can be used in blind mode, and to our knowledge, this mode is specific to this system. Katai [7] explains that blind mode is very important for students understanding. He says that "Visualizing information that has extra meanings for human viewers can obstruct them in following strict computer algorithms".

Like Alvis Live! [3], AlgoTouch provides the notion of index, and facilitates populating arrays. But it uses the opposite philosophy of the "What You See Is What You Code" concept defined in this system where the user codes and sees "live" the results. With it, the teacher does not write a single line of code. When executing an algorithm, AlgoTouch can be seen as an animation tool. Finally, it automatically produces program code in a pseudo language.

Unlike MatrixPro [6] which has been designed to demonstrate general data structures and algorithms, AlgoTouch is dedicated to designing simple algorithms on one or more arrays.

UUhistle [12] is more that a visualization system and therefore has some similarities with AlgoTouch. Indeed a student can "take the role of the computer as executor of a program in order to learn about program dynamics". With AlgoTouch, a user can also take this role but in order to build the program on-the-fly. It is a "Program by Demonstration" tool [1]. With it, the teacher does the work and the code is produced automatically.

6. STATUS AND FUTURE WORK

The implementation of the system has been conducted in several steps. At each step, the author defined new functionalities based on his teaching experience and on exercises from his course. While under development, a simple version of AlgoTouch (without macros) has been shown to students. The students could see the execution of some standard array algorithms they had to program: sum of array elements, searching for a subsequence, main loop for insertion, selection, bubble sort and partitioning (used in QuickSort). The author could see how the system could help explaining algorithms and then modify some features.

A prototype implementation of AlgoTouch has been completed and is currently available for testing and evaluation purposes. Two seminars were organized for teachers (about 25) from five computer science dept of two French universities. During the second seminar, the author could demonstrate the system on an interactive whiteboard. A questionnaire was used to evaluate the system both as an electronic whiteboard (direct manipulations only) and as a programming assistant (recording and generating the program). Fifteen responses were collected. Concerning the tool as an electronic whiteboard, 14 responses indicate that the system will be useful (10) or very useful (4) for teachers. The strengths are its interactivity, the blind mode and the index visualization. The weaknesses are mainly on the interaction with the graphical interface. Concerning the tool as a programming assistant: 13 think that the system is useful for the teacher (9) or very useful (4). Only two responses indicate that the system is not useful for the teachers. The strengths of this part of the system are: executing pieces of code, decomposing a problem into macros and visualizing missing code. The weaknesses are the lack of functions, no way to edit the code and the need for a better graphical interface.

Work in the near future will concentrate on further testing of usability and effectiveness with first year students. The results from these studies will then be used to refine the interface and functionalities of the system.

In parallel, we intend to work on the following points: (1) develop new features: new types (char, string, boolean, float), (2) enhance user interactions: new gestures, program animation.

The author wants to thank Prof. Dan Lewis from Santa Clara University (California) for proof-reading this paper.

7. REFERENCES

[1] A. Cypher. *Watch what I Do: Programming By Demonstration*. MIT Press, 1993.

[2] M. Guzdial. Programming environments for novices. *Computer science education research*, 2004:127–154, 2004.

[3] C. D. Hundhausen and J. L. Brown. What you see is what you code: A "live" algorithm development and visualization environment for novice learners. *Journal of Visual Languages & Computing*, 18(1):22–47, 2007.

[4] C. D. Hundhausen, S. F. Farley, and J. L. Brown. Can direct manipulation lower the barriers to computer programming and promote transfer of training?: An experimental study. *ACM Transactions on Computer-Human Interaction (TOCHI)*, 16(3):13, 2009.

[5] K. Kahn. How any program can be created by working with examples. *Your wish is my command*, pages 21–44, 2001.

[6] V. Karavirta, A. Korhonen, L. Malmi, and K. Stålnacke. MatrixPro - A tool for on-the-fly demonstration of data structures and algorithms. In *Proceedings of the Third Program Visualization Workshop*, pages 26–33, The University of Warwick, UK, July 2004.

[7] Z. Katai. Selective hiding for improved algorithmic visualization. In *Proceedings of the 2014 Conference on Innovation & Technology in Computer Science Education*, ITiCSE '14, pages 33–38, New York, NY, USA, 2014. ACM.

[8] C. Kelleher and R. Pausch. Lowering the barriers to programming: A taxonomy of programming environments and languages for novice programmers. *ACM Comput. Surv.*, 37(2):83–137, June 2005.

[9] B. Meyer. *Touch of Class: learning to program well with objects and contracts*. Springer, 2009.

[10] D. C. Smith. Pygmalion: An executable electronic blackboard. In *Watch what I do*, pages 19–48. MIT Press, 1993.

[11] J. Sorva, V. Karavirta, and L. Malmi. A review of generic program visualization systems for introductory programming education. *Trans. Comput. Educ.*, 13(4):15:1–15:64, Nov. 2013.

[12] J. Sorva and T. Sirkiä. Uuhistle: A software tool for visual program simulation. In *Proceedings of the 10th Koli Calling International Conference on Computing Education Research*, Koli Calling '10, pages 49–54, New York, NY, USA, 2010. ACM.

FrenchPress Gives Students Automated Feedback on Java Program Flaws

Hannah Blau
School of Computer Science
University of Massachusetts Amherst
blau.hannah@acm.org

J. Eliot B. Moss
School of Computer Science
University of Massachusetts Amherst
moss@cs.umass.edu

ABSTRACT

We created an Eclipse plug-in called FrenchPress that partially automates the task of giving students feedback on their Java programs. It is designed not for novices but for students taking their second or third Java course: students who know enough Java to write a working program but lack the judgment to recognize bad code when they see it. FrenchPress does not diagnose compile-time or runtime errors, or logical errors that produce incorrect output. It targets silent flaws, flaws the student is unable to identify for himself because nothing in the programming environment alerts him.

FrenchPress diagnoses flaws characteristic of programmers who have not yet assimilated the object-oriented idiom. Such shortcomings include misuse of the `public` modifier, fields that should have been local variables, and instance variables that should have been class constants. Other rules address the all too common misunderstanding of the boolean datatype. FrenchPress delivers explanatory messages in a vocabulary appropriate to the student's current level.

This paper reports preliminary results of a formative evaluation of FrenchPress conducted in a Fall 2014 data structures and algorithms course. User satisfaction survey responses indicate that among the students who received substantive diagnostic suggestions from FrenchPress, the percentage who were motivated to modify their program varied from 36% to 64% on four different assignments.

Categories and Subject Descriptors

K.3.2 [**Computers and Education**]: Computer and Information Science Education—*Computer science education*; D.2.5 [**Software Engineering**]: Testing and Debugging—*Diagnostics*; D.3.2 [**Programming Languages**]: Language Classifications—*Java*

Keywords

Eclipse plug-in, educational technology, program analysis, static analysis

1. INTRODUCTION

Anyone who has taught a programming course at the freshman or sophomore level knows how difficult and time-consuming it can be to address issues of program style in student submissions. Even if the instructor discusses numerous examples of well-written code in class, many students ignore or mangle these templates when they write their own programs. Often the class is so large that the teaching assistant/grader can spend only a few minutes on each program, checking to see if it produces the expected output for selected test inputs. This naturally leads students to conclude that a good program is one that has the desired input/output behavior, and it matters not how they achieve that behavior. A student could get a perfect grade on all his assignments and still be writing poor code.

When the teaching assistant does take the time to inspect student programs, issues of subjectivity arise. Judgments of code quality are hard to pin down, all the more so if multiple TAs are employed for different sections of the same course or over time. The potential for inconsistency makes the instructor reluctant to assign much weight to program style in calculating grades. If the student loses only a few points for a poorly written program, he will have little motivation to follow the corrections he receives from the teaching assistant. He might even dismiss these comments as a reflection of the TA's idiosyncrasies. The student could reach upper level courses before he gets an instructor whose grading policy enforces good programming practices. By this point the student might already have developed bad programming habits. These bad habits carry over into advanced classes where they are a hinderance for the student and a headache for the instructor.

To address this problem we developed FrenchPress, a static analysis tool that partially automates the task of giving students feedback concerning their Java programs. Students get guidance to make improvements without depending on the instructor or the teaching assistant to review their code. Our target population is not complete beginners but students taking their second or third undergraduate Java course: students at the level of an introduction to data structures and algorithms, who know enough Java to write a working program but lack the judgment to recognize bad code when they see it. We chose Java because it has been widely adopted for undergraduate curricula in object-oriented programming. Our goal is not to diagnose compile-time or runtime errors, or logical flaws that produce incorrect output. We are after the silent flaws — flaws the student is unable to identify for himself because he gets no feedback from the programming environment to alert him that a problem exists. Such shortcomings include misuse of the `public` modifier, fields that should have been local variables, and instance variables that should have been class constants. These flaws are characteristic of programmers who have not yet assimilated the object-oriented idiom. Other diagnostic rules target the all too common misunderstanding of the boolean datatype.

FrenchPress is easy to use for both students and instructors. The instructor does not have to write a model solution or customized diagnostics for each assignment. The analysis applies to any compilable Java program. The Eclipse plug-in integrates seamlessly into the student's development environment. The student can get feedback as he works, so he can iteratively improve the code before submitting his project. We conducted a classroom trial of FrenchPress in a data structures and algorithms course during the Fall 2014 semester. User satisfaction survey responses indicate that among the students who received substantive diagnostic suggestions from FrenchPress, the percentage who were motivated to modify their program varied from 36% to 64% on four different assignments.

2. RELATED WORK

Advanced beginner students of Java are not well served by the program analysis tools created in the past decade. Existing style checkers (Expresso [5]) and automatic assessment systems (CourseMarker [3], BOSS [6]) developed in academic institutions are aimed at students just learning to program. Expresso is a pre-compiler for Java programs that helps novices avoid common mistakes that can lead to incomprehensible compiler messages or unexpected runtime behavior. Expresso will flag errors such as unbalanced parentheses, braces, and brackets; confusion of `=` and `==`; and misplaced semicolons. The Environment for Learning to Program (ELP [11]) does both dynamic and static analysis, but only on program snippets submitted by students to complete fill-in-the-gap exercises in the introductory Java course. ELP checks for unused variables, unused parameters, redundant logical expressions, numeric literals that should be named constants, and other stylistic blunders. ELP performs a structural similarity analysis between the student's code and the instructor's model solution(s) for the exercise. This approach only works with fill-in-the-gap exercises because they are so short there is relatively little room for structural variation. The Java Critiquer [9] addresses localized stylistic issues, including boolean expressions, increment operators, unnecessary parentheses, and floating point data types. The Java Critiquer [8] can analyze only one class file at a time. FrenchPress handles more challenging assignments, involving multiple class definitions, that students would encounter in their second or third Java course.

The MIT system described in [10] tackles a class of problem FrenchPress does not cover: logic errors that cause incorrect output. MIT's system gives automated feedback to novice Python programmers. To formulate feedback for a programming exercise, it requires a reference solution for the exercise and a set of corrections for mistakes the instructor anticipates students will make. The system gives hints to help the student transform his program into one that matches the expected behavior. The instructor controls how much of a hint she wants to give the student, ranging from the line number of an error to a suggestion of exactly what

transformation to make on the original code. The suggested transformations may improve program correctness but do not generally improve program style.

On the other end of the spectrum, program analysis tools such as FindBugs [2, 4] and PMD [8] are geared for large-scale professional projects. Their bug reports assume a sophisticated understanding that college students are unlikely to attain in their first year of exposure to Java. Professional tools do not look for, and consequently do not find, the program flaws FrenchPress catches, precisely because the errors of an experienced software engineer are not those of a second-semester student. FrenchPress is similar in spirit to systems such as Stench Blossom [7] that alert programmers to *code smells*, questionable program features that indicate the code should be refactored or redesigned. FrenchPress flaws can be considered code smells specific to advanced beginner Java programmers.

3. OBJECTIVES

The main objectives of the FrenchPress project are:

1. Give the student effective and useful feedback without increasing TA or instructor workload.

2. Make it easy for the student to run the diagnostic tool, so he can iteratively improve his program before the final submission.

3. Liberate the instructor from the burden of writing customized design checks from scratch for each programming exercise.

3.1 Effective feedback

Many of the programming best practices articulated in books such as *Effective Java* [1] evolved in the context of projects with multiple team members producing software destined to be maintained and enhanced for several years. This perspective is essentially meaningless to a student who works no longer than two weeks on any assignment and who knows neither he nor anyone else will ever look at his code again after he gets his grade. The feedback we give this student must be relevant for his situation, not some hypothetical situation of large-scale software development.

Giving effective feedback means formulating messages in language the student can understand, even if that entails glossing over the subtleties. Giving effective feedback also means that the incidence of false positives must be kept to a minimum. A false positive occurs when FrenchPress delivers feedback that is inappropriate for the student's program: a diagnostic rule triggers when it should not have. Students at the advanced beginner level in Java would not be able to distinguish between a true flaw and a false report. They might respond to a spurious feedback message by modifying their program in a way that makes it worse, not better. This would undermine their trust in the tool's suggestions and they would stop using it. A false negative occurs when FrenchPress skips over a student mistake that could have been corrected: a diagnostic rule fails to trigger when it should have. False negatives are less of a problem than false positives for a user population of inexperienced programmers. As these students were not receiving much stylistic feedback from their instructors, if FrenchPress misses an opportunity to be helpful the student is no worse off than he was before he installed the software.

3.2 Easy for the student

Even when the professor or TA takes the time to write comments on submitted assignments, that feedback might come too late to be of interest to the student. We feel it is essential to integrate the tool into the student's development environment so he can run the diagnostics while still working on his program. We decided to implement FrenchPress as an Eclipse plug-in: the student can easily install the software and run it repeatedly as he changes and improves his code. Eclipse is a widely used development environment and has a well-established and free mechanism for software distribution. We created an update site for FrenchPress to take advantage of the *Install New Software* and *Check for Updates* features in Eclipse. The student runs FrenchPress by selecting a menu item in the Package Explorer view. He can choose to analyze a single `.java` file, or all the `.java` files in the `src` folder of his Java project. FrenchPress writes a feedback file for each `.java` file it analyzes. The plug-in creates a `frenchpress` folder in the student's Java project and stores all its feedback files there. The student can review the feedback whenever he wishes. Figure 1 shows a screenshot of FrenchPress.

3.3 Easy for the instructor

In designing a pedagogic program analysis system, we face a tradeoff between its range of applicability and the quality of its feedback. If the diagnostics are tailored to a specific programming exercise, the system can give detailed feedback because the course instructor has a good idea of what she expects to see in a student solution. Some educational tools (for example, [11] and [10]) require a substantial effort from the instructor in the form of customized diagnostic checks or a model solution for each programming assignment. Conscious of the many claims on the time of both professors and teaching assistants, we sought an approach that would be less labor-intensive for them while still offering a benefit to their students. We opted instead for a generic tool that demands nothing from the instructor, and has no knowledge of what problem the student is attempting to solve.

There is a wide range of emphasis in CS2 courses, as evidenced by the multiplicity of textbooks on offer to teach data structures in Java. FrenchPress diagnostics are not limited to a particular course syllabus. The rules described in Section 4 embody principles of good programming that are appropriate for assignments from any of these textbooks.

4. DIAGNOSTICS

The current version of the FrenchPress prototype comprises seven diagnostic rules. We chose these rules by examining a set of student programs submitted for the data structures and algorithms course. We identified flaws that are amenable to automated analysis and frequent enough to be worth investing our effort. Some of FrenchPress's rules overlap with the diagnostics of earlier pedagogic systems including the Java Critiquer [9]. We wanted a well-rounded set of diagnostics that would cover commonly occurring flaws in CS2 student submissions, whether or not those flaws had been addressed in previous work. To implement these rules, the plug-in crawls the abstract syntax tree, exploits Eclipse's type hierarchy and call graph search functions, and performs data flow analysis. Some of these questionable programming practices reveal the student's poor grasp of the object-oriented programming paradigm. Others are stylistic blunders one might see in any programming language.

If the student's `.java` file contains flaws of multiple types, FrenchPress presents feedback in the order of the rules listed below. We grouped the rules into four broad categories so that explanatory messages about related concepts would be displayed together. We ordered the categories according to our judgment of their severity. Misconceptions about the use of variables and access modifiers seem to us more serious in their potential consequences than redundant boolean expressions or unexpected `for` loop control variables. We want to first draw the student's attention to the issues we consider to be more significant. For each diagnostic we include below an example of the feedback FrenchPress gives the student. If no diagnostic rules are triggered the student gets a message congratulating him on his good work.

4.1 Misuse of fields

Advanced beginner Java programmers do not always understand the significance of fields in a class definition. They might declare something as an instance variable but then use it as a class constant. Or they declare fields that are unrelated to the class's data representation; these are really local variables that have been inappropriately promoted to the status of instance or class variables. Perhaps this habit is a vestige of high school programming classes where they were encouraged to declare all the variables at the top of the program.

4.1.1 Field could have been a local variable.

A field could be made local if, in every method that uses the variable, it is always written before it is read, and it is read at least once. The same variable name might appear in several different methods but it is used as a local variable in each of them. An example of feedback follows; the numbers in parentheses are line numbers in the `.java` file.

```
Variables such as
    game (8)
    m (9)
are declared at the class level but appear to
function as local variables. Each of these
variables could be declared locally in each
method where it is used. To find all the places
a variable is used, select the variable name
and Eclipse will highlight every occurrence
of that variable.
```

4.1.2 Instance variable could have been a static final constant.

The instance variable is initialized to a constant expression and never modified thereafter.

```
Instance variables such as
    numTrials (4)
could be declared static final (class constants)
because they are initialized to a constant value
and never changed later.
```

4.2 Misuse of the public modifier

CS2 students often do not attach much importance to the principle of hiding the details of a class's data representation and internal methods. They routinely declare instance variables `public` or make a method `public` even though it is

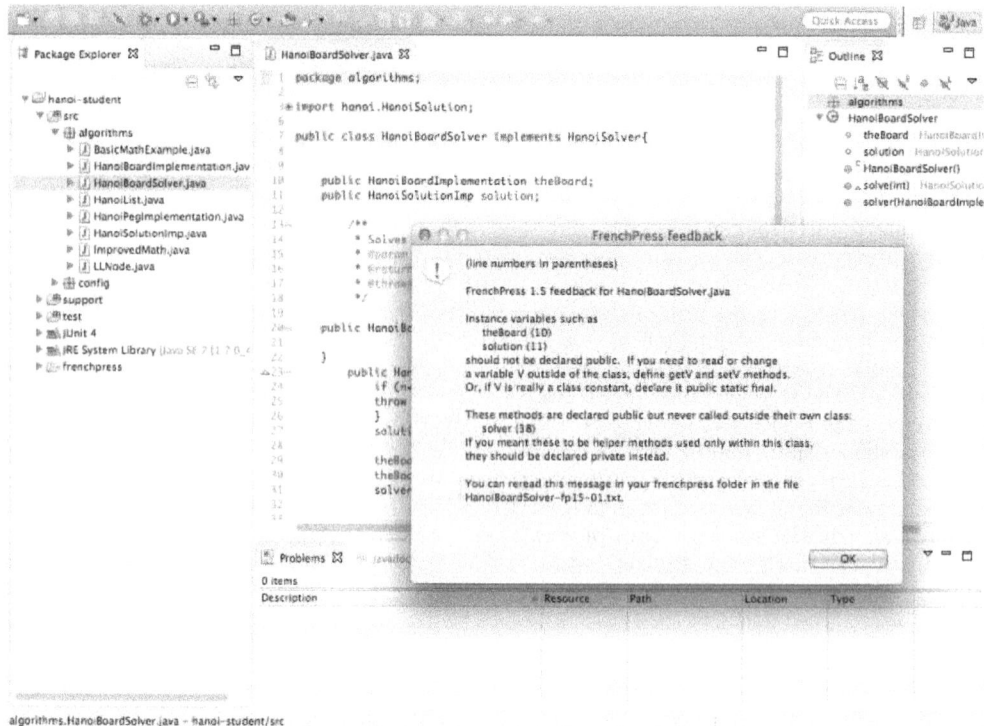

Figure 1: Screenshot of FrenchPress feedback

not part of the API for the class. This is understandable in the case where the student is working on his program alone (true for most CS2 projects) and has no intention of re-using his code after the due date of the assignment. Nevertheless we try to remind students of better programming practices.

4.2.1 Instance variable declared public

The student should define getter and setter methods instead of exposing the class's instance variables.

```
Instance variables such as
    count (8)
should not be declared public.  If you need to
read or change a variable V outside of the
class, define getV and setV methods. Or,
if V is really a class constant, declare it
public static final.
```

4.2.2 Non-static method declared public

If a `public` method is not called outside of its class, it does not need to be `public`. (This rule does not trigger if the method is inherited from a superclass or required by an interface the class implements.)

```
These methods are declared public but never
called outside their own class:
    moveRec (23)
If you meant these to be helper methods used only
within this class, they should be declared private
instead.
```

4.3 Misunderstanding booleans

The boolean data type seems to baffle some students more than other primitive data types. FrenchPress recognizes two forms this misunderstanding can take in student code.

4.3.1 Integer variable used as a boolean flag

In some cases the student declares an integer variable but uses it as a boolean flag. A integer variable is suspect if it never gets any value other than 0 or 1, is compared to 0 or 1 in at least one expression, and never compared to any other values.

```
Variables such as
    Check (27)
are declared int but appear to function as boolean
flags. Instead of giving them the values 1 and 0,
declare them as boolean and give them the
values true and false.
```

4.3.2 Redundant boolean expressions

Boolean expressions that compare a boolean variable to the constants `true` or `false` will be familiar to anyone who has read student code.

```
Boolean expressions such as
    isLegalMove(move) == false (11)
    temp.hasRings() != true (63)
are redundant and can be shortened.  If B is a
boolean expression,
B == true or B != false means the same thing as B
B != true or B == false means the same thing as !B.
```

4.4 Inappropriate for loop control

Students occasionally use an instance variable or a constructor/method parameter as a loop control variable. Perhaps this reflects a misconception that their code is more economical or efficient if they re-use variables instead of declaring a new `int i` in their `for` loop.

```
Instance variables such as
```

```
numPeople (39)
```
should not be used as for loop control variables.
It is preferable to use a separate variable as in,
for (int i = ...).

5. FRENCHPRESS CLASSROOM TRIAL

We conducted a classroom trial of FrenchPress in a Fall 2014 data structures and algorithms course. The trial covered four programming assignments. For each assignment, students enrolled in the trial were asked to analyze at least one, preferably more, of their `.java` files before submitting their program to be graded. After the assignment due date, the students responded to a short online user satisfaction survey. They were rewarded for their cooperation by a small amount of extra credit towards their final grade in the course. The number of study participants varied slightly from one assignment to the next, as a few students forgot to use the plug-in or skipped the survey for a particular project but then re-engaged on the following one. We had to weed out responses from students who completed the survey even though they had not run FrenchPress on their program. The number of legitimate survey responses varied during the trial from a low of 43 to a high of 47.

Table 1 summarizes survey responses for the four assignments to the question, "Did the FrenchPress feedback for this assignment lead you to change your program?" *No Flaws* indicates that the student chose the option "French-Press found no flaws in my program". Certainly we do not expect FrenchPress to influence the student's coding choices if he did not get any substantive feedback on the files he selected to analyze. Since each student could decide for himself how many of his `.java` files he wanted to examine with FrenchPress, the amount of diagnostic feedback to which the student was exposed depended in part on how zealous he was in running the plug-in. We wanted to give students some leeway so they would not drop out of the study because they found the requirements of participation too time-consuming.

The second and third columns of Table 1 show the percentage of all survey respondents who say they did/did not change their program in light of the feedback they received from FrenchPress. The *Yes* response declined from a high of 54% on the first assignment to a low of 11% on the final assignment. The fourth column of the table calculates the *Yes* response as a percentage of those students who said FrenchPress found flaws in their code: *Yes / (Yes + No)*. This measure ranges from 64% on the first assignment in the study to 41% on the final assignment, but it does not show a smooth decrease in between. The sharp decline from Project 1 to Project 2 might reflect the fact that the students' initial enthusiasm for new software has worn off. By the end of the classroom trial, fewer participants were getting substantive feedback from FrenchPress but a good proportion of those who got feedback were still motivated to modify their code. If FrenchPress is achieving its educational goals, we would expect the frequency of feedback to decline over time as students learn to avoid the mistakes they were making when they first starting using the plug-in. We have not yet scrutinized the trajectory of each individual in the study population to confirm or contradict this explanation of the survey data.

The most frequently triggered rule is 4.2.2, a method declared public for no apparent reason. However, we suspect that many of these feedback messages are not on point be-cause in fact the method is not called anywhere, in the class where it is defined or outside of that class. Students sometimes define getter and setter methods that are not needed in the program, but they include the methods anyway for completeness. There might also be methods that are not called anywhere because the student changed his mind as the program evolved and forgot to delete code that had become useless. We need to refine this rule to distinguish between methods that are called only within the class where they are defined, and methods that are not called at all.

6. FUTURE WORK

The feedback FrenchPress currently offers is rudimentary. For the simpler rules such as `for` loop control, perhaps the two- or three-sentence message FrenchPress now displays is adequate. More subtle rules such as *field should have been local variable* or *integer variable should have been boolean* demand more explanation. The next phase of FrenchPress development will provide a two-tier system of feedback. In addition to the short message FrenchPress now delivers, students will have the option to open a new window and read a more detailed writeup including an example.

We also realized over the course of the classroom trial that the term "flaw" can be offensive to students who are proud of their programming skills. We believe the vocabulary of "suggesting improvements" instead of "finding flaws" will be more readily accepted by our intended audience.

We have ordered FrenchPress's diagnostic rules to reflect our judgment of their relative importance for the student's understanding of Java. Another professor may have a different opinion about the best way to order multiple feedback messages. In a future version of the plug-in we would like to give the course instructor the power to change the order of the rules or to disable rules she does not want her students to see.

Our original plan included two rules that fall into the category of misconceptions about object-oriented programming. Many inexperienced Java programmers have only a shaky grasp of the concept of inheritance. Some students appear to confuse *Is-a* with *Has-a*: they use inheritance when composition would be suitable. For example, they create a class that extends `ArrayList` when they really should have given their class an `ArrayList` instance variable. Our rule would signal an inappropriate inheritance relationship when a subclass does not override any method of its superclass. An exception to this rule would be a subclass that implements an interface the superclass does not implement. This rule would catch cases in which the student declares his class to extend a Java library class, or makes spurious inheritance relationships between two classes of his own devising.

Another error we have observed in some student programs is a constructor that does not stop at constructing an object but tries to run the entire program by calling instance methods. This anomaly is difficult to detect with static analysis but we could at least warn the student if his constructor calls instance methods that are neither private nor final.

We eliminated these two rules from the FrenchPress prototype because they seemed less applicable to CS2 as it is now taught at our institution. The class size of our data structures and algorithms course continues to increase year after year. This has forced a move to automated grading of submissions based solely on input/output behavior. Automated grading requires greater uniformity in the submitted

Table 1: Did FrenchPress feedback lead student to change the program?

	No Flaws	Yes	No	Yes if Flaws
Project1	16%	54%	30%	64%
Project2	30%	25%	45%	36%
Project3	34%	32%	34%	48%
Project4	73%	11%	16%	41%

programs than might have been the case five or ten years ago when the submissions were graded by TAs. The CS2 professor provides a starter project for each assignment that the student imports into Eclipse. The student may add classes or methods but must not deviate from the program structure expected by the automated tests.

Obviously one is more likely to see design flaws when the student is given the freedom and the responsibility to organize his program as he sees fit. To become a competent programmer, the student must progress from filling in the missing pieces of a pre-existing structure to creating the structure for himself. FrenchPress could be helpful as the student is struggling to make that transition, whether it occurs in his second programming course or not until the third. When the plug-in is deployed in a smaller class that can afford to give students more flexibility, we will implement the inheritance and constructor rules.

7. CONCLUSION

Many existing automated assessment systems are designed to help students get through their first Java course, as they are struggling with the mechanics of the language. When students graduate to the next level of instruction they outgrow these tools because they have made, and learned from, most of the beginner mistakes. Students in their second or third Java course are not ready for professional strength diagnostics from FindBugs and comparable program analysis systems. The errors detected and the explanations offered fly over the head of the CS2 student. We have developed FrenchPress for the population of advanced beginners in Java who are now dependent on their instructors and teaching assistants for helpful feedback on their programs.

Implemented as an Eclipse plug-in, FrenchPress can be readily incorporated into many different undergraduate programming courses. The system will support student learning in any educational environment, but particularly those in which the teaching staff have difficulty providing individualized attention to all the students. These include community colleges, where instructors have no teaching assistants, and public universities, where large class sizes outstrip limited personnel resources. Automated feedback will also facilitate distance learning: the student can get guidance on his program anytime and anywhere he needs it. Whether at a community college or a four-year institution, introductory CS courses become "gateway courses" where a significant percentage of women and under-represented minorities quit the discipline—often because they lack confidence in their skills. By improving the delivery of instructional feedback in these courses, FrenchPress will contribute to the retention of at-risk students.

8. ACKNOWLEDGMENTS

R. Moll, W. R. Adrion, B. Lerner, and Y. Smaragdakis contributed valuable insights to the conception and development of FrenchPress. We are grateful to colleagues who graciously allowed us to collect data in their classrooms: J. Allan, D. A. M. Barrington, M. Corner, W. Lehnert, G. Miklau, and T. Richards.

9. REFERENCES

[1] J. Bloch. *Effective Java*. The Java Series. Addison-Wesley, Second edition, 2008.

[2] FindBugs 3.0.0. *http://findbugs.sourceforge.net/*.

[3] C. A. Higgins, G. Gray, P. Symeonidis, and A. Tsintsifas. Automated assessment and experiences of teaching programming. *Journal on Educational Resources in Computing*, 5(3):5, 2005.

[4] D. Hovemeyer and W. Pugh. Finding bugs is easy. *SIGPLAN Not.*, 39(12):92–106, 2004.

[5] M. Hristova, A. Misra, M. Rutter, and R. Mercuri. Identifying and correcting Java programming errors for introductory computer science students. In *SIGCSE '03: Proceedings of the 34th SIGCSE technical symposium on Computer science education*, pages 153–156, New York, NY, 2003. ACM.

[6] M. Joy, N. Griffiths, and R. Boyatt. The BOSS online submission and assessment system. *Journal on Educational Resources in Computing*, 5(3):2, 2005.

[7] E. Murphy-Hill and A. P. Black. An interactive ambient visualization for code smells. In *Proceedings of the 5th International Symposium on Software Visualization*, SOFTVIS '10, pages 5–14, New York, NY, USA, 2010. ACM.

[8] PMD 5.2.3. *http://pmd.sourceforge.net/*.

[9] L. Qiu and C. Riesbeck. An incremental model for developing educational critiquing systems: Experiences with the Java Critiquer. *Journal of Interactive Learning Research*, 19(1):119–145, 2008.

[10] R. Singh, S. Gulwani, and A. Solar-Lezama. Automated feedback generation for introductory programming assignments. In *Proceedings of the 34th ACM SIGPLAN Conference on Programming Language Design and Implementation*, PLDI '13, pages 15–26, New York, NY, USA, 2013. ACM.

[11] N. Truong, P. Roe, and P. Bancroft. Static analysis of students' Java programs. In *ACE '04: Proceedings of the sixth conference on Australasian computing education*, pages 317–325, Darlinghurst, Australia, 2004. Australian Computer Society, Inc.

Questions on Spoken Language and Terminology for Teaching Computer Science

Ira Diethelm
Carl von Ossietzky University
Computer Science Education
Oldenburg, Germany
ira.diethelm@uni-oldenburg.de

Juliana Goschler
Carl von Ossietzky University
Institute of German Studies
Oldenburg, Germany
juliana.goschler@uni-oldenburg.de

ABSTRACT

Spoken and written language are key factors for communication, especially for teaching and learning in general and for all subjects. In K-12 schools, 'being fluent with information technology', 'CS fluency and competency', 'computer literacy' and 'computational literacy' are terms for learning objectives of ICT, computer science courses that refer to skills in CS as well as to reading and speaking. But in most cases, the term 'language' in the context of CS refers to programming languages or formal languages. This paper is neither on programming languages nor on students' knowledge or (their wrong) usage of certain terms. We would like to raise awareness for the problem area of spoken language and proper terminology for teaching and learning CS. As a first step, we provide definitions of terms and aspects of theory related to this problem domain to start a meta-discourse on spoken language for teaching CS. We present some observations from different perspectives as examples for the need of further research. We then derive a list of research questions to open the research area of 'CS classroom language', structuring it from different perspectives.

Categories and Subject Descriptors

K.3.2 [**Computer and Information Science Education**]: specified by: computer science education, computer literacy

General Terms

Theory

Keywords

terminology; CS classroom language; meta-discourse

1. INTRODUCTION

All students and teachers need a proper use of terminology and spoken or written language in class. For the subject of CS, they need specific terms to communicate about topics of

ITiCSE'15, July 6–8, 2015, Vilnius, Lithuania.
Copyright is held by the owner/author(s). Publication rights licensed to ACM.
ACM 978-1-4503-3440-2/15/07 ...$15.00.
DOI: http://dx.doi.org/10.1145/2729094.2742600.

our science in class and also outside in everyday life. Therefore it is astonishing that many curricula only marginally mention the linguistic requirements.

Although it is generally agreed that language skills in CS are very important, there is very little research about the use of terminology in CS. This is different in other domains: in natural science, many educational standards or papers about scientific or mathematical literacy address language skills in terms of talking about science. Our nearest neighbors in educational research have a long tradition of investigating the proper use of terminology in science and maths classes. They make a distinction between knowledge and language skills, and they are able to measure them separately [13].

There is a need of general language and communication skills in computer science, as stated in [1], but there seems to be little awareness of problems with the use of terminology in CS classes. Only Holmboe [11, p. 158] states that "Teachers and teacher trainers in computer science need to pay more attention to the linguistic or semiotic aspects of the subject. [...] students show a lack of *metalinguistic consciousness*. They seem to be unfamiliar with the thought that a term does not have a predefined meaning which is uniform to all users of a given natural language." We'd like to contribute to the metalinguistic consciousness in the research area of CSE and bring these aspects more into focus.

The next section provides a conceptualization of central terms belonging to this field. There we refer to several aspects of theory from the natural sciences and linguistic research. This leads to the first set of general research questions in section 3. Afterwards, we structure the problem area from several perspectives and develop more detailed questions. There, we also give some concrete examples of problems with terminology use in CS classes that we discovered in several small studies that need further investigation to approach a quite empty research area. Most of all, this paper's purpose is to be a motivation and an invitation to reflect on the linguistic influences in our research, and to apply new insights to established parts of our research area.

2. DEFINITIONS OF TERMS

First of all, when entering a more or less new domain of research, we need some definitions. According to Wittgenstein "the meaning of a word is its use in language" (PI §43, see [20, p. 126]), so for us, a term is a word that represents a certain conception of a special subject matter in the disciplinary context. All terms and their usage together form the language of a disciplinary context. A technical term then connects a word with an object in a meaningful context in a certain discipline, see [13, p. 383], in a sense of a so-called 'semiotic triangle'.

'Terminology' is the body of all terms relating to a particular discipline, e.g. electronic engineering. It is also used for the science of terms in general. The word 'terminology' is also often used synonymously with 'language' in the context of discipline-specific language. In other disciplines the terms 'discipline-specific' or 'domain-specific' language refer to the spoken language about topics in certain domains like the natural sciences, economy, or law.

But in our discipline these terms are already linked with different meanings. In CS, they refer to special (formal) languages that have been developed for special uses in particular application domains of CS and are used for human-machine communication and machine-machine communication. So the terms 'domain-specific' and 'discipline-specific language' can easily be misunderstood.

The term 'scientific language' often refers to the discipline-specific language used by scientists of a certain discipline to communicate research results and to teach at university.

'CS classroom language' could be a term that, on the one hand, focuses on the spoken or written language used by humans to communicate about CS in the context of teaching and learning CS as a subject in school, but on the other hand it is a term that is not already taken. In our conception, this kind of language is a summary of the scientific language and as well as the everyday language to communicate about CS in classrooms. Therefore, it is not only the sum of all terms of the discipline (also called lexis), but it also contains the usage of these terms in disciplinary contexts.

2.1 Classroom Discourse

The term 'classroom discourse' according to [12, p. 261] refers to "all forms of discourse that take place in the classroom. It encompasses the linguistic as well as the nonlinguistic elements of discourse. The former includes the language used by the teacher and the learners, as well as teacher-learner and learner-learner interactions. The latter includes paralinguistic gestures, prosody, and silence - all of which are integral parts of the discourse. The linguistic and non-linguistic elements constitute the observable dimension of classroom discourse."

There are two different types of classroom discourse: traditional and non-traditional lessons. According to [4] "On one hand, traditional lessons refer to the using of a three-part sequence: teacher initiation, student response, and teacher evaluation or follow-up (IRE or IRF)". Lemke describes this format as 'triadic dialogue' [16]. Non-traditional lessons, on the other hand, mean the sequence of talk in classrooms does not fit an IRE structure on account of a changed educational goal (see [4, p. 31]). In traditional lessons, teachers dominate the class discussions and their students have fewer opportunities to ask their own questions. Therefore, Lemke [16] and others advise teachers to use a less controlling type of discourse to encourage student participation to the greatest extent. For CS classes it should be investigated to what extent these types of classroom discourses occur or if there are more and different types of classroom discourses.

2.2 Language and Learning

In educational contexts, ee take it as given that learning in a constructivistic sense by conceptional growth and concep-

tional change is linked strongly to terms and their conceptualizations. Many researchers have written on the relationship between language and learning. According to Driver et al. knowledge and understandings "are constructed when individuals engage socially in talk and activity about shared problems or tasks. Making meaning is thus a dialogic process involving persons-in-conversation, and learning is seen as the process by which individuals are introduced to a culture by more skilled members" [24, p. 654].

Thus, the term 'language' is difficult to use when talking about CS in class. As computer scientists, our internalization of this term usually refers to 'programming language' and not to spoken language because we are not used to it.

Starting from Piaget and Bruner, Vygotsky [21] and others recognized a relationship between learning a science and learning a language and emphasized the social function of language in learning processes. Rincke [19] summarizes this sociocultural perspective on learning: "language plays a key role when students are introduced into new ways of thinking and talking about the world. In this view, the process of internalizing new ideas or new languages originates in the social plane. Individuals construct their meaning with respect to the social language which they experience in the given situation." It is necessary to distinguish between the development of spontaneous concepts (i.e. children learning everyday language) and scientific concepts (i.e. institutionalized or specialized language). Learning and teaching therefore depend on social interaction, and this certainly involves 'face-to-face interaction mediated by speech' in classrooms. Speech plays a critical role in children's learning and in the processes of assistance and teaching.

2.3 Socio-cultural view in CS

For the research area of CS education, Tennenberg and Knobelsdorf describe in [23] the sociocultural cognition theory as a summary of theories that "view minds as cultural products, biologically evolved to be extended by tools, social interaction and embodied interaction in the world." They also refer to Vygotsky and others, but they only mention tools and programming languages, but do not mention any relation between spoken language and learning in classrooms.

Also, Murphy et al. [17] and Corney et al. [5] who investigated the "ability to 'Explain in Plain English'" do not draw connections between their research and linguistic aspects of these explanations or the terminology used for it. Both groups of authors conclude that non-programming activities like code-reading and explaining code correlate or even support code-writing and recommend a mix of code-writing and code-reading (which implicates the process of explanation and discussion of the meaning of that piece of code). Their findings can also be explained with the sociocultural perspective on learning and language use in class.

However, a relationship between language and social context corresponds with the common constructivistic view on learning in CS education. But in linguistics and educational sciences, there is also a debate if this relationship between thought and language concepts exists at all, and if it does, what comes first.

2.4 Ambiguity and Metaphors in CS

Ambiguity is a big problem in computer science education. The terminology of CS consists of many so-called 'dead metaphors' that are not noticed anymore by computer scientists. They are 'lived by' [15].Just take the following examples: 'packet', 'string', 'protocol', 'cloud', 'stack', even 'program' and 'model'. They all are ambiguous terms; they all have one meaning in everyday life and a different one in CS. They are not metaphors anymore; they are the scientific terms. Their meaning depends on the person who uses these terms and on the context.

The use of metaphors in CS was the subject of Busch's PhD-thesis [3], which provided a detailed and comprehensive insight into the metaphors of CS in general and for teaching CS as well. There he suggests three steps for using metaphors for teaching CS [p. 125]:

1. Clarification of the meaning of the term in other non-CS contexts

2. Speculation about possible meanings of that term in CS, and also about what it would certainly not mean

3. Development of the CS-related meaning of the term.

2.5 Meta-discourse

A way to handle problems with terminology explicitly in class is the teaching method of using a 'meta-discourse' whose "aim was to engage students in a discussion about language including syntactic and semantic features of informal everyday talk and of formal scientific use" [19]. It was described in detail by Lemke and is influenced by Mortimer and Scott [19], who distinguish two social languages used in the classroom: the 'scientific language' and 'spontaneous everyday language' [16]. For concerns of immigrants in school, Gogolin and Lange suggest in [10] to distinguish not only between 'everyday language' and 'scientific language', but also 'educational language'.

Brown and Ryoo [2] see "language as symbolic of cultural affiliation", and discuss "how being faced with detailed scientific language can impact students' opportunities to learn". They propose "viewing science teaching and learning from a position that understands that science teaching, if taught without respect to language learning, may promote issues of cultural conflict for minority students and limit students' conceptual understanding". This is an important point in light of the recent discussion about heterogeneous classes and inclusive teaching of pupils with special needs in regular schools. And it is also important for teaching students who have different mother tongues (such as immigrants) and who therefore have to use a second language in class [10]. For them, a 'meta-discourse' to clarify the meanings and usage of terms in class is even more important.

3. GENERAL QUESTIONS

By now, with these definitions and this review of literature, some general research questions already arise about teaching computer science in schools (see also [8]):

1. What terms are used to communicate about content, concepts and facts of CS in respect to certain topics and certain target groups of learners? What is the overall lexis for teaching CS and how can it be structured?

2. How do CS teachers and their students use these terms when speaking and writing about a certain CS concept and how does their terminology and language differ?

3. What is a suitable set of terms and definitions for CS teaching for introducing and applying a certain concept in CS classes?

4. How can classroom discourses be structured to support CS learning?

These questions map four main aspects of language in class: the terms (1.), their usage (2.), recommendations for terms (3.), and recommendations for their usage (4.).

These questions also address several different perceptions and point to possible different conceptions of the content structure of our discipline in educational contexts.

When we ask questions about terms from Computer Science and their usage in class we realize that we cannot answer them without knowing the perspective: Who talks? Who uses the term? And in what context? Who is listening? What's written in the scientific books and in textbooks? And what terms are used how in the curriculum? Who else uses these terms in other related contexts?

The next sections will take a closer look into the general questions from different perspectives: the scientific perspective, the classroom perspective, and the curriculum perspective.

4. SCIENTIFIC PERSPECTIVE

A first step into this perspective is the clarification of science content, the terms, definitions, and their usage in scientific contexts. In many cases, this is the basis for the concepts of CS that are taught in school for a given topic. This means that the following questions have to be answered:

1. Which CS principles and concepts are related to this topic?

2. Which genesis, function and different meaning do the related scientific terms in different scientific contexts have, and in what context do they occur here?

3. Which terms are used in scientific publications and textbooks and which of them could hinder or support learning due to the narrow meaning of the word or parts of it?

4. What kind of metaphors are involved in this part of CS and which of them are ambiguous or dead metaphors?

For the natural sciences, Slisko and Dykstra [22] pointed out the question whether or not there exists a precise scientific terminology that is ready to use or if the meaning for terms is varied and always has to be negotiated. They agree with the second opinion and illustrate that there is no agreement on the meaning of central terms among scientists and between texts. They show that terms are used inconsistently and they connect this finding with teacher education. They see two problems: "(1) one of relying on the notion of a standard interpretation of terms and concepts and (2) the other of whether or not one can actually tell students what they should know in such a way that they can actually understand."

For CS, this means investigating not only CS lessons but also scientific texts and textbooks for university classes and for primary and secondary schools as well. To support CS at school, we should discuss the usage of special terms for special purposes in school. We should conduct research on suitable and unsuitable scientific terms, their different meanings and metaphors in books and also in other publications.

4.1 Example: 'Algorithm' in Textbooks

In a first small survey, we found varying definitions for the term 'algorithm' in CS textbooks for secondary schools. We discovered that there are no clear definitions given for parts of the terminology. Very often, terms are only explained in context without a clear definition for general use. Just to get an idea of the problem, here we show two brief examples for 'algorithm' (translated from German) from two German textbooks for secondary schools:

From a textbook for grade 9/10:

> An algorithm is a process instruction consisting of a finite sequence of unambiguous executable instructions. If the conditions are equal, executing an algorithm will always produce equal results.

From a second textbook for grade 6/7:

> For a robot to follow some instructions you have to
> - use the elementary instructions that he knows
> - tell him clearly and unambiguously what to do
> - and in what order he has to do it
> - give instructions he can execute
> - give complete instructions only
>
> Sequences of instructions meeting these conditions are called algorithms. An algorithm is a finite sequence of elementary, unambiguous and executable instructions.

These two definitions vary a lot from the definitions you may find in scientific textbooks for students at the university level or even the one from Wikipedia (which many pupils and teachers use to approach a new topic). The reasons for these differences may be reasonable with respect to the different ages of the target group. But nevertheless with this small example it becomes noticeable that much research on the descriptions and terms used in textbooks for secondary schools is needed. This kind of research should lead to recommendations for writing CS textbooks as well.

5. CLASSROOM PERSPECTIVE

In classrooms, the acting persons are teachers and students. Thus, from a constructivistic point of view, teachers and students also have to negotiate the meaning of terms.

From a linguistic perspective, this not only means looking at the teacher but also observing and respecting the terms students use in class and providing opportunities to develop their everyday language as well as their scientific language.

The investigation of the four general questions from section 3 from the students' perspectives means answering the questions not only for the average student but also for students of both gender and with very different backgrounds:

1. How do the learners experience the given topic in everyday life or in class? How do they talk in everyday language about it? And what terms do they use for it?

2. Which scientific concepts and terms do the students use to explain related phenomena?

3. What conceptions do they have already for the terms that are used by scientists to explain it and especially for those that the teacher plans to use in class?

5.1 Teacher's Perspective and Lesson Design

Another very important factor in CS education is teacher education. As CS is not a compulsory subject in many countries and CS education in school does not have a long tradition, the educational backgrounds and self-conceptions of the CS teachers might be very different [18]. Some of them might have a specific degree in CS (M.Sc.), others might have a specific teachers' degree (M.Ed.) that includes courses in pedagogy and psychology. But even for teachers with a background in pedagogy and psychology, instruction and reflection on topics like language, language use and language varieties, bi- and multilingualism are rare or nonexistent in their studies.

"Consequently, the teachers will differ substantially regarding their subject domain knowledge, their pedagogical knowledge and their pedagogical content knowledge. Therefore they might work on very different abstraction levels or apply very different teaching methods for the same topic of the curriculum" [9]. And they will use different terms to teach these concepts. Thus, from this point of view, the teachers' perspectives on a certain topic, including their usage of terminology and conceptions of each term have to be taken into account very closely.

The teacher's perspective can be seen as a key factor for the design of lessons as well as for educational research. This means answering the following questions:

1. What conceptions do the teachers have regarding lesson design and teaching CS in general? What kind of classroom discourse do they prefer?

2. What conceptions do they think their students might have to explain a given concept? And what terms do they expect the students to use?

3. What terms do teachers use to explain a certain phenomenon and the related concept of CS?

4. What is their conception of the terms that are used for this in scientific literature or textbooks?

To investigate these questions in more detail according to a 'CS classroom language' it would be very interesting to analyze lesson designs according to this next set of questions:

1. Who uses what terms in what meaning at what point in the lesson?

2. How does the conceptualization of a certain term take place?

3. How does the meaning of a term shift from one year to another in a sense of a spiral curriculum?

5.2 Example: Course Keywords

In a small survey we asked teachers to name five keywords they would choose to tag their CS course (fig. 1 left). And we asked the same teachers for five keywords their students would use to tag the same course (fig. 1 right). We did not ask the students but only the teachers for the different perspectives. For each of both sets of answers (N=64) we created a tag cloud using the usual algorithm and the tool 'R' to visualize the relative prominence of each keyword.

When comparing these tag clouds, a few things become obvious: First, teachers and students would use different keywords to tag the same course. Second, the teachers are aware of this difference.

We also asked the same teachers if they see any problems with terminology in their classes. There were a few answers

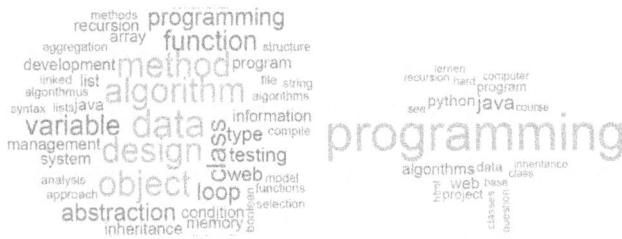

Figure 1: Teacher's and Students' keywords

where teachers' and students' keywords varied a lot and the same teacher stated that he or she does not perceive any problems with terminology. Some also made statements like: "I thought there wouldn't be any, but now that you ask I perceive some."

It would be very interesting to compare these tag clouds with those of their students. And sure, it is necessary to investigate the meaning of the listed terms and what teachers and students mean when they use words like 'programming'.

5.3 Students' View

Last but not least, we will have to take a closer look at all papers ever written on students' perceptions, conceptions and misconceptions. We cannot go into detail here, as that would require another paper. But for every paper we'll have to ask about what terms are used, what is *said*, and what is *meant*. How and in what context have these misconceptions been discovered? Who judged whether the statements of students were 'wrong' or 'right' and what is the conception of him or her regarding a special term? And are the categorizations made reliable and repeatable? Are students' statements really wrong or do they only describe the same concept in other words? Then, aren't they rather a good occasion for a fruitful classroom discussion?

6. CURRICULUM PERSPECTIVE

In this section we would like to give several examples from this problem domain from the perspective of the social demand on a CS concept or learning objective. We have to think about some viewpoints of stakeholders giving different answers to the question *why* this part of CS or this topic or special example should be taught in school and *how*. We should reflect on these points of view as well and take them into account when investigating CS terms and the use of a 'CS classroom language'.

For all papers that contain policies and requirements of CS in school we additionally could question the language and terms used:

1. What terms are used to make statements about CS at school, about its rationale, its content, concepts and facts? And how are these terms related in these documents?

2. How do these terms influence CS teachers and their lessons, e.g. through nation wide written tests?

3. What statements are made about CS terminology?

4. What kind of recommendations do these documents give for CS classroom language explicitly or implicitly?

6.1 Computational Thinking

'Computational thinking' appears to be one of the accepted goals of CS courses in general. Wing defined it as "a kind of analytical thinking, and it shares with mathematical thinking for problem solving, with engineering for modeling and design constrained by the real world, and with scientific thinking for understanding computability, intelligence, the minds and human behavior. The essence of computational thinking is abstraction that can be automated, which is what computing is about." [25]. Hu discusses in [14] many different meanings of this term but no definition we found refers to the expression of this kind of thinking in terms of a perceivable classroom discourse.

The "operational definition of computational thinking" of the CSTA [6] lists the following supporting skills of computational thinking that are connected to language in class:

Formulating problems in a way that enables us to use a computer and other tools to help solve them
The ability to communicate and work with others to achieve a common goal or solution

So, further research is needed to define these skills in detail and to find out how a classroom discourse should be structured to support computational thinking. Computational thinking also should lead to 'computational classroom discussions'. Lessons that aim at computational thinking should be investigated according to the four questions above and from section 3 as well.

6.2 CS Curricula

As an example for CS curricula, the CSTA curriculum from 2003 formulates the social demand of communicating *about* IT as follows: Students at grade 2 will

communicate about technology using developmentally appropriate and accurate terminology

This is the one and only competency in the CSTA curriculum that refers directly to terminology to speak *about* CS. The demand to communicate *with the use* of information technology can be found in that document several times.

The new computing curriculum from the UK [7] does not refer to terminology or spoken language directly but lists a few competencies that require them: Students should be able to

understand and explain the quantitative dimensions of a problem
describe how internet search engines find and store data
[are] able to explain how [a procedure] works and how to test it
explain how instructions are stored and executed within a computer system
explain how data of various types can be represented and manipulated in the form of binary digits including numbers, text, sounds and pictures

These two curricula show that a classroom discourse *about* CS is far out of focus. But if we want to achieve goals like 'computational thinking' we definitely should pay much more respect to the usage of human language in class. The German Curriculum of the GI even contains two separate parts explicitly for communicational competencies ('communicate and cooperate' and 'reason and evaluate'). There are many direct and indirect references to terminology in other parts of the curriculum as well.It would be interesting to find out how teachers handle these requirements of the use of a 'CS classroom language' and how they grade these competencies, if they do.

7. CONCLUSION

In each section of this paper we tried to point out the importance of human language for learning and teaching computer science. We gave definitions and summaries of related theories. And most of all we showed what has been omitted in CS education research and showed some starting examples to fill the gap. There is much work to be done in the next years, but we feel confident that this kind of research has potential to support the classroom discourse as well as the scientific discourse. It can help to solve some open problems and see existing solutions from a different angle, e.g the discussions about programming languages in class and about misconceptions.

All questions stated in this paper get a new dimension in the case of all kinds of minority students: non-native speakers or in the case of inclusive teaching of disabled students. How do *they* describe the meanings in *their* everyday language, what terms do *they* use, and what differences in grammar do they use? Teachers should be aware of the obstacles they create with spoken scientific language in CS classes and even more of the problems they can cause by inconsistent use of terms.

In the case of CS as a compulsory subject, we should not only focus on the fun and benefit our subject brings to the schools, but we should also reflect on the pain it can cause for those that are not 'digital natives' and cannot 'speak CS fluently'.

There is much work to do and many investigations to conduct. This paper provides the first steps into a research area that has been out of focus for too long.

8. REFERENCES

[1] T. Beaubouef. Why computer science students need language. *Reviewed Papers inroads - The SIGCSE Bulletin*, 35(4):51–54, 2003.

[2] B. A. Brown and K. Ryoo. Teaching science as a language: A 'content-first' approach to science teaching. *Journal of Research in Science Teaching*, 45(5):529—553, 2008.

[3] C. Busch. *Metaphern in der Informatik. Modellbildung - Formalisierung - Anwendung*. Deutscher Universitäts-Verlag, Wiesbaden, 1998.

[4] C. B. Cazden. *Classroom discourse: the language of teaching and learning*. Heinemann, Portsmouth, NH, 2nd edition, 2001.

[5] M. Corney, S. Fitzgerald, B. Hanks, R. Lister, R. McCauley, and L. Murphy. 'explain in plain english' questions revisited: Data structures problems. In *Proceedings of the 45th SIGCSE*, pages 591–596. ACM, 2014.

[6] CSTA. Operational definition of computational thinking for K-12 education, 2011.

[7] Department of Education UK. Computing programmes of study for key stages 1 - 4, 2013.

[8] I. Diethelm and J. Goschler. On human language and terminology used for teaching and learning CS/ Informatics. In *Proceedings of the 9th WiPCSE*, pages 122–123. ACM, 2014.

[9] I. Diethelm, P. Hubwieser, and R. Klaus. Students, teachers and phenomena: Educational reconstruction for computer science education. In R. McCartney and M.-J. Laakso, editors, *12th Koli Calling conference on computing education research*, Tahko, 2012.

[10] I. Gogolin and I. Lange. Bildungssprache und Durchgängige Sprachbildung. In S. Fürstenau and M. Gomolla, editors, *Migration und schulischer Wandel: Mehrsprachigkeit*, pages 263–280. VS-Verlag, Wiesbaden, 2011.

[11] C. Holmboe. Conceptualization and labelling as cognitive challenges for students of data modelling. *Computer Science Education*, 15(2):143–161, 2005.

[12] N. H. Hornberger, editor. *Encyclopedia of Language and Education, Volume 6: Knowledge about Language*. Springer US, Boston, MA, 2008.

[13] H. Härtig, C. Pehlke, H. E. Fischer, and A. Schmeck. Sind Fachsprache und Fachwissen bezogen auf Physik unterscheidbar? *Zeitschrift für Didaktik der Naturwissenschaften*, 18:381—390, 2012.

[14] C. Hu. Computational thinking: what it might mean and what we might do about it. In *Proceedings of the 16th ITiCSE*, pages 223–227. ACM, 2011.

[15] G. Lakoff and M. Johnson. *Metaphors we live by*. University of Chicago Press, Chicago, 2003.

[16] J. Lemke. *Talking Science: Language, Learning, and Values*. Language and Classroom Processes. Ablex Publishing Corporation, 1990.

[17] L. Murphy, S. Fitzgerald, R. Lister, and R. McCauley. Ability to 'explain in plain english' linked to proficiency in computer-based programming. In *Proceedings of the 9th ICER*, pages 111–118. ACM, 2012.

[18] L. Ni and M. Guzdial. Who AM I?: understanding high school computer science teachers' professional identity. In *Proceedings of the 43rd SIGCSE*, pages 499–504. ACM, 2012.

[19] K. Rincke. It's rather like learning a language: Development of talk and conceptual understanding in mechanics lessons. *International Journal of Science Education*, 33(2):229–258, 2011.

[20] J. Schulte. *Wittgenstein: an introduction*. SUNY series in logic and language. State University of New York Press, Albany, N.Y, 1992.

[21] P. Scott. Teacher talk and meaning making in science classrooms: a vygotskian analysis and review. *Studies in Science Education*, 32:45–80, 1998.

[22] J. Slisko and D. I. Dykstra. The role of scientific terminology in research and teaching: Is something important missing? *Journal of Research in Science Teaching*, 34(6):655–660, 1997.

[23] J. Tenenberg and M. Knobelsdorf. Out of our minds: a review of sociocultural cognition theory. *Computer Science Education*, 24(1):1–24, Jan. 2014.

[24] S. Vosniadou. *International Handbook of Research on Conceptual Change*. Educational Psychology Handbook. Taylor & Francis, 2010.

[25] J. M. Wing. Computational thinking and thinking about computing. *Philosophical Transactions of the Royal Society A: Mathematical, Physical and Engineering Sciences*, 366(1881):3717–3725, Oct. 2008.

How Challenging are Bebras Tasks? An IRT analysis based on the performance of Italian students

Carlo Bellettini
Dept. of Computer Science
Università degli Studi di Milano
Milan, Italy
bellettini@di.unimi.it

Violetta Lonati
Dept. of Computer Science
Università degli Studi di Milano
Milan, Italy
lonati@di.unimi.it

Dario Malchiodi
Dept. of Computer Science
Università degli Studi di Milano
Milan, Italy
malchiodi@di.unimi.it

Mattia Monga
Dept. of Computer Science
Università degli Studi di Milano
Milan, Italy
monga@di.unimi.it

Anna Morpurgo
Dept. of Computer Science
Università degli Studi di Milano
Milan, Italy
morpurgo@di.unimi.it

Mauro Torelli
Dept. of Computer Science
Università degli Studi di Milano
Milan, Italy
torelli@di.unimi.it

ABSTRACT

This paper analyses the results of the 2014 edition of the Italian Bebras/Kangourou contest, exploiting the Item Response Theory statistical methodology in order to infer the difficulty of each of the proposed tasks starting from the scores attained by the participants. Such kind of analysis, enabling the organizers of the contest to check whether or not the difficulty perceived by pupils was substantially different from that estimated by those who proposed the tasks, is important as a feedback in order to gain knowledge to be used both in ranking participants and in organizing future editions of the contest. We show how the proposed analysis essentially highlights that the 63% of tasks was perceived at the same level of difficulty estimated by those who proposed them, but a 37% of tasks were either easier or more difficult than expected.

Categories and Subject Descriptors

K.3.2 [**Computers and Education**]: Computer and Information Science Education—*Computer Science Education*

Keywords

informatics and education, learning contests, Bebras, Kangourou of Informatics

1. INTRODUCTION

Several contests focusing on the informatics discipline[1] have been organized worldwide in the last decades. Such

---

[1]We choose the term *informatics* to denote the field elsewhere named computing, computer science, and so on.

ITiCSE'15 July 04–08, 2015 Vilnius, Lithuania
Copyright 2015 ACM 978-1-4503-3440-2/15/07 ...$15.00
DOI: http://dx.doi.org/10.1145/2729094.2742603

events, typically arranged on a regular basis, mainly result from two attitudes of mind: one focused in selecting students particularly talented in the field (this attitude is notably reflected in the Informatics Olympiads), and another one aimed at spreading the basic concepts of the discipline to a vast audience of students, starting from the belief that such concepts should be taught even in the first stages of the educational system. Within this second vein, the Bebras contest [1, 7] is a competition organized on an annual basis in several countries since 2004, with an average number of participants higher than half a million in the recent editions.

The core of the Bebras contest organization is an annual international workshop gathering participants from all the involved countries, with the aim of proposing and jointly tuning an ample set of tasks. From such pool each country chooses a number of tasks to set up the local competition. Tasks are divided into six areas (such as algorithms, data structures, and so on) and their difficulty level is scored in the scale (easy, medium, hard), with the idea of proposing in each contest a suitable mix of tasks having different difficulty and belonging to different areas of informatics. Students are given a fixed amount of time to solve tasks, either choosing an answer from a set of four alternatives, or using an interactive interface based for instance on dragging and dropping items. Bebras questions should be small and moderately challenging tasks that enable an entertaining learning experience. The criteria for good tasks have been surveyed in [2], thus they well deserve a new name, *tasklets*: in general they should be fun and attractive, independent of specific curricular activities, be adequate for contestants' age and the solution should take on average three minutes.

A correct assessment of the task difficulty is particularly important, as even partial failure in this job can result in a non-heterogeneous set of tasks proposed to pupils, with the effect of letting participants perceive the contest as too difficult or too easy, and ultimately not appealing. However, evaluating the difficulty of a task is actually not easy. Thus, after the conclusion of the competition it is advisable to infer the perceived task difficulty starting from the participants' performance (see also [3, 13]), in order to tune choices and strategies in the next competitions.

This paper shows the results of such an analysis on the

scores of the 2014 edition of the Italian competition, relying on the statistical techniques in the domain of Item Response Theory (IRT) [8, 4]. IRT is routinely used to evaluate massive educational assessment studies like OECD's PISA (Programme for International Student Assessment), and [9] used it to find psychometric constructs common to a set of tasklets of the German 2009 Bebras.

The paper is organized as follows: Sect. 2 illustrates the specific features of the Italian Bebras/Kangourou and the data collected in the 2014 contest; Sect. 3 describes our approach to IRT in order to model and measure the difficulty of the Bebras tasks; Sect. 4 shows and discusses the results of our analysis; finally, Sect. 5 draws some concluding remarks and outlines further refinements of the work.

2. DATA FROM BEBRAS/KANGOUROU

In Italy the competition is jointly organized with the Kangourou community [10] since 2013. In the 2014 edition, 684 teams (2736 pupils) participated in the contest, divided into four age groups: *Benjamin* (grades 6–7, ages 11–12), *Cadet* (grades 8–9, ages 13–14), *Junior* (grades 10–11, ages 15–16) and *Student* (grades 12–13, ages 17–18)[2]. Table 2 summarizes the composition and performances of the participating teams, detailed according to the corresponding age group.

In this paper we report some data about the quizzes of the last edition[3]: the name of the tasklets in Table 4 are the Bebras identifiers (with three extra quizzes), a + at the end of the name indicates that the quiz was proposed as an open question, a * that the question was significantly changed with respect to the Bebras one which inspired it. The Italian version of the contest contained 16 or 17 tasks for each age group with a time limit of 45 minutes (2700 seconds).

Compared to the international Bebras, the Kangourou flavour has a significant difference: it is a competition among teams of four pupils. In 2013 we realized that proposing exactly the same (translated from English) quizzes resulted in a too easy contest because the four team members can work in parallel and exploit a coordinate effort. This "team aspect" is in our opinion something valuable that we decided to preserve even after we joined the Bebras community. In the last two editions we thus changed the tasklets slightly with respect to the ones proposed to the international Bebras contestants, mostly by transforming multiple choice questions in open or interactive ones. In the latter case, partial scores are in general admitted, since the chance to make some minor mistakes may be relevant. In this analysis, answers with partial score are considered incorrect.

Since a lot of work is needed to organize and implement the contest (although tasklet delivery is computer based), a tasklet is usually proposed to more than one category, with different difficulty: for example, (see Table 4) `2014-CA-07` was used for both Benjamins and Cadets, and considered of medium difficulty for the younger contestants and easy for the older ones. In the analysis, such tasklets are repeatedly

---

[2]The equivalence between groups and grades/ages slightly changes from country to country. Moreover, some countries also consider the *Mini* age group (grades 3–4, ages 8–10).

[3]All the Italian tasklets are available to any visitor at `http://test.kangourou.it`. Although each quiz has a flag of the country of origin, the mapping between the Italian name and the Bebras id might not be evident. Please contact the authors if you need to connect the two terminologies.

considered, since the results by a category of contestants on a task are independent from the results by another category.

3. AN IRT MODEL FOR THE CONTEST

"Le mérite en toutes choses est dans la difficulté" [4] says Aramis in the *Three Musketeers*, Dumas' masterpiece. But how to survey the difficulty of a Bebras tasklet? A rough measure is the analysis of the results ([13, 3]): the rate of wrong answers is certainly correlated to the difficulty of a quiz. However what was difficult for some, could result easy for someone else: in other words, just taking into account the wrong answers is not enough, because it could happen that the sample of students to which the tasklet was proposed was biased towards excellence or mediocrity. Thus, we tried to measure the difficulty with a more sophisticated model. To this end, we resorted to IRT [8], a well established psychometrics approach to evaluate tests (as a set of quiz *items*) in which several parameters are taken into account: the difficulty of a quiz, but also the *ability* of the solver. In fact, we adopted a model in which we consider the ability θ of a team and the probability p to answer correctly a quiz as a function of θ. The function associated to each tasklet is a sigmoid characterized by three parameters:

$$p(\theta) = \eta + \frac{(1 - \eta)}{1 + e^{-\alpha \cdot (\theta - \delta)}} . \qquad (1)$$

In function (1) the parameter η gives the minimum probability to guess the answer correctly even when the ability is very low: this is indeed the case of multiple choice questions, in which there is always the possibility to correctly guess when giving a random answer. The parameter δ models the *difficulty*: when η is zero, the probability will be > 0.5 only if the ability of a team is greater of the item difficulty. The last parameter, α, gives a measure of how a small change in the ability is reflected by a change in the probability: it represents the *discrimination* of a question.

The pictures in Figure 1 show the Item-Response curves for the same tasklet proposed to different categories. The value of δ moves the curve on the horizontal axis: the quiz resulted more difficult for the Benjamins (it needed an ability > 0.39 to have positive odds), the other categories have a decreasing δ. The discrimination α changes less and resulted higher for Students. The value of η reflects a multiple choice question with four alternatives (it is not exactly 0.25 since it is the product of stochastic fitting, see Sect. 4). The dotted lines use a fixed $\eta = 0$ to show how the curve would change if a multiple choice quiz would be changed to an open one.

We aimed at fitting this IRT model with the data collected during the Kangourou contest, that is 11483 quizzes, given by 684 teams. We designed a hierarchical statistical model following [6] and our regression analysis adopted a Bayesian approach: the data are fitted with respect to a probability model of all the unknown parameters and this model is then simulated and sampled with a Markov Chain Monte Carlo (MCMC) algorithm [5], in order to get the posterior prob-

---

[4]*"The merit of all things lies in their difficulty."*: Aramis refers to his new activity of writing a poem in verses of one syllable. *"Add to the merit of the difficulty that of the brevity, and you are sure that your poem will at least have two merits."*, notes d'Artagnan: Bebras tasklets share some merits with Aramis' poem!

Age group	Teams	Students	Tasks	Tot. score	Max.	Min.	Avg.	Std.	Avg. time (s)
Benjamin	145	580	16	62	49	11	25.70	8.23	2620
Cadet	207	828	17	68	57	4	29.30	10.45	2661
Junior	181	724	17	68	62	8	25.70	9.04	2689
Student	151	604	17	68	56,5	8	26.39	11.70	2694

Table 1: **A synthesis of the students' performance in the 2014 edition of the Italian Bebras contest. The columns "Tot. score", "Max.", "Min.", "Avg.", and "Std." report respectively the maximum attainable score, the actual maximum and minimum ones, and the average and standard deviation of scores. Finally, the column "Avg. time" shows the average time (out of 45 minutes) used by teams, measured in seconds.**

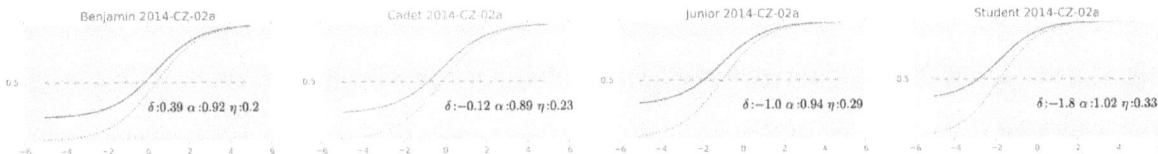

Figure 1: **Item-Response curves of the same tasklet proposed to different categories.**

ability distributions of latent variables conditioned on the observed data.

Let T and Q be the set of teams and quizzes, and denote by i and j an item in T and Q, respectively. Each (observed) answer y_n is modeled with a random variable drawn from a Bernoulli distribution with parameter p_n dependent on δ_j, η_j, α_j and computed according to (1):

$$y_n \sim \mathrm{Ber}(p_n) \quad 1 \leq n \leq 11483.$$

The model needs also the *a priori* distributions of the parameters, for $j \in Q$ and $i \in T$:

$$\theta_i \sim N(0, s_\theta), \qquad \delta_j \sim N(m_{\delta_j}, s_\delta),$$
$$\log(\alpha_j) \sim N(0, s_\alpha), \qquad \eta_j \sim \mathrm{Beta}(1, c_j),$$

where N and Beta denote respectively the Gaussian and Beta distribution, and c_j is the number of choices for the multiple choice question j or 1000 if the question is an "open" one. We did not want to make strong assumptions about the hyper-parameters of normal distributions: we used 0 as a reference point of ability, and 1 as a reference point of discrimination and we fixed their means accordingly. The variances, however, are again modeled with weakly informative distributions[5]: $s_\theta \sim \mathrm{Cauchy}(0, 5)$, $s_\delta \sim \mathrm{Cauchy}(0, 5)$, and $s_\alpha \sim \mathrm{Cauchy}(0, 5)$, where Cauchy denotes the Cauchy distribution. Instead, the prior distribution of the mean of δ is chosen according to the estimation of the difficulty given by the authors of the tasklet.

$$m_{\delta_j} \sim \begin{cases} \mathrm{Cauchy}(-1, .5) & \text{if } j \text{ marked as easy}, \\ \mathrm{Cauchy}(0, .5) & \text{if } j \text{ marked as medium}, \\ \mathrm{Cauchy}(1, .5) & \text{if } j \text{ marked as hard}. \end{cases}$$

3.1 Model implementation

We implemented the model with Stan [11], a probabilistic programming language for Bayesian statistical inference. The main parts of the program are in Listings 1 and 2: it is virtually a transposition with Stan syntax of the statistical model described above. However, we used a couple of

---

[5]The choice of a Cauchy distribution is suggested in [12, 6] as a good default for regression coefficients which can concentrate their mass around their median, but have tails that are so fat that the variance is infinite.

```
data { // observed data
  /* ... */
  int<lower=0,upper=1> y[N]; // results
  int<lower=1,upper=T> ii[N]; // team for y[n]
  int<lower=1,upper=Q> jj[N]; // quiz for y[n]
  real<lower=-1, upper=1> m_step[Q];
  // wrong answers for multiple choices
  real<lower=0> c[Q];
}
parameters { // latent parameters
  vector[T] theta_raw;    // ability
  vector[Q] delta_raw;    // difficulty
  vector[Q] alpha_raw;    // discrimination
  real<lower=0, upper=1> eta[Q]; // guessing

  real<lower=0, upper=pi()/2> s_theta_unif;
  real<lower=0, upper=pi()/2> s_delta_unif;
  real<lower=0, upper=pi()/2> s_alpha_unif;
  real<lower=-pi()/2, upper=pi()/2> m_delta_unif[Q];
}
transformed parameters { // computed from parms and data
  vector[T] theta;    // ability
  vector[Q] delta;    // difficulty
  vector[Q] alpha;    // discrimination
  real<lower=0> s_theta;
  real<lower=0> s_delta;
  real<lower=0> s_alpha;
  vector[Q] m_delta;

  // reparameterization (see Stan manual, chapter 19)
  // faster than s_theta ~ cauchy(0, 5);
  s_theta <- 5*tan(s_theta_unif);
  s_delta <- 5*tan(s_delta_unif);
  s_alpha <- 5*tan(s_alpha_unif);

  // faster than theta ~ normal(0, s_theta);
  theta <- s_theta * theta_raw;
  alpha <- s_alpha * alpha_raw;

  for (j in 1:Q) {
    // faster than m_delta ~ cauchy(m_step, .5);
    m_delta[j] <- m_step[j] + 0.5 * tan(m_delta_unif[j]);
    // faster than delta ~ normal(m_delta, s_delta);
    delta[j] <- m_delta[j] + s_delta * delta_raw[j];
}}
```

Listing 1: **Stan program (minor parts omitted) implementing our model of task difficulty: data and parameters.**

```
model { // statistical model
 vector[N] p;

 for (n in 1:N) {
  p[n] <- eta[jj[n]] + (1 - eta[jj[n]]) *
   inv_logit(exp(alpha[jj[n]]) *
            (theta[ii[n]] - delta[jj[n]]));
 }

 theta_raw ~ normal(0, 1);
 alpha_raw ~ normal(0, 1);
 delta_raw ~ normal(0, 1);
 eta ~ beta(1, c);
 y ~ bernoulli(p);
}

generated quantities {
 // other interesting posterior values
  vector[Q] diff;
  vector[K] m_thetas;
  /* ... */
}
```

Listing 2: Stan program (minor parts omitted) implementing our model of task difficulty: model and generated quantities.

reparameterizations of Cauchy and Gaussian distributions, as suggested in Ch. 9 of [12]: this reduced the computation time from about 25 hours to 3, for a session with 40000 iterations[6].

4. RESULTS

Running a Stan program produces a sequence of samples for all the modeled parameters and the other generated quantities. The theory behind MCMC algorithms guarantees that, as the number of iterations approaches infinity, the samples are derived from the true posterior distributions of interest. No universal threshold to convergence exists across all problems: for convergence diagnostics Stan provides the Gelman-Rubin statistic $\hat{R}$. The basic idea is to use multiple independent chains to check for lack of convergence, assuming that if they have converged, by definition they should appear very similar to one another; at convergence $\hat{R} = 1$. We obtained stable results (that is, $\hat{R} = 1$ for all parameters in our model) with four chains with 10000 iterations each. The first 5000 samples were used for warming up the algorithm, and the remaining samples were thinned discarding every second one. In total we got 10000 samples that we used to draw the posterior distribution of the parameters. Stan also provides a measure of the "effective sample size" (*i.e.*, the number N_{eff} of independent samples with the same estimation power as the N autocorrelated sample) for each parameter: this can be used to estimate the *standard error* as *standard deviation*/$\sqrt{N_{eff}}$.

The parameter we wanted to estimate is the difference between the average ability $\bar{\theta}_k$ of a category and the difficulty δ_j of a tasklet. The samples resulting from the Stan model give the posterior distribution of all the θ and δ: as a generated quantity we also computed the distribution of the difference between the average θ for each category and the δ of a tasklet (see Figure 2). When the difficulty of a quiz is approximately similar to the ability of a category, we should get a mean close to 0. A negative mean indicates a difficult quiz (on average, ability was less than difficulty), and a positive mean an easy one. The values of the differences are collected in Table 4. We fitted two slightly different models: a "big" one in which we considered a θ for each team

(thus $\bar{\theta}$ is the average across all the teams of a category), and a "small" one in which all the teams of a category were aggregated (thus the observed answer of a tasklet has the multiplicity of the number of teams in a given category). We classified a tasklet as hard or easy when the absolute value of the difference was greater than 0.5. As Table 4 shows, the results of the classification are highly consistent in the two models; in 14 cases out of 67, however, they differ: the data do not support clearly the same classification in the two models. Interestingly, in 25 cases out of 67 (37%), the classification does not correspond to the authors' one: as remarked in Sect. 1 and also shown by previous research [3, 13] it is not easy to estimate the difficulty upfront.

4.1 Model checking

We checked how our results are correlated with rough measures of failures and scores. The correlations for the "big" model, shown in Figure 3, are good, especially if (second row of the picture) four outliers are ignored. Partially surprisingly, instead, is the fact that the time spent in tasklet is almost uncorrelated with the difficulty measured by the model. The corresponding values of correlations (without outliers) for the "small" model are 0.87, 0.87, 0.02.

4.2 Discussion

The analysis points out some facts.

Very few tasklets (Benjamin 2014-JP-05a, Cadet 2014-CH-02, Cadet and Junior 2014-PL-07+, Cadet and Junior 2014-FR-01) were perceived easier than expected by authors. In three cases out of four, the problem underlying the tasklet is not trivial (sorting networks, generation of a sentence by a grammar, topological sorting) but the tasklets themselves refer to rather simple instances.

However — when the perceived difficulty is different — it is in most cases greater than the expected one. This often happened for tasklets proposed in the original Bebras form but with rescaled difficulty (Benjamin 2014-BE-16b, Benjamin 2014-DE-04, Benjamin 2014-SE-04, Benjamin and Cadet 2014-SK-07), but also for modified ones (Cadet 2014-AU-03a, Cadet and Junior 2011-CH-06[7], Student 2014-CH-07, Student 2011-DE-09, Student 2014-CA-01, Student 2014-CH-06, Student 2014-RU-06). In particular, replacing a set of few alternatives with an open question often results in a problem with too many issues to be considered; for instance, this happens when the correct solution is counterintuitive (as in 2014-RU-06) or one has to find the good way to approach the problem (as in 2014-SE-04): in fact, devising the right approach is much harder than detecting the right answer when it is listed. For a few tasklets (2014-CA-07, 2014-DE-04, 2014-SE-04, 2014-AU-03a), some discontinuity in the level of perceived difficulty appears. Indeed each of them proposes a minor obstacle that appears to hinder only the youngest categories: understanding the problem in 2014-CA-07 is not difficult per se, but the execution is a bit long and error-prone; in 2014-DE-04 three answers (out of four) can be excluded, but the correct one can only be obtained assuming some hypothesis that is actually omitted in the text, thus a doubt may arise; the solution of 2014-SE-04 is immediate only after one detects a special property which is only implicit in the text of the tasklet; the correct answer for 2014-AU-03a is counterintuitive: to answer

---

[6]All the Stan programs, data, and further graphics are available at: https://bitbucket.org/mmonga/bebrastan

[7]This tasklet resulted also much more difficult than expected for Benjamins.

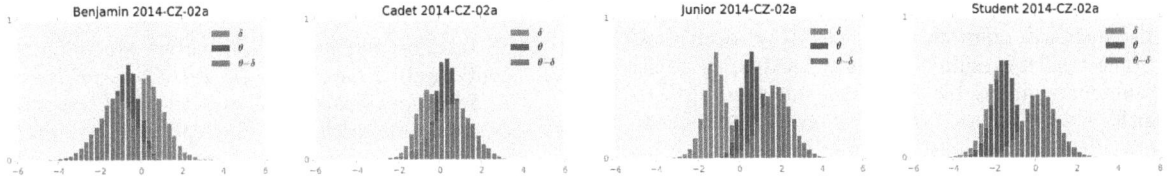

Figure 2: Examples of posterior distributions of δ_j (in red), $\bar{\theta}_k$ (in blue), and $(\bar{\theta}_k - \delta)$ (in green).

Tasklet	mods	Benjamin a.d.	Benjamin perceived difficulty	Cadet a.d.	Cadet perceived difficulty	Junior a.d.	Junior perceived difficulty	Student a.d.	Student perceived difficulty
2014-CZ-02a		e	**h** $(-2.4 \pm 0.9; -1.1 \pm 0.1)$	e	**m** $(0.5 \pm 0.0; -0.3 \pm 0.3)$	e	e $(1.8 \pm 0.0; 0.6 \pm 0.1)$	e	me $(0.2 \pm 0.0; 1.4 \pm 0.0)$
2014-CZ-08		e	e $(0.9 \pm 0.0; 1.2 \pm 0.0)$						
2014-JP-03		e	e $(34.0 \pm 7.9; \; 40.0 \pm 6.2)$						
2013-BE-16b		e	**hm** $(-0.7 \pm 0.3; -0.1 \pm 0.2)$						
2014-CA-05		e	**m** $(0.0 \pm 0.0; 0.2 \pm 0.1)$						
2014-FR-04	*	e	**h** $(-3.7 \pm 0.0; -2.7 \pm 0.0)$						
2014-JP-05a		m	**e** $(2.2 \pm 0.0; 2.3 \pm 0.0)$	e	e $(3.4 \pm 0.0; 2.9 \pm 0.0)$				
2014-CA-07	+	m	**h** $(-1.4 \pm 0.0; -0.6 \pm 0.0)$	e	em $(0.6 \pm 0.0; 0.3 \pm 0.0)$				
2014-DE-04		m	**h** $(-2.2 \pm 0.0; -2.7 \pm 0.2)$	e	em $(0.5 \pm 0.0; -0.3 \pm 0.0)$				
2014-SE-04		m	**h** $(-1.7 \pm 0.0; -2.5 \pm 0.3)$	e	em $(0.7 \pm 0.0; -0.3 \pm 0.1)$				
2014-SK-07		m	**h** $(-1.8 \pm 0.0; -1.4 \pm 0.2)$	e	m $(0.5 \pm 0.0; 0.1 \pm 0.0)$				
2014-CH-02		h	h $(-1.1 \pm 0.0; -0.7 \pm 0.0)$	m	**e** $(1.3 \pm 0.0; 0.9 \pm 0.0)$	e	e $(3.2 \pm 0.0; 2.0 \pm 0.0)$		
2014-RU-03		h	h $(-2.3 \pm 0.0; -2.2 \pm 0.1)$	m	m $(0.1 \pm 0.0; -0.4 \pm 0.0)$	e	e $(2.1 \pm 0.0; 1.0 \pm 0.0)$		
2014-AU-03a	+	h	h $(-3.3 \pm 0.0; -2.6 \pm 0.0)$	m	**h** $(-0.7 \pm 0.0; -1.2 \pm 0.0)$	e	em $(1.0 \pm 0.0; 0.5 \pm 0.0)$		
Disegni		h	h $(-14.0 \pm 1.5; \; -5.2 \pm 0.4)$	m	**h** $(-1.5 \pm 0.0; -4.0 \pm 0.3)$	e	em $(0.9 \pm 0.0; -0.3 \pm 0.1)$		
2011-CH-06	+	h	h $(-6.1 \pm 0.2; \; -140.0 \pm 130.0)$	m	**h** $(-2.1 \pm 0.0; -2.6 \pm 0.0)$	e	**h** $(-1.1 \pm 0.0; -1.1 \pm 0.0)$		
2014-PL-07	+			h	**em** $(0.8 \pm 0.0; 0.2 \pm 0.0)$	m	**e** $(2.0 \pm 0.0; 0.7 \pm 0.0)$	e	me $(-0.4 \pm 0.0; 0.6 \pm 0.0)$
2014-FR-01				h	h $(0.0 \pm 0.0; -0.4 \pm 0.0)$	m	**e** $(1.8 \pm 0.0; 1.2 \pm 0.0)$	e	e $(0.9 \pm 0.0; 2.0 \pm 0.0)$
2014-FI-04				h	h $(-0.7 \pm 0.0; -2.0 \pm 0.1)$	m	em $(1.6 \pm 0.0; 0.4 \pm 0.0)$	e	e $(1.1 \pm 0.0; 2.3 \pm 0.0)$
2014-HU-02				h	h $(-0.8 \pm 0.0; -2.1 \pm 0.2)$	m	em $(0.9 \pm 0.0; -0.3 \pm 0.1)$	e	me $(0.3 \pm 0.0; 1.3 \pm 0.0)$
2014-CH-07	+			h	h $(-1.9 \pm 0.0; -2.1 \pm 0.0)$	m	mh $(-0.2 \pm 0.0; -0.9 \pm 0.0)$	e	**h** $(-2.2 \pm 0.0; -0.5 \pm 0.0)$
Cruci				h	h $(-50.0 \pm 16.0; \; -33.0 \pm 9.9)$	h	h $(-3.4 \pm 0.0; -3.6 \pm 0.0)$	h	h $(-5.2 \pm 0.0; -3.1 \pm 0.0)$
2011-DE-09	*					h	h $(-2.8 \pm 0.0; -2.5 \pm 0.0)$	m	**h** $(-4.5 \pm 0.0; -2.2 \pm 0.0)$
2014-CA-01	*					h	h $(-1.5 \pm 0.0; -2.2 \pm 0.0)$	m	**h** $(-2.6 \pm 0.0; -1.1 \pm 0.0)$
2014-CH-06	*					h	h $(-1.9 \pm 0.0; -2.5 \pm 0.0)$	m	**h** $(-3.0 \pm 0.0; -1.2 \pm 0.0)$
2014-RU-06	+					h	h $(-2.1 \pm 0.0; -2.5 \pm 0.0)$	m	**h** $(-3.5 \pm 0.0; -1.8 \pm 0.0)$
2014-SI-04						h	h $(-1.9 \pm 0.2; \; -17.0 \pm 14.0)$	m	**h** $(-2.9 \pm 0.1; -1.6 \pm 0.1)$
2014-TW-04	+							h	hm $(-1.7 \pm 0.0; -0.2 \pm 0.0)$
Critto								h	h $(-2.6 \pm 0.0; -1.0 \pm 0.0)$
2014-IT-05	+							h	h $(-4.1 \pm 0.1; -3.7 \pm 0.9)$
2013-BE-15a								h	h $(-2.1 \pm 0.0; -2.0 \pm 0.2)$
2013-FR-05								h	h $(-2.8 \pm 0.0; -1.5 \pm 0.0)$

Table 2: Difficulty classification of tasklets (easy, medium, or hard): for each category the first column is the difficulty given by the authors (a.d.), the second (perceived difficulty) the output of the big and small models (in bold when it differs from authors' one). For each classification the value of $\bar{\theta}_k - \delta_j$ is given, within Monte Carlo Standard Error. Values in *italics* are outliers. The mods column indicates if the tasklet was modified w.r.t. the Bebras original (see Sect. 1).

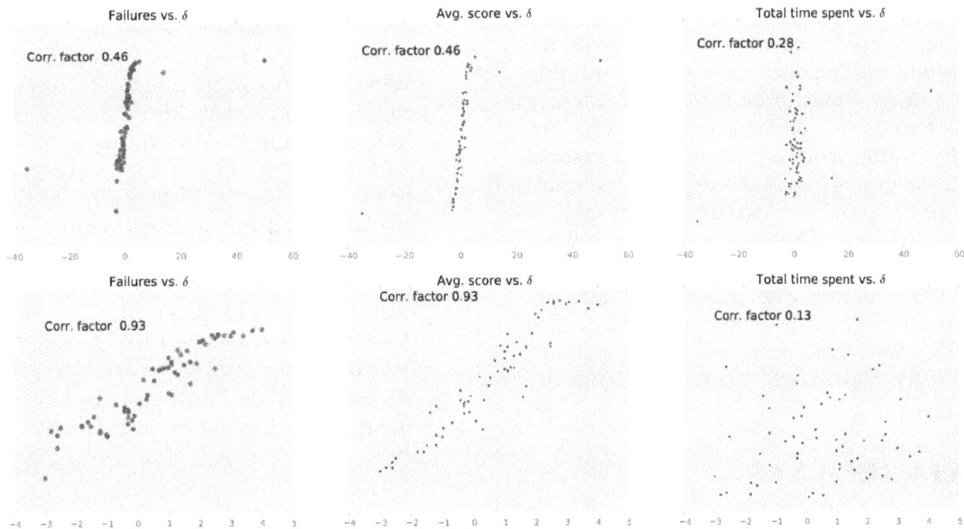

Figure 3: Correlations between δ and failures, average score, and total time spent in a tasklet. In the second row outliers are ignored.

correctly one needs to build the right algorithm (the original, multiple choice, question would probably result much easier). Some tasklets resulted generally hard, with no significant differences among the categories, but were classified by the authors with different difficulty levels (`2011-CH-06`, `2014-CH-07`, `Cruci`, `2011-DE-09`, `2014-CA-01`, `2014-CH-06`, `2014-RU-06`). Most of them were significantly changed from the original form, and hence admitted partial scores. However, in the analysis presented here we considered only full-score answers as correct.

5. CONCLUSIONS

Assessing the difficulty of tasks in an informatics contest aiming at spreading the discipline has a critical importance in order to avoid letting participants perceive the contest as too difficult or too easy, and thus not appealing. As several studies have pointed out, such estimation is not easy to carry out. Thus it is advisable to reconsider a proposed set of tasks *after* the competition ends, using the attained scores in order to infer the difficulty actually perceived by participants, compare it with the difficulty initially estimated by those who proposed the same tasks and gain knowledge in order to tune the future contest editions. This paper presents the results of an analysis aimed at inferring the perceived difficulty of tasks proposed in the 2014 edition of the Italian Bebras/Kangourou competition, based on the scores of more than 2000 participants. Such analysis, exploiting the methodology of IRT, highlights a substantial match between planned and perceived difficulty, meanwhile also emphasizing that in roughly one third of the cases the tasks were either easier or more difficult than expected. In the future we plan to further refine the analysis, also in view of providing an automated version of the workflow to be executed shortly after the contest ends but before the process of checking answers and ranking participants. However we can already infer some suggestions to better estimate the difficulty of tasklets. First, rescaling the difficulty proposed by the Bebras community according to the greater ability of team w.r.t. an individual is in general a good idea, but that should be done carefully because this criterion is not always applicable: not for all tasklets it is possible to work in parallel, thus the time needed may not decrease; replacing a set of few alternatives with an open question may result in a problem with too many issues to be considered. Second, assigning the same tasklet to a different category with varied level of difficulty is in general fair, except in the cases of tasklets just requiring special competences usually reached at a certain age (this is related very often to a high value of the α parameter). The teams of a younger category will not be able to solve it despite the team effort, and for the teams of an older category they are too easy. Last, many tasks appear to be too hard for every category, but often they called for partial scores that were not considered in this analysis. A refinement of this hypothesis could give more insights also on this issue.

6. ACKNOWLEDGMENTS

We would like to thank all the Bebras community for the great effort spent in producing exciting tasklets. Their Italian version saw also the fundamental contribution of Lorenzo Repetto, Fabrizio Carimati, Angelo Lissoni, and all the staff of the Italian Kangourou.

7. REFERENCES

[1] V. Dagienė. Sustaining informatics education by contests. In *Proc. of the 4th Int. Conf. on Informatics in Secondary Schools - Evolution and Perspectives: Teaching Fundamentals Concepts of Informatics*, pages 1–12, Berlin, Heidelberg, 2010. Springer-Verlag.

[2] V. Dagienė and G. Futschek. Bebras international contest on informatics and computer literacy: Criteria for good tasks. In R. T. Mittermeir and M. M. Sysło, editors, *Informatics Education - Supporting Computational Thinking*, volume 5090 of *LNCS*, pages 19–30. Springer Berlin Heidelberg, 2008.

[3] V. Dagiene, L. Mannila, T. Poranen, L. Rolandsson, and P. Söderhjelm. Students' performance on programming-related tasks in an informatics contest in Finland, Sweden and Lithuania. In *Proc. of the 2014 Conf. on Innovation & Technology in Computer Science Education*, pages 153–158, New York, NY, USA, 2014. ACM.

[4] M. Forišek. Using item response theory to rate (not only) programmers. *Olympiads in Informatics*, 3:3–16, 2009.

[5] D. Gamerman and H. F. Lopes. *Markov chain Monte Carlo: stochastic simulation for Bayesian inference*. CRC Press, 2006.

[6] A. Gelman and J. Hill. *Data Analysis Using Regression and Multilevel- Hierarchical Models*. Cambridge University Press, 2007.

[7] B. Haberman, A. Cohen, and V. Dagiene. The beaver contest: Attracting youngsters to study computing. In *Proc. of the 16th Annual Joint Conference on Innovation and Technology in Computer Science Education*, pages 378–378, New York, NY, USA, 2011. ACM.

[8] R. K. Hambleton and H. Swaminathan. *Item Response Theory: Principles and Applications*. Springer-Verlag, 1985.

[9] P. Hubwieser and A. Mühling. Playing PISA with Bebras. In *Proc. of the 9th W. in Primary and Secondary Computing Education*, pages 128–129, New York, NY, USA, 2014. ACM.

[10] V. Lonati, M. Monga, A. Morpurgo, and M. Torelli. What's the fun in informatics? Working to capture children and teachers into the pleasure of computing. In I. Kalaš and R. Mittermeir, editors, *Informatics in schools: contributing to 21st century education. Proc. of the Int. Conf. on Informatics in Schools: Situation, Evolution and Perspectives*, volume 7013 of *LNCS*, pages 213–224. Springer-Verlag, 2011.

[11] Stan. http://mc-stan.org/, 2014.

[12] Stan Development Team. *Stan Modeling Language. User's Guide and Reference Manual*, Oct. 2014. Stan Version 2.5.0.

[13] W. van der Vegt. Predicting the difficulty level of a Bebras task. *Olympiads in Informatics*, 7:132–139, 2013.

Changing Culture: Educating the Next Computer Scientists

Deborah Adshead
Department of Computing
Sheffield Hallam University
Sheffield, United Kingdom
d.adshead@shu.ac.uk

Charles Boisvert
Department of Computing
Sheffield Hallam University
Sheffield, United Kingdom
c.boisvert@shu.ac.uk

David Love
School of Computing
Leeds Beckett University
Leeds, United Kingdom
david.love@leedsbeckett.ac.uk

Phil Spencer
Department of Education
Sheffield Hallam University
Sheffield, United Kingdom
phil.spencer@shu.ac.uk

ABSTRACT

Since 2012 the United Kingdom has fundamentally reformed its computing teaching: the subject matter, the reliance on university specialists, even the subject name has changed. We describe the response at Sheffield Hallam University, which has been to involve academic staff from both the Department of Education and the Department of Computing, forming the Centre for Computing Education.

The aim of our integrated approach is to help support the transformation from 'ICT' to 'Computing'. Through the Centre's work, a new generation of young teachers and trainees are being supported to embrace the cultural change. The growing use of tools and resources we provide, the visits, events, and teacher support network is strengthening the curricular shift in many schools.

However, the challenge remains to reach schools who, so far, struggle to engage with the depth of change in the curriculum. Whilst still young, we believe that our integrated approach can continue to make a strong contribution to the teaching of computing at K-12 level in the UK.

Categories and Subject Descriptors

K. Computing Milieux [**K.3 COMPUTERS AND EDUCATION**]: K.3.2 Computer and Information Science Education—*Subjects: Computer science education*

General Terms

K-12 Computer Science Education

Keywords

Computing at Schools, Computer Science Education, Secondary Education, K-12 Teacher Training

1. INTRODUCTION

In 2012 the United Kingdom (UK) Government began a response to industry calls to radically change the teaching of Information and Communications Technology (ICT) in schools in England and Wales [1, 7]. This ambitious programme aims to change not just the skills of teachers involved in computing education [9], but also to radically change the teaching *culture*. Teaching in ICT was limited in mainstream schools to productivity applications, with the technical subject a preserve of specialist institutions; such teaching of non-technical ICT would end completely within England and Wales [10, 11]. The 'Network of Teaching Excellence in Computer Science', forged new links between Universities and schools. Even the subject name changed to 'Computing' to reflect the new approach [4, 22].

With a long history of primary and secondary teacher training, Sheffield Hallam University has been involved in the 'Computing at Schools' programme since the Government initiative was announced. An almost unique feature of the response from Sheffield Hallam University, however, has been in the involvement of academic staff from both the Departments of Education and the Department of Computing.

The engagement by staff from both Departments has also focused on in-school delivery of special lessons and knowledge transfer rather than simply supporting the changes to the new teacher training requirements.

This has given academic staff in the Department of Computing a track-side view of the changes in computing education. Altogether the intended changes amount to a radical alteration of the culture of computing education in England and Wales. But has the new culture penetrated all schools and is it reflected in student applications?

2. CONTEXT AND WORDING

To make it very clear for a global audience, we will refer to different levels of education, not by some national education standard, but by age. By "K-12" we mean all pre-university education from kindergarten to (typically at 18) 12th grade; within this, primary education is up to 11 years old, and secondary the older half to 18. Post 18, higher education is to obtain a first degree (undergraduate), or a higher degree (postgraduate).

In the UK most teachers undertake a one-year qualifying postgraduate diploma, the *Post-Graduate Certificate in Ed-*

ucation (PGCE): which we will refer to, for simplicity, as "teacher training" or "initial teacher training". Education is also offered to qualified teaching staff, to improve their skills or support them in a changing environment, through formal *Continuous Professional Development* (CPD).

This vocabulary established, we can describe the recent history of IT Education in the UK. The teaching of computing in schools has a long and distinguished history in the UK, including for example the creation of the BBC microcomputer, made specifically for school education in 1981 [8, 3]. But as in many other countries, the curriculum shifted to teaching the day-to-day, office applications of computing under the name of *Information and Communications Technology* (ICT); by the mid-2000s the disastrous consequences of poor computing K-12 education were clear, with a crisis in undergraduate recruitment in the field and a mismatch between teaching and student expectations. Computing academics and professionals lobbied for change and in 2011, the UK Department for Education responded with a challenge, and their demands were made into a reality in a matter of months, by introducing code in the curriculum of secondary schools. To signify the change, 'ICT' was renamed 'computing'.

The recent changes to the national curriculum to introduce increasing amounts of computing across the key stages have created considerable amounts of both concern and positive anticipation. Concern, due to the lack of training and support which the teaching profession are receiving to allow them to deliver this new curriculum and positive anticipation, because for many of us, teaching some 'real' computing is something that we have been wanting to do for some time. As a subject ICT has, for some time been a poisoned brand for a number of reasons: not least that it was a 'simple' subject that anyone can teach. The speech by the UK Secretary of State for Education, Michael Gove, in January 2012 demanding change [13] was seen as the final nail in the coffin for ICT.

3. AN INTEGRATED ANSWER FROM SHU

3.1 An Enthusiastic Response

But the very short interval between the announcement of the curriculum changes and the delivery in school created a difficult task for schools. This difficulty was greatly exacerbated by the historic paucity of teachers trained in the tools and methods of computer science; and of the general lack of staff with a basic knowledge of computer science [7, Chapter 7]. Nonetheless, *ad hoc* links had developed between individual IT teachers or secondary schools and academics within the Departments of Education or Computing over previous years. Instead of formalising a response to schools from only one Department, staff within the two Departments worked together to deliver a combined 'Computing at Schools' programme as soon as the government initiative was announced. A pilot scheme was developed in May 2012 to test the viability of our proposal. The joint-venture was very productive and eventually was named, to help identify our work for enquiring schools, the *Centre for Computing Education*. In this paper, for simplicity, we will attribute joint education work from the two departments to that Centre, even though much was initiated before the Centre for Computing Education was officially formed.

We believe that our joint response to these school needs at Sheffield Hallam University holds lessons for any higher education academic wishing to get involved in K-12 Computing education. The teaching context of computer science within a University is very different from that of secondary schools, and academics within the Department of Computing had to pick up skills very familiar to those in the Department of Education. Simultaneously, academics from the Department of Computing could bring a broad subject expertise to colleagues in the Department of Education: an expertise which has been a necessary support in the rapid re-development of the teacher training programme.

As the possibility of supporting schools transitioning from ICT to computing became clear, the response of colleagues in the Department of Computing was enthusiastic. Staff offered their time and resources in many areas, proposing ways to engage the children using mobile technologies, robotics, unplugged activities, original uses of Scratch and many more, and to host classes in the university as well as deliver sessions in schools.

A third characteristic of our involvement in schools comes from the students. Student engagement in K-12 education is not new: and indeed the Department for Education has long been engaged in mentoring student activities with schools [2]. In addition the University also has structures in place to employ students on a casual basis, for example as Student Ambassadors welcoming and giving tours to young visitors or newcomers, and a formal Hallam Award scheme to support students' engagement outside their studies.

Initial meetings led to a proposition that would link all of the above: the relationship with schools; the involvement of Education and Computing staff; the support of student volunteers; and the double offer of travelling to schools, and welcoming pupils on the University site. To allow the involvement of students, the respective roles of school staff, university lecturers and students were clearly defined: school staff would always remain present to manage their pupils and ensure the respect of school child protection obligations; university staff prepared resources and tools — hardware, software, teaching materials — demonstrated them to volunteer students in advance of the sessions to help them prepare, and led the sessions with pupils. Students, paid per-hour for their involvement, also assisted in supporting pupils during lessons. The aims were to ensure that when working with technology that is unusual in schools, any difficulties with hardware and software, or any complexity, such as programming syntax, that would be a barrier to the purpose of the session, could be ironed out quickly with help, allowing the pupils to focus on higher learning goals; but also to provide much-needed role models for the school children.

Finally, the Education staff joined in the visits and complemented them with offers of regional meetings to support teachers in post, continuous professional development to improve their level of qualification, placement for new trainee teachers, and a new qualification to train teachers in computing. In all, including the pilot sessions in May 2012, we have delivered: 8 sessions to 5 different schools in the summer 2012; 18 sessions in the academic year 2012–13 to the same schools plus a further 7 schools; and 20 in 2013–14, adding 8 more schools to our portfolio. The programme is ongoing this academic year.

Therefore the engagement by staff on all sides went much further than simply delivering a specific action within their

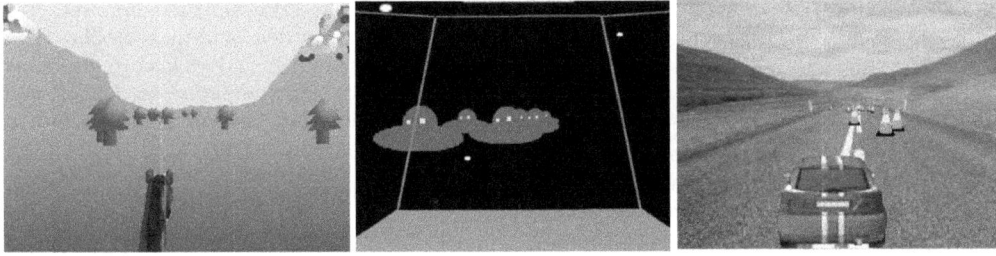

Figure 1: multiple themes to support pupils' creation

role: we all became involved in support of change, working to understand the new teaching demands from teachers, supporting their training requirements, as well as the more common, in-school delivery of special lessons and knowledge transfer.

3.2 Our Offer to Teachers: Some Examples

Some examples of the events offered will illustrate the diversity and multiple aim of our offer to schools. These examples are taken among the more frequent and popular events, but an exhaustive list would be beyond the scope of this paper.

3.2.1 Scratch 3D

Scratch is well known in schools and it may not be apparent why school pupils and teachers need more intervention to learn the language. But our visits show that its use, although common, remains limited to shallow, repetitive uses of the software. The aim of our visits is to counter the expectation that Scratch is extremely limited, and help pupils and teachers alike to break into more creative and diverse uses of Scratch which link to computational thinking.

To spur the interest of pupils we created a set of resources that simulate 3D in scratch. The material provided includes some ready code, but also ready art (Figure 1), because pupils often spend more time drawing than programming, missing out on learning to control their systems' behaviour. The students' involvement is precisely to help ensure that pupils do not get stuck in a rut [21, 16, 18], and exploit the ideas further with original uses.

The pupils typically start by closely following the guidance they receive. From it they are able to make diverse animations and games. A final activity is for those who wish to present their ideas to their class.

The session is more difficult to manage than using robots — the project challenges the pupils, but also the volunteer students, who need to understand the 3D simulation in greater depth.

3.2.2 Racing Robots

The most popular lessons, repeated in many schools since 2011, has been programming small robots. The robots used (Pololu 3PIs) were chosen for their sturdiness and simplicity. As well as the robots, we make available laptops ready configured with the development environment.

Students are able to iron out any problems that result from handling the environment, being used to this already, making the experience much more enjoyable for the pupils

Figure 2: Pololu 3PI Robot (Source: Pololu Corporation [6])

Figure 3: Robots at the Ready

as this minimises the frustration of having exciting tools but too many barriers to use them.

Two typical problems that pupils work out are to ensure the robot goes in a roughly straight line (a genuine problem in a real world of motors, gearing, dust and voltage drops, as opposed to tracing lines on digital images!), and can carry a load — a marble, carefully balanced on the two batteries (shown in Figure 2) — without dropping it as the robot speeds up, slows down, and turns around . This culminates into a race between the robots, to find which can carry the load to a line and back without dropping it (Figure 3).

The session is very successful with pupils and motivates them to shift from visual, drag-and-drop coding tools like Scratch, to coding in C. Additional support is required to ensure that the children's focus is on debugging, not on correcting syntax errors. Nonetheless, several school teachers have since chosen to use the same robots in their schools, in new computing lessons or through in-school clubs.

3.2.3 FIRST Lego League

The 'status' of in-school clubs, however, illustrates one of the key weaknesses of the UK 'Computing at School' programme. In 2006 the UK Government created the *After-School Science and Engineering Clubs* (ASSEC's) programme, designed to inspire pupils aged 11–14 to learn about science and engineering [24]. The activity of these clubs has been co-ordinated and supported by the *Science, Technology, Engineering and Mathematics Network* (STEMnet), a UK charity partly supported by Government funding.

In schools where ASSEC clubs are well-established, the 'Computing at School' activities have largely been folded into the existing clubs. Where no previous ASSEC club exists, a new in-school club is usually created (and sometimes then linked to the ASSEC programme). Confusion over programme delivery is hardly novel, but it does lead to challenges in supporting the broader 'Computing at School' objectives.

The teaching background of staff supporting ASSEC clubs is largely design technology [24, pp. 19–20]: traditionally in the UK a very different teaching discipline to computing. So while many STEM ambassadors (external volunteers co-ordinated, trained and monitored by STEMnet) come from a broad range of engineering and computing disciplines, the in-school support for ASSEC clubs has historically been much narrower. Therefore while robotics and computing activities may be popular with pupils, schools must often rely on teachers voluntarily picking up skills in a new field.

Using peer-support through the *Continuing Professional Development* (CPD) programmes at Sheffield Hallam is one approach to ensuring the continued success of 'computing' clubs in school). Another is to link into national (and international) competitions based around engineering and computing to provide both a framework for supporting the teachers — and additional self-learning resources for the pupils.

At Sheffield Hallam we have been involved in the FIRST Lego League since 2013, acting as regional host in the UK. Originating in the United States, but now well-established internationally, the FIRST Lego League is an international competition involving an annual 'challenge': part of which is solved by Lego robots solving a fixed set of problems, and part of which involves presenting a broader engineering solution to the challenge topic [20, 19]. The running of the national League in the UK is co-ordinated by the *Institution for Engineering and Technology* (IET): the body overseeing the professional regulation of electrical and computing engineers in the UK [12].

Since schools work on the first round of the FIRST Lego League over a period of roughly three months, this activity offers the potential for substantial links between schools and staff inside the University. At present, however, much of this potential has yet to be realised. Teams established before Sheffield Hallam took over the Sheffield regional event only rarely ask for support from the University. Teams that do ask for support however, would prefer regular (usually weekly) engagement along the lines of the ASSEC clubs. But while STEMnet offers comprehensive support and training of STEM ambassadors (including managing the extensive documentation required for volunteers to work in UK schools), finding a similar support structure for the 'Computers at School' programme has been difficult.

Practically, this means that all students who want to work with schools on a regular basis for the FIRST Lego League have to become STEM ambassadors first. While this is not a tremendous burden (and indeed offers the students many other opportunities), it does lead to questions over the long-term viability of 'Computers at School' clubs. Especially when a 'competing' support structure in overlapping disciplines that already exist.

3.3 Our Offer to Students

As well as supporting schools with sessions on school grounds and here on site at the University, it was also seen as important to involve students currently studying for computing related degrees at the University. We have already mentioned the importance of providing a larger pool of support for delivering sessions, but involving the students is also invaluable for them, and we work to maximise that value.

Students with some programming experience are recruited at intervals throughout the year to act as paid mentors. Some also volunteer unpaid for the Hallam award — a university award given for voluntary work. Both then attend Masterclasses in the subject material prior to taking part in any teaching activities, and sessions are divided as evenly as possible amongst the trained students based on their availability and their interests.

Since 2012, we have recruited over 70 students to participate in delivery of the sessions. Many of those involved are undergraduate, but some postgraduate students at Master or (more rarely) PhD level are also involved. The direct involvement of students in delivering the sessions has many benefits: it provides students with valuable work experience to add to their CVs; it helps reinforce the students' skills and subject knowledge as they practice them in a different context and at a simpler level; it fosters a peer learning environment with students helping each other, and meeting across the usual barrier of level of study and detailed specialisms.

Some students are considering the idea of becoming computing teachers in schools themselves, and for those, the volunteering or hourly-paid opportunities are a way to test the waters of a school teaching environment before committing themselves to teacher training.

3.4 Providing Teacher Education

The main problem for school Computing, is the lack of specialist teachers who are able to deliver the topic with confidence. As we have said, most teachers who were teaching ICT are not Computing specialists [7, *op. cit.*], so finding ones with computing qualifications is a considerably difficult thing to do.

From the outset of the involvement in the Computing at Schools initiative, staff at Sheffield Hallam University were committed to developing a support structure to the schools that would benefit not only the school children who would be attending taught sessions but would also help to cultivate a culture of professional development for the teachers. This takes two main forms

1. Continuous development for teachers already in post, who need to retrain into computing from ICT — and sometimes from unrelated specialisms altogether [7, Chapter 7, *op. cit.*].

2. A one-year teacher training qualification, in the new Computing discipline, for incoming teachers.

3.5 CPD of Established Teachers

Whilst it is not a requirement to be involved in the initiative, the teachers of the participating schools are offered several opportunities to support their development from ICT to Computing specialists. This activity, is limited by the amount of time staff are given to attend such sessions as well as the funding given to schools to allow teachers to undergo training; but the Centre for Computing Education aims to provide a diverse offer to reach the broadest possible audience.

At the simplest level, all the resources — handouts, software tools, information about the practice — resulting from the visits are made available to teachers, open to re-use and adaptation for later classes. Between other results, this open culture has facilitated the adoption of robots by two of the schools, and the development of local computing clubs to use them.

Further, building on its positive working relationships with a large number of secondary schools, the University's Department of Education acts to support via a range of CPD events. It leads a regional 'hub' for the 'Computing at School' programme, periodically hosting the 'Computing at School' meetings and different outreach workshops. These enable us to support schools with new ideas, resources and activities.

Finally, teachers are encouraged to attend weekend and evening workshops delivered by the joint Centre for Education in Computing. Through these, teachers who are not qualified in the subject can develop their knowledge and obtain a qualification validated by the *British Computer Society* (BCS[1]); but those who are already knowledgeable in Computing can also become 'master teachers', and support training of new teachers, also with the approval of the BCS.

3.6 Training New Teachers

However, while Government funding has increased the number of teacher training positions in Computer Science, intervening changes in the national teacher training programme has led to an overall decrease in the number of student teachers [25]. Thus there is a concern that we will not be able to produce sufficient new teachers to meet the requirements of schools in the area.

This being said, we do have a cohort of 15 teachers who are currently studying a PgCert in Education with a focus on computing. Students are also placed in schools that may not have specialist staff — deliberately to facilitate the exchange of technical knowledge, as well as support the development of teaching skills. This has been a positive experience for all as we have not only looked into pedagogical and theoretical issues, but it has allowed the formation of a group of schools who are offering further support to other schools in the area.

The strong development of teacher training is very much a result of the concerted action of the Centre for Computing Education over the past three years. Take the case of current teacher trainee, Emily (not her real name). As an undergraduate student at the university, Emily was interested in the lack of role models for girls who, like her, would be interested in studying computing; she was also on the lookout for paid work while studying. This double interest

found a natural home when, in her final year, she joined the pool of students mentors.

Her commitment to education only strengthened as she visited schools and welcomed children in the University helping with robot races, 3D scratch, mobile development lessons for secondary schools. Through these visits she also met with experienced teachers and with the teacher training staff, and this academic year she is completing her own teacher training, having reinforced her professional interest thanks to the mentoring opportunities provided by the Centre.

4. SHIFTING THE CULTURE OF COMPUTING

As we explained in the introduction, the Centre for Computing Education was created in response to the UK government and industry hoping to not just improve the school curriculum, but to radically change the teaching of computing [2, 1]. This begs the question, are we contributing to such an ambitious change within England and Wales?

On the one hand, a radical transformation of the culture has taken place, which we have witnessed rather than initiated. In the short years before government changed the curriculum in 2012, industry was asking for such change. Academics were also concerned by a recruitment crisis[2]; the poor computing knowledge of their intake, and changing student demand clearly indicated the need for the change to a more science-based computing education. In the same period that saw changes to the school curriculum, student intake filled increasingly technical computer science courses, making them unexpectedly popular. We cannot attribute the new interest of students in computer science to the government initiative: their curriculum was not affected by it, as changes were proposed as they left school. The cultural change is therefore broader and more complete than any government-led initiative, and the agents of that change are multiple.

Yet the transformation is incomplete. In schools, the main concern is less with those schools who engage actively with the university, but with the many others who do not, for whatever reason. Many choose to ignore the need to support their staff through the change, still hoping that simple investment in recent hardware will magically solve the problem of teaching Computing, just as they did with 'technological toolery' in earlier ICT [17]. But tools by themselves are not enough [5]. Unless these staff can be reached and supported, there may be a clear two-tier situation in schools as far as the delivery of computing is concerned, with some schools under-performing or even, for those that are able to do so opting out of computing and thus ignoring a major branch of modern science.

The culture shift that industry, government and academics have all been working for is therefore in progress. We are, as Prof. Peyton-Jones describes in his campaigning work, in *"the ground war"* [15]: the struggle to train and disseminate the new ideas [14]. This would not happen without a multi-aimed approach to simultaneously recruit students, improve secondary education, lift the standard of school computing and counter the illusion that computing is IT.

---

[1]The British Computer Society is the professional body devoted to *"study and practice of Computing"* in the UK [23], acting as the main chartering body for computing and IT professionals outside the IET.

[2]For instance, the UK computer science student numbers in 2013–2014 are still only a two-thirds of the equivalent number in 2003–2004 [26, Table 3].

Our multi-dimensional work finds a new challenge in the extension of coding to primary schools. Announced in 2013, coding in the primary school curriculum is an even greater challenge than for secondary school teachers, given that these schools do not employ subject specialists. Our response adapted the work started with secondary schools, through sessions that are shorter, more active, and carefully consider the level at which the children can work. In primary school sessions, we also gave students a greater role as they prepared and led unplugged activities, sessions on Scratch, and on using Scratch with Microsoft Kinect sensors. In this context, our integrated approach is helping support the culture change in progress. It provides, for example, the flexibility necessary to adapt to the needs of primary school teachers and start supporting them.

Through the work of our Centre for Computing Education, more teachers don't just buy, but use, the tools and resources provided — and develop Computing teaching materials. The visits, events, and Computing at School support network is strengthening the curricular shift in many schools. A generation of young teachers is being trained that is embracing that cultural change, and their placements are already influencing a new approach to the topic.

Nevertheless, despite our successes there is still a way to go. The pupils who have experienced the new curriculum are not yet old enough to apply to Higher Education establishments. There still remains the challenge of reaching those schools who, by failing to engage with the changes in the curriculum through a shift in their culture, run the real risk of failing to support pupils who increasingly need the skills to fully comprehend, and to fit in to, an ever more technological world and workplace.

5. REFERENCES

[1] C. at Schools Working Group. *Computer Science: A Curriculum for Schools*. Mar 2012.

[2] S. Bevins, M. Brodie, and E. Brodie. The views of five participating undergraduate students of the student associates scheme in England. *Teacher Development*, 14(1):29–44, 2010.

[3] T. Blyth. *The Legacy of the BBC Micro*. NESTA, 2012.

[4] P. Bradshaw and J. Woolard. Computing at school: An emergent community of practice for a re-emergent subject. In *International Conference on ICT in Education*, 5-7 July, Rhodes, Greece, 2012.

[5] D. Catlin and J. Woollard. Educational robots and computational thinking. In *Proceedings of 4th International Workshop Teaching Robotics, Teaching with Robotics & 5th International Conference Robotics in Education*, pages 144–151, Padova, Italy, July 2014.

[6] P. Corporation. Pololu 3pi robot. https://www.pololu.com/product/975.

[7] Excellence in Science, The Royal Society, and The Royal Academy of Engineering. Shut down or restart? the way forward for computing in UK schools. Technical Report DES2448, 2012.

[8] J. Fitzpatrick. An interview with Steve Furber. *Communications of the ACM*, 54(5):34–39, May 2011.

[9] D. for Education. *Subject Knowledge Requirements for Entry in to Computer Science Teacher Training: Expert Group's Recommendations*. 2012.

[10] D. for Education. National curriculum in england: Computing programmes of study — key stages 1 and 2. Technical Report DFE-00171-2013, 2013.

[11] D. for Education. National curriculum in england: Computing programmes of study — key stages 3 and 4. Technical Report DFE-00191-2013, 2013.

[12] I. for Engineering and Technology. FIRST LEGO League (FLL) UK and Ireland. http://firstlegoleague.theiet.org.

[13] M. Gove. Michael Gove speech at the BETT Show 2012, 2012. http://bit.ly/1D6xG5e.

[14] V. Grout and N. Houlden. Taking computer science and programming into schools: The Glyndŵr/BCS Turing Project. *Procedia — Social and Behavioral Sciences*, 141(0):680–685, 2014.

[15] S. P. Jones. The computing at school working group. In *Proceedings of the 18th ACM Conference on Innovation and Technology in Computer Science Education*, page 1, Canterbury, England, UK, 2013.

[16] J. M. Lavonen, V. P. Meisalo, M. Lattu, and E. Sutinen. Concretising the programming task: A case study in a secondary school. *Computers & Education*, 40(2):115–135, 2003.

[17] D. Lovell-Badge. *The Pathology of Educational Change: a Case Study of the Management of Information Technology in an FE/HE Institution*. PhD thesis, City College, Norwich, 1996.

[18] O. Meerbaum-Salant, M. Armoni, and M. Ben-Ari. Habits of programming in Scratch. In *Proceedings of the 16th Annual Joint Conference in Innovation and Technology in Computer Science Education*, pages 168–172, Darmstadt, Germany, 2011.

[19] A. Melchior. *Evaluation of the FIRST LEGO League "Senior Solutions" Season*. Center for Youth and Communities, Brandeis University, 2013.

[20] A. Melchior, T. Cutter, and F. Cohen. *Evaluation of the FIRST LEGO League*. Center for Youth and Communities, Brandeis University, July 2004.

[21] C. Rader, C. Brand, and C. Lewis. Degrees of comprehension: Children's understanding of a visual programming environment. In *Proceedings of the ACM SIGCHI Conference on Human Factors in Computing Systems*, CHI '97, pages 351–358, Atlanta, USA, 1997.

[22] S. Sentance, S. Humphreys, and M. Dorling. The network of teaching excellence in computer science and master teachers. In *Proceedings of the 9th Workshop in Primary and Secondary Computing Education*, pages 80–88, New York, USA, 2014.

[23] T. B. C. Society. Our role and purpose. http://www.bcs.org/category/6988.

[24] S. Straw, R. Hart, and J. Harland. *An Evaluation of the Impact of STEMNET's Services on Pupils and Teachers*. NFER, Nov. 2011.

[25] U. UK. *The Impact of Initial Teacher Training Reforms on English Higher Education Institutions*. Oct. 2014.

[26] U. UK. *Patterns and trends in UK higher education 2014*. 2014.

Semi-Automatic Assessment of Unrestrained Java Code*

A Library, a DSL, and a Workbench to Assess Exams and Exercises

David Insa   Josep Silva
Universitat Politècnica de València
Camino de Vera, s/n
46022 Valencia, Spain
{dinsa,jsilva}@dsic.upv.es

ABSTRACT

Automated marking of multiple-choice exams is of great interest in university courses with a large number of students. For this reason, it has been systematically implanted in almost all universities. Automatic assessment of source code is however less extended. There are several reasons for that. One reason is that almost all existing systems are based on output comparison with a gold standard. If the output is the expected, the code is correct. Otherwise, it is reported as wrong, even if there is only one typo in the code. Moreover, why it is wrong remains a mystery. In general, assessment tools treat the code as a black box, and they only assess the externally observable behavior. In this work we introduce a new code assessment method that also verifies properties of the code, thus allowing to mark the code even if it is only partially correct. We also report about the use of this system in a real university context, showing that the system automatically assesses around 50% of the work.

1. INTRODUCTION

Assessment is an integral part of instruction, as it determines whether or not the goals of education are being met. When assessment works best, it provides diagnostic feedback both to students and teachers. Therefore, it provides both means to guide student learning and essential information for both the learner and the teacher about the learning process.

In the psychology education area, it has been proved that most students often direct their efforts based on what is assessed and how it affects the final course mark (see, e.g., [4],

[Chapter 9]). As a consequence, continuous assessment during a course can be used to direct and enhance the learning process. However, providing quality assessment manually for even a small class requires an important effort. When the class size grows, the amount of assessed work has to be limited or rationalized in some other way.

This is the reason why many efforts have been made to produce tools and techniques for the *automatic assessment* (AA). In fact, this has been a hot topic for a long time [7], and there are in the literature many different ways for the teacher to define tests, resubmission policies, security issues, and so forth.

AA has been traditionally focussed on multiple-choice exams. Most of the work has been done in that area, mainly improving the scanning process, allowing recognition of students annotations (e.g., permitting to alter the annotated answer by annotating the "error" circle and handwriting the letter of the correct answer next to the appropriate row), or enabling automated reading of a limited set of handwritten answers, thus minimizing the need for a human intervention.

Another area of special interest is the correction of programs written by students. Most of the work has focussed on restricted programs, where the student has to select different (finite) options in a GUI to construct a program, or it is based on output comparison. Most advanced AA systems compile the student code, execute it, and compare the result with the correct answer. Random test generation can be also used reducing the number of false positives.

Unfortunately, checking the output of the student's code, even if we compare all possible outputs, is often not enough to ensure a quality assessment. This is illustrated in Example 1.1.

EXAMPLE 1.1. *An exercise says: Implement a class "Car".* *Cars have an attribute* `numberPlate` *that can be obtained* *with method* `getNumberPlate()`. *We can assume that this* *exercise is part of a wider model to represent a garage.*

```
      SOLUTION 1                    SOLUTION 2

class Car {                   class Car extends Vehicle {
  int numberPlate;
  Car(int np){                  Car(int np){
    numberPlate = np;             super.numberPlate = np;
  }                             }
  int getNumberPlate(){         int getNumberPlate(){
    return numberPlate;           return super.numberPlate;
  }                             }
}                             }
```

*This work has been partially supported by the EU (FEDER) and the Spanish *Ministerio de Economía y Competitividad (Secretaría de Estado de Investigación, Desarrollo e Innovación)* under grant TIN2013-44742-C4-1-R and by the *Generalitat Valenciana* under grant PROMETEOII2015/013. David Insa was partially supported by the Spanish Ministerio de Educación under FPU grant AP2010-4415.

While both solutions could be acceptable for a first-year student, the first solution is unacceptable for a second-year student. Solution 2 is more maintainable and reuses code via inheritance. Solution 1 does not make use of inheritance, and thus it can be wrong when an object "Car" should behave as a "Vehicle". However, both cars have the same attributes and methods, and thus for most tests, they will always produce the same output. In this example, a teacher would not be interested in the output, but in one specific property of class "Car" (i.e., it extends class "Vehicle").

Another important restriction of output comparison is that they just return the whole code as correct or the whole code as wrong. No intermediate mark is possible. The reality is however different: Teachers normally divide an exam into small appraisable pieces. For instance, using inheritance could be assigned a value of 3 points over 10, thus, `Solution 1` should be marked with 7 points.

Moreover, output comparison is very sensible to small errors. For instance, if the student accidentally changes `return numberPlate` by `return numberPate`, then all output comparison based methods will mark the exam with 0 points. Nevertheless, many teachers would see the typo as something not important or just due to lack of time, and they would mark the exam with, e.g., 9 points. Of course, output comparison methods cannot handle programs that do not compile (e.g., because a semicolon is missing).

Our approach goes beyond output comparison, and it can assess unrestrained code (i.e., the student can freely use the complete programming language without restrictions). In particular, our technique can automatically assess the code not only from the final output, but also checking whether the own source code fulfills any properties desired by the teacher (e.g., definition of a particular class hierarchy, implementation of interfaces, existence of a particular field, etc.). Concretely, we have developed an assessment library that uses the abstraction and advanced meta-programming features of Java to allow properties verification. Based on this library, we have developed a domain specific language (DSL) for the specification of automatic exam assessment templates. And we have also developed a system that integrates the DSL into a workbench with GUIs and facilities for AA of unrestricted Java programs.

We believe that our approach opens a new line of research in AA, and we have made the library, DSL, tools and the source code open and free. In contrast to many other approaches [7], it has not been designed as a tool for a specific Java programming course useful for a single teacher, but a tool that can be widely used, configured and augmented to design any Java exam or exercise and to automatically assess batteries of exams.

It is important to note that we call our tool *semi-automatic* even though it is as automatic as the other tools and systems available in the bibliography that claim that they are automatic. We want to remark that not all programming exercises can be automatically assessed. In the general case, AA is an undecidable problem, and thus no fully-AA-system can be constructed. For instance, a program that does not terminate cannot produce an output. And it must be stopped. For this program, it is not possible to know whether it is really non-terminating or just inefficient, because determining non-termination is by itself an undecidable problem. Other programs simply do not compile, they are syntactically wrong, and thus no dynamic analysis can be done with

them. For all these kinds of problems, human (teacher) intervention is needed to correct the program or just to assign a mark.

Our system also performs output comparison. It automatically compares the output of the exam with the expected solution. It also uses test generation to compare the output with many different inputs. But, as a new feature, it also validates arbitrary properties of the code. Whenever human intervention is needed, the system prompts the teacher with the available information showing the problem found, and both the student's exam and the solution.

We summarize the main contributions of our work:

- An assessment Java library with abstraction methods for the verification of properties in Java code.

- A DSL built on top of the library for the specification of exams and their corresponding assessment templates.

- A semi-automatic assessment tool for Java exams and exercises based on output comparison via tests generation and verification of properties.

- A report on teachers assessment problems identified with our tool.

2. RELATED WORK

Pears et al. [12] classify the tools that support teaching programming into four groups: (1) visualization tools, (2) AA tools, (3) programming support tools, and (4) microworlds.

Focussing on AA tools, the main area of interest has been automatic marking of multiple-choice exams. This is of special interest in university courses with a large number of students, and the problem has been solved and solutions implanted in almost all universities. Some remarkable systems of this kind are [14, 6].

A second kind of AA tools is based on *visual algorithm simulation exercises* [9]. These tools use advanced GUIs that control all possible (finite) actions of the student regarding a particular problem (e.g., sorting an array). In visual algorithm simulation exercises, a learner directly manipulates the visual representation of the underlying data structures to which the algorithm is applied. The learner manipulates these real data structures through GUI operations with the purpose of performing the same changes on the data structures that the real algorithm would do (e.g., a student can simulate the steps of Quicksort using the GUI, and the system can assess every single movement using the real quicksort algorithm) [9].

In this paper we focus on a third kind of AA tool that has been less investigated: AA of source code. In this area, almost all approaches are based on output comparison (see, e.g., [13, 5], and the four surveys [2, 1, 10, 7]). The general idea is to compile the students code, execute it with a predetermined set of inputs, and compare the outputs with the expected results. The most advanced systems [15, 8, 3] also use random test case generation and some sort of model (often the correct algorithm) to compare the results. Some of these systems are language independent. This is possible because they use the compiler as a parameter, and they just compare the results.

Unfortunately, there are very few works that perform code analysis to mark exams. Two exceptions are [11] and [16].

In both approaches, the idea is to measure the similarity of the student code to the pool of known solutions. Similarity is computed with a graph representation of the code.

A comparison of the most important AA tools can be found in [7]. Other previous reviews are [2, 10, 1].

Our approach also uses output comparison with automatic test generation. But, in contrast to many of the related work, we do not use a pool of known solutions, a model, or a graph. We use a solution to the exam provided by the teacher. We compile it and use it as an oracle to generate test cases. Moreover, our generated tests are not completely random, they are based on an analysis of path conditions to maximize code coverage.

Another important difference of our approach is the property verification module. We are not aware of any other technique that uses a DSL to specify properties that can be automatically validated and assigned a mark. Finally, another feature that is completely novel, is the possibility to mark an exam that does not compile.

3. THE SYSTEM IN A NUTSHELL

Our automatic assessment system, including libraries, the DSL specification, the workbench, manuals, the source code, and examples, is free and publicly available at:

http://www.dsic.upv.es/~jsilva/teaching/ASys/

We describe here its functionality and architecture, and we refer the interested reader to the project website for implementation details. Essentially, our system performs three different assessment phases:

1. *Compilation*: To identify compilation errors.
2. *Analysis*: To check whether the specified requirements are properly implemented.
3. *Testing*: To identify runtime errors.

Phases 1 and 3 are already implemented and reported in other works (see, e.g., [15, 8, 3]) so we will explain here phase 2, which is a novel contribution of our work. We just want to remark that, for phases 1 and 3, our system is not limited to a set of predefined tests to check some provided finite input-output pairs. Contrarily, our system can generate any arbitrary number of test cases. For this, the system inputs the solution of the exam (in Java), and iteratively generates them. Then, tests are used with a battery of Java exams, so that, the output of exams is checked against the output of the compiled solution. Tests implemented manually can also be used in the testing phase.

Phase 2 is our most important contribution. To implement the analysis phase, we first implemented a Java metaprogramming library with assessment functions, and a DSL on top of the library for the specification of assessment templates. Because the DSL is compliant with Java, it is directly executable by an assessment engine that can automatically verify the properties in the template against a given exam. In the next sections we describe the library, the DSL, and the workbench that integrates all of the components.

3.1 The assessment library

One of the most important contributions of our work is our assessment library, because it is per se a tool to create assessment systems. It is a Java library with heavy use of reflection that provides an API composed of 77 methods

that can be used to inspect and analyze Java source code. The library provides a class called "Inspector" that internally makes all the abstraction. This class provides several methods to query and manipulate the meta information in order to check properties of the code.

EXAMPLE 3.1. *Some methods of the library, useful to determine whether a given property is satisfied, follow:*

- ```
  public boolean checkType(Field field,
                           TypeVariable<?> genericType)
  ```
  Checks whether the type of a given field is the generic type given as second argument.

- ```
  public boolean checkGenericType(Field field,
                                  int[] indices)
  ```
  Checks whether a given field contains a generic type in a specified position (e.g., in Map< T, Map<S, R>> the indices [1, 0] stands for the generic type S).

- ```
  public Method getDeclaredMethod(Class<?> clazz,
          String methodName, Class<?>[] paramTypes,
          Class<?> returnType, boolean allowWrappers)
  ```
  Returns the method with the given name, parameters and return value. It can allow a wrapper as any parameter or returned value instead of the primitive ones.

- ```
  public Class<?> getSuperClass(Class<?> clazz)
  ```
  Returns the superclass of a given class.

EXAMPLE 3.2. *Given the code in Solution 1 of Example 1.1, with the library, we can automatically check whether class "Car" extends class "Vehicle" with the following code:*

```
public boolean checkCarExtendsVehicle() {
  Class<?> carClass = inspector.getClass("Car");
  Class<?> vehicleClass = inspector.getClass("Vehicle");
  boolean carExtendsVehicle =
      inspector.checkSuperClass(carClass, vehicleClass);
  return carExtendsVehicle;
}
```

where methods inspector.checkSuperClass *and* inspector.getClass *are provided by the library and have the obvious meaning.*

The assessment library is used by our system, but it is an independent piece of work that can be used in other systems and projects. Therefore, we have made it available independently as an standard Java library. The library is publicly accessible at: http://www.dsic.upv.es/~jsilva/teaching/ASys/library/.

3.2 The assessment DSL

With the assessment library, we have created a DSL that allows teachers to programmatically assess Java exams and exercises. The DSL allows us to load a Java program (e.g., an exercise) and check whether it has been implemented correctly. For instance, we can check the correct use of inheritance, interfaces, abstract classes, etc.

In particular, the DSL provides mechanisms to specify properties and assign marks to them. Each exam is assigned with a set of evaluation pieces, and each evaluation piece is associated with one property that we want to check, and a

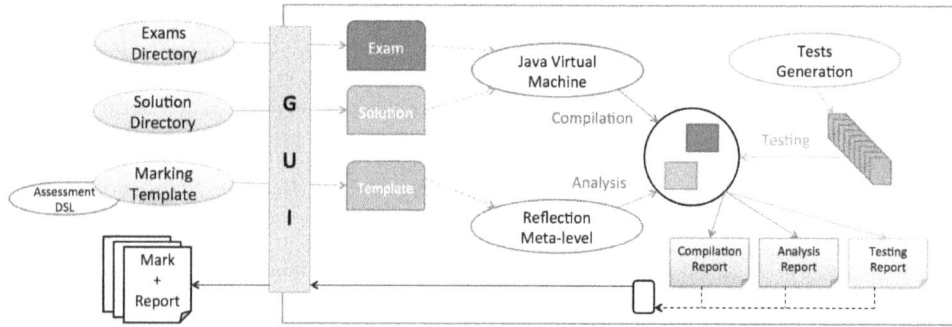

Figure 1: Architecture of ASys

mark that is assigned if the property holds. Properties can be specified using the library API.

When properties hold, the correction can be done automatically, assigning the specified mark to each property. When a property fails, the system can be configured to either assign a mark (e.g., 0 points), or work semi-automatically: the teacher is prompted with the source code that caused the problem, the explanation of the property that fails, and a form to assign a mark and a review for this failing property. The DSL also gives support to this behavior.

Concretely, all functionality of the DSL (creating assessment templates formed from evaluation pieces) has been accompanied with a GUI, so that teachers can graphically create assessment templates and include properties and marks using buttons and text boxes.

Due to lack of space, we refer the reader to the project website for explanations and examples of the DSL.

3.3 The assessment workbench

Our semi-automatic assessment system is called ASys (which stands for Assessment System). The architecture of ASys is depicted in Figure 1. The input of the system is (i) a path to the directory with the exams to be assessed, (ii) a path to the directory with the solution to the exam, and (iii) a marking template specified with the assessment DSL that defines how to mark the exam.

The output of the system is, for each exam, a report that specifies the final mark together with a detailed list of the problems found. This output is useful for both the teacher and the student, and thus, each report is duplicated and presented in two different ways: one for the teacher with information useful to automate the marking and publication of marks, and another for the student, with learning feedback explaining the problems encountered. Concretely, the report is composed of information from the system and the teacher about compilation errors (compilation), unsatisfied properties (analysis), and runtime errors (testing).

In order to understand how this triple report is built, we can see the data flow diagram (DFD) of the system depicted in Figure 2. Dark boxes with **Exam**, **Exam solution**, and **Assessment template** are the inputs provided by the user. They correspond to those in Figure 1. Following the paths in the DFD, one can easily understand that there are three different phases highlighted with the **Phase 1**, **Phase 2**, and **Phase 3** boxes. These phases correspond to the three modules in the architecture: **Compilation**, **Analysis**, and **Testing**.

One could think that the three phases are executed sequentially. That is, the exam is compiled once, then, the generated code is analyzed, and, finally, it is tested to find runtime errors. This sequential behavior is the one used in previous tools (without the analysis phase, which is novel). However, our system works differently.

We repeat the three phases every time that the teacher modifies the code; and this happens every time that an error (either compilation error, unsatisfied property, or failing test) is identified. Hence, the general schema in the DFD is: `find one error` → `prompt the teacher` → `recompile the whole exam` → `check *all* properties` → `check *all* tests`. This is repeated until no more errors are found. This schema:

- allows the teacher to correct (and mark) any part of the code when an error is found. He/she can correct a single error, more than one error, or even the complete exam at once. Then, Asys will check again that everything is correct.

- prevents the teacher to introduce errors. For instance, once a property A has been already corrected by the teacher, the correction of property B could make A to fail again. But this is not a problem, because Asys recompiles and verifies all properties again.

Figure 4 shows a screenshot of ASys when reporting an error: "*class QuadrangularPrism should extend class Square*". In the left window, we can see (in different tabs) the source code of the student (automatically showing the cause of the error). This code must be modified by the teacher to solve the problem. For this, at the right window, we can see the original source code of the student, and the solution. Once corrected, at the bottom, the teacher can assign marks to the problems encountered, and reviews, which will be included in the final report for the student. Reviews are (optionally) used to provide feedback explaining the cause of the error. Observe that several (independent) marks and reviews can be added to the same property (e.g., because several problems are encountered). Note also that "review" is a listbox. It contains all previous reviews for this property. This is very useful when correcting several exams, because once a problem is identified and a review introduced, it can be reused in different exams. This significantly speeds up the assessment, because after a few exams, the errors are often repeated once and again; and the teacher only has to clic and select to automatically assign a review and a mark.

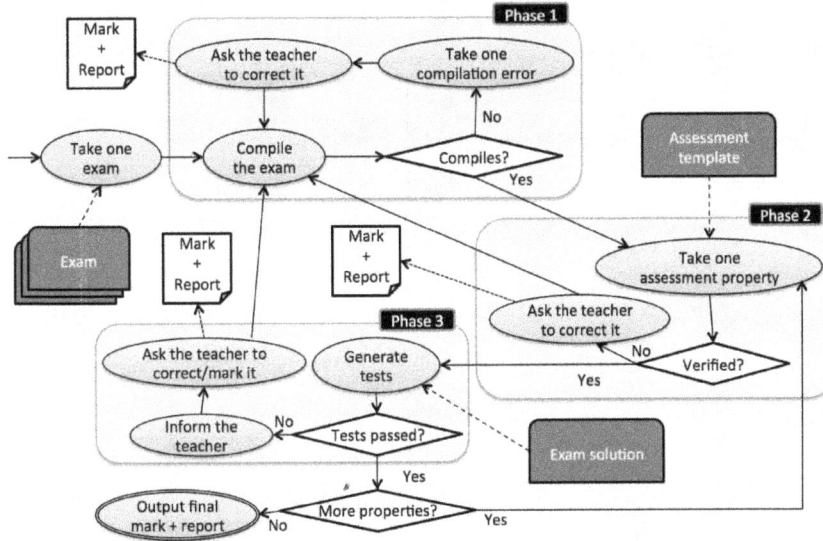

Figure 2: Data Flow Diagram of ASys

4. A USE CASE

The use case reported in this section is not an artificial one. It is a real example performed by different teachers (different from the authors) in a real university exam. Three Java exams were done during a second year university course at Universitat Politècnica de València. There were 5 teachers and 381 students involved. As normally, each of the teachers assessed a subset of the exams, and they published the marks. Then, we asked them to assess again the exams with ASys. Results are summarized in Figure 3.

In the table, each row is a different exam. The meaning of the columns is the following: Column #Exams contains the number of exams to be assessed. Column #Properties contains the number of properties in the assessment template. Column Automatic represents the percentage of properties automatically corrected by Asys (without teacher intervention). Column Average Mark contains the average mark of all exams (this is computed for the teachers assessing alone and assessing with Asys). The standard deviation of the marks is computed in column Standard Deviation. Finally, column Difference computes the difference in absolute value and percentage between the two average marks computed.

The first important conclusion is that ASys is able to automatically perform almost half of the assessment work (48%). Moreover, it is important to note that the average mark obtained with ASys and without ASys is different. The difference is small in two exams (less than 3%), but it is significant in the third exam (more than 21%). We studied with the teachers the causes of these differences. In almost all cases they were due to errors of the teachers in the first (manual) assessment, and in a few cases they were due to small differences in the interpretation of the assessment criteria (e.g., unspecified details that were penalized with -0,1 the first time and with -0,2 the second time).

The errors in the first teacher assessment were due to (1) wrong code introduced by the students in classes not involved in the exercise (and thus, no revised by the teacher and no penalized), (2) type errors not affecting the result, (3) incorrect use of interfaces, (4) code that is correct but it is marked as wrong because it is surrounded by wrong code, (5) correct code very difficult to understand even for the teacher, (6) introduction of dead code, or even (7) errors of the teacher when marking (this happened massively in the third exam and produced the difference of 21.93%: One teacher wrongly marked one question for all students).

In the same way that we, teachers, make mistakes when programming, we also make them when correcting a program. Tool assistance can help not only to make part of the work automatically, but also to improve the quality of our assessment. In this way, ASys allowed to identify many assessment errors, and, at the same time, it introduced a systematic (partially automatic) methodology to assess the exams, providing also reports for the student and the teacher.

5. CONCLUSIONS

We have presented a new tool for semi-automatic assessment of Java code. This tool introduces a new analysis

	#Exams	#Properties	Teachers with Asys			Teachers without Asys		Difference	
			Automatic	Average Mark	Standard Deviation	Average Mark	Standard Deviation	Absolute	%
Exam 1	129	7	67%	6.66	3.77	6.49	3.71	-0.17	-2.62%
Exam 2	129	10	34%	3.99	3.26	3.88	3.47	-0.11	-2.84%
Exam 3	123	7	43%	4.45	3.09	5.7	2.97	+1,25	+21,93%
Total	381	Average	48%	5.03	3.37	5.36	3.38	+0,32	+5,49%

Figure 3: Performance results obtained after assessing real exams with ASys

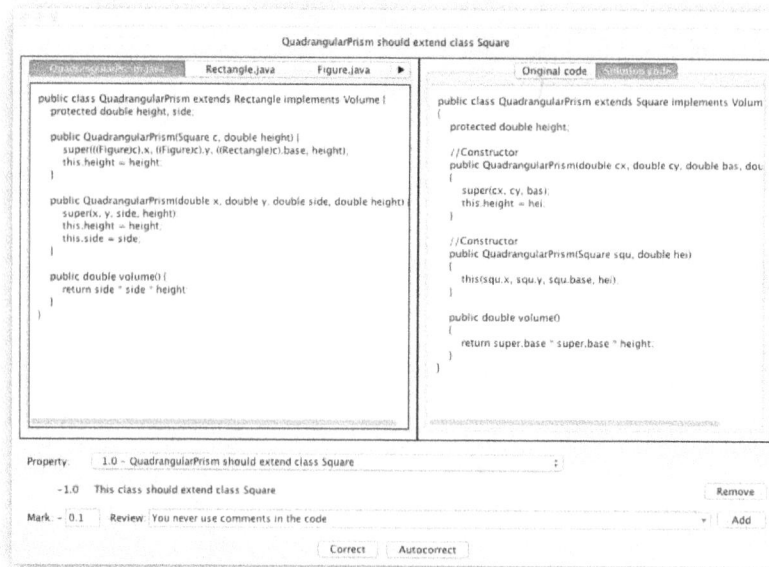

Figure 4: Screenshot of ASys

phase that can verify properties and assign a mark to them. The tool is built using a DSL defined over a new meta-programming library defined to assess Java code. The new system has been used in the university with very good results. It was able to assess more that 380 exams with several different problems including compilation errors.

As already reported in [7], it is surprising, and quite disappointing, to see how few AA systems are open-source, or even otherwise (freely) available. In many papers, it is stated that a prototype was developed but we were not able to find the tool. In some cases, a system might be mentioned to be open source but you need to contact the authors to get it. This is the cause why we are reinventing the wheel, implementing the same assessment systems once and again. For this reason, we made our system, DSL, and library open-source and publicly available, so that other researchers can reuse it or join efforts to further developing it.

6. REFERENCES

[1] K. A Rahman and M. Jan Nordin. A review on the static analysis approach in the automated programming assessment systems. In *National Conference on Programming 07*, 2007.

[2] K. Ala-Mutka. A survey of automated assessment approaches for programming assignments. In *Computer Science Education*, volume 15, pages 83–102, 2005.

[3] C. Beierle, M. Kula, and M. Widera. Automatic analysis of programming assignments. In *Proc. der 1. E-Learning Fachtagung Informatik (DeLFI ',03)*, volume P-37, pages 144–153, 2003.

[4] J. Biggs and C. Tang. Teaching for Quality Learning at University : What the Student Does (3rd Edition). In *Open University Press*, 2007.

[5] P. Denny, A. Luxton-Reilly, E. Tempero, and J. Hendrickx. CodeWrite: Supporting student-driven practice of java. In *Proceedings of the 42nd ACM technical symposium on Computer science education*, pages 09–12, 2011.

[6] R. Hendriks. Automatic exam correction. 2012.

[7] P. Ihantola, T. Ahoniemi, V. Karavirta, and O. Seppala. Review of recent systems for automatic assessment of programming assignments. In *Proceedings of the 10th Koli Calling International Conference on Computing Education Research*, pages 86–93, 2010.

[8] H. Kitaya and U. Inoue. An online automated scoring system for Java programming assignments. In *International Journal of Information and Education Technology*, volume 6, pages 275–279, 2014.

[9] M.-J. Laakso, T. Salakoski, A. Korhonen, and L. Malmi. Automatic assessment of exercises for algorithms and data structures - a case study with TRAKLA2. In *Proceedings of Kolin Kolistelut/Koli Calling - Fourth Finnish/Baltic Sea Conference on Computer Science Education*, pages 28–36, 2004.

[10] Y. Liang, Q. Liu, J. Xu, and D. Wang. The recent development of automated programming assessment. In *Computational Intelligence and Software Engineering*, pages 1–5, 2009.

[11] K. A. Naudé, J. H. Greyling, and D. Vogts. Marking student programs using graph similarity. In *Computers & Education*, volume 54, pages 545–561, 2010.

[12] A. Pears, S. Seidman, C. Eney, P. Kinnunen, and L. Malmi. Constructing a core literature for computing education research. In *SIGCSE Bulletin*, volume 37, pages 152–161, 2005.

[13] F. Prados, I. Boada, J. Soler, and J. Poch. Automatic generation and correction of technical exercices. In *International Conference on Engineering and Computer Education (ICECE 2005)*, 2005.

[14] M. Supic, K. Brkic, T. Hrkac, Z. Mihajlovic, and Z. Kalafatic. Automatic recognition of handwritten corrections for multiple-choice exam answer sheets. In *Information and Communication Technology, Electronics and Microelectronics (MIPRO)*, pages 1136–1141, 2014.

[15] S. Tung, T. Lin, and Y. Lin. An exercise management system for teaching programming. In *Journal of Software*, 2013.

[16] T. Wang, X. Su, Y. Wang, and P. Ma. Semantic similarity-based grading of student programs. In *Information and Software Technology*, volume 49, pages 99–107, 2007.

Planting Bugs: A System for Testing Students' Unit Tests

Samuel A. Brian   Richard N. Thomas   James M. Hogan   Colin Fidge

School of Electrical Engineering and Computer Science
Queensland University of Technology
Brisbane, Qld. Australia

+61 7 3138 2736   +61 7 3138 9328   +61 7 3138 2870

s.brian@qut.edu.au   r.thomas@qut.edu.au   j.hogan@qut.edu.au   c.fidge@qut.edu.au

ABSTRACT

Automated marking of student programming assignments has long been a goal of IT educators. Much of this work has focused on the correctness of small student programs, and only limited attention has been given to systematic assessment of the effectiveness of student testing. In this work, we introduce SAM (the *Seeded Auto Marker*), a system for automated assessment of student submissions which assesses both program code and unit tests supplied by the students. Our central contribution is the use of programs seeded with specific bugs to analyse the effectiveness of the students' unit tests. Beginning with our intended solution program, and guided by our own set of unit tests, we create a suite of minor variations to the solution, each seeded with a single error. Ideally, a student's unit tests should not only identify the presence of the bug, but should do so via the failure of as small a number of tests as possible, indicating focused test cases with minimal redundancy. We describe our system, the creation of seeded test programs and report our experiences in using the approach in practice. In particular, we find that students often fail to provide appropriate coverage, and that their tests frequently suffer from their poor understanding of the limitations imposed by the abstraction.

Categories and Subject Descriptors

J.1 [**Computer Applications**]: Administrative Data Processing – *Education*. K.3.1 [**Computing Milieux**]: Computer Uses in Education – *Computer-Assisted Instruction (CAI)*. K.3.2 [**Computing Milieux**]: Computer and Information Science Education – *Computer Science Education*.

General Terms

Measurement, Languages, Verification.

Keywords

Automated Assessment; Technology in Education; Unit Testing.

1. INTRODUCTION

IT educators have long attempted to automate grading of student programming assignments, with tools emerging as early as the late 1960s [1]. Most of these tools, including many in current use, focus on the assessment of (often small scale) student programs, particularly those which might appear in a CS1 or CS2 course. As

industry has demanded greater expertise in software engineering from IT graduates, so educators have given greater attention to the important skill of unit testing – especially automated testing in the context of agile development. Yet while canonical unit tests are often employed as a means to ensure the correctness of student program code, far less attention has been given to assessing the quality of the tests produced by the students themselves. At the Queensland University of Technology (QUT) we have developed SAM (the *Seeded Auto Marker*), a tool that allows us to test both student programs *and* their associated tests, scoring the programs with respect to the bugs identified by our own test cases, and scoring the student test cases with respect to their success in detecting errors intentionally introduced into an otherwise correct model solution. In this paper, we describe our approach, the tool itself and how it is used in practice to assess programs and tests.

This general approach has been used at QUT since 2009 in the third software development unit students encounter in the bachelor degree, with SAM, the present tool, introduced in 2014. The unit, entitled *Software Development*, covers modern programming practices, following the introduction of CS1/CS2 level material in the pre-requisite units. Java is the programming language used, complementing earlier studies of Python and C#. Software Development is intended to produce skilled developers capable of contributing to a software engineering team, as required in a subsequent unit that covers agile software development practices. In 2014 over 250 students completed the unit.

The topics covered in Software Development include the core Java language, application programming interfaces (APIs) and the Java library, unit testing (JUnit) and test-driven development (TDD), source control systems, design patterns and refactoring, simple graphical user interface programming and event handling, database connectivity, and simple concurrency. This wide range of topics is taught from the unifying perspective of programming in the large as a software development professional, and distinguished from earlier CS1/CS2 material.

Students complete two major programming assessment tasks in this unit and both are assessed using the testing tool. The first assignment is completed individually and involves writing a small object-oriented program to solve a specified problem. In 2014 this was a simple simulation of a water release system for a dam. Students were provided with a framework for the assignment and were required to implement two classes that conformed to the interface specifications provided. This approach helps to re-inforce the concept of abstraction [2] and simplified the design of the testing tool [3]. Students were also required to develop a suite of JUnit tests for their code. Student submissions include their code for the required classes and the JUnit tests for those classes.

The second, larger, assignment is completed in pairs and involves some GUI and database programming. Students are again provided with an initial framework for the assignment and with interfaces to which their classes must conform. In the second assignment, students are meant to follow a test-driven development approach to writing their software.

In 2014 the second assignment was to write a simulation of a car parking lot, monitoring the flow of cars into and out of the lot and the time they spent parked. The simulator had to cater for issues such as different sized parking spaces (e.g., car and motorcycle); only allowing cars to enter the car park if a parking space was available; allowing vehicles to queue and wait for spaces but with a finite length of queue and finite patience that drivers were willing to wait. For more detail about how these assignments are managed see our previous publication, *What vs. How: Comparing Students' Testing and Coding Skills* [4].

In both assignments, the effectiveness of unit tests carried a significant weight of the overall marks. For the first assignment, effectiveness of unit tests was worth 40%, the implementation (passing instructor-provided unit tests) was 35%, and code and documentation quality was 25%. In the second assignment the model implementation was worth two-thirds and the GUI implementation was worth one-third of the total mark. For the model implementation, effectiveness of unit tests was worth 25% of the mark, implementation 30%, code quality 15%, and pair process 30%. This means that the ability to effectively implement unit tests contributed to 13% of the students' final grade in the unit, which mapped well to the intended learning outcomes.

This paper is organised as follows. The extensive history of automated marking systems for programming assignments is reviewed briefly in Section 2. In Section 3, we describe our system and the marking process in detail, leading into Section 4, in which we consider the crucial question of buggy program code as a test case for unit tests. This section includes a number of examples of the choice of defect, and the results obtained. We conclude in Section 5 with further discussion of the approach and consideration of future work.

2. PREVIOUS WORK

Automated program grading tools fall into two main categories: tools that attempt to evaluate the correctness of submitted programs; and tools that attempt to evaluate the quality of submitted programs [5]. In a number of cases tools span both categories. The focus of our work is on the first category, evaluating the correctness of programs, though our work differs markedly from its predecessors in its approach to assessing unit tests.

Many of these tools, for example BOSS2 [6], CourseMarker [7] and Oto [5] focus just on the submitted program, testing its correctness using functional and/or unit testing. This may be appropriate for introductory subjects that wish to focus on programming and problem solving, but it is limiting for subjects that require students to implement their own test suites.

Other tools, such as ASSYST [8] focus on functional testing, determining if the submitted test data provides adequate test coverage of the submitted program. This is suitable for small programs but for larger programs it is useful to be able to identify the particular methods that are causing errors rather than just identify an incorrect result.

Tools such as AutoGrader [3], Marmoset [9] and Web-CAT [10] assess unit tests submitted with a program but limit their testing to comparing the results of student submitted unit tests against those of the instructor-supplied tests when run against the submitted program. This is useful in finding errors in the student program that are not identified by the student's own tests but does not evaluate the overall effectiveness of student-supplied tests in identifying other defects.

Like ProgTest [11], our SAM tool not only compares student and instructor tests when run against the student's program, but also runs the student tests against a sample solution. This allows the students' tests to be assessed more thoroughly, particularly in cases where students submit unit tests for methods not fully implemented in their programs. This corresponds to the expectation of TDD that tests will be written first. While the majority of students are expected to complete all aspects of assignments, there will inevitably be some students whose submissions are incomplete. Valid tests submitted by the student may fail on their own program code, but pass when run against the sample solution.

A key feature of our tool is that it uses a suite of erroneous programs to more fully assess the student's unit tests. Each erroneous program contains a *single error* that should be caught by at least one of the unit tests. (The erroneous programs are generated by the instructor guided by our own unit tests, which are produced by following TDD practices while implementing the sample solution.) The student's unit tests are then executed against each of the erroneous programs, and the tool determines the number of errors found by their test suite. This provides a rigorous evaluation of the student's unit tests as the tool can determine how many known errors were identified.

Several studies, as reported by Buffardi and Edwards [12], have identified that students are reluctant to adopt TDD. By placing a strong emphasis on TDD in lectures and laboratory sessions, by allocating a significant percentage of marks to writing unit tests, and by rigorously evaluating the effectiveness of unit tests, we are trying to encourage students to adopt TDD and its practices. We have found that the unit tests submitted by students in the second assignment are markedly improved compared to those submitted in the first assignment [4]. This does not guarantee that students are following TDD, but does at least demonstrate an improvement in their ability to effectively test their programs, which in itself is a useful outcome for a unit intended to produce skilled software developers. SAM provides a mechanism to allow unit tests to be rigorously evaluated without placing too large a burden on the academic staff marking the assignments.

3. TESTING TOOL

Our approach was to automate as much of the assignment marking process as was feasible, leaving only assessment of code quality to manual intervention—though even here the process was supported. The four automated steps are extraction, compilation, execution and results processing.

The first step is to extract the students' source code files from the submitted zip archives. A basic check of the presence of the required files is then performed. Submissions that failed this check often contained misnamed files or an unexpected file hierarchy, and were manually reorganised.

The compilation of each student's source code can be performed in two ways. One method is to compile all the student's source code together, just as the student would have on their own computers, which is required if the assignment specification is flexible in how it allows the students to develop their solutions. This method, however, does not detect violations of the assignment's API specifications—potentially causing run-time errors later where the problem is harder to find.

An alternative method is to compile the source files individually against the pre-compiled solution, detecting API problems at compile time. A common violation of the API specification is the students' introduction of extra public variables or methods, which is only a minor issue if the public fields are used by classes that are under the students' control only, but is a major problem when student unit tests that expect these public fields are run against the marker's solution which does not have them [4]. In these cases, the failed compilation logs allow the offending unit tests to be identified and removed from students' code. Also, a stubborn marker can look at the student's code to see if it is possible to modify the unit test to use public methods or fields from the published interface. This allows part marks to be given for identifying valid test cases, even if the unit test is implemented incorrectly. Deleting the offending unit tests or modifying them requires manual editing of the student's submission, but deleting offending tests takes much less time than attempting to modify tests. These problems arise frequently even though students are provided with a tool to check for compile-time errors and the structure of their code archives before submission.

The execution step involves running sets of unit tests and piping the output to files. Figure 1 shows how a student's tests and implementation are separated and used in three different kinds of tests: (i) the student's implementation against the solution unit tests assessing the correctness of the student's program code for the implementation mark; (ii) the solution implementation against the student's unit tests—ensuring basic correctness of the student's unit tests; and (iii) the broken implementations against the student's unit tests—assessing the effectiveness of student-supplied tests in finding defects. Both steps (ii) and (iii) are used to calculate the unit test mark.

Some issues may inadvertently emerge in the testing of broken implementations, with student tests relying on a correct implementation for a loop condition disrupted by the planted bug. Timeout conditions are thus an essential part of the process.

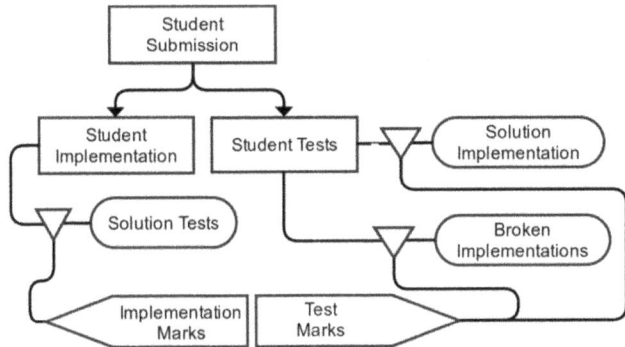

Figure 1. Student Submission Execution Process

The final automated step is the processing of the test results. The logs of unit test outputs are scraped for the raw results: the number of tests passed out of the tests performed. The mark given for students' implementation code is simply proportional to the fraction of our solution tests passed.

Calculating the mark for the students' unit testing code is more involved as a successful test suite will have at least one failed unit test for each broken implementation (true positives), but the students' tests that incorrectly fail the solution implementation (false negatives) must also be considered. A 'broken' implementation is considered to have been detected if a student's test suite shows more failed tests than when the student's tests are

run against the solution implementation, and a mark can then be awarded that is proportional to the fraction of broken implementations detected.

4. EXAMPLE SCENARIO

In the 2014 car park assignment, students had to implement four classes to complete the model: a `CarPark` class, a `Vehicle` abstract class, and `Car` and `MotorCycle` classes that extend `Vehicle`. The required test suite consisted of `CarParkTests`, `CarTests`, and `MotorCycleTests` classes, where the `Vehicle` class is tested indirectly through the subclasses.

For instance, one student's submitted implementation of the model passed 21 of 56 unit tests from the marker's solution `CarParkTests`, 7 of 9 from `CarTests`, and 48 of 53 from `MotorCycleTests`. By weighting these results to 7, 1, and 4 marks respectively, the total implementation mark is calculated as shown in Table 1 as 7.026/12.

Table 1. Solution Tests vs. Student Implementation

Test Class	Tests		Marks	
	Passed	Out Of	Score	Out Of
`CarParkTests`	21	56	2.625	7
`CarTests`	7	9	0.778	1
`MotorCycleTests`	48	53	3.623	4
			TOTAL: 7.026	12

With our solution implementation, the student submission's test suite passed 19 of 22 tests in `CarParkTests`, 0 of 33 in `CarTests`, and 30 of 30 in `MotorCycleTests`, as per Table 2.

Table 2. Student Tests vs. Solution Implementation

Test Class	Passed	Out Of
`CarParkTests`	19	22
`CarTests`	0	33
`MotorCycleTests`	30	30

The anomaly of every unit test in `CarTests` failing the solution implementation suggests some fundamental misunderstanding of the assignment specification. In this case, two `Car` objects were constructed before each `CarTests` unit test was run, the second with an invalid argument (the `-1` below):

```
@Before
public void setUp() throws Exception {
  carTest = new Car("C1", 1, true);
  carTest2 = new Car("C2", -1, false);
}
```

This invalid argument caused an exception to be thrown by our solution implementation, but not the student's own implementation which failed to check it (causing at least one of the failures against the solution `CarTests` where it passed 7 of 9 tests).

The tests that failed in the results described in Table 2 are false negatives, and were used as a reference to compare the results of the submission's tests run against our broken implementations. Two suites of broken implementations were constructed for marking: *brokenVehicles* and *buggyCarParks*. As the students were not instructed which test class (`CarTests` or `MotorCycleTests`) would be used to test broken implementations in *brokenVehicles*, both were evaluated. Three scenarios occurred when determining if a bug in a broken implementation had been detected by the students' tests.

47

In a 'broken' variation of the solution implementation titled *brokenVehicles_Fails_Vehicle_enterParkedState_NoThrow_IncorrectState*, one exception check was removed from the `enterParkedState` method. When run against the student's `MotorCycleTests`, it resulted in one more failure (29/30) than when the student's tests were run against our solution implementation (30/30), meaning that the student's unit test suite successfully detected the bug (as shown in Table 3).

Table 3. Test results that show more failures than reference (bug detected)

Test Class	Passed	Out Of	Reference	Detected
CarTests	0	33	0	*No*
MotorCycleTests	29	30	30	*Yes*

Another of our broken implementations is *brokenVehicles_Fails_CarConstructor_IncorrectCarSize* which fails to correctly set the "small car" Boolean flag which is passed as an argument to the `Car` constructor. An equal number of failures occurred with this broken implementation as with the reference results (shown in Table 4), which means that the student's tests failed to detect the bug.

Table 4. Test results that show failures that equal reference (bug not detected)

Test Class	Passed	Out Of	Reference	Detected
CarTests	0	33	0	*No*
MotorCycleTests	30	30	30	*No*

Lastly, our *brokenVehicles_Fails_Vehicle_Constructor_NoThrow* broken implementation resulted in *fewer* failures (Table 5) because the exception check that is absent is the one that caused all of the submission's `CarTests` to fail previously. The bug is considered undetected by the student when this scenario occurs.

Table 5. Test results that show fewer failures than reference (bug not detected)

Test Class	Passed	Out Of	Reference	Detected
CarTests	33	33	0	*No*
MotorCycleTests	30	30	30	*No*

By applying this process to all of the broken implementations, the student submission's tests were found to detect 14 of 27 bugs from *brokenVehicles*, and 4 of 17 bugs from *buggyCarparks* (including 1 broken `Car` subclass). These results are weighted to 2 and 3 marks respectively, resulting in the marks in Table 6.

Table 6. Student Tests vs Broken Implementations

Broken Implementation Suite	Broken Implementations		Marks	
	Detected	Out Of	Score	Out Of
brokenVehicles	14	27	1.037	2
buggyCarParks	4	17	0.706	3
		TOTAL:	1.743	5

When the automatic process is complete and a submission has been given a mark for its implementation and unit tests, the manual marking step must be performed. As part of SAM, manual marking is aided by providing a comment box and mark entry boxes for additional criteria such as code quality and GUI functionality, quality, and testing, from which the total mark can be calculated (see Figure 2). The tool allows a compressed archive to be created of the whole directory containing a student's compilation logs, raw test results, and a marking rubric pre-filled with the marks and comments, all of which may be returned to the student.

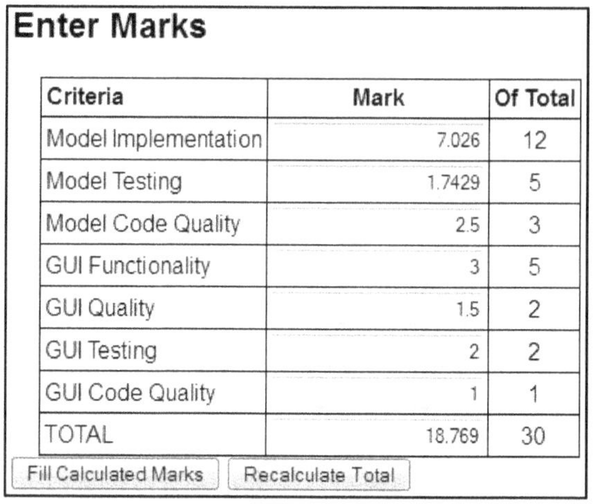

Enter Marks

Criteria	Mark	Of Total
Model Implementation	7.026	12
Model Testing	1.7429	5
Model Code Quality	2.5	3
GUI Functionality	3	5
GUI Quality	1.5	2
GUI Testing	2	2
GUI Code Quality	1	1
TOTAL	18.769	30

[Fill Calculated Marks] [Recalculate Total]

Figure 2. Final Mark Calculation Screen

5. BUGGY IMPLEMENTATIONS

This section provides two examples of deliberate errors used to assess the effectiveness of student-submitted unit test suites. The examples cover the simple case of a unit test that depends on just the method being tested and a more complex case where the unit test calls more than one method. Each example shows the "buggy" method, a unit test that detects the error, and a student test for the method that failed to detect the error.

In the simple case where a unit test only calls the method being tested, a failure is a clear indication that the bug has been identified. The constructor of the `Vehicle` class was required to throw an exception if the arrival time argument was zero or negative, meaning that the vehicle arrived *before* the first minute the car park was open. The commented-out condition below is the one we removed to 'break' the method.

```
public Vehicle(String vehID, int arrivalTime)
   throws VehicleException  {
//if (arrivalTime <= 0) {
// throw new VehicleException("Vehicle " +
// vehID + ": arrival time must be strictly
//  positive");
//}
 this.vehID = vehID;
 this.arrivalTime = arrivalTime;
 // ... other initialisation
}
```

The following unit test will catch this error because the `Vehicle` constructor no longer throws the `VehicleException` that is expected by the test.

```
@Test (expected = VehicleException.class)
public void testCarConsExceptionZero()
  throws VehicleException {
 Car c = new Car("brokenZero", 0, true);
}
```

The following unit test is an example of a student test that did not catch the error. It is a simple error: the student did not anticipate the exception to be thrown.

```
@Test
public void testCarZeroIsSatisfied()
  throws VehicleException {
 Car c = new Car("XYZ012", 0, true);
 assertFalse(c.isSatisfied());
}
```

Here, our buggy code will detect the incorrect unit test as the test will *not* fail when the tool expects it to.

A more complex situation occurs when a unit test calls two or more methods. When evaluating the test it is difficult to determine which buggy method caused the test to fail. The `Vehicle` class has a method `exitParkedState`, which causes the vehicle to exit the car park after earlier parking successfully. One of our buggy versions of this method introduced an off-by-one error. The second condition, underlined below, should be < and not <=.

```java
public void exitParkedState(int departureTime)
throws VehicleException {
  String msg = "";
  if (this.inQueue || !this.parked) {
    msg = " in queue or otherwise not parked";
    throw new VehicleException("Vehicle " +
                        this.vehID + msg);
  }
  if (departureTime <= this.parkingTime) {
    msg = ": departure time cannot be earlier than";
    msg += " parking time";
    throw new VehicleException("Vehicle " +
                        this.vehID + msg);
  }
  this.departureTime = departureTime;
  this.parked = false;
}
```

The following unit test will catch the error because the buggy code will throw an exception when `exitParkedState` is called, causing an error in the JUnit runner as the Exception is not expected,indicating to the tool that the bug was identified.

```java
@Test
public void testExitParkedValidDepartOnParking()
throws VehicleException {
  this.testMC.enterParkedState(PARK_ON_ARRIVAL,
                        DURATION);
  this.testMC.exitParkedState(PARK_ON_ARRIVAL);
  assertTrue("Park=Departure",
          !this.testMC.isParked());
  assertEquals("Park=Departure", PARK_ON_ARRIVAL,
          testMC.getDepartureTime());
}
```

The following unit tests are examples of student tests that did not catch this error. In this case the student had thought to check for off-by-one errors, but was unable to translate this idea into a correctly structured test with the appropriate logic, with the result that their tests did not identify the real bug.

```java
@Test (expected = VehicleException.class)
public void testExitParkedValidDepartOnParking()
throws VehicleException {
  this.testMC.enterParkedState(PARK_ON_ARRIVAL,
                        DURATION);
  this.testMC.exitParkedState(PARK_ON_ARRIVAL);
}
```

```java
@Test
public void testExitParkedValidDepartOnParking()
throws VehicleException {
  this.testMC.enterParkedState(PARK_ON_ARRIVAL,
                        DURATION);
  this.testMC.exitParkedState(PARK_ON_ARRIVAL+1);
  assertTrue("Park=Departure",
          !this.testMC.isParked());
  assertEquals("Park=Depart", PARK_ON_ARRIVAL+1,
          testMC.getDepartureTime());
}
```

In this situation, the tool can determine that the student has not identified the incorrect logic of the broken program, and this is correctly reflected in the mark calculated by the tool. However, one challenge is that the student's test calls *two* methods – `enterParkedState` and `exitParkedState`. When using the instructor-supplied tests to assess the student's program, the tool cannot determine *which* of the methods caused the error, and so cannot provide detailed feedback beyond recording the fact that the test did not detect the error.

6. CONCLUSIONS

In this work, we have introduced a new tool, SAM, developed to assess automatically student programming assignments and their associated unit tests. In contrast to many previous approaches (see Section 2) our approach pays particular attention to the problem of unit testing, and in particular the problem of assessing the effectiveness of unit tests in detecting known defects. Following the strategy we introduced earlier [4], we assess unit tests against a suite of variations on the model solution, otherwise correct implementations seeded with a single known defect.

Use of the tool has provided a number of insights into the problems experienced by intermediate students transitioning from CS1 and CS2 sized exercises to those approximating contributions needed in a professional project. Among the more important of these themes are:

- Weak test coverage overall;
- Misconceptions about the role of unit testing and the primacy of the object abstraction; and
- Diffuse and redundant test cases.

As we discussed previously [4], however, the approach does lead to significant improvements in performance between the first and second assignments in the unit. The use of SAM has allowed far better feedback to be provided, and fewer manual interventions in the marking process. Improvements to the system for 2015 will include a more sophisticated submission checking system, placing the responsibility for structural correctness on the students and reducing the tedious manual fixes that have been required to date.

7. AVAILABILITY

The SAM program is available at https://bitbucket.org/samuelbr/automarker-inb370 as a Python script with a web interface. The tool can be configured for Java programming assignments that are structured as described in this paper.

8. ACKNOWLEDGMENTS

We wish to thank Dr. Andrew Craik, now at IBM Canada, for developing the original assignment marking scripts upon which SAM has been based. We would also like to thank Lawrence Buckingham (QUT) for his contributions to the testing and development of the original marking scripts and SAM.

9. REFERENCES

[1] Hext, J. B. and Winings, J. W. An automatic grading scheme for simple programming exercises. *Commun. ACM*, 12, 5 (May 1969), 272-275.

[2] Schmolitzky, A. "Objects first, interfaces next" or interfaces before inheritance. In *Proceedings of the Companion to the 19th annual ACM SIGPLAN conference on Object-oriented programming systems, languages, and applications* (Vancouver, BC, Canada, 2004). ACM.

[3] Helmick, M. T. Interface-based programming assignments and automatic grading of java programs. In *Proceedings of the 12th annual SIGCSE conference on Innovation and technology in computer science education* (Dundee, Scotland, 2007). ACM.

[4] Fidge, C., Hogan, J. and Lister, R. What vs. How: Comparing Students' Testing and Coding Skills. In *Proceedings of the 15th Australasian Computing Education Conference (ACE 2013)* (Adelaide, Australia, January, 2013). Australian Computer Society, Inc.

[5] Tremblay, G., Guerin, F., Pons, A. and Salah, A. Oto: A Generic and Extensible Tool for Marking Programming Assignments. *Software Pract. Exper.*, 38, 3 (March 2008), 307-333.

[6] Joy, M., Griffiths, N. and Boyatt, R. The boss online submission and assessment system. *J. Educ. Resour. Comput.*, 5, 3 (September 2005), 2.

[7] Higgins, C., Hegazy, T., Symeonidis, P. and Tsintsifas, A. The CourseMarker CBA System: Improvements over Ceilidh. *Education and Information Technologies*, 8, 3 (September 2003), 287-304.

[8] Jackson, D. and Usher, M. Grading student programs using ASSYST. In *Proceedings of the 28th SIGCSE technical symposium on Computer science education* (San Jose, California, USA, 1997). ACM.

[9] Spacco, J., Hovemeyer, D., Pugh, W., Emad, F., Hollingsworth, J. K. and Padua-Perez, N. Experiences with marmoset: designing and using an advanced submission and testing system for programming courses. In *Proceedings of the 11th annual SIGCSE conference on Innovation and technology in computer science education* (Bologna, Italy, 2006). ACM.

[10] Edwards, S. H. Teaching software testing: automatic grading meets test-first coding. In *Proceedings of the Companion of the 18th annual ACM SIGPLAN conference on Object-oriented programming, systems, languages, and applications* (Anaheim, CA, USA, 2003). ACM.

[11] Souza, D. M. d., Maldonado, J. C. and Barbosa, E. F. ProgTest: An environment for the submission and evaluation of programming assignments based on testing activities. In *Proceedings of the 24th IEEE-CS Conference on Software Engineering Education and Training* (May 22-24, 2011). IEEE Computer Society.

[12] Buffardi, K. and Edwards, S. H. Exploring influences on student adherence to test-driven development. In *Proceedings of the 17th ACM annual conference on Innovation and technology in computer science education* (Haifa, Israel, July 3-5, 2012). ACM.

Evaluation of Source Code with Item Response Theory

Marc Berges
TUM School of Education
Technische Universität München
Arcisstr. 21, 80333 München, Germany
berges@tum.de

Peter Hubwieser
TUM School of Education
Technische Universität München
Arcisstr. 21, 80333 München, Germany
peter.hubwieser@tum.de

ABSTRACT

The analysis of source code produced by novice programmers could provide interesting insights into their learning progress, particularly in introductory programming courses. Yet, as the programming ability of a person is assumed to be quite complex, it is not likely that it would be observable directly in its total. Instead, we regard those abilities as latent psychometric constructs and apply the methodology of item response theory (IRT) to assess their manifestations. In preparatory work, we had identified a list of items that represent the central concepts of object-oriented programming. In this paper we propose a methodology that allows the evaluation of coding abilities by analyzing the application of those concepts. We demonstrate this methodology by exemplarily analyzing source code that was produced during programming projects. The results provide interesting information about the difficulty of the concepts' application and the distribution of the respective coding abilities among the students.

Categories and Subject Descriptors

K.3.2 [**Computer and Information Science Education**]: Computer science education

Keywords

programming novices; code analysis; item-response theory

1. INTRODUCTION

A few years ago, we have introduced a preliminary programming course for the freshmen of computer science at our university [9]. These courses offered a broad research field for the investigation of source code that was written by students with well-known levels of programming experience in a closely controlled setting.

Although the direct evaluation of source code is difficult, several methodologies for assessing programming abilities from code have been presented, e.g. qualitative analysis of students' solutions [13], measures of code quality [8] or investigations about misconceptions [16].

Yet, due to its complexity, we do not assume that any programming ability could be measured in a direct way. Nevertheless, we could regard certain attributes of the source code as manifestations of latent psychometric constructs according to the principles of item response theory. More detailed, we could treat the application of certain structural elements like loops, conditional statements or inheritance operators as positive responses on certain items (e.g. "existence of loops"). In consequence, the probability of such positive responses in dependence on the item difficulty and the estimated person abilities could be described by certain psychometric models, e.g. the Rasch Model.

In the research project of this paper, we have applied the item response theory to evaluate coding abilities of freshmen on the basis of items gathered from their source code.

2. RELATED WORK

The analyzing and scoring of object-oriented code is a central topic in educational research ever since object-oriented programming has been taught in introductory courses in computer science.

For example, Börstler et al. proposed in [5] three categories for the evaluation of object-oriented example programs according to certain criteria like content, style or modeling. Sanders and Thomas introduced in [16] a check-list for scoring object-oriented programs by investigating concepts and misconceptions in object-oriented programming. In contrast, an automatic approach is conducted in [17], based on a framework for static code analysis of students' programs. For this, Truong et al. summarized common poor programming practices and common logical errors from literature. Additionally, they conducted a survey among teaching staff and students. The framework is working on a XML basis and enables the students to get feedback on their programs and rate them automatically.

Currently, there are several tools for educational purposes that assess code in an automatic way. Many work online like the one introduced in [18]. In [10] the scoring of the International Olympiad in Informatics is investigated. Kemkes et al. score the code with 1 if it runs successfully on a given set of input data. Otherwise it is scored with 0. In addition, they compared this methodology to other scoring schemes with the help of item response theory. Finally, they state that the simple scoring is the most applicable if an automatic scoring is needed.

ITiCSE'15, July 6–8, 2015, Vilnius, Lithuania.
Copyright ©️ 2015 ACM 978-1-4503-3440-2/15/07 ...$15.00.
DOI: http://dx.doi.org/10.1145/2729094.2742619.

One solution for the problem of a simple assessment system could be to investigate the syntax elements of a programming task with an open solution. A recent example is the research presented in [12]. The authors investigated differences in the correct solutions of students. For this purpose, they define a taxonomy that distinguishes the code according to structure, syntax and presentation. Structure means different control flow in the code, syntax means differences in the code with the same control flow structure. Finally, presentation means variation in the identifier names or number of white-spaces for example.

Some additional tools and algorithms for student assessment in computer science courses are presented in [19]. Winters and Payne conducted an item-response analysis on students' score data that was gathered during the semester. Additionally, existing tools were evaluated and the advantages of such a methodology for the process of identifying suitable items were pointed out.

3. BACKGROUND

In classical test theory (CTT), the construct of interest (e.g. student abilities) is considered to be measured directly by item scores, yet this might be error-prone. This straight-forward approach is not suitable for measuring such complex constructs as programming abilities. In contrast, the item response theory (IRT) regards the constructs of interest as latent psychometric constructs that cannot be measured directly. Nevertheless, the probability of correct answers depends from those constructs in a certain way: $P(X_{ik} = 1|\theta_i, \beta_k) = f(\theta_i, \beta_k)$, where θ_i is the parameter of person i, representing the manifestation of the psychometric construct, β_k the parameter of item k, representing its difficulty, and $f(\theta_i, \beta_k)$ a function that is determined by the psychometric model (e.g. the Rasch Model (RM), see below)

The latent construct might be uni- or multi-dimensional. Depending on the theoretically based assumptions of the structure of the psychometric construct, different mathematical models can be applied according to IRT.

A logistic model with one parameter (1pl) was introduced by Rasch [15]. The basic idea of the Rasch model is that the probability of solving an item is determined by the difference of a person's ability in the latent dimension θ and the difficulty of the item itself (β).

There are three model restrictions related to the Rasch model: the items have to be locally stochastically independent, fulfill specific objectivity, and measure one latent construct [1, pp. 20].

Basically, there are two approaches in the item analysis. First, a set of homogeneous items has to be found that is conducted to one latent psychometric construct. Second, the itemset has to be fit to a proper item response test or model, respectively. For these purposes, there are several tests.

The nonparametric tests for the Rasch model that are based on a Markov Chain Monte-Carlo algorithm are a suitable test framework for small sample sizes. Basically, the lack of data is reduced by simulating data matrices that have equal row and column sums than the estimated dataset. For that purpose two columns of the original matrix are randomly chosen. Afterwards, the rows with different values are randomly changed. This procedure leads to a new matrix with equal margins. As the algorithm needs the matrices to be independent of the initial matrix and to occur with

the same probability, not all simulated matrices can be used for the calculation [11, pp. 4]. For the nonparametric tests a valid Rasch model is assumed. in a valid Rasch model the row and column sums are a sufficient statistic and because of that matrices with different values but equal row and column sums can be compared.

The general idea behind the nonparametric tests is the comparison of all item pairs [14]. A violation in homogeneity can be assumed if there are more unequal item pairs in the observed matrix than in the simulated ones. So, the test compares the observed test statistic with simulated test statistics [11]. For the characterization of a latent construct, a set of homogeneous items is necessary.

The local stochastic independence has to be proven for validating the Rasch model. On the one hand, the items are not allowed to be too similar. With regard to two items, this can be expressed by the number of equal response patterns. In contrast to the assumption of homogeneity, violation of the local stochastic independence is expressed by too many equal response patterns.

On the other hand, violation of the local stochastic independence can be a result of a learning effect within the items; participants answer on one item is dependent of the solution of another one. For this reason, only those patterns that are both answered correctly are summed. The local stochastic independence is important to find items for a proper test framework. For the definition of the latent dimension, dependent items can be useful as well.

If the ratio of the items' number and the number of participants is suitable, parametric tests can be applied. Generally, all these tests are based on the assumption that the model is valid in every sub population that is grouped by chance. So, if there is no significant difference in the parameters if the investigated population is separated into two groups the model is assumed to be valid. Especially, if there are other measures like previous knowledge or gender aspects, these criteria should be used for finding different groups [1, p. 63].

The first test is the Likelihood Ratio Test (LRT). For the test, the likelihood is calculated for the estimated parameters of each group and for the complete population as well. Afterwards, the likelihoods are compared. If the estimated parameters fit the model in the subgroups as well as in the complete population, the model is assumed to be valid. Otherwise it would be better to estimate the parameters for each single group and calculate separate models [7, pp. 86].

Another test for the model fitting that is based on the idea of separating the population into two groups is the Wald-test. In contrast to the LRT, the standard Wald-test is comparing the items directly. So, the standard Wald-test can identify items that violate the model assumptions [7, pp. 89].

4. COURSE DESIGN

In autumn 2008 we developed a course at our university for the freshmen studying Computer Science (CS) [9]. It takes place just before the first semester. All the students starting their studies are invited during their enrollment process. The participation is voluntarily. The necessity of the course results from the German lecture system at universities. During the semester there are mainly lectures with only very little time for practical experiences. Nevertheless, it is officially communicated that it would be possible to study CS without any prior programming knowledge, which implies that students without such prior knowledge should be accommodated somehow, too. Therefore we have developed and installed specific programming courses for this purpose that take place before the first semester.

All students were asked at the registration to self-assess their prior programming experience in one of three levels: (1) "I have no experience at all", (2) "I have already written programs", (3) "I have already written object-oriented programs".

Based on this information we tried to compose the groups – 6 to 15 participants each – as homogeneously as possible. The demands of the programs the students should realize differed according to their respective level of programming experience. The students of the first level were asked to program a "Mastermind" game. The groups of level 2 should realize a tool for managing results from a sports tournament (e.g. a football league). The groups of the 3rd level should program a version of the dice game "Yahzee".

The course took two and a half days. All participants worked on their own (instead of in teams), because we wanted to investigate the individual learning outcome. However, the students were actively encouraged to talk to each other. The material was presented in the form of worksheets that contained all the required information. Additionally, each group was coached by an experienced student as a peer tutor. The students were encouraged to approach the tasks in a self-directed learning process. So, the tutors were responsible for helping the students to understand the worksheets and tools, but they were advised not to give any assistance (or instruction) on programming itself. We suggested that the students use BlueJ due to the reasons mentioned by Bergin [4] for their first steps in programming. Towards the end of the course, they had the choice to switch over to Eclipse.

5. DATA COLLECTION

Based on a concept extraction from the materials of the underlying course, a list of 21 concepts was formed according to the method described in [3]: *access modifier (AM), array (AR), assignment (AG), association (AC), attribute (AT), class (CL), conditional statement (CS), constructor (CO), data encapsulation (DE), datatype (DT), inheritance (IN), initialization (IS), instance (IT), loop statement (LO), method (ME), object (OB), object orientation (OO), operator (OP), overloading (OV), parameter (PA), and state (ST)*. For the final concept list, four of them are eliminated because of different reasons. OO is eliminated because it is provided by design of Java. CL and DT are excluded because it cannot be distinguished between "implementation by the students" and "implementation forced by the IDE". Finally, IT is the same as OB and because of that only OB is included into the list.

For the calculation of a model in the item-response theory, a set of items is needed. In [3] the concepts mentioned above, were split up into observable items in the code. These items cover all observable aspects that are related to a specific concept. The list below presents these items, formulated as questions which can be 1-rated if the code answers the item with "yes", or 0-rated otherwise. The abbreviations in front of each item points to the underlying concept. The items included in the final model are underlined.

IN1 Is there inheritance from existing classes?
IN2 Is the code using a manually created inheritance hierarchy?

ME1 Is there a method call in the code?
ME2 Is there a method declaration?
ME3 Is there a return value in a method?
AG1 Is an assignment used in the code?
CO1 Is there a declaration of a new constructor?
CO2 Is there a call of a constructor?
ST1 Is it possible to save the state of an object?
ST2 Is it possible to change the state of an object?
ST3 Is it possible to use the state of an object?
AC1 Is there an association between classes in the code?
AC2 Is there any use of associations between classes?
DE1 Is the visibility of the attributes other than public or default?
OP1 Is the assignment operator used?
OP2 Are there any logical operators used in the code?
OP3 Are there any other operators used, apart from the assignment or logical operators?
AR1 Are there arrays with pre-initialization declared in the code?
AR2 Are there arrays without pre-initialization declared in the code?
AR3 Is there any access of the elements of an array in the code?
AR4 Is there an initialization with *new*?
AR5 Are methods of the class `Arrays` used in the code?
IS1 Is there an explicit initialization of the attributes?
PA1 Is there a method call with parameters in the code?
PA2 Are there any method declarations with parameters used?
PA3 Are the parameters of a method declarations used in the method body?
AT1 Are there attributes declared in the code?
AT2 Are attributes of other classes accessed?
AT3 Are attributes of class accessed within this class?
CS1 Is there an IF-statement without ELSE?
CS2 Is there an IF-statement with ELSE?
CS3 Is there a SWITCH-statement?
OB1 Is there a declaration of any object?
OB2 Is a declared object used in the code?
OB3 Is there a reference to its own object using *this*?
OV1 Is there a declaration of an overloaded method?
OV2 Is there an overloaded method used in the code?
LO1 Is there a use of loops?
AM1 Are the access modifiers *public, private* or *protected* used with attributes or methods?

During the investigation, the students were asked to implement a small project on the basis of an assignment that did not include explicit questions on programming. Nevertheless, the resulting programming code contains the responses on these questions. This is why we can assume the code-items to be assignments posed to the participants.

In total 321 datasets, gathered from 2008 to 2011, are included in this research project. Each dataset consists of the personal data and a vector with the responses on all code items.

6. RESULTS

The main goal of this research project was to develop and evaluate a methodology for assessing personal coding abilities from source code. For this purpose, we had to find a model that would describe the measured outcomes in a suitable way. Additionally, we had to validate the model by evaluating its outcomes.

6.1 Model Validation

The first step towards a valid item set for a Rasch model is to identify items that violate the preconditions of the Rasch model. First, all items that are related to the same structural element as others are eliminated. For example, both items ST1 and AT1 need a variable declaration in the code to be 1-rated. More precisely, this affects the items AG1, ST1, ST2, ST3, and OB1.

As all the tests that rely on dividing the population or item set into two parts need differing items in both parts of the population, the trivial items are removed in advance. An item is said to be trivial if it is either 1-rated for almost all or almost none of the participants. For that reason a limitation level of 0.01 is defined for this study. In particular, this affects only the item OP1, which deals with the use of an assignment operator.

Due to the large number of items in comparison to the number of participants at the beginning, the calculation of an exact test on local stochastic independence and homogeneity is not possible. Because of that, the non-parametric tests are applied. First, the item set is reduced to those items that are homogeneous.

Starting with the 33 items after the exclusion process, all items that violate the homogeneity criterion are eliminated. In the first run the items DE1, OP2, IS1, AR5, CS2, CO1, AR4, CS3, OV1, AR1, PA2, PA3, ME2, and IN1 violate the homogeneity criterion. The selection criteria for which items are eliminated is the frequency of the dependent items. Thus, DE1 has the most dependencies, while IN1 has the least. In general, all pairs of dependent items are listed and the items are removed from that list one by one until the list is empty; then, no dependencies are left. Afterwards, a new set of simulated matrices is calculated based on the new item set. The second run results in elimination of AR3, AR2, LO1, OB3, ME1, AC2, AT1, AT3, ME3, PA1, and AC1. Once again, the items are ordered by their number of dependencies. After a third and fourth elimination run, the items AM1 and CS1 are removed from the item set. In the end the remaining items are homogeneous. Now, as the item set has been reduced to six items, the exact tests can be applied for justifying the nonparametric tests. The Martin-Löf test is conducted on the resulting item set. Here, the p-value is 0.66. Thus, the items are assumed to be homogeneous and locally stochastically independent. After that, the two test statistics presented in [2] are calculated. For the general goodness-of-fit test statistic G^2, a value of 62.1 is the result. Additionally, the χ^2 test statistic X^2 results in a value of 139.4. Both are not significant for 13 degrees of freedom to a level of 0.05 in the χ^2-distribution. Again, the H_0-hypothesis is rejected and the items are assumed to be homogeneous.

Following the test on homogeneity, the items that violate local stochastic independence in the way of being too similar in their results have to be found. Actually, only the item OB2 is dependent on another item and is, therefore, eliminated from the result set. Last, the learning aspect of the local stochastic independence is tested. Here, no item violates the presumption.

The resulting item set with the items IN2, CO2, OP3, AT2, and OV2 is valid with regard to the presumption of the Rasch model.

After validating the presumptions of the Rasch model, fitting of the data and a valid model are calculated for the given data. The likelihood-ratio test has a p-value of 0.5 for the first pre-knowledge splitting criterion (pre-knowledge level 1 vs. pre-knowledge levels 2&3). The test is not significant and, because of that, the model is assumed to be valid. A look at the Wald test for the items also shows no significant model violations (p<0.05). For both tests we have to assume a vector that splits the population into two parts. For this reason students' self-assessments of the previous knowledge (pk) concerning programming is chosen as a separator and, additionally, gender is chosen to find differences. Concerning the students' previous knowledge, two levels are put together and compared with a third level to get two groups. No model violations can be found for all three combinations. Gender as a separation criterion is not applicable as only 19% of the participants were female. As mentioned in [11, p. 99], the two groups should be almost of equal size.

Concerning the gender aspect, a closer look at the different items with separated participant groups show the violations in the model fit. For that reason, all items are split by gender. Afterwards for each group the items are tested if they are trivial. Due to the small group size of the female participants, a ratio of 0.01 is too small as it is less than one person. Because of that, the limit is set to 0.02, which means that at least one person has to have a different answer than the others. The problem occurs with the item OP3, where there is less than 0.02 different answers for the female group. Additionally, the item IN2 has a value of only 0.03 for the female participants. Nevertheless, this is not critical for the test. All other items have a distribution between the answers of 0.3 and 0.7 (CO2 and OV2) and 0.5 for both groups (AT2).

As described above, the Rasch model is a one-parametric test model where the items only differ in their level of difficulty. To show that another model with more estimated parameters does not fit better, a two-parametric test model is calculated and both models are compared. The comparison coefficients AIC and BIC [6] to get two groups have almost the same values. The two-parametric model provides no advantage by introducing an additional parameter.

6.2 Model Interpretation

After fitting the dataset to a valid Rasch model, the next paragraphs present the results of the model. In Figure 1 the item characteristic curves for all items that are included in the model are shown. According to the definition of the Rasch model, they only differ in their level of difficulty. This is expressed in the figure by a shift on the x-axis, which shows the latent parameter on a scale of -10 to 10. All curves are parallel and only differ in the value of the latent parameter at the probability of 50% for rating a code item with "yes" (1). The probability that an individual with a specific value of the latent parameter has solved a specific item is drawn on the y-axis.

By definition, the item parameters sum up to 0. The items OP3 and IN2 have values of -5.4 and 5.0, respectively. The item that is closest to the average of 0 for the investigated population is AT2 (0.84). The use of attributes of other classes, either direct or by using a method, indicate participants with an average ability in coding, concerning the investigated items. Interestingly, all items except AT2 and OV2 have the same distance between each other. In general, Figure 1 presents a ranking of the items. The simplest item is OP3, which represents the use of arithmetic operators. The underlying concept is simple to code and all projects

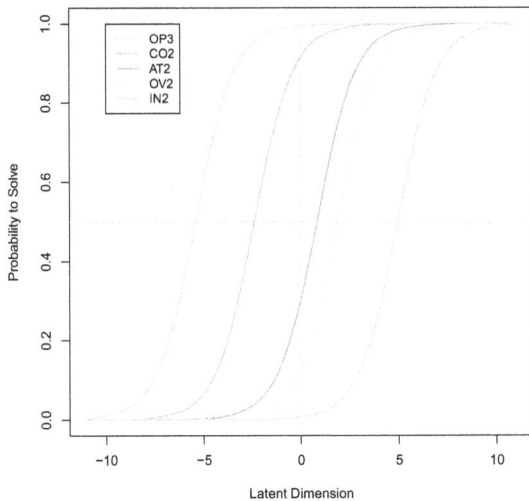

Figure 1: Item characteristic curves (ICC) of all items included in the Rasch model

need calculations. As a result, the position within the items is not surprising. The next concept in the ranking is CO2, which indicates the use of a constructor or an initialization of an object. Again, the underlying concept is easy, but the basic object-oriented notions have to be implemented as well. Next, the items AT2 and OV2 indicate the use of interrelations between classes. As mentioned above, the first one represents the use of foreign methods and attributes. The second one represents the use of overloaded methods. Regarding the last item IN2 (use of an own class hierarchy), these two items represent more advanced concepts of object orientation. Thus, the item set contains representatives of simple coding concepts that can be related to the procedural paradigm, as well as representatives of advanced object-oriented notions.

In general, if the Rasch model is valid, the marginals of the underlying dataset are a sufficient statistic. Because of that, each possible person score is related to a person parameter. For mathematical reasons the parameters for the margins 0 and 5 cannot be estimated, but have to be interpolated. The mean value of the person parameters is 0.11; the median is -0.92.

Actually, there is a medium correlation (0.42) between the self-assessment of the students' previous knowledge and their person parameters (p-value $\ll 0.01$). Regarding gender of the participants, females (-0.13) have a lower – but not significant – average person parameter than male students (0.26). On the other hand, the self-assessment has a significant difference (p-value $\ll 0.01$) in the person parameters. The students with previous knowledge have a mean value of 1.06, while those without any previous knowledge have a mean value of -0.93.

In addition to students' previous knowledge and their gender, lines of code are another measurement that can be conducted on the source code. In particular, the projects differed a lot in their complexity. There were projects with only a few lines of code (min. 6 LOC) and some with more than one thousand lines of code (max. 1330 LOC) containing a

GUI and other features . The mean value of project size regarding the lines of code is 212.7 LOC. For all participants, the median is 129 LOC, while the first quartile is 73 LOC and the third is 275 LOC. Furthermore, the projects developed by those with previous knowledge have significantly (p-value $\ll 0.01$) more lines of code. The mean value for those with pre-knowledge is 253.2 LOC versus 160.7 LOC for those without pre-knowledge. Regarding the person parameters of the Rasch model, there is no correlation (0.07) to the lines of code.

7. DISCUSSION

The resulting model contains only five items. Except OP3 which deals with arithmetic operators, the items are related to the object-oriented paradigm. As shown in Figure 1, the most simple one is the use of operators (OP3) followed by calling a constructor (CO2) and accessing attributes of other classes. The difficulty of this item is close to the use of overloaded methods (OV2). The most difficult item according to the Rasch model is the use of manually created inheritance hierarchies (IN2).

Generally, there are more homogeneous item sets than the presented one. The order of removing dependent items is important for the resulting item set. Here, the number of dependencies built the criterion. This results in a broad item set. In further research other criteria could be taken into account.

Concerning the evaluation of programmers, the person parameters of the model are of interest. As mentioned above, the participants had to assess their own previous knowledge. This self-assessment correlates with the results of the model. Furthermore, there is a significant difference in the use of the items between those with previous knowledge to those without any previous knowledge.

In addition to the code items we calculated the lines of code (LOC). Again, there is a significant difference between the previous knowledge levels. But, the person parameters of the model have no correlation to the lines of code. Concerning the lines of code, the projects produced by the participants without any previous knowledge are more similar than those produced by the other participants. Nevertheless, even in the group without any previous knowledge, there are projects with more than 500 LOC.

8. FUTURE WORK

Validating whether the items really measure the programming ability as the latent dimension is difficult to proof. In fact, the items only cover a part of programming ability as some concepts that are not mentioned in the material for the preprojects are missing. Additionally, the facet of problem solving that is a large part of the programming ability cannot be assessed by a simple structural analysis.

Although the model is fitting the data, there still remain some problems. Obviously, there are different kinds of difficulty concerning the code items. On the one hand, there are concepts that are difficult in a common understanding and there are concepts that force the programmer to recognize its use for a better programming code. So, this distinction implies two different kind of programming abilities and because of that more than one dimension. The investigation of the relationship of these dimensions is content of future work.

Another problem we figured out, is the dependence of some items on the programming assignments. Especially, some force specific concepts like *inheritance* while others do not. So, to create a generally valid model for programming assessment the assignments have to be chosen in a proper way so that no concept is privileged.

During the model fit tests we found several items that did not fit the model and because of that were excluded from the model. In a future research it would be important to find a way either to include the concepts by identifying other code items or by extending the investigated population.

9. CONCLUSION

We have shown in this paper that the investigation of source code with the help of item response theory could provide interesting outcomes. Yet, it seems difficult to find appropriate assignments that show the persons' programming abilities. The most common way is to provide small coding tasks that assess a specific part of that ability. Nevertheless, if the application and especially the combination of different concepts should be assessed this methodology does not work. Although, our method still has to be improved, the a posteriori identification of programming concepts in a bigger assignment might allow figuring out the complete facets of programming. Additionally, small tasks can be assessed as well at the time a general assessment tool based on item-response theory is conducted.

10. REFERENCES

[1] R. J. d. Ayala. *The theory and practice of item response theory*. Methodology in the social sciences. Guilford Press, New York, 2009.

[2] D. J. Bartholomew. *Analysis of multivariate social science data*. Chapman & Hall/CRC statistics in the social and behavioral sciences series. CRC Press, Boca Raton, 2nd edition, 2008.

[3] M. Berges, A. Mühling, and P. Hubwieser. The Gap Between Knowledge and Ability. In *Proceedings of the 12th Koli Calling International Conference on Computing Education Research - Koli Calling '12*, pages 126–134, New York, 2012. ACM Press.

[4] J. Bergin, K. Bruce, and M. Kölling. Objects-early tools: a demonstration. In *Proceedings of the 36th SIGCSE technical symposium on Computer science education*, pages 390–391, New York, 2005. ACM.

[5] J. Börstler, Henrik B. Christensen, Jens Bennedsen, M. Nordström, Lena Kallin Westin, J. E. Moström, and Michael E. Caspersen. Evaluating OO example programs for CS1. In *Proceedings of the 13th annual conference on Innovation and technology in computer science education*, pages 47–52, New York, 2008. ACM Press.

[6] K. P. Burnham and D. R. Anderson. *Model selection and multimodel inference: A practical information-theoretic approach*. Springer, New York, 2nd edition, 2002.

[7] G. H. Fischer and I. W. Molenaar. *Rasch Models: Foundations, recent developments, and applications*. Springer, New York, 1995.

[8] B. Hanks, C. McDowell, D. Draper, and M. Krnjajic. Program quality with pair programming in CS1. In *Proceedings of the 9th annual SIGCSE conference on Innovation and technology in computer science education*, volume 36, pages 176–180, New York, 2004. ACM Press.

[9] P. Hubwieser and M. Berges. Minimally invasive programming courses: learning OOP with(out) instruction. In *Proceedings of the 42nd ACM technical symposium on Computer science education*, pages 87–92, New York, 2011. ACM Press.

[10] G. Kemkes, T. Vasiga, and G. Cormack. Objective Scoring for Computing Competition Tasks. In R. Mittermeir, editor, *Informatics Education – The Bridge between Using and Understanding Computers*, volume 4226 of *Lecture Notes in Computer Science*, pages 230–241, Berlin, 2006. Springer.

[11] I. Koller and R. Hatzinger. Nonparametric tests for the Rasch model: explanation, development, and application of quasi-exact tests for small samples. *InterStat*, 11:1–16, 2013.

[12] A. Luxton-Reilly, P. Denny, D. Kirk, E. Tempero, and S.-Y. Yu. On the differences between correct student solutions. In *Proceedings of the 18th ACM conference on Innovation and technology in computer science education*, pages 177–182, New York, USA, 2013. ACM Press.

[13] M. McCracken, V. Almstrum, D. Diaz, M. Guzdial, D. Hagan, Y. B.-D. Kolikant, C. Laxer, L. Thomas, I. Utting, and T. Wilusz. A multi-national, multi-institutional study of assessment of programming skills of first-year CS students. In *Working group reports from ITiCSE on Innovation and technology in computer science education*, Working Group Reports, pages 125–180, New York, 2001. ACM Press.

[14] I. Ponocny. Nonparametric goodness-of-fit tests for the rasch model. *Psychometrika*, 66(3):437–460, 2001.

[15] G. Rasch. *Probabilistic models for some intelligence and attainment tests*. University of Chicago Press, Chicago, 1980.

[16] K. Sanders and L. Thomas. Checklists for grading object-oriented CS1 programs: concepts and misconceptions. In *Proceedings of the 12th annual SIGCSE conference on Innovation and technology in computer science education*, pages 166–170, New York, 2007. ACM Press.

[17] N. Truong, P. Roe, and P. Bancroft. Static analysis of students' Java programs. In *Proceedings of the 6th conference on Australasian computing education*, pages 317–325, Darlinghurst, 2004. Australian Computer Society, Inc.

[18] A. Vihavainen, T. Vikberg, M. Luukkainen, and M. Pärtel. Scaffolding students' learning using test my code. In *Proceedings of the 18th ACM conference on Innovation and technology in computer science education*, pages 117–122, New York, USA, 2013. ACM Press.

[19] T. Winters and T. Payne. What Do Students Know?: An Outcomes-based Assessment System. In *Proceedings of the first international workshop on Computing education research*, pages 165–172, New York, 2005. ACM Press.

Computational Thinking and Child Performance in a Preschool

Gustavo Abreu Caetano
FACCAMP & UNASP
R. Guatemala, 167, Jardim América
Campo Limpo Paulista, SP, Brazil
55 11 4812-9400

gustavo.caetano13@gmail.com

Osvaldo Luiz de Oliveira
FACCAMP
R. Guatemala, 167, Jardim América
Campo Limpo Paulista, SP, Brazil
55 11 4812-9407

osvaldo@faccamp.br

ABSTRACT
Computing has been viewed as a basic activity and should be studied starting in preschool. This work investigates (1) the ability of children attending preschool (3 to 6 years old) to compute with a ludic model of computation and (2) whether there is a correlation between the ability to compute and the performance of children in preschool. The ludic computing model, specially designed for children, is proposed and used in experiments with 41 children attending preschool. The results indicate that the ability to use the proposed model to compute varies with the age of the child and that there is a correlation between this ability and the school performance of the child.

Categories and Subject Descriptors
K.3.2 [**Computers and Education**]: Computer and Information Science Education - *Computer Science Education.*

Keywords
Computational Thinking, Preschool, Kindergarten.

1. INTRODUCTION
Similar to reading, writing, and performing arithmetic operations, the ability to compute has been considered as a basic, fundamental, and essential ability of people [15]. Assuming the principle of the fundamental nature of the activity of computing, studies have been proposed to understand what it means and to analyze the practices derived from it [5].

The term Computational Thinking (CT) has been associated with studies reporting experiments that examine the educational advantages of using computational tools and concepts to think about various domains of knowledge. CT has also been associated with studies not necessarily directed toward formal education but to all people, encompassing ideas and tools, such as CS Unplugged, LEGO Mindstorms, SCRATCH and APP Inventor [6, 13]. In general, studies on CT employ an intuitive notion of computation and aim to export to other domains of knowledge artifacts well known and studied in the field of Computer Science: problem solving, programming, simulation, modeling, game design etc.

Since CT is associated with many contexts and activities, the term CT needs to be defined to avoid possible misunderstandings

ITICSE '15, July 04 - 08, 2015, Vilnius, Lithuania
Copyright 2015 ACM 978-1-4503-3440-2/15/07...$15.00
http://dx.doi.org/10.1145/2729094.2742592

regarding the sense in which we use it. In this study CT refers to the mental activities required to deal with a model of computation. As will be seen in Section 4 these activities involve abstraction, calculation, design and reading.

This study develops and uses a ludic model of computation, called World of the Treasure, consisting of characters, scenarios and objects. Objects in the model of computation World of the Treasure cause transformations in characters. These transformations are understood as functions in the sense of mathematical functions. A child computes something in World of the Treasure operating with functions. The model of computation World of the Treasure is designed in a way that the child deals with mathematical functions, but need not be aware of the mathematical formalities and procedures of functions.

he aim of this study is to investigate the ability of children attending preschool (3 to 6 years old) to compute and verify whether there is a correlation between the ability to compute on the proposed model and the performance of children in preschool.

The remainder of this paper is organized as follows. Section 2 describes the elements that comprise the model of computation, World of the Treasure. Section 3 shows the relation between World of the Treasure, mathematical functions and possible computational activities to be performed. Section 4 shows what ability a child should have to use the proposed model to compute. The conducted experiment to test the child's ability to use the model to compute is detailed in Section 5. Section 6 presents the results, and Section 7 describes related works. Section 8 highlights the main conclusions, summarizes a few of our views on the work performed and notes directions for further research.

2. MODEL OF COMPUTATION: WORLD OF THE TREASURE
World of the Treasure (WT) was inspired by the Mario video games of the Japanese company Nintendo. WT consists of characters, objects and scenarios and is represented in two ways: (1) printed on paper, as illustrated in Figure 4(a–b) and (2) more concretely, as in theater, with scenarios, real objects and actors playing characters, as illustrated in Figure 6(a).

Characters in WT can perform actions such as jump, walk, run, rotate, and increase and decrease in size. Objects can cause changes in the characters or can be captured by them. Scenario items are used in WT to compose an "atmosphere" for the environment. For example, Figures 4(a–b) shows the character Joe, a mushroom and a thorn object in a countryside scenario. The character Joe performs the action of running. When passing by the mushroom object, the object causes a transformation that increases the character's size. When passing by the thorn object, the object causes a transformation that reduces the character size. Figure 6(a) shows an actor playing the character Joe, a scenario consisting of a checkerboard carpet and objects that are chocolate coins. The character can walk on the carpet and capture chocolate coins.

3. FUNCTIONS, WORLD OF THE TREASURE AND COMPUTATIONAL ACTIVITIES

Objects in WT can cause transformations in the characters. These transformations can be seen as mathematical functions. In general, an object can induce a function $f : P \rightarrow P$, where P is the set of characters. Thus, for example, the mushroom in Figure 4(a) induces a function f that takes a character of the set P (domain) and produces a larger character in the set P (image). Similarly, the thorn in Figure 4(b) induces a function g that takes a character of the set P and produces a smaller character in the set P. Figures 1(a) and 1(b) use Venn diagrams to illustrate the functions f and g. Figure 1(c) shows the Venn diagram corresponding to the composite function $g (f (p))$ for $p \in P$.

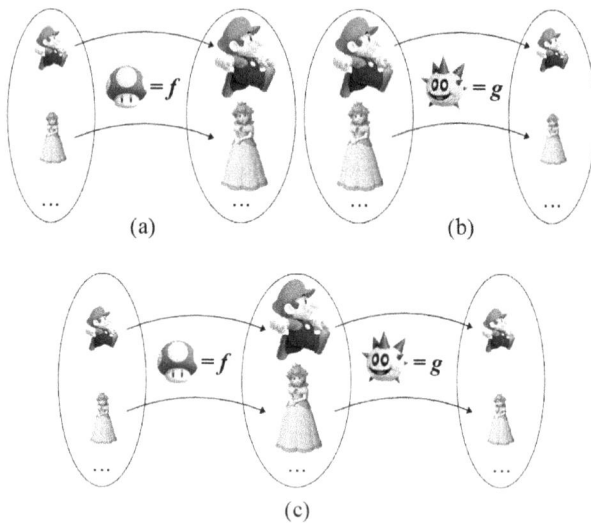

(a)   (b)

(c)

Figure 1. Transformations produced by objects in WT can be seen as mathematical functions, represented here by Venn diagrams: (a) The function f expresses the transformation performed by the mushroom object. (b) The function g expresses the transformation performed by the thorn object. (c) Representation of the composite function $g (f (p))$. The ellipsis (...) indicate the presence of other elements in the set P that are not shown here due to a lack of space.

Several types of computing activities can be performed in WT, among which we highlight the following:

- *Type 1 Activity*: The child must infer what a function does based on elements of the domain and their corresponding images. For example, observing the size of the character Joe before he passes by the mushroom (domain element) and the increase in the size of the character Joe after he passes by the mushroom (image), the activity consists of inferring what is the transformation that the mushroom produces (function) (Figure 2(a)).

- *Type 2 Activity*: The child must calculate the value of a function (image) based on an element of the domain and the knowledge of what the function does. For example, the child must calculate what will happen to the character Joe after he passes by the mushroom. This calculation can be made based on (1) the transformation made by the mushroom and (2) who and how is the character before he passes the object mushroom (domain) (Figure 2 (b)).

(a)   (b)

Figure 2. Type 1 and Type 2 computational activities in WT: (a) Type 1 – Infer what a function does; (b) Type 2 – Calculate the image of a function.

Another type of computing activity that can be performed in WT is the designing ("programming") of a function to perform a task (or transformation). For example, consider the concrete scenario consisting of a checkerboard carpet with quadrants of different colors, with one actor playing the character Joe and being initially placed at the center front quadrant, and chocolate coins in the treasure chest near the right rear quadrant (Figure 3(a)). A map printed on paper (Figure 3(b)) shows the initial position of the character and quadrants containing "bombs". If the character occupies a quadrant containing a bomb, he dies. Having the ability to give verbal instructions to an actor ("turn", "move to the quadrant of the color <color name>"), a task to be designed is to develop a trajectory that makes the character pass, quadrant by quadrant, from its initial position to the position where the treasure chest of chocolate coins is.

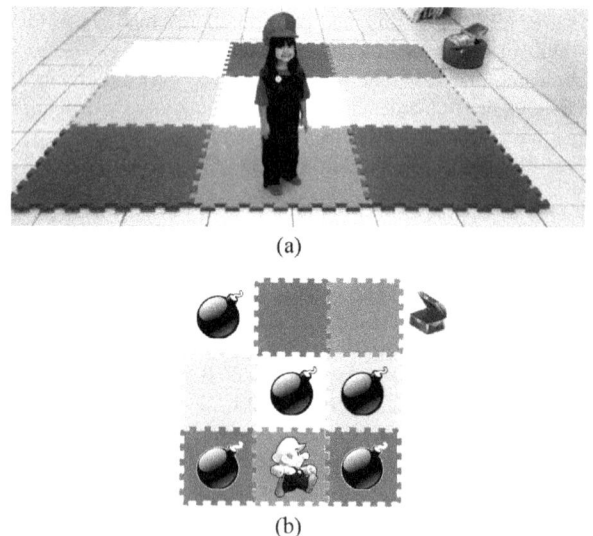

(a)

(b)

Figure 3. Type 3 computational activity in WT: Design a function for an actor performing a task in a concrete scenario: (a) the concrete scenario and (b) a map. The child should read the map and give verbal instructions to an actor.

4. ABILITY THAT A CHILD SHOULD HAVE TO COMPUTE IN THE WORLD OF THE TREASURE

Different types of activities in WT demand different abilities in a child. Four abilities can be highlighted:

- *Abstraction*: This ability is mainly required in Type 1 activities. The process of analyzing the domain and the image of a function, discovering regularities, and generalizing to infer what a function does demands the ability to abstract.

- *Calculation:* This ability is mainly required in Type 2 activities. Type 2 activities require calculating the value of a known function, also having knowledge of an element of the domain of the function.

- *Designing ("programming") and Verbalization*: This ability is mainly required in Type 3 activities. The activity that leads to a description of how a task should be performed requires the ability to design. In WT, the task description is not written but is spoken; hence, the ability to verbalize is also required.

- *Reading*: Type 1, 2 and 3 activities require the abilities of reading. This occurs because to perform an activity, the child must read and understand the elements of WT, printed on paper or represented concretely.

5. MATERIALS AND METHODS
5.1 Test of Child's Ability to Compute

We developed a test based on the WT activities to measure a child's ability to compute. The test was previously validated in a pilot experiment applied to five children who did not participate in the final experiment. Small problems were fixed in the test, and it was improved. The test consists of eight questions and is divided into three parts. Parts 1 and 2 have questions concerning WT printed on paper, and Part 3 has questions concerning WT represented concretely.

Part 1 (questions 1–3) mainly evaluates the child's ability to abstract and to calculate. Each question in this part has one or two Type 1 activities followed by a Type 2 activity. Figure 4 illustrates a question in this part of the test. Analyzing Figures 4(a) and 4(b), the child must be able to abstract what the mushroom and thorn objects do to the character Joe (Type 1 activity). Considering what has been abstracted and the situation proposed in Figure 4(c), the child has to calculate the transformation of the character Joe after he passes, in sequence, by the mushroom and thorn objects (Type 2 activity). The answer is given by the choice of a card among five possible alternatives. The card chosen as the answer should be pasted in the space reserved for the response (Figure 4(c)).

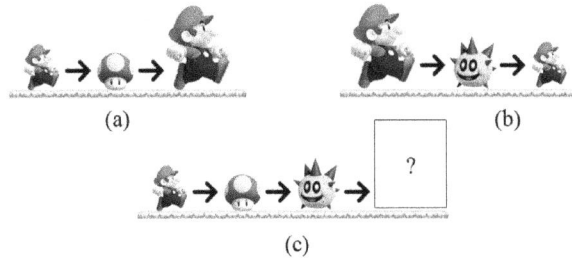

Figure 4. Example of a question from Part 1 of the Test: (a)–(b) The child must abstract what the mushroom and thorn objects do to the character Joe. (c) The child has to calculate the transformation of the character Joe.

Part 2 (questions 4–5) mainly evaluates the child's ability to design and verbalize (Type 3 activities). Each question in this part involves the design and verbalization of instructions to make the character Joe perform a route in a maze, deviating from obstacles, to achieve the goal of arriving at the castle. Figure 5 illustrates a question in this part of the test. The child must verbalize the sequence of instructions (run, jump, and squat) for the character to accomplish the task. The experimenter should note the child's answer.

Part 3 (questions 6–8) also evaluates the child's ability to design and verbalize. While the questions in Part 2 referred to WT printed on paper, the questions in this part refer to WT concretely represented. Each question in this part involves the concrete scenario, consisting of checkerboard carpet with different colors, one actor playing the character Joe, and a map containing quadrants that are empty or that contain objects, such as a "bomb" or a chocolate coin. The child must design and verbalize instructions ("turn", "move to the quadrant of color <color name>", "get a chocolate coin", "drop a chocolate coin") that make the character walk quadrant by quadrant, deviating from "bombs" and collecting chocolate coins along the way.

Figure 5. Example of a question from Part 2 of the Test. The child must design and verbalize a sequence of instructions (run, jump, and squat) to make the character Joe move through the maze, deviating from obstacles, to reach the goal of arriving at the castle.

The task of questions 6 and 7 is to develop a trajectory that makes the character come out of its initial position, deviating from "bombs", and achieve the goal of reaching a treasure chest of chocolate coins. The trajectory of Question 6 is simpler than the trajectory of Question 7, and these questions can each be answered by a single block sequence of instructions. Question 8,

59

illustrated in Figure 6, is slightly more complicated than questions 6 and 7 because it imposes the design of the repetition of three blocks of instruction sequences. The child should instruct the character to obtain chocolate coins on the carpet and to bring them to the treasure chest. However, there is the restriction that the character must take one coin at a time, which requires the child to think and design three blocks of instruction sequences, one for each chocolate coin.

5.2 Subjects

A total of 41 children attending a preschool participated in the survey. Table 1 shows the profile of participants organized into two groups by age. The number of participants represented 13% of the preschool population of the school surveyed. The participants were randomly selected among children whose parents expressed written consent for them to participate in the experiment.

Table 1. Profile of the experiment participants. Ages are shown in decimal notation (e.g., 4.5 represents the age of four years and six months).

Group	Gender, n (%)		Age, years		
	Female	Male	Range	Mean	Median
I	12 (55)	10 (45)	3.0 ⊢ 4.5	3.9	3.9
II	10 (53)	09 (47)	4.5 ⊢ 6.0	5.4	5.2

(a)

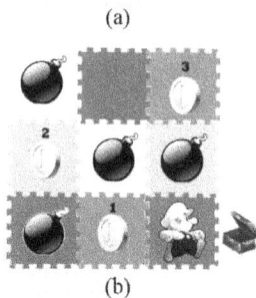

(b)

Figure 6. Example of the question from Part 3 of the Test. The child must design and verbalize a sequence of instructions ("turn", "move to the quadrant of color <color name>", "get a chocolate coin", and "drop a chocolate coin") to repeat the action to collect chocolate coins and to bring it to the treasure chest one coin at a time.

5.3 Experimental Setup

One room was specially prepared for the experiment to be conducted in. The children, one by one, took part in the experiment in individual sessions designed to avoid bias caused by communication between children. Additionally, to avoid bias

caused by the fatigue of the child, the experimental sessions were conducted in two phases, one involving the questions in Parts 1 and 2 and the other phase involving the questions in Part 3. Two experimenters attended all experimental sessions. Each experimental session was performed in approximately 5 minutes and followed the procedure outlined below: (1) the experimenters welcomed the child into the room, dedicating time for the child to integrate with the environment and to be motivated to compute in the WT. Concrete objects and dolls were used to assist in the setting and in the motivation of the child. (2) The questions were submitted one by one. For each question, an experimenter described the question and requested a response from the child. The other experimenter observed the interaction of the child and noted the answers. (3) The experimenters performed a debriefing and offered chocolate coins as a gift for the child.

Aiming to minimize interference in the routine of the children and of the school, the experimental sessions took place over three weeks in the summer of 2014.

6. RESULTS

A score from 0 (completely wrong) to 8 (completely correct) was assigned as result of the test done by a child. Table 2 shows the mean and standard deviation obtained by the groups of children aged 3 (inclusive) up to 4.5 years old and 4.5 (inclusive) up to 6 years old.

Student's t-test at 1% significance was used as a statistical measure of the significance of the difference between of the means obtained by the two groups. For the population studied, the t-test suggests that there is a significant difference between the means obtained by the two groups ($t(39) = 2.75$, $p\text{-value} \le 0.01$). In this case, the mean obtained by the older age group (Group II) were significantly higher than the mean obtained by the younger age group (Group I).

Table 2. Mean (0−8) and standard deviation of the results obtained by the two groups of children.

Group	Range (age)	n	Mean (0−8) ± SD
I	3.0 ⊢ 4.5	22	6.20 ± 1.20
II	4.5 ⊢ 6.0	19	7.20 ± 1.12

A score to the academic performance of the child was assigned by teachers of the preschool. The scores were described in the Likert scale, having been assigned 2 (very weak), 4 (weak), 6 (regular), 8 (good) and 10 (very good). A correlation analysis was performed between the test score and performance of children in the preschool. As a statistical measure for correlation, was used the Pearson product-moment correlation coefficient, also known as Pearson's r. This coefficient is a measure of the linear correlation between two variables. For the population studied the t-test at 1% significance, used as a statistical measure of significance for Pearson's r, suggests a strong positive correlation between the academic performance of the children and the score obtained by them in the test. Table 3 lists values of Pearson's r in each group for correlations between the academic scores and the test scores. Figure 7 shows the scatter plots of the obtained correlations.

Table 3. Pearson's *r* coefficient for correlation between academic scores and test scores.

Group	Pairs	Pearson's *r*	*t*	*p*-value
I	22	0.86 (strong)	7.44	0.0001
II	19	0.74 (strong)	4.51	0.0003

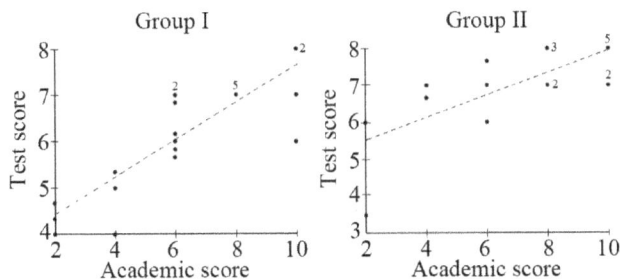

Figure 7. Scatter plot of the correlation between academic scores and test scores. The numbers indicate the amount of coincident points.

Finally, we highlight the following result. We observed a statistically significant difference in the percentage of correct answers in the World of the Treasure printed on paper (questions 1−5, mean = 78%, SD = 19%) and the World of the Treasure concretely represented (questions 6−8, mean = 91%, SD = 22%) ($t (39) = 2.82$, *p-value* ≤ 0.01).

7. RELATED WORK

The idea that computers and various computational artifacts can be used as a tool for thinking about non-computational domains is old and has roots in the work of Papert [9]. The term Computational Thinking (CT), first used by Wing [15], has been used in this sense today. Research in this field has been intense and include studies to investigate what CT is and what we can do with it [5], analyze students' pre-instructional ability to develop algorithms [1], investigate CT in elementary [2, 4, 12], middle [14, 16] and high schools [11]. A review of the state of the art of CT in K-12 is presented in [3]. This work differs from previous ones by the fact of using a model of computation to explicit and to delimit what is understood by CT in context of this study.

Two works are closely related to this study. It is reported in [7] a statistical evidence of a correlation between mental ability to compute and student performance in four undergraduate courses at a university. It is reported in [8] an experimental study that shows a significant correlation between the student's ability to compute and his/her academic performance in a primary school. The main difference of this work to [7] and [8] is the type of model of computation used. While [7] and [8] use a model of computation based on Turing Machines, this study presents a ludic model of computation in which computing activities are activities involving computation of mathematical functions, without that the children are aware that they are dealing with mathematical functions.

8. CONCLUSION

This work assumes the principle that computing is a basic activity required to the processes of all domains and things. This work relies on the generality of mathematical functions to achieve the universality necessary to a computational concept be applied to various domains. The World of the Treasure, employed in this study, is an enjoyable environment that invites the child to work with functions to calculate, reason to infer meanings and solve problems. The agenda of preschool education covers various subjects and areas such as Language, Mathematics, Movement, Nature, Society, perception of identity, and the notion of autonomy. The development of a learning method that exercises the computational aspects present in various subjects has the potential to improve preschool education.

The percentage of correct answers in the test, 77% for the younger group and 90% for the older group, indicates that the child from the preschool has good ability to compute with computing models like World of the Treasure, which has a certain level of abstraction. Even in activities considered more complex, as the repetition of blocks of instruction sequences, the younger group had a good percentage of correct answers (81%).

The highest percentage of correct answers in World of the Treasure concretely represented than in the World of the Treasure in paper, and the finding that the ability to compute on the proposed model vary with the age of the child reflect the Cognitive Theory of Piaget [10]. These results should be taken into consideration when designing approaches that make explicit the computational perspective on learning subjects from the preschool agenda.

The verification of the existence of significant correlation between the ability to compute on the proposed model and the performance of child in a preschool reinforces the validity of the principle that the ability to compute is fundamental. Future studies are needed to determine the cause of this correlation and to verify if teaching-learning methods that make explicit the computational perspective can improve the performance of children in preschool.

Finally, we observe that this paper presents statistical evidence regarding the population studied. The results presented motivate check whether they remain valid for other groups of children attending preschool.

9. ACKNOWLEDGMENTS

We would like to thank all subjects who volunteered for the experiment for their invaluable contribution to this work.

10. REFERENCES

[1] Dwyer, H., Hill, C., Carpenter, S., Harlow, D. and Franklin, D. 2014. Identifying Elementary Students' Pre-instructional Ability to Develop Algorithms and Step-by-Step Instructions. *Proceeding of the 45th ACM Technical Symposium on Computer Science Education* (Atlanta, Georgia, USA, March 05 - 08, 2014). SIGCSE'14. ACM, New York, NY, 511-516. DOI= 10.1145/2538862.2538905.

[2] Feaster, Y., Ali, F., Zhai, J. and Hallstrom, J. O. 2014. Serious Toys: three years of teaching computer science concepts in K-12 classrooms. In *Proceedings of the 2014*

Conference on Innovation & Technology in Computer Science Education (Uppsala, Sweden, June 23 - 25). ITiCSE'14. ACM, New York, NY, 69-74. DOI=10.1145/2591708.2591732.

[3] Grover, S. and Pea, R. 2013. Computational Thinking in K–12: A Review of the State of the Field. *Educational Researcher* 42, 1, 38-43.

[4] Hill, C. 2014. Computational Thinking Curriculum Development for Upper Elementary School Classes. In *Proceedings of the Tenth Annual Conference on International Computing Education Research* (Glasgow, Scotland, UK, August 11 - 13, 2014). ICER'14. ACM, New York, NY, 151-152. DOI=10.1145/2632320.2632327.

[5] Hu, C. 2011. Computational Thinking: what it might mean and what we might do about it. In *Proceedings of the 16th Annual Joint Conference on Innovation and Technology in Computer Science Education* (Darmstadt, Germany, June 27 - 29, 2011). ITiCSE'11. ACM, New York, NY, 223-227. DOI=10.1145/1999747.1999811.

[6] Imberman, S. P., Sturm, D. and Azhar, M. Q. 2014. Computational Thinking: expanding the toolkit. *Journal of Computing Sciences in Colleges* 29, 6 (Jun. 2014), 39-46.

[7] Oliveira, O. L. 2012. Statistical Evidence of the Correlation between Mental Ability to Compute and Student Performance in Undergraduate Courses. In *Proceedings of the 17th Annual Joint Conference on Innovation and Technology in Computer Science Education* (Haifa, Israel, July 03 - 05, 2012). ITiCSE'12. ACM, New York, NY, 111-115. DOI=10.1145/2325296.2325326.

[8] Oliveira, O. L., Nicoletti, M. C. and Cura, L. M. 2014. Quantitative Correlation between Ability to Compute and Student performance in a Primary School. In *Proceeding of the 45th ACM Technical Symposium on Computer Science Education* (Atlanta, Georgia, USA, March 05 - 08, 2014). SIGCSE'14. ACM, New York, NY, 505-510. DOI=10.1145/2538862.2538890.

[9] Papert. S. 1993. *Mindstorms: children, computers, and powerful ideas*. 2ⁿᵈ ed. Basic Books, New York, USA.

[10] Piaget, J. and Inhelder, B. 1972. *The Psychology of the Child*. Basic Books, New York, USA.

[11] Settle, A., Franke, B., Hansen, R., Spaltro, F., Jurisson, C., Rennert-May, C. and Wildeman, B. 2012. Infusing Computational Thinking into the Middle- and High-School Curriculum. In *Proceedings of the 17th Annual Joint Conference on Innovation and Technology in Computer Science Education* (Haifa, Israel, July 03 - 05, 2012). ITiCSE'12. ACM, New York, NY, 22-27. DOI=10.1145/2325296.2325306.

[12] Touretzky, D. S., Marghitu, D., Ludi, S., Bernstein, D. and Ni, L. 2013. Accelerating K-12 Computational Thinking using Scaffolding, Staging, and Abstraction. In *Proceeding of the 44th ACM Technical Symposium on Computer Science Education* (Denver, Colorado, USA, March 06 - 09, 2013). SIGCSE'13. ACM, New York, NY, 609-614. DOI=10.1145/2445196.2445374.

[13] Turbak, F., Pokress, S. C. and Sherman, M. 2014. Mobile Computational Thinking with APP Inventor 2. *ACM Journal of Computing Sciences in Colleges* 29, 6 (Jun. 2014), 15-17.

[14] Werner, L., Denner, J., Campe, S. and Kawamoto, D. C. 2012. The Fairy Performance Assessment: Measuring Computational Thinking in Middle School. In *Proceedings of the 43rd ACM technical symposium on Computer Science Education* (Raleigh, North Carolina, USA, February29–March 3, 2012). SIGCSE'12. ACM, New York, NY, 215-220. DOI=10.1145/2157136.2157200.

[15] Wing, J. 2006. Computational Thinking. *Communications of the ACM* 49, 3 (Mar. 2006), 33-35. DOI=10.1145/1118178.1118215.

[16] Yadav, A., Mayfield, C., Zhou, N., Hambrusch, S. and Korb, J. T. 2014. Computational Thinking in Elementary and Secondary Teacher Education. *ACM Transactions on Computing Education 14*, 1 (Mar. 2014), 1-16.

Design and Preliminary Results
from a Computational Thinking Course

Dennis Kafura
Virginia Tech
kafura@cs.vt.edu

Austin Cory Bart
Virginia Tech
acbart@vt.edu

Bushra Chowdhury
Virginia Tech
bushrac@vt.edu

ABSTRACT

This paper describes the design and initial assessment of a general education course in computational thinking for non-computer science majors. The key elements of the course include multidisciplinary cohorts to achieve learning across contexts, multiple languages/tools, including block-based and textual programming languages, repeated exposure to the underlying computational ideas in different forms, and student-defined projects using real world ("big") data to heighten motivation through self-directed contextualized learning. The preliminary multi-methods assessment shows that the course engendered high levels of motivation, achieved key objectives for learning in and across contexts, largely affirmed the choice of languages/tools, and supported, though less strongly than anticipated, the motivational effects of real-world data.

Categories and Subject Descriptors

K.3.2 [**Computer and Information Science Education**]: Computer Science education, Curriculum – *computational thinking, problem-based learning, engagement, group work.*

General Terms

Measurement, Design, Experimentation.

Keywords

Computational Thinking; Big Data; Student Engagement; Interdisciplinary Cohorts.

1. INTRODUCTION

Believing that a computational mode of thought is valuable to all members of society, our university recently included learning objectives for computational thinking in its general education requirements that must be met by all graduating students. Informed by a national report [1] , Wing's writing [2], and the Computer Science Teachers Association (CSTA) [3] among others, the university considered computational thinking to be:

The intellectual skills rooted in the ability to conceive of meaningful information-based representations that can be effectively manipulated using an automated agent (e.g., a computer).

ITiCSE'15, July 6–8, 2015, Vilnius, Lithuania.
Copyright © 2015 ACM 978-1-4503-3440-2/15/07…$15.00.
http://dx.doi.org/10.1145/2729094.2742593

In this paper we describe the innovative pedagogical approach and technology support for an Introduction to Computational Thinking course and present early results, both quantitative and qualitative, from a first offering of the course in Fall 2014. In particular, we focus in this paper on:

- innovative progressive course design in which core concepts are encountered several times in different contexts (Section 2),

- multidisciplinary "cohorts" to foster collaborative learning and learning across contexts (Section 3),

- "big data" to enhance the students' sense of realism and utility, not just interest (Section 4),

- technology support for cohort interaction and access to big data through block-based programming, all in an extended web-based ebook framework (Section 4), and

- preliminary multi-methods assessment of motivation and how helpful, useful, and interesting different elements were to students (Section 5).

We believe that the conclusions (Section 6) are valuable to others in computer science education, especially to those teaching computational thinking or introductory computer science courses.

The course we created both draws on and is distinct from other approaches that teach computational thinking, offer an introduction to computer science, or use big data. As a single course our approach differs from the inclusion of computational thinking modules into several required courses in a curriculum (e.g. general education[4], architecture [5], or the humanities [6]). As a general education course we differ from the inclusion of computational thinking into courses that target a specific discipline (e.g., sciences [7], computer science [8], humanities [9], and biology [10]). We draw on the ideas of other computational thinking or introductory computer science courses intended for all students. Some courses used teams (e.g., [11]), included social impacts (e.g.,[12]), or employed block-based programming (e.g., [13]). All of these elements are integrated in our course. We share the spirit of the "fluency" approach [14] but trade depth for breadth (e.g., we include only three of the ten "fluency" concepts.) We share with the media computation approach [15] the idea of providing a unifying, open-ended resource (images and sound in media computation vs. big data in our course). However, we believe that big data is seen by students as "useful" which is more engaging than media computation which is seen as "interesting" [16]. Our course shares with [17] the sense of engaging students with real world data. What we offer is that the data and questions to be answered are decided by the student and are not pre-determined assignments. Though we are using big data our goal is to teach computational thinking *using* big data as opposed to the goal of "data science" courses where big data is itself the object of study. We have in common with [18] the assessment of big data approaches though we also include quantitative methods and are focused on computational thinking rather than an introduction to computer science course. We also have a shared view with courses that used block-based programming (Snap!, Scratch, or App Inventor). What we add to a block-based programming approach is the connection to realistic big data sources, the ability to embed the programming in an ebook form to better integrate learning materials (see Section 4), and automated, guiding feedback through program analysis.

2. COURSE DESIGN

2.1 Learning Objectives and Dispositions
Four learning objectives for computational thinking were defined at our university. Students are required to:

1. Formulate problems and find solutions using computational or quantitative thinking in their field of study.
2. Give examples of the application to, and discuss the significance of, computational thinking in at least two different knowledge domains.
3. Apply computational methods to model and analyze complex or large scale phenomena.
4. Evaluate the social and political impact of computing and information technologies

In meeting these learning objectives the course design was also influenced by the CSTA's "dispositions or attitudes" that a computational thinker should exhibit [3]:

- "Confidence in dealing with complexity
- Persistence in working with difficult problems
- Tolerance for ambiguity
- The ability to deal with open ended problems
- The ability to communicate and work with others to achieve a common goal or solution."

Though defined for K-12 education, these dispositions seem equally relevant to university-level students. The first four dispositions influenced our use of student-defined big data projects where complexity, difficulty, ambiguity and open-endedness are present. The last disposition influenced our use of multi-disciplinary cohorts.

2.2 Content
The structure of the course is shown in Table 1. Though shown as a separate component the social impacts topic is woven throughout the course. A more complete description of this aspect of the course is beyond the scope of this paper.

The computational modeling topic uses NetLogo [19], a multi-agent development and simulation environment. Typical student work involves a student selecting a model relevant to their major from the library of pre-defined models in diverse areas (e.g., art, biology, sciences, games, mathematics, networks, social science, and system dynamics). Each student reads the description of the model and performs computational simulations by varying the model's parameters and observing the model's visualizations. Students in a cohort demonstrate and explain their models to each other. Finally, the cohort collectively and each student individually identify the properties for a model's abstraction and the programming constructs that manipulate these properties (via calculation, decision, and iteration). Through this work students begin to see the role of abstraction, the programming elements that determine the model's behavior, and the relevance of these computational techniques to many areas of study.

The fundamentals of algorithms topic uses a custom version of Blockly, a block-based programming language. Typical student work initially involves assembling specialized blocks to perform visually interesting computations (e.g., guiding an avatar through a maze using decisions and iteration). Subsequent classwork (in cohorts) and homework (individually) progressively involves the full Blockly environment and our custom "big data" blocks which connect students to realistic data streams. The current example data streams are in meteorology (weather forecasts), economics (stock market prices), geosciences (earthquake reports), and sociology (crime statistics). Initial algorithms constructed in Blockly use decision and iteration to calculate properties (e.g., averages) of data in simple lists while later algorithms involve more complex logic to filter and transform lists and data with more complex structure (e.g., the equivalent of Python lists and dictionaries). Blockly allow students to gain confidence in their ability to construct algorithm before having to cope with the syntactic detail of a textual programming language. An important aspect of Blockly is that the Python code for a Blockly algorithm can be rendered at the student's request. This makes the transition from Blockly to Python a more progressive step for learners.

Table 1: Course Topics

Topic (Length)	Description
Computational Modeling (4 weeks)	Model-based investigation of how complex global behavior arises from the interaction of many "agents", each operating according to local rules. Students use case-based reasoning and encounter basic computation constructs in a highly supportive simulation environment.
Fundamentals of Algorithms (2 weeks)	Study of the basic constructs of programming logic (sequence, decisions, and iteration) and program organization (procedures). A block-based programming language is used to avoid syntactic details. Students can see how these constructs are expressed in Python.
Data-intensive Inquiry (7 weeks)	Project-based exploration of complex phenomena by algorithmically manipulating large-scale data from real-world sources. Students construct algorithms in Python using a supportive framework for accessing the data.
Social Impacts (2 weeks)	Explore and discuss contemporary societal issues involving computing and information technology.

The data intensive inquiry topic introduced students to a carefully selected subset of Python. Initial student work involves cutting and pasting the Python code generated for previous Blockly exercises into a standard Python programming environment (e.g., IDLE or Spyder). This environment offers an important, authentic programming experience to offset any perceived penalty in usefulness that students perceive in Blockly. Students are initially encouraged and progressively discouraged to refer to the Python code automatically generated for algorithms written in Blockly. Generation of basic visualizations (line graphs, scatter plots, histograms) via a Python library is incorporated into the student work. Finally, students propose, complete and present a multi-week project that takes advantage of a big data source related to their major. Big data has become pervasive in almost all disciplines, so learning to work with it is an authentic, relevant experience for students that can be customized for each student while maintaining a common context in the class.

The organization of these three topics is progressive, meaning that each core concept is encountered in three different contexts. Students see the use of abstraction and algorithms (sequence, decision, iteration, functions) in the computational modeling topic by exploring the NetLogo programming of a model of their own choosing. They encounter these same elements again in the fundamental of algorithms topic where they modify and create algorithms in the context of a block-based programming language extended to access and manipulate big data. Finally, the same elements are seen a third time in the data-intensive inquiry topic where a major project is completed in a text-based programming language (Python).

Both Blockly and Python have been extended to use CORGIS (Collection of Real-time, Giant, Interesting, Situated) [20], a publicly available gallery of big data sources designed for educational use by novice students. The CORGIS project has many real-world datasets including geological sciences, history, psychology, social media, and many more. All of the CORGIS datasets are examples of big data – each having some aspect of high volume, high velocity, or high variation. The sense of what constitutes "big" must be interpreted, of course, in relation to the capability of the students involved. The CORGIS collection is an open-source project with tools to rapidly create new data sources for students.

3. PEDAGOGICAL APPROACH

The course work is organized to achieve a balance between context-based learning and learning across contexts. Context-based learning provides students with a motivating framework for their learning [21]. In particular, if computational thinking is embedded in the disciplinary material of a student's major there is greater likelihood that the student will appreciate the relevance of computational thinking to their own needs and goals. In addition, the meaning of aspects of computational thinking may be more clearly learned in context because it is related to knowledge with which the student may already be familiar. However, there are equally important reasons to learn across contexts. The notion of transference refers to the ability to use in some context what has been learned in a different context. Transference is especially relevant to computational thinking because it is a generic skill that can be applied in many different situations. Learning across contexts enhances the ability of a student to recognize in new situations the applicability of computational thinking. Furthermore, by seeing computational thinking concepts in different contexts it is more likely that the student has gained a clear notion of these concepts. Also, the student may develop a deeper appreciation for different ways of knowing by appreciating how techniques relevant to the values and practices of their primary discipline are also relevant to the values and practices of other disciplines.

Context-based learning is achieved by allowing each student to specialize major aspects of their work to be relevant to their discipline or interests. As an individual, a student self-directs the selection of a computational model to explore and the selection, exploration, and completion of a project relevant to their major field of study. To support students' self-direction we have used the CORGIS tools to quickly create new data sources for students who could not find a suitable library in the existing collection.

Learning across contexts is achieved by organizing students into interdisciplinary [22] cohorts that foster collaborative learning [23]. Each cohort contains students with 4 or 5 different majors. Students will perform all class room activities within these groups. Students also collaborate virtually using the course book, a custom-built, interactive web-based platform with embedded coding activities and real-time, shared text writing (similar to Google Docs). Collaborative learning also relates to each student's role in their cohort [23]. As a member of the cohort, a student is responsible for:

Presentation: describing to the other cohort members the significance of the project they have selected.

Interaction: asking questions and providing feedback about the projects of other cohort members, thereby gaining insight into how computational techniques are used across disciplines.

Support: helping other members of the cohort with the mechanics of the tools and frameworks that are common across projects.

The assumption is that collaboratively learning computational thinking within interdisciplinary cohorts will foster "learning across contexts". The expectation is that regular interaction with peers from different disciplines will provide students an opportunity to share and listen to others perspective. This will help students to form an understanding of how computational thinking applies in other disciplines.

4. TECHNOLOGICAL INNOVATION

A key technological element of this class is an open-source e-textbook platform named "Rhinestone", based on the popular Runestone project [24]. Rhinestone is a port of Runestone from the Web2py web framework to the Flask web framework, making it easier to extend Rhinestone with new features and directives to support the general education needs of our classroom.

Rhinestone's biggest extension is automatic, continuous server-side storage of all student work as changes occur. This extension uses HTML5 local storage features to robustly backup data on the client in the case of disconnection and reducing the responsibility of students to manage their work. Another new feature is top-level support for collaboration. This extension allows members of a cohort to collaborate in the style of Google Docs. The underlying technology is Google MobWrite [25], a real-time communication library that provides differential synchronization between multiple users. Third, rather than being interleaved as in the Runestone model, the content of the book is divided into two dynamically linked sections – the readings (largely static content meant to be the definitive material of the course) and the class/home work (largely interactive problems and exercises that are completed by students).

Rhinestone also fully-integrates support for Blockly [26], a block-based visual programming language by Google that is based loosely on Scratch. The block-based nature of Blockly empowers students to focus on the semantics of their algorithm rather than its syntax. Moreover, Blockly blocks compile directly to JavaScript, making it runnable from the browser. These blocks can also be directly rendered as Python source code, which helps students transition from the high-level block-based programming to more authentic text-based coding. Our implementation of Blockly is more than just a coding environment - static program analysis and unit testing is used to deliver just-in-time, guided feedback that gives students contextualized assistance. An instructor identifies constraints for a question that are then matched with a hint – e.g., if students neglected to use an iteration block when processing a list of data, the environment links to the iteration chapter in the book.

With the support of CORGIS client libraries, the CORGIS blocks access rich data streams with apportioned complexity. For instance, particularly massive datasets can be sampled down for development purposes, switching to "full" mode on demand. Similarly, data sources that rely on an external, ever changing real-time source (such as weather, social media, or earthquake data) can be cached locally for access in an "offline mode", avoiding problems with students' internet connection and ensuring reproducibility during development and testing. When students have finished their development, the "online" access mode is used instead. Because students are encouraged to find their own dataset, they have a more personalized, engaged experience with their programming in comparison to a single set of instructor-provided data, even if that instructor-provided data is realistic.

5. PRELIMINARY RESULTS

5.1 Methods

The preliminary results from the first offering of the class in the Fall 2014 semester include an analysis of student motivation and the use of cohorts. Survey results are from 20 students in the class, 30% female and 70% male, representing an 80% respondent rate for the class as a whole. There was very little overlap between majors, with students in psychology, mechanical engineering, mathematics, theatre, university studies, and other disciplines. To assess the motivational impact of our pedagogical approaches and technological innovations, we surveyed students with the MUSIC Model of Academic Motivation Inventory (MMAMI). MMAMI is a validated instrument for measuring students' beliefs related to the five key components of the MUSIC model [27]. The version used in our course consists of 26 statements that students responded to on a 6-point Likert scale (ranging from "Strong Disagreement" to "Strong Agreement"). The responses are then averaged into subscales relating to each of the components of the MUSIC model – eMpowerment, Usefulness, Success, Interest, and Caring. Examples of the statements include:

"The knowledge I gain in this course is important for my future."

"I enjoy completing the coursework."

Students were also surveyed on the different learning resources used in this course using a 4-point Likert scale. In particular, they were asked how helpful the resources were to their learning, their expectation of the usefulness of the resource to their long-term goals, and the interestingness of the resource. These questions asked about students' experiences listening to lecture, reading the online textbook, getting help from the instructors in class, and working with their cohorts, NetLogo, Blockly, Python, and real-world data.

To better understand the quantitative data, qualitative data about the class was also collected by observing students working in cohorts during class time and by interviewing 9 students of the class at the end of semester. The following sections describe the findings of both quantitative and qualitative data of the study.

5.2 Analysis of Quantitative Data

As a baseline measure of success, the results from the MUSIC inventory suggest that students were overall motivated in this course. Students reported high average scores in all five areas of the MUSIC model, with no strong standard deviation. The results, shown in Figure 1, indicate that students "Agreed" in the belief that they were empowered, able to succeed, cared for, and that the

course was interesting and useful. Our interpretation of this data is that, at a minimum, this course was successful in engaging students.

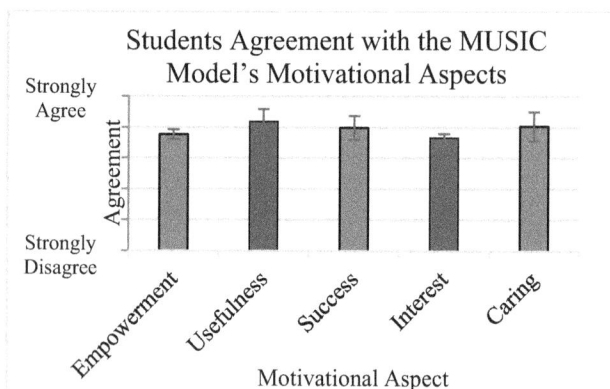

Figure 1: MUSIC Model Results

The follow-up surveys were useful in divining the sources of this engagement. The survey data is presented for helpfulness (Figure 2), usefulness (Figure 3), and interestingness (Figure 4).

The cohort model was a significant factor in motivation with students citing it as helping their learning (Figure 2) while also being both interesting (Figure 3) and useful (Figure 4) to their long-term goals. In fact, students' cohorts were considered almost as useful as the assistance from instructors. Critically, no students thought that the cohort model was valueless, making the value of the collaborative learning experience very clear. Similarly, the negative results from the textbook and lectures, compared to the positive results from the cohort and instructors, reinforce the expanding literature on the value of active learning techniques compared to traditional lecture models.

In terms of the languages, Python was an unsurprisingly popular component of the course, with high positive results for most students. This matches recent literature on Python's suitability for introductory programming experiences. A more interesting result is for Blockly – students perceived it as being useful to their learning (and moderately interesting), but recognized that it had little long-term usefulness. This matches with the use of Blockly as "training wheels" for Python, meant to be gracefully discarded as the students gain familiarity with algorithmic concepts and are prepared to cope with Python's syntax.

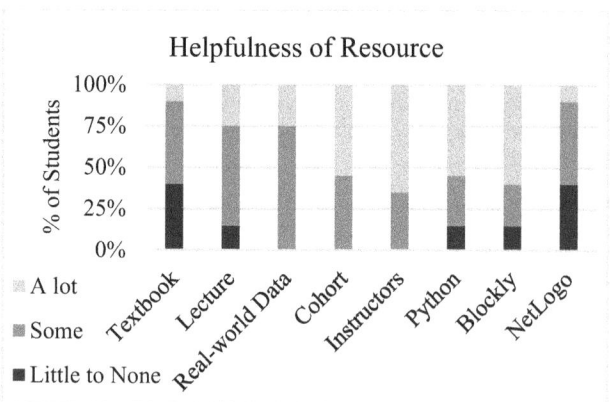

Figure 2: Survey Results on Helpfulness

The results related to NetLogo are more ambiguous – although few students found it very uninteresting, few reported it as very interesting or very useful to their long-term goals. There are positives and negatives to the use of NetLogo within this course that we are still exploring.

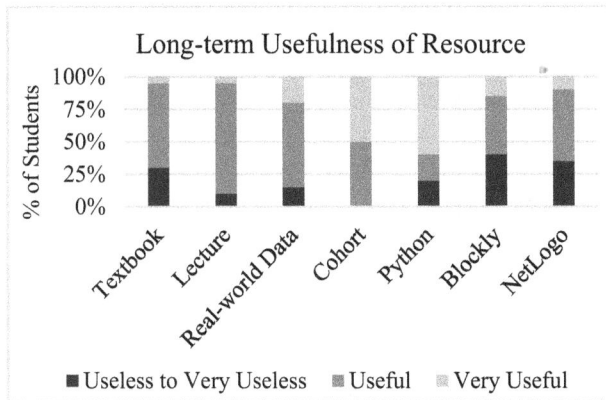

Figure 3: Survey Results on Usefulness

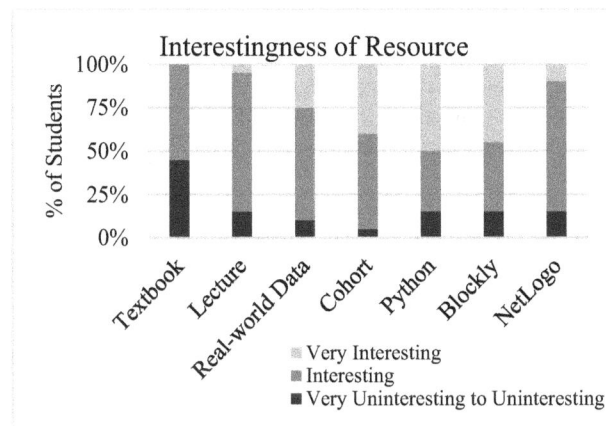

Figure 4: Survey Results on Interestingness

5.2 Analysis of Qualitative Data

Group observations (13 hours) and interviews with students (9 students) suggest that working in a cohort was beneficial. While some class activities were designed to be collaborative, students in their cohort usually worked on individual problems. If a student got stuck with a problem s/he would ask other members in their cohort for help. In some cohorts a more active student would inquire if other members were stuck with a problem. Students felt it was easier to ask help from peer members because they were at the same level of learning.

"It's nice to have other people that are in a similar level of learning to you so you can bounce ideas off each other as opposed to get an explanation from someone who already know the materials and is trying remember what it is like not know the material. So it's getting a better explanation from someone that is closer to where you are… "(Student1)

Help usually was offered in the form of explanation instead of providing the answer.

"If we are doing individual work we usually break off and solve the problems. If we have difficulty we ask the other members. Usually if we get an explanation that is more about the concept as opposed to the individual problem we had. So say if we got a problem with 'if' statement, we get an explanation on why our 'if' statement wasn't working as opposed to the right way to write that individual 'if' statement. There is more learning the 'whys' as opposed to the 'what' I guess"(Student 1)

Forming cohorts with students from different disciplines allowed students to better understand the application and implications of CT across disciplines.

"It offered different perspectives. When we were working with Netlogo and how we chose a view point, like a program that we can relate to our major. I know the biology major did one on AIDS and how it spreads and the other two on voting and voting habits. And I did something on networking… it was good to open up and see different perspectives and how programs can be applied to different focuse" (Student 7)

"Since we all are working on different projects it is kind of interesting to see what we can do with the data. So like while my one is working on voting habits and government, I think one of the other guys is comparing literature and it is just like how you can approach problems in different ways…" (Student 4)

Apart from understanding concepts, students also found cohort members useful in locating technical resources or explaining how to use certain features of a course resource.

"In the beginning of the Blockly program, the airplane, the diagram, all of that – I really did not know how to do it. It was easy, but I really did not know how to start it. So I asked my team member how to start. He explained to me how to start and after that I was able to do it easily. So it was basically getting to know the basics of how to start the program and then I was able to do it." (Student 5)

Students also appreciated the presence of the instructor and co-instructor.

"The basic understanding, solidifying the basic understanding of the underlying principles of programming –that is not something most people (instructor) will go over, at least at this level I guess. Having that explained with someone there, who knows the material and is willing to explain it further, that was just really helpful…" (Student 1)

Students of this class stated that taking this CT class has helped them realize the role of computation in their major.

"Taking this course I now realize how much the modeling that we do in python is being used by people in my major and is seen as a valuable skill to employers …I did not know (before taking this course) how thorough and how much it would tie into my major until I took the class…"(Student 3)

6. CONCLUSIONS

This paper has outlined the design of a general education university course in computational thinking. The quantitative and qualitative assessments provide early evidence supporting key course design decisions and the achievement of important learning objectives. First, the course engendered a high level of student motivation and engagement. We see this as an especially critical finding for a general education course. Second, the multidisciplinary cohorts were seen as helpful to learning and useful to student's long-term goals. Importantly, the qualitative data indicates that the cohorts fostered learning across disciplines, a key learning objective. Third, the preliminary analysis of the qualitative data also indicates that students made gains on another key learning objective - a deeper appreciation for the use of computation in their own disciplines. Fourth, the use of Blockly and Python were largely supported by the assessment while the use of NetLogo is more ambiguous and requires further study. We had expected the assessment to more prominently support the use of real-world data. While helpful overall the response was weaker than for the multidisciplinary cohorts and instructors. We believe that the small negative view of the real-world data on measures of interestingness and usefulness may be due to the repeated use of overly simplified big data on exercises and assignments. We have plans to introduce more varied and more successively realistic examples of big data in the next offering of the course and to observe the effect of this change.

7. ACKNOWLEDGMENTS

We thank Jason Riddle and Omar Saleem for preparing big data resources and Shelli Fowler for use of the TLOS Learning Studio as our classroom. This work was supported in part by NSF Grant TUES-1444094.

8. REFERENCES

[1] National Research Council, Report of a Workshop on the Scope and Nature of Computational Thinking: National Academy Press, 2010.

[2] J. M. Wing, "Computational thinking," *Communications of the ACM*, vol. 49, pp. 33-35, 2006.

[3] International Society for Technology Education. 2011, Computational Thinking Teacher Resources (Second Edition ed.). Available: http://www.iste.org/docs/ct-documents/ct-teacher-resources_2ed-pdf.pdf?sfvrsn=2

[4] L. Perkovik, et al., "A framework for computational thinking across the curriculum," Proceedings of the Fifteenth Annual Conference on Innovation and Technology in Computer Science Education, Bilkent, Ankara, Turkey, 2010.

[5] N. Senske, "A Curriculum for Integrating Computational Thinking," presented at the ACADIA Regional Conference 2011 Lincoln, Nebraska, 2011.

[6] C. Kuster, et al., "Developing Computational Thinking Skills across the Undergraduate Curriculum," presented at the 44th Annual Midwest Instruction and Computing Symposium (MICS'11), Duluth, MN, 2011.

[7] S. Hambrusch, et al., "A multidisciplinary approach towards computational thinking for science majors," Proceedings of the 40th ACM Technical Symposium on Computer Science Education, Chattanooga, TN, USA, 2009.

[8] D. Kafura and D. Tatar, "Initial experience with a computational thinking course for computer science students," Proceedings of the 42nd ACM Technical Symposium on Computer Science Education, Dallas, TX, USA, 2011.

[9] A. Ritz, "Evolution of a Computational Thinking Course," Presentation to CS6604 Class, Ed., ed, 2013.

[10] H. Qin, "Teaching computational thinking through bioinformatics to biology students," Proceedings of the 40th ACM Technical Symposium on Computer Science Education, Chattanooga, TN, USA, 2009.

[11] W. Booth, et al. (2013, Computational Thinking: Building a Model Curriculum. 11pp. Available: https://ciiwiki.ecs.baylor.edu/index.php/Computational_Thinking:_Building_a_Model_Curriculum.

[12] T. J. Cortina, "An introduction to computer science for non-majors using principles of computation," Proceedings of the 38th ACM Technical Symposium on Computer Science Education, Covington, Kentucky, USA, 2007.

[13] T. Li and T. Wang, "A Unified Approach to Teach Computational Thinking for First Year Non–CS Majors in an Introductory Course," IERI Procedia, vol. 2, pp. 498-503, 2012.

[14] L. Snyder, Fluency with Information Technology, 6th ed., Addison-Wesley, 2014.

[15] M. Guzdial, "A media computation course for non-majors," SIGCSE Bull., vol. 35, pp. 104-108, 2003.

[16] M. Guzdial and A. E. Tew, "Imagineering inauthentic legitimate peripheral participation: an instructional design approach for motivating computing education," Proceedings of the Second International Workshop on Computing Education Research, Canterbury, United Kingdom, 2006.

[17] R. E. Anderson, et al., "Introductory programming meets the real world: using real problems and data in CS1," Proceedings of the 45th ACM Technical Symposium on Computer Science Education, Atlanta, Georgia, USA, 2014.

[18] T. T. Yuen and K. A. Robbins, "A Qualitative Study of Students' Computational Thinking Skills in a Data-Driven Computing Class," Trans. Comput. Educ., vol. 14, pp. 1-19, 2014.

[19] U. Wilensky, "Modeling Nature's Emergent Patterns with Multi-Agent Languages," in Center for Connected Learning and Computer-Based Modeling, ed. Northwestern University: Available at: http://ccl.northwestern.edu/papers/2013/mnep9.pdf, 2013.

[20] A. C. Bart, et al., "Motivating Students with Big Data: CORGIS and MUSIC," in Splash-E, Portland, Oregon, USA, 2014.

[21] D. I. Cordova and M. R. Lepper, "Intrinsic motivation and the process of learning: Beneficial effects of contextualization, personalization, and choice," Journal of Educational Psychology, vol. 88, pp. 715-730, 1996.

[22] L. R. Lattuca, et al., "Does interdisciplinarity promote learning? Theoretical support and researchable questions," The Review of Higher Education, vol. 28, pp. 23-48, 2004.

[23] P. Dillenbourg, "What do you mean by collaborative learning?," Collaborative-learning: Cognitive and Computational Approaches., pp. 1-19, 1999.

[24] B. Miller and D. Ranum, "Runestone interactive: tools for creating interactive course materials," Proceedings of the First ACM Conference on Learning @ Scale, Atlanta, Georgia, USA, 2014.

[25] N. Fraser, "Differential synchronization," Proceedings of the 9th ACM Symposium on Document Engineering, Munich, Germany, 2009.

[26] Blockly Website. (2014. Available: https://developers.google.com/blockly/

[27] B. D. Jones and G. Skaggs, "Validation of the MUSIC Model of Academic Motivation Inventory: A measure of students' motivation in college courses," in International Conference on Motivation, Frankfurt, Germany, 2012.

Supporting Computational Algorithmic Thinking (SCAT): Exploring the Difficulties African-American Middle School Girls Face while Enacting Computational Algorithmic Thinking

Jakita O. Thomas
Spelman College
350 Spelman Lane, SW Box 1257
Atlanta, GA 30314
1+404-270-5880
jthoma41@spelman.edu

ABSTRACT

Computational algorithmic thinking (CAT) is the ability to design, implement, and assess the implementation of algorithms to solve a range of problems. It involves identifying and understanding a problem, articulating an algorithm or set of algorithms in the form of a solution to the problem, implementing that solution in such a way that it solves the problem, and evaluating the solution based on some set of criteria. This paper introduces CAT as explored through the Supporting Computational Algorithmic Thinking (SCAT) project, an on-going longitudinal between-subjects research project and enrichment program that guides African-American middle school girls (SCAT Scholars) through the iterative game design cycle resulting in a set of complex games around broad themes. This paper explores the difficulties SCAT Scholars face while using CAT capabilities in the context of game design as described by the Scholars themselves in online journals.

Categories and Subject Descriptors

K.3.2 [**Computers and Education**]: Computer and Information Science Education

General Terms

Algorithms, Design

Keywords

Computational algorithmic thinking; game design; middle-school; girls; African-American

1. INTRODUCTION

This research makes explicit a critical aspect of computational thinking through its focus: the design, development, and implementation of algorithms to solve problems where an algorithm is defined as "a well-ordered collection of unambiguous and effectively computable operations that, when executed, produces a result and halts in a finite amount of time"

[34]. Computational algorithmic thinking (CAT) is the ability to design, implement, and assess the implementation of algorithms to solve a range of problems. It involves identifying and understanding a problem, articulating an algorithm or set of algorithms in the form of a solution to the problem, implementing that solution in such a way that it solves the problem, and evaluating the solution based on some set of criteria. CAT has roots in Mathematics [30], through problem solving and algorithmic thinking [20]. CAT lies at the heart of Computer Science, which is defined as the study of algorithms [34]. CAT embodies the ability to think critically and creatively to solve problems and has applicability in a range of areas from Computer Science to cooking to music [16, 29, 42].

Supporting Computational Algorithmic Thinking (SCAT) is a longitudinal between-subjects research project exploring how African-American middle-school girls develop CAT capabilities over time in the context of game design. SCAT is also a free enrichment program designed to expose middle school girls to game design. The goals are: 1) to explore the development of computational algorithmic thinking over three years in African-American middle-school girls as they engage in iterative game design, and 2) to increase the awareness of participants to the broad applicability of computational algorithmic thinking across a number of industries and career paths. Spanning three years, participants, called SCAT Scholars (or just Scholars), develop CAT capabilities as they design more and more complex games. Scholars design games around the theme "games for social change" and use game design as a platform to explore and address a range of issues that the Scholars and/or their communities face on a local, regional, national, or global scale. Issues that Scholars have designed games to address include bullying, environmental sustainability, animal rights, gun control, texting while driving, and other cultural and social issues.

SCAT Scholars begin the program the summer prior to their 6th grade year and continue through their 8th grade year. They engage in 3 types of activities each year (also called a SCAT Season): 1) a two-week intensive game design summer camp; 2) Two (2) six-week technical workshops where Scholars implement the games they have designed using visual and programming languages (e.g., SCRATCH, GameMaker, Unity) in preparation for submission to national game design competitions (e.g., National STEM Video Game Challenge); and 3) field trips where Scholars learn about applications of CAT in different industries and careers. This paper aims to explore the following research questions: *What difficulties do Scholars face as they engage in computational algorithmic thinking?*

While there is a great deal of research that examines how to engage students in computational thinking and learning in Computer Science (CS) or that focuses on how game design improves IT fluency, algorithmic thinking, collaboration, programming capability, and broader participation from under-represented groups, there is a scarcity of research that focuses on understanding and describing how the development of CAT happens over time as a complex cognitive capability [32, 24, 36, 40, 23, 13, 6, 18, 19, 28]. Furthermore, there is less research that focuses on understanding how the development of these kinds of complex cognitive capabilities can impact not only how we leverage game design to teach and support students as they develop these capabilities, but also how we define and measure the learning that happens during that development.

We begin to address this research question by examining the online journals of SCAT Scholars collected during the first year, or Season, of SCAT. The next section of this paper will provide the background context that grounds the research. Then, the SCAT learning environment, including the scaffolds that support Scholars as they engage in game design, will be described. Next, we will describe the data collection and analysis methods, followed by a description of findings from our analysis of the first Season of online journal data. Finally, we will discuss what these findings not only suggest about supporting CAT capabilities, but also how they inform the project going forward as it moves through the second year of data collection.

2. BACKGROUND

The National Research Council [25], in their report entitled *A Framework for K-12 Science Education: Practices, Crosscutting Concepts, and Core Ideas*, outlines eight practices as being "essential elements of the K-12 science and engineering curriculum". Among them are: defining problems, developing and using models (physical or mathematical models and prototypes), planning and carrying out investigations, analyzing and interpreting data, using mathematics, information & computer technology and computational thinking, designing solutions, engaging in argument from evidence, and obtaining, evaluating, and communicating information. While the major competencies that students should have by the 12th grade and sketches regarding how that competence should progress are described, the NRC identifies that those sketches are based on The Committee on a Conceptual Framework for New Science Education Standards' judgment as "there is very little research evidence as yet on the developmental trajectory of each of these practices" (p. 3-6).

As a domain, engaging in game design aligns with the eight practices outlined by the NRC [25]. The iterative game design lifecycle involves several phases, which are also iterative [15], as shown in Figure 1. During brainstorming, game designers generate many ideas for games and present those ideas. Once an idea is selected, paper-and-pencil drawings are created, called storyboards that include demo artwork. Playtesting is next, which involves bringing actual players from the target user group in and observing them as they play the game (or engage with the storyboard) in real time, getting feedback about the game experience to inform the design of the game [15, 13]. Next, game designers create a playable physical prototype using paper-and-pencil and/or craft materials, which is playtested. Then, a rough software prototype is created which models some aspect(s) of core gameplay. Then follows more playtesting. Next comes creating the design document, which outlines every aspect of the game and how it will function. This is followed by implementing

the game with playtesting throughout implementation. Finally, quality assurance testing is done with continued playtesting.

Game design has been chosen as the domain for a number of reasons. First, game design is a domain with which middle-schoolers have a great deal of familiarity as consumers [18, 17]. The Pew Internet & American Life Project's survey revealed that among young people, ages 12 – 17, 97% of respondents play

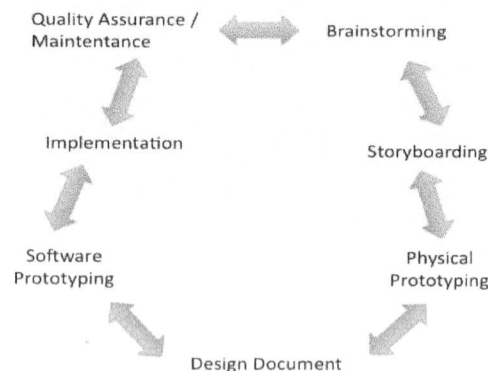

Figure 1. The Game Design Cycle

video games [22]. As such, this domain can provide motivation as learners "look under the hood" of their favorite games to understand how they are designed and implemented. Second, game design is centered around the iterative design, representation, and implementation of algorithms, which makes it an ideal domain to understand and describe the development of CAT over time [12]. Third, based upon industry practices, game designers iteratively move from game conceptualization to production and release over time [15], making game design an ideal domain for conducting longitudinal studies. Lastly, game design is a domain in which African-American women are grossly under-represented [10]. Of the 97% of young people who stated they played games in the Pew Institute's survey, over 94% of girls play video games with little difference in the percentages by race, ethnic group, or socio-economic status [22]. However, women represent only about 10 – 12% of the game design workforce, and Latinos and African-Americans comprise less than 5% combined [31].

The acquisition and development of skills, capabilities, and practices involves the changing of declarative knowledge, or independent pieces of factual knowledge, to procedural knowledge, or connected knowledge that forms a process for carrying out a skill [2, 1]. Applied in context and/or among a community, a process evolves into a practice [27, 21]. While skills, or abilities refer to what one can do in the present, capabilities refer to what one can learn to do with instruction and support, or scaffolding [3, 4, 38, 9, 35]. However, moving learners from capability to ability requires several things [9, 24, 36]. First, learners need opportunities to make connections between their experiences and the knowledge or skills they are learning. Second, learners need enough time to learn and develop skills and capabilities so that they can use them flexibly in appropriate situations. Third, learners should be supported as they attempt to represent problems at higher levels of abstraction. Finally, learners should be encouraged to monitor their learning and should be supported as they learn meta-cognitive strategies.

3. SCAT LEARNING ENVIRONMENT

The facilitator plays a major role in the development of Scholars' CAT capabilities in the SCAT learning environment as she serves first as the primary modeler and then as a just-in-time coach [11]. In addition, the facilitator leads and supports discussions that help Scholars as they think through their designs, helps them make connections across dyad experiences and problems as they design and implement their games, and models the kinds of questions Scholars should be asking themselves and their peers as they develop algorithms for their game designs, move through the iterative game design cycle, and reflect on their use of CAT [19]. As dyads work on their game designs, she walks from group to group asking them questions about their designs, helping them identify problems and issues, illustrating for them how to use the Design Notebook and other tools and resources provided to them to help them design their games, and serving as a sounding board for dyads as they design. Although the facilitator is a critical component to the SCAT learning environment, she cannot be with every group or individual all the time. To help overcome that limitation and to help Scholars develop more expert CAT capabilities, the Design Notebook has been created to coach Scholars as they engage in CAT through game design. The Design Notebook has been integrated into SCAT activities, affording Scholars multiple opportunities to develop CAT capabilities while working individually and collaboratively in dyads.

The Design Notebook contains paper-and-pencil based tools that coach groups and individuals in the ways cognitive apprenticeship suggests [11, 30] by using a system of scaffolds [24, 36]. Each scaffold in the system supports groups and individuals in a particular way and addresses a particular difficulty that learners may face when engaging in complex cognitive skills, processes, and capabilities like designing an experiment, interpreting and applying the experiences of experts, or engaging in CAT. The system of scaffolds has 5 parts [24, 36]. First, tool sequences make process sequence visible. This scaffold addresses the structuring of tools to suggest a high-level process that learners are engaging in. Second, within each tool, structured questioning or statements make the task sequence clear. This scaffold addresses prompts, which are questions or statements used to focus learners' attention as they are carrying out or reflecting on a task. Third, for each prompt in the sequence, hints are provided. Hints are task-specific/domain-specific questions or statements used to refine a task. Fourth, for each prompt in the sequence, examples are provided. Examples are exemplars that can be used to model a process or a specific step of a process. Fifth, for some tasks in the sequencing, a template or chart to help with lining up one's reasoning is provided.

Given that Scholars will be able to move through the iterative game design cycle at their own pace, it is likely that those Scholars or dyads who are further along in the game design cycle will be able to scaffold dyads who are not as far along [38, 33, 24, 36, 27]. In addition, different Scholars will bring different perspectives to the dyad, which will contribute to greater understanding by the dyad. The literature shows that small group collaboration and discussion has many benefits [14, 19, 33, 8, 39, 7, 5].

4. CAT IN SCAT

As mentioned previously, game design is all about algorithms, and computational algorithmic thinking is enacted in a number of places throughout the game design cycle. The game design cycle itself is an algorithm consisting of seven phases as described in Section 2, BACKGROUND. In addition, as Scholars move through the phases of the game design cycle, they engage in computational algorithmic thinking. For example, during the Storyboarding phase, Scholars engage in computational algorithmic thinking as they draw stills that depict the gameplay for the user from beginning to end as well as the non-visual elements of the game. In fact, the storyboard is the first enactment of CAT as it visually describes many of the game's algorithms. During the Physical Prototyping phase, Scholars articulate the rules and procedures of the gameplay, which are the primary algorithms that govern gameplay and how players engage with the game. The implementation phase involves Scholars not only articulating algorithms in SCRATCH to implement gameplay functionality and behavior, but also adapting and implementing SCRATCH algorithms (e.g., creating a scrolling screen, keeping score, enacting a timer, detecting and responding to a collision between objects, etc.). As Scholars move through the phases of the game design cycle, they articulate the algorithms in their games more and more specifically as they move toward a more fully functional game.

5. METHOD

This section presents the setting, participants, and data collected and analysis for this work.

5.1 Setting and Participants

This longitudinal between-groups research takes place at Spelman College in Atlanta, GA and various locations around the metro-Atlanta area. Spelman College is a private, liberal arts, Historically Black College for women located in Atlanta, Georgia. Spelman College has been a leader in training minorities and women in Science, Technology, Engineering Mathematics, and Computer Science (STEM+CS) areas, with about one third of the students majoring in these fields. Currently at Spelman College, 97% of the students are African-American, of whom approximately 35% are majoring in STEM+CS fields. Each season, Scholars participate in the three activities described earlier: two-week summer camp, workshops, and field trips. This paper focuses on data collected during SCAT Season 1, which ran from July 2013 – May 2014. During that season, we worked with 20 African-American 6th grade girls. Of these SCAT Scholars, 95% had never used SCRATCH, and none of the Scholars had ever engaged in the game design cycle in this way to design novel games.

5.2 Data Collection and Analysis

We collected various data including Scholar artifacts (Design Notebooks, storyboards, design documents, physical prototypes, software prototypes, presentations, etc.), video observations (both whole class and small group), semi-structured interviews, pre- and post-surveys (of students and parents), online journals, and end of season online evaluations (questionnaire). While we are in the midst of analysis for all of these different data for Season 1, this paper will focus on the online journal data that each SCAT Scholar completed every time they met for SCAT activities (excluding field trips).

Each day during the two-week summer camp and each week during the two 6-week game design workshops, Scholars individually made entries into their online journals. This journal was created using a Google form to make capturing the responses in a spreadsheet easier. The online journal was used as a tool to help Scholars describe what they set out to accomplish for the day and to reflect on the victories and difficulties faced over the course of the day that allowed them to accomplish their goal or hindered them from meeting their goal. In addition, Scholars also reflected on what they liked and disliked about the day's activities, and had the opportunity to provide additional comments about the day's activities, the next day's/week's activities, or the experience overall. The online journal consisted of the following questions: *What was your group's goal for today? What did you like about today? What did you dislike about today? What was easy for you today? What was difficult? Any other comments?* During the last fifteen minutes of each SCAT activity day, Scholars would individually make an entry into their online journal. To analyze the online journal data, which included over 300 entries, we took several passes over the data engaging in content analysis, identifying emergent themes. In particular, we focused on the question *What was difficult?* to better understand how Scholars described the difficulties they faced while engaging in computational algorithmic thinking in the context of game design.

6. FINDINGS

This section presents findings based on our analysis of the online journal data, which Scholars completed at the end of each SCAT meeting (every day during the two-week summer camp and each week for 12 weeks during the two 6-week workshops). In particular, we will describe and discuss the most prevalent themes that emerged as a result of our analysis, focusing on the difficulties that Scholars described in their online journals as they engaged in CAT in the context of game design. We will also include actual Scholar responses that align with each category of difficulty.

6.1 Articulating Algorithms to Describe User Actions and Related Gameplay Functionality or Behavior

Scholars' experienced the most difficulty as they attempted to articulate algorithms to describe user actions and gameplay functionality or behavior. Responses described this difficulty in two ways: either 1) figuring out how to build a set of blocks in SCRATCH (i.e., articulating an algorithm) that would allow the game to respond or behave in an appropriate way based on some aspect of the game that the Scholar dyads designed (e.g., "Getting ghouls to move right" or "Fixing the money so that the character collects it every time"), or 2) remembering how to articulate common SCRATCH algorithms (e.g., "Creating the timer" or "Changing to the next level").

6.2 Describing Aspects of the Game Design More Specifically

Over the course of the two-week summer camp, Scholars brainstormed ideas for games, selected a game idea, and engaged in storyboarding and physical prototyping that game idea. As mentioned earlier, each subsequent phase required Scholars to be more and more specific in describing aspects of the game design in order to move through that phase. As such, Scholars often experienced difficulty with articulating that specificity as they moved from phase to phase (e.g., "Coming up with the actual game and trying to think about the details" or "Writing our formal elements").

Scholars also play-tested each other's games. This playtesting involved Scholar dyads moving together to playtest their peers' games and leaving feedback about questions they had about how the games worked, things they liked about the games, things they did not like, and any changes they would suggest for their peers to make to their games. Following playtesting, dyads reviewed the feedback from their peers and often engaged in a whole group discussion about that feedback with the facilitator so that they could interpret the feedback and identify how they would iterate on their games to address the feedback. As a result, Scholars began to think about the design of their games from the perspective of the player instead of from their own perspective as designers, which often demanded that they be more specific in how they described their rules, procedures, and other aspects of gameplay. This transition from viewing the design of their games from their own perspective to that of the player proved to be a difficult transition for many Scholars (e.g., "Trying to see me and my partners game in someone else's point of view because we know the game but someone else may not…" or "Finishing our prototype was so hard because it was hard to make sure that someone who did not know how to play could play with no problems without us there to help them with any problems they had. But also [we] had to make sure that it wasn't confusing or difficult to figure out so we had to be extremely careful").

In addition, Scholars were expected to design and implement at least one level of their game over the course of Season 1. However, many Scholar dyads were able to begin implementing additional levels over the course of the season. As they began implementing those additional levels, many dyads realized that they had not described those levels in enough detail during the storyboarding and physical prototyping phases to implement them in SCRATCH (e.g., "Thinking about level two was [kind] of hard" or "Getting ideas for level 2"). Dyads found that they often had to revisit the brainstorming, storyboarding, and/or physical prototyping phases to describe the game and gameplay (including the rules and procedures) with enough specificity to then implement the additional level(s) using SCRATCH.

6.3 Understanding the Difference Between Rules and Procedures

Scholars experienced a great deal of difficulty understanding the difference between rules and procedures, where rules define game objects and allowable actions by the players (i.e., what players can and cannot do) and procedures define the methods of play and the actions that players can take to achieve the game objectives (i.e., who does what, where, when, and how) [15]. The facilitator guided the Scholars as a group through several discussions over the course of the summer camp about the difference between rules and procedures, and that discussion was revisited during the workshops as feedback during playtesting brought the distinction between the two back to the fore. However, Scholars described understanding the difference between the two as a difficulty they faced, especially during the summer camp (e.g., "It was difficult trying to figure out what to put on the rules because the steps and rules kept getting me confused", "coming up with procedures and rules", or "understanding the difference between rules and procedures was difficult for me").

6.4 Collaborating Within Dyads

Scholars worked in dyads to design and implement their games, and many Scholars described collaborating with their partner as a difficulty they had to overcome (e.g., "working with my partner", "what was difficult was when my partner and I weren't coming together with ideas", or "It was difficult to come up with solutions that both my partner and I agreed on"). Many of the Scholars expressed during whole group discussions that they had never worked with a partner before the SCAT program or, if they had, their previous group experiences had not been positive. Some of those collaborative difficulties seemed to arise because of conflicting personalities (i.e., two dominant personalities not being able to agree on who will do what or one dominant personality not allowing a quiet personality to be involved) (e.g., "Trying not to completely take over everything and let my partner do some things"), the social awkwardness of 6th grade girls (for instance, two Scholars who are friends outside of SCAT are not partners and one becomes jealous of the friendship that her friend is developing with her partner), as well as having little prior experience engaging in group work prior to SCAT (e.g., "The easiest thing today was coming up with ideas when we actually put our thoughts together").

6.5 Assessing Algorithms That Behave in Unexpected Ways and Adapting Those Algorithms

Dyads often play-tested their own games as they designed and implemented them. This might involve reviewing a storyboard for flow or running the game in SCRATCH. When their games behaved in unexpected ways, dyads had to figure out what went wrong and how they would fix it; in other words, they had to debug their games. Debugging their games involved assessing the algorithms they had designed and/or implemented and adapting those algorithms in ways that better aligned with expected outcomes based on the game design. Many scholars expressed difficulty engaging in that assessment and adaptation to debug their games (e.g., "...fixing some of the problems with the game was somewhat challenging" or "learning what was wrong with our game" or "The bugs in the game made today somewhat difficult" or "It was very hard trying to fix...parts of the game").

7. DISCUSSION AND FUTURE WORK

This paper presented computational algorithmic thinking and the SCAT project. In addition, this paper described the difficulties Scholars faced enacting CAT in the context of game design as described in their online journal entries. Our analysis uncovers areas where Scholars need additional support.

We have begun to address some of these areas through changes to the Design Notebook. For example, to help Scholars better articulate algorithms to describe user actions and related gameplay functionality or behavior, we created the *Algorithm Design Template*. This template helps Scholars not only describe in a step-by-step way the actions they want the user to perform and the resulting behavior that the game should display, but it also helps Scholars connect those action/result pairs to implementation blocks in SCRATCH.

Another example includes adapting the Design Notebook to help Scholars better distinguish between rules and procedures, with a particular focus on helping them better articulate procedures during game design. We updated the *Procedures of My Game Design* Page to make the definition of procedures more salient and distinct from rules and to guide Scholars better through the creation of their rules. This Design Page reminds Scholars that procedures describe who does what, where, when, and how. It also prompts them to describe the starting action of the game,

how action progresses during the game, what actions end gameplay, and special actions a player might take in unusual game situations (e.g., providing a get out of jail free card).

The *Algorithm Design Template* and the *Procedures of My Game Design* Pages were piloted as a part of the Design Notebook during the Season 2 summer camp held this past June.

As we continue our full analysis of SCAT Season 1 data while collecting Season 2 data, we will be looking for additional opportunities to not only better support Scholars through the difficulties they face using CAT in the context of game design over the remaining years of the project, but also to understand how these difficulties may change and, in some cases, resolve themselves over time (e.g., Scholars find it easier to collaborate because of their experiences in SCAT as well as their natural growth and maturity). We will also be looking for additional difficulties that arise and suggestions that data will make about how to better support those difficulties.

8. ACKNOWLEDGMENTS

We are grateful for the generous support of the National Science Foundation (DRK-12 1150098).

9. REFERENCES

[1] Anderson, J. R. (2000). Cognitive Psychology and Its Implications: Fifth Edition. New York: Worth Publishing.

[2] Anderson, J. R., Greeno, J. G., Kline, P.J. & Neves, D.M. (1981). Acquisition of problem-solving skills. In J. R. Anderson(Ed.), *Cognitive skills and their acquisition*. Hillsdale, NJ: Lawrence Erlbaum Associates.

[3] Bandura, A. (1994). Self-efficacy. In R. J. Corsini (Ed.), *Encyclopedia of psychology* (2nd ed., Vol. 3, pp. 368-369). New York: Wiley.

[4] Bandura blog entry. *Ability and Capability*. Downloaded from Bandura's blog, http://des.emory.edu/mfp/AbilityCapability.html.

[5] Barron, B. (2003). When smart groups fail. *Journal of the Learning Sciences*, 12, 307-359.

[6] Barnes, T., Richter, H., Chaffin, A., Godwin, A., Powell, E., Ralph, T., Matthews, P. & Jordan, H. (2007). Game2Learn: A study of games as tools for learning introductory programming. In Proc. of SIGCSE2007.

[7] Barron, B., Schwartz, D.L., Vye, N.J., Moore, A., Petrosino, A., Zech, L., Bransford, J. D. & The Cognition and Technology Group at Vanderbilt (1998). Doing with understanding: Lessons from research on problem- and project-based learning. *Journal of the Learning Sciences*, 7(3&4), 271-311.

[8] Bayer, A. (1990). Collaborative-apprenticeship learning: Language and thinking across the curriculum, K-12. Mountain View, CA: Mayfield..

[9] Bransford, J. D., Brown, A.L., & Cocking, R. R. (1999). *How people learn: Brain, mind,experience, and school*. Washington, DC: National Academy Press.

[10] Brathwaite (2009). Interview on Women, Games and Design. Downloaded from Applied Game Design blog, http://bbrathwaite.wordpress.com/2009/01/07/interview-on-womengames-and-design/.

[11] Collins, A., Brown, J.S., & Newman, S.E. (1989). Cognitive apprenticeship: Teaching the crafts of reading, writing, and mathematics. In L.B. Resnick (Ed.), *Knowing, learning, and*

instruction: essays in honor of Robert Glaser, 453-494. Hillsdale, NJ: Lawrence Erlbaum Associates.

[12] Crawford, C. (2010) How to Think: Algorithmic Thinking, In the *Journal of Computer Game Design* v.7.

[13] DiSalvo, B. J., Guzdial, M., Mcklin, T., Meadows, C., Perry, K., Steward, C. & Bruckman, A. (2009). Glitch Game Testers: African American Med Breaking Open the Console. In Proc of DiGRA 2009.

[14] Feltovich, P.J., Spiro, R.J., Coulson, R.L., & Feltovich, J. (1996). Collaboration within and among minds: Mastering complexity, individually and in groups. In T. Koschmann (Ed), *Computer systems for collaborative learning*, Hillsdale, NJ: Lawrence Erlbaum, 25-44.

[15] Fullerton, T., Swain, C., and Hoffman, S. (2004). Game Design Workshop: designing, prototyping and playtesting games. San Francisco, CA: CMP Books.

[16] International Society for Technology in Education – National Education Technology Standards (2007). *NETS for Students 2007*, downloaded from http://www.iste.org/standards/netsfor-students/nets-student-standards-2007.aspx.

[17] Irvine, M. (2008). "Survey: 97 Percent of Children Play Video Games". Downloaded from The Huffington Post, http://www.huffingtonpost.com/2008/09/16/survey-97-percent-ofchil_n_126948.html.

[18] Kafai, Y. B. (2006). Playing and Making Games for Learning: Instructionist and Constructionist Perspectives for Game Studies. In *Games and Culture*, 1(1), pp. 36-39.

[19] Koschmann, T., Kelson, A.C., Feltovich, P.J., & Barrows, H.S. (1996). Computer-supported problem-based learning: A principled approach to the use of computers in collaborative learning. In T.D. Koschmann (Ed.), *CSCL: Theory and practice of an emerging paradigm* (pp. 83—124). Hillsdale, NJ: Lawrence Erlbaum.

[20] Kramer, Kramer, D. (2002). *Algorithms Should Mind Your Business*, downloaded from http://www.outsourcing-russia.com/docs/?doc=680ssification. *J. Mach. Learn. Res.* 3 (Mar. 2003), 1289-1305.

[21] Lave, J., & Wenger, E. (1991). Situated learning: Legitimate peripheral participation. Cambridge, UK: Cambridge University Press.

[22] Lenhart, A., Kahne, J., Macgill, A. R., Evans, C. & Vitak, J. (2008). Teens' gaming experiences are diverse and included significant social interaction and civic engagement. Report 202-415-4500 for the Pew Internet & American Life Project: Washington, D.C.

[23] Maloney, J., Burd, L., Kafai, Y., Rusk, N., Silverman, B., and Resnick, M. (2004). Scratch: A Sneak Preview. Second International Conference on Creating, Connecting, and Collaborating through Computing. Kyoto, Japan, pp. 104-109.

[24] Owensby, J.N. (2006). Exploring the Development and Transfer of Case Use Skills in Middle-School Project-*Based Inquiry Classrooms*. Completed Dissertation, Georgia Institute of Technology. Proquest (1115125971).

[25] National Research Council (2011). A Framework for K-12 Science Education: Practices, Crosscutting *Concepts, and Core Ideas*. Washington, DC: The National Academies Press.

[26] Nersessian, N.J. (2008) *Creating Scientific Concepts*. Cambridge, MA: MIT Press.

[27] Palincsar, A. & Brown, A. (1984). Reciprocal teaching of comprehension-fostering and comprehension-monitoring activities. *Cognition and Instruction*, 1, 117 – 175.

[28] Papert, S. (1993). The children's machine: Rethinking school in the age of the computer. New York: Basic Books.

[29] Polya, G. (1973). How to Solve It: A New Aspect of Mathematical Method, 2nd Edition. Princeton, NJ: Princeton University Press.

[30] Puntembekar, S., & Kolodner, J. L. (1998). The Design Diary: Development of a Tool to Support Students Learning Science By Design. Proc of the Interational Conference of the Learning Sciences '98, 230-236.

[31] Plutzik, N. (2010). "So, Only White Men Can Be Game Designers?" Downloaded from the NPR All Tech Considered blog, http://www.npr.org/blogs/alltechconsidered/2010/03/if_youre_not_white_and_male_yo.html.

[32] Repenning, A. and Ioannidou (2008). Broadening Participation through Scalable Game Design, ACM Special Interest Group on Computer Science Education Conference, (SIGCSE 2008), ACM Press.

[33] Roschelle, J. (1996). Learning by collaborating: Convergent conceptual change. In T. Koschmann (Ed.). *CSCL: Theory and practice of an emerging paradigm*, Mahwah, NJ: Lawrence Erlbaum, 209-248.

[34] Schneider, G. M. & Gersting, J. L. (2010). *Invitation to Computer Science, 5th Edition*. Boston, MA: Course Technology, Cengage Learning, 4-16.

[35] Tabak, I. (2004). A complement to emerging patterns of distributed scaffolding. *The Journal of the Learning Sciences, 13*(3), 305-335.

[36] Thomas, J.O. (2008). Scaffolding Complex Cognitive Skill Development: Exploring the Development and Transfer of Case Use Skills In Middle-School Project-Based Inquiry Classrooms. VDM Publishing.

[37] Thomas, J. O. (2014). Supporting Computational Algorithmic Thinking (SCAT): Development of a complex cognitive capability in African-American middle-school girls, ACM Special Interest Group on Computer Science Education Conference, (SIGCSE 2014), ACM Press.

[38] Vygotsky, L. S. (1978) Mind and society: The development of higher mental processes. Cambridge, MA: Harvard University Press.

[39] Wells, G. & Chang-Wells, G. L. (1992). *Constructing knowledge together*. Portsmouth, NH: Heinemann.

[40] Werner, L., Campe, S., & Denner, J. (2005). Middle school girls + games programming = Information technology fluency. ACM special interest group in information technology education (SIGITE). Newark, NJ.

[41] Wing, J.M. (2006). *Computational Thinking*. In CACM Viewpoint, March 2006, pp. 33-35.

[42] Wing, J.M. (2010). "Computational Thinking". Presented at the Centre for Computational Systems and Biology, Trento, Italy, December 2010.

Using Unity to Teach Game Development: When You've Never Written a Game

Paul E. Dickson
Ithaca College
Computer Science Department
953 Danby Rd.
Ithaca, NY 14850, USA
pdickson@ithaca.edu

ABSTRACT

Video games are ubiquitous and our students want to learn how to make them. As computer science professors we see incorporating games into our curricula as a great way of increasing student excitement, increasing retention, and teaching communication skills. The problem many of us face though is how to teach game development when you have never written a game. Searches of articles and course offerings from other colleges does not provide a lot of clarification on what is the best environment for teaching such a course. The solution that we have found after many attempts is to build a game development course around the Unity game engine, and in this paper we describe how we arrived at this decision. Unity is easy to learn, free, cross-platform, a real game engine, and known in the field of game development but not discussed in computer science literature with regard to this type of course.

Categories and Subject Descriptors

K.3.2 [**Computers and Education**]: Computer and Information Science EducationComputer Science Education

General Terms

Design

Keywords

Game development, computer science education, Unity game engine, game programming

1. INTRODUCTION

Courses on game design and development keep popping up in computer science programs. The reasons for their inclusion vary and include improving program retention [1, 3, 15, 18, 19], team building [2, 16], and teaching project management [1, 3] among others. The value of such a course

ITiCSE'15, July 6–8, 2015, Vilnius, Lithuania.
Copyright © 2015 ACM 978-1-4503-3440-2/15/07 ...$15.00.
http://dx.doi.org/10.1145/2729094.2742591.

to teach a skill that our students need can be obvious, but if you are tasked with building just such a course, how do you go about it if you are not someone who has built games?

The purpose of this paper is to try to provide insights into building a stand-alone game development course so that the next person without the proper background who has to build such a course can avoid the mistakes that we made. Our experience is that trying to design the course from scratch can be daunting. Do you have students build games from scratch or do you use game development software? Do you want your course to focus on design, development, or a combination of the two? How easily can someone who does not build games get up to speed sufficiently to teach students the fundamentals of building games?

In this paper we describe our experience building a stand-alone game development course using the Unity [20] game engine[1] and the failures that led to our decision to use Unity. We present the structure of a course that can easily be modified to emphasize whatever a given department would like to emphasize, be it design or development. The existence of Unity is well known within the game development community but is unknown outside the community, perhaps because it is so well known that no one considers it necessary to record for those outside the community. Proof of how unknown it is outside of game development programs is that it was not even considered by Ritzhaupt when he was trying to put together an inexpensive game course in 2009 [17] and settled on Torque game engine [7] because it was only $100 for an old version, never considering Unity despite it being free for education. Further proof that Unity is not well known outside of the game development community is shown by how few references to it can be found when searching databases of computer science publications.

Unity is not the industry standard, is less likely to directly correspond to what employers in the gaming industry are looking for than is the Unreal Engine [12], and is generally not used in dedicated game development programs because it is not the industry standard. The reason that Unity is an excellent choice for a stand-alone game development course is that it has a shallow learning curve. If you are only going to have one course related to building games and you want your students to build games by the end of the semester, then you really need to use a game engine with a shallow learning curve so that students can focus on building games.

---

[1] A game development engine is a software framework that handles all aspects of game development, including sound, rendering, physics, etc.

Unity is also a good choice because it is cross-platform, is free, and can be used to build real games and not just toy games for the classroom.

2. BACKGROUND

When weighing the options for developing a game course that will fit into a computer science curriculum, you first need to have some understanding of what is available and what terms mean. The first issue is the focus of the course. In the United States game design usually means the design of the game and focuses on story, mechanics, look, etc., which is enough material to easily take an entire semester without going into too great detail. Game development is the counterpart to design and focuses on implementation of a game design and is closer to software engineering. If your goal is to have students leave a course with a playable game, there must be a greater emphasis on development.

In this paper we will often make references to students creating "playable games". It is hard to quantify success when students are building varied games. In two-thirds of a semester students can build a 3D version of mine sweeper that can be played for hours or 5-10 minutes of content in an adventure game; both are successful games. When describing a game as playable, we mean that students have created a mechanic for a game with only minor bugs that connects art assets to the mechanic and lays out some introduction (story/list of game controls) that introduces how to play the game. This means that a square shooting squares at circles that disappear when hit and increase a score is not a playable game but the same game with multiple levels, each of which includes an increasing number of targets to hit within a time limit, that includes instructions and a scoreboard would be.

In our department we offer a game design course that is intended for non-majors that cannot count toward a computer science degree as well as a 3D game development course open to majors and non-majors that can count toward a computer science degree. In this paper we discuss the 3D game development course. The course is considered stand alone as the design course is not a prerequisite and the material it covers has little to no effect on this course. The prerequisites for the development course is either the design course or CS1, meaning that little to no programming experience is required for this course. The development course is part of the Game Development minor we offer and a small percentage of the students in the course are interested in working in game development after college.

The goal of the course is to give students exposure to game development using software that is at least similar to what is found in industry. We focus on problem solving, project planning, working with an SDK, and teamwork and see this course as a way of exciting and motivating students who are not as excited by traditional computer science courses. Before we discuss what led us to use a game development engine, we will give a brief background because the advantage of using a development engine is one of the big things we learned from this process.

After a decision has been made to teach a game development course, the first major question faced is what environment to use to build the games. Do you use a toy engine designed for ease in the classroom like was done using GameMaker [3], RPG Maker [1], or Alice [22]? Do you try to build your own engine as was done with Labyrinth [5] or CAGE [21]? Do you build games using Flash [6] or decide to jump in with a full environment like XNA [10, 13] or a full engine like Unreal [12]?

If the goal of the course is to give students game development experience, then you have to give them a game development engine to work with or, as we discovered, the entire semester will be spent building infrastructure. While it is possible to build an engine that students can use [5, 21], they will end up learning a system that they will never see again after the course. We want our students to have experience with a real engine so that they have a real skill if they decide to pursue a job in game development. This leaves engines like Unreal [12], XNA [14], and Unity[20]. All three of these are free for use in an academic setting.

The Unreal engine can be used to create beautiful games and is used on many AAA[2] titles but has a steep learning curve[3]. We had not seen examples of it being used in courses other than those for game development majors, and our students who had used it to develop on their own did not speak well of it. Microsoft's XNA has a lot going for it in that it can be used to develop for Xbox and has been used in an academic setting [10, 13] but is as much an environment as a game engine. Discussion with Linhoff revealed that not many of the students in the first upper-level game development course using XNA were able to get their games onto Xbox; we did not want our students to work all semester toward this goal only to be unable to reach it. XNA also requires students to run visual studio, which does not work well for us as half of our students own Macs.

We decided to use Unity because it is cross-platform and our students who had used it spoke highly of it. It can also be used to develop for any platform including web (some specific licensing fees apply for specific platform compilation) and has been used in academia to develop a casual game [4]. It is a 3D engine with plugins to allow it to be used as a 2D engine. On the downside it is not a mainstay of the industry and only borderline AAA game titles have been released in it. Like the other game engines, Unity does not require a faculty member to develop any specific tools/modules for students to be able to use it to build games. Scripting in Unity can be done in C# or JavaScript so it is not tightly tied to a language that may not fit a department.

3. HOW NOT TO TEACH GAME DEV.

Our first three attempts at game development courses were at an institution with a lot of interest from students for such a course and with no other courses that related to building games. It is not the same institution where the successful game development course described in this paper was created.

---

[2] AAA is the title used to refer to the highest production value games made with the largest budgets. These games typically only come out of major game studios and all have large promotions.

[3] Unreal 4 is supposed to have a shallower learning curve than previous versions of the engine. It was only released for the general public in March 2014 and made free for education in September 2014. After the acceptance of this paper Unreal 4 was released for free to the general public in March 2015. We have yet to experiment with Unreal 4.

3.1 First Attempt, Xcode and iPhone

The first time we created a game development course, we decided that building for mobile devices was the best idea. Our thought was that having a restrictive device with limited input would stop our students from being too ambitious. We believed that our students' background in C/C++ would enable them to easily pick up Objective-C and build directly for the iPhone. As an added advantage our students would easily be able to show off what they created to others and this would motivate them to strive further in the course. Anyone who has any experience with iPhone development or game development will find this logic and the assumption that our goal was possible within a semester to be comical considering that many of the students in the course had only taken CS1. In our defense it was 2009 and app development was only beginning to take off in academia.

The students learned an enormous amount in this course; unfortunately it was mainly about iPhone development and the problems inherent to working with hardware. While many of the students ended up with things that were halfway playable and could be called games, the course was not really about game development. The most successful group of students managed to build an engine for building tower defense games. We would highly recommend avoiding this route.

The problem with this approach is that for students to get a feel for game development, they need an environment that they can easily use to create games so that the focus is on getting things in the game to work right and not just to work at all. Even if our students had had a background in app development on the iPhone, they would have spent most of the semester trying to build a basic game loop with art-connected assets and not a game that would be played.

3.2 Second Attempt, Bali and iPhone

Our second attempt at a game development course showed that we drew the wrong conclusion from our first attempt: we thought that an easier app development environment would be the answer. We were still blinded by how cool it would be for our students to show off their apps on a handheld device. The software we used was called Bali (it was later renamed Cabana before the company was bought by twitter and the software was discontinued) and made it possible to build apps by wiring together modules in a visual programming environment. Bali made it possible to teach basic app development pieces in 5 minutes that took an hour in Xcode.

Students were able to build games more successfully but were fighting the development software. Many of the groups of students spent most of their time trying to connect art with assets in their games. Again, students were spending more time building a game environment than games. It became obvious that a game development engine was required if students were to spend their time working on games. What we had really been doing was teaching a bad game engine development course.

3.3 Third Attempt, Unity

The third attempt was a 3-week intensive game development course that was open to students who had been in either of the first two attempts. Students took only this one class and the entire class worked to build one game. We decided to use a game development engine because of our experience with our previous two attempts and decided to use Unity because some students in the course had used it. The results were surprisingly good and all students agreed that having a real game engine was far better than trying to use generic software.

Greater progress was made on this game than any of those from the previous semesters despite the students having to learn and use Unity in a short time. The fact that a game engine includes everything needed to link player, art, and environment made a huge difference for what students could accomplish. For the first time students saw what it meant to build a game. This conclusion will be obvious to anyone with experience in this field and possibly should have been obvious to us before we made our first attempt, but it was not and is not obvious from the literature.

4. HOW TO TEACH GAME DEV.

After the previous three attempts and a move to a new institution, we came up with a successful way of teaching game development that included basing the course around the Unity game engine. Being at a new institution led us to reconsider the goal of the course; in our case the goal is game development, not game design. The students eligible for the course have taken our CS1 course or our game design course that is primarily for non-majors. Our previous attempts showed us that using a game engine was the right decision for this type of course.

Once the decision was made to use a game engine, we revisited available options. We wanted to make sure the course was in an environment that students might use again, and our options were Unity, XNA, and Unreal. Our campus has a large percentage of Mac users and at least 50% of the students who take our game development course use Macs. For this reason we decided not to consider XNA seriously because of the software issues associated with getting students to dual boot their machines. We decided against Unreal because of the learning curve associated with it despite its prevalence in industry. A large percentage of the students in our game development course have only taken our CS1 course in Python. We are not a tech school and what we cover in CS1 is less comprehensive than the average CS1 course (our CS2 finishes the concepts of a tech school CS1 course and is in Java). We believe that doing the course in Unreal would make it impossible for the non-majors in the class, who have no formal programming experience, to complete the course.

Based on our past experience with Unity and the above logic, we decided to use it for our course. We thought that would be easy enough to learn so that our students could just focus on building game for most of the semester. We describe here how we learned Unity and built a course that would achieve our goals in one semester.

4.1 Learning Unity

We wanted to develop our course around a book with solid examples that could act as a guide for both us and our students. The best book we have found for Unity is *Unity 3.x Game Development Essentials* [8]. A single game is built over the course of the book, with each chapter introducing a new concept and aspect of the game. All code examples are written in both JavaScript and C#. The book is out of date because Unity is now on version 4[4] but the author of the book has been good about updating the book material on his website [9]. It is a very quick read for anyone with programming experience and gives enough details for even beginning programmers with little to no experience.

This book quickly gives insight into colliders, particle systems, etc. for anyone without game development experience without talking down to those who know what they are doing. Without going through the entire book, we were able to intuit how Unity works for game development. Working through the book gives enough background to teach a course in Unity.

One area of concern partially addressed above is the rapid development of Unity and the effect this has on finding up-to-date materials to work with. Unity has begun to outpace the authors updates of the book. Unity's active online community has made it relatively easy to find tutorials to show how to update the code from the book to handle new features and changes in Unity. Should a new version of the book not be forthcoming, a viable alternative would be to base the course around one of the series of online tutorials that builds a complete game. Many of these tutorials include all assets to be used and provide the insight into how Unity works in a similar manor to how the current book does if with less detail.

4.2 Structure of the Course

The basic structure for the course appears below. Decisions made were based on our students and our goals for the course and can be easily modified while keeping the same basic structure. Our goal with this course is to give students a taste of game development while emphasizing project management, working with others, working with an SDK, and problem solving. The first part of the course focuses on teaching the students to use Unity and the second focuses on students working in groups to develop real games. The class meets 4 times a week: 3 lectures and 1 lab per week while students are learning Unity and 2 lectures and 2 in-class work days while students are working on final project games.

4.2.1 Students Learning Unity

The method we used to have students learn Unity is similar to the one that we used to learn Unity: we had the students work through the book. Specifically, we had the students work through chapters 1-9. The concepts covered in these chapters were 3D basics, scripting, building 3D environments, player controllers, interactions (collisions and rigid bodies), inventory, instantiation, particle systems, and menus. Each week a new chapter/concept was introduced and the example from the book was recreated with the reasoning behind why things were being done explained. Students were required to recreate what was done in class for 80% of the points for lab assignments and add new and creative pieces for the other 20%.

The 80%/20% breakdown on points was very successful and we would recommend trying it regardless of what you choose to emphasize in the course. The type of student who is drawn to game development tends to have a more creative bent. The final 20% with its freedom really excited these students. For example, one assignment required them

to build a wall that they could shoot down. For the final 20% students were allowed to change this game, each change giving them 10% up to a possible 20%. I had students make the gun act as a machine gun, fire palm trees, fire multiple projectiles, and change the color of the block hit. In each case the student was required to look into how different parts of the code worked in detail to figure out how to make changes. Throughout this first part of the semester students pushed themselves to learn more so that they could make fun additions, which taught them how to look things up and problem solve with Unity before they started working on their final project games, which required these skills.

During this process of working through the chapters, students built a basic game in which they controlled a character that could run around an island that they built and could play various mini-games.

4.2.2 Final Project Game

In the second part of the course (about two-thirds of the semester), students worked in groups to build final project games. We let students decide what games they wished to build and work together in groups of 3-4. This project was run as a fairly standard project in a project-based course, with students required to develop project plans, present milestones (in our case vertical slices[5]), usability test, and present final work. The lectures for this part of the course covered a wide variety of topics. Some specific aspects of game development that students would likely need were discussed as well as a very brief introduction to Maya [11], a modeling program that can be used to create assets for any game engine. Time was also spent discussing aspects of the game development industry such as development team roles and the development process.

Each group decided who would perform what roles and what they would need to do to finish the game. For non-majors who may have struggled with the first part of the course where they were learning how to program, this meant that they could shift to other aspects of development that were strengths and leave the coding to those with a stronger background without it hurting their group.

The assignments for this part of the course all relate to keeping students on track to finish the final project games. They include students submitting game ideas, project plans, vertical slices, usability tests, the final game, and weekly update reports on who accomplished what.

5. RESULTS

This course has now been taught twice and both times every group in the class was able to successfully build a playable game for the final project, which is significantly better than the less then 50% of the groups that had succeeded in previous courses. Over the two semesters there were 38 students and of those students there were two withdrawals from the course (one withdrew from the college) and one failure; none of these students was a CS major. This course appears to have had no effect on major retention or

---

[4]Unity 5 was released while this paper was in process and during the teaching of the third iteration of the course.

[5]In game development a vertical slice is a snapshot chunk of a game in which every aspect of the game is implemented though the game is not complete. In a first-person shooter game, this could be a section of a level that a player can run around in, showing all movement, and in which only one weapon and one bad guy are implemented to show the basics of the game.

on recruiting majors but a number of the students from the course added minors in our department. Exact figures as to the number of minors added cannot be given because of how we count minors. We have seen no evidence that students diverted attention from other courses.

All students built their games for the web even though Unity supports compilation for more platforms[6]. Students have built platformers (Figure 1), casual games (Figure 2), and survival horror games (Figure 3) among others.

Figure 1: Platformer game.

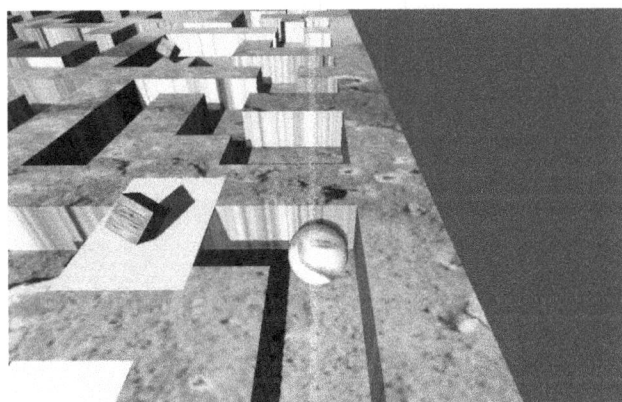

Figure 2: Casual game.

The variety of these games show that students are free to build games of their choosing instead of being limited to modifying a first-person shooter or similar style game. The differences in games between groups that decided to build their own assets (Figure 1) and those that decided to buy assets (Figure 3) are noticeable and showed the class the importance of artwork and the need to plan for asset development in the game development process.

6. DISCUSSION AND CONCLUSIONS

Based on our experience, Unity is a good option for teaching a stand-alone game development course. Choosing to teach game development without a game engine is a bad idea unless you have very technical students with a good background or the goal of your course is to build a game

---

[6]Students may have complied for other platforms on their own but we have only viewed/graded the web versions.

Figure 3: Survival horror game.

development engine. Because Unity is easy to learn, students can pick it up in under half a semester, which leaves more than half a semester to focus on whatever topic you feel is important (game design, project management, etc.). Using Unity makes it possible for every student who takes to course to finish it with a real game. We believe that the brief discussion of our failed attempts to create a game development course are instructive about what is important while building this type of a course.

7. REFERENCES

[1] Tiffany Barnes, Heather Richter, Eve Powell, Amanda Chaffin, and Alex Godwin. Game2learn: Building cs1 learning games for retention. In *Proceedings of the 12th Annual SIGCSE Conference on Innovation and Technology in Computer Science Education*, ITiCSE '07, pages 121–125, New York, NY, USA, 2007. ACM.

[2] Quincy Brown, Frank Lee, and Suzanne Alejandre. Emphasizing soft skills and team development in an educational digital game design course. In *Proceedings of the 4th International Conference on Foundations of Digital Games*, FDG '09, pages 240–247, New York, NY, USA, 2009. ACM.

[3] Kajal Claypool and Mark Claypool. Teaching software engineering through game design. In *Proceedings of the 10th Annual SIGCSE Conference on Innovation and Technology in Computer Science Education*, ITiCSE '05, pages 123–127, New York, NY, USA, 2005. ACM.

[4] Daniel V. de Macedo and Maria Andréia Formico Rodrigues. Experiences with rapid mobile game development using unity engine. *Comput. Entertain.*, 9(3):14:1–14:12, November 2011.

[5] Joseph Distasio and Thomas Way. Inclusive computer science education using a ready-made computer game framework. In *Proceedings of the 12th Annual SIGCSE Conference on Innovation and Technology in Computer Science Education*, ITiCSE '07, pages 116–120, New York, NY, USA, 2007. ACM.

[6] Anthony Estey, Jeremy Long, Bruce Gooch, and Amy A. Gooch. Investigating studio-based learning in a course on game design. In *Proceedings of the Fifth International Conference on the Foundations of Digital Games*, FDG '10, pages 64–71, New York, NY, USA, 2010. ACM.

[7] GarageGames. Torque 3d | products | garagegames.com. http://www.garagegames.com/products/torque-3d. Accessed: 2014-12-16.

[8] Will Goldstone. *Unity 3.x Game Development Essentials*. Packt Publishing, 2011.

[9] Will Goldstone. Unity book - 3.x game development essentials. http://unitybook.net/, Mar 2015.

[10] James Harris. Teaching game programming using xna: What works and what doesn't. *J. Comput. Sci. Coll.*, 27(2):174–181, December 2011.

[11] Autodesk Inc. 3d animation software, computer animation software | maya | autodesk. http://www.autodesk.com/products/autodesk-maya/overview. Accessed: 2014-07-24.

[12] Epic Games Inc. Unreal engine technolog | home. https://www.unrealengine.com/. Accessed: 2014-07-24.

[13] Joe Linhoff and Amber Settle. Teaching game programming using xna. In *Proceedings of the 13th Annual Conference on Innovation and Technology in Computer Science Education*, ITiCSE '08, pages 250–254, New York, NY, USA, 2008. ACM.

[14] Microsoft. Download microsoft xna game studio 4.0 from official microsoft download center. http://www.microsoft.com/en-us/download/details.aspx?id=23714. Accessed: 2014-07-24.

[15] Briana B. Morrison and Jon A. Preston. Engagement: Gaming throughout the curriculum. In *Proceedings of the 40th ACM Technical Symposium on Computer Science Education*, SIGCSE '09, pages 342–346, New York, NY, USA, 2009. ACM.

[16] Yolanda Rankin, Amy Gooch, and Bruce Gooch. The impact of game design on students' interest in cs. In *Proceedings of the 3rd International Conference on Game Development in Computer Science Education*, GDCSE '08, pages 31–35, New York, NY, USA, 2008. ACM.

[17] Albert D. Ritzhaupt. Creating a game development course with limited resources: An evaluation study. *Trans. Comput. Educ.*, 9(1):3:1–3:16, March 2009.

[18] Timothy E. Roden and Rob LeGrand. Growing a computer science program with a focus on game development. In *Proceeding of the 44th ACM Technical Symposium on Computer Science Education*, SIGCSE '13, pages 555–560, New York, NY, USA, 2013. ACM.

[19] Kelvin Sung. Computer games and traditional cs courses. *Commun. ACM*, 52(12):74–78, December 2009.

[20] Unity Technologies. Unity - game engine. http://unity3d.com/. Accessed: 2014-07-24.

[21] Juha-Matti Vanhatupa. Game engines in game programming education: Experiences from use of the cage game engine. In *Proceedings of the 11th Koli Calling International Conference on Computing Education Research*, Koli Calling '11, pages 118–119, New York, NY, USA, 2011. ACM.

[22] Linda Werner, Shannon Campe, and Jill Denner. Children learning computer science concepts via alice game-programming. In *Proceedings of the 43rd ACM Technical Symposium on Computer Science Education* SIGCSE '12, pages 427–432, New York, NY, USA, 2012. ACM.

An Experimental Project Course to Prepare Students for Agile Web Application Development

Nicholas K. Clark
Dept of Computer Science
and C4I Center
MS4B5 George Mason University
Fairfax, VA 22030
+1-703-993-1743
nclark1@c4i.gmu.edu

John Mark Pullen
Dept of Computer Science
and C4I Center
MS4B5 George Mason University
Fairfax, VA 22030
+1-703-993-1538
mpullen@c4i.gmu.edu

Christopher D. Bashioum
Defense Intelligence Information
Enterprise (DI2E) Framework
3076 Centreville Rd
Herndon, VA 20171
+1-703-464-9020
Chris.Bashioum@di2e.com

ABSTRACT

Commercial software development today is dominated by the dramatic growth of Web/Internet-delivered information, combined with development techniques that feature rapid creation of reliable, maintainable application software. Staying current with these technologies is a constant challenge in any computer science curriculum. This paper reports on a pilot project course for six computer science fourth-year undergraduates that addressed this challenge in a synergistic way, to the benefit both of the participating students and of a government sponsor. The project created a new, open-source implementation of the Common Map API (CMAPI). It was accomplished using agile development techniques, intensive team activities, and advice from an industry CMAPI expert. Three one-month "sprints" resulted in a working, open-source system that met the needs of the sponsor and provided an excellent learning experience for all concerned. The approach used should be considered for inclusion in every undergraduate computer science curriculum.

Categories and Subject Descriptors

D.2.2 [**Software**]: Software Engineering – *evolutionary prototyping.*

General Terms

Design, Economics, Management, Reliability, Verification.

Keywords

Open source, web application, agile development.

1. INTRODUCTION

Today's commercial software development is dominated by the dramatic growth of Web/Internet-delivered information, combined with Web application (webapp) development techniques that feature rapid creation of reliable, maintainable application software. Staying current with these technologies is a constant challenge in any computer science curriculum. Similar concerns also challenge government-sponsored software systems development, which has tended to fall behind the commercial

world in recent years. This paper reports on a pilot project course for computer science fourth-year undergraduates that addressed both of these challenges in a synergistic way, to the benefit both of the participating students and of a government sponsor.

The sponsor in question, Defense Intelligence Information Enterprise (DI2E) Framework [6], is chartered to develop and maintain a common supporting information environment to be shared among networked software systems of the United States' military Services (Army, Navy, Air Force, Marines, and other related components). The DI2E Framework seeks to build on advantageous commercial and open-source software technologies and development techniques, providing timely capabilities to support those needs in the Defense Intelligence Environment.

As part of their effort to take advantage of the latest commercial technologies and development techniques, the DI2E Framework program office has supported student activities in plugfesting. Plugfests are events where rapid development/integration of networked software components is undertaken, based on open standards and generally also on open-source components. In this way they are able to explore software alternatives at relatively low cost while also nurturing a new generation of capable software developers.

The program office indicated an interest in sponsoring some of our students involved in plugfesting to undertake a related challenge, beyond the scope of a single plugfest: reimplementation of the Common Map API (CMAPI) outside of the Ozone Widget Framework (OWF) [16] where they had originally supported its development. The intended purpose was to demonstrate the broad utility of the CMAPI. They also agreed to provide the student project with an advisor having high expertise in both the CMAPI and contemporary software development methods.

The opportunity to implement the CMAPI as a student project was extremely attractive. The project would necessarily involve a team of several students, working collaboratively and employing the most appropriate commercial rapid development techniques as we understood them. It would be a challenging project that could draw on the technical strengths of our students while teaching them a great deal about methods for effective networked software development in a context broader than a typical one- or two-student senior project. Moreover, the sponsor was prepared to pay the students' course tuition plus a stipend and the project would produce published, open source software, which attracted the attention of some of our better and more employment-oriented students. This created a great educational opportunity that also met the sponsor's intention to demonstrate the broad utility of

CMAPI at a relatively modest development cost. We were able to recruit six students to undertake the project, which we cast as a one-semester project course executed in three "spirals" structured as "sprints" [21].

The first two authors of this paper are university faculty, who were responsible for conducting the project course; the third author served as the DI2E Framework advisor, formed an integrated team with the faculty members, and assisted in mentoring the students. The remainder of this paper is organized as follows: section 2 describes the Common Map API that formed the specification for the student project, section 3 describes how the project (and thus the course) was organized, and the next section describes how the three sprints were conducted. This is followed by a concluding section, describing how the CMAPI was demonstrated during the DI2E Plugfest, how the project course was carried out, and how it benefited the students while achieving the sponsor's goals.

2. COMMON MAP API

In today's online environment, a "map", or "web-map" is a graphic object that represents layers of geospatial data, metadata (e.g., URLs), or images in either two or three dimensions for human viewing and interaction [14]. The Common Map Application Program Interface (CMAPI) is a specification that codifies a standard way for data search/manipulation widgets (defined below) to be able to communicate with map widgets over a publish/subscribe (pub/sub) mechanism. The following text is paraphrased from the CMAPI specification itself [5]:

- Many programs and projects create webapps that search for or manipulate data, then present the results on a map. The CMAPI provides a standard that allows end-users or developers to combine data search/manipulation web apps from any vendor with map web apps from other vendors.

- The API is intended to work with any pub/sub based inter-widget communication mechanism. Messages are sent to the appropriate channels (as defined in [5]), and the map updates its state accordingly. Other widgets interested in knowing the current map state can subscribe to these messages as well.

2.1 Widgets and Web Applications

With HTML5 and the current web development mindset, the web browser can be thought of as the new application platform [22, 25], where windows or iFrames on a browser are similar to processes in an operating system (OS), and interwindow or interwidget communication within the browser is similar to interprocess communication (implemented by APIs) on an operating system.

The World-Wide Web Consortium (W3C) Mobile Web Application Best Practices Recommendation [23] defines a web application as "a Web page … or collection of Web pages delivered over HTTP which use server-side or client-side processing (e.g. JavaScript) to provide an "application-like" experience within a Web browser. Web applications are distinct from simple Web content … in that they include locally executable elements of interactivity and persistent state." The W3C Packaged Web Apps (Widgets) Recommendation [24] further defines widgets as "full-fledged client-side applications that are authored using Web standards such as [HTML] and packaged for distribution. They are typically downloaded and installed on a client machine or device where they run as stand-alone applications, but they can also be embedded into Web pages

and run in a Web browser. Examples range from simple clocks, stock tickers, news casters, games and weather forecasters, to complex applications that pull data from multiple sources to be "mashed-up" and presented to a user in some interesting and useful way." In other words, a widget is a "packaged" webapp. A map webapp or widget is one that is designed to render both map images, and features as layers on top of the map images.

According to the World Wide Web Consortium (W3C) Web App Working Group: "The word *widget* is used to mean many things … A W3C Widget is specifically a packaged web application of any degree of complexity" [26]. Widgets often are implemented using HTML, CSS, and JavaScript or ECMAScript. According to the W3C Rich Web Client working Group: "Development of modern Web applications … depends on Web browsers supporting interaction between contexts, similar … to supporting inter-process communication in operating systems" [8]. In other words, communications among widgets.

2.2 Ozone Widget Framework

Four "patterns" of interwidget communication exist [27]: 1) message oriented, 2) shared memory, 3) Remote Procedure Call (RPC), and 4) pub/sub. There are also two "scopes" of interwidget communications: 1) single user/single browser, 2) multi-user/multi-browser. The Ozone Widget Framework (OWF) is a JavaScript based set of tools that implements the pub/sub pattern and single user/single browser scope of interwidget communications, and describes itself as "a web application for composing other lightweight web applications called 'widgets'. It is basically an extensive web portal engine, with the unusual characteristic that the content within the portal (i.e. the widgets) is decentralized. It includes a secure, in-browser, publish-subscribe eventing system, allowing widgets from different domains to share information. The combination of decentralized content and in-browser messaging makes OWF particularly suited for large distributed enterprises with legacy stovepipes that need to combine capability 'at the glass'." [16]

2.3 Project Purpose

Although DI2E managers believed that CMAPI could be applied in whatever technology implemented any of the communications patterns or scopes identified above, prior to the course described here the only extant CMAPI implementations required the OZONE Widget Framework (OWF) inter-widget communication platform technology. The sponsor's problem was to demonstrate CMAPI's applicability to various current platform technologies by implementing it in all four patterns and two scopes. However, due to time constraints, it was determined that implementing it using standard JavaScript and HTML5 cross-domain messaging technology (pub/sub pattern) with the two scopes would be sufficient to provide the required demonstration.

3. PROJECT AND TEAM ORGANIZATION

This course was unusual in that it also was a sponsored project run by our C4I Center [4], which undertakes research projects related to military information technology. It was structured to meet on a weekday evening like our other fourth-year undergraduate courses but the students were paid as if they were working ten hours per week in one of our laboratories, an arrangement normally considered only for graduate students but highly motivational to our undergraduates.

We recruited six students by means of email, sent to all potentially interested students we could identify. The students followed a less formal, hybrid development methodology that borrowed from agile development techniques commonly found in Extreme Programming/XP [2], Scrum [21], Crystal [3], and Dynamic systems development method (DSDM) [20]. The students were organized into three teams of two. Based on a student suggestion, team members were rotated after each one-month sprint so each student experienced working with three others. The whole group, including faculty mentors, met weekly and was joined by our DI2E-provided advisor once or twice per month. Each sprint was concluded by a session where the advisor reviewed the running code presented by each team. This was consistent with best industry practices [21] and proved highly effective, in that students produced a working, open-source system posted on the open source repository GitHub [9] at the end of the third sprint. They named the system uMap (Universal Map). Heavily based on other open-source components, the resulting system has an innovative design and complexity well beyond that which could have been expected from individual students, especially in such a short timeframe.

To facilitate project management and coordination, the students used a set of open source collaboration tools. These tools made communication and coordination easier since most of the work was done in pairs working at different locations. In addition to scheduled weekly meetings, students met outside of class to work independently and all other coordination was done virtually. Collaboration tools used included:

- *Redmine:* A flexible project management webapp that includes project wikis, discussion forums, issue tracking, time tracking, and integration with source control management systems
- *Git:* A distributed version control system
- *Jenkins:* A continuous integration tool, Implemented for the third sprint
- *Google Docs:* Although not open source, the free 'shared-document editing service' provided by Google was used extensively for collaborating on documents, demo plans and presentations

4. DESIGN AND CODING SPRINTS

The sponsor did not provide a formal requirements document. The primary functional requirement was simply to implement the CMAPI outside of the OWF environment and do so using some form of inter-process/widget communication with the capability for single user or multi-user interaction.

4.1 Sprint 1: System Organization

Sprint 1 objectives:
- Understand and refine the requirements
- Explore alternative widget frameworks
- Explore inter-process/widget communication paradigms
- Define a system design concept by using exploratory prototypes
- Define components to use in Sprint 2

Students were advised that they should use any open source or commercial off-the-shelf (COTS) options available to minimize development effort and maximize simplicity and reusability. Each student pair selected an existing alternative widget framework to evaluate, demonstrate and critique. These included web-based framework/APIs jQuery [13] and the Dojo Toolkit [7] as well as a

native application framework using GTK+ [11]. The discussions led students to agree on using a web-based approach with web browsers as the clients rather than native applications. They agreed that this approach would be simpler to develop and was instantly more portable to different platforms. Feedback from the industry advisor supported this approach with a suggestion of using web based clients with widgets in the form of iFrame objects running within browsers.

The students proceeded to evaluate communications paradigms for use between components with each student pair evaluating implementations of one of RPC, Message Passing (including pub/sub), and Shared Memory. These discussions produced two artifacts to facilitate the spiral 1 designs. The first was a common vocabulary of the system components as shown in Figure 1. The second was a set of criteria for evaluating the characteristics of communication components based on: real time 'across browser' support (message subscribe), ability to handle intermittent connections/disconnections, existence of at least one robust implementation, availability of multiple implementations, ease of use in a virtualized environment, support for multiple web browsers, ease of binding to a data storage provider, and having an open source license other than GPL.

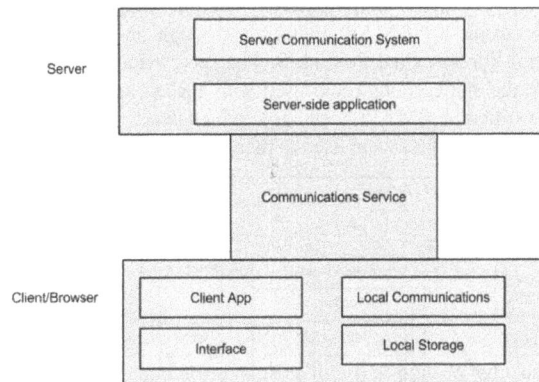

Figure 1. Common Vocabulary

The final product for each of the three teams in Sprint 1 was a system design with prototype demonstration. Teams One and Two produced fundamentally similar designs that only differed in the choice of persistent storage structures and specific Javascript libraries for communicating message traffic. They both included the capability for multiple widgets in a single browser instance as well as multiple user/browser connections. Both also required a local publish/subscribe capability within the single browser in addition to a library for client to server communication. Team Three's design abandoned the notion of multiple widgets within a single browser window and focused on multiple users in separate browser instances. Team Three also used a direct connection between each browser instance and a message queue server which utilized an in memory data storage server for persistence. All teams limited the scope of their initial prototype to implementing one or two functions of the CMAPI as a proof of concept. There was no formal code review of the initial prototypes since the objective was to use "throw-away" code to identify components to be used in the system design.

The group as a whole learned several important lessons from evaluating each of the three teams' designs. From Team Three, we learned that using direct connections from the browser to the queuing server in a wire-level format was overly complex in implementation. The group agreed the approach using web sockets through an intermediate web server as presented by the other teams was more efficient. However, Team Three's use of the in-memory data storage provided by Redis [19] was viewed by all as a more efficient solution for server side storage and solved issues with storage performance identified by other groups. All of the groups also identified some aspects of the CMAPI that were vague to implement and would require input from the industry expert. From an educational view, the teams working on competing system designs proved a useful way to explore design ideas and encourage involved discussion.

The system design that went into Sprint 2 is shown in Figure 2. It was composed of components from among the different teams' designs. The students elected to include support for multiple widgets in a single browser as well as multiple user/browser support in their architecture. The client-side design included a Map Abstraction layer that enabled publish-subscribe type API calls to underlying map implementations such as Google Maps, OpenLayers, Leaflet, or ESRI's ArcGIS. The content displayed on the map was to be stored locally and managed by a Content Manager (CM), which would store and track the data referenced from the CMAPI messages such as overlayIDs and featureIDs. Other widgets could communicate with the map and content manager using the CMAPI messages through an Open Source Javascript library called PubSubJS. The server side used Node.js to serve the static content and used web sockets to both receive and transmit the CMAPI messages, which were also stored in Redis. REST services were used to manage access control.

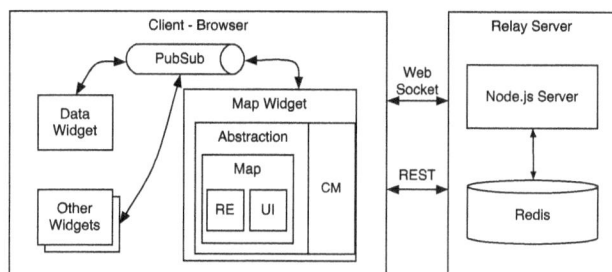

Figure 2. Sprint 1 System Design

4.2 Sprint 2: Solving the Hard Problems

The purpose of Sprint 2 was to identify the critical sub-components of the system design from Sprint 1 and build them into a working prototype. Sprint 2 was the most ambitious in terms of the amount of work needed to meet the objectives as it involved identifying and solving the harder, lower-level design problems. Some schedule and priority changes were necessary mid-sprint to address challenges encountered.

Sprint 2 objectives:

- Implement client-side code such as Content Manager for local storage, abstraction layer for Leaflet and ESRI, core set of map functions from CMAPI, and extending PubSubJS to provide publisher and source information
- Implement server code for inter-browser sharing of data leveraging Node.JS and Redis, including web server implementation for all REST calls to manage access to virtual rooms, and web sockets for pub/sub calls and JSON format for the data,
- Create and maintain documentation artifacts for design decisions and user documentation
- Build test cases and test harnesses

For Sprint 2, teams were no longer building competing system designs. Instead, each team focused on one part of the system. They naturally divided work into server and client components. With most of the complexity present in the client side, two teams focused there while one team worked on server side components.

On the client side, the map abstraction layer required an underlying geospatial component that renders geospatial information passed via the CMAPI into a visual map representation. The geospatial information referenced in the CMAPI can include a variety of types of information including points, lines, polygons, and images inside of container overlay and feature objects. It was not required that the students build their own map rendering system; they explored open source implementations such as Leaflet [15], Google Maps [10], and also the commercial ESRI ArcGIS for Javascript [1]. One team focused on the map implementation using Leaflet and ESRI in parallel. Leaflet was selected because it was designed for simplicity, ease of use, and performance, while ESRI's ArcGIS option was attractive as a COTS product.

During development, the map team discovered that the complexity of implementing two separate underlying map renderer libraries was greater than expected. They also encountered difficulty in implementing the Leaflet map renderer within the abstraction layer. They found that Leaflet's simplicity was actually a drawback in that it abstracted too much of the required functionality and thus would have required more development work. The group re-evaluated the available options and chose to focus on the Google Maps API for Sprint 2 because of its superior set of available references and examples, and to leave the ESRI implementation to Sprint 3. The group also pushed the Content Manager development into Sprint 3 and kept the local content storage directly within the abstraction layer.

Coordination of progress and scheduling became a challenge for the group during Sprint 2. Multiple discussion forum threads about development of different components were ongoing, but some students had trouble in conveying their progress and did not adopt a clear timetable for completion. Also, some students were so focused on their specific development that they had not considered the effort required for integration and testing with the overall system. The schedule for the Sprint 2 demonstration with the industry expert needed to be extended to allow time to address these issues. To address future coordination issues, one team leader was assigned to monitor and coordinate.

Although a delay of one week was needed to complete integration and testing, the final demonstration for Sprint 2 showed a working prototype to our CMAPI industry expert. The demo included both single user interaction within a single browser and multi-user/browser support leveraging Google Maps API version 3. All of the critical components were implemented for this demo. During this Sprint, the system design as shown in Figure 3 was altered to accommodate challenges with implementing decisions made in Sprint 1: the Content Manager was integrated directly into the map abstraction layer, and PubSubJS was replaced with another open source project called Porthole to support intra-browser communication among widgets and overcome issues with browser security on cross-domain communication [18].

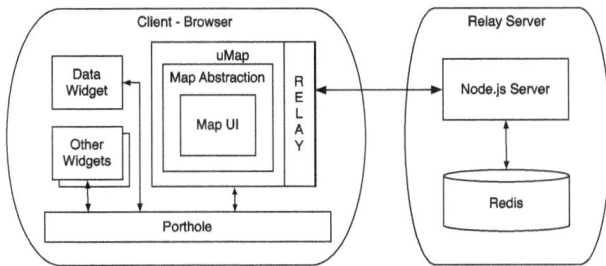

Figure 3. Sprint 2 Design as Implemented

4.3 Sprint 3: Working uMap System

Sprint 2 succeeded in building the critical components; however, there was still considerable work to build a polished product. The overall goal of the project, to be completed at the end of Sprint 3, was a demonstration of the complete system with the project sponsor.

Sprint 3 Objectives:

- Full support of the CMAPI with Google Maps renderer
- Support ESRI ArcGIS Javascript map renderer
- Fully integrate components
- Continuous integration testing environment
- OWF interoperation

Continuous integration development environments are an industry practice in which active developers merge new code with the main development branch at regular (and short) intervals [8]. Once the new code is merged, regression tests are performed, often nightly and through an automated system that notifies developers when a test fails. This approach is beneficial because it can catch problems early, reduce the amount of time tracing the change that caused the error, and reduce overall development time.

In Sprint 3, the student groups agreed that testing and continuous integration was an important early priority. A continuous integration build environment was created using the open source software, Jenkins [12]. Since a lot of the testing was based on client user interface interaction that would normally take place in a web browser, PhantomJS (a scriptable headless browser testing API that allows for fully automated tests without an actual web browser or user [17]) was used to facilitate testing. Image captures of rendered artifacts were automatically compared to saved images of the expected output, and when an inconsistency between the two was found during nightly testing, the developers were notified of the failure by email.

Aided by the testing environment, development time was reduced and the components were successfully integrated. This included a new room manager interface on the client that utilized the already implemented REST access control interface on the server, which enabled users to identify themselves and create, join, or leave a virtual room. When joined to a room, the client will send and receive CMAPI messages only within that room, allowing multiple users to carry on virtual geospatial chats (i.e., editing and manipulating shared maps) in different rooms simultaneously.

Demonstrating the robustness of the CMAPI was an important goal for this project. To that end, it was important to demo CMAPI features rendered on more than one underlying map visualization product. One team member focused on this implementation and in the final product we had the capability to plot features onto both Google Maps version 3 and ESRI ArcGIS

maps. However, the ESRI implementation was completed only at proof of concept level; uMap used Google Maps for the full multi-user demonstration.

uMap's conformity with the CMAPI specification was also demonstrated via interoperability with some extant CMAPI widgets within the OWF environment. This was accomplished by creating a custom OWF-based "uMap Relay Widget." This widget relayed CMAPI messages between OWF based map widgets and the uMap server. Thus, when users using the uMap browser client would manipulate geospatial information on their maps, the OWF users could see the same information and vice versa.

At the end of Sprint 3, the teams disbanded and all six students worked extensively on the demonstration script and plan for a final presentation to our sponsors at the DI2E Framework. Their hard work paid off in a successful demonstration of uMap that included extensive documentation, Google and ESRI map implementations, multi-browser virtual room support, and interoperability with all existing OWF CMAPI Widgets. The project sponsors were pleased with the success of the project both in representing the robustness of the CMAPI standard and identifying areas that were difficult to implement outside of OWF, such as the scheme used to generate unique identifiers for overlays and features. They also expressed interest in further development of some features that were not included in the Sprint 3 design such as the ability for late joiners to a room to catch up with previously transmitted information.

The final product, uMap, is an open source implementation of the CMAPI. The uMap framework of tools provides real-time network collaboration between operators, which OWF does not. uMap includes a mapping provider widget which supports Google Maps and ESRI. Other mapping providers are possible. The map provider natively uses the network relay tools to provide the network collaboration features such as editing maps with other users in a virtual room. It supports all applicable features in the CMAPI 1.1 standard. A uMap example interface is shown below in Figure 5. The uMap code is available on GitHub at https://github.com/gmuc4i/umap. An example implementation is available at http://styx.c4i.gmu.edu:3000/.

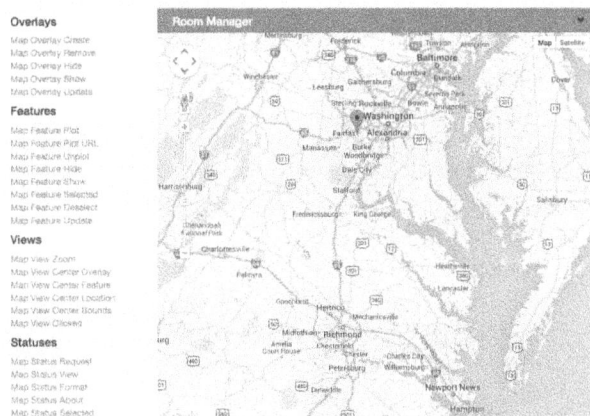

Figure 5. uMap Example User Interface

5. CONCLUSIONS/FUTURE WORK

The project met its multiple goals: students learned a great deal about webapp programming and agile/team development; faculty learned effective ways of teaching these things; and the sponsor achieved the sought confirmation of the generality of CMAPI along with some caveats about the same.

Sprint 3 of the uMap project was completed two weeks before the DI2E Plugfest 2014, a major event that was hosted at our university. The sponsor encouraged our students to participate in the event and demonstrate uMap. The DI2E Plugfest includes a subevent called the "Mashup Challenge" where government-sponsored integration teams integrate the interoperable applications provided by industry participants and made available through the "DI2E Storefront," a repository of such applications. The students built a mashup (an interoperating group of webapps) around the uMap. Their mashup involved a scenario where intelligence analysts collaborate using uMap to track the movement of a suspected terrorist and an illegal arms shipment. They leveraged several data query services present in the DI2E Storefront and visually collaborated using different map products through uMap. The result drew considerable positive attention by government and industry attendees at the plugfest event.

Web programming and software development by agile teams both have emerged as important areas for mastery by computer science students. The project described in this paper demonstrated conclusively a creative approach to introducing these current topics into the upper-division curriculum. Our students grasped the new approaches eagerly and performed admirably. The ability to also meet a current business need and provide financial support to students while exploring this approach were additional benefits that will not necessarily be available to other faculty who expand the computer science curriculum into these areas. However, we believe that one key aspect of our work is essential to the computer science curriculum: the state of practice in software development has come to a point where effective mastery at the baccalaureate level requires that student participate in small, well-structured teams solving current real-world problems. We therefore intend to develop a regular fourth-year elective project course similar to the one described above, but with a requirement for local industry guidance rather than a supporting sponsor. We encourage computer science faculty members from other institutions to consider doing the same.

Toward this end, we offer these organizing principles for an agile webapp development project course:

1. Begin with worthwhile, well-defined problem set and knowledgeable representative user or surrogate user
2. Build on available open-source and COTS, in Web environment
3. Insist on a small team (4 to 8) per product
4. Employ short, high-intensity sprints (3 or 4 in semester) producing documented, running code products presented to engaged audience at end of sprint
5. Within teams, have students work in pairs (or maybe triples) that rotate for each sprint
6. Define sprint products at beginning of each sprint and monitor progress in weekly team meetings with faculty
7. Expect success but watch for stumbles and involve team in immediate remediation

6. ACKNOWLEDGMENTS

Our thanks to DI2E Framework Program Office for its support.

7. REFERENCES

[1] ArcGIS API for Javascript. Retrieved December 31, 2014 from https://developers.arcgis.com/javascript/jsapi/
[2] Beck, K., Extreme Programming Explained: Embrace Change. Addison-Wesley Longman Publishing Co., Inc., Boston, MA, 1999
[3] Cockburn, A. Crystal clear: a human-powered methodology for small teams. Addison- Wesley Professional, 2005
[4] Center of Excellence in Command, Control, Communications and Computing, Retrieved December 23, 2015 from http://c4i.gmu.edu
[5] Common Map API Specification. Retrieved December 26, 2014 from http://www.cmap.org
[6] Defense Intelligence Information Enterprise (DI2E). Retrieved December 23, 2014 from http://www.dtic.mil/ndia/2014system/16835WedTrack6Azizian.pdf
[7] Dojo Toolkit. Retrieved December 23, 2014 from http://dojotoolkit.org
[8] Duvall, P., S. Matyas, and A. Glover. Continuous Integration: Improving Software Quality and Reducing Risk. Pearson Education, 2007.
[9] GitHub, Inc. open source repository. Retrieved December 23, 2014 from https://github.com
[10] Google Maps API. Retrieved December 25, 2014 from https://developers.google.com/maps/
[11] GTK+, The GIMP Toolkit. Retrieved 23 December 2014 from http://dojotoolkit.org
[12] Jenkins. An open source continuous integration server. Retrieved December 23, 2014 from http://jenkins-ci.org/
[13] jQuery, Retrieved December 23, 2014 from http://jquery.com
[14] Kraak, M. & A. Brown (eds). Website accompanying Web Cartography: developments and prospects. Retrieved December 31, 2014 from http://kartoweb.itc.nl/webcartography/webbook
[15] OpenLayers. Retrieved December 25, 2014 from http://openlayers.org
[16] Ozone Widget Framework, Retrieved 26 December 2014 from https://github.com/ozoneplatform/owf
[17] PhantomJS. Headless scriptable WebKit with JavaScript API. Retrieved December 26, 2014 from http://phantomjs.org
[18] Porthole. JavaScript Library for Secure Cross Domain iFrame Communication. Retrieved 25 December 2014 from http://ternarylabs.github.io/porthole/
[19] Redis. Retrieved December 23, 2014 from http://redis.io
[20] Stapleton, J. DSDM: The Method in Practice. Addison-Wesley Longman Publishing Co., Inc., Boston, MA, 1997
[21] Sutherland, J. Scrum: the Art of Doing Twice the Work in Half the Time, Crown Business, New York, 2014
[22] W3C, Browser Technologies, Retrieved 31 December, 2014 from http://www.w3.org/wiki/BrowserTechnologies
[23] W3C, Mobile Web Applications Best Practices, W3C Recommendation 14 December 2010. Retrieved December 31, 2014 from http://www.w3.org/TR/2010/REC-mwabp-20101214/
[24] W3C, Packaged Web Apps (Widgets)-Packaging and XML Configuration (Second Edition), W3C Recommendation 27 November 2012. Retrieved December 31, 2014 from http://www.w3.org/TR/2012/REC-widgets-20121127/
[25] W3C, Rich Web Client Activity. Retrieved December 26, 2014 from http://www.w3.org/2006/rwc/Activity
[26] W3C, Widget/Webapp Definition. Retrieved 26 December 2014, http://www.w3.org/2008/webapps/
[27] Zusak, I, M. Ivankovic, and I. Budeselic, A Classification Framework for Web Browser Cross-Context Communication. Retrieved December 26, 2014 http://arxiv.org/abs/1108.4770

Teaching Git on the Side – Version Control System as a Course Platform

Lassi Haaranen and Teemu Lehtinen
Department of Computer Science
Aalto University, School of Science
Espoo, Finland
{lassi.haaranen, teemu.t.lehtinen}@aalto.fi

ABSTRACT

The ability to use version control systems is a highly desired skill in the software industry and the need to teach it has been recognized in the literature. Git, and other version control systems, have previously been used by instructors in classrooms to distribute exercises, to facilitate assessment, and as a platform for project collaboration and teamwork. Using version control brings benefits to instructors, e.g. by lowering the need for administrative tasks, as well as to students, e.g. by providing experience with standard software industry tools.

We describe how to incrementally present features of Git and incorporate them into the course workflow. We present a case study of running a large (ca. 200 students) course utilizing Git and evaluate the results both from instructor's and learner's point of view. Our evaluation shows, that a distributed version control system can be used successfully to disseminate course materials and facilitate exercise submissions.

Categories and Subject Descriptors

K.3.2 [**Computers and Education**]: Computer and Information Science Education—*Computer science education*

Keywords

version control, Git, course management, software engineering

1. INTRODUCTION

In order to be a part of the global community writing software - one must know how to interact with that community. The ability to use version control systems is increasingly important. However, this essential skill is not necessarily a part of computer science curricula. We sought out to remedy this situation by investigating how version control could be taught simultaneously with other topics, in our case, web software development.

Skills to use version control systems are not only crucial from the point of view of development but are also very desirable when seeking employment in the industry. Since a lot of software nowadays is written by teams – version control is an important factor in communicating with other developers and team members.

Our main contributions are a method and evaluation on how to use a distributed version control system as a platform for disseminating course material. Related to this, we describe how distributed version control system features were introduced incrementally during a course. In addition, we surveyed students' perceptions towards this approach.

Our approach places a strong emphasis on *authentic use* of version control, as opposed to practising it separately. Workflows similar to what we chose are used widely both in the industry as well as in open source projects. Our main contributions are:

- Describing a way to use Git as a course platform

- Presenting an approach to introduce and teach Git concepts alongside main course content

- Evaluating our approach from students' and instructors' perspective

In Section 2 we review the relevant literature regarding the use of version control systems in software industry and in education. Section 3 explains the course context in which the case study was conducted and details our approach. Next, in Section 4, we evaluate our approach, and finally, in Section 5, we discuss the results.

2. RELATED WORK

Different version control systems can be broadly divided into two categories: *centralized* (VCS) and *distributed* (DVCS) [8]. Centralized systems have a distinct single version of the project representing the latest stage of development, shared amongst all users, with possible access restrictions. In distributed systems, there is no one place that is "more official" than the other. All repositories contain a history of the project and features can be incorporated from any developer's repository to anyone else's repository.

We'll review relevant literature from two points of view. First, by looking at the trends in the software industry and especially what are their expectations of graduates. And secondly, we will look at various ways (D)VCS have been incorporated into programming/software engineering courses.

2.1 Version Control Systems and Industry Expectations

Decentralized version control systems have gained popularity in recent years and many software projects are moving from centralized to distributed workflows. De Alwis and Sillito [3] have found benefits perceived to come from a decentralized workflow. These include items such as providing first-class access for all developers, simple automatic merging (of changes), and support for offline operations.

Using VCS and collaborating with team members are essential skills for software engineers. This fact is also reflected on research on the abilities of graduates when entering the workforce. Team skills, collaboration and tools to support those are often mentioned as needing improvement [1].

Radermacher and Walia [9] conducted a literature review detailing differences of industry expectations and graduates' abilities. They identified frequently mentioned deficiencies in the literature, including written communication, project management, software tools, and teamwork. All of those relate to, in one way or another, using VCS and how software is created in teams.

2.2 Version Control Systems in Computing Education

Subversion[1] (a centralized VCS) has been used [2] to manage course material between multiple instructors on a course reducing administrative efforts in a CS1 course. In addition, it was used to facilitate student participation in group projects with benefits of detecting freeloaders in groups and providing individualized feedback. Anecdotally, students liked working with version control.

Another VCS that has gained popularity in industry is *Git*[2]. It has been used to introduce (D)VCS in computing courses. For example, Kelleher [6] describes how he used Git and other free to use services to disseminate learning material on a course. In addition to the typical benefits of (D)VCS, he mentions that this worked as a way to introduce standard industry practices to students.

Lawrance et al. [7] also used cloud based hosting and Git as a platform for their course. They detail their experiences with Git with computer science majors and other engineering majors, concluding that version control should be considered fundamental in programming and not in software engineering from a curriculum point of view.

DVCS emphasises collaboration and multiple people working on the same codebase, so it is often introduced for group projects. Isomöttönen and Cochez [4] detail their experiences using Git based on a survey done on students and their own experiences. They observed some students having difficulty on particular aspects of Git (e.g. creating accidental sub-repositories, branches). They also noted that some students not comfortable in command-line interfaces (CLI) started confusing Git commands to CLI commands. Graphical interfaces could be used to avoid this problem, but it too has been observed confusing novices in VCS – and using CLI might be preferred by students [6].

3. COURSE CONTEXT AND APPROACH TO GIT

This section details the course for our case study. First, the context of the course is outlined. Afterwards, we describe how different DVCS concepts were introduced and how Git was used as a course platform.

3.1 Course Description

The topic of the course in question was web software development with the emphasis on programming and the distributed nature of web. For the course it is recommended that students have taken a CS2 course and a course in databases, however this is not enforced and students can enroll to the course without fulfilling beforehand the prerequisites. The course had 225 enrolled students, mostly third year bachelors in computer science and some masters in related fields. The computer science curriculum at Aalto University includes VCS concepts before this point of the studies but due to the diverse background of students we could not assume that all students had had practical experience with it. It was presumed that all students aiming for software development related careers will need VCS skills in professional life. The course was staffed by one lecturer and one teaching assistant.

The course spanned two periods (ca. four months). The first period offered two weekly lectures and a weekly exercise session arranged for personal advice in exercises. Lecture materials and exercises were distributed using Git and submitting exercises utilized Git as well. The obligatory exercises included diverse programming tasks in JavaScript and Python. The second period mainly involved project work in groups, also facilitated by Git. However, the student projects fall outside the scope of this paper.

3.2 Git on The Course

The course employed three important online web tools for students. First, Git repository hosting was enabled via a web service running GitLab[3]. It is a service that enables extra features to Git, e.g. merge requests and forking projects. Second, A+ [5] learning management system (LMS) allowed automatic grading and feedback for the exercises. Finally, student questions were encouraged in the Piazza[4] discussion board service. These tools were already integrated for common student access.

We introduced features of Git and GitLab gradually as the course progressed. The first two exercises were solely focused on introducing these tools to the students – the first lecture also included a demonstration on how to solve those exercises.

The features we chose to include are frequently used or considered essential. This enabled us to have an *authentic workflow* throughout the course while slowly increasing the students' vocabulary of DVCS concepts. The concepts that we introduced (in the order they were presented) were: `local & remote repository`, `fork`, `clone`, `add & commit`, `push`, `upstream repository`, `merge`, `branch`, `merge conflicts`, and `merge request`. The following subsections and Figure 1 detail the concepts and usage of Git and GitLab.

---

[1] https://subversion.apache.org/
[2] http://git-scm.com/

[3] https://about.gitlab.com/
[4] https://piazza.com/

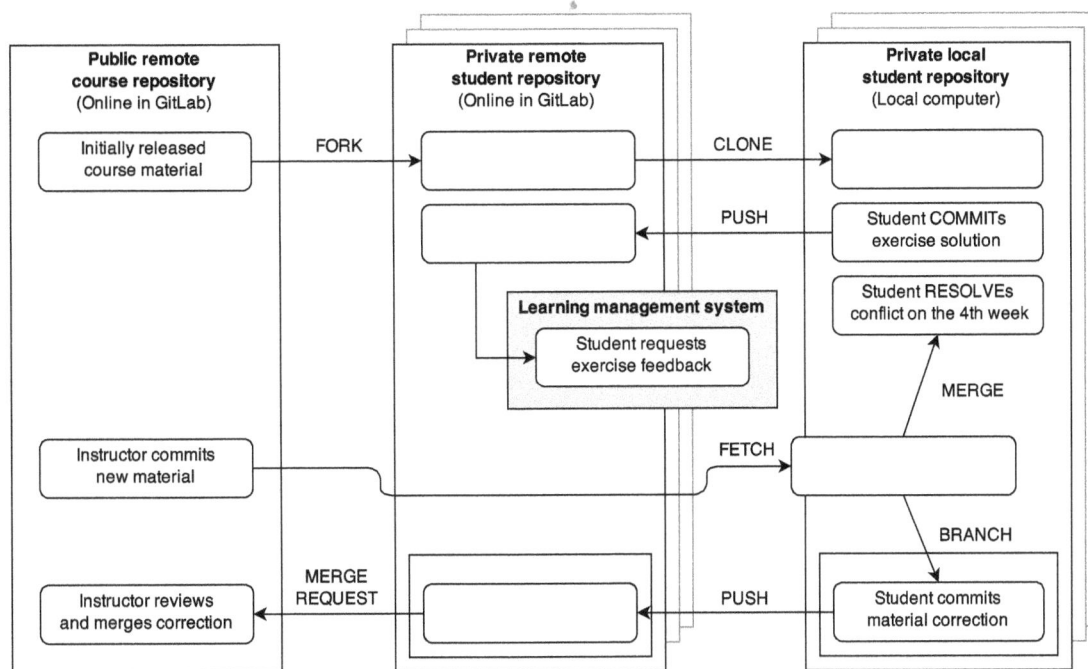

Figure 1: Data flows between course and student Git repositories

Fork and Repository

Generally forking enables building on another software project or suggesting changes to it without the extra work and risk of access control for the original project. Forking does not require access to change the original code. We will return to the topic of suggesting changes later.

The first exercise was to **fork** the public course repository to a private remote repository using GitLab web interface. Students also had to open access for a 'course agent' account to their new repository. This account enabled automatic assessment of student work. Finally students had to confirm their success by entering the repository URL to the LMS – where it was automatically assessed.

Clone

The second exercise started with students **cloning** their own private remote repository to a local work repository on their computer. The course only provided instruction and examples for using Git from command line. Git for Windows includes a terminal simulation that offers a command line interface similar to OS X, Linux or other Unix flavors.

The repository included lecture slides in HTML, code examples, and materials for exercise rounds. In the beginning of the course the available material covered the first two lectures and the first three exercise rounds.

Commit and Push

The second exercise was to change a few lines in an HTML file and **add**, **commit**, and **push** those changes to the private remote repository. When the students were ready, they opened the LMS to request automatic feedback and grading for the exercise. The same workflow was used for the remaining exercises that pertained to the core content of the course.

Further exercises were only delivered via Git and comprised of instructions in HTML and related resources, such as template code and unit tests. Grading requests were limited to ten per exercise.

Pushing to private remote repository did not alone invoke grading and could be done to just store changes online. Having the material in a remote repository enabled the student to clone the environment to different computers, enabling working in multiple locations.

Fetch and Merge from Upstream Repository

A forked software project can be synchronized with the original project from which it was forked. This is necessary to include new code from the original project that was added after forking it. In Git, the concept is to merge two branches. The original repository is conventionally called upstream.

On the second week, instructions for updating the course material in the students' remote and local repositories were given in the LMS. To get the latest lecture slides and exercise rounds, students had to add the public course repository as an **upstream remote**, **fetch** new commits from there and **merge** those changes to their local repository's master branch. The instructors published new material weekly and improvements without delay.

Merge Conflicts and Resolving Them

When Git merges two branches or pulls remote changes to a cloned repository it will try to automatically incorporate commits from the two sources. In the case when the commits overlap Git will create a conflict and needs manual decisions to resolve it.

On the fourth week, we introduced an *intentional* change to a file students had edited in the second exercise which caused a merge conflict that had to be resolved manually. At the same time, information and instructions for merge conflict were announced in the LMS. During their next material

Question	Answer type
Q1 Please choose what best describes your attitude towards using Git on the course	Scale 1-5 (1 negative, 5 positive)
Q2 Choose what best describes your previous experience before the course with Git	{No/Some/A lot of} previous experience
Q3 Where have we succeeded so far?	Text
Q4 Name and explain what areas you think most need improvement on the course.	Text
Q5 General Feedback	Text

Table 1: Questions pertaining to Git in the survey

update, students noticed the `merge conflict` and had to `resolve` it by editing a new version to keep.

Git prevents committing changes when conflicts are present. This means that students were forced to resolve the conflict in order to submit further exercises. In addition to the written instructions we also had a quick demonstration during a lecture how resolving conflicts in Git can be done.

Merge Request and Contributing to Material

Apart from the required activity, extra points to the exam were awarded for corrections to course material. This was possible using the method for suggesting changes to the upstream project. Instructions for creating a correction branch to student repository and opening a `merge request`[5] in Git-Lab were posted to the discussion board. The instructors reviewed and accepted merge requests from the students. Once accepted, the corrections were immediately available for all students.

4. EVALUATION

We studied the success of using Git as a course platform and how successful we were teaching Git alongside the main course content. We used a mixed method approach combining data from two sources:

- A *feedback survey* collected after the individual exercises and exam was completed by the students. It included both numeric answers as well as free text responses.

- *Git usage data* from the students' forked repositories. The data included commit times and messages separately for merges and for exercise content.

An anonymous feedback questionnaire was opened to students after individual exercises and exam were completed. Table 1 summarises the questions and answer options related to Git. The questionnaire included other items as well, e.g. previous experience in other technologies used in the course.

4.1 Survey Results

In the survey students were asked to rank their attitude towards different aspects of the course with a 5 point likert scale (1=negative, 3=neutral, 5=positive). A total of 141 students answered the questionnaire, giving the survey response rate of 63 %. Using Git on the course scored the average of 4.58, which was the highest of among all asked items[6]. As seen from Table 2, the reception to Git was very

positive, only two students ranked it negatively whilst the vast majority ranked it very positively. It is also worth noting that most of the students had some experience in Git, while roughly a third had no previous experience at all, as seen in Table 3. Previous experience and attitude towards Git did not correlate.

N=141	1	2	3	4	5
Q1	2 (1 %)	0	10 (7 %)	31 (22 %)	98 (70 %)

Table 2: Students perceptions towards using Git on the course

N=141	None	Some	A lot
Q2	40 (28 %)	79 (56 %)	22 (16 %)

Table 3: Students' experience with Git before the course

Of the 141 responses to the survey 99 contained text detailing what students felt was positive about the course (Q3), 72 filled in text for something needing improvement (Q4), and 45 wrote something in the general feedback section (Q5).

Two raters first classified textual answers based on whether an item referred to Git and/or VCS in general and the way Git was utilized and taught (Cohen's $\kappa = 0.84$). Those items that did not include Git in particular but described direct effects of Git as a course platform were included as well. Conflicts on ratings were resolved through discussion. After each feedback item, regardless of whether it was written for Q3, Q4, or Q5, the item was rated through discussion to either positive, neutral, or negative. Table 4 presents how use of Git was perceived in the freeform feedback.

	Q3 (N=99)	Q4 (N=72)	Q5 (N=45)
Positive	25 (25 %)	0	2 (4 %)
Neutral	1 (1 %)	4 (6 %)	2 (4 %)
Negative	0	5 (7 %)	0
Total	26 (26 %)	9 (13 %)	4 (9 %)

Table 4: Number of positive, neutral, and negative comments regarding Git to Q3, Q4, and Q5

The textual answers reflected the numerical ones and overall were very positive. They highlighted the benefits students perceived for using Git in this manner, such as its suitability as a platform and usefulness of it:

> "Also using git for course material reduced file management by a lot and made submitting solutions fast and simple"

---

[5]In GitHub – similar service to GitLab – these are known as pull requests

[6]Other items were Lectures (avg. 3.93), Exercises (avg. 4.20), Lecture Quizzes (avg. 3.49), Piazza (avg. 3.79), and Exercise sessions (avg. 3.40)

"Using git was very educative! I've used it before but learned a lot of ROUTINE through this course."

"Introduction to git was really useful for me!"

Authenticity and importance of (D)VCS in the software industry was also remarked by multiple answers, e.g.:

"I started using git for work at the same time I started the course, and using it during the exercises has certainly improved my learning curve."

"Usage of Git and Tests was really good. It felt like doing things properly."

4.2 Student Participation

One of the benefits of choosing a distributed version system was that it enabled student participation on the course material with an authentic workflow. Students were encouraged to submit corrections via merges and merge requests to the official course material in the cases where they spotted clear errors or omissions. These were reviewed by instructors and if deemed appropriate merged into the material. 11 (ca. 5 %) students submitted corrections that were merged. Most of these corrections were fixing minor errors, e.g. spelling mistakes and missing semicolons in code examples. This was also highlighted in one feedback:

"The lecture slides are good, and i like that they are in git and everyone can fix issues with them"

However, some of these commits also modified the content and highlighted the power of collaboration and power of DVCS. As an example, it was stated on a lecture slide on October 29th that HTML5 specification was to be used on the course, even though it was not officially finalized yet. However, the specification had been finalized a day before the lecture and a student submitted a correction removing the mention of draft status a day after the lecture in question.

4.3 Git Log Data

We analyzed the log data from students' Git usage in order to determine if students had adopted the concepts and if our approach had major effects on drop outs.

Three students had interacted in the LMS without forking the repository. Four students had successfully forked their own repository but for unknown reason did not complete the next steps. 217 (96 %) students had cloned their local repository, committed changes and pushed them to their remote repository. 197 (88 %) students had merged updated material from the public course repository. Out of these only 3 less, 194 students, had resolved the introduced merge conflict.

Table 5 presents the number of students committing on each exercise round. Passing two last rounds was not required to pass the course but passing them contributed towards a better grade. The numbers of students committing declined steadily, which is consistent with normal drop off rate.

Round	1	2	3	4	5	6	7
Students	217	212	207	206	199	184	177

Table 5: Number of students committing on each exercise round (completing exercises)

Since it is normal and expected that some students do not finish this course, as seen in previous years. It is difficult to estimate to what degree, if any, the introduction of Git contributed to student dropout. Anecdotally, two students informed that they would drop the course citing busyness with other courses as the reason. The median of commits per student over the exercises was 31 of which 4 were merges. This helps to build routine before starting to work in a project group using DVCS.

Rounds 4 and 5 required updated course material but more students have completed these exercises than have merged the material. We found out that 15 students (7 %) had copied the new material inside their repository and did not use the merge ability of Git. They made a detour rather than learning a new concept. At the same time, they avoided the merge conflict.

4.4 Drawbacks and Difficulties

Though the majority of textual feedback related to Git was positive there was negative feedback as well. The feedback commented on the difficulty of learning Git, desire for more exercise, and questioned the suitability as a course platform:

"Understanding Git was quite hard in the beginning."

"I was happy to learn a bit GIT, even though I'm still not 100% happy with my ability to use it & it seemed to slow down some of the exercise & lecture handling."

"Git could always be explained better, because despite the seeming simplicity it is quite complicated version control system, especially compared to something like SVN."

"More git exercises would be great, but I suppose I will get familiar with it whilst doing the project."

In our university many, but not all, lecturers post slides to a portal that also contains other information on the courses, such as deadlines and schedules. The fact that we did not do so was dominant in the neutral/negative feedback received:

"Lecture slides should be uploaded to [University Portal]."

"It would be convenient if lecture slides were also available in [University Portal] (and thus accessible with mobile devices)."

"using [University Portal] to deliver course related news alongside it would have been a nice addition"

We also ran into the issue faced by others [4], that some students, especially those with a Windows background, had problems grasping the command line interface. However, these problems were relatively minor and were easily resolved in the open exercise groups.

The biggest hurdle in using Git that we noticed during exercise sessions and in online forum discussions, was the fact that our GitLab only supported authentication through SSH keys. We did not collect statistics on this but approximately a fifth of the students had trouble setting up the SSH key on the machine where they intended to work. However, this was overcome with additional instruction and help. Since that was a one time operation, it did not present challenges later on.

4.5 Instructors' Point of View

As others [2] have pointed out already, we also found managing course assets through Git beneficial by simplifying our workflow. Moreover, the contributions that students made to the material were advantageous – it is not likely that we would have been able to detect and correct all the details that got corrected. It is also worth pointing out that student corrections appeared rapidly – sometimes even during lectures.

Enabling students to participate through merge requests provided an authentic use case for Git – it was comparable to contributing to an open source project or collaborating in a company. We believe that it is through these kinds of interactions – facilitated by tools used in industry – that enable students to learn essential skills the industry desires that might not otherwise be part of the curriculum.

Incorporating Git in this manner did have a technical cost beforehand. Before the course we spent considerable time and effort planning how different systems would work together and how we might introduce those to students. We believe it is this effort on designing and implementing the workflow used in the course that was key to its success.

Presenting DVCS concepts incrementally enabled us to answer questions, resolve problems, and add instructions when problems were encountered. Git (and other DVCS) is often introduced to students as a tool for group work – and multiple people working on the same codebase can be confusing, e.g. leading into merge conflicts. By removing others and having students first practise Git in their individual repositories one source of confusion was removed.

5. DISCUSSION

Overall the use of Git as a platform was very well received and worked well for both instructors and students alike. We conclude that our approach worked well – though improvements to it can and should be made.

The biggest objection from students was the fact that lecture slides were only available in Git. From instructors' point of view the slides being in Git was ideal, since it was always the latest version and improvements from students were easy to incorporate. Though it is worth noting, that this scheme only works due to the fact that the slides were created in a text format (HTML) and not as a binary one.

We also view that our approach was well suited to our needs. By presenting Git concepts incrementally and with ample instruction it did not seem to have been an obstacle. Though based on the textual feedback, more opportunities to practise Git usage (perhaps in more varied ways) might have been helpful.

There were a few students that "worked around" the need to merge changes from the public repository. We did not have any technical checks to enforce that students had to get the files from the public repository – though in future we might do this. Working around and committing provided files (presumably by cloning the public repository somewhere and copying them) is not a good practise and requires more effort in the long run.

We suspected that using Git would not be met with hostility. However, we were surprised by the almost overwhelmingly positive reaction by students. This also aligns with the anecdotal evidence from Clifton et al. [2] that students like working with VCS. Also from instructors' point of view, the approach proved to be ideal to manage course assets and collaborate.

There are also validity issues that need to be addressed. Because the survey was conducted after the exercises the population is biased, it is likely that only those who completed the exercises (and thus had used Git throughout the course) were included. Naturally, those who answered the anonymous questionnaire are self-selected possibly increasing the bias.

Future Work

In the future it would be interesting to analyze students' repositories in more detail, for instance, looking at the times when they committed changes and comparing those to the times when they requested grading. Additionally, we have approximately 7000 commit messages collected during the course that might reveal additional insights to our approach when analyzed further.

One particular area of interest that we plan to investigate in future is the students group project that was completed after the individual exercises. We have collected Git log data from this course's group projects as well as previous years' instances where Git was only introduced after the individual exercises.

6. REFERENCES

[1] A. Begel and B. Simon. Struggles of new college graduates in their first software development job. In *ACM SIGCSE Bulletin*, volume 40, pages 226–230. ACM, 2008.

[2] C. Clifton, L. C. Kaczmarczyk, and M. Mrozek. Subverting the fundamentals sequence: using version control to enhance course management. In *ACM SIGCSE Bulletin*, volume 39, pages 86–90. ACM, 2007.

[3] B. De Alwis and J. Sillito. Why are software projects moving from centralized to decentralized version control systems? In *Cooperative and Human Aspects on Software Engineering, 2009. CHASE'09. ICSE Workshop on*, pages 36–39. IEEE, 2009.

[4] V. Isomöttönen and M. Cochez. Challenges and Confusions in Learning Version Control with Git. In *Information and Communication Technologies in Education, Research, and Industrial Applications*, pages 178–193. Springer, 2014.

[5] V. Karavirta, P. Ihantola, and T. Koskinen. Service-oriented approach to improve interoperability of e-learning systems. In *Advanced Learning Technologies (ICALT), 2013 IEEE 13th International Conference on*, pages 341–345, July 2013.

[6] J. Kelleher. Employing git in the classroom. In *Computer Applications and Information Systems (WCCAIS), 2014 World Congress on*, pages 1–4. IEEE, 2014.

[7] J. Lawrance and S. Jung. Git on the cloud. *Journal of Computing Sciences in Colleges*, 28(6):14–15, 2013.

[8] G. Lionetti. What is version control: Centralized vs. dvcs, 2012. http://blogs.atlassian.com/2012/02/version-control-centralized-dvcs/. Accessed 29.12.2014.

[9] A. Radermacher and G. Walia. Gaps between industry expectations and the abilities of graduates. In *Proceeding of the 44th ACM technical symposium on Computer science education*, pages 525–530. ACM, 2013.

A Game Engine in Pure Python for CS1: Design, Experience, and Limits

John Aycock
Dept. of Computer Science
University of Calgary
ICT 602, 2500 University Dr. NW
Calgary, AB, Canada T2N 1N4
aycock@ucalgary.ca

Etienne Pitout
Dept. of Computer Science
University of Calgary
ICT 602, 2500 University Dr. NW
Calgary, AB, Canada T2N 1N4
et.pitout@gmail.com

Sarah Storteboom
Computational Media Design
University of Calgary
ICT 602, 2500 University Dr. NW
Calgary, AB, Canada T2N 1N4
sstorteboom@gmail.com

ABSTRACT

Games are being increasingly used to create compelling assignments for students learning programming, and Python is often used as an initial programming language. To that end, we present a game engine written in pure Python. Not only does the engine integrate seamlessly with what students already know about Python, but the game engine code itself is not a "black box" – it is readable and approachable for beginning students. We report on two years' worth of experience using our game engine in CS1 for both regular assignments as well as "master classes," the engine's design, and its limits.

Categories and Subject Descriptors

K.3.2 [**Computers and Education**]: Computer and Information Science Education; K.8.0 [**Personal Computing**]: General—*games*

General Terms

Design, performance

Keywords

Games; game engines; Python; turtle graphics; education

1. INTRODUCTION

When teaching CS1 using Python 3, our goal was to get students – especially the newcomers to programming – engaged right from the first lecture. Ideally, we wanted to introduce programming in a straightforward visual way, then be able to build on that foundation throughout the course.

There is a limited amount of time remaining in a course's first lecture once administrative details are covered. The introduction to anything programming-related during the first lecture must be short, easy to communicate, and easy to understand.[1] We decided to use "turtle graphics" for this purpose. Turtle graphics [1, 10] date back decades and were an integral part of the Logo programming language. The basic concepts are extremely easy to describe, taking a few minutes at most in our experience, and Python comes with a turtle graphics module in its library already [13] that is fully cross-platform. Some Python textbooks also incorporate use of the turtle module [9].

A typical first assignment for our students is to draw a picture with turtle graphics, given certain constraints on the type of scene, the number of objects in the scene, and so on. This acclimatizes students to programming Python and the computing environment, and helps students build confidence in their programming ability where necessary.

But this paper is not about getting students in CS1 started in Python and turtle graphics. Instead, this paper is the story of what happens *next*.

Python, although well suited for many applications, is not the fastest programming language. Furthermore, the turtle module is not designed for high performance either. In fact, it can be rather glacial: as a reference point, drawing a 50x50 square using the turtle module at its default settings on a recent machine[2] takes 0.710 s. Hiding the turtle, a common optimization, only reduces that to 0.703 s.

An effective means of engaging students is through game-related assignments, and the challenge was how to construct games that performed with any semblance of speed, given a combination of slow language and slow turtle. One option was to simply retire the turtle and switch midstream to a prebuilt, high-performance game engine, but this was distasteful pedagogically. Surely there must be a way to make games, and build incrementally on students' knowledge of Python and the turtle module.

In the remainder of this paper we describe the game engine we constructed using Python and the turtle module to do just that. The next section discusses the game engine's design, and Section 3 talks about two years' experience using the game engine. Section 4 looks at how far the engine can be pushed, and Sections 5 and 6 detail related work and our conclusions, respectively.

---

[1]There are, of course, practical considerations involved in having students programming in the first lecture; details of the system we built to support this have been reported elsewhere [2]. The game engine we describe here is not dependent on that earlier work.

[2]Python 3.4.0 on Linux Mint 17, Intel Core 2 Duo at 3.16 GHz with 8 GiB RAM and local display; times reported are the arithmetic average of 5 runs.

ITiCSE'15, July 6–8, 2015, Vilnius, Lithuania.
Copyright © 2015 ACM 978-1-4503-3440-2/15/07 ...$15.00.
http://dx.doi.org/10.1145/2729094.2742590.

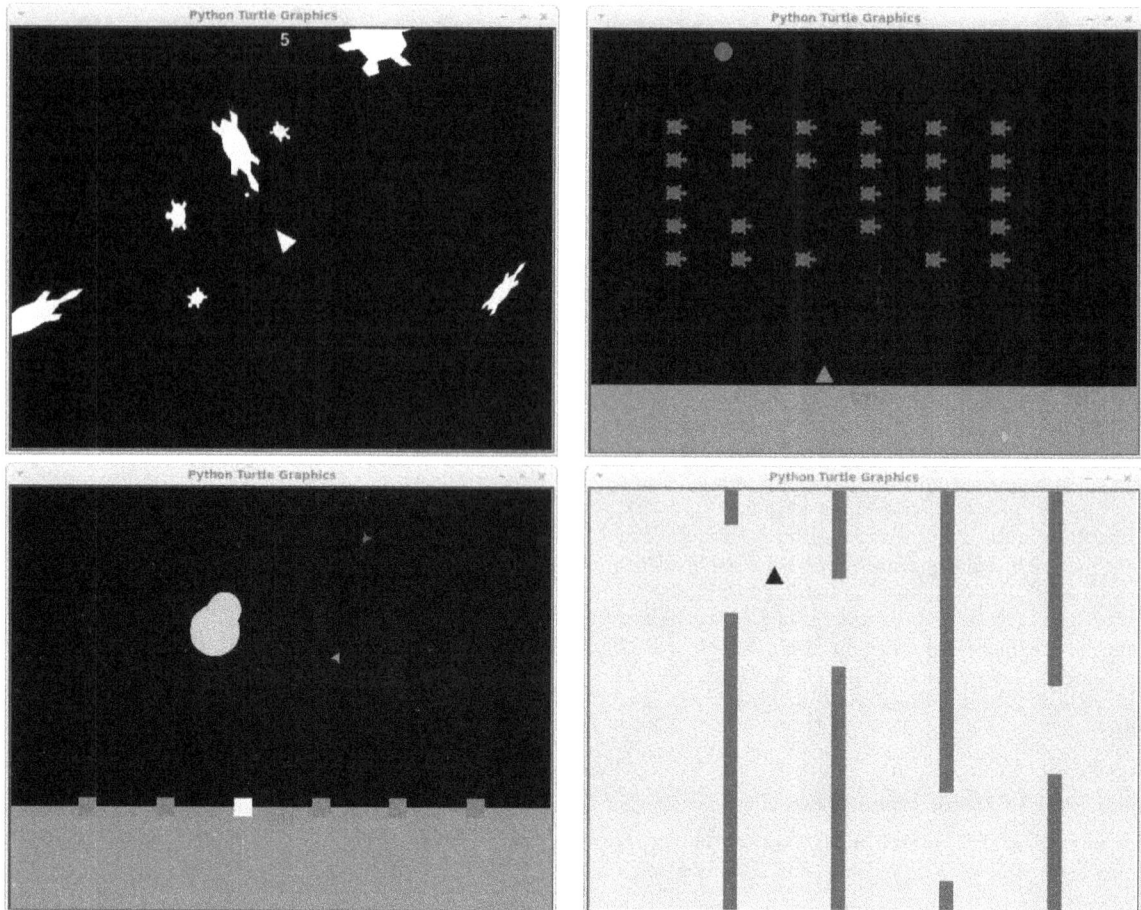

Figure 1: Computer games (re)created using the game engine

```
import engine

class Box(engine.GameObject):
    def __init__(self):
        super().__init__(x=0, y=0,
                         deltax=+1, deltay=0,
                         shape='square',
                         color='red')

engine.init_screen(width=640, height=480)
engine.init_engine()
box = Box()
engine.add_obj(box)
engine.engine()
```

```
import engine

class Circle(engine.GameObject):
    def __init__(self, deltax, deltay):
        super().__init__(0, 0, deltax, deltay,
                         shape='circle', color='blue')

def keyboard_cb(key):
    if key == 'space':
        L = [ (0,1), (0,-1), (1,0), (-1,0) ]
        for i in range(len(L)):
            (deltax, deltay) = L[i]
            obj = Circle(deltax, deltay)
            engine.add_obj(obj)
    elif key == 'q':
        engine.exit_engine()

engine.init_screen(width=640, height=480)
engine.init_engine()
engine.set_keyboard_handler(keyboard_cb)
engine.engine()
```

Figure 2: Moving box example, with named arguments shown for readability (left); and a more extensive example (right) that responds to keyboard input with a simple kaleidoscope-like effect

2. DESIGN

The key to creating our game engine was to identify turtle module drawing operations that executed very quickly. These ultimately allowed us to move (and eventually animate) game objects without flickering by drawing a new game object image and then erasing the old one, even in lieu of support for sprites or multiple buffering. The game objects in our game engine module wrap this functionality in a class cleverly called `GameObject`. The game engine is coupled to these objects, invoking their various methods as needed.

The full API is given in Appendix A. Despite its small size, we have used its basic functionality to build pastiches of both classic games and modern casual games. Figure 1 shows our re-creations of *Asteroids* (1979), *Space Invaders* (1978), *Missile Command* (1980), and *Flappy Bird* (2013).

A simple example of using the game engine is shown in Figure 2 (left), where a game object is subclassed to create a moving box. One of the design goals was that it should be easy to use game objects without much code, and so a lot of functionality is provided in game objects by default, such as moving and performing out-of-bounds checks. Figure 2 (right) shows a more involved example with control flow. (The game engine's freely-available software distribution includes many more tutorial examples.)

From a high level, our game engine design is comparable to standard game engines [5, 8]. A game loop, in conjunction with functionality in the game objects, moves objects, performs collision detection, and handles I/O events. An important optimization is broad phase collision detection [5], that reduces the number of game objects that must be checked for collisions each game time step from the worst case $O(\frac{n^2}{2})$. This is implemented efficiently in Python by registering game object (sub)classes that can possibly collide; given two game objects, a tuple of their classes are used to quickly index into a dictionary and decide whether or not to proceed with a more expensive collision test. The speed will vary with the game and platform, naturally, but with the configuration mentioned in the Introduction, the game engine can sustain 29–30 frames (updates) per second running a demo with 100 moving balls, and over 60 FPS with 50 moving balls.

3. EXPERIENCE

Our game engine has been used in different ways in two CS1 classes over the last two years. Even though the CS1 course was for computer science majors, the majority of students in each class were non-majors (we suspect due to scheduling issues), but this means that our experience is generalizable to both majors and non-majors.

3.1 Assignments and Exercises

The debut of the game engine saw it used for an assignment involving a version of the *Missile Command* game code. Students were provided with an implementation of the game intentionally containing bugs and lacking some features, and they were given a series of "bug reports" ranging from the trivial to the challenging. For example:

Bug #1. The code has a syntax error (someone made a modification and didn't test it!). Fix it.

Bug #3. There should be six cities, not two.

Bug #4. Add a `draw_stars` function that randomly draws 25 stars (points) at random locations in the background. Call it from an appropriate place in the game code.

Bug #10. Add some simple game AI to demo mode so that the demo-mode "player" is not shooting randomly.

This assignment was intended to give students practice understanding and working with code they didn't create, a common task in practice.

We used the game engine more extensively in the second year's CS1 course. It was used for several small, optional practice exercises such as making a square "ping-pong" back and forth across the screen, and creating the "stepping feet" motion optical illusion [3]. The large assignment using the game engine was creating a version of *Flappy Bird* from scratch. Here, code for other games using the game engine were provided, as well as a YouTube video we made showing a sample solution in action.

One nice property of using the games that ties it in with lectures is that the game objects give a concrete set of examples with which to explain object-oriented concepts. Another nice property relates back to our initial goal, that the students' knowledge of turtle graphics is built on incrementally. Besides the engine using Python's turtle module, many things the students needed to code built on the turtle commands they were already familiar with, such as drawing backgrounds, rendering title screens and scores, and tracing out polygons for use as game object shapes.

3.2 Master Classes

Each instance of the CS1 course, we have run a "master class," for want of a better term. This is an optional session scheduled outside normal lecture and tutorial time, typically taking around 90 minutes. It usually draws a subset of the most keen students in the course, in our experience. The idea is to walk through the game engine code in detail, and explain the design considerations and design tradeoffs that were made – in other words, this exposes beginning students to a programmer's thought process, and the multitude of considerations that are made for every line of code written.

One important thing we stress is that the game engine design, despite having been written by their instructor, is *not* a perfect one. Rather, it is a design that has evolved over time and use, and there are a variety of tradeoffs that have been made, and different ways that the engine's code could be expressed (invariably involving different tradeoffs).

It could be argued that, in terms of explaining the game engine code and its evolution, that we have a distinct advantage over anyone trying to reproduce our master class. It wouldn't be obvious, for instance, that `GameObject.heading` was a very late addition that suddenly became necessary; or, that there used to be code to get the game time steps elapsed that was a) never incremented due to a bug, and b) completely and utterly unused in any of the games (it was removed from the game engine in the end). However, even without that knowledge, there are still many discussion points in the game engine code that can be leveraged by other instructors:

- Coupling and cohesion. Should the game object and the game engine code be in the same module, and what are the tradeoffs in coupling the two together?

- What should and should not be an object. The game engine proper is not contained in a class, although

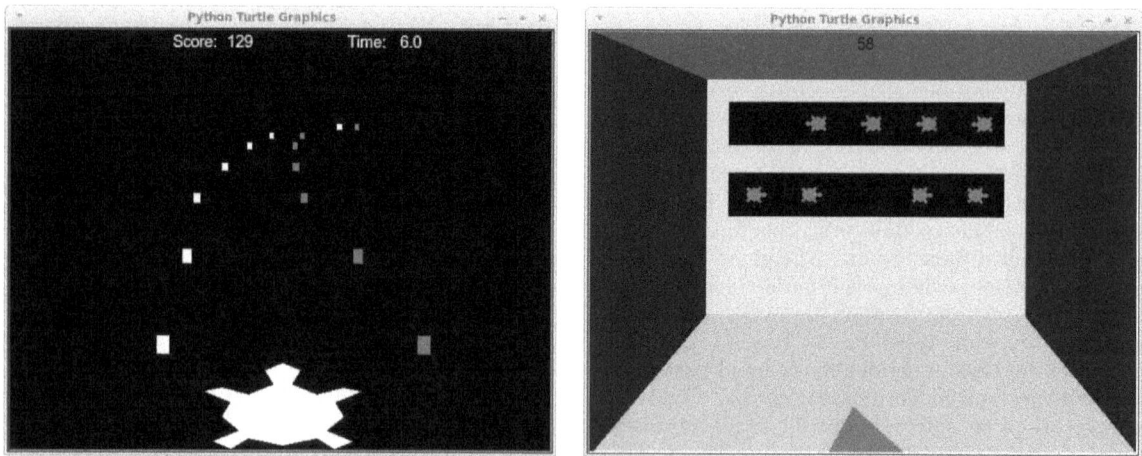

Figure 3: Games beyond 2D

the game state it keeps is placed in a singleton object for easy (re)initialization. Design issues that can be discussed here include the everything-is-an-object philosophy versus objects-are-one-tool-of-many, as well as the more prosaic explanation of what a singleton *is* and why it can be useful even if only one instance can exist.

- Class design. Why break functionality into many small methods (for overriding), and how does a designer anticipate possible future uses?

- Naming and name space issues: why certain "internal" variables are prefixed with underscores, and whether or not certain names within the module are appropriate. For example, should the redundant-sounding `engine.engine` be changed to `engine.run` to better reflect its purpose?

- Documentation, and drawing attention to current or potential future trouble spots with "XXX"-tagged comments.

- Controlling garbage collection. Beyond the basic discussion of what garbage collection is lies considerations of when (or if) objects are destroyed; game objects have an explicit deletion method rather than relying on the fickle `__del__` mechanism. This also leads into a discussion of language specifications, and how different language implementations may vary in practice.

- Data structure issues. This includes efficient usage, as in the dictionary previously mentioned for collision detection (the worst-case time is also an opportunity to introduce computational complexity), but also hard-to-debug problems like deleting from lists that are being traversed.

- Abstraction benefits and drawbacks. There are the advantages of using the turtle module that have already been mentioned, but also the drawbacks – performance is one, but also not all needed functionality may be exposed by an abstraction. The game engine reluctantly dips into the layer underlying the turtle module, Tkinter, to extract all keyboard events; this illustrates an unfortunate, but pragmatic, reality.

These are all points we have covered in our master classes, and undoubtedly other instructors can find more or different ones in their critical code readings.

4. EXPLORING THE LIMITS

Finally, we wanted to see how far we could push the game engine's capabilities. One obvious extension is to move beyond 2D games into so-called "2.5D," which we did by developing a version of the racing game *Night Driver* (1976) as well as a shooting gallery game; both are shown in Figure 3.

An unintended side effect of the engine's design that we partially used in the shooting gallery game was the drawing order of objects. Game objects created and added into the game engine earlier render before later ones, meaning that we can control which objects are in the foreground and background. This was explored much more extensively in the construction of a tile-based background (Figure 4, left). In this example, each background tile is a separate game object, and they scroll infinitely behind the spacecraft in the center, with their direction depending on the spacecraft's orientation. This demonstrates that the game engine supports a large number of active game objects (181, in this case), and could be used for any game with a tile-based map.

As hinted at with the optical illusion mentioned in the last section, the engine can be used for creating things other than games, too. Figure 4 (right) shows a narrative animation created with the game engine. The stick figure and bird are composed of multiple line segments, whose positions are encoded as key frames. We wrote code to do tweening between the key frames to create the animations. The trees shown are each a single large polygon, which are being used to demonstrate parallax scrolling.

5. RELATED WORK

We are probably well past the point where the use of games in education must be justified. They have been used with resounding success at all levels of university CS curriculum [6, 14]. Instead, we focus our related work discussion on the game engine and its use.

Our work is most similar in spirit to Luxton-Reilly and Denny, who made a CS1 game framework in Java [7]. Theirs is based on Swing, roughly the equivalent of Tkinter; cer-

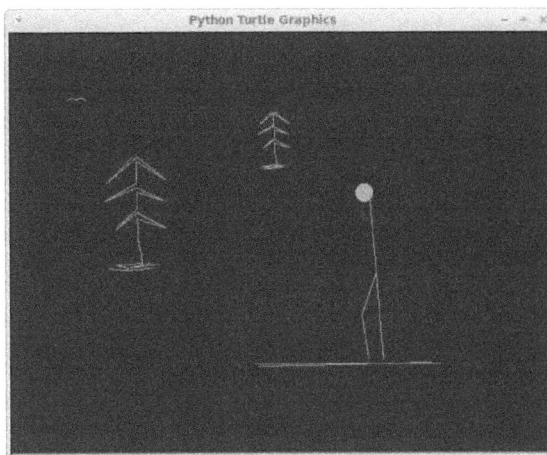

Figure 4: Many moving objects, and narrative

tainly we had many more technical challenges getting a game engine working well atop a higher level of abstraction than this, and their framework seems only to have been used for assignments. There have been various graphical frameworks for Python (e.g., [12]), but we are unaware of any that integrate well with the standard Python libraries and that build on what the students know in the way our game engine does.

Outside the academic realm, Python is used as a scripting language for some game engine projects. Space precludes us from listing them all, but typically Python is used in these in conjunction with a fast underlying library or non-Python game engine. For example, pygame is built on top of the SDL library [11], and cocos2d uses OpenGL [4]. From an educational point of view, none present a small enough API for CS1, nor a small code base that can be dissected the way ours can. They also do not directly build on students' knowledge.

6. CONCLUSION

Despite technical performance challenges, Python 3 and its turtle graphics module can be used to create a game engine that can support a wide range of games for use in CS1. The fact that the engine itself is written in Python has also allowed us to walk through its design and evolution with students. As future work, we would like to do a formal evaluation of the benefits of this approach in general and the game engine in particular. Our game engine is freely available from `http://www.cpsc.ucalgary.ca/~aycock`; it comes with 13 small tutorial examples, and nine larger game and demonstration examples.

7. ACKNOWLEDGMENTS

The first author's research is supported in part by the Natural Sciences and Engineering Research Council of Canada. Thanks to Andre Berthiaume for helpful comments.

8. REFERENCES

[1] H. Abelson and A. A. diSessa. *Turtle Geometry: The Computer as a Medium for Exploring Mathematics.* MIT Press, 1980.

[2] J. Aycock. μPython: Non-majors programming from the very first lecture. In *17th ACM Annual Conference on Innovation and Technology in Computer Science Education*, pages 345–350, 2012.

[3] M. Bach. "Stepping feet" motion illusion. `http://michaelbach.de/ot/mot-feetLin/index.html`, 2004. Retrieved 17 December 2014.

[4] cocos2d. `http://python.cocos2d.org/`. Retrieved 19 December 2014.

[5] J. Gregory. *Game Engine Architecture.* A K Peters, 2009.

[6] S. T. Leutenegger. A CS1 to CS2 bridge class using 2D game programming. *Journal of Computing Sciences in Colleges*, 21(5):76–83, 2006.

[7] A. Luxton-Reilly and P. Denny. A simple framework for interactive games in CS1. In *40th ACM Technical Symposium on Computer Science Education*, pages 216–220, 2009.

[8] S. Madhav. *Game Programming Algorithms and Techniques.* Addison Wesley, 2014.

[9] B. N. Miller and D. L. Ranum. *Python Programming in Context.* Jones and Bartlett, 2nd edition, 2013.

[10] S. Papert. *Mindstorms: Children, Computers, and Powerful Ideas.* Basic Books, 1980.

[11] Pygame. `http://www.pygame.org/wiki/about`. Retrieved 19 December 2014.

[12] B. Stephenson and C. Taube-Schock. QuickDraw: Bringing graphics into first year. In *40th ACM Technical Symposium on Computer Science Education*, pages 211–215, 2009.

[13] turtle – turtle graphics. `http://docs.python.org/3.4/library/turtle.html`. Retrieved 16 December 2014.

[14] K. Villaverde and B. Murphy. Senior project: Game development using Greenfoot. *Journal of Computing Sciences in Colleges*, 27(4):159–167, 2012.

APPENDIX

A. GAME ENGINE MODULE CONTENTS

The game engine is 284 lines of Python 3 code. Here we present the API for the game engine and the game engine objects that it manipulates; the code itself has been omitted.

```
def init_screen(width, height):
```
This should be called once only, before anything in this module is used.

```
def init_engine(delay=_ENGINEDELAY):
```
(Re)initializes the game engine. Only one game engine may exist at any one time. The optional parameter specifies a delay added to each game time step, in seconds; the value may be a floating point number.

```
def add_random_event(prob, fn):
```
Defines a callback function that is invoked with probability *prob* at each time step. Multiple random event callback functions may be registered at the same time. The probability must be a float in the range [0.0, 1.0].

```
def set_keyboard_handler(fn):
```
Sets callback function to invoke when a key is pressed. The function is passed the name of the key pressed as a string. Only one keyboard handler may be registered at a time.

```
def set_mouse_handler(fn):
```
Sets callback function to invoke when the mouse button is pressed. The function is passed the x and y coordinates where the mouse was clicked. Only one mouse handler may be registered at a time.

```
def register_collision(class1, class2, fn):
```
Instructs the game engine to invoke the callback routine *fn* when a collision is detected between an instance of *class1* and an instance of *class2*. Note that there is no ordering guaranteed for how game objects are tested for collision, so both combinations of *class1*/*class2* and *class2*/*class1* will need to be registered.

```
def add_obj(obj):
```
Adds a GameObject-derived object instance to the game.

```
def del_obj(obj):
```
Removes a GameObject-derived object instance from the game.

```
def exit_engine():
```
Instructs the game engine to exit on the next time step.

```
def engine():
```
Starts the game engine running.

```
class GameObject:
    def __init__(self, x, y, deltax, deltay,
                 shape, color):
```
Instantiates a game object at position (x, y) with the given shape and color, to move by $(deltax, deltay)$ each time step.

```
    def heading(self):
```
Returns the direction the object should be facing. By default, this is towards where the object will be moving.

```
    def draw(self):
```
Draws the object at its current (x, y) coordinates.

```
    def delete(self):
```
Invoked to delete an object.

```
    def erase(self):
```
Removes the object's image on screen.

```
    def update(self):
```
Invoked to update the object's image on screen, a draw-new-then-erase-old sequence.

```
    def move(self):
```
Invoked to move the object's (x, y) position on each time step.

```
    def isstatic(self):
```
Returns a Boolean value: True (static, unmoving object), or False (the default, a moving object).

```
    def isoob(self):
```
Returns True/False to indicate if the object is out of bounds or not. By default, the screen height/width and the object's (x, y) position are used to determine this.

```
    def step(self):
```
Called by the game engine each time step to allow the game object to update accordingly. The object's age (in game time steps) is updated and, if it's a moving object, invokes methods to perform the move and update. Moving out of bounds causes the object to be deleted from the game.

Facilitating Programming Success in Data Science Courses through Gamified Scaffolding and Learn2Mine

Paul Anderson, Thomas Nash, and Renée McCauley
College of Charleston, Charleston, SC, USA
{AndersonPE2, NashTF, McCauleyR}@cofc.edu

ABSTRACT

This paper discusses the learning strategies adopted in a publically available, cloud-based learning environment, Learn2Mine, which facilitates student-progress as they solve data science programming problems. The learning system has been evaluated over three consecutive terms. Learn2Mine was initially introduced in an introductory course and pilot-tested for usability and effectiveness in Fall 2013. Students reported positive opinions on usability and effectiveness of the system in their completion of programming assignments. In Spring 2014, Learn2Mine was evaluated in an upper-level data mining course by comparing student submission rates and amount of programming accomplished for a group with access to the tool versus one without access. The group with access to Learn2Mine had an average assignment submission rate of 84%, while the group without had an average submission rate of only 48% (difference significant at $p < 0.01$). In Fall 2014, a controlled experiment was conducted in an introductory data science course: one group of students worked on a multi-part programming task with support of scaffolding and gamification as implemented in Learn2Mine, while the other section did not. The group with access performed significantly better in overall task completion ($p < 0.01$).

Categories and Subject Descriptors

K.3.2 [**Computing Milieux**]: Computers and Education - Computer and Information Science Education

General Terms

Human Factors

Keywords

Data mining, data science, programming, R, Python, gamification.

1. INTRODUCTION

As of 2015, the field of data science is just over a decade old and still lacks engaging data science (DS) and analytics software aimed at teaching aspiring data scientists to explore and find patterns in large datasets. As the field depends on knowledge from so many diverse fields, a tool/environment that integrates this knowledge could be particularly useful. Learn2Mine is an environment that satisfies these needs and one of few environments developed with the goal to educate data scientists.

ITICSE '15, July 04 - 08, 2015, Vilnius, Lithuania   Copyright 2015
ACM 978-1-4503-3440-2/15/07...$15.00
http://dx.doi.org/10.1145/2729094.2742597

Learn2Mine is an open-source, cloud-based gamified learning system that can be used to scaffold learning through incremental programming assignments in data science. Learn2Mine is publically available for use via an Internet browser as well as for download and local installation.

Learn2Mine, with its gamified scaffolding approach, has been evaluated over three consecutive terms, in two DS courses required in an undergraduate DS major: an introductory DS course and an upper-level data mining course.

Learn2Mine is in its third version, having been used, tested and evaluated by students and instructors and refined by developers based on evaluation results. Section 2 provides details on relevant background work. Section 3 provides a brief overview of the learning system and a summary of the pilot-implementation of Learn2Mine (version 1) in an introductory DS course in Fall 2013. Section 4 discusses the Spring 2014 use and evaluation of the system (version 2) in teaching an upper-level data mining course. Section 5 provides details of a controlled experiment evaluating the effectiveness of the gamified scaffolding features of Learn2Mine (version 3) in teaching the introductory DS course in Fall 2014. Section 6 provides a discussion of the implications of the findings, and Section 7 summarizes the conclusions and suggests future work.

2. BACKGROUND

The primary goal in development of Learn2Mine was to provide an educational environment for teaching DS. In satisfying this need, a secondary goal was to produce a learning system that students would find both useful and enjoyable. To increase enjoyment, gamification was employed. Previous studies from within the computing education community have reported various benefits from the use of games or game elements in learning software systems. Boyce, Campbell, Pickford, Culler and Barnes [2] found that adding game elements to learning software resulted in increased motivation and higher learning gains in computational thinking among high school and college students. Iosup and Epema [4] found that the gamification of course software for an undergraduate course in computer organization and a graduate course in cloud computing was correlated with an increase in the percentage of passing students and in students' participation in voluntary activities and challenging assignments. Lee, Ko and Kwan [5] found that including assessments in games resulted in independent, self-directed learners voluntarily playing longer, completing more levels, and completing levels faster.

Another goal was to produce a system that would scaffold students through the learning process. Learn2Mine makes large problems accessible by allowing students to complete them incrementally, providing immediate feedback, and allowing students to retry problems until they achieve success. Linder, Abbott, and Fromberger [6] found that the pedagogy of scaffolding was effective in teaching software design. They found that using small, individual assignments that later assignments built upon was more effective than the use of a single semester-long project for teaching design. Vihavainen, Vikberg, Luukkainen, and P. rtel [8] found scaffolding learning with their TestMyCode system to be useful to both students and instructors in a programming course. Their system feedback was supportive of students and freed the teaching assistants from having to repeatedly answer many of the same questions. As a result, instructors could focus on more complex person-to-person scaffolding. The automated grading feature allowed both students and teachers to monitor progress.

3. THE Learn2Mine ENVIRONMENT

3.1 Overview

Learn2Mine is a cloud-based learning system that can be used by anyone interested in DS and its related sub-disciplines. This learning system minimizes the need for local computing resources as it can be used through this institution's portal. However, the system is open-source and available for download through a github site that provides instructions on how to use, contribute, or deploy locally. For the learner, Learn2Mine reduces the need for sophisticated programming skills before one begins to learn data science by providing lessons that teach programming and data science concurrently.

Learn2Mine employs elements of game-playing (gamification: badges, points, competition, leader board, etc) to encourage engagement and reward successful completion of tasks similar to what can be gleaned from gaming. With Learn2Mine, users are given immediate feedback and receive visual rewards in terms of notifications and badges which mark progress. Users unlock the ability to earn a "Learned" status on more lessons with each one they complete through manipulation of provided code or the creation of solutions from scratch. Game-playing aspects, such as experience bars and badges, were designed to be unobtrusive and allow learners not interested in the game playing to easily ignore the gaming aspects.

Learn2Mine offers lessons in the form of a progressively built skill tree that includes many common DS algorithms, such as k-nearest neighbors, naïve Bayes classifier, k-means clustering, neural networks, and market basket analysis, among others. Learn2Mine allows users to program in either R or Python programming languages. The system provides gamified scaffolding, but the learner can skip over subproblems to answer the main problem directly.

For an instructor, Learn2Mine provides a record of student activities including time on task, number of submissions, record of completion, and scores on tasks. The instructor can monitor student progress as students work through lessons. Learn2Mine grades lessons and presents the student with immediate feedback allowing them to progress without having to stop and wait for availability of the instructor or teaching assistant, through office hours or email, for assistance. This frees up the instructor to give more meaningful guidance and instruction to individual students, enabling the instructor to function as a guide as the student explores the material. Learn2Mine also allows any user to add new lesson content. Content can be extended to include any exercises that involve command-line driven, interpreted programming. A user can easily create a lesson through a form-driven interface and create a course that generates a link through which students can enroll in the course.

3.2 Courseware

At present Learn2Mine includes more than 30 DS lessons; each lesson consists, typically, of 3 – 10 subproblems. Subproblems provide opportunities for students to solve smaller problems that collectively solve an overall problem that is the goal of the lesson.

Subproblems are intended to provide scaffolding and build student confidence. They enforce the concepts of problem-decomposition and unit testing. Through solving subproblems the student incrementally solves the main problem associated with the lesson. However, a student can opt to solve the main problem directly, without going through the subproblems.

Students can stop in the middle of a lesson, saving the status of their progress until they have time to return. Students are allowed to retry subproblems and lessons. After successfully completing a lesson, a user is issued a corresponding badge for that lesson. Some of the badges have additional levels (learned versus mastered), and further, some of the lessons provide open-ended evaluation (i.e., an accuracy score) that can be used to rank an individual student.

Learn2Mine provides structured lessons in commonly used DS algorithms. As an example, a run-through of learner interaction proceeds as follows:

1. Log in and Select a lesson from a skill tree or list of lessons on Learn2Mine "Lessons" page.
2. Read lesson requirements and Implement solution through Learn2Mine or a standard programming environment, such as Rstudio, IDLE, PyCharm, etc.
3. Submit (and possibly resubmit) solution to subproblem or the final problem directly through Learn2Mine which provides immediate feedback for the student indicating the status of the submission including:
   (i) For a runtime error, the system reports the error generated by the R or Python runtime environment.
   (ii) For code that executes, but does not perform correctly, then a customizable report that provides feedback and guidance, can be sent to the user
   (iii) For a correct solution, a message of congratulations is displayed.
4. Completion of problem when the user successfully completes the last (overall) problem, followed by a badge being awarded and displayed at the bottom of the screen. Skill trees, experience bars, etc. are also updated.

3.3 Pilot Implementation

In Fall 2013, Learn2Mine was pilot-tested for usability in an introductory DS course, a course that has no prerequisites and assumes no prior programming experience. This course introduces knowledge discovery techniques, with an emphasis on computer-based tools for the analysis of large data sets. Topics include the DS process and inductive data-driven modeling. Concepts and theory required for completing assignments were covered in a lecture/discussion classroom setting. Learn2Mine was used throughout the term to complete programming-based homework assignments.

The goal of the pilot implementation was to evaluate the pedagogical usability of the system, including its ease-of-use and its effectiveness in supporting students as they work through programming projects. As this pilot-test was the initial introduction of the Learn2Mine system, developers interacted daily with student users through a private Facebook group. There were thirty-five students enrolled in two sections of the course.

This initial use of Learn2Mine was evaluated in two ways. An anonymous five-statement post-term survey collected student agreement (1 = Strongly Disagree, 2 = Disagree, 3 = Neutral, 4 = Agree, 5 = Strongly Agree) on the usefulness of Learn2Mine's automatic feedback and retry-system, its use of badges and skill-trees on motivation, and student willingness to use the learning system in other courses. The median student response on all questions was Agree, and a statement about the usefulness of "the ability to retry assignments improved my ability to learn and understand the material" received the highest overall positive response. Twenty-four students responded to a request for open-ended comments on the overall system – many of these comments suggested improvements to the system that were implemented in version 2. The details of the pilot implementation and evaluation are available in [1].

4. IMPACT OF Learn2Mine IN TEACHING DATA MINING

In Spring 2014, Learn2Mine version 2 was used to support learning in an upper-level, data mining course (demographic information shown in **Table 1**). Popular approaches to teaching this course include the use of tools (e.g., Weka [3]) and a programming-centric approach. In Spring 2013 and Spring 2014, a programming-centric approach was used. A single instructor taught the course in both terms using the same textbook and covering the same topics: an introduction to a data mining programming language, unsupervised learning, supervised learning, and optimization. Written homework, exams, and programming assignments were used in both terms to assess student achievement. Programming assignments were completed throughout both course offerings, but in Spring 2014, the instructor was able to assign 11 assignments rather than only 4 as done 2013. The instructor also believes that the 2014 assignments required a deeper understanding of the content than those in 2013. He attributes both of these advances to the use of Learn2Mine, which scaffolded student progress through immediate automatic feedback and allowed them to retry problems.

During the spring 2013 semester, the problems used were directly from the required textbook, *Machine Learning: An Algorithmic Perspective* by Stephen Marsland [7]. The textbook was chosen specifically because it integrated Python code directly into the chapters, and many exercises required modification of author-supplied Python code. As the students had two years of programming experience, including a semester of Python programming before taking the data mining course, the instructor believed that this book with its use of Python code would increase the accessibility of the material for students over other texts that did not include code. However, students in 2013 found the exercises quite challenging and appeared to flounder on many of them. In 2014, the instructor rewrote the exercises to include a series of subproblems to guide students through solution of the subproblems to solve a more complex overall problem. These problems were added to Learn2Mine, provided automatic feedback on subproblems, and allowed students to retry problems as many times as they wished or until they generated correct answers. This scaffolding approach through Learn2Mine was used throughout the term to support the programming assignments from the text.

To demonstrate the differences in assignments with and without scaffolding as manifested in Learn2Mine, consider the programming assignments associated with studying decision trees used in 2013 and 2014, based on those in the Marsland textbook. The book presents a discussion of and the code for a fundamental decision tree algorithm, with several related exercises. Below are three example exercises on decision trees that were assigned in the Spring 2013 course:

> Problem 6.5 – The CPU dataset in the UCI repository is a very good regression problem for the decision tree. You will need to modify the decision tree code so that it does regression, as discussed in Section 6.3.2. You will also have to work out the Gini impurity for multiple classes.

Problem 6.6 – Modify the implementation to deal with continuous variables, as discussed in Section 6.2.5.

Problem 6.7 – The misclassification impurity is $N(i) = 1 - \max P(w_j)$. Add this into the code and test the new version on some of the datasets above.

Contrasting the 2013 (above) and 2014 programming assignments, **Figure** 1 illustrates how Marsland's decision tree problems were adapted using a scaffolding approach. This approach guides the student through the development of important components of the complete algorithm, such as the ability to calculate the entropy of a set. Students are instructed to submit implementations that are required to adhere to the given function and return signatures. At any time the student may skip to the last problem and complete the entire assignment in a way of their own choosing. Subproblems are supplied to guide the students toward correct solutions; subproblems are graded, so students know if they are making progress. Graded subproblems provide a mechanism to award partial credit at the discretion of the instructor. The instructor may also manually award partial credit or modify grades that do not adhere to style guidelines.

The decision tree lesson (Figure 1) begins by asking the students to implement a function to return the entropy of a set. Students are then encouraged to implement a function to calculate the specific conditional entropy. This is extended into a more general version of this function that computes the conditional entropy for all of the possible values of a categorical variable. This demonstrates how complicated functions can be broken up into subproblems designed to promote experiential learning. The remainder of the lesson follows a similar pattern, guiding the students through the development of code to calculate information gain and the optimal split given a set of categorical variables. The final problem is required for completion of the lesson, though partial credit can be awarded at instructor discretion. This final problem asks the students to implement the fundamental decision tree algorithm which can be implemented as a composition of previous subproblems that have been tested and are known to function properly.

For the decision tree problem, the submission rate (i.e. the percentage of students that submitted a solution to the assignment) in 2013 was 60%, while in 2014 the submission rate was 90%. Over all programming exercises, there were significant increases in submissions rates in 2014 (with Learn2Mine) over that observed in 2013 (without Learn2Mine). In 2014, the average submission rate over the eleven programming assignments was 84%, while in 2013 the average submission rate over the four programming assignments was only 48% (significant difference tested with two proportion z-test, $p < 0.01$). In 2013, only two assignments had a submission rate above 50%; it is not known if the other 50% of students attempted the exercises at all, but it is known that they did not submit solutions. In 2014, a large majority (78% or more) of students submitted solutions for all exercises except for the final exercise of the term. Also, the average score on submitted solutions increased 10 percentage points from 2013 to 2014.

Table 1. Demographic information of 22 students who completed data mining course in Spring 2014.

Major		Gender		Class	
CS-related	**Other**	**Female**	**Male**	**Fresh/ Soph**	**Junior/ Senior**
21 (95%)	1 (5%)	4 (18%)	18 (82%)	3 (14%)	19 (86%)

5. IMPACT OF Learn2Mine IN TEACHING INTRODUCTORY DATA SCIENCE

In Fall 2014, there were two sections of the introductory DS course, the same course in which Learn2Mine was initially introduced in Fall 2013. In 2014, Learn2Mine version 3 was used to facilitate programming completion in the both sections of the introductory DS course. As mentioned previously, this course requires hands-on experience with statistical inference and data mining programming (R Statistical Computing Language).

As discussed in Section 3.3 the 2013 evaluation was for usability and effectiveness. In 2014, a controlled study was designed to compare the effectiveness of receiving feedback on programming assignments through scaffolding and gamification, as implemented in Learn2Mine, to programming without such feedback.

5.1 Participants

Participants were the 37 students in the two sections of the introductory data science course in Fall 2014, who attended class on the day that the experiment was conducted. The students across the two sections were similar in background and course grades earned so far in the class. There were 19 students enrolled in the section that did not receive feedback after completion of each subproblems, and 18 enrolled in the section that did.

Table 2: Demographic information for 45 students who completed the introduction to data science course in Fall 2014.

Major		Gender		Class	
CS-related	Other	Female	Male	Fresh/ Soph	Junior/ Senior
17 (38%)	28 (62%)	17 (38%)	28 (62%)	20 (44%)	25 (56%)

5.2 Methods

The study was conducted about two-thirds of the way through the semester. Students in both sections of the course had used the Learn2Mine tool as part of the course prior to the study. The same instructor taught the two sections and students had studied the same content and worked the same problems.

For this study, the students in each section of the course were treated differently in terms of access to features of Learn2Mine. Both groups used Learn2Mine with its features of automatic grading and feedback and ability to retry solutions. However, only one group was provided full-access to Learn2Mine's features of scaffolding and gamification. Students in both groups were presented the same in-class programming assignment that had 4 subproblems (A, B, C, and D). These corresponded to different functions necessary for computing the posterior probability of a Naïve Bayes Classifier. The subproblems were (A) write a function to compute the empirical priors, (B) write a function to compute the likelihood of a specific value, (C) write a function that computes the likelihood for a set of values, and (D) compute the posterior probabilities. Subproblem A can be completed independently of subproblem B and C. Subproblem D is dependent on A, B, and C. The assignments in each of the two section were identical in every way except that one section was provided with the option of receiving intermediate feedback and associated gamified content on parts A, B, C, and D through Learn2Mine, while the other was not. All students were able to receive full credit and receive automatic grading on the entire assignment by submitting a completed and correct set of answers to all subproblems.

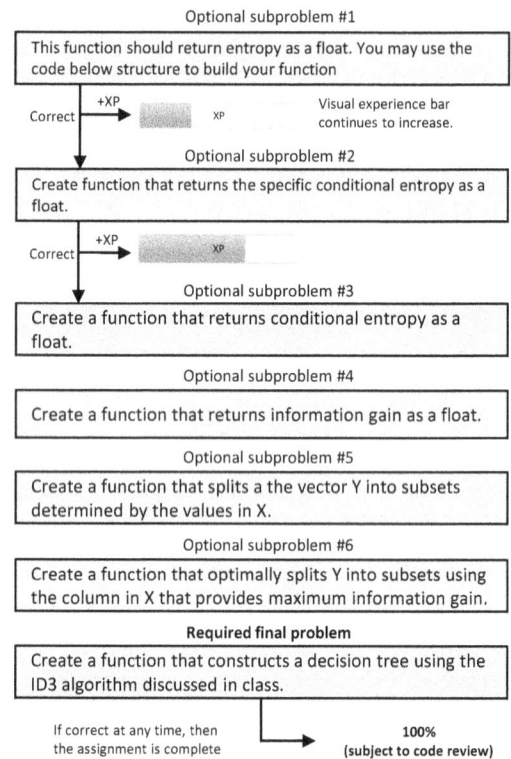

Figure 1: General lesson decision tree lesson workflow.

This study compares results of a programming assignment that is broken up into multiple parts and autograded at the completion of the entire problem, with an approach that offers grading and feedback after each subproblem is completed. Specifically, students in the gamified and scaffolded section were encouraged to try and retry the individual problems until they were successful. Both sections were encouraged to skip subproblems they deemed unnecessary to completing the final problem.

The data for the experiment was collected during a single class period of 1 hour and 15 minutes. After a short introduction of the assignment by the instructor, the students worked independently for an hour. In both sections, the instructor moved through the class guiding individuals, providing mini-lectures to subgroups of students, and answering questions. The progress of both groups was then recorded after an hour of work. The students were then prompted to give their written comments on the system.

5.3 Quantitative Results

The results of this study are shown in Table 3. While the number of students involved is small, applying the Freeman-Halton extension of the Fisher exact probability test showed a significant difference at $p < 0.01$ in completion rates for students using the scaffolded and gamified approach over those who did not. This supports our theory that access to scaffolding and gamification as implemented in Learn2Mine improved completion rates, and therefore, we believe it improved understanding and learning. While these results are not definitive, they are suggestive that the Learn2Mine system provides beneficial support in completion of the programming assignments.

Table 3: Results of study. Two students in the section without scaffolding and gamification did not complete any of the assignments successfully.

Access to scaffolding & gamification	n	Number of Students Completing Each Subproblem			
		A	B	C	D
No	19	16 (84%)	12 (63%)	1 (5%)	0 (0%)
Yes	18	18 (100%)	17 (94%)	14 (78%)	8 (44%)

5.4 Qualitative Results

In the last 15 minutes of the study session, students were asked to provide written comments about their use of the learning system in completing the assignment.

18 of 19 students in the group that were not given access to scaffolding and gamification provided written comments, while 9 of 18 students in the group with access provided comments. Comments from both groups were analyzed and classified. One classification identified comments as reflecting positive, negative or both positive and negative opinions about use of Learn2Mine in completing the task. Table 4 provides an overview of comments in terms of groups, numbers and classification.

Table 4: Summary of the student feedback reflecting positive, negative or a mix of both positive and negative opinions about the use of Learn2Mine is completing the task. Comments that did not fit into these classes are counted under Other.

Access to scaffolding & gamification	n	Classification			
		Positive	Negative	Positive & Negative	Other
No	18	3 (16%)	5 (28%)	4 (22%)	6 (33%)
Yes	9	2 (22%)	0 (0%)	5 (56%)	2 (22%)

Due to lack of space, a single comment in each category from students in each group is shown next:

With scaffolded learning and gamification:

Positive: *I really like the way Learn2Mine is set up. It's helpful the way that the problems are broken up into smaller and more manageable/understandable pieces. It's also helpful that it offers feedback on incorrect answers and shows the instructor's output. All of this helps me to troubleshoot my own work and try to figure it out on my own. And the badges at the end are fun to get :)*

Positive and negative: *Breaking up problems and testing code step by step makes it a lot easier to follow whats happening. Sometimes felt like at the end of the assignments I didn't really learn much of the language since I mostly plugged things in instead of generating the code myself, but I still got the overall concepts.*

Without scaffolded learning and gamification:

Positive: *I really liked that I was building the final long program instead of working on little functions and having you give us the really long one at the end. I could understand better how the entire thing comes together in the end instead of changing things in the code. We created it ourselves. Yes. It was harder but I think I understand the code better. We were still able to check ourselves along the way just like in the other method, but with this way I could see me connection between each step. I wasn't trying to figure out each step individually as if it were all separate problems.*

Negative: *I think assignments are much more effective for practicing and learning a new concept when you are able to check*

your work along the way. It is overwhelming to have a mutli-step assignment with no way to make sure you're completely each step correctly or at least heading in the right direction. It is reassuring to see that you are correctly understanding the assignment as you are in the process of completing it rather than at the very end.

Positive and negative: *I liked this lesson. It was more difficult but it made me think harder and play around until I got the correct answer. However, without the individual submissions it was hard to tell if you actually got the correct answer without your confirmation.*

Six students in the group that had access to scaffolding and gamification provided comments that were constructive in suggesting possible improvement to Learn2Mine. Three of these constructive comments were actually part of larger comments classified as being both positive and negative (see Table 4).

Constructive:

...some of the error reports were hard to understand. If they were more specific as to where my error was, it might have made the code easier to fix and help me understand why I needed to fix it/what I did wrong. (This constructive comment is part of a large comment classified as being Positive and Negative.)

Six of the 18 comments provided by students who did not have access to scaffolding and gamification did not fit into any meaningful category. Due to lack of space, they are not presented here, but some appeared to be "brown-nosing" tactics and others general complaints.

6. DISCUSSION OF ALL RESULTS

After examining the results of the Spring 2013 offering of the Data Mining course, it was apparent that the programming assignments did not have their intended impact on student learning. The initial motivation behind choosing the textbook for the course was to find a book that integrated Python – a language the students learned in a previous class – with the algorithms discussed in the course. It was believed that this would increase the accessibility to the programming side of the course. After reviewing the data, however, only an average of 50% of the students were able to complete and submit the programming assignments. This corresponds to approximately the top 50% of the students, as one might expect. Those students who did attempt the programming assignments performed well, averaging a score of 80%. Students' questions and comments suggest that it was the need to modify the author's code – the very reason the book had been chosen - that was actually a barrier to participation!

This finding in Spring 2013 was part of the impetus for designing and developing the Learn2Mine environment to guide students through data mining exercises via gamified scaffolded learning. After keeping the other aspects of the course as constant as expected from one term to another, the Learn2Mine environment with scaffolded and gamified learning increased the average submission rate from 48% to over 84%.

While the lecture and exam material remained relatively unchanged from 2013 to 2014, the number of programming exercises assigned increased, and we believe the complexity of those assignments also increased from 2013 to 2014. For example, the decision tree programming assignment in 2014 required students to implement the fundamental algorithm from scratch, as opposed to simply changing selected components (2013), which we observed students doing without fully understanding the algorithm itself. The increase in complexity is hard to quantify, but instructor experience leads us to believe this. The 2014 offering also introduced all of the students to a new language (R), which, after its introduction, was an optional component of the assignments. Specifically, on lessons that were not R specific, the students were allowed to complete programming assignments using either Python or R. This increased the workload of the instructor who would need to program both solutions into the system to enable this functionality. By the end of the semester, all of the students were submitting their assignments in R, indicating that it was possible to develop adequate proficiency in a new data mining language to complete the required assignments. Moreover, the number of programming assignments jumped from 5 in 2013 to 11 in 2014.

In the fall of 2014, we attempted to isolate an aspect of Learn2Mine that we believed was contributing to student success. Specifically, we hypothesized that the scaffolding and gamification elements of a Learn2Mine lesson were responsible for higher completion rates, which we believe relates to learning, or else we wouldn't make the assignments at all! We conducted a controlled experiment, wherein two sections were given the same assignment with and without access to gamified scaffolded learning. The results support our hypothesis that these aspects of the Learn2Mine system increase completion rate. We believe this correlates with higher levels of understanding and learning by the students. This is based on the assumption that the Bayesian classification lesson is representative of a standard lesson.

The qualitative data (comments) are interesting in at least three regards. (1) Across both groups (with and without gamified scaffolded learning), students indicated that the scaffolded approach of solving subproblems and immediate feedback in the Learn2Mine system is desirable. (2) A small number of student comments mentioned the non-scaffold related gamification features of the environment. This lack of acknowledgment could be due to the unobtrusiveness of the other gaming aspects (badges, etc.) or due to the perceived greater value of the scaffolding. (3) Some comments focused on the lesson content, indicating that this system does not remove the need for thoughtfully created exercises and the need for talented instructors.

7. CONCLUSION AND FUTURE WORK

Learn2Mine has been shown to be beneficial in teaching programming-centric DS courses. In introductory and upper-level applications, Learn2Mine has been found to be beneficial in providing scaffolding and immediate feedback beneficial to students as they progress through programming assignments. The environment also allowed the instructor to make more programming assignments than was previously possible without Learn2Mine. Moreover, Learn2Mine was shown to improve the submission rate, depth, and breadth of programming assignments. Additional studies are planned to determine the extent to which these results generalize. To evaluate the generalization of these results, two other state universities in the USA have committed to using Learn2Mine in their data mining and pattern recognition courses.

Currently, Learn2Mine is available for any user to try. The software is fully open source and is under the MIT License. The open source github repository (https://github.com/Anderson-Lab/Learn2Mine-Main) contains all of the source code for other institutions to deploy their own customized systems if they desire; however, it is possible and even encouraged for these institutions to add their functionality to the main Learn2Mine server directly. Learn2Mine is actively being developed, and improvements and bug fixes are ongoing. The data science community is invited to use the system and suggest additional enhancements.

8. ACKNOWLEDGMENTS
Our thanks to the Learn2Mine development team that has included Clayton Turner, Jake Dirksheide, others. The authors acknowledge funding from the SC EPSCoR/IDeA GEAR:Research Experiences (PI: P. Anderson).

9. REFERENCES

[1] Anderson, P., Turner, C., Dierksheide, J. and McCauley, R. An extensible online environment for teaching data science concepts through gamification, in *Proceedings of the 44th Annual Frontiers in Education Conference (FIE'14)*, October 22-25, 2014, Madrid, Spain, pp 1336 - 1343.

[2] Boyce, A., Campbell, A., Pickford, S., Culler, D. and Barnes, T. Experimental evaluation of BeadLoom game: how adding game elements to an educational tool improves motivation and learning, in *Proceedings of the 16th annual conference on innovation and technology in computer science education (ITiCSE'11)*, June 27-29, 2011, Darmstadt, Germany, pp. 243-7.

[3] Hall, I. Frank, M., Holmes, E., Pfahringer, G., Reutemann, B., Witten, P. The WEKA data mining software, *SIGKDD Explor.*, vol. 11, no. 1, 2009.

[4] Iosup, A. and Epema, D. An Experience Report on Using Gamification in Technical Higher Education, in *Proceedings of the 45th Technical Symposium on Computer Science Education (SIGCSE'14)*, March 5-8, 2014, Atlanta, GA, USA, pp. 27-32.

[5] Lee, M.J., Ko, A.J., and Kwan, I. In-game assessments increase novice programmers' engagement and level completion speed, in *Proceedings of the International Computing Education Research Workshop* (ICER'13), August 12–14, 2013, San Diego, California, USA, pp. 153-160.

[6] Linder, S.P., Abbott, D. and Fromberger, M.J. An instructional scaffolding approach to teaching software design, *Journal of Computing Sciences in Colleges*, 21(6), June 2006, pp. 238-250.

[7] Marsland, S., 2009, *Machine learning: An Algorithmic Perspective*, Chapman & Hall/CRC, Boca Raton, Florida, 390pp.

[8] Vihavainen, A. Vikberg, T., Luukkainen, M. and Pärtel, M. Scaffolding students' learning using Test My Code, in *Proceedings of the 18th Conference on Innovation and Technology in Computer Science Education* (ITiCSE'13), July 1–3, 2013, Canterbury, England, UK, pp. 117-122

Applied Computer History: Experience Teaching Systems Topics through Retrogames

John Aycock
Department of Computer Science
University of Calgary
ICT 602, 2500 University Drive NW
Calgary, AB, Canada T2N 1N4
aycock@ucalgary.ca

ABSTRACT

Computing history need not be dry, useless, or boring. We describe a computer science course we taught, *Retrogames*, that used old computer games' implementation throughout to explain techniques and systems topics that modern students are not typically exposed to in any depth, ideas that are still applicable in both game and non-game settings. As a side effect, students also learned about how development was done and problems were solved in highly-constrained environments, which gave them useful tools to add to their toolbox.

Categories and Subject Descriptors

K.3.2 [**Computers and Education**]: Computer and Information Science Education; K.2 [**Computing Milieux**]: History of Computing—*hardware, software, systems*; K.8.0 [**Personal Computing**]: General—*games*

General Terms

Algorithms, design, performance

Keywords

Games; retrogames; history; system design; programming techniques

1. INTRODUCTION

History may be thought to have limited usefulness in a fast-changing area like computer science, but one critical reason why historical, constrained computing systems matter to contemporary students is that some techniques from old, constrained environments are still in use today. We describe a course we taught to highlight this: *Retrogames*. We used the implementation of old games as a vehicle to explain modern computer science techniques that students wouldn't necessarily get exposed to in any depth during their degree.

Retrogames was offered as a one-semester[1] computer science course at the 4th-year (senior) undergraduate computer science level. The recommended prerequisite was our third-year operating systems course. *Retrogames* quickly filled up to its capacity of 30 students, even though it was clearly advertised as a systems course.

There is an additional benefit to this historically-based approach: learning creative ways to solve problems. All too often, computer science students now learn in what are essentially unconstrained software, hardware, and development environments. Even our "low-level" assembly course uses Raspberry Pi boards with a baseline configuration of 512 MiB of memory – hardly minimalist. These may sound like curmudgeonly rantings, but in fact something very important has been lost in students' education. The nature of that something has been observed by various people within the computing profession, and it was also expressed very eloquently by the composer Stravinsky [21, p. 87]: '...my freedom will be so much the greater and more meaningful the more narrowly I limit my field of action and the more I surround myself with obstacles. Whatever diminishes constraint, diminishes strength.' Put less lavishly, necessity is the mother of invention, and modern students are rarely if ever challenged to think this way, something *Retrogames* addresses.

It is important to highlight what this course is *not*. It is not a traditional computer history course. It is not a "history of games" class, a course which – at our institution – is already offered by the arts and humanities. It is not about just playing old games, nor is it just using games in a regular course, e.g., as assignments. This retrogames class is a technical, low-level systems course and can serve a variety of roles: an effective capstone course for systems-oriented students, a complementary course for a game curriculum, or simply an interesting computer science option.

The techniques we covered in *Retrogames* are below, with detail added for some that are less obvious:

- Memory management (handling not enough memory, too much memory, and preserving memory state)

- Extensibility through external data (managing slow, incompatible I/O devices and screen updating; program designs; embedded languages and a lead-in to interpretation)

- Interpretation

---

[1]13 weeks, 150 minutes per week.

- Data compression (text, static images, full-motion video)

- Procedural content generation

- Copy protection

- Code obfuscation

- Code optimization

Some examples are helpful to explain our approach. Looking at interpretation, text adventure games like *Zork* often didn't run directly on the hardware, but instead were interpreted by a virtual machine [4]. We use this and other interpreted retrogames to explain how different types of interpreter are constructed ("classic" interpreters vs. direct and indirect threading), instruction set design choices (stack- vs. register-based designs, code and data alignment, inline arguments), as well as allocation of bits/bytes within an instruction set. This applies to modern settings because a lot of popular programming languages are still interpreted, yet most students would not otherwise encounter interpreters dissected to this level of detail.

As another example, we presented games that used external data, initially from the point of view of managing a plethora of dumb terminals (via `termcap`). This naturally leads into screen update algorithms and the value of exploiting differences in data, program designs that incorporate external data in different ways, and eventually into interpretation. The modern applications are software distribution using differences (e.g., [1]), code internationalization, and embedded scripting languages.

The modern applications were deliberately chosen to be *non*-game examples, to drive the point home that these are general techniques that apply beyond the scope of games (although many of them are still used in some way in games). Where possible, modern examples were selected to be surprising, such as use in malicious software or examples of dual-use technology. For instance, code obfuscation is used for legitimate software protection but also by malware [6].

Of course, we used more game examples than just *Zork*. In total, there were 50 game examples on multiple platforms spanning the years 1973–1993, with most in the 1980s. These were not necessarily historically significant games, and in fact some were fairly obscure, but they were all chosen for aspects of their implementation.

One advantage to retrogame examples is that they tend to be simple. Given examples for teaching are often abstracted for pedagogical reasons anyway, using old games means that this abstraction is effectively already done, and students can be shown a "real" example in its entirety.[2]

We begin with related work, then move to the student experience. From there, Sections 4 and 5 discuss theoretical and practical aspects underlying the course and its design, respectively, followed by the grand conclusion.

2. RELATED WORK

The closest related work is history of computing (HoC) courses, although we have not found any that make historical games the focus as we have, much less the games' implementation.

Nakano et al. [15, p. 28] observe that technical content in an HoC course can make it 'more interesting to computer

science students and more relevant to the curriculum', but also note that few HoC courses do this. Indeed, there are some outliers like [7, 18] but more seem to follow the recommendation in [10, p. 7] suggesting 'written examinations, short essays, and a major essay would properly assess an experience in the history of computing' rather than programming. Even compared to the cases of the hands-on [7, 18], we think the student interest is enhanced by our use of games throughout.

A commonly-cited motivation for learning the HoC is one that is backwards-looking: learning from the past, avoiding repeated mistakes [10, 13, 15, 17]. While we do not disagree with this, we argue that it does not go far enough by showing students (as we do) that these techniques are still useful in a modern setting and giving students techniques to add to their toolbox, thus making the history content practical in a very tangible way.

The potential of games to both interest students as well as cover a broad range of computer science topics has been realized by others, too (e.g., [5]), although we are unaware of any use of historical game implementation.

3. STUDENT EXPERIENCE

Students were evaluated based on in-class game presentations, two programming assignments, a term project, and small written homework assignments.

The point of the student game presentations was to extend the range of games seen in the course, and at the same time applying the retrogame review criteria they themselves collectively decided upon. We had the game reviews done in pairs based on an idea from Fullerton [9] about watching someone else play a game and comparing it to one's own experience. The games the students chose ranged widely across years and platforms; one pair even lugged in a vintage stand-up arcade cabinet! Students were also advised to keep their game selection classroom-appropriate: no *Custer's Revenge*, no *Leisure Suit Larry*, no *Night Trap*, no *1*77, and so on.[3]

The two assignments were a balance of game- and systems-related. The first was retrogame code analysis: locating and modifying a number of elements in the Atari 2600 *Chase the Chuck Wagon* game; sample questions from this assignment are in Appendix A. The second assignment was a modern application of old techniques, internationalizing a small program and extending it with an embedded scripting language.

The term project was to produce a retrogame. Some did this on actual retro hardware, while others produced a retrogame using a modern system/language such as Unity or Java/C++. There were a variety of genres represented, including Roguelikes, JRPGs, fighting games, and platformers.

Finally, there were a number of small homework assignments, short activities that were submitted in writing via email, and that provided either some learning experience or preparation for in-class discussions. We stressed the experiential learning component when possible: we wanted students to not just learn about the past abstractly, but to experience it. The homework assignments are listed in Appendix B, and some examples involved reading back issues

---

[2]An observation hinted at by [13].

[3]Finding out more regarding unfamiliar titles here is left as a not-safe-for-work exercise for the interested reader.

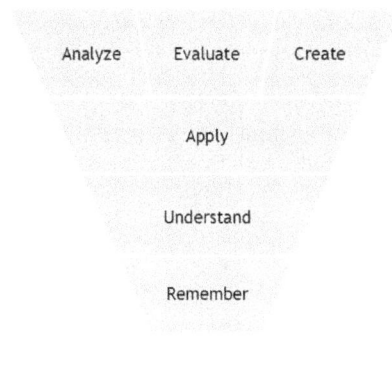

Figure 1: Bloom's taxonomy

of *Byte*, interacting with a shell using a low-baud-rate simulator we wrote,[4] and using a line editor.

Further to the experiential learning, we were fortunate in that our campus library maintains a special collection of videogames including retrogames. The library staff equipped a room for us as a home arcade for one class, where students could play games on the original equipment, much of which was discontinued before they were born. A number of the students commented that they enjoyed the hands-on session in the library, and we followed it up with comparative and reflective homework assignments.

The positive student experience is borne out by the results of the anonymous student course evaluations, which had a 72% response rate. Our institution asks students twelve questions, each on a seven-point Likert scale, and our faculty collects written comments as well. Quantitatively, *all* mean responses for *Retrogames* exceed those for the comparison group of 4th-year courses within both the computer science department *and* the faculty (which includes six departments). The lowest mean rating on any question was 6.32/7; particular questions of note were with regards to overall instruction (mean 6.63/7) and 'I learned a lot in this course' (mean 6.53/7). The written comments were also supportive, from the short 'Material was VERY interesting' to the long:

> 'The material was all very relevant to CPSC [computer science] generally, lots of cool ideas presented, interesting ways to approach all sorts of problems, in addition to cool historical stuff.'

> 'This course felt like it tied together many of the comp. sci courses I'd taken previously but in an extremely engaging manner which added much more relevance and meaning to material I'd previously dismissed. [...] It was in itself very informative but most valuable in how it linked into my degree so far and is one of the most important courses I've ever taken because of this.'

4. THEORETICAL ASPECTS

We realized that *Retrogames* offered an unusual opportunity from the viewpoint of educational theory, specifically

---

[4]We also used this in class later to demonstrate screen update algorithms.

the (revised) Bloom's taxonomy [2], illustrated in Figure 1. Normally in a course where students are presented with new material, we would expect them to remember, understand, and apply the new knowledge at a minimum. However, we assumed (correctly) that students would already be familiar with games, and thus could be pushed to higher levels of Bloom's taxonomy for game-related tasks. We chose two to focus on: defining what a retrogame *is*, and choosing retrogame review criteria.

For the retrogame definition, students needed to analyze and evaluate existing games to create a definition... which was new knowledge that got fed back into the taxonomy, because students needed to remember/understand/apply that definition in the selection of retrogame examples for presentations and in their own retrogame term projects. Similarly for the retrogame review criteria, students had to analyze game reviews and apply their retrogame definition to create their own criteria. Again this was new knowledge that they needed to apply to evaluate retrogames for in-class reviews. For non-game systems material, our expectation was for students to function at remember/understand/apply as usual.

To better reflect this duality, the course had two "tracks" – games and systems – and most lectures were divided up accordingly, with one student game presentation (game track) followed by the remainder as traditional lecture time (systems track).

Bloom aside, the key theoretical question the *students* needed to resolve at the start of the course was a definitional one: what is a retrogame? To show some of the subtleties, a straightforward approach would simply define a retrogame as an old game, and in fact some authors do just that [16, 22]. But when exactly does "old" end, and does that point change over time? Is an old game played on a modern computer under emulation still a retrogame? Is a newly-created game running on old hardware a retrogame? What about a new game, on new hardware, with retro design elements? From the instructional point of view, we needed to be mindful that a definition should allow students' term projects to be retrogames in some sense, and also that the game examples used for the course should be firmly in the retro category.

Given that the majority of our game examples were from the 1980s, we naïvely expected that they would be safe from any retrogame definition the students collectively arrived at. Unsurprisingly, considering the age of the students, most wanted the definition of retrogame extended relatively late, into the late 1990s. Some held, however, that "retro" ended with the video game crash in the mid-1980s, which presented an unexpected problem.

Following this class discussion, we proposed a common retrogame definition that would resolve most of the issues, although ultimately the students had to agree to differ on the target range of years. Figure 2 illustrates the definition. A game is presented as a "black box." If that game is indistinguishable from a game in the target range of years, *regardless of the technology used inside the box*, then the game is a retrogame (cf. the Turing test [23]). One possible retrogame criterion suggested by students, nostalgia, can be an excellent game design criterion but isn't part of the definition, because it is subjective and not necessarily felt by all students.

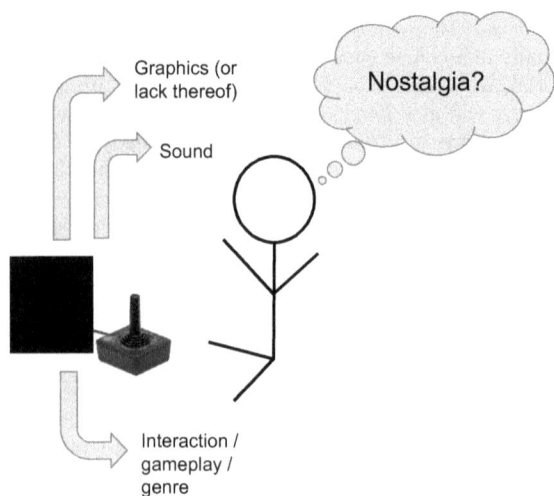

Figure 2: "Black box" retrogame definition

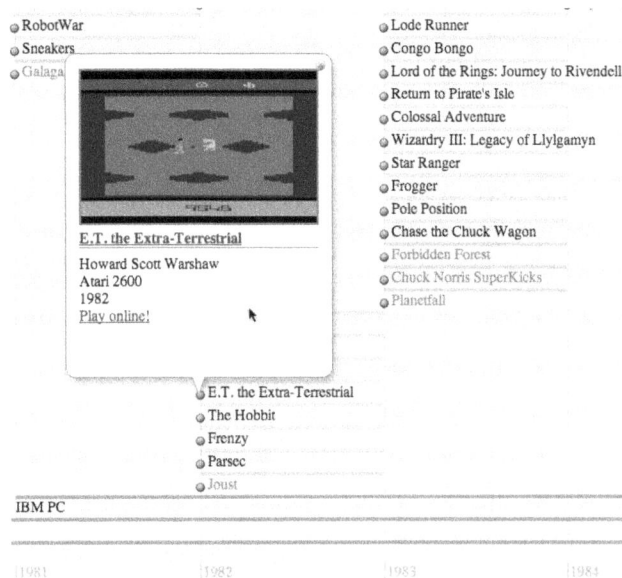

Figure 3: Interactive retrogame timeline

Students' temporal distance from old games led them to make a number of observations we had not considered, too. For example, they observed the limited color palette, and the severe difficulty and punishment in old games.

5. PRACTICAL ASPECTS

There were three major practical aspects to consider when preparing this course.

First, there was the question of how to organize the material. No nice chronological presentation seemed possible, as game examples for any given systems technique could come from many different years. We therefore followed the order of topics listed in the Introduction, but to supply context for the students, we set up an interactive timeline on the course web site with links to information for each game (Figure 3).[5] Games from student reviews were posted on the timeline in

[5]Using the timeline from SIMILE Widgets [19].

a different color, to stand out, and the availability of some major platforms was also shown for reference.

Second, copyright issues needed to be considered, because even though some games might be considered "abandonware," they would still be subject to copyright. Events in two countries have facilitated a solution. Recent changes to Canadian copyright law finally added an explicit fair-dealing exemption for education, for one; for another, the Internet Archive fortuitously unveiled their "Console Living Room" [11] just before the start of *Retrogames*, which permits old games to be played in-browser – the Internet Archive had previously secured a DMCA exemption in order to archive old software [12]. We also had someone from our university's Copyright Office give a presentation to the students regarding what was and was not permissible.

Third, how did we get the material? There was no extant textbook to base this on. It was the result of over a year of research we did,[6] involving traditional information-gathering for generating leads to promising retrogames, static and dynamic assembly code analysis, source code analysis (when available; both of games and emulators), in-emulator hypothesis testing, and creating reconstructions and visualizations. The good news for anyone not wanting to make a similar time investment is that our research will be published in a forthcoming book [3]. It is not necessary to be a "gamer" to teach this course, and in fact we are not particularly adept at gameplay ourselves.

While bits of our experience have been woven throughout this paper, one area we would particularly look to improve upon in future offerings of this course is the student game presentations. Because the presentations ran through the majority of classes during the semester, by the time we noticed problems cropping up, it was too late to change things without affecting students who had already presented. The game presentation criteria, based on students' reading of existing game reviews, tended to lack depth at times – a problem also identified by Fernández-Vara [8]. Some more preparatory readings on game analysis for students would be helpful, along with some steering of the in-class discussion when students are creating their review criteria, would help address the problem. We also suggest leading with an instructor-provided game review first (in class or as a video) to provide an example to guide students.

6. CONCLUSION

Historical video games can be applied in a very practical and compelling way to teach modern ideas. The *Retrogames* course gives students an appreciation for developing code under different constraints, a set of tools and ideas that have modern applications, and experiences with an earlier time in computer science. As future work, we would like to conduct a formal assessment of the course and its effectiveness. We leave the last word on *Retrogames* to the students, from their anonymous written course evaluations:

> 'Offer it more often or give it more time, since there is even more to cover and it has all been hugely useful and inspiring.'

> 'I like this course and wished it was a year long.'

[6]One particularly difficult area to get primary source material for is retrogame software protection, interestingly, because often the surviving versions of games are the cracked ones.

7. ACKNOWLEDGMENTS

Thanks to Jerremie Clyde and Dylan Tetrault for setting up the library "arcade," Rowena Wake from the Copyright Office for the class presentation, and Kate Beamer from Research Services for clearing certain statements and data used in this paper with respect to ethics approval. The joystick (Figure 2) and Bloom's taxonomy images are from Wikimedia Commons and are in the public domain. The *E.T.* thumbnail is copyright Atari Interactive, Inc.

APPENDIX

A. RETROGAME ANALYSIS ASSIGNMENT

These are some sample tasks for the first assignment, analysis of *Chase the Chuck Wagon*. Chapter 2 of Montfort and Bogost [14] was suggested as pre-reading, and using the excellent Stella emulator/debugger [20] was recommended. To underscore the level of difficulty, students were solving these tasks using a combination of static and dynamic analysis on the game's undocumented 6507 (6502) assembly code. Typical students would have seen ARM, x86, or SPARC assembly prior to this course, but not 6502.

- Find the location in memory of the timer that's displayed on screen. Change it to read 1234.

- Find the location in memory of the player's score that's displayed on screen when the food bowl drops between levels. Change it to read 5678.

- Find the locations of the four levels' playfield data in memory, i.e., the wall layout of the mazes.

- Prove that you found the correct answer for the last task by writing a program in any programming language that takes the game cartridge ROM image as input, extracts the relevant data, and prints out an ASCII rendition of the maze walls for the levels.

- Change the code so that the score is incremented by 10 instead of by 1.

- Find the lookup tables in the code that point to the four levels' playfield data.

- There is a 30+ year old bug in the game. If the timer's value is greater than 99, it will display the timer value but the player loses a life when only the last two digits of the timer value count down to 0. Verify the bug and identify where it is in the code.

- Change the code so that the timer is decremented by 2 instead of by 1.

- Find the location in memory that is used to keep track of how long the dog is paralyzed after being hit by the bone.

- Change the code so that the dog is *not* paralyzed after being hit by the bone. (It's okay if it still plays the annoying sound.)

There were several bonuses available. One was to produce a complete documented disassembly of the game code, and another was to fix the identified bug – nontrivial because ROM space had to be found to add code.

B. HOMEWORK

The homework assignments used in *Retrogames* are below, edited to remove administrative minutia and campus-specific details.

- Read Chapter 2 of Juul's *A Casual Revolution* (MIT Press, 2009). In your own words, summarize what a casual game is. *Rationale: for class discussion, is there an overlap between casual games and retrogames?*

- Play at least two games that you think are "retro", and play one that you think should not be retro. Think about what separates the retro from non-retro.

  Summarize the games you played, their year of release, and whether or not our definition worked, e.g.

  ```
  Combat   Atari 2600, 1977   retro
  Karateka   Apple II, 1984   retro

  World of Warcraft   Windows, 2004   not retro
  ```

  We'll return to the definition itself in the next class.

- Have a look at one or more game review sites online. List 2–3 game review criteria you would want to see used for in-class game presentations.

- Compare the specifications (CPU, memory, graphics, sound, storage) for two home game consoles that were contemporaries in the 1970s or 1980s.

- Pick one of the two consoles you used for Homework 4. Find the specs for your smartphone (or tablet/laptop if you don't have a smartphone) and calculate how many times more memory, storage, and screen resolution it has. Watch your units!

- Experience retrocomputing by perusing one or two issues of *Byte Magazine* from the late 1970s or early- to mid-1980s (available at the Internet Archive). Provide 2–3 observations about how the computing environment differed back then compared to now. (You may find the ads as enlightening as the articles, by the way.)

- Experience working over a low-speed connection. Open a terminal/ssh window to 80x24 on the department Linux machines and run

  ```
  /usr/bin/baudy -b 1200
  ```

  This is a program I modified to simulate different baud rates. Another common one would be 300 baud instead of the 1200 above.

  Some suggested things to try:

  - Do a full listing of some longish directory.

  - Compare how different full-screen programs refresh the screen. vim and emacs (-nw may be required so it doesn't open a separate window) are fairly smart; try scrolling just a few lines up or down, or half a screen. (Obviously, use a longish file for this.) Then try the pagers more and less to see how they handle it. top is another one to watch the updates on.

Send 2–3 observations/thoughts about your experiences trying this.

- Many old games were written using a line editor. Experience this by using `ed` on a Unix-based system (Mac OS X even has this) to edit a file.

  If you want the full experience, do this in `baudy` at 1200 baud or lower, and try writing a short program.

  Submit 2–3 observations/thoughts about your experiences trying this.

- Play one or more of the games you tried on the original machines at the library in an emulator – what is the difference, if any, between the experiences? which do you prefer?

- Recall your experience playing with the different game controllers in the library. How do you think the controller affects the games you would create for a platform, and how would it affect porting an existing game (it may be helpful to remember the cases where you saw/played the same game on different platforms), if at all?

- Read Chapter 2 of Maher's *The Future was Here: The Commodore Amiga* (MIT Press, 2012). Briefly summarize how the Amiga made *Boing* possible.

- This is the last homework exercise, and it's best done at the end of the course – note the late due date. I encourage you to think about it even if you don't need the marks.

  Do you have a different opinion of retrogames now than you did at the beginning of the course? If so, how?

C. LUDOGRAPHY

177. Macadamia Soft. PC-88 and Sharp X1, 1986.

Chase the Chuck Wagon. Spectravision. Atari 2600, 1983.

Custer's Revenge. Mystique. Atari 2600, 1983.

Leisure Suit Larry [in the Land of the Lounge Lizards]. Sierra On-Line. Various platforms, 1987.

Night Trap. Sega. Various platforms, 1992.

Zork [I]. Infocom. Various platforms, 1980.

D. REFERENCES

[1] S. Adams. Software updates: Courgette. `http://dev.chromium.org/developers/design-documents/software-updates-courgette`. Retrieved 13 August 2014.

[2] L. W. Anderson, D. R. Krathwohl, P. W. Airasian, K. A. Cruikshank, R. E. Mayer, P. R. Pintrich, J. Raths, and M. C. Wittrock, editors. *A taxonomy for learning, teaching, and assessing*. Longman, 2001.

[3] J. Aycock. *Retrogame archeology: Exploring old computer games*. Springer. To appear.

[4] M. S. Blank and S. W. Galley. How to fit a large program into a small machine. *Creative Computing*, 6(7):80–87, July 1980.

[5] B. Burns. Teaching the computer science of computer games. *Journal of Computing Sciences in Colleges*, 23(3):154–161, Jan. 2008.

[6] C. Collberg and J. Nagra. *Surreptitious software: Obfuscation, watermarking, and tamperproofing for software protection*. Addison-Wesley, 2010.

[7] G. M. Draper, R. R. Kessler, and R. F. Riesenfeld. A history of computing course with a technical focus. In *40th ACM Technical Symposium on Computer Science Education*, pages 458–462, 2009.

[8] C. Fernández-Vara. *Introduction to Game Analysis*. Routledge, 2014.

[9] T. Fullerton. *Game Design Workshop: A playcentric approach to creating innovative games*. CRC Press, 2nd edition, 2008.

[10] J. Impagliazzo, M. Campbell-Kelly, G. Davies, J. A. N. Lee, and M. R. Williams. History in the computing curriculum. *IEEE Annals of the History of Computing*, 21(1):4–16, 1999.

[11] Internet Archive. The console living room. `https://archive.org/details/consolelivingroom`. Last accessed 15 August 2014.

[12] Internet Archive. Internet Archive helps secure exemption to the Digital Millenium Copyright Act. `https://blog.archive.org/2006/11/29/internet-archive-helps-secure-exemption-to-the-digital-millennium-copyright-act/`, 29 November 2006.

[13] J. A. N. Lee. "Those who forget the lessons of history are doomed to repeat it" or, Why I study the history of computing. *IEEE Annals of the History of Computing*, 18(2):54–62, 1996.

[14] N. Montfort and I. Bogost. *Racing the Beam: The Atari video computer system*. MIT Press, 2009.

[15] H. Nakano, M. G. Styles, and G. M. Draper. A call for champions: Why some 'history of computing' courses are more successful than others. *ACM Inroads*, 4(1):26–28, Mar. 2013.

[16] J. Newman. *Videogames*. Routledge, 2nd edition, 2012.

[17] J. A. Rupf. Teaching the history of computing (painlessly). *Journal of Computing Sciences in Colleges*, 20(2):212–218, Dec. 2004.

[18] P. J. Schielke. Old hardware new students: Using old computing machinery in the modern classroom. *Journal of Computing Sciences in Colleges*, 29(4):74–79, Apr. 2014.

[19] SIMILE Widgets. Timeline: Web widget for visualizing temporal data (version 2.3.1). `http://www.simile-widgets.org/timeline/`. Last accessed 16 August 2014.

[20] Stella: A multi-platform Atari 2600 emulator. `http://stella.sourceforge.net/`. Last accessed 15 August 2014.

[21] I. Stravinsky. *Poetics of music in the form of six lessons*. Harvard University Press, 1970. Trans. A. Knodel and I. Dahl.

[22] J. Suominen. The past as the future? Nostalgia and retrogaming in digital culture. *Fibreculture Journal*, 11, 2008. Retrieved 14 August 2014.

[23] A. M. Turing. Computing machinery and intelligence. *Mind*, LIX(236):433–460, Oct. 1950.

Gender Gap in Academia: Perceptions of Female Computer Science Academics

Katrina Falkner
first.last@adelaide.edu.au
School of Computer Science
The University of Adelaide
Adelaide, South Australia,
Australia, 5005

Claudia Szabo
first.last@adelaide.edu.au
School of Computer Science
The University of Adelaide
Adelaide, South Australia,
Australia, 5005

Dee Michell   Anna Szorenyi   Shantel Thyer

first.last@adelaide.edu.au
Department of Gender Studies and Social Analysis
School of Social Sciences
The University of Adelaide
Adelaide, South Australia, Australia, 5005

ABSTRACT

Despite increased attention from Universities and Industry, the low representation of female students in Computer Science undergraduate degrees remains a major issue. Recognising this issue, leading tech companies have established strong and committed diversity initiatives but have only reached up to 17% female representation in their tech departments. The causes of the reduced attraction and retention of female students are varied and have been widely studied, advancing the understanding of why female students do not take up or leave Computer Science. However, few analyses look at the perceptions of the females that have stayed in the field. In this paper, we explore the viewpoints of female academics and postgraduate students in Computer Science with various undergraduate backgrounds and pathways into academia. Our analysis of their interviews shows the influence of family, exposure, culture, sexism and gendered thought on their perceptions of the field, and of themselves and their peers. We identify that perceptions of identity conflict and a lack of belonging to the discipline persist even for these high-performing professionals.

Categories and Subject Descriptors

K.3.2 [**Computing Milieux**]: Computers and Education-Computer and Information Science Education

Keywords

Computer Science Education, Gender Diversity

1. INTRODUCTION

The benefits of gender diversity in Computer Science have been intensely studied over the last decade [19]. Existing studies show that a diverse company fares better financially and is more innovative: companies with at least three women serving on the board of directors had, in 2007, a 16% return on equity, as opposed to an average 11.5%; return on sales was 16.8%, as opposed to an average of 11.5% [13]. The presence of women in a team has been shown to be the major predictor of team intelligence, with the teams that scored highest on team intelligence tests having 50% women [28]. However, despite this recognition, and of significant recent efforts in changing curricula [14] and addressing stereotypes [24, 16], the underrepresentation of women in Computer Science still remains a crucial problem.

Currently, about 20% of Computer Science (CS) faculty in the US are female [30]. Top IT companies report lower percentages of women in their tech staff, with Apple reporting 20% [1], Google 17% [11], and Facebook 15% [8]. Many reasons have been identified for female students not picking up CS or for their leaving CS careers once employed. A plethora of studies analyse these issues in detail, including the perception of CS as a male dominated field [16, 25], the lack of identification with the 'geek' stereotype [16], self-efficacy [7], and the lack of organisational support [20].

In this paper, we explore the thoughts and perceptions of high-performing women who have stayed in Computer Science academia, with the aim of identifying the support, family and societal structures, and personal strategies that have allowed them to become successful despite the barriers identified above. The women who are currently working in CS academia are a highly accomplished group who have already survived a series of selections: self-selection following self-efficacy issues as above, unconscious bias and stereotype threat [19], as well as selection from educational and employing institutions. Our analysis of interviews with Computer Science academics and PhD students identifies the influence of family, exposure and culture on the perception that these accomplished Computer Scientists have of the field of Computer Science, and of themselves within the field.

We identify that gender-specific issues relating to the view of who a Computer Scientist *is* persist, and that within this high-performing cohort, concerns over not belonging and fraudulence remain, with stereotypical images of the discipline continuing to define how we see ourselves.

2. RELATED WORK

A large number of studies exist in the literature that focus on the reasons why female students do not take up or leave Computer Science [16, 17, 23]. These reasons include, among others, the perception of CS as a male dominated field [16, 17, 21], the lack of female role models [17, 16], (lack of) exposure to computers early in life [16], media and societal portrayal of CS as a male profession [16, 25], the lack of identification with the 'geek' stereotype [5, 16, 17], and the perception of interest in computers as negative among others. Another key factor is self-efficacy, with studies showing that female students consistently think of themselves as less competent than their male counterparts, despite equal or superior academic performance [18, 27], resulting in a negative perception of CS and computers, and of endorsing and strengthening the stereotype that men are "just better" at CS than women [16, 27].

Self-efficacy, defined as the extent or strength in an individual's beliefs in their capability of successfully completing a task and goal [2] has been shown to contribute to perceptions of career-efficacy in CS and thus to the reasons why female students do not take up or leave Computer Science [15, 17, 21]. Some studies show that females attribute their CS success to chance and hard work; women in CS attribute failure to (unchangeable) inability [16], and take personal responsibility for their failures [16]. Seymour and Hewitt [23] identified a process of discouragement, in which female students consistently doubt their abilities, have a reduced capacity to deal with set-backs and are significantly more dependant on reassurance from peers and lecturers. Moreover, some studies suggest that the perception of self-efficacy decreases over time [27], implying that female CS graduates might end up being less confident of their abilities when they graduate than when they started their CS degree. These symptoms are similar to impostor syndrome, in which individuals feel fraudulent despite being successful in their career or their tasks [10]. Individuals with impostor syndrome will attribute their success to luck, compensatory hard work, and external factors such as physical attractiveness or likeability [6, 10]. They are also highly sensitive to failures in tasks, especially in the case when peers, family and superiors have been consistently praising them: the presence of failure implies that they are not as good as suggested by the praise, therefore invalidating the praise and endorsing the feelings of fraudulence [6].

Few studies have focused on women pursuing an academic career in Computer Science, and thus we include here studies that focus on engineering and science. Among the top 100 US Universities, only 8.8-15.8% of tenure-track positions in math intensive fields are held by women, with full professor positions in engineering only held by less than 5% female [4]. Studies show that the causes of such disparities are numerous and subtle. Valian [26] finds that two concepts drive the disparity between women and men's careers in sciences: gender schemas and accumulation of advantages. Gender schemas are implicit or individual factors that affect males in academia (e.g., unintentional biases, outmoded institu-tional structures [20]), which lead to males accumulating small advantages that lead to bigger gains. Other studies show that 52% of women in Sciences would leave their jobs at a critical 'fight or flight' moments, and most women that leave academic careers have cited institutional blockage (tenure clock vs biological clock) and gender separation of labor (e.g., women being assigned more teaching) [12].

Fox [9] identifies key social-organizational factors that influence women's progress in academic careers: frequency of talking to faculty about research, ratings of aspects and positions within the department, the department climate, and the levels of interference of family issues on work. The analysis shows that 44% of the interviewed women academics spoke less than weekly about research with people in their faculty, and that women report a significantly lower sense of inclusion, belonging, and recognition received from faculty.

3. METHODOLOGY

In this paper, we undertake a quantitative and qualitative analysis of interviews with female postgraduate students and academics within Computer Science, in order to explore their key perception of gender in relation to their discipline, and their experiences of gender and gender-bias in their transition from student to expert in their field. We explore the identification of their gendered perceptions, including the analysis of the impact of societal, family and peer pressures on their development as Computer Scientists, and their identification as Computer Scientists. The research questions that we ask are: (i) *how do these women see gender as an influence on their perception of Computer Science as a discipline, and on their identity as Computer Scientists?* and (ii) *how have their interactions with society, family and their peers influenced their choices?*.

3.1 Research Method

An instrumental case study is a suitable approach for answering our research question as it allows us to use a particular case as an illustration to identify and elaborate on the perception of gender in relation to Computer Science. Case studies capture the complexities of a phenomenon; such detailed observations cannot be captured in surveys or experimental designs [22]. A typical interview cohort consists of 10-15 participants, to support deep analysis of variation of experience and understanding [3].

This project has adopted a mixed-method case study design where both quantitative and qualitative data were collected. The data were subjected to grounded theory analysis, starting with a process of open coding, before proceeding to axial coding. Grounded theory involves the establishment of a coding framework and analysis environment derived from the data itself. Grounded theory differs from other types of qualitative analysis in that a specific, structured coding framework is not employed. The first stage in grounded theory development is open coding, where the data is broken down into distinct segments in order to obtain the full collection of ideas and concepts present in the data, without regard to how it will be used. Subsequently, axial coding is employed, where the coding framework developed during the open coding stage is refined and reorganised into specific categories, informed by theoretical frameworks and comparison within the data. There are significant advantages in the adoption of a grounded theory approach, in contrast to directed content analysis with an established coding framework, including removing the potential to force fit observations into existing categories and misclassification.

In our project, we undertook a pilot stage refining an initial set of interview questions derived from the literature, before conducting a series of in-depth semi-structured interviews with our participant cohort. Participants were sought from current female postgraduate students and current female academics within a School of Computer Science, with 12 participants agreeing to participate in interviews of approximately 1 hour in duration. The participants represented a diverse cross section in terms of background, with all but two having completed their undergraduate studies at different institutions, representing a combination of 7 different countries. We refer to all as female academics in the following, with the understanding that the term captures both females who are appointed as academics and those that are on an academic track, pursuing postgraduate studies.

Each interview followed a distinct question sequence, interspersed with relevant follow up questions designed to allow the participants to share their experiences of gender and gendered thought in their perception of Computer Science as a discipline. The questions were deliberately open ended, and asked participants to share their perceptions, and the key influences and reactions from their support groups.

1. What is your area of expertise in CS?

2. What was your perception of CS and ICT before you chose to focus your study in this area?

3. What influenced you to choose the area of CS/ICT to pursue your study?

4. What were your friends and families reaction to you pursuing this area of study?

5. What are the advantages/disadvantages of being in a minority group whilst studying this degree?

6. In what ways do you think CS can improve in order to attract more women into this area?

7. What would you want to say to young women who are considering a career in CS?

8. In what ways has the degree lived up/failed to meet your expectations?

9. Where do you see your future in CS?

The basic unit of analysis in this project was coding units [29], including sections of text responses, of any size. Within the open coding stage, sections of text, such as a sentence, word or phrase, were coded while the selection represented a single idea or concept related to gender and perceptions of gender. In excess of 500 individual interview responses from 12 participant interviews were coded using the qualitative software NVivo (version 10) defining an initial set of 27 distinct codes. The researcher methodically worked through the student reflections, coding their observations either to existing nodes within the framework or to a newly created node, identifying a description of the newly created node and exemplar. During the axial coding state, the researcher worked in collaboration with the project team to iteratively refine the established codes into categories, merging codes where appropriate and in agreement, and identifying discipline-specific categories as derived from the data.

4. QUANTITATIVE ANALYSIS

In their discussions relating to their perceptions and experiences of Computer Science, and the origins of their perceptions, our participants identified several areas associated with gender. Further, the interview participants identified strategies that they felt could act to negate or obviate current negative experiences (total count = 49).

Interview participants identified both positive and negative associations with gender in their perceptions of Computer Science both as a discipline in general and as their discipline of choice, although with a stronger emphasis in the discussion on negative associations. Participants identified positive experiences or beliefs (Table 1) that promoted their sense of belonging within the field, typically associated with their natural talents for STEM (associating with Computer Science or Mathematics specifically), or an interest in creative problem solving. Participants identified experiences or perceptions of positive gendered thought associated within their position in the discipline, typically associated with benefits that they perceived were a natural consequence of their gender, for example, stereotypical beliefs that women were specifically well suited to specific roles needed within the discipline, or benefits in terms of supportive roles they played within discipline teams. The interview participants further identified the crucial nature of external sources of support in their decision to pursue Computer Science as their discipline, with a stronger emphasis on family support.

Table 1: Positive experiences of gender association (total count = 95).

Category	Freq	%Freq
Sense of Belonging	*30*	*31.58%*
Natural Fit	20	21.05%
Excellence	7	7.37%
Respect	3	3.16%
Gendered Thought	*24*	*25.26%*
Positive Support	*20*	*21.05%*
Positive Family Support	12	12.63%
Positive Societal Support	8	8.42%
Increased Confidence	*1*	*1.05%*

With the majority of gender associations identified as negative, Table 2 presents a broader and deeper range of experiences or perceptions suggested by the participants. Within the negative context, gendered thought appears as a dominant factor, where participants were freely identifying multiple examples of negatively-associated gendered perceptions of ability within Computer Science, or aptitude for STEM as general area. Participants clearly identified the *lack of a sense of belonging* as a negative experience - in their negative discussions of this category, participants primarily discussed specific examples of feeling isolated, or at odds with what their perceptions of a Computer Scientist should be or act like. They reported experiences or perceptions where they indicated a sense of fraudulence - where they were not really acting as a Computer Scientist should, or not achieving results similar to their male counterparts - a surprising emphasis given the highly competent and successful nature of the interview participants, however consistent with previous studies on imposter syndrome [10].

Table 2: Negative experiences of gender association (total count = 204).

Category	Freq	%Freq
Gendered Thought	57	27.94%
Sense of Not Belonging	57	27.94%
Identity Conflict	35	17.16%
Fraudulance	19	9.31%
Unnatural Fit	3	1.47%
Negative Support	41	20.10%
Sexism	20	9.80%
Negative Societal Support	15	7.35%
Negative Family Support	6	2.94%
Perception of Challenge	24	11.76%
Gender Imbalance	19	9.31%
Lack of Confidence	6	2.94%

Negative support was also a significant contributing category in the interview discussions, including explicit identification of sexism or sexist behaviour within the field, and negative feedback or messages from their society and their families. Participants discussed Computer Science as a field with many challenges, and clearly identified gender imbalance as a significant and visible issue.

5. QUALITATIVE ANALYSIS

5.1 Influence and Support

The interviewed academics identified a range of positive family and societal support that allowed them to pursue a career in Computer Science. Participants reported that it was the economic benefit of the field that drove their families in supporting or encouraging them to become Computer Scientists. Careers in Computer Science are seen as "good jobs", with a "good future" and thus parents strongly encourage their daughters to pursue them:

> "My parents choose this topic for me, because it was very hard, and they knew that I could get a good job out of this."

Another driver for the positive family support is the perceived novelty and value of technology; however, specific benefits of technology are not identified nor used as drivers for support. One participant notes:

> "(my father) thought this was the thing to do. He could see this was an excellent area for future development."

while another observes:

> "My parents are from the commerce side, but they are very interested in the new technological things."

Computer Science is similarly perceived in society as a "good" career to be in, as a participant notes:

> "They see IT as an excellent path for anyone to go into; engineering and IT are definitely seen as being a good career to be in."

It is important to highlight that the drivers for positive support to pursue a Computer Science career are very broad, and are focused on the perceived economic benefits or the novelty of ICT. In contrast, the discouragement received by participants is gender specific, with family or society perceiving that Computer Science is either not a suitable career for a female, or that other, more suitable careers, such as teachers or doctors, exist:

> "My parents wanted me to do something like physics, and they wanted me to become a teacher."

or, as another participant notes,

> "My mother was very keen on me doing medicine, she thought that was a good job for a girl."

In other cases, the negative support is focused on ensuring that females focus on building a family and a home, at the expense of building a career:

> "There is still an attitude with many societies, that women stay at home."

Moreover, the simplified perception of Computer Scientists does not match traditional gendered expectations:

> "you are expected to get married, not sit in front of a computer."

There is also a conflict between work-life balance in an academic career and the various family-building pressures:

> "My parents are still not happy. Because I will be doing research for 5-10 years and only work on that. They would like me to get married, have children."

5.2 Identity and Sense of Belonging

We found a similar contrast when looking at positive and negative identification with Computer Science, in that the positive association with Computer Science was typically very broad, whereas the negative associations are generally Computer Science specific and more gendered. The ability to perform well in Maths and STEM disciplines in high-school was perceived by many as one of the main positive association points with Computer Science, as one participant notes:

> "I was good at maths, I have always been good at maths."

For another participant, there is a sense of pride associated with being good at a difficult subject such as mathematics:

> "I liked mathematics, so computer sciences has a good relationship with the mathematics background so I was rather interested in the theoretically side of computer science. That is the reason I chose computer science, because it is like a realisation of mathematics (...) the mathematics stream is very hard. It is difficult to get in."

The negative associations to Computer Science focus on perceived gender-specific traits that are seen as incompatible with the Computer Scientist identity. These include working with people, the perceived lack of coding skills in females, but also the way the Computer Science field views female interests. One participant notes that her desire to communicate and interact is incompatible with the Computer Science identity:

> "I like working with people. That's a disadvantage for me with Computer Science."

For another participant, this gendered perception of women as good communicators has undesired outcomes:

> "The assumption was that women are good at customer service, with me being more technical though, I seemed to be pushed into areas I didn't want to pursue."

The perception that female-associated traits or desires are not suitable to Computer Science extends beyond communication and working collaboratively:

> "The things that attract women are seen as lesser (...) What I see is engineers putting down 'Human Factors'. One of the greatest challenges is touch screen, how we use things, but its put down as less important than say networking or operating systems."

In some cases the participant herself suggests that females are in general not technically skilled, but that regardless there are opportunities within the field even for them:

> "It's probably best to attract people who are technically skilled. Trying to attract people who are not good at that area, is really not a good idea. I suppose to attract more women, you have to inform them about what computer science actually is, it's more than technical there are a whole range of different activities within Computer Science you can be part of."

The above stereotypical views of Computer Science and of the 'geek' or CS identity imply that these accomplished Computer Scientists will always view themselves as outsiders, both through their own thoughts, but also through the actions of others. The Computer Scientist who knows she is technically skilled will not belong in the group of other female Computer Scientists, by default perceived as having less skills; the communicator who likes to work in large projects does not feel accepted by what she perceives is the Computer Science culture; the human factors researcher feels that her work is not important and not accepted by the community because it is not 'geeky' enough.

5.3 Imposter Behaviours

The lack of a sense of belonging and of a positive identification with Computer Science also leads to imposter behaviours, with 67% of participants reporting feelings of fraudulence. In some cases, the imposter thoughts are gendered:

> "The girls are always doing documentation you have nothing to do with the implementation. You just write things. The boys do things quicker than us."

Another participant's imposter thoughts are focused on the need for persistence, hard work, and luck to have a successful career:

> "Don't be afraid of the competency of the men, because sometimes you can think better than the men. I think if you persist you will have a good future, you are the minority group and sometimes they want the females."

whereas another participant focussed on likeability as a key to success:

> "I think the best part is that you are always a princess. It is very simple to communicate with a male, and they like to help you. It is a very good atmosphere."

Around 40% of participants reported on the need of flawless excellence to either succeed or to feel that they belong:

> "I think, it is similar in other fields that women are not always as powerful than men, unless they are very excellent they cannot achieve that level."

6. DISCUSSION

An identity for Computer Scientists that is at odds with how women see themselves presents a significant problem for our discipline. Research has demonstrated that lack of alignment with stereotypes - the image of the discipline - can have a significant, negative impact on recruitment strategies [5], despite gender. Specifically, women and men who embody the stereotype of our discipline may struggle to recruit those that see themselves as *other*. However, with promise, research has also indicated that offering a different image of a group that is a better fit, or more closely aligned with self image, may encourage others to consider themselves becoming part of the group.

While the participants in our study were aware, in general, of the gender imbalance within the field before entering it, they did not see this as a significant issue. They had confidence in their abilities, stemming from their capability in related STEM areas, and fostered by family support associated with financial and stability means. However, their experiences within the discipline have resulted in the development of a clear identify of the discipline that does not represent who they are. This result demonstrates that our embodiment of stereotype, in many cases associated with gender, associated with our discipline is not just an external perception, but is a present and clear issue *within* our discipline.

In our interviews, we asked participants to identify what they saw as possible strategies to address these concerns. In addition to expected commentary regarding recruitment and mentoring opportunities - of which we are supportive - participants consistently identified the lack of a clear identity as a concern. The most prevalent focus in the discussion of strategies, identified by 80% of the participants, was on defining and effectively communicating what Computer Science is. The main points identified as part of a Computer Science identity are problem solving, and the fact that it is more than 'technical' coding. One participant notes:

> "I suppose to attract more women, you have to inform them about what Computer Science actually is, it's more than technical"

This lack of a clear, positive message from our discipline has resulted, in their perception, in continued attention to negative, media-driven stereotypes. This represents a further call for action to challenge, both without and within our discipline, the image of our discipline, and behaviour within our own environments that narrows our perceptions of who we are.

7. CONCLUSION

In this paper, we have presented the analysis of interviews with a range of female academics and near academics in Computer Science, identifying persistent gendered perceptions of their discipline and their place within the discipline. We have identified that although confident in their general capabilities in STEM, lack of confidence in their specific abilities within Computer Science pervades, and that the image or sense of identity of what it means to be a computer scientist conflicts with how these women see themselves.

8. REFERENCES

[1] Apple, Inc. Inclusion inspires innovation. https://www.apple.com/diversity/, 2015. Last accessed January 2015.

[2] A. Bandura. *Self-efficacy*. Wiley Online Library, 1994.

[3] A. Berglund and M. Wiggberg. Students learn cs in different ways: Insights from a empirical study. In *Proceedings of iTiCSE'06*, pages 265–269, 2006.

[4] S. J. Ceci and W. M. Williams. Sex differences in math-intensive fields. *Current Directions in Psychological Science*, page 0963721410383241, 2010.

[5] S. Cheryan, V. C. Plaut, P. G. Davies, and C. M. Steele. Ambient belonging: how stereotypical cues impact gender participation in computer science. *Journal of personality and social psychology*, 97(6):1045, 2009.

[6] P. R. Clance and S. A. Imes. The imposter phenomenon in high achieving women: Dynamics and therapeutic intervention. *Psychotherapy: Theory, Research & Practice*, 15(3):241, 1978.

[7] J. S. Eccles, A. Wigfield, and U. Schiefele. Motivation to succeed. 1998.

[8] Facebook, Inc. Building a more diverse facebook. http://newsroom.fb.com/news/2014/06/building-a-more-diverse-facebook/, 2015. Last accessed January 2015.

[9] M. F. Fox. Women and men faculty in academic science and engineering: Social-organizational indicators and implications. *American Behavioral Scientist*, 53(7):997–1012, 2010.

[10] H. K. Gediman. Imposture, inauthenticity, and feeling fraudulent. *Journal of the American Psychoanalytic Association*, 1985.

[11] Google, Inc. Our workforce demographics. http://www.google.com.au/diversity/at-google.html#tab=tech, 2015. Last accessed January 2015.

[12] S. A. Hewlett et al. *The Athena factor: Reversing the brain drain in science, engineering, and technology*. Harvard Business School Watertown, MA, 2008.

[13] L. Joy, N. M. Carter, H. M. Wagner, and S. Narayanan. The bottom line: Corporate performance and womenâĂŹs representation on boards. *Catalyst*, 3, 2007.

[14] M. Klawe, T. Whitney, and C. Simard. Women in computing—take 2. *Communications of the ACM*, 52(2):68–76, 2009.

[15] S. Lewis, C. Lang, and J. McKay. An inconvenient truth: The invisibility of women in ict. *Australasian Journal of Information Systems*, 15(1), 2008.

[16] J. Margolis and A. Fisher. *Unlocking the clubhouse: Women in computing*. MIT press, 2003.

[17] I. Miliszewska, G. Barker, F. Henderson, and E. Sztendur. The issue of gender equity in computer science–what students say. *Journal of Information Technology Education: Research*, 5(1):107–120, 2006.

[18] P. Moorman and E. Johnson. Still a stranger here: Attitudes among secondary school students towards computer science. In *ACM SIGCSE Bulletin*, volume 35, pages 193–197. ACM, 2003.

[19] B. Nelson. The data on diversity. *Communications of the ACM*, 57(11):86–95, 2014.

[20] C. on Maximizing the Potential of Women in Academic Science, E. (US), C. on Science, and P. P. (US). *Beyond bias and barriers: fulfilling the potential of women in academic science and engineering*. Natl Academy Pr, 2007.

[21] M. R. Roberts, T. J. McGill, and P. N. Hyland. Attrition from australian ict degrees: why women leave. In *Proceedings of the Fourteenth Australasian Computing Education Conference-Volume 123*, pages 15–24. Australian Computer Society, Inc., 2012.

[22] M. Sandelowski. Sample size in qualitative research. *Research in Nursing & Health*, 18(2):179–183, 1995.

[23] E. Seymour and N. M. Hewitt. *Talking about leaving: Why undergraduates leave the sciences*, volume 12. Westview Press Boulder, CO, 1997.

[24] C. M. Steele. Whistling vivaldi: And other clues to how stereotypes affect us (issues of our time) author: Claude m. steele, publisher. 2010.

[25] E. M. Trauth, S. Nielsen, and L. Von Hellens. Explaining the it gender gap: Australian stories for the new millennium. *Journal of research and practice in information technology*, 35(1):7–20, 2003.

[26] V. Valian. *Why so slow?: The advancement of women*. MIT press, 1999.

[27] M. Volman and E. van Eck. Gender equity and information technology in education: The second decade. *Review of Educational Research*, 71(4):613–634, 2001.

[28] A. W. Woolley, C. F. Chabris, A. Pentland, N. Hashmi, and T. W. Malone. Evidence for a collective intelligence factor in the performance of human groups. *Science*, 330(6004):686–688, 2010.

[29] Y. Zhang and B. Wildemuth. *Application of social research methods to questions in information and library science*, chapter Qualitative analysis of content, pages 308–319. Westport Conn: Libraries Unlimited, 2009.

[30] S. Zweben and B. Bizot. 2013 taulbee survey. *COMPUTING*, 26(5), 2014.

Gender Differences in Factors Influencing Pursuit of Computer Science and Related Fields

Jennifer Wang
Google Inc.
1600 Amphitheatre Pkwy
Mountain View, CA 94043
+1-310-866-3258
jennifertwang@google.com

Hai Hong
Google Inc.
1600 Amphitheatre Pkwy
Mountain View, CA 94043
+1-310-866-3258
haihong@google.com

Jason Ravitz
Google Inc.
1600 Amphitheatre Pkwy
Mountain View, CA 94043
+1-310-866-3258
ravitz@google.com

Marielena Ivory
Google Inc.
1600 Amphitheatre Pkwy
Mountain View, CA 94043
+1-310-866-3258
mivory@google.com

ABSTRACT

Increasing women's participation in computer science is a critical workforce and equity concern. The technology industry has committed to reversing negative trends for women in computer science as well as engineering and information technology "computing" fields. Building on previously published research, this paper identifies factors that influence young women's decisions to pursue computer science-related degrees and the ways in which these factors differ for young men. It is based on a survey of 1,739 high school students and recent college graduates. Results identified encouragement and exposure as the leading factors influencing this critical choice for women, while the influence of these factors is different for men. In particular, the influence of family is found to play a critical role in encouragement and exposure, and outreach efforts should focus on ways to engage parents.

Categories and Subject Descriptors

K.3.2 [**Computers and Education**]: Computer and Information Science Education – *computer science education.*

Keywords

Gender differences; factors; high school; college; encouragement, perceptions; self-confidence; K-12 education.

1. INTRODUCTION

Previous studies that examined the factors that motivate students to pursue studies or careers in technology typically: 1) had small sample sizes, 2) were conducted with students from a particular institution or geographic region, and 3) measured 2-3 independent variables. Our study: 1) surveyed 1,739 young men and women, 2) used a nationally-representative population, 3) considered 91 variables identified in the literature, 4) grouped these into factor scores, and 5) controlled for all significant variables in our analysis. Our analyses allowed us to rank the influence of each variable on young women's decisions to study computer science (CS), along with engineering or information technology (IT) fields. Social encouragement was determined to be one of the most powerful influencers on the decision to pursue these fields—considerably stronger for women than for men. This paper focuses specifically on gender differences in the way such factors influence the decision to pursue computing and related fields.

ITICSE '15, Jul 04-08, 2015, Vilnius, Lithuania
ACM 978-1-4503-3440-2/15/07.
http://dx.doi.org/10.1145/2729094.2742611

2. RELEVANCE

According to the National Science Foundation [16] Science and Engineering Indicators, women make up only 26% of Computer Science and Mathematical Science professionals in the United States. These numbers are even more stark when considering that while degree conferment for the proportion of women in science, technology, engineering and mathematics (STEM) is trending upward, the proportion of women in computer science, specifically, has declined to 18% from a 37% peak in the mid-1980s [17]. In addition to issues related to equity and workplace diversity, the lack of female participation in computer science exacerbates a problem with labor supply shortages: the overall need for computing professionals has severely outstripped the number of graduates entering the workforce [16]. Moreover, evidence has shown that more diverse teams produce better products. Page [19], for example, found that when solving complex problems, diversity of skills, perspectives, and abilities leads to a better outcome. This has further motivated industry to officially address its lack of diversity.

A wealth of research has investigated factors that influence girls' interest in STEM and CS (e.g., [8,11]). Studies on gender differences showed that women more often ranked their most important life goal as "helping other people" [3], which may be an important influence for girls. Societal influences include a lack of female STEM characters in television and pop culture [2], negative stereotypes about girls' abilities, and negative perceptions about computing as a course of study or career option (e.g., [4]). Parental encouragement to study science and mathematics increases the likelihood of a young adult pursuing [7] and persisting in STEM careers [6]. However, parents' evaluation of their children's abilities differs by gender—in particular, this translates to differences by child gender in parents' perceptions and encouragement of their child's interest in STEM fields (e.g., [5]). Families purchase more STEM games or manipulative materials for boys than for girls [13], and parents of boys believe that their children like science more than parents of girls, more often overestimating their child's science ability than do parents of girls [5].

Girls can develop more positive perceptions of CS-related fields if they receive encouragement at home [12,15]. In a survey of scientists, Sonnert [21] found that women were more likely than men to mention a parent as an influencer, and that fathers were more often cited as influencers than mothers were.

3. DATA SOURCES

To ensure a statistically relevant study with a high level of confidence (95% or better) and a small margin of error (5% or less), 1090 young women and 649 young men were surveyed in accordance with the following:

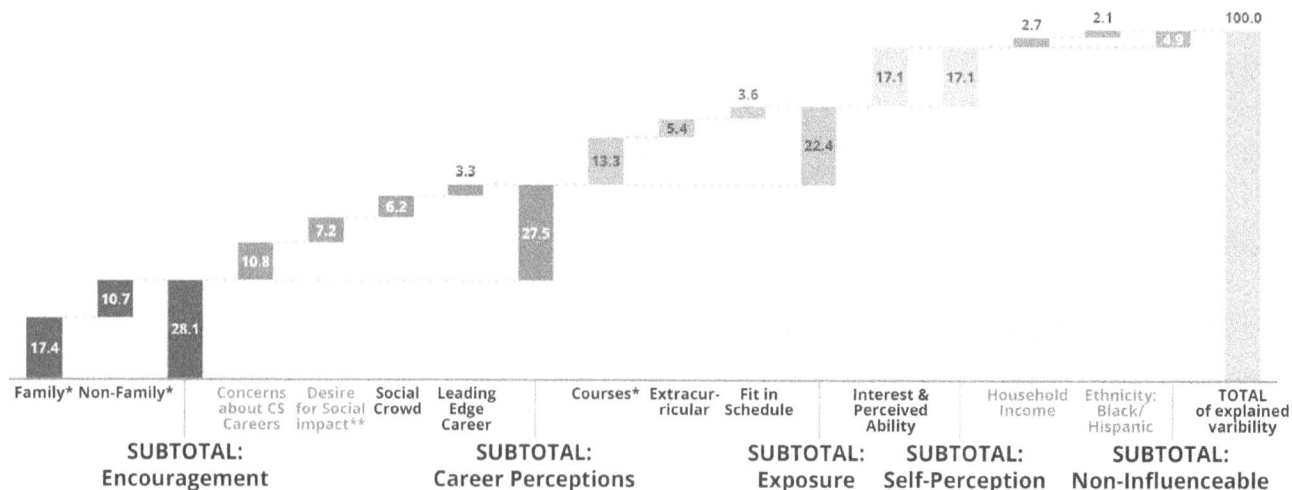

Figure 1. High school model for percentage contribution of factors influencing a girl's choice to study computer science and related fields (n = 527, Pseudo-R2 = 60.5%, * significantly more influential for girls than boys, ** significantly more influential for boys than girls).

- Geographically and academically diverse, across the US
- 50% high school, 50% recent college graduates
- 50% interested in or had studied a computing-related field

4. METHODS

As a first step, we reviewed existing studies in order to: a) determine a comprehensive set of influencing variables, b) identify strengths and limitations and incorporate best practices from previous studies, and c) refine our study's hypothesis around influencing variables. Our review resulted in 91 statistically relevant variables with the potential to influence a decision to pursue a computer science or related mathematics, IT or engineering degree.

The survey was developed to measure the 91 variables' influence on the dependent variable: interest in studying CS and related fields or not. The survey was given online to participants.

Participants were initially recruited via Research Now and their partners' panels of high school juniors and seniors and recent college graduates. To supplement low response rates on the panels (< 5%), particularly from high schoolers and men, river sampling was used to solicit participants via online banner ads with incentives and snowball referrals with small monetary incentives were used by asking respondents to refer others, particularly computer science women. Women and those interested in or who had studied computer science were oversampled for this study. To obtain a nationally-representative sample, quotas for age and gender were used and data on ethnicity and geographical region were weighted after data collection.

Using factor analysis [10], all 91 variables were combined into 25 factors used concurrently to control for highly correlated variables. To control for related influences and fairly evaluate competing factors, the survey results were analyzed using logit regression—a form of statistical modeling used to predict binary outcomes [1]. We used logit regression to rate the importance of factors in predicting interest in pursuing the computing-related fields. We used this analysis to measure the strength of the relationship between dependent variables (wanting to pursue a CS-related degree) and independent variables (e.g., the life experiences and opportunities that may lead to that choice).

5. RESULTS

Results suggest the high school model for girls' influencers has a very high Pseudo-R2, as shown in Figure 1. The influencing

factors contribute to 60.5% of the dependent variable—an exceptionally high score that translates to reasonably accurate influence modeling. Our study found that encouragement and exposure are key controllable indicators for whether or not young women decide to pursue a computing-related degree. The top four influencing factors for young women—and notable gender differences related to these factors—were as follows:

5.1 Social Encouragement

Social encouragement includes positive reinforcement from family, teachers, and peers, and for the high school model, comprises 28.1% of the explainable factors influencing a young woman's wanting to pursue a computing-related degree. Encountering this encouragement in an extracurricular setting also has a large impact. Our findings suggest encouragement from non-family (11%) is almost as important as familial support (17%) for young women (see Figure 2). Overall, encouragement from family (parents and siblings) as well as from non-family (teachers, role models, peers, and media) contributed significantly more to girls' decisions to pursue a computing-related degree when compared to boys.

Figure 3 shows that, across the various types of social encouragement, CS girls were most likely to be encouraged by their mother, father, sibling, teacher, or friends and peers. On the other hand, non-CS girls were least likely to receive encouragement from all except their teacher. And, of particular note is the discrepancy within genders: the discrepancy between encouragement received for CS girls and for non-CS girls was much larger compared to the discrepancy between encouragement for CS boys and for non-CS boys. In other words, of those who were not interested in CS-related fields, boys were more likely to be encouraged while of those who were interested in CS-related fields, girls were more likely to be encouraged.

For both the high school and the college model, the occupation of parents was statistically insignificant when controlling for other variables. Although parents with computing backgrounds may offer more encouragement, what seems to matter most is encouragement, not whether this encouragement was from someone with technical expertise. This is particularly important since even though encouragement is much more important to young women than to young men (Figure 2), young women are less likely than young men to receive that encouragement (in any form). Furthermore, while encouragement from family is the most

High school model

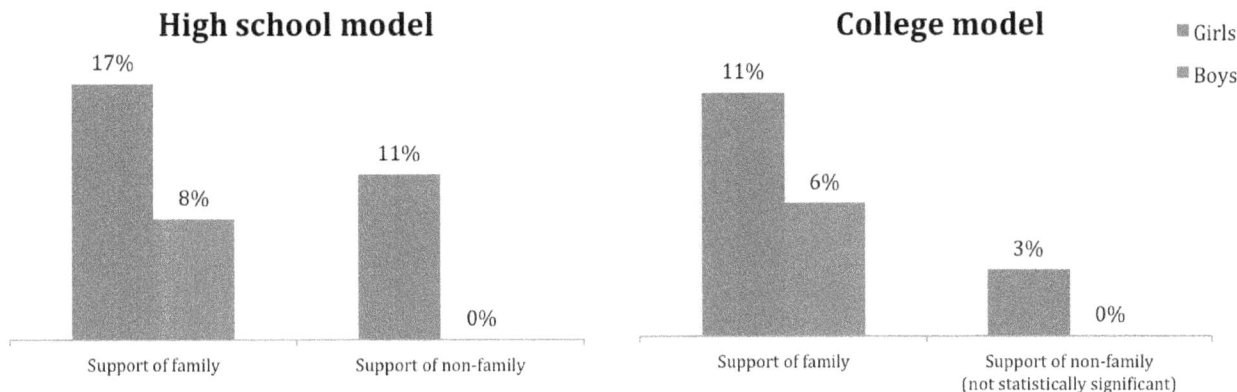

17%

8%

11%

0%

Support of family   Support of non-family

College model

■ Girls

■ Boys

11%

6%

3%

0%

Support of family   Support of non-family
(not statistically significant)

Figure 2. Total percentage contribution to choosing to study computer science of the variables support of family and support of non-family for males and females (n = 846 for high school and n = 893 for college, Nagelkerke R^2 = 56.8%).

influential variable overall and is more important for young women than for young men (17% vs. 8%), there is an even larger discrepancy in the influence of encouragement received from non-family members (11% for females vs. 0% for males; Figure 2).

Figure 4 shows the differences in parent encouragement received for both women and men college graduates. Not surprisingly, most CS graduates received encouragement from parents. However, of the non-CS graduates, only 12% of women vs. 21% of men received encouragement from mothers, and similarly, only 19% of women vs. 30% of men received encouragement from fathers. As discussed above for high school students, similar discrepancies were found for those not interested in computer science and related fields. Thus, of those interested in CS, more girls are encouraged than boys while of those not interested in CS, more boys are encouraged than girls, and our analyses show that encouragement is a highly influential factor for girls (Figure 1).

The major takeaway is that efforts to increase girls' interest in computing should include a parent education component, so that they know how to actively encourage their daughters. Parents who are not in technology fields need to know that their words and actions have an impact, and should feel confident encouraging their daughters to try out computing.

5.2 Career Perceptions

Another key finding concerns the familiarity with and perception of computing as having diverse applications and a broad potential for positive societal impact. At 27.5%, a high school girl's perception of computer science and its associated careers is the second most potent explainable factor influencing the pursuit of a computer science degree.

Specifically, interest in a career with social impact was negatively influential for both boys and girls, but significantly more influential for boys than girls at the pre-college level. This

means that boys are significantly more likely to not want to study CS-related fields than girls if they were interested in a career with social impact. On the other hand, the social crowd in CS courses was significant only for girls, steering girls away from CS if the social crowd was not like them. And, of the college graduates population, 44% of young women who majored in computer science believed that first year computer science courses were geared towards male interests.

Furthermore, perceptions from role models is a much stronger influencer for women than for men, as shown in Figure 5. Of the college graduates, more women CS majors strongly agree that "Role models gave me a good impression of CS" than men CS majors. On the other hand, many more women non-CS majors strongly disagreed with the statement, even compared to men non-CS majors. Thus, women may be more strongly impacted than men by role models in the field.

The negative potential associated with flawed or incomplete career perceptions is twofold: 1) not understanding computing fields makes an informed decision more difficult and, 2) an incomplete perception of the discipline actively dissuades young women from considering it. The end result is that young women unfamiliar with computer science and its broad applications have difficulty visualizing it outside the narrow scope often presented in popular media. They may be unable to perceive computer science-related careers as fulfilling both the academic passion (inventing, problem solving, exploration, etc.) and the intangible,

Encouragement

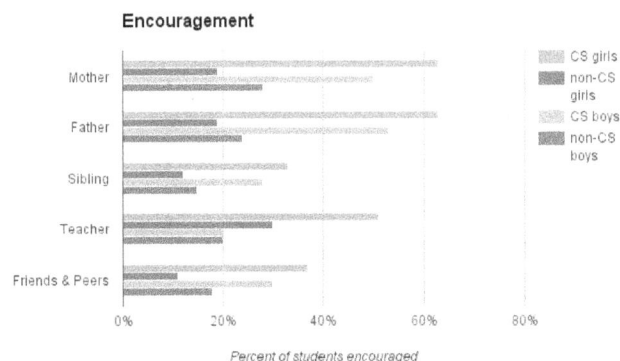

Mother

Father

Sibling

Teacher

Friends & Peers

0%   20%   40%   60%   80%

CS girls
non-CS girls
CS boys
non-CS boys

Percent of students encouraged

Figure 3. Percent of high school students encouraged, by gender and interest in CS-related fields (n = 846).

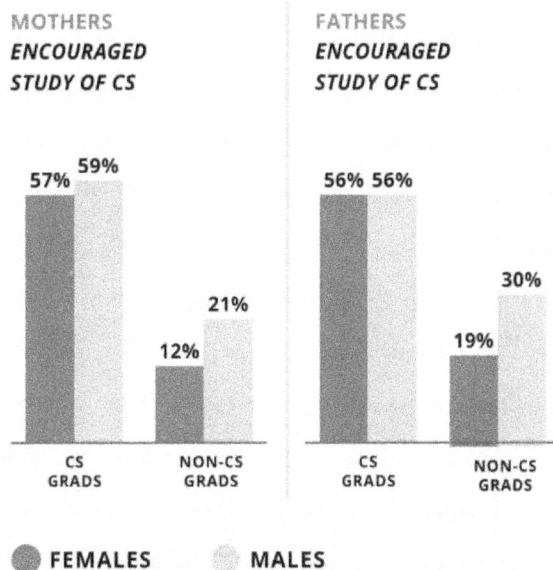

MOTHERS
ENCOURAGED STUDY OF CS

FATHERS
ENCOURAGED STUDY OF CS

57% 59%

12% 21%

56% 56%

19% 30%

CS GRADS   NON-CS GRADS   CS GRADS   NON-CS GRADS

● FEMALES   MALES

Figure 4. Percent of college grads whose parents encouraged study of computer science (n = 893).

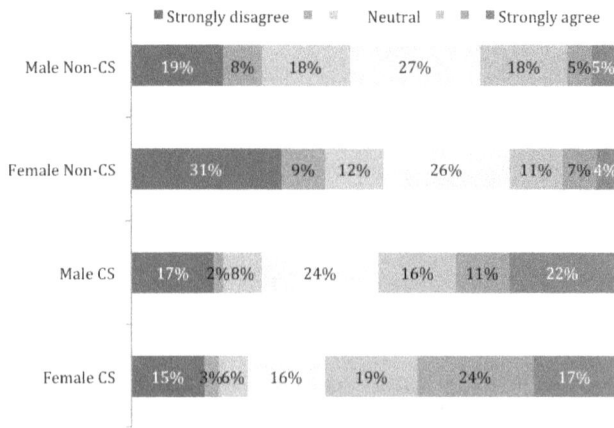

Figure 5. Percent of college grads and their agreement with the statement "Role models gave me a good impression of CS" (n = 893).

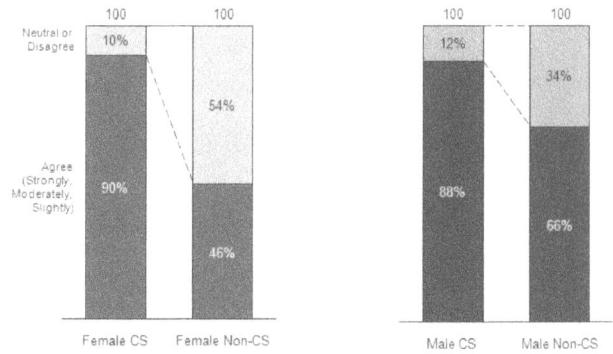

Figure 7. College graduates' agreement with the statement "I think I understand the difference between computer science and IT" (n = 893). Note the discrepancy between females and males in the non-CS group.

social passions (helping people, conservation, medical breakthroughs, etc.) that make a profession personally rewarding. Thus, limited and negative perceptions around what CS involves and who does CS narrow participation in the field. It is important to show the broad applications of CS as well as diverse computer scientists.

5.3 Academic Exposure

The ability to participate in computer science courses and activities accounts for 22.4% of the explainable factors influencing whether girls say they want to pursue a computer science-related degree. This includes participation in structured (e.g., graded studies) and unstructured (e.g., after-school programs) activities.

Importantly, having taken a CS course before college plays a significantly larger role for girls than boys in choosing to study CS-related fields. And, influential factors for high school girls only included logistical and social aspects of participation; scheduling issues and courses not counting for requirements as well as lack of friends in the courses influenced girls to not take CS courses. Thus, exposure, utility, and broad participation in CS courses may be key for increasing the number of girls pursuing computer science.

Among the college population, those who had the opportunity to take the Advanced Placement (AP) Computer Science A exam

were 46% more likely to pursue a computing major. This is particularly true for women, who are 38% more likely to pursue a computing degree after having taken AP Computer Science in high school. Yet, in high school, girls interested in computer science most often cite not having space in their schedules or classes being full as reasons for not having taken computer science.

In addition to examining the influence of AP coursework specifically, the study controlled for varying high school curricula (e.g., no computer science classes, compulsory classes, and elective classes) and the accessibility of extra-curricular programs (e.g., clubs and camps) and found that, regardless of how they were exposed, young women who had opportunities to engage in learning about computer science were more likely to consider computing-related degrees than those without those opportunities.

Furthermore, among college graduates who did not major in CS, a larger percentage of women than men were not able to recall the availability of CS classes (AP and non-AP), extracurricular CS classes, extracurricular CS clubs, and CS camps (see Figure 6). This shows that there is a greater lack of awareness of CS opportunities among women when compared to men. Following this, Figure 7 shows that of those who did not major in CS, a larger percentage of women than men indicated that they disagreed that they understood the difference between IT and CS, while a larger percentage of men than women in CS indicated that they strongly agreed with the statement.

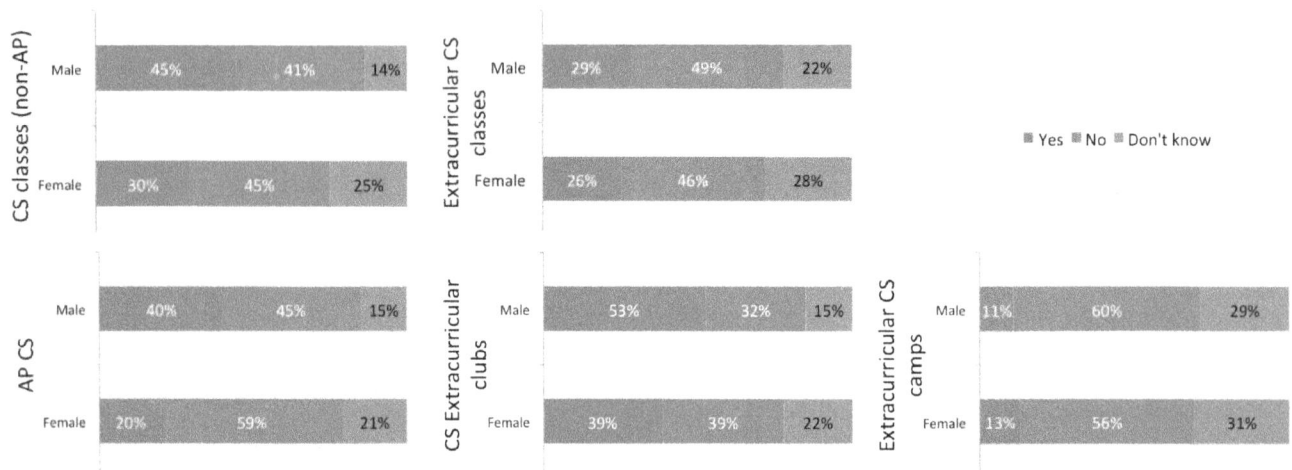

Figure 6. Non-computer science major college graduates' recall of availability of computer science opportunities in high school (n = 893).

"I Love Math" | "I Love Problem Solving" | "I love taking things apart to see how they work" | "Theoretical and abstract problems are interesting"

Neutral or Disagree

	Female CS	Female Non-CS	Female CS	Female Non-CS	Female CS	Female Non-CS	Female CS	Female Non-CS
Neutral or Disagree	24%	55%	12%	36%	25%	55%	29%	46%
Agree (Strongly, Moderately, Slightly)	76%	45%	88%	64%	75%	45%	71%	54%

	Male CS	Male Non-CS	Male CS	Male Non-CS	Male CS	Male Non-CS	Male CS	Male Non-CS
Neutral or Disagree	35%	44%	12%	20%	17%	33%	25%	27%
Agree (Strongly, Moderately, Slightly)	65%	56%	88%	80%	83%	67%	75%	73%

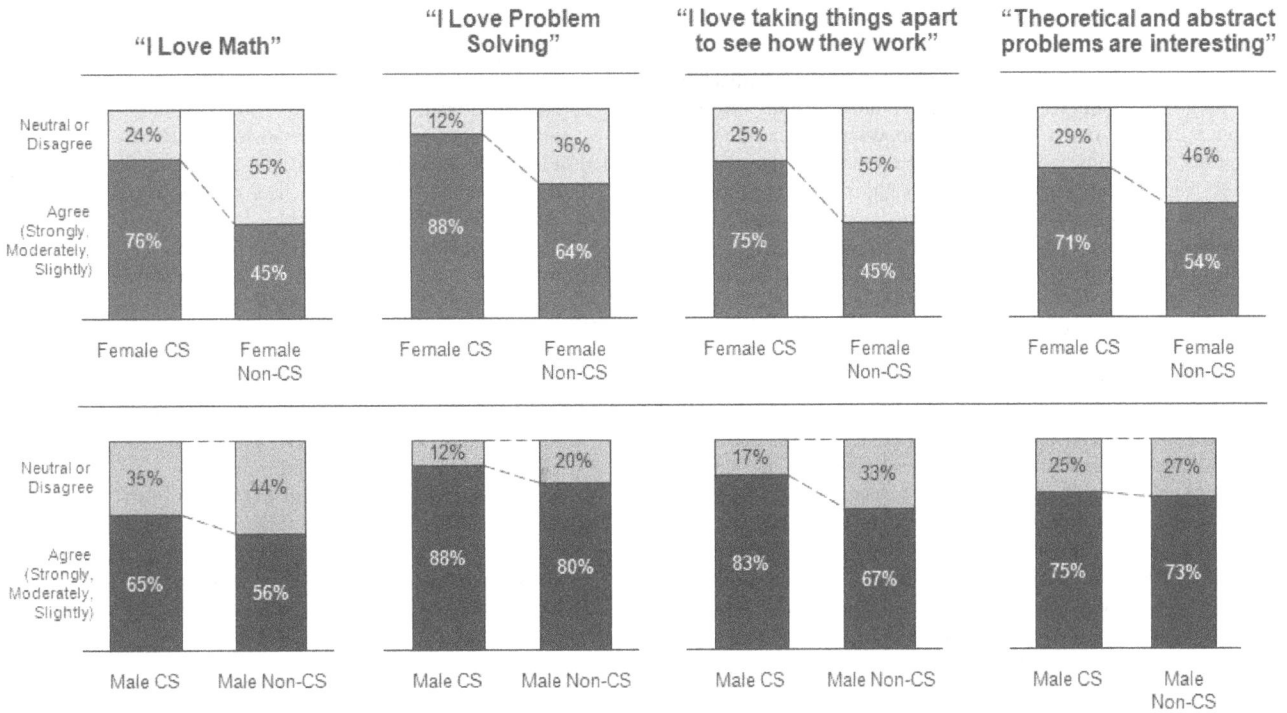

Figure 8. College graduates' agreement with various statement about their interests and personalities (n = 893). The discrepancy between CS and non-CS females is often greater than the discrepancy between CS and non-CS males.

We also found that scholarships for studying CS were significantly more influential for women than men. This provides an important practical implication that offering scholarships to women is a means of broadening awareness, exposure, and participation.

The key takeaway is that the specific type of participation is statistically insignificant when measured against having been exposed in some way. This seems to be a case of "anything is better than nothing." Early exposure to computer science is important because familiarity with a subject can generate interest and curiosity while establishing a sense of competency. Moreover, even a basic understanding of computing provides insight into viable career paths within the field and how those careers can be leveraged to achieve personal goals. Increasing awareness through exposure, encouragement, and support can help provide a broader and more complete picture of computer science as relevant to girls' lives and help widen participation.

5.4 Self-Perception

Finally, girls' interest in and perceptions of their own proficiency in mathematics and problem-solving significantly influence their wanting to pursue a computing-related education. In the high school model, this perception comprises 17.1% of the explainable factors. No significant differences in this factor were found between girls and boys, though of high schoolers interested in CS and related fields, girls were more likely than boys (81% vs 66%) to agree that they were "always in the top or 'honors' math classes." Among college students who had studied CS, women were significantly more likely than men (76% vs. 65%) to agree with the statement "I love math" (see Figure 8).

This positive self-perception provides internal encouragement in the form of ongoing confidence in one's abilities. Families and educators can foster positive self-perception by encouraging interest in mathematics and tinkering and creating safe opportunities for girls to explore and build these skills.

The high influence of self-perceptions confirms previous studies on the influence of self-confidence on students'

persistence, career interests, etc. (e.g., [9,14,18,20,23]), which have shown that girls usually have lower self-confidence than boys. As a consequence, girls' lower confidence discourages them from pursuing these fields. Furthermore, encouragement has been found to help increase confidence [22], and shows the interrelatedness of the various influencing factors. Thus, self-perception is a key factor in choosing to study CS for both genders, with interest and confidence in technical subjects potentially more influential for girls.

6. SIGNIFICANCE

Our study addresses a major societal issue that speaks to the concerns of advocates for women and workforce development. Our findings offer actionable recommendations by identifying the top factors influencing women to study computing fields.

The study found most of the decision-making to pursue computer science-related fields, including engineering and IT, occurs before a young woman begins college; once she enters college, application requirements and variable interdependence are so tightly coupled that the decision becomes less malleable. As a result, the factors with the most influence are associated with pre-college experiences.

The most heartening outcome of the study is the limited role that uncontrollable factors play in influencing the pursuit of a computer science degree. For example, for high school girls, uncontrollable factors like household income and ethnicity contribute to only 4.9% of the explainable factors—statistically insignificant when compared to factors that can be controlled. Not only do uncontrollable factors play a limited role in explaining a young woman's decision to pursue a computer science-related degree, the controllable factors of encouragement and exposure are the largest influencers.

Exposure to and the ability to enroll in computer science courses in- or out-of-school are critical to girls pursuing CS in college. Encountering encouragement in an extracurricular setting may have a large impact because it fosters peer encouragement and places computing in a social context. Accordingly, parents have a key role to play in giving girls the experience and confidence to pursue interests in these fields—either by advocating for computer science and related classes in their children's schools or by identifying opportunities in the local community (or online) to explore their learning. Parents and families can foster positive self-perception by encouraging interest in mathematics and tinkering and creating safe opportunities for girls to explore and build these skills.

Our research suggests it is important to help parents and educators learn how to draw attention to the wide applicability of computing to a variety of fields. The negative potential associated with flawed or incomplete career perceptions is two-fold: 1) not understanding computing fields makes an informed decision more difficult and 2) an incomplete perception can actively dissuade young women from considering one of these fields. The end result is that young women unfamiliar with computer science and its broad applications may have difficulty visualizing it outside the narrow scope often presented in popular media. They may be unable to perceive computer science-related careers as fulfilling both the academic passion (inventing, problem solving, exploration, etc.) and the intangible, social passions (helping people, conservation, medical breakthroughs, etc.) that make a profession personally rewarding.

The bottom line is that the factors most related to female participation in computing are actionable, and understanding the differences between the way such factors influence men and women will help inform our approaches to taking action. That's not to say this is a problem that can be solved easily, but it is a problem that can be tackled with deliberate and directed action focused on encouragement and exposure.

7. ACKNOWLEDGEMENTS

We acknowledge the contributions of our colleagues: Iveta Brigis, Sarah Chavis, Heather Thorne, Eduardo Samuel, and others. We also thank Applied Marketing Science for assistance with instrument development, data collection, and analyses.

8. REFERENCES

[1] Anderson, J. A. (1982). Logistic regression. *Handbook of Statistics*. North-Holland, New York, 169-191. Retrieved from http://www.schatz.sju.edu/multivar/guide/Logistic.pdf

[2] Achtenhagen, L., Johansson, A., & Picard, R. (2007). The Promotion of Entrepreneurship in the Audio-Visual Media (esp. TV): Final Report for the European Commission, Enterprise and Industry Directorate-General. Retrieved from http://ec.europa.eu/enterprise/policies/sme/files/support_mea sures/av/media_study_en.pdf

[3] Barth, J., Todd, B., Goldston, D., & Guadagno, R. (2010). *An Integrated Approach to Choosing Technical Careers: Gender Differences in Life Goals for College Students.*

[4] Benyo, J., & White, J. (2009). New Image for Computing: Report on Market Research. Boston, MA: WGBH Educational Foundation and the Association for Computing Machinery. Retrieved from http://www.zephoria.org/files/NICReport.pdf

[5] Bhanot, R.T. & Jovanovic, J. (2009). The Links Between Parent Behaviors and Boys' and Girls' Science Achievement Beliefs. *Applied Developmental Science*. Philadelphia, PA. 42-59.

[6] Dabney, K. P., Chakraverty, D., & Tai, R. H. (2013). The Association of Family Influence and Initial Interest in Science. *Science Education, 97*(3), 395-409.

[7] Fan, X. & Chen, M. (2001). Parental Involvement and Students' Academic Achievement: A Meta-Analysis. Retrieved from http://rd.springer.com/article/10.1023/A:1009048817385

[8] Fisher, A., & Margolis, J. (2002). Unlocking the Clubhouse: the Carnegie Mellon Experience. *ACM SIGCSE Bulletin, 34*(2), 79-83. Retrieved from http://dl.acm.org/citation.cfm?id=543836

[9] Fox, M. F., & Firebaugh, G. (1992). Confidence in Science: The Gender Gap. *Social Science Quarterly*.

[10] H. H. Harman. (1976). *Modern factor analysis*. Chicago, IL: University of Chicago Press.

[11] Hill, C., Corbett, C., & St Rose, A. (2010). Why So Few? Women in Science, Technology, Engineering, and Mathematics. Washington, DC: American Association of University Women. Retrieved from http://files.eric.ed.gov/fulltext/ED509653.pdf

[12] Ing, M. (2014). Can Parents Influence Children's Mathematics Achievement and Persistence in STEM Careers?. *Journal of Career Development, 41*(2), 87-103. Retrieved from http://jcd.sagepub.com/content/41/2/87

[13] Jacobs, J. E., & Bleeker, M. M. (2004). Girls' and Boys' Developing Interests in Math and Science: Do Parents Matter? *New Directions for Child and Adolescent Development.* 5–21.

[14] Lent, R. W., Brown, S. D., & Larkin, K. C. (1986). Self-efficacy in the Prediction of Academic Performance and Perceived Career Options. *Journal of Counseling Psychology, 33*(3), 265.

[15] Miller, J. D., & Kimmel, L. G. (2012). Pathways to a STEMM Profession. *Peabody Journal of Education, 87*(1), 26-45.

[16] National Science Foundation. (2012). Science and Engineering Indicators 2012. Washington, DC. Retrieved from http://www.nsf.gov/statistics/seind12/c0/c0i.htm

[17] National Center for Education Statistics (2012). Degrees conferred by degree-granting institutions. Washington, DC. Retrieved from http://nces.ed.gov/programs/digest/d12/tables/dt12_318.asp

[18] O'brien, V., Martinez-Pons, M., & Kopala, M. (1999). Mathematics Self-efficacy, Ethnic Identity, Gender, and Career Interests Related to Mathematics and Science. *The Journal of Educational Research, 92*(4), 231-235.

[19] Page, S. E. (2008). *The Difference: How the Power of Diversity Creates Better Groups, Firms, Schools, and Societies*. Princeton University Press.

[20] Shashaani, L. (1994). Gender-differences in Computer Experience and Its Influence on Computer Attitudes. *Journal of Educational Computing Research,11*(4), 347-367.

[21] Sonnert, G. (2009). Parents Who Influence Their Children to Become Scientists: Effects of Gender and Parental Education. *Social Studies of Science.* 927-941. Retrieved from http://sss.sagepub.com/content/39/6/927

[22] Stake, J. E. (2006). The Critical Mediating Role of Social Encouragement for Science Motivation and Confidence Among High School Girls and Boys. *Journal of Applied Social Psychology, 36*(4), 1017-1045.

[23] Wilson, B. C. (2002). A Study of Factors Promoting Success in Computer Science including Gender Differences. *Computer Science Education, 12*(1-2), 141-164.

A Computer Science Linked-courses Learning Community

Amber Settle, John Lalor, Theresa Steinbach

DePaul University

243 S. Wabash Avenue

Chicago, IL 60604

(312) 362-8381

asettle@cdm.depaul.edu, jlalor@mail.depaul.edu, tsteinbach@cdm.depaul.edu

ABSTRACT

Previous work has shown that factors such as student engagement and involvement can impact progress for computer science majors. One promising approach for improving student engagement is learning communities, which have a long history in academia but are relatively uncommon in computing. In this article we describe a linked-courses learning community for women and men of color majoring in development-focused computing degrees. We provide logistical information about the first offering of the learning community and assess the effectiveness of the community via a student survey. Our results show that students in the learning community are more likely to report that they have support for success in computer science courses and that they are a part of a community of programmers.

Categories and Subject Descriptors

K.3.2 [**Computer and Information Science Education**]: Computer science education

Keywords

Attitudes; CS1; confidence; community; engagement; programming; Python

1. INTRODUCTION

The Computing Research Association reports the number of new undergraduate computing majors has steadily risen the last five years [24]. There is, however, evidence that the number of college graduates with computer science degrees is failing to match demand [7]. This suggests that retention efforts, particularly for underrepresented groups, remain important. It has been shown that computing experiences affect a student's perception and attitude about the field, which enable or inhibit pathways in the discipline [18].

Computing educators have devoted considerable time and energy to improving the student experience in introductory programming courses, and particularly CS1 classes, since these courses are often the first experience students have in the computer science

major. The efforts at improving CS1 courses have in many cases resulted in lower failure rates, better retention, and in some cases better gender balance [1]. These changes are welcome since introductory programming classes can have a strong impact on student perceptions of the computer science major. For example, it has been demonstrated that students' self-assessment of their ability level impacts their decision to major in computer science [10]. Researchers have also found that student attitudes and beliefs about computer science were more varied in their first than in their last year [15]. Factors such as limited faculty-student engagement and involvement with other students in the major have been shown to have a higher impact on underrepresented groups in computing, such as women [9].

An approach that has shown promise in improving students' sense of belonging is linked-course learning communities [12]. The origin of learning communities dates back to a six-year experiment at the University of Wisconsin in 1927 [12], and numerous models have been developed. In a linked-course learning community, students simultaneously enroll in courses from different disciplines or interdisciplines that are connected in content, purpose, and organization [5]. Learning communities intentionally restructure the curriculum to connect students and faculty [12]. The community is designed to provide students with an integrative and collaborative learning environment, with the aim of enhancing student achievement, reducing attrition rates, and increasing student and faculty enthusiasm [5]. Other issues that learning communities attempt to address are inadequate levels of interactions among students and between students and faculty [13].

While learning communities have a long history, there is relatively little to be found in the computing education literature about them. A recent article described a living-learning community in existence since 2010 at the Pennsylvania College of Technology [11]. The Penn College learning community has improved academic performance, increased student interaction, and improved retention [11]. As a part of a selective merit scholarship program aimed at increasing the number of women in engineering and information technology, the University of Maryland Baltimore County also has a living-learning community, although that aspect of the diversity program is not extensively discussed in associated publications [17]. Further, there are learning communities in existence at several institutions that have a focus on computing or other STEM disciplines, including Rochester Institute of Technology, Syracuse University, and Purdue University. But prior to our project there were no published articles discussing technology-focused linked-courses learning communities or evaluating the effectiveness or impact of such a learning community. This is surprising given that recent recommendations for learning communities suggest

ITICSE '15, July 04 - 08, 2015, Vilnius, Lithuania

Copyright is held by the owner/author(s). Publication rights licensed to ACM.

ACM 978-1-4503-3440-2/15/07…$15.00

http://dx.doi.org/10.1145/2729094.2742621

that they be intentionally engineered around combinations of courses likely to be taken by students in clusters of majors [13].

In this article we describe the first instance of a linked-courses learning community for men of color and women majoring in a development-focused computing degrees that require Python as the introductory language. During the first quarter of the 2014-2015 academic year the authors created a linked-courses community for two required first-term courses in four development-focused computing majors. The students recruited for the learning community were enrolled in a content-based course (a CS1 course) and a liberal studies course focused on the digital divide. The planning for the learning community was described in a previous article [19]. Here we describe first instance of the linked-courses learning community, including the recruitment procedures used to enroll students, the courses chosen for the project, demographics for students enrolled in each of the courses, and the activities that were a part of the co-curricular and extra-curricular components of the community. We then describe the assessment of the learning community, providing results of a survey administered to all students taking the CS1 course that was a part of the linked-courses learning community. We conclude with future plans.

2. LEARNING COMMUNITY

Linked-courses learning communities are unusual in the computing education literature so we begin by describing the logistics of the community. The first section describes the process of recruiting students for the community. We briefly describe the two courses in the community, and the demographics of the students who enrolled in the learning community. We conclude the section with details of the co-curricular and extra-curricular activities arranged for the community.

2.1 Recruitment

The learning community discussed here is targeted at first-quarter freshman. As a result, the recruitment for the community has to begin prior to the students' first quarter at the university. In an attempt to reach the broadest group of students, we began recruitment for the community with admitted students, that is, students who have been accepted to DePaul but not yet committed to attend the university.

We were assisted in this endeavor by a mentoring program for prospective students that has existed since 2004 [20]. In this program prospective students are matched with faculty mentors as soon as they are admitted into a major in the College of Computing and Digital Media (CDM). The faculty mentors make regular contact with the students to answer any questions they have about the curriculum or academics at DePaul. The goal is to provide prospective students with early faculty contact, which helps them to make more informed decisions about enrollment.

As a part of the learning community project we requested that all men of color and women (of any ethnicity) who were admitted to the computer science (CS), math and computer science (math and CS), computer game development (gaming), or information assurance and security engineering (IASE) programs be assigned to either the first or third author in the prospective student mentoring program. Beginning in February 2014, the staff in CDM shared with us the names and email addresses of the targeted students. There were in total 281 students meeting the requirement, 66 of which were female. We contacted each of the

students by email, informing them about the learning community and encouraging them to consider joining the community if they chose to attend DePaul. We also attended the Admitted Student Day in March 2014, which is an in-person event for admitted students and their families. The students and their families attend information sessions and have tours of the campus.

As of May 1, 2014 there were 23 women and 74 men of color in one of the four targeted majors who placed deposits indicating that they intended to enroll at DePaul. The first and third authors again reached out to those students, informing them about the logistics of summer orientation sessions and asking them to consider being a part of the learning community. The third author also attended summer orientation sessions to help recruit students for the learning community.

Unfortunately despite our extensive efforts we were unable to fill the two classes in the learning community solely with men of color or women in one of the four majors. Beginning in August 2014 both classes were opened to any CDM student who needed to take them. In total there were 21 students enrolled in both classes, and thus in the learning community. There were three white male students who enrolled in both courses, thus placing them into the learning community, although they were not specifically targeted into the recruitment for the community.

2.2 Courses and Demographics

In this section we describe the courses in the learning community and the demographics of students in each course.

2.2.1 Courses

The courses chosen for the project are required in each of CS, math and CS, gaming, and IASE to ensure that community is appealing for students and does not require undo effort to join. Each of the majors are ones in which students are expected to become strong programmers and have a significant number of courses focusing on application development in the curriculum. The students are also first-quarter freshman who have additional first-year requirements.

Students declaring any of these majors have two choices for their first programming course. Students with little or no programming experience are directed to take a Python programming sequence that makes no assumptions about prior experience. CSC 241: Introduction to Computer Science I and CSC 242: Introduction to Computer Science II focus on problem solving and application development in Python. The relatively simple syntax of Python allows the introduction of significant and interesting problems early in the course and provides the future developers targeted by the class with frequent opportunities for problem solving. The problem-solving approach in the class is enhanced by an extra 90-minute weekly lab section. The section is supervised by a graduate assistant, and during the session the students collaboratively solve programming exercises. Students who have earned a strong grade (above a B-) in at least one semester of a high-level programming language are directed to take a more accelerated Python course. CSC 243: Python for Programmers covers much of the material from CSC 241/242 but does so in a single quarter. The Python sequences use several interventions recommended in the literature, including closed labs with collaborative activities (in CSC 241/242), differentiated courses for novice and experienced programmers, and engaged and enthusiastic faculty [2, 3, 8, 16]. The first author served as the instructor for the CSC 241 in the learning community.

Additionally, every freshman at DePaul is required to take a Chicago Quarter class. These classes are designed to acquaint first-year students with DePaul and the metropolitan community, neighborhoods, cultures, institutions, organizations, and people of Chicago. Each course has a Chicago-centric theme around which the academic topics are organized, and the courses come in two types: LSP 110: Discover Chicago or LSP 111: Explore Chicago. Explore Chicago classes begin meeting when the regular quarter starts in early September, but meet for an extended class session. Each class is required to have multiple excursions into the city to see neighborhoods, institutions, and organizations relevant to the academic focus of the course. The course has standardized reading and writing requirements which are met using discipline-specific material designed by the instructor. The courses also have a "Common Hour," which addresses issues of transition for first-year students, including academic success skills and educational and career planning [6]. Students participating in the linked-courses community were enrolled in a section of LSP 111 entitled "The Digital Divide." This Explore Chicago class explores the social issues surrounding access to information and communications technology (ICT). The third author was the lead instructor for the course, and she was assisted by a student mentor from CDM as well as a staff mentor.

2.2.2 Student demographics
As mentioned previously there were 21 students enrolled in the linked-courses learning community as of the start of the first quarter in the 2014-2015 academic year in September. There were also 8 students in the Digital Divide class who were not in CSC 241, and 9 students in the CSC 241 class who were not in the Digital Divide class.

In the learning community there were 4 female students and 17 male students. There were 5 white students, 6 Latino/a students, 6 Asian students, 3 African-American students, and a multiracial student. A white male student enrolled in both courses dropped CSC 241 early in the quarter, and a multiracial male originally in the learning community switched to the accelerated Python course. This reduced the size of the learning community to 19.

In the learning community there were 14 students majoring in CS, 5 students majoring in one of the gaming concentrations, 1 student majoring in math and CS, and 1 student majoring in mathematics. The students who left the learning community were CS majors.

2.3 Activities
A variety of activities were planned to facilitate the forming of an academic support group – an open house in week three of the quarter at the Chicago Quarter instructor's home, study sessions for the CS 1 midterm and final, a game day to celebrate the end of midterms at the CS1 instructor's home, group seating for the women and men's opening basketball tournament, an introduction to the school's new physical computing lab and two employer visits with the assistance of the Career Center. As previously mentioned, there were students enrolled in both courses that were not part of the learning community. These students were also invited to all of the events. Participation varied from one to a dozen students in each of these activities. It is interesting that no one student participated in all activities and all but three students participated in at least one activity.

3. EVALUATION
The goal of the linked-courses learning community is to engage the students in an effort to improve their feelings of belonging and confidence, improve their study habits, and ultimately, improve their retention in the courses and degree program. To measure whether students experienced a change in attitudes and habits during the quarter the learning community was in place a survey developed by the authors was administered. The survey is based on previous surveys of attitudes toward computer science [4, 14, 22, 23].

The survey has 33 questions that measure attitudes toward computing and programming, answered on a 5-point Likert scale, with 5 = strongly agree and 1 = strongly disagree. There was also one question that asked students about their utilization of resources for learning computing. There the students were asked to rank the resources from 1 to 8, with 1 being the most frequently used resource. A complete list of the questions is not provided here due to space limitations, but the survey can be found in its entirety in previous publications [19, 21].

The survey was administered pre-quarter and post-quarter in all CS1 Python classes during the first quarter of the 2014-2015 academic year. The survey was administered during a class session following a protocol approved by the DePaul Institutional Research Board (IRB). The student IDs were requested so that pre- and post-quarter responses could be matched. Once the two surveys were connected, identifying information was discarded.

3.1 Demographics
Due to logistical issues there were more surveys completed post-quarter than pre-quarter.

3.1.1 Pre-quarter
There were 59 pre-quarter surveys returned by all CSC 241 students. Of the pre-quarter responses there were 46 males (78%) and 13 females (22%). There were 47 responses from first-quarter students (80%), 1 response from a second-quarter student (2%), 3 responses from third-quarter students (5%), and 7 responses from students in their fourth quarter and beyond (12%). There were 33 responses from computer science majors (56%), 4 from IASE majors (7%), 10 from game development majors (17%), 2 from other CDM majors (3%), 9 from other majors (15%), and 1 undecided (2%). GPA information was reported only by the 12 students in their second quarter and beyond. There were 5 students reporting a GPA of 3.5 – 4.0 (42%), 2 students reporting a GPA of 3.0 – 3.5 (16.5%), 3 students reporting a GPA below 3.0 (25%), and 2 students not providing an answer (16.5%).

There were 17 pre-quarter surveys returned by students in the learning community. Of these 14 (82%) were male and 3 (18%) were female. All of the students were in their first quarter, and the GPA question was not relevant for them. There were 11 responses from computer science majors (65%), 1 response from an IASE major (6%), 4 responses from game development majors (24%), and 1 response from another major (6%).

125

3.1.2 Post-quarter

There were 171 responses to the post-quarter survey. Of the post-quarter responses there were 138 males (81%), 31 females (18%), and 3 people who did not specify their gender (2%). There were 138 responses from first-quarter students (81%), 6 responses from second-quarter students (4%), 6 responses from third-quarter students (4%), and 21 responses from students in their fourth quarter and beyond (12%). There were 100 responses from computer science majors (58%), 11 IASE majors (6%), 25 game development majors (15%), 7 other CDM majors (4%), 24 other majors (14%), and 4 undecided (2%). Again, GPA information was reported only by the 33 students in their second quarter and beyond. Of these 16 students reported a GPA of 3.5 – 4.0 (49%), 8 students reported a GPA of 3.0 – 3.5 (24%), 5 students reported a GPA below 3.0 (15%), and 4 students did not provide an answer (12%).

There were 15 post-quarter responses from students in the learning community. There were 11 responses from men (73%) and 4 responses from women (27%). All of the students were in their first quarter, and the GPA question was not relevant. There were 9 responses from computer science majors (60%) and 6 responses from game development majors (40%).

3.2 Attitude Questions

The responses to the attitude questions were analyzed using a one-way ANOVA test to determine if the changes pre-quarter to post-quarter were statistically significant. We performed the test between the pre- and post-quarter survey responses, with a null hypothesis of "Taking the introductory Python class did not affect students' responses regarding ____," with the blank representing each question.

There were statistically significant results among the learning community students either pre- or post-quarter (but not between the pre- and post-quarter responses) on questions 29 and 33. Q29 is "I have a lot of support that will help me to succeed in computer science courses," and Q33 is "I have had good teachers in my computer science courses." The results for the entire CSC 241 population and the learning community students are presented in Table 1.

Table 1. Significant pre- and post-quarter responses

Q	Pre	LC-Pre	Post	LC-Post	Result
29	4.00	4.64	3.84	4.64	$F(1,44) = 11.27$, p = .001
33	3.97	4.57	3.84	4.42	$F(1, 44) = 9.611$, p = .01

When considering changes between the pre- and the post-quarter responses in the entire CSC 241 population, there were statistically significant differences on five questions, namely 10, 13, 14, 24, and 32. Q10 is "It would make me happy to be recognized as an excellent student in computer science." Q13 is "I'll need programming for my future work." Q14 is "Knowing programming will help me earn a living." Q24 is "I feel isolated in computer science courses." Q32 is "My family is happy that I am taking computer science courses." The results are presented in Table 2.

There was one significant difference between the pre- and post-quarter responses from the learning community students. On question 25, which is "I am part of a community of programmers." On Q25 the CSC 241 population had a pre-quarter mean of 3.031 and a post-quarter mean of 2.718. The learning community students had a pre-quarter mean of 3.928 and a post-quarter mean of 4.143. This is a result with $F(1,44) = 11.97$, p = 0.001.

Table 2. Differences over time for CSC 241 population

Q	Pre	Post	Result
10	4.369	4.696	$F(1, 45) = 10.95$, p = .001
13	4.348	4.543	$F(1, 45) = 5.985$, p = .01
14	4.478	4.696	$F(1, 45) = 4.482$, p = 0.03
24	2.326	1.891	$F(1, 45) = 7.627$, p = .008
32	3.978	4.348	$F(1, 45) = 10.58$, p = 0.002

We considered several subpopulations of the CSC 241 students to determine if there were statistically significant differences in their responses. The groups we considered were male versus female students, students in particular quarters, students who reported particular GPAs, and students by major. There were 4 statistically significant differences for students in particular quarters, 8 statistically significant differences for students with certain reported GPAs, 1 statistically significant result by gender, and 9 statistically significant results by major. Due to space limitations not all of these results are presented here.

The only result for which there were statistically significant responses for male versus female students was on question 6, which is "I have a lot of self-confidence when it comes to programming." The responses were statistically significant pre- or post-quarter but the changes over the quarter were not statistically significant. Pre-quarter males had a mean of 4.029 and pre-quarter females had a mean of 3.167. Post-quarter males had a mean of 4.058, and post-quarter females had a mean of 3.500. This is a result with $F(1, 44) = 8.822$, p = .005.

The significant results for first-quarter versus other students included results on questions 13 and 28. Q13 has been previously stated. The following lists the significant differences between first-quarter students and two other populations on Q13.

Table 3. Differences in future utility of programming

Group 1	Group 2	Result
Qt1=4.566	Qt2=3.333	$t(77) = 2.9293$, p = .004
Qt1=4.566	Qt4+=4.000	$t(84) = 2.2096$, p = .029

Q28 is "Computing offers diverse and broad opportunities." The following table shows the significant differences between first-quarter students and two other student levels on Q28.

Table 4. Differences in perception of breadth of computing

Group 1	Group 2	Result
Qt1=4.553	Qt2=3.667	$t(77) = 2.5206$, p = 0.014
Qt1=4.553	Qt3=3.667	$t(77) = 2.5206$, p = 0.014

3.3 Resource Question

There were no significant differences among the entire CSC 241 population or among the learning community students either pre- or post-quarter or between the pre- and post-quarter responses with respect to their utilization of resources for learning computing.

When the subpopulations in the subsection above were considered, the only significant difference found was by quarter. Students in their first quarter had significant differences in their responses regarding self-study with respect to third- and fourth-quarter students. The differences were significant pre- or post-quarter but not over time. The following table presents those results. Recall that students ranked answers to this question from 1 to 8, with a lower number meaning a higher utilization of it.

Table 5. Significant differences in reported use of self-study

Group 1	Group 2	Result
Qt1=3.118	Qt3=5.667	$t(77) = -2.176, p = .03$
Qt1=3.118	Qt4+=4.500	$t(84) = -2.040, p = .04$

4. DISCUSSION

There were some results presented in the previous section that provide evidence that the learning community is effective. There were also some results from the general CSC 241 population that do not directly speak to the effectiveness of the learning community but are nevertheless interesting. We conclude this section by discussing the limitations of this study.

4.1 Effectiveness of the Learning Community

Students in the learning community were more likely than the general CSC 241 population to indicate both pre- and post-quarter that they have a lot of support to help with success in computer science courses. It is notable that the response to the question about support did not change pre- to post-quarter, which suggests that being recruited for the learning community, and not participating in the learning community, had the largest effect in terms of perceived support. It should also be noted that the response to the question about support decreased pre- to post-quarter among the general CSC 241 population, although not significantly. The responses pre- and post-quarter were stable for the learning community students, although again the result is not statistically significant.

Learning community students were also more likely to indicate that they had good teachers for their computer science courses than the general CSC 241 population. Both groups of students had a lower post-quarter response than their pre-quarter response about quality computer science teachers, although neither change was statistically significant.

The learning community students were more likely to indicate both pre- and post-quarter that they were a part of a community of programmers, and the change pre- to post-quarter was both positive and statistically significant. This provides evidence that participating in the learning community improved the students' perception of belonging to a community of programmers, which was one of the goals of the project.

4.2 Other Results

There were several pre- to post-quarter changes in the general CSC 241 population, indicating some general effects of having taken the CS1 course. Students were more likely to agree post-quarter that they would like being recognized as an excellent student in computer science, that they would need programming for their future career, that knowing programming will help them to earn a living, and that their family is happy about them taking computer science courses. Also, the general CSC 241 population was more likely to disagree with the statement "I feel isolated in

computer science courses" post-quarter. It would appear that the CS1 courses without the added benefit of the learning community are already having a positive impact on students.

The results also showed the female CSC 241 students are less confident about their programming ability than male students. Here it was difficult to obtain any results about the impact of the learning community since the female population in the learning community was so small.

There were also results that showed first-quarter students were more likely to believe that programming would be necessary for their future work than second- and fourth+-students and more likely to believe that computing offers diverse and broad opportunities than second- and fourth+-quarter students. Finally, first-quarter students were also more likely to utilize self-study than students in their third- and fourth+-quarters. The learning community results were not significantly different from the CSC 241 population as a whole.

4.3 Limitations

There are some limitations to this study. Some of the questions posed in the survey are sensitive in nature, and participants may have chosen to not complete those portions of the survey causing their data to be discarded in the analysis. Students were asked to provide their student IDs as a part of the survey to enable verification that only those students who completed both parts were included in the analysis, and this may have led students to not participate in the survey. The evaluation of the learning community is based on self-reported values provided by participants, and care must be taken when interpreting the results. Additionally, though care was taken in choosing survey questions and choices that are unambiguous, there is a risk that the participant may have misinterpreted the questions or choices. Further the learning community population is relatively small, making it difficult to determine if there were impacts of the learning community of some of the subpopulations considered.

5. CONCLUSION AND FUTURE WORK

The results of the survey administered to students taking the CS1 class and to students in the learning community provide evidence for the effectiveness of the community in making students feel supported and part of a community. Students in the learning community were more likely to indicate that they have a lot of support to help be successful in computer science courses and that they are a part of a community of programmers. The result regarding support suggests though that being recruited for the learning community had a larger impact than participating in the community.

Because the learning community was relatively small it was difficult to determine if the project was successful in achieving some of its goals. There were only four women in the community, so measuring if there were any statistically significant changes for female students pre- to post-quarter was not possible. For this and other reasons we intend to offer the learning community again in the first quarter of the 2015-2016 academic year. Obtaining more data from learning community participants will enable better evaluation of the effectiveness of the approach. We are also interested in comparing the retention of learning community students in their chosen major as compared to other students taking CSC 241 at the same time. We are currently working on obtaining IRB approval for this extension of the project.

There are several things that we would like to modify when we offer the learning community the next time. First, it would be ideal if the enrollments in both classes were restricted to students in the learning community. It was somewhat distracting to have students who were not in the learning community in the courses, something that the learning community participants commented on. Further, we were unable to implement several extracurricular activities that we feel would have been beneficial, most notably a mentoring program pairing upperclassmen with students in the learning community. It is our hope that with more lead time this program can be implemented.

6. REFERENCES

[1]   Alvarado, C., Lee, C.B., and Gillespie, G. 2014. New CS1 pedagogies and curriculum, the same success factors? In *Proceedings of the 45th ACM Technical Symposium on Computer Science Education* (Atlanta, Georgia, USA, March 2014).

[2]   Barker, L.J.,McDowell, C. and Kalahar, K. 2009. Exploring Factors that Influence Computer Science Introductory Course Students to Persist in the Major. *Proceedings of the 40th ACM Technical Symposium on Computer Science Education* (Chattanooga, Tennessee, USA, March 2009).

[3]   Boyer, K.E., Dwight, R. S., Miller, C.S., Raubenheimer, C.D., Stallmann, M.F., and Vouk, M.A. 2007. A Case for Smaller Class Size with Integrated Lab for Introductory Computer Science. In *Proceedings of the 38th ACM Technical Symposium on Computer Science Education* (Covington, Kentucky, USA, March 2007).

[4]   Bruckman, A., Biggers, M., Ericson, B., McKlin, T., Dimond, J., DiSalvo, B., Hewner, M., Ni, L., and Yardi, S. 2009. "Georgia computes!": Improving the Computing Education Pipeline. In *Proceedings of the 40th ACM Technical Symposium on Computer Science Education* (Chattanooga, Tennessee, USA, March 2009).

[5]   Cargill, K. and Kalikoff, B. 2007. Linked Psychology and Writing Courses Across the Curriculum. *The Journal of General Education*, 56:2, pp. 83-92.

[6]   Chicago Quarter, First-Year Program, DePaul University, http://liberalstudies.depaul.edu/FirstYearProgram/ChicagoQuarter/index.asp, accessed December 2014.

[7]   Code.org stats, http://code.org/stats, accessed December 2014.

[8]   Cohoon, J.. 2002. Recruiting and retaining women in undergraduate computing majors. *SIGCSE Bull.* 34, 2 (June 2002), 48-52.

[9]   Cohoon, J.M. and Aspray, W.F. 2006. *Women and information technology: Research on underrepresentation.* MIT Press: Cambridge, MA.

[10]   Dorn,B. and Tew, A.E. 2013. Becoming Experts: Measuring Attitude Development in Introductory Computer Science. In *Proceedings of the 44th ACM technical symposium on Computer Science Education.* (Denver, Colorado, USA, March 2013).

[11]   Gorka, S., Helf, M., and Miller, J. 2014. Implementing a living-learning community in information technology. In *Proceedings of the 15th Annual Conference on Information Technology Education* (SIGITE '14). ACM, New York, NY, USA, 153-158.

[12]   Kellogg, K. 1999. Learning Communities. ERIC Digest. http://eric.ed.gov/?id=ED430512.

[13]   Johnson, K.E. 2013. Learning Communities and the Completion Agenda. *Learning Communities Research and Practice*, 1:3.

[14]   Lamb, R.L, Annetta, L, Meldrum, J., and Vallett, D. 2012. Measuring Science Interest: Rasch Validation of the Science Interest Survey. *International Journal of Science and Mathematics Education.* 10:3 (June 2012), 643-668.

[15]   Lewis, C., Jackson, M.H., and Waite, W.M. 2010. Student and faculty attitudes and beliefs about computer science. *Commun. ACM* 53, 5 (May 2010), 78-85.

[16]   Newhall, T., Meeden, L., Danner, A., Soni, A., Ruiz, F., and Wicentowski, R. 2014. A Support Program for Introductory CS Courses that Improves Student Performance and Retains Students from Underrepresented Groups. In *Proceedings of the 45th ACM Technical Symposium on Computer Science Education.* (Atlanta, Georgia, USA, March 2014).

[17]   Rheingans. P., Brodsky, A., Scheibler, J., and Spence, A. 2011. The Role of Majority Groups in Diversity Programs. Trans. Comput. Educ. 11, 2, Article 11 (July 2011).

[18]   Schulte, C. and Knobelsdorf, M. 2007. Attitudes towards Computer Science-Computing Experiences as a Starting Point and Barrier to Computer Science. In *Proceedings of the Third International Workshop on Computing Education Research* (Atlanta, Georgia, USA, September 2007).

[19]   Settle, A., Lalor, J., and Steinbach, T. 2015. Reconsidering the Impact of CS1 on Novice Attitudes. In *Proceedings of the 45th Annual SIGCSE Technical Symposium on Computer Science Education.* (SIGCSE '15). ACM, New York, NY, USA.

[20]   Settle, A., Pieczynski, S., Friedman, L., Kizior, N. 2013. Evaluating a Prospective Student Mentoring Program. In *FECS 2013: The International Conference on Frontiers in Education: Computer Science and Computer Engineering*, (Las Vegas, Nevada, USA, July 2013).

[21]   Settle A. and Steinbach, T. 2014. Building a Linked-Courses Learning Community for Introductory Development Majors. In *Proceedings of the International Conference on Frontiers in Education: Computer Science and Computer Engineering* (Las Vegas, Nevada, USA, July 2014).

[22]   USG Student Computing Survey, http://dl.dropboxusercontent.com/u/2635522/USG%20Student%20Survey.pdf, accessed December 2014.

[23]   Wiebe, E.N., Williams, L, Yang, K. and Miller, C. 2003. Computer Science Attitude Survey, Dept. of Computer Science, North Carolina State University, TR-2003-1, http://www4.ncsu.edu/~wiebe/www/articles/prl-tr-2003-1.pdf.

[24]   Zweben, S. 2013. Computing Degree and Enrollment Trends. http://cra.org/govaffairs/blog/wp-content/uploads/2013/03/CRA_Taulbee_CS_Degrees_and_Enrollment_2011-12.pdf.

VIGvisual: A Visualization Tool for the Vigenère Cipher

Can Li, Jun Ma, Jun Tao,
Jean Mayo, Ching-Kuang
Shene
Department of Computer
Science
Michigan Technological
University
Houghton, MI
{canli,junm,junt,jmayo,shene}@mtu.edu

Melissa Keranen
Department of Mathematical
Sciences
Michigan Technological
University
Houghton, MI
msjukuri@mtu.edu

Chaoli Wang
Department of Computer
Science & Engineering
University of Notre Dame
Notre Dame, IN
chaoli.wang@nd.edu

ABSTRACT

This paper describes a visualization tool VIGvisual that helps students learn and instructors teach the Vigenère cipher. The software allows the user to visualize both encryption and decryption through a variety of cipher tools. The demo mode is useful and efficient for classroom presentation. The practice mode allows the user to practice encryption and decryption. VIGvisual is quite versatile, providing support for both beginners learning how to encrypt and decrypt, and also for the more advanced users wishing to practice cryptanalysis in the attack mode. Classroom evaluation of the tool was positive.

Categories and Subject Descriptors

K.3.2 [**Computers and Education**]: Computer and Information Science Education—*Computer science education, information systems education*

General Terms

Algorithms, Security

Keywords

Cryptography; visualization

1. INTRODUCTION

The Vigenère cipher appeared in the 1585 book *Traicté des Chiffres* by Blaise de Vigenère. It is a simple cipher, but for nearly three centuries the Vigenère cipher had not been broken until Friedrich W. Kasiski published his 1863 book [7]. Charles Babbage also broke the cipher with a similar technique in 1846, although he never published his work. Currently, the Vigenère cipher has become a standard topic in many textbooks [4, 8, 10].

ITiCSE'15, July 6–8, 2015, Vilnius, Lithuania.
Copyright © 2015 ACM 978-1-4503-3440-2/15/07 ...$15.00.
DOI: http://dx.doi.org/10.1145/2729094.2742589.

Well designed pedagogical tools are very useful in helping students understand concepts and practice needed skills. While there are tools available [1, 2, 9], most of them only provide interfaces for encryption and decryption without showing the process, and very few include cryptanalysis. VIGvisual is designed to address this issue by providing an environment so that it can be used in the classroom and for self-study. It is able to animate the Vigenère cipher with a variety of cipher tools, all of which are available for students to practice encryption and decryption with error checking. Furthermore, VIGvisual also helps students learn how to break the Vigenère cipher. VIGvisual uses Kasiski's method and the Index of Coincidence method for keyword length estimation, and the χ^2 method with frequency graphs for keyword recovery. To the best of our knowledge, only [2] offers a similar capability; however, it is just an interactive cryptanalysis environment. VIGvisual goes one step further by offering a more comprehensive visualization component with tools and animation not only for cryptanalysis but also for beginners to learn and practice the Vigenère cipher.

In the following, Section 2 discusses the course in which VIGvisual was used and evaluated, Section 3 presents an overview of VIGvisual, Section 4 has our findings from a classroom evaluation, and Section 5 is our conclusion.

2. COURSE INFORMATION

VIGvisual was used in a cryptography course, MA3203 Introduction to Cryptography, that is offered out of the Department of Mathematical Sciences at Michigan Technological University. It is a junior level course that gives a basic introduction to the field of cryptography. This course covers classical cryptography, the Data Encryption Standard (DES), the Advanced Encryption Standard (AES), the RSA algorithm, discrete logarithms, hash functions, and elliptic curve cryptography. For each cryptosystem, we study how it was designed, why it works, how one may attack the system, and how it has been used in practice.

Understanding classical cryptography is essential to any introductory cryptography course, and one of the major classical cryptosystems is the Vigenère cipher. The Vigenère cipher is a generalization of the monoalphabetic shift cipher, which has a keyword length of one. This cipher is very difficult to present in class because of the long pieces of text that need to be used in order to illustrate the algorithm in a meaningful way. Because VIGvisual was used in the course, students were able to see the encryption algorithm demonstrated quickly. This allowed for a more thorough study of the most interesting aspects of the cipher, which are the decryption techniques and attacks. The attack component covers Kasiski's method, the index of coincidence method, and the χ^2 method.

3. SOFTWARE DESCRIPTION

VIGvisual supports Linux, MacOS and Windows and has three modes, Demo, Practice and Attack. The Demo mode helps the user visualize the process of encryption and decryption with animation. The Practice mode allows the user to practice encryption and decryption with error checking. The Attack mode offers a chance for the user to learn how to break the Vigenère cipher with Kasiski's and the Index of Coincidence (IOC) methods, followed by the χ^2 method to recover the unknown keyword.

3.1 The Demo Mode

VIGvisual starts with the Demo mode (Figure 1). The top portion has input fields for plaintext, keyword and ciphertext. The user starts a new session with New and enters a plaintext-keyword pair or a ciphertext-keyword pair, or uses RandPT and RandCT to automatically generate a random plaintext-keyword pair and a random ciphertext-keyword pair. This is followed by clicking Encrypt or Decrypt to encrypt or decrypt the entered message. By default, the keyword is repeated and aligned with the original word structure. Clicking Align switches to the view of breaking the plaintext/ciphertext to align with the keyword length.

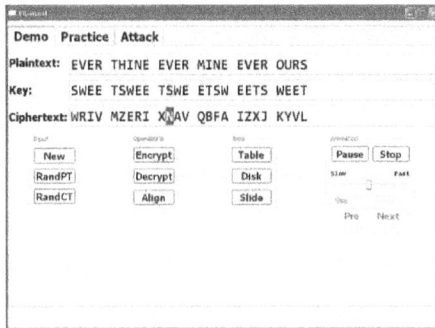

Figure 1: Screenshot of the Demo Mode

The user uses Start and Stop to start and stop an animation, the slider to select an animation speed, and Pre and Next to move to the previous and next position. The corresponding plaintext letter, keyword letter and ciphertext letter are shown in different colors in an animation.

The user may bring up one or more tools with buttons Table, Disk and Slide. Figure 2(a) shows the Vigenère table. The plaintext letter under consideration and its column use one color, the corresponding keyword letter and its row use a different one, and the ciphertext letter is at the intersection of the plaintext column and keyword row. The cipher disk has two concentric disks stacked together (Figure 2(b)). The bottom (*resp.*, top) disk, the *stationary* (*resp.*, *movable*) one, represents the plaintext (*resp.*, ciphertext) letters and is fixed (*resp.*, rotatable). The user rotates the movable disk so that the keyword letter aligns with the letter A of the stationary disk. Then, the corresponding plaintext and ciphertext letters align together. Figure 2(c) has the Saint Cyr Slide. The upper part is fixed while the lower part

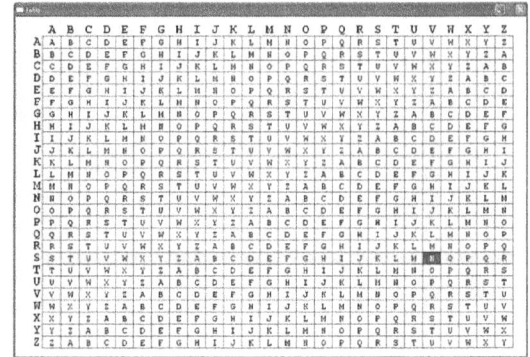

(a) Vigenère Table

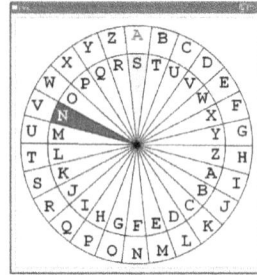

(c) Saint Cyr Slide

(b) Cipher Disk

Figure 2: Cipher Tools

can be moved left or right. The table rows and columns, the movable disk and the bottom slide change according to the triplet of plaintext letter, keyword letter and ciphertext letter. Thus, the instructor has a demo tool for classroom use and the students have a clear view of how the Vigenère cipher performs encryption and decryption.

3.2 The Practice Mode

Click the Practice tab to enter the Practice mode (Figure 3). All three tools are available. The user clicks Encrypt or Decrypt to start a new session, and uses Random to generate a random plaintext-keyword or ciphertext-keyword pair, New to start a new session, Redo to redo the current session, and Align to align the plaintext or ciphertext using the keyword length. Then, the user enters a keyword (if Random is not chosen) followed by the expected ciphertext or plaintext. The user may stop at anywhere and click the Check button to check the result. Incorrect letters are marked in red or with question marks if the positions are left as blank. The Answer field shows the correct answer.

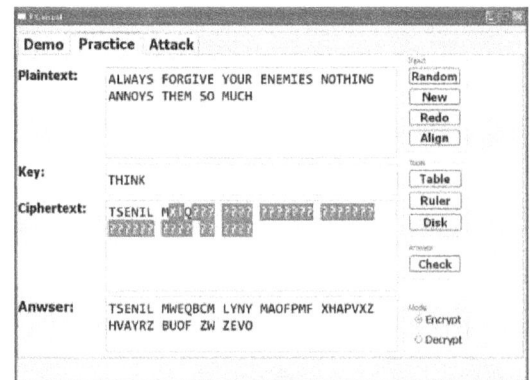

Figure 3: Screenshot of the Practice Mode

3.3 The Attack Mode

Click the `Attack` button to enter the `Attack` mode. The user clicks `Random` to randomly generate a ciphertext or `New` to start a new session and enter a new ciphertext (Figure 4). The process of breaking a message has two steps: keyword length estimation and keyword recovery. This process may not always be successful, and several iterations may be needed. VIGvisual has several `Hint` buttons in all windows under the `Attack` tab, each of which brings up a hint window to either explain what the window and/or algorithm is or provide a chance for the user to do simple exercises.

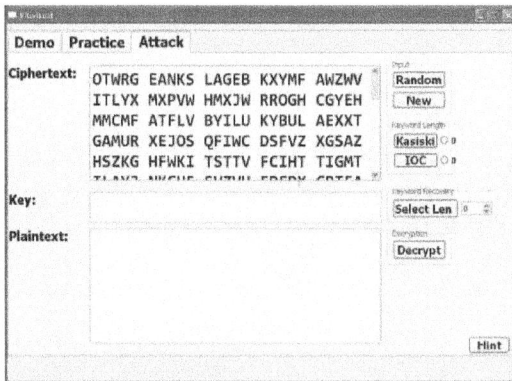

Figure 4: Screenshot of the Attack Mode

3.3.1 Kasiski's Method

VIGvisual provides two methods for keyword length estimation: Kasiski's method and the Index of Coincidence method. The user clicks `Kasiski` to use Kasiski's method. VIGvisual searches the given ciphertext for repeated substrings of length 3 (*i.e.*, trigraph) to 20, computes the distance between each pair of adjacent repeated substrings, finds the factors of this distance, and counts these factors.

Kasiski suggested that the factors that occur most often may be good estimates of the length of the keyword [7]. The `Kasiski` window shows a table in which each row has a distance value and the factors of this distance (Figure 5(a)). The bottom of this table (Figure 5(b)) shows the count of each found factor. The user clicks a factor, which will be shown in yellow, to select that length. This length appears to the right of the `Kasiski` button in the `Attack` tab. Repeated substrings are shown on the right panel of the `Kasiski` window along with their positions and distances. Clicking those repeated substrings can have them highlighted in the original ciphertext. Note that even though "ab" appears in "abcd" and "abce", only the longest repeated one "abc" is reported.

3.3.2 The Index of Coincidence Method

The concept of Index of Coincidence (IOC) was proposed by William F. Friedman in 1922 [3]. The IOC of a string is the probability of having two identical letters in that string. A typical English string without spaces and punctuation has an IOC around 0.068 while a random string of the 26 English letters has an IOC around 0.042. If a plaintext is encrypted by a single letter, the ciphertext is a shift of that letter, and its IOC is equal to that of the plaintext. Therefore, if keyword length is k, we may divide the ciphertext $C_1 C_2 C_3 \cdots C_n$ into k cosets $S_1, S_2, \ldots, S_k$ where $S_i = C_i C_{i+k} C_{i+2k} \ldots (1 \leq i \leq k)$, and each S_i is encrypted

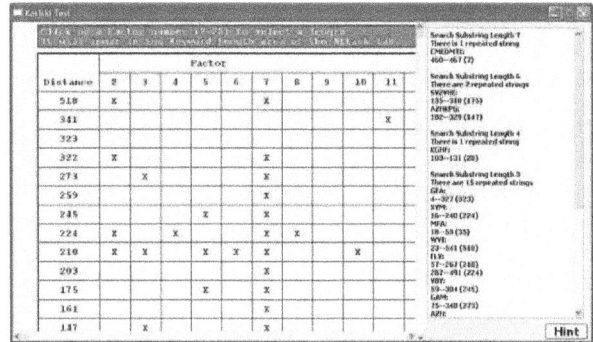

(a) Top Portion

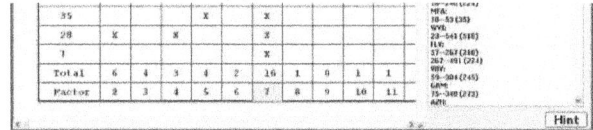

(b) Bottom Portion

Figure 5: Screenshot of the Kasiski Window

by the same letter with an IOC close to 0.068. To apply this idea, for each $1 \leq k \leq n$, we may divide the ciphertext into k cosets, calculate the IOC of each coset, and calculate the average of the k IOC values. If k is the correct length, each individual IOC is close to 0.068 and their average would also be close to 0.068. The estimated keyword length is the value of k that produces the highest average IOC.

Click the `IOC` button to bring up the `IOC` window. VIGvisual displays a table (Figure 6). Each row corresponds to a possible keyword length in the range of 1 and 20, and the columns display the cosets, their IOC values, and the average. The highest three average IOC values are shown in blue. The user chooses a high average and clicks the length to export this value to the `Attack` window.

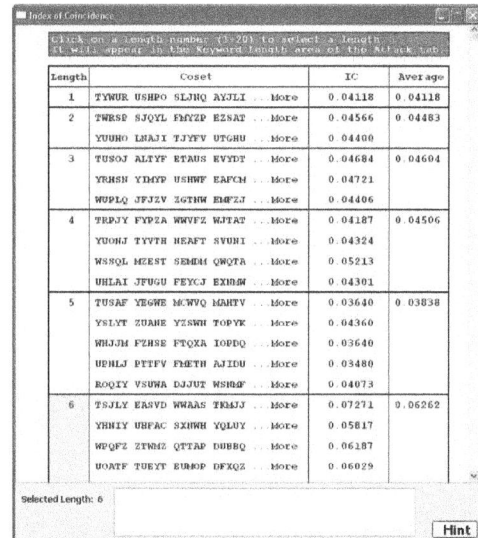

Figure 6: Screenshot of the IOC Window

3.3.3 Keyword Recovery

Once a length estimation is known, the user moves on to keyword recovery. The user clicks the circular button next to the estimated keyword length obtained by Kasiski's method or the IOC method to make it available in the `Select Len` field, or modifies this value to her choice. Then, the user clicks the `Select Len` button to recover the keyword.

VIGvisual uses the χ^2 method to recover the keyword. Assuming the estimated length k is correct, the ciphertext is divided into k cosets, each of which is encrypted by a single letter. Each coset is shifted one position to the right in a cyclic way. After each shift the letter frequency is computed and compared against the typical English letter frequency. Let F_i and f_i ($1 \leq i \leq 26$) be the English letter frequency and calculated letter frequency of letter i, respectively. The χ^2 is defined as follows:

$$\chi^2 = \sum_{j=1}^{26} \frac{(f_i - F_i)^2}{F_i}$$

A lower χ^2 value means the letter frequency of a particular shift matches the English letter frequency better. Hence, the letter corresponding to the shift that yields the smallest χ^2 is very likely to be the correct letter in the keyword.

The `Keyword Recovery` window displays a table (Figure 7). Each column of this table corresponds to a keyword letter and has the χ^2 values of each shift with the smallest one in blue. The letter corresponding to the smallest χ^2 is shown in the column heading. The bottom of this window shows the English letter frequency graph in black. The user may click a coset to modify its keyword letter and a letter on the horizontal axis of the frequency graph to examine its frequency graph. The keyword changes accordingly and the frequency graph of that letter appears. The user may click on every letter and investigate the difference between the English letter frequency and the frequency of the selected letter, and pick the best match by examining all frequency graphs. This step is required as the shift corresponding to the smallest χ^2 value may not be the best choice, and shifts corresponding to other smaller χ^2 values must be examined.

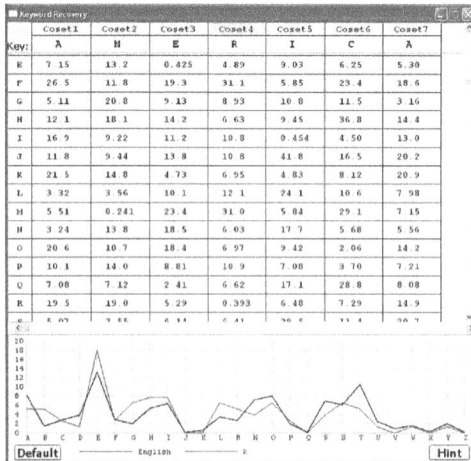

Figure 7: Screenshot of the `Keyword Recovery` Window

Any changes applied to the keyword will also be shown in the `Keyword` field in the `Attack` tab. Finally, the user clicks the `Decrypt` button to decrypt the ciphertext using the current recovered keyword and makes further changes to the keyword in the `Keyword Recovery` window if needed.

4. EVALUATION AND ASSESSMENT

Our survey consists of two parts, a set of 14 questions and eight write-in comments. Choices available are 5:strongly agree, 4:agree, 3:neutral, 2:disagree, and 1:strongly disagree. We collected 25 valid forms. The distribution of majors was as follows: 1 in computer network and system administration (CNSA), 5 in electrical and computer engineering (EE/CpE), 13 in computer science, 1 in mathematics (Math), 1 in chemical engineering, and 4 undeclared.

4.1 General Discussion

This paper uses $\alpha = 0.05$ as the level of significance for all statistical decisions. Our survey showed that 10 and 11 students used the table and slide for their work, and two chose to use the cipher disk. During the evaluation period, on average students used the tool for 13.2 minutes to understand the cipher with standard deviation 7.1 and confidence interval (6.1,20.3). Table 1 has the remaining questions.

Table 1: Survey Questions

Q_1	The `Demo` mode helped better understand
Q_2	The `Practice` mode helped better understand
Q_3	VIGvisual helped identify the parts that were not understood
Q_4	VIGvisual enhanced the course
Q_5	`Kasiski` helped understand the topic
Q_6	`IOC` helped understand the topic
Q_7	χ^2 helped understand the topic
Q_8	VIGvisual helped understand attack
Q_9	The `Demo` mode helped self-study
Q_{10}	The `Practice` mode helped self-study

Q_1 and Q_2 asked if the `Demo` mode and the `Practice` mode helped the students better understand the encryption and decryption processes. The means, standard deviations and confidence intervals were 3.88 and 3.6, 0.6 and 0.87, and (3.64,4.12) and (3.26,3.94). This reflected that the `Practice` mode was not as helpful as the `Demo` mode for this simple cipher. Q_3 asked the students if VIGvisual helped identify the parts of the Vigenère cipher that they did not understand. The mean, standard deviation and confidence interval were 3.8, 0.65 and (3.55,4.05). Thus, VIGvisual helped students learn the Vigenère cipher. As a result, the rating of Q_4, which asked if VIGvisual enhanced the course, is reasonably high with mean, standard deviation and confidence interval 4.24, 0.52 and (4.04,4.44).

Q_5 to Q_8 asked students to assess if the Kasiski, IOC, χ^2 and the `Attack` components helped them understand the topics. Table 2 has a summary. While the χ^2 question (Q_7) received a lower mean of 3.52, the answer to Q_8 has a higher mean of 4.24. This indicated that although the χ^2 component may not help students better learn than Kasiski and IOC do, the students actually understood more after using VIGvisual. Note that we cannot reject the means of Q_5 (3.96) and Q_6 (3.88) being 4 with p-values 0.832 and 0.503, respectively, and the mean of Q_7 being 3.75 with a p-value of 0.148.

4.2 Further Statistical Analysis

The ratings of questions were loosely related to each other. The highest correlation was 0.713 between Q_9 and Q_{10}, and the correlations for question pairs (Q_1, Q_2), (Q_3, Q_9), (Q_5 Q_6), (Q_6, Q_{10}), (Q_7, Q_9), (Q_7, Q_8) and (Q_8, Q_9) were all larger than 0.5. This suggested that ratings of Q_5 to Q_{10} had a positive trend. It is interesting to note that the correlations between Q_4 and other questions was mostly neutral,

Table 2: Ratings of the Kasiski, IOC and `Attack` Components

	Q_5 Kasiski	Q_6 IOC	Q_7 χ^2	Q_8 `Attack`
Mean	3.96	3.88	3.52	4.24
St Dev	0.93	0.88	0.77	0.52
CI$^-$	3.59	3.53	3.22	4.04
CI$^+$	4.33	4.23	3.82	4.44

Confidence Interval = (CI$^-$,CI$^+$)

Table 3: Test Scores

	Quiz 1	Quiz 2
Mean	3.94	5.94
St Dev	1.25	0.35
CI	(3.5,4.37)	(5.8,6.0)

as all the correlations were small, which indicated that the higher rating 4.24 of "if VIGvisual enhanced the course" was independent of ratings of other questions.

Since the student body consisted of several disciplines (*e.g.*, computer science, electrical and computer engineering, chemical engineering and mathematics), we would like to know if students from different disciplines reacted differently. We only grouped students into computer science (CS) and students not in computer science (non-CS). Since the questions may correlate with each other as mentioned earlier, the questions were also grouped into four groups: **(1)** Q_1, Q_2, Q_3 – the Demo, `Practice` modes were helpful and VIGvisual helped identify parts that were not understood, **(2)** Q_5, Q_6, Q_7 – the Kasiski, IOC and χ^2 components were helpful in general, **(3)** Q_9, Q_{10} – the Demo and `Practice` modes were useful in self-study, and **(4)** all questions are in a single group. MANOVA (Multivariate ANOVA) was applied to each of the question groups. In addition, we used ANOVA to investigate the difference between the student groups for Q_4 – if VIGvisual enhanced the course. While the assumptions of MANOVA (*i.e.*, normality and heteroscedasticity) are stronger than those of ANOVA, MANOVA is reasonably robust in our case [5, 6].

We used the general linear model (GLM) of R to perform all tests at $\alpha = 0.05$. The computed p-values of the four groups were 0.842, 0.805, 0.511 and 0.502. This suggested that the ratings from CS and non-CS groups did not vary significantly. The ANOVA result for Q_4 did not suggest difference at $\alpha = 0.05$ either. However, the p-value (0.068) is smaller for this question. In summary, we did not find a significant variation among disciplines and question groups.

4.3 A Test Scores Comparison

A quiz of six problems that address all aspects of the Vigenère cipher was given after the classroom lecture. Then, we discussed VIGvisual and made the software available. One week later a second quiz was given. This quiz has three questions similar to those in the first quiz and three ciphertexts for the students to practice cryptanalysis. The first ciphertext is trivial and can be broken directly using VIGvisual. The second is still easy, but VIGvisual yields a keyword with one incorrect letter. The third is not so trivial because VIGvisual yields a keyword with three incorrect letters, and the students must work a bit harder to break the ciphertext correctly. Both quizzes have a full score of 6 points (*i.e.*, one point per problem). We collected 33 papers from each quiz, and the results are shown in Table 3. The t-values of comparing the means obtained in various t-tests were all larger than 8.5 with p-values nearly 0, and Cohen's d is 2.18. This suggested that the difference between the means is significant and the effect size is large. As a result, we concluded that the software contributed to student learning significantly.

4.4 Student Comments

There were eight write-in questions asking students to make suggestions for further development. We focused on the following issues: whether the layout is useful, whether the Demo mode is more helpful than blackboard work, whether the Kasiski's method, IOC method and the `Keyword Recovery` component enhance learning, whether new features should be added, and software installation issues.

The layout was generally welcomed with comments like *"The layout is well done, the tab separation keeps everything organized and each section is clearly labeled"* and *"Everything was clearly findable. Never got confused"*. Students agreed that the system functioned well and was easy to use.

The Demo mode vs. blackboard question received some interesting comments. Most students indicated VIGvisual is useful; but a few of them believed "in depth things come from the board" or the "procedures". Here is a list of student comments in various aspects: *"The program was much better than the blackboard since it was faster and easier to understand"*, *"I prefer the more visual demonstration"* and *"The demo was better than the use of the chalk board since it was more organized and isolated."*.

Since Kasiski, IOC and keyword recovery components require a significant amount of information and require additional knowledge to be used properly, we expected students may encounter some difficulty in comprehending the system. However, most students were satisfied. The following are typical comments: *"It [Kasiski] was a little confusing due to the table layout, but it made sense after I figured it out"*. *"The Kasiski Test tabs was my favorite function of VIGvisual"*, *"It [IOC] helped me to understand cosets better"*, *"Having the full [IOC] table enhanced my ability to understand because it showed more than just the answer"*, *"If it is your first time seeing IOC, it will be hard. If you have a prior understanding, it makes sense"*, *"The `Keyword Recovery` window made it easy to see why a keyword was likely to be correct"*, and *"[Keyword Recovery] was a little hard to understand, but the Hint button helped a lot"*.

As for new features, the most wanted one is resizable windows and more extensive hints and explanations. Very few students encountered problems installing the system. Those who had problems were mainly due to improperly installed libraries on Mac and some unknown issues on Windows 8.x. VIGvisual ran on Linux and Windows 7 and XP well.

4.5 Self-Study Investigation

We also invited students who did not take our course for a 2-stage self-study. This small scale survey was used to determine if there was a difference between classroom and self-study with our tool. There were two stages, each stage took about one week. In Stage 1, volunteers were asked to find resources to learn the Vigenère cipher, including Kasiski's and IOC methods. At the end of Stage 1, students evaluated their progress and completed six quiz problems.

133

In Stage 2, students were provided with VIGvisual and our web-based tutorial. At the end of this stage, students filled in the evaluation form and completed three quiz problems on cryptanalysis.

We collected seven completed survey forms from 11 volunteers. Volunteers were usually highly motivated, and, as a result, they received nearly perfect scores in both quizzes. They spent on average 14.29 minutes to understand the cipher with a confidence interval of $(6.16, 22.41)$, which is similar to that of the students in our course. On the other hand, the median of the total time spent on the tool is about 41 minutes, which is much higher than that of the students in our course. We used median instead of average because there was a volunteer who used a very long time to practice cryptanalysis. Except for one volunteer who used the disk and slide, all others used the table.

Table 4: Self-Study Survey Results

	Q_1	Q_2	Q_3	Q'_4	Q_5	Q_6	Q_7	Q_8
Class μ	3.88	3.60	3.80	4.24	3.96	3.88	3.52	4.24
Class σ	0.60	0.87	0.65	0.52	0.93	0.88	0.77	0.52
μ	3.86	3.71	4.00	4.29	4.29	4.29	4.00	4.29
σ	0.69	0.76	1.29	0.76	0.76	0.95	0.89	1.11
CI$^-$	3.35	3.15	3.04	3.73	3.73	3.58	3.28	3.46
CI$^+$	4.37	4.27	4.96	4.85	4.85	4.99	4.72	5.11
p-value	0.95	0.75	0.71	0.88	0.36	0.33	0.23	0.97

μ: mean σ: standard deviation Confidence Interval: (CI$^-$,CI$^+$)

Since this survey was about self-study, questions in Table 1 related to classroom presentation were removed. A summary of this self-study results is given in Table 4 in which Q'_4 is the version of Q_4 for self-study. The "Class μ" and "Class σ" rows have the mean values and standard deviation obtained from our classroom survey (Section 4.1 and Table 2). No extensive hypothesis testings were performed because of small sample size. It is interesting to note that Q_1 to Q'_4 were rated similarly in both surveys. On the other hand, students involved in self-study rated our tool higher than those enrolled in our class. Regardless of the sample size issue, t-tests for comparing the means did not suggest any significant differences because the p-values in Table 4 are all larger than 0.1, suggesting no presumption against the null hypothesis (*i.e.*, the corresponding means being equal). Write-in comments were not very different from those obtained from the classroom survey. Hence, we have reasonable evidence to believe that the difference may be small.

5. CONCLUSIONS

This paper presented a visualization tool VIGvisual for teaching and learning the Vigenère cipher. With this tool, instructors are able to present all details of the cipher and a complete cryptanalysis procedure using Kasiski's and the IOC methods for keyword length estimation and the χ^2 method for keyword recovery. The animation and cipher tools help students see the "flow" of the cipher, learn the concepts and practice the cryptanalysis steps with VIGvisual. Evaluation results showed that VIGvisual was effective in the classroom presentation and for student self-study. In particular, after using the tools, the students learned cryptanalysis better and gained understanding of the cipher.

Based on the student comments, the most needed extensions are **(1)** resizable windows, **(2)** making the Vigenère table rows shaded in an alternating way so that it is more readable, **(3)** considering an extension or modification to the Keyword Recovery window so that the frequency graph can work alone rather than as part of the χ^2 method, **(4)** extending the error checking in the Practice mode so that errors can be reported on-the-fly, **(5)** adding the autocorrelation analysis for keyword estimation, and **(6)** developing a web-based version so that the system would be more "portable" as suggested by some students.

VIGvisual is a part of larger development of cryptography visualization tools supported by the National Science Foundation. In addition to VIGvisual, SHAvisual for the Secure Hash Algorithm, DESvisual for the DES cipher, AESvisual for the AES cipher, RSAvisual for RSA cipher, and ECvisual for the elliptic curve based ciphers are available online. Tools, evaluation forms, and installation and user guides for Linux, MacOS and Windows can be found at the following link, from which a complete tutorial of the Vigenère cipher, including cryptanalysis, is available:

www.cs.mtu.edu/~shene/NSF-4.

6. REFERENCES

[1] Cryptool. http://www.cryptool.org.

[2] M. E. Dalkilic and C. Gungor. An Interactive Cryptanalysis Algorithm for the Vigenere Cipher. In *Proceedings of the First International Conference on Advances in Information Systems*, pages 341–351, 2000.

[3] W. F. Friedman. *The Index of Coincidence and Its Applications in Cryptanalysis*. Riverbank Laboratories, 1922.

[4] J. Hoffstein, J. Pipher, and J. H. Silverman. *An Introduction to Mathematical Cryptography*. Springer, 2008.

[5] K. Ito. On the Effect of Heteroscedasticity and Nonnormality Upon Some Multivariate Test Procedures. In P. R. Krishnaiah, editor, *Multivariate Analysis II*. Academic Press, 1969.

[6] K. Ito and W. Schull. On the Robustness of the T^2 Test in Multivariate Analysis of Variance When Variance–Covariance Matrices Are Not Equal. *Biometrika*, 51:71–82, 1964.

[7] F. W. Kasiski. *Die Geheimschriften und die Dechiffrirkunst*. Mittler und Sohn, 1863.

[8] D. Salomon. *Data Privacy and Security*. Springer, 2003.

[9] D. Schweitzer and L. Baird. The Design and Use of Interactive Visualization Applets for Teaching Ciphers. In *Proceedings of IEEE Information Assurance Workshop*, pages 69–75, 2006.

[10] W. Trappe and L. C. Washington. *Introduction to Cryptography with Code Theory*. Prentice-Hall, 2002.

Acknowledgements

The authors are supported by the National Science Foundation under grants DUE-1140512, DUE-1245310 and IIS-1456763.

The Impact of Learning Style Adaptivity in Teaching Computer Security

Mohammad Alshammari[1], Rachid Anane[2], Robert J. Hendley[1]

[1]School of Computer Science, University of Birmingham, UK

{m.t.m.alshammari, r.j.hendley}@cs.bham.ac.uk

[2]Faculty of Engineering and Computing, Coventry University, UK

r.anane@coventry.ac.uk

ABSTRACT

Teaching computer security is one of the most challenging tasks in computer science, because of the need to successfully integrate abstract concepts and practical applications. Several e-learning systems have been developed to address this issue. However, they usually provide the same material in the same sequence irrespective of the characteristics of the students, such as their knowledge level and learning style. In this paper, an approach to learning style adaptivity is proposed for the teaching of computer security. An e-learning system was developed to provide more personalised and adaptive learning, based on the information perception style of the Felder-Silverman model. This is the dimension of learning style, which has received the least attention in published research. In the approach, a personalised sequence of learning material is generated based on an individual learning style. The approach is evaluated in order to determine its effectiveness in learning provision. An experiment conducted with sixty subjects produced significant results. They indicate that matching computer security learning material, according to the learning style of the students, yields significantly better learning gain and student satisfaction than without matching.

Categories and Subject Descriptors

K.3.1 and K.3.2 [**Computers and Education**]: Computer Uses in Education- *Computer-assisted Instruction (CAI)*; Computer and Information Science Education- *Computer Science Education*

General Terms

Experimentation, Human Factors

Keywords

Computer Security Education, Adaptivity, E-learning Systems, Learning Style

1. INTRODUCTION

Computer security is often considered one of the most relevant and challenging topics in computer science. Teaching computer

ITICSE '15, July 04 - 08, 2015, Vilnius, Lithuania.
Copyright 2015 ACM 978-1-4503-3440-2/15/07...$15.00
http://dx.doi.org/10.1145/2729094.2742614

security is a complex task. In a traditional setting, the complexity of teaching computer science courses in general, and computer security courses in particular, arises from the requirement of combining theoretical concepts with applications and examples, all within the constraints of lecture schedules and laboratory resources [19,20]. Another source of difficulty stems from the requirement to meet the needs of all the students in classroom learning. Some students may also find the classroom setting distracting or too rigid.

E-learning systems can, to some extent, alleviate this complexity by offering learning opportunities anytime and anywhere. These systems are expected to support better, more student-centric instruction and enable more self-paced and self-directed learning. They provide learning material and content in several forms such as hypermedia, animation and virtual laboratories. For example, Hu and Wang have introduced a virtual laboratory environment for computer security education; it allows students to perform different hands-on exercises [15]. Tele-Lab IT Security is a tutoring system that provides different security exercises and tasks augmented with background concepts [16]. More innovative tools have been also proposed, such as the CyberCIEGE game; it supports the teaching of computer security in an engaging process [11].

Although traditional e-learning systems offer useful learning environments, they are not flexible enough [20]. They provide the same material and tasks in the same sequence irrespective of the characteristics of students - such as their knowledge, abilities and learning style. Moreover, the learning process can be time consuming, inefficient and less effective. An independent approach to studying taken by students may lead to poor decisions on what and how to study. In addition, pedagogical aspects need to be carefully considered so that systems do not focus exclusively on technical issues but also on well-defined instructional design models [19].

Several instructional approaches have been proposed in computer science in order to make the educational process more effective and to meet the needs of students. Adaptation of learning material based on knowledge and learning style has been the subject of intensive research [7]. For example, the SQL-Tutor is an intelligent e-learning system that customises the sequence of SQL lessons based on the knowledge level of students [21]. An approach that takes into account the learning style in order to provide instructional recommendations to students has also been represented by the eTeacher system for teaching artificial intelligence [23]. The Protus system combines knowledge level and learning style to personalise learning material for teaching Java programming [18].

The deployment of these systems, among others, has produced promising results in enhancing the learning and the satisfaction of students for different computer science topics [1]. However, few attempts have been made in the domain of computer security [1,19]. Furthermore, learning style adaptivity is still a controversial issue; it is not always evident how to provide adaptation based on learning style [6]. These issues need to be addressed in order to make computer security education more effective.

This paper presents an initial investigation into the impact of learning style adaptivity in teaching computer security using e-learning systems. An adaptive approach based on learning style is proposed. It customises the sequence of learning objects for each student based on their learning style.

An evaluation of the approach's effectiveness in terms of learning gain and student satisfaction is also provided. All students go through the same learning objects with the same allocated time. However, the system generates different sequences of the learning objects to match the learning style of each student. By varying the order of the learning objects, it is possible to undertake a more controlled set of experiments.

The next section reviews existing work on learning styles, and puts it into the context of computer security. Section 3 gives an outline of the proposed approach of learning style adaptivity. Section 4 describes the evaluation method. Section 5 presents the results. Section 6 offers a critical discussion of the work, and Section 7 summarises the work and draws some conclusions.

2. LEARNING STYLE

Learning style is defined as "characteristic cognitive, affective, and psychological behaviours that serve as relatively stable indicators of how learners perceive, interact with, and respond to the learning environment" [17]. Several studies have emphasised the importance of learning style in order to improve learning [13,17]. More importantly, it is argued that computer science education should support many different learning styles [22]. Several approaches have been proposed to support the teaching of topics in computer science, such as programming and databases, by adapting learning material according to different learning style models [1,18,21,23]. However, the lack of studies in learning style adaptivity that are based on well-designed experimental evaluation calls for more research [1].

Although a large number of learning style models and frameworks have been introduced [10], the Felder-Silverman model is the most widely used and preferred model in science and engineering education [1,2]. It provides comprehensive details on its components and identifies a teaching style for each component [13]. It also comes with a reliable and validated learning style assessment instrument [14].

The information perception style (sensory-intuitive) is an important component of the Felder-Silverman model [13]. It is argued by some researchers that it is the most important learning style [12]. Conversely, it has received the least attention in published research [1,9]. An investigation of how to provide adaptation based on this style is highly desirable; in addition, its effectiveness in e-learning systems, particularly the teaching of computer security, needs to be evaluated.

The information perception dimension of learning style is concerned with the type of learning material (abstract/concrete) with which an individual student will learn best and also with the best order in which to present material. Students are classified into two categories: sensory and intuitive. Sensory students prefer facts, problem solving by standard methods and real-world examples; intuitive students prefer principles, theories and mathematical models [13]. Sensory students may benefit more from concrete information; intuitive students may learn better with abstract concepts. Felder and Silverman define sensing and intuition as follows: "Sensing involves observing, gathering data through the senses; intuition involves indirect perception by way of the unconscious—speculation, imagination, hunches. Everyone uses both faculties, but most people tend to favour one over the other." [13].

In the linkage between the information perception style and computer security education, students should grasp scientific concepts besides their applications through hands-on activities and concrete examples [19]. In addition, students find the hybrid approach of theory and practice in a computer security course more appealing and exciting [24]. The information perception style is appropriate for dealing with this issue in providing appropriate learning material when taking into account abstract conceptualisation and concrete experience. Furthermore, the incorporation of this approach offers a solution to the debate over how to offer instruction: from abstract concepts to concrete examples, or from examples to concepts.

The next section presents the proposed approach. It personalises the sequences of learning material for each student based on their information perception style.

3. LEARNING STYLE ADAPTIVITY

A specific adaptivity approach based on the information perception style is proposed for computer security education. Personalised learning paths through learning material are generated in an e-learning system [3]. Learning material is represented at two levels. Level one contains a number of learning units. A learning unit focuses entirely on one topic of the course. Each learning unit contains a set of interrelated learning objects in level two [5]. The learning objects are annotated to support adaptation to match the information perception learning style - following the Felder-Silverman model [13]. The main aim is to provide an appropriate combination and ordering of concrete and abstract learning objects.

Figure 1 depicts an example of the course, and how learning paths are generated for sensory and intuitive students. Sensory students study concrete learning objects first and then interact with abstract learning objects (i.e., concrete-to-abstract). It implies that examples and practical activities will be presented first and then followed by concepts and mathematical models when teaching each learning unit. In contrast, intuitive students interact with abstract learning objects first, and then study concrete learning objects (i.e., abstract-to-concrete). Concepts and mathematical models are presented first; followed by examples and practical activities.

A basic computer security course is built and represented in the adaptive e-learning system. It contains two learning units: symmetric key encryption and key-exchange protocols. The symmetric key encryption unit contains four learning objects (concept, example, mathematical notation and interactive tool).

The key-exchange protocols unit has two learning objects (concept and example).

Each learning unit incorporates concrete and abstract learning objects, which will ensure that sensory and intuitive learning styles are equally supported when generating learning paths. Concrete learning objects provide direct practical experience by performing a new task or by presenting a real-world example. A screenshot of a concrete learning object as provided by the system is presented in Figure 2. Abstract learning objects present the mathematical models, principles and concepts of a specific subject of computer security.

It should be noted that this approach is, to some extent, generic; it can be adapted to many application domains by providing personalised sequence of learning material. It is not limited to the computer security domain only.

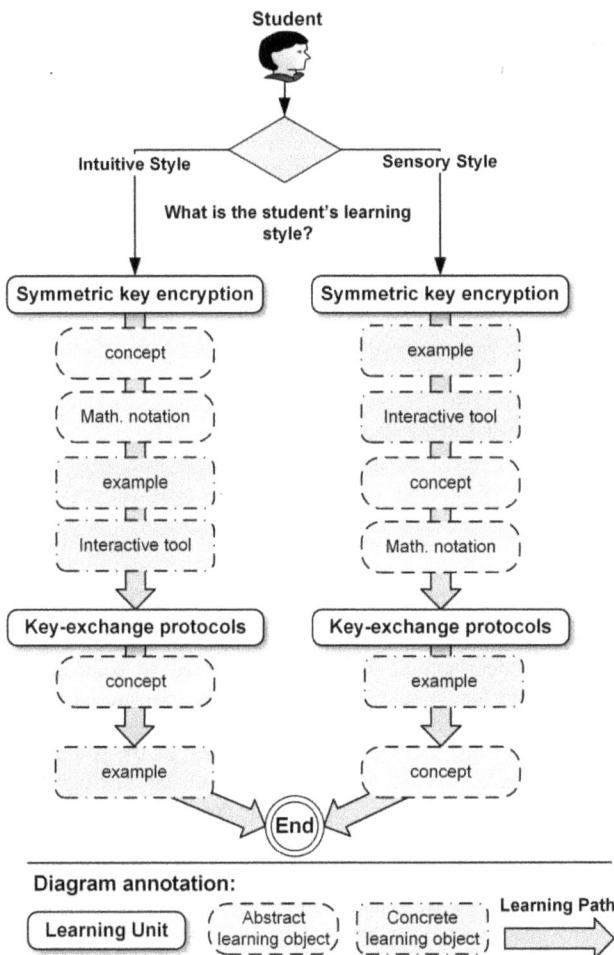

Figure 1. Generation of learning paths for sensory and intuitive students.

4. EXPERIMENTAL EVALUATION

A controlled experiment in a higher education learning environment was conducted in a computer laboratory in order to evaluate the proposed approach. Eight experimental sessions were conducted; each session lasted for about 75 minutes. An important point is that computer security was not part of the subjects'

curriculum; the students were encouraged to take part in the experiment to learn a new topic.

A between subjects design, in which each subject experiences only one condition, was used to avoid the problems of carryover and learning effect from one condition to another.

Figure 2. A concrete learning object example as provided by the adaptive e-learning system.

The next sections provide the research hypotheses, data collection tools and experimental procedure. They are prerequisites for any well-conducted and controlled experiment.

4.1 Hypotheses

Two hypotheses were put forward for this study based on the information perception style. The hypotheses are formulated as follows:

Hypothesis 1. Matching computer security learning material and the information perception style of students yields significantly better learning gain than without matching.

Hypothesis 2. Matching computer security learning material and the information perception style of students yields significantly better student satisfaction than without matching.

According to these hypotheses, the variables were classified into two types: independent and dependent variables. Two independent variables were manipulated to test the dependent variable: (1) an experimental group who interacted with an e-learning system that matched learning material and the information perception style (matched group), and (2) a control group who interacted with an e-learning system that mismatched learning material and the information perception style (mismatched group).

Learning gain and student satisfaction (i.e., the dependent variables) were measured to provide insight into the effectiveness of adaptivity based on the information perception style in computer security education.

4.2 Data Collection

Three data collection tools are used. A subset of the Index of Learning Style (ILS[1]) questionnaire, based on the Felder-Silverman model, containing 11 questions was used to identify the information perception style [13]. The tool is considered reliable and valid for identifying the learning style of students [14].

Pre and post-tests were developed and subjectively evaluated by three computer security experts to measure the learning gain (post-test – pre-test). Recalling, understanding and applying learning factors were taken into account when developing the questions of the tests. Both tests were similar except for the formulation of some questions, their order and the answer options. They were multiple-choice questions with four options for each question. Incorrect answers were penalised in order to discourage random guessing following the strategy developed for standardised tests (such as the SAT[2] test). The strategy is to deduct $100/(n-1)$ percent of the value of the question, where n is the number of answer options. There were 10 multiple-choice questions in each test, and the value of each question is 10.

Student satisfaction was measured by the e-learner satisfaction questionnaire tool (ELS) which can be found in [25]. The tool is a questionnaire that measures satisfaction in terms of four components including the system interface, learning community, learning content and system personalisation. Three components (i.e., interface, content and personalisation) were taken into account; their related 13 questions were used with 7-point Likert scale with anchors ranging from "strongly disagree" to "strongly agree". An example related to satisfaction with the learning content in the ELS tool is: '*the content provided by the e-learning system is easy to understand*' [25].

4.3 Experimental Procedure

The subjects were first introduced to the main objectives of the experiment and informed of the procedure. They were asked to access the e-learning system via an Internet browser. They completed a demographic data form and the ILS questionnaire using the system. Then, the system randomly assigned subjects to experimental (matched) or control (mismatched) groups, and then they completed a pre-test. The pre-test involved answering a set of questions related to computer security.

The subjects then started the process of learning and completed all the learning objects related to symmetric key encryption and key-exchange protocols, but in a different sequence according to their matched or mismatched learning style. At the end of the learning session, they completed a post-test, followed by the e-learner satisfaction questionnaire tool (ELS) [25]. This ended the procedure.

5. RESULTS

The experiment was completed successfully by 60 male subjects. There were 29 subjects in the matched group and 31 subjects in the mismatched group. The subjects were undergraduate computer science students. The mean age of the subjects was 25. In the experiment, there were more sensory students (72%) than intuitive students (28%). Few subjects had strong characteristics of the information perception style for both categories: sensory and intuitive. However, the majority of the subjects had mild to moderate characteristics. The distribution of sensory and intuitive

students somewhat matches other studies according to their samples [14]; there are often more sensory students than intuitive students.

5.1 Learning Gain

The learning gain (i.e., post-test score – pre-test score) and the post-test results of the matched group were higher than those of the mismatched group as presented in Figure 3. The maximum learning gain score was 66, which is the same for both groups.

In order to test the significance of the learning gain, a null hypothesis was put forward indicating that the matched and the mismatched groups are different in terms of the pre-test (prior knowledge). An independent sample t-test at the alpha level .05 was calculated to test the null hypothesis. It indicates that there was no significant difference between the two groups in terms of the pre-test, p>.05. It should be also noted that computer security was a new topic to 95% of the experimental subjects, based on their self-assessment. Therefore, the null hypothesis is rejected; differences between the study groups can be neglected and the significance of the learning gain can be conducted.

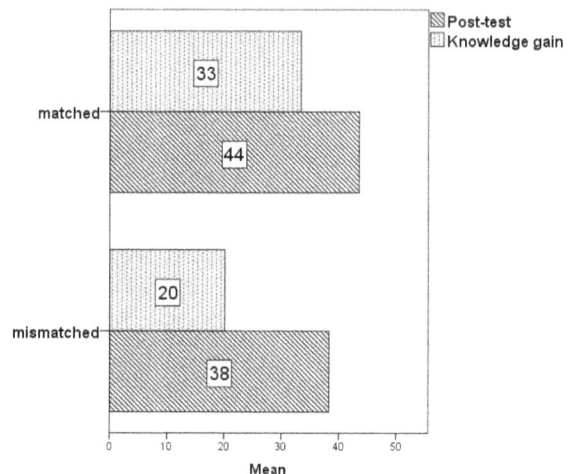

Figure 3. Learning gain and post-test results for the matched and mismatched groups.

An independent sample t-test was conducted to compare the learning gain for the matched group and the mismatched group. There was a significant difference in the learning gain scores for the matched group and the mismatched group, p<.05. Hypothesis 1 is therefore confirmed, and it can be concluded that matching learning material to the information perception style yields significantly better learning gain than without matching, with medium to large effect (d=.57).

A further analysis was conducted to test the difference between sensory and intuitive students in terms of learning gain. Figure 4 shows that in general the matched group had greater learning gain for both sensory and intuitive students than the mismatched group. Therefore, matching learning material and the information perception style is beneficial for both sensory and intuitive students.

Concerning affinity with learning style, the learning gain scores of the students who have mild sensory and intuitive characteristics in both the matched and mismatched groups were relatively the same. Balanced treatments for students who have mild preferences may be more suitable than either matching or mismatching learning style and learning material. As the affinity with learning

---

[1] http://www.engr.ncsu.edu/learningstyles/ilsweb.html

[2] https://sat.collegeboard.org/home

style increases, the learning gain for the matched group was higher than the mismatched group. For example, moderate sensory and intuitive students in the matched group had better learning gain than moderate sensory and intuitive students in the mismatched group. However, a comparison between students who had a strong affinity with their learning style could not be made; very few subjects had strong sensory and intuitive characteristics in the experimental sample.

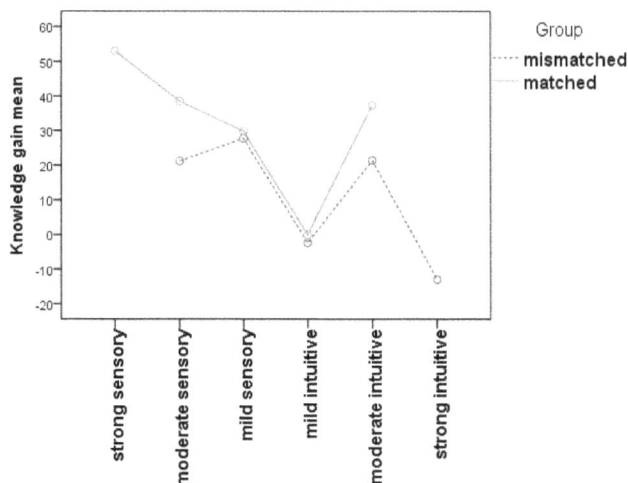

Figure 4. Learning gain of sensory and intuitive students.

5.2 Student Satisfaction

General student satisfaction was evaluated using the e-learner satisfaction questionnaire tool (ELS) [25]. Three components of the ELS tool were taken into account including the system interface, the learning content and the system personalisation; satisfaction for each component was also calculated. An independent sample t-test was conducted; it indicates that the matched group (M=6.17) had significantly higher general student satisfaction scores than the mismatched group (M=5.35), p<.05. Hypothesis 2 is also confirmed.

Table 1 indicates that the matched group had higher student satisfaction mean scores in terms of the system interface, the learning content and the system personalisation than the mismatched group. It may imply that the satisfaction of students even for elements that are not directly related to learning such as the interface is higher when matching the information perception style and learning material.

Table 1. Students' satisfaction scores.

Component	Matched group	Mismatched group
System interface	5.93	5.12
Learning content	6.14	5.41
System personalisation	6.10	5.45

5.3 Additional Findings

The correlation between learning gain and student satisfaction variables was tested. It was found that the relationship between the two variables was non-monotonic. Hence, it can be suggested that there is no clear correlation between the learning gain and student satisfaction. A Pearson correlation coefficient test was computed to assess the relationship between learning gain and time spent on learning. There was a weak, positive correlation which was not statistically significant, r(58)=.23, p> .05.

A Spearman rank correlation coefficient test was also computed to investigate the relationship between age and learning gain as well as the relationship between age and time spent on learning. There was a weak, negative correlation between age and learning gain variables, which was statistically significant, $r_s(58)$=-.27, p< .05. There was also a very weak, negative correlation between age and time spent on learning, which was not statistically significant, $r_s(58)$= - .07, p> .05.

6. DISCUSSION

In contrast with some published studies [8,10], the findings of this work confirm the view that the adaptation of learning material based on learning style does have an effect on learning gain. These results are in line with the outcome of many related research programmes [18,23]. More specifically, it was demonstrated that matching computer security learning material with the students' information perception style yields significantly better learning gain. It should be noted that the learning gain is related to the short-term learning effect where students completed the post-test immediately after the experiment. This finding cannot however be generalised to cover the long-term learning effect. A study with a wider scope is currently being carried out, which will incorporate the students' existing knowledge level into the adaptation model.

In this study, other relevant factors were also investigated. It was found that there was a positive correlation between the learning gain and the time spent on learning. Although it may be the case that the more students spend their time on learning, the higher their learning gain, the correlation between learning gain and time spent was weak and was not significant. In addition, a negative but significant correlation between learning gain and age was found. This might imply that the older the student the lower the learning gain. Furthermore, the time spent on learning decreased with age. These particular results may be specific to the experimental sample. With respect to student satisfaction, the results reveal that student satisfaction is higher when the computer security material is matched with student information perception style. However, there was no correlation between learning gain and student satisfaction. This may point to the potential use of learning style as a motivational factor in enhancing the experience of the students [1].

It is expected that the results can, to some extent, be generalised to other topics in computer security, such as Data Encryption Standards (DES) [4] and Kerberos protocols. Furthermore, since the proposed approach effectively enhances learning and contributes to better computer security education, its application could be beneficial in other computer science topics such as programming and databases. This potential generalisation could provide an opportunity for exploring further the range of the characteristics of the information perception dimension: mild, moderate and strong. This could also encourage a more refined and creative approach to the design, implementation and deployment of learning objects. The research would also benefit from a more heterogeneous sample of subjects, who would be exposed to a larger set of learning objects.

Although the information perception dimension of learning style might be considered the most important [12], other learning style dimensions should also be integrated into the proposed approach in order to enhance the learning process. Moreover, the cognitive and meta-cognitive skills of the students can be enriched by encouraging more collaborative work, and by enabling students to monitor their learning performance and learning style profiles.

This paper reports on one of the few studies where the information perception style is explicitly applied in the domain of computer security education. This work has also the merit of offering a resolution to the on-going debate, in teaching, between the exclusive application of an abstract-to-concrete approach or a concrete-to-abstract approach. It provides a compromise by adopting an appropriate approach according to the learning style of each student.

7. CONCLUSION

In this paper, an approach of learning style adaptivity was proposed for computer security education. In the approach, a personalised sequence of learning material was generated for each student based on the information perception dimension of learning style. This involved providing a concrete-to-abstract sequence of learning material to sensory learners, and the generation of the sequence of abstract-to-concrete material for intuitive students.

The approach was evaluated by a controlled experiment with sixty subjects. There were positive findings in terms of learning gain and student satisfaction when matching learning material to the learning style of students. It indicates that this approach can contribute to better computer security education. It may be also useful in other computer science topics such as programming and databases. Moreover, it is suggested that the fixed teaching approach such as abstract-to-concrete or concrete-to-abstract will not always be beneficial for all students. The findings have however revealed that the teaching approach should match the students' preferences.

The main limitations of the experiment were that it was based on a short-term study with a limited number of computer security learning objects and with a relatively small group of subjects. Future research will extend the proposed approach to incorporate other learning factors such as cognitive and meta-cognitive skills and the abilities of students. It will also involve a long-term evaluation.

8. REFERENCES

1. Akbulut, Y. and Cardak, C.S.Adaptive educational hypermedia accommodating learning styles: A content analysis of publications from 2000 to 2011. *Computers & Education 58*, 2 (2012), 835–842.
2. Alshammari, M., Anane, R., and Hendley, R.Adaptivity in E-Learning Systems. *The 8th International Conference on Complex, Intelligent, and Software Intensive Systems (CISIS 2014)*, (2014), 79–86.
3. Alshammari, M., Anane, R., and Hendley, R.An E-Learning Investigation into Learning Style Adaptivity. *The 48th Hawaii International Conference on System Sciences (HICSS-48)*, (2015), pp11–20.
4. Anane, R., Purohit, K., and Theodoropoulos, G.An Animated Cryptographic Learning Object. *Computer Graphics, Imaging and Visualisation, 2008. CGIV'08. Fifth International Conference on*, (2008), 61–68
   http://www.cs.bham.ac.uk/research/projects/lemsys/DES/.
5. Anane, R.The Learning Object Triangle. *Advanced Learning Technologies (ICALT), 2014 IEEE 14th International Conference on*, (2014), 719–721.
6. Brusilovsky, P. and Millán, E.User models for adaptive hypermedia and adaptive educational systems. *The adaptive web*, (2007), 3–53.
7. Brusilovsky, P.Adaptive Hypermedia for Education and Training. *Adaptive Technologies for Training and Education*, (2012), 46.
8. Buch, K. and Sena, C.Accommodating diverse learning styles in the design and delivery of on-line learning experiences. *International Journal of Engineering Education 17*, 1 (2001), 93–98.
9. Chrysafiadi, K. and Virvou, M.Student modeling approaches: A literature review for the last decade. *Expert Systems with Applications 40*, 11 (2013), 4715–4729.
10. Coffield, F., Moseley, D., Hall, E., and Ecclestone, K.*Learning styles and pedagogy in post-16 learning: A systematic and critical review.* Learning and Skills Research Centre London, London, 2004.
11. Cone, B.D., Irvine, C.E., Thompson, M.F., and Nguyen, T.D.A video game for cyber security training and awareness. *Computers & Security 26*, 1 (2007), 63–72.
12. Felder, R.M., Felder, G.N., and Dietz, E.J.The effects of personality type on engineering student performance and attitudes. *Journal of Engineering Education 91*, 1 (2002), 3–17.
13. Felder, R.M. and Silverman, L.K.Learning and teaching styles in engineering education. *Engineering education 78*, 7 (1988), 674–681.
14. Felder, R.M. and Spurlin, J.Applications, reliability and validity of the index of learning styles. *International Journal of Engineering Education 21*, 1 (2005), 103–112.
15. Hu, D. and Wang, Y.Y.Teaching Computer Security using Xen in a Virtual Environment. *Information Security and Assurance, 2008. ISA 2008. International Conference on*, (2008), 389–392.
16. Hu, J., Meinel, C., and Schmitt, M.Tele-lab IT Security: An Architecture for Interactive Lessons for Security Education. *Proceedings of the 35th SIGCSE Technical Symposium on Computer Science Education*, ACM (2004), 412–416.
17. Keefe, J.W.Learning style: An overview. *Student learning styles: Diagnosing and prescribing programs*, (1979), 1–17.
18. Klasnja-Milicevic, A., Vesin, B., Ivanovic, M., and Budimac, Z.E-Learning personalization based on hybrid recommendation strategy and learning style identification. *Computers & Education 56*, 3 (2011), 885–899.
19. Konak, A., Clark, T.K., and Nasereddin, M.Using Kolb's Experiential Learning Cycle to improve student learning in virtual computer laboratories. *Computers & Education 72*, 0 (2014), 11–22.
20. Marsa-Maestre, I., De La Hoz, E., Gimenez-Guzman, J.M., and Lopez-Carmona, M.A.Design and evaluation of a learning environment to effectively provide network security skills. *Computers & Education 69*, (2013), 225–236.
21. Mitrovic, A.An intelligent SQL tutor on the web. *International Journal of Artificial Intelligence in Education 13*, 2 (2003), 173–197.
22. Rößling, G., Joy, M., Moreno, A., et al.Enhancing Learning Management Systems to Better Support Computer Science Education. *SIGCSE Bull. 40*, 4 (2008), 142–166.
23. Schiaffino, S., Garcia, P., and Amandi, A.eTeacher: Providing personalized assistance to e-learning students. *Computers & Education 51*, 4 (2008), 1744–1754.
24. Sharma, S.K. and Sefchek, J.Teaching information systems security courses: A hands-on approach. *Computers & Security 26*, 4 (2007), 290–299.
25. Wang, Y.-S.Assessment of learner satisfaction with asynchronous electronic learning systems. *Information & Management 41*, 1 (2003), 75–86.

RBACvisual: A Visualization Tool for Teaching Access Control using Role-based Access Control

Man Wang,
Jean Mayo,
Ching-Kuang Shene
Dept. of Computer Science
Michigan Technological
University
Houghton, MI
{manw,jmayo,shene}
@mtu.edu

Thomas Lake,
Steve Carr
Dept. of Computer Science
Western Michigan University
Kalamazoo, MI
{thomas.l.lake,
steve.carr}@wmich.edu

Chaoli Wang
Dept. of Computer Science
and Engineering
University of Notre Dame
Notre Dame, IN
chaoli.wang@nd.edu

ABSTRACT

This paper presents RBACvisual, a user-level visualization tool designed to facilitate the study and teaching of the role-based access control (RBAC) model, which has been widely used in companies to restrict access to authorized users. RBACvisual provides two graphical abstractions of the underlying specification. Policies can be input and modified graphically or using text-based files. Students can use an embedded Query system to answer commonly asked questions and to test their understanding of a given policy. A Practice subsystem is also provided for instructors to assign quizzes to students; the answers can be sent to the instructor via email. We also present the results of an evaluation of RBACvisual within a senior-level course on information security. The student feedback was positive and indicated that RBACvisual helped students understand the model and enhanced the course.

Categories and Subject Descriptors

k.3.2 [**Computers and Education**]: Computer and Information Science Education—*Computer science education, information systems education*

Keywords

Security, visualization

1. INTRODUCTION

Within organizations and companies, it has always been critical, yet challenging to associate privileges and responsibilities with different positions. In the 1970s, computer applications were developed to implement access constraints according to job positions. The role-based access control

models were simple and application-specific. The first general-purpose RBAC model was proposed by Ferraiolo and Kuhn [4] in 1992. Based on this model, Sandhu et al. [7] introduced an RBAC framework in 1996. Later, a U.S. national standard for RBAC was proposed and accepted in 2004. Now the model is widely used in modern industry. As the RBAC model gains more and more popularity, understanding the model and using it to design policies to fulfill security goals has become increasingly important.

Visualization has been applied to some access control models. Schweitzer et al. developed a visualization system to enable active learning about the HRU (Harrison, Ruzzo, Ullman) and Take-Grant models of access control [9]. Hallyn and Kearns developed DTEEdit and DTEView for graphical analysis of DTE specifications [6]. DTEEdit and DTEView do not have pedagogical goals. Visualization and animation have also been applied in many areas of security education [1, 3, 8, 9, 10, 11]. This paper describes RBACvisual that aims to enhance the pedagogy of the RBAC model. It allows students to create, modify, and analyze policies graphically. Students can practice RBAC policy design without taking time to learn the details of a security specification language. RBACvisual can import and export human-readable text-based policies. Analysis is via three graphical representations of a policy or via a query subsystem. Instructors may use a test module that requires students to answer questions about policies and then sends student answers to the instructor by email. The system is not tied to the underlying operating system and currently runs under Linux and MacOS. RBACvisual was tested in a senior-level course on computer security.

The remainder of this paper is organized as follows: Section 2 provides the background of the computer security course where RBACvisual was evaluated, Section 3 presents our tool, Section 4 has a detailed study of our findings from student evaluation, and Section 5 has our conclusions.

2. COURSE INFORMATION

RBACvisual was used in a Computer Security course, offered by the Department of Computer Science at Michigan Technological University. It is a senior-level course that gives a basic introduction to topics in computer security. The access control component covers the Role-Based Access Control (RBAC), Domain Type Enforcement (DTE), and

Bell-LaPadula (BLP) models. The course also covers secure coding in C, cryptography, key management, authentication, malicious logic, and intrusion detection.

Most students were computer science majors who took the course as an elective. The class in which the evaluation was conducted included twenty-seven students.

Students were given paper and pencil exercises on the RBAC model as part of the regular course homework. For this first use of RBACvisual, students were additionally given extra credit if they used the tool to solve their assignment questions. The problem was to evaluate some simple policies via a series of questions. A quiz feature (described in Section 3.5) was used in the take-home final exam. A survey was distributed for students to participate in voluntarily.

3. SOFTWARE DESCRIPTION

Roles

	cust	dev	pres	qc	sales
cathy	X				
charles	X				
dave	X	X			
dot		X			
patty			X		
quinn				X	
sam					X

Objects

	/	/path	/path/to	/path/to/db	path/to/evidenc	/path/to/files	/path/to/tests
cust				x,r,w			
dev							r,w
pres					r,w		
qc							x
sales				x,r,w		-r | r,w	

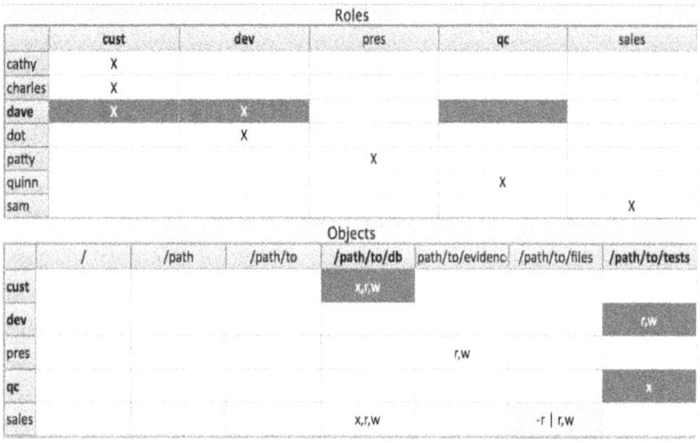

Figure 1: User Interface (with Matrix View)

RBACvisual is a visualization tool designed to facilitate the study and teaching of the Role-Based Access Control (RBAC) model. It implements the RBAC model in Core and Hierarchical forms [5]. The basic concept of Core RBAC is that users as well as permissions to objects (files and directories) are directly assigned to roles based on their job functions. Therefore, users' membership to roles determines if they have access to objects in the system. Core RBAC allows the user-to-role assignment and role-to-object permission to be many-to-many. Based on Core RBAC, Hierarchical RBAC additionally supports a role hierarchy. A hierarchy is mathematically a partial order defining a seniority relation between roles, whereby senior roles acquire the permissions of their juniors, and junior roles acquire the user membership of their seniors [5]. We denote the senior role as r_1 and junior role as r_2. Let $U(r)$ be the set of users assigned to role r and $P(r)$ be the permissions of role r. We define the inheritance relation $>$ such that $r_1 > r_2$ if and only if $U(r_1) \subseteq U(r_2)$ and $P(r_1) \supseteq P(r_2)$.

RBACvisual supports two types of files: specification files (.rbac) and visualization files (.rbacvis). A specification file contains text that describes role inheritance, user-to-role assignments and role-to-object permissions. A visualization file stores the graphical information of the visualization, and implicitly the underlying specification, so that the same arrangement and layout can be retrieved later. The visualization focuses on the interpretation of the user-to-role and role-to-object relationship combined with the role hierarchy.

3.1 Visualization

Two different views, the Matrix View and the Hierarchy View, are available to examine a policy. Figure 1 has an example of the Matrix View. The top matrix is for the user-to-role assignment and the bottom matrix shows the role-to-object permissions.

Figure 2 shows the Hierarchy View, which consists of two parts. The Role Hierarchy Section with green background constructs a graph based on the role hierarchy. The Object Hierarchy Section with red background shows the hierarchy of objects in the file system. Green nodes represent roles, red nodes represent objects, and yellow nodes representing users are located around their role nodes. An edge is drawn from node r_1 to node r_2 when node r_1 inherits node r_2[1]. All inheritance relationships are extracted from the policy and are depicted by an edge. If the inheritance is not specified explicitly in the policy file, the edge line is dashed.

3.2 Analysis Mode

In the Matrix View in Figure 1, users, roles and objects are shown as headers of the tables. Clicking on a user (*i.e.*, dave) highlights the roles (*i.e.*, cust, dev, qc) this user occupies based on direct assignment and any defined role hierarchy and thus highlights the accessible objects. Likewise, clicking on an object highlights users and roles that have access to it. In the bottom table, the permissions of roles to objects are listed. The content follows the format "-r| permissionset"[2] when the permission applies to the objects underneath and is highlighted in yellow. When the permissions do not apply to objects underneath, the format will simply be "permissionset".

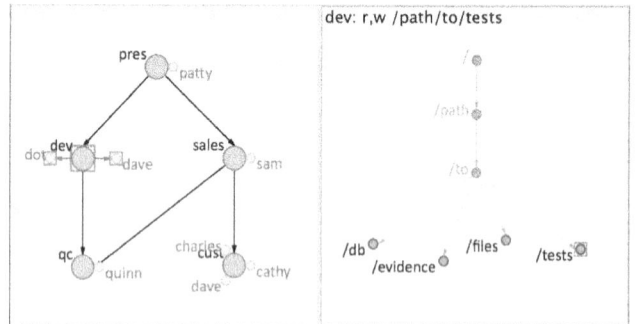

Figure 2: Role Node Highlight without Inheritance

As for the Hierarchy View, clicking on a node of interest will highlight the user and object nodes the role can access. Explicit read, write and execute permissions can be found in the top left corner of the Object Hierarchy Section. When a user node is clicked, the roles to which the user is assigned and the objects that can be accessed through those roles are highlighted. Clicking on an object node will highlight the roles and users that have access to the object.

Functions in the Highlight Nodes section in a toolbox (not shown) allow users to configure the highlight scheme of role nodes. Highlighting can be configured to include or exclude

[1]Edges inferred by transitivity in the role hierarchy are removed to reduce visual clutter.

[2]The permissionset can be any subset of r,w,x where r stands for read, w for write, x for execute. Thus, if granting read and write permissions, the permissionset should be "r, w".

the role hierarchy. When the hierarchy is included, highlighting shows the users assigned to the role and the objects the role has access to from itself as well as through the inheritance relation. User nodes are visible by default but can be turned off to reduce the clutter in the graph.

Figure 2 shows an example of clicking on a role node. When the Without role hierarchy option is selected, each of the role nodes can be turned on and off by clicking on it. In Figure 2, role dev is turned on. Therefore, its user nodes dot and dave and object node /path/to/tests are highlighted by red frames while all other nodes are off (gray).

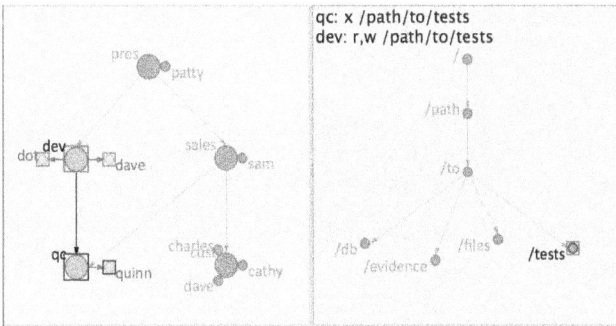

Figure 3: Role Node Highlight with Children

With the role hierarchy turned off, multiple nodes can also be turned on. All users and objects accessible by highlighted nodes will be highlighted. While highlighting a single node provides information directly from the policy specification, highlighting multiple nodes allows a study of the combined permissions of many roles.

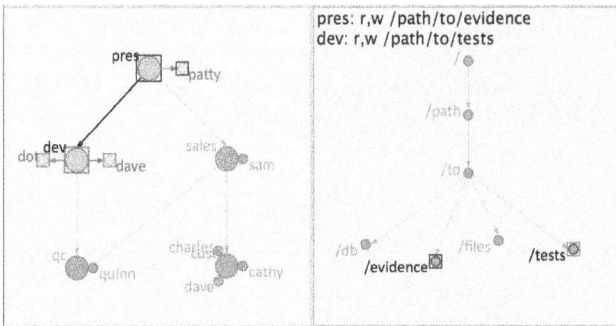

Figure 4: Role Node Highlight with Parents

It is also possible to configure the Highlight Nodes section in the toolbox so that role inheritance is involved. Choices of highlighting the children, parents, or both children and parent role nodes of the clicked role node are available. Different from the mode without hierarchy, this mode only allows one role node to be selected at a time. Along with the selected node, role nodes with the selected inheritance relation will be highlighted in blue frames. User nodes and object nodes will be highlighted in red frames if directly accessible from the clicked role or in blue frames if accessible from blue-framed roles. Figures 3 and 4 depict the nodes related to role dev. The highlighting in the left view shows that the child and parent role nodes of dev are qc and pres, respectively. The right view shows that dev and qc both have access to /path/to/tests with different permissions and pres additionally has access to /path/to/evidence. Likewise,

when a user node is clicked, the roles it is assigned to and the objects accessible from those roles will be highlighted. When an object node is clicked, the roles and users that have access to the object are highlighted.

3.3 Edit Mode

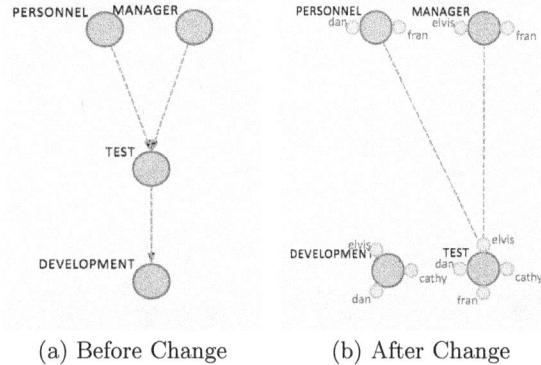

(a) Before Change   (b) After Change

Figure 5: Edit mode

Both views allow building a policy from scratch and editing the policy graphically. In the Matrix View, the table cell values can be changed. In the Hierarchy View, a context menu (not shown) can be used for editing the properties of each node. The toolbox provides a dialog to modify, add, or delete any element of the user-to-role or permission-to-role assignment. Addition and removal of any role, user or object are also available. In this mode, any edit applied will cause immediate update of relations and depict the effect. Figure 5 shows the role hierarchy of a policy before and after user assignment to roles. Before the assignment, the role hierarchy was suggested as dashed lines based on the permissions of roles to objects; no users are assigned to roles. After modification, users elvis, cathy and dan are assigned to DEVELOPMENT while elvis, cathy, dan and fran are assigned to TEST. That is, the users of TEST are no longer a subset of the users of DEVELOPMENT. Hence, there is no suggested inheritance relation between them in Figure 5 (b).

3.4 Specification and Query

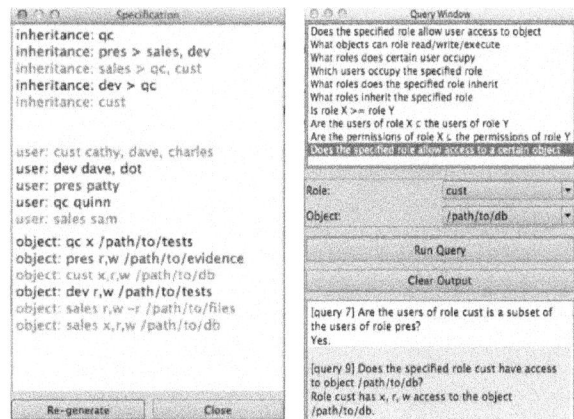

(a) Specification Diagnosis   (b) Query

Figure 6: Specification and Exercise Modules

The Specification Window in Figure 6 (a) shows the text-based specification of the existing policy. It can be edited via graphical operations on views or textual edit within the window. Changes will be reflected immediately. The Query Window in Figure 6 (b) contains questions commonly asked about an RBAC policy. Parameters for certain questions can be configured on the interface and answers to questions can be found in the bottom field, with the most recent answer being highlighted.

3.5 Practice and Test

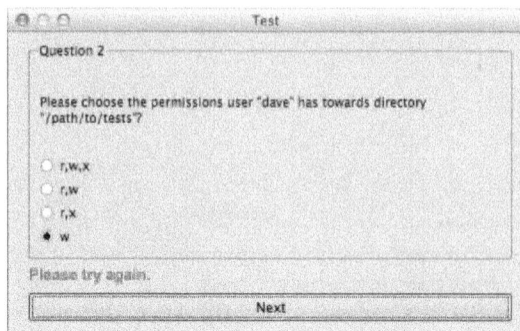

Figure 7: Multiple Trial Quiz Mode with Wrong Answer

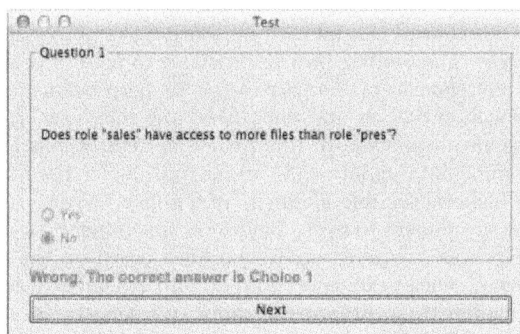

Figure 8: Self-test Quiz Mode with Wrong Answer

RBACvisual allows an instructor to give a series of questions (or a "quiz") to students. Three quiz modes are available which control how a student may progress through the questions. The questions are configurable so that instructors can use their own questions to achieve various teaching goals. All the questions are multiple-choice questions. Instructors specify the quiz mode and the questions that comprise the quiz through a file that adheres to a prescribed format (given in the Instructor Manual). Instructors can share the question file with their students and a test can be started by importing the question file into the system through a dialog.

RBACvisual supports three quiz modes. The first mode is Traditional Mode where students' answers will be sent at the end of the quiz. The quiz moves forward after the first response to each question. The second mode is Multiple Trial Mode. In this mode, students are allowed to try multiple times until they get the correct answer to a question. The number of attempts for each question will be stored. Figure 7 shows an example of the interface when a wrong answer is chosen. The third option is Self-test Mode. Correct answers will be shown to the students after a choice has been confirmed for a question, as depicted in Figure 8.

A dialog confirming the submission will show up as the last step of any test. The system will attempt to bring up

Thunderbird to send answers to the instructor. If Thunderbird is not installed, a warning dialog will show up indicating where the answer file is stored and the student will be able to send the email manually. In this case, the answer file will include the student user ID and be encrypted using the instructor's public key. Instructors later can retrieve the readable answer files by applying their private keys. Encryption helps ensure a submitted file was generated by a particular student. With the unique user ID stored and encrypted, it would be difficult for a student to submit a file with the identity of another student. However, students can still take a quiz multiple times (and change their answers) if time allows. The vulnerability of this approach to cheating is similar to a take-home exam. For Multiple Trial Mode and Self-test Mode, the quiz is intended as a practice for students and there is no intention to prevent cheating. Our goal is to let students practice and know the answers for self-evaluation and to let instructors know that a student took the quiz and how the student performed.

4. EVALUATION

Table 1: Rating Questions

Q1	Matrix View helped understand RBAC
Q2	Hierarchy View helped understand RBAC
Q3	Toolbox made it easy to create/edit policy
Q4	Context Menu in Hierarchy View is convenient for policy editing
Q5	Query helped study RBAC policy
Q6	RBACvisual made correct modification on policies easier
Q7	Matrix View was intuitive and clear
Q8	Hierarchy View was intuitive and clear
Q9	Hierarchy View helped understand role inheritance
Q10	Colors used can distinguish different items
Q11	Width of edges was reasonable
Q12	Understood RBAC better after using the tool
Q13	The tool helped find mistakes in my policy
Q14	RBACvisual enhanced the course
Q15	The software was easy to use
Q16	How long did it take you to understand the RBAC model by using the software
Q17	How many times did you use the software
Q18	How long did you use this software in total

The RBACvisual evaluation included two parts: 18 rating questions and seven write-in comments. The rating questions are listed in Table 1. The first 15 rating questions study the effects of RBACvisual. The choices are: 1:strongly disagree, 2:disagree, 3:neutral, 4:agree, and 5:strongly agree. Q16, Q17 and Q18 study the time participants spent on the tool. The choices for Q16 are 1:less than 5 mins, 2:5-10 mins, 3:10-15 mins, 4:15-30 mins and 5:more than 30 mins. The choices for Q17 are 1:once, 2:1-3 times, 3:3-5 times, 4:5-10 times, and 5:more than 10 times. The choices for Q18 are 1:less than 5 mins, 2:5-15 mins, 3:15-30 mins, 4:30-60 mins, and 5:more than 1 hour. This evaluation was conducted in a senior-level Computer Security course. For this first use of RBACvisual, students were given extra credit if they used the tool to solve their assignment questions. A survey was distributed at the end of the semester for students to participate in voluntarily. We collected eight valid forms from students, five of whom major in Computer Science, one in Computer Systems Science, one in Software Engineering, and one in Computer Engineering.

4.1 General Discussion

Table 2 has the means, standard deviations and confidence intervals (at 95% significance level of mean) of rating questions Q1 to Q15. The ratings of questions are no less than 3.88. Their overall mean value is 4.34 with a standard deviation 0.69, suggesting that the feedback to the tool was positive in general. Q6 and Q13 have the lowest mean of 3.88 with standard deviation of 0.99 and 0.64, respectively. Q6 investigates whether the tool makes the correct modification of policies easier. The lower scores it received might be because some modifications did not introduce big changes in visualization and thus some efforts should be taken to examine the changes. Q13 probably shares the same reasoning when changes are applied and it is hard to tell the correctness of a change as it depends on the users' intention, which is hard to detect. The means and confidence intervals of Q7 and Q8 are 4.29 and 4.57, (3.92, 4.65) and (4.18, 4.97), indicating that students generally thought the Matrix View and the Hierarchy View were intuitive and clear. Q1, Q2, Q12 and Q14 received scores no less than 4.13. This suggests that RBACvisual helped students understand the RBAC model better and enhanced the course. Q3, Q4 and Q15 on the easiness of using the tool were rated over 4.25 and thus showed that the tool was easy to use.

Table 2: Mean (μ), Standard Deviation (σ) and Confidence Interval

	Q1	Q2	Q3	Q4	Q5	Q6	Q7
μ	4.38	4.25	4.38	4.25	4.38	3.88	4.29
σ	0.52	0.89	0.74	0.89	0.74	0.99	0.49
CI^-	4.02	3.64	3.86	3.64	3.86	3.19	3.92
CI^+	4.73	4.86	4.89	4.86	4.89	4.56	4.65

	Q8	Q9	Q10	Q11	Q12	Q13	Q14	Q15
μ	4.57	4.86	4.57	4.29	4.13	3.88	4.25	4.63
σ	0.53	0.38	0.79	0.76	0.64	0.64	0.46	0.52
CI^-	4.18	4.58	3.99	3.73	3.68	3.43	3.93	4.27
CI^+	4.97	5.00	5.00	4.85	4.57	4.32	4.57	4.98

Confidence Interval = (CI^-, CI^+)

The last three questions (Q16 to Q18) are about the usage of the tool. Table 3 has the distribution of answers. On Q16, 62.5% of students selected Choice 2 and 37.5% chose Choice 4. This implies that all students were able to understand the RBAC model within 15 minutes. As for Q17, the distribution indicates that half of the students used the tool for one to three times and all of them used the tool for less than 5 times. Answers to Q18 suggest that 75% of the students used the tool for less than 30 minutes while there were some students who used the tool for up to one hour.

Table 3: Usage Distribution

	Choice1	Choice2	Choice3	Choice4	Choice5
Q16	0	62.5%	37.5%	0	0
Q17	12.5%	50%	37.5%	0	0
Q18	12.5%	25%	37.5%	12.5%	12.5%

4.2 Statistical Analysis

We were interested in knowing the rating correlation of each question pair. To this end, the Spearman rank correlation test was applied to the first 15 questions. We found 16 out of the 105 question pairs had a p-value less than the level of significance $\alpha = 0.05$. This means that nearly 85% of the question pairs did not have a significant monotonic correlation. Moreover, all Spearman ρ's between Q10 and other questions were insignificant, meaning the rating of the use of colors is likely to be independent of the rating of other questions. Figure 9 shows the 16 pairs with the value of ρ shown on each edge. It is clear that the ratings of Q2, Q3, Q5, Q6, Q8 and Q11 were very closely inter-related with a Spearman ρ value of at least 0.78. Therefore, the Hierarchy View, Query, easy policy modification, and policy creation/editing were rated similarly in a monotonic way. Q5, Q12, Q13 and Q9 formed a linear chain with $\rho(Q5,Q12) = 0.839$, $\rho(Q12,Q13) = 0.820$ and $\rho(Q9,Q13) = 0.764$. This indicated that if a student rated "Query helped study RBAC policy" (Q5) higher this student would very likely provide higher ratings to questions "RBACvisual helped understand RBAC better" (Q12), "RBACvisual helped find mistakes" (Q13), and "Hierarchy View helped understand role inheritance" (Q9). It is interesting to note that the Spearman ρ between "RBACvisual enhanced the course" (Q14) and "RBACvisual was easy to use" (Q15) is 0.4 with a p-value of 0.374. As a result, we cannot reject the null hypothesis, which means there was no statistically significant monotonic correlation between the rating of Q14 and the rating Q15. On the other hand, the two high Spearman ρ dangling pairs $\rho(Q6,Q14) = 0.882$ and $\rho(Q3,Q15) = 0.794$ were perhaps coincidences. We also

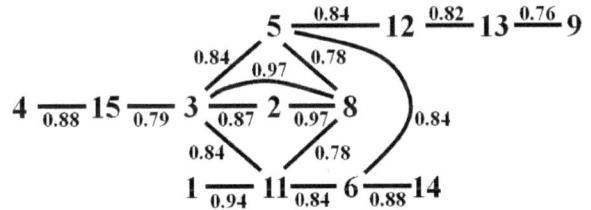

Figure 9: Graph of Significant Spearnman Correlation Pairs

used a Student's t-test to compare the differences among ratings. While the sample size is small, Student's t-test is rather robust and still can be used in this study [2]. We first looked at the "helped" question group (Q1, Q2, Q5, Q9, Q13). Pairwise t-test shows that except for pairs (Q5,Q9) and (Q9,Q13) with p-values 0.03 and 0.00, respectively, all other p-values were larger than 0.1. This suggested that except for (Q5,Q9) and (Q9,Q13), the null hypothesis (that the questions were rated equally) cannot be rejected. The p-value for pair (Q7,Q8) is 0.17, and, hence, students rated the Matrix View and the Hierarchy View equally even though the means were 0.429 and 0.458, respectively. Finally, we looked at three summary questions "Understood RBAC after using the tool" (Q12), "RBACvisual enhanced the course" (Q14), and "The software was easy to use" (Q15). The mean values of Q12, Q14 and Q15 were 4.13, 4.25 and 4.63, respectively, and the p-values for (Q12, Q14), (Q12, Q15) and (Q14,Q15) were 0.60, 0.03 and 0.08, respectively. Therefore, the rating difference between Q12 and Q15 is statistically significant, and students considered ease of use higher than improved understanding of RBAC after using the tool. Since only 13 out of 105 pairwise t-tests were significant and many question pairs were not directly related, the rating differences would be small. Coupled with high ratings of questions, we conclude that the evaluation results were very positive for this sample.

4.3 Student Comments

The seven write-in questions were designed to gather suggestions from participants for further improvement. The aspects include: representation in visualizations, the effects of in-class demo of the tool, new feature suggestions, and performance and installation of the tool.

The overall feedback to visualization representations was positive. Some students stated "*I enjoy this view when looking at who has permissions quickly. I can click on what I need to know and it will light up anything corresponding to.*", "*This was the best part. The hierarchy showed the role dominance and which users belonged to which roles very clearly.*", and "*The hierarchy view helped me understand what roles are ranked higher and lower than one another.*" Some issues were mentioned: (1) to add header scrolling in the matrix view; and (2) presentation of permissions to objects that fits the visual theme better than the text presentation.

The in-class demo received neutral feedback. For the students who sent evaluation forms back after final exams, it was hard to remember the in-class demo afterwards, and they generally gave a neutral feedback. For the feedback received on time, the feedback was positive. Students mentioned "*I think the most advantage is [that] I am involved and get a helpful feedback quickly.*", and "*I think the most helpful part is being able to click on elements and see the relations between roles, users and objects.*"

Students also provided some general comments for further improvement. They suggested: (1) the Matrix View should have multiple selections that allow comparisons; (2) Keyboard shortcuts should be supported; and (3) the specification should be directly editable in the Specification Window. No performance or installation issues were reported.

In summary, we found that students who rated "Query helped study RBAC policy" tend to give high ratings to "RBACvisual helped understand RBAC better", "RBACvisual helped find mistakes" and "Hierarchy View helped understand role inheritance". We also found that students rated the Matrix View and the Hierarchy View equally. Combined with the high ratings of questions and students comments, we believe that RBACvisual effectively helped students understand and the instructor teach the RBAC model better with intuitive visual representation.

5. CONCLUSIONS

The paper presents a tool RBACvisual which is designed to facilitate the teaching and self-learning of the Role-Based Access Control model. Students can practice RBAC policy design without taking time to learn the details of a security specification language. They can also take quizzes or run the query subsystem to evaluate their understanding of the RBAC model and an individual policy. Instructors can use the tool during lecture to discuss complex examples and easily demonstrate the effect of policy modifications.

Our evaluation showed that RBACvisual was effective in helping students understand the model better and enhancing the course. The general feedback was positive with mean value of 4.34 and standard deviation of 0.69 for all questions. As suggested in the feedback, we will improve the tool as follows: (1) allowing multiple selections in Matrix View; (2)

supporting keyboard shortcuts; and (3) making the Specification Window directly editable.

RBACvisual is a part of larger development of security visualization tools supported by the National Science Foundation. Besides RBACvisual, DTEvisual for the Domain Type Enforcement access control model and MLSvisual for Multilevel Security have been developed. Visualization tools for UNIX, tutorials for each model, and the ability to run programs under a given policy will be available in the future. The tool, user guide and demonstration video are accessible at the following URLs:

acv.cs.mtu.edu/RBACvisual.html
www.vimeo.com/109193019

6. REFERENCES

[1] J. R. Crandall, S. L. Gerhart, and J. G. Hogle. Driving Home the Buffer Overflow Problem: A Training Module for Programmers and Managers. In *Proceedings of National Colloquium for Information Systems Security Education*, 2002.

[2] J. C. F. de Winter. Using the Student's *t*-test with Extremely Small Sample Sizes. *Practical Assessment, Research & Evaluation*, 18(10):1–12, 2013.

[3] D. Ebeling and R. Santos. Public Key Infrastructure Visualization. *The Journal of Computing Sciences in Colleges*, 23(1):247–254, 2007.

[4] D. Ferraiolo and R. Kuhn. Role-Based Access Control. In *Proceedings of NIST-NCSC National Computer Security Conference*, pages 554–563, 1992.

[5] D. F. Ferraiolo, R. Sandhu, S. Gavrila, D. R. Kuhn, and R. Chandramouli. Proposed NIST Standard for Role-based Access Control. *ACM Transactions on Information and System Security*, 4(3):224–274, 2001.

[6] S. Hallyn and P. Kearns. Tools to Administer Domain and Type Enforcement. In *Proceedings of USENIX Conference on System Administration*, pages 151–156, 2001.

[7] R. S. Sandhu, E. J. Coyne, H. L. Feinstein, and C. E. Youman. Role-Based Access Control Models. *IEEE Computer*, 29(2):38–47, 1996.

[8] D. Schweitzer and W. Brown. Using Visualization To Teach Security. *The Journal of Computing Sciences in Colleges*, 24(5):143–150, 2009.

[9] D. Schweitzer, M. Collins, and L. Baird. A Visual Approach To Teaching Formal Access Models In Security. In *Proceedings of National Colloquium for Information Systems Security Education*, 2007.

[10] J. Tao, J. Ma, M. Keranen, J. Mayo, and C.-K. Shene. ECvisual: A Visualization Tool for Elliptic Curve Based Ciphers. In *Proceedings of ACM Technical Symposium on Computer Science Education*, pages 571–576, 2012.

[11] J. Tao, J. Ma, J. Mayo, C.-K. Shene, and M. Keranen. DESvisual: A Visualization Tool for the DES Cipher. *The Journal of Computing Sciences in Colleges*, 27(1):81–89, 2011.

Acknowledgements

This work was supported in part by the National Science Foundation under grants DUE-1140512, DUE-1245310 and IIS-1456763.

The Exploring Computer Science Course, Attendance and Math Achievement

Daniel W. Lewis
Santa Clara University
Santa Clara, CA 95053
1-408-554-4449
dlewis@scu.edu

Lisa Kohne
SmartStart Evaluation & Research
Irvine, CA 92604
1-949-396-6053
lkohne@smartstartecs.com

Timothy Mechlinski
SmartStart Evaluation & Research
Irvine, CA 92604
1-949-396-6053
tmechlinski@smartstartecs.com

Mariana Schmalstig
SmartStart Evaluation & Research
Irvine, CA 92604
1-949-396-6053
mschmalstig@smartstartecs.com

ABSTRACT

Exploring Computer Science (ECS) is a high school curriculum that was designed to be more inclusive and engaging for all students, especially women and students of color who have typically been under-represented in the discipline. The course uses an inquiry-based approach that is expected to improve students' problem solving skills. Students who enrolled in ECS at ten high schools in San Jose, California were monitored over a three-year period to investigate possible relationships between participation in ECS, attendance rates, and scores on standardized math tests. Results show a statistically significant difference between ECS participants and their peers in both areas for two of three project years. Additional study is recommended to explore whether there is a causal relationship.

Categories and Subject Descriptors

K.3.2 [Computer and Information Science Education]: Computer Science Education

General Terms

Measurement, Achievement, Performance, Experimentation.

Keywords

Pre-college, high school, pre-AP, curricula, math, attendance.

1. INTRODUCTION

In 2010, the authors began an NSF project to establish Exploring Computer Science (ECS) [2] at ten suburban public high schools from three school districts in the greater San Jose, California area. ECS is a pre-Advanced Placement (AP) course providing an introduction to the breadth of computer science. Assignments and instruction are inquiry and equity based and designed to be socially relevant and meaningful for diverse students.

1.1 ECS and Problem Solving

ECS develops problem solving skills throughout the six units of the curriculum. Unit 1 (Human Computer Interaction) establishes a problem-solving foundation by showing how "intelligent" machine behavior is simply algorithms applied to useful representations of information and by exploring what makes certain tasks easy or difficult for computers versus humans. Unit 2 (Problem Solving) develops the basic steps of problem-solving, including the problem statement, algorithm design, implementation, testing, and verification. The unit also explores selected topics in discrete mathematics such as Boolean logic, functions, sets, graphs, and the binary number system. Exercises are presented that illustrate the value of abstraction in solving programming problems. Unit 3 (Web Design) reinforces abstraction through the hierarchical and structured design of Web pages using HTML and CSS. In Unit 4 (Programming), students develop algorithms and programming solutions to a variety of problems using Scratch and see the benefits and limitations of different data structures when used as a fundamental organizing principle in the design of solutions. Unit 5 (Computing and Data Analysis) explores the use of computers to translate, process and visualize data in order to find patterns and test hypotheses. Much of this is put in practice in Unit 6 (Robotics) to build and program a robot to solve a required task.

1.2 ECS Teachers

The Santa Clara County Office of Education requires computer science to be taught by math-certified teachers. Participating schools were therefore selected by their respective district office based on the interest and availability of math teachers in their schools who were not needed to teach math courses. Five teachers participated in a four-week professional development workshop during the summer of 2010. Of those, three began to teach ECS in 2010-11, one began in 2011-12, and one was reassigned to a different course just before school began. Seven additional teachers received training in the summer of 2011. Six of those began teaching ECS in 2011-12 and one was reassigned. Ultimately, ECS was offered at each of ten high schools by the fall of 2011.

ITICSE '15, July 04 - 08, 2015, Vilnius, Lithuania
Copyright 2015 ACM 978-1-4503-3440-2/15/07…$15.00
http://dx.doi.org/10.1145/2729094.2742598

Only four of the teachers had previously taught a computer science course; one of those had previously worked in industry as a software engineer. All received stipends for attending the training. A second NSF grant provided teachers with academic-year stipends and computer science graduate students as in-class teaching assistants for three years starting in the fall of 2011.

1.3 ECS Students

Over the course of the project, 755 ECS students from grades 9 through 12 were monitored to compare their attendance rate to the overall average by school. In addition, scores on the math portions of the California STAR Test (CST) taken by 532 ECS students in grades 9 through 11 were compared to scores of non-ECS students attending the same schools. (12th graders don't take CST exams.) All students self-selected to enroll in ECS since it was offered only as an elective. Demographics varied from one school to another. In total, however, 20% of the ECS students were female, 58% Asian, 22% Caucasian, 12% Hispanic, and 3.6% African American.

1.4 ECS and Curriculum Standards

SRI International received an NSF grant to develop mappings of the unit objectives and computational practices of the ECS curriculum to several state and national standards [11]. SRI hired an experienced ECS teacher with a credential in mathematics to develop the initial mappings, and then had the mappings reviewed by external experts, including other ECS teachers and computer science content specialists.

ECS was mapped to many of the mathematical practice objectives in the Common Core State Standards (CCSS): making sense of problems and persevering in solving them, abstract and quantitative reasoning, constructing viable arguments and critiquing the reasoning of others, mathematical modeling, and the strategic use of appropriate tools. ECS was also mapped to several mathematical content objectives: creating equations, building functions, understanding independence and conditional probability, making references and justifying conclusions, and interpreting categorical and quantitative data.

The mappings simply reflect personal judgments informed by years of experience, but serve to recognize the relationship between ECS and mathematics that motivates this study.

The CCSS were not available at the time the ECS course was offered during this study. Although the data presented here does not reflect the results of content tests that were specifically designed to assess CCSS, the mapping done suggests that ECS participation may have further beneficial impacts for students taking a math curriculum founded on the CCSS mathematical practice objectives.

2. RELATED RESEARCH

In the Los Angeles Unified School District, where it was originally created, females, African Americans and Latinos who had taken ECS exhibited significantly higher AP CS participation rates than the national and California averages [9].

Tracy et al [7] have recommended problem solving as a fundamental and important skill needed in mathematics and other subjects:

Instructional programs from prekindergarten through grade 12 should enable all students to build new mathematical knowledge through problem solving; solve problems that arise in mathematics and in other contexts; apply and adapt a variety of appropriate strategies to solve problems.

Their data supports evidence of a relationship between inquiry-based strategies used in the classroom and students' math problem-solving.

Other early studies investigated the effects of computer programming in LOGO on student achievement in mathematics. Milner [3] suggested that 5th grade students could learn the concept of a variable through programming and that it helped them to develop problem-solving skills. Noss [4] found that LOGO programming improved elementary school students' understanding of the geometric concepts of angle and length, especially for girls. Clements and Battista [1] studied 3rd grade children and reaffirmed that LOGO had a positive effect on their geometric conceptualizations, but also that their responses during discussions were more mathematically coherent and abstract.

More recently, the programming environment Bootstrap has been used to teach middle school students about algebra and coordinate geometry by having them develop their own video games. Schanzer et al [6] and Wright [8] found that Bootstrap provided statistically significant improvements on standard algebra word problems and function composition problems, and extensive anecdotal evidence that Bootstrap builds student confidence in mathematics.

An unpublished investigation, "Computer Science Course May Improve Math Scores," (February 2013) [Pirmann, personal communication] found that high school students who took computer science performed better on the Pennsylvania System of School Assessment (PSSA) math test. Before implementing computer science, between 76% (2006) and 79% (2007) of students were scored above "Below Basic" on the PSSA. After implementing computer science (as a module of other technology courses, or as a full course), the percent of students scoring in this same range increased to between 83% (2008 and 2009) and 90% (2012).

3. METHODS

Independent sample t-tests were applied to attendance data to compare the mean percent attendance of students in ECS classes to non-ECS students in all participating schools. To compare math CST scores across ECS and non-ECS students, a simple random sample of non-ECS students was taken to match the size of the ECS group (n=539). The math CST data was analyzed using a series of independent sample t-tests, comparing ECS participants to non-ECS students disaggregated by each of the following variables:

- Year of participation
- School
- Grade level
- Math CST test
- Gender

In addition, a factorial ANOVA was conducted that compared ECS participation for students based on the combination of their grade level and the math CST test they took. Finally, a multiple linear regression was conducted to control for the confounding variable of course acceleration (whether a student is in a standard course for her grade level or a higher-level course). Students were classified according to when they took their math CST test:

Accelerated:	Non-Accelerated:
Alg II – 9th Grade	Alg I – All Grades
Summ. Math – 9th, 10th Grade	Geom – All Grades
	Alg II – 10th, 11th Grade
	Summ. Math – 11th Grade

For all tests, means, standard deviations, and *p*-values are presented. In general, in accordance with social science convention, any *p*-value of .05 or less is considered statistically significant and is marked with an asterisk (*) in the graphs and tables.

4. ATTENDANCE

The possibility of a direct relationship between attendance rate and increased math achievement was not investigated in this study. However, higher attendance rates were expected to increase overall academic performance, and thus we were interested to learn if ECS students had higher attendance rates than non-ECS students.

Table 1 shows the ECS student attendance by school compared to the overall attendance rate of the high school for the 2010-11, 2011-12, and 2012-13 school years. Empty cells correspond to

years in which a particular school did not offer ECS. Results vary considerably depending on the school; however, the overall trend is that students enrolled in ECS had higher attendance rates compared to students not enrolled in ECS.

In each of the three years that ECS was offered at these schools, the mean ECS student attendance rate was higher than the mean overall attendance rate across schools. The gap between the mean ECS attendance rate and the mean overall attendance rates increased each year. Boldface and shading are used to highlight entries in the table where ECS students' attendance rates exceed the corresponding school average by five percentage points or more. In 2011-12 and 2012-13 the mean attendance rate for ECS classes across all schools was significantly higher than for the schools as a whole.

Table 1. ECS Student Attendance by School

	2010-11		2011-12		2012-13	
	Overall school	ECS students	Overall school	ECS students	Overall school	ECS students
Evergreen Valley	97.2%	98.3%	99.6%	98.7%	98.0%	98.1%
Independence	-	-	95.2%	98.2%	97.2%	97.2%
Oak Grove	94.2%	95.5%	93.4%	**99.0%**	95.0%	**100.0%**
Pioneer	96.2%	95.1%	95.5%	96.1%	96.2%	97.3%
San Jose High	-	-	93.8%	96.7%	95.5%	96.6%
Santa Clara	-	-	98.3%	96.4%	95.3%	96.7%
Santa Teresa	-	-	98.7%	98.5%	95.8%	96.9%
Silver Creek	-	-	95.1%	98.3%	-	-
Adrian Wilcox	-	-	96.4%	98.4%	91.7%	**96.3%**
Willow Glen	-	-	95.8%	96.5%	96.7%	97.2%
Average	95.87%	96.30%	96.18%	97.68%	95.71%	97.37%
Difference in attendance rates	+0.43 percentage points		+1.5 percentage points		+1.66 percentage points	
p-value	*p* = .38		*p* < .03*		*p* < .02*	

5. MATH ACHIEVEMENT

Math CST scores of ECS and non-ECS students in 2010-11, 2011-12, and 2012-13 were compared to assess whether there is a relationship between participation in ECS and achievement in math.

Students were not tracked from year to year, and therefore the evaluators were not able to distinguish between students who had never taken ECS and those who had taken it prior to a particular project year. The most likely impact of this is that a relatively small number of former ECS students were counted as non-ECS students in subsequent years, potentially causing the relationship between ECS and math achievement to appear smaller than it actually is. Data for one school in 2010-11 was removed due to a small ECS sample size (n=6) and because the teacher only taught half of the ECS curriculum.

5.1 Overall Scores

When aggregated across all three years, of the 1071 students, those who were enrolled in ECS had scores that were significantly higher than non-ECS students (t = 6.2, *p* < .01). Overall, ECS students' mean CST score was 359 (s.d. = 84.4), while non-ECS students' mean score was 330 (s.d. = 68.2). When each year of the program was considered on its own, the same statistically significant difference was found for 2011-12 (*p* < .01) and 2012-13 students (*p* < .01). No significant difference was found for 2010-11 (*p* = .20) students, but this is not surprising considering the small sample size for that year (only two sections of ECS were included in the analysis). Overall, the data demonstrate an increasing difference over time between mean CST score for ECS and non-ECS students across the program. Figure 1 shows that scores were lower in 2010-11, and 29 and 40- points higher for ECS students than the comparison group for the following two years respectively (standard deviations are in parentheses).

Comparison group   ECS students

365
(73.8)   346
(83.2)   331
(65.5)   360*
(81.3)   322
(67.5)   362*
(87.1)

2010-11
(n=128)   2011-12
(n=429)   2012-13
(n=511)

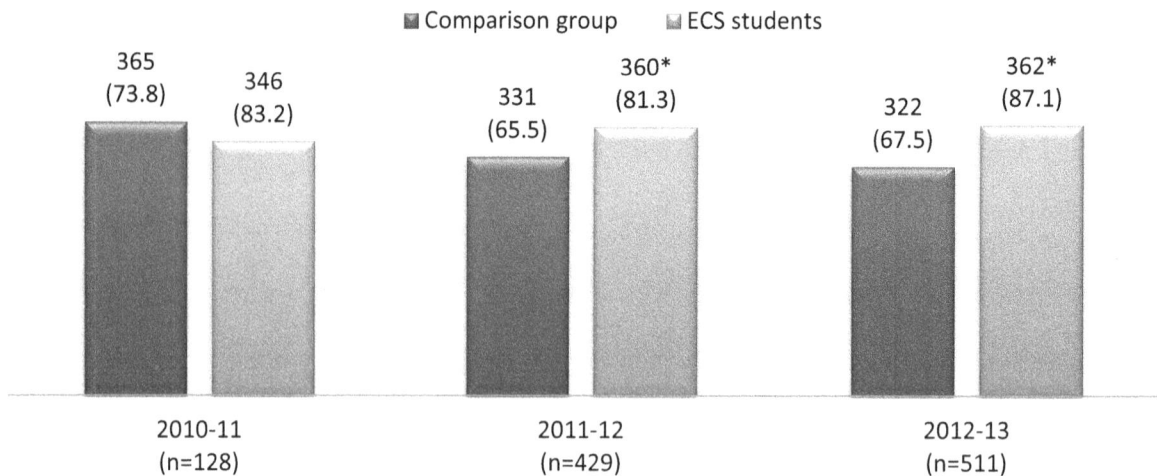

Figure 1. CST scores for ECS students and comparison group by academic year, all schools.

5.2 Scores by Grade Level

Differences in CST scores were also assessed by categorizing data by students' grade level to determine whether a relationship exists with ECS participation. The analysis demonstrated that across all project years ECS students had higher CST scores at each grade level (9, 10, and 11) compared to non-ECS students. Overall, there appears to be a correlation between participation in ECS and students' CST scores regardless of their grade level. The difference in CST score was largest for 9th graders (42 points, $p < .01$) and smallest for 11th graders (13 points, $p < .10$), with 10th graders in the middle (29 points, $p < .01$), as shown in Figure 2 (standard deviations are in parentheses).

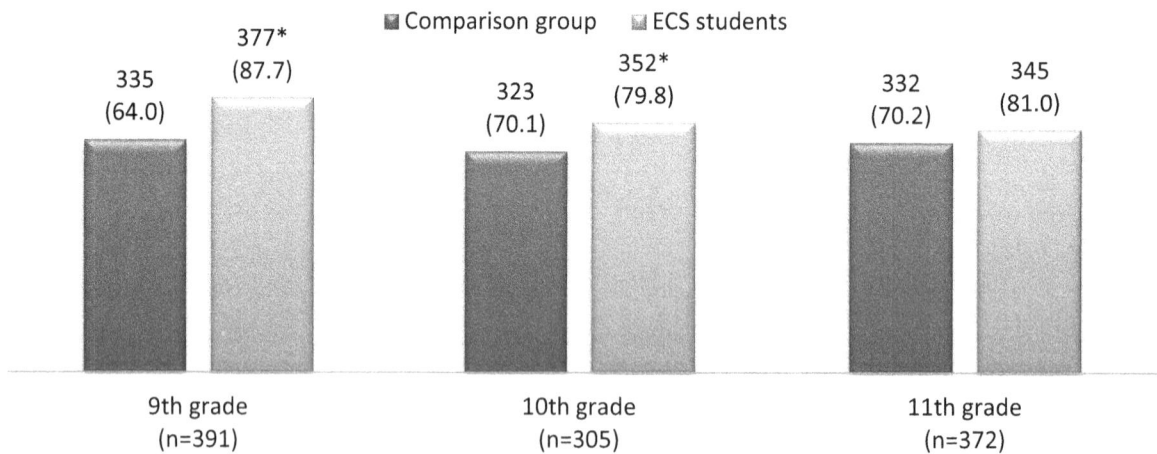

Comparison group   ECS students

335
(64.0)   377*
(87.7)   323
(70.1)   352*
(79.8)   332
(70.2)   345
(81.0)

9th grade
(n=391)   10th grade
(n=305)   11th grade
(n=372)

Figure 2. CST scores for ECS students and comparison group by grade level, all schools

5.3 Scores by CST Math Test

Differences in CST scores were additionally assessed by categorizing CST data by math subject to assess whether a relationship exists between participation in ECS and understanding of various math subjects. As shown in Figure 3, ECS students who took the Algebra II ($p < 01$), or Summative Math ($p < .05$) CST scored significantly higher than non-ECS students. With the highest mean difference, students in ECS who took the Algebra II test scored 49 points higher than non-ECS students. The differences for Geometry and Algebra I were not statistically significant; Geometry ECS students scored 8 points higher than the comparison group ($p = .23$), while Algebra I ECS students had a mean score 10 points lower than the comparison group across all project years ($p = .23$).

■ Comparison group   ▨ ECS students

314
(58.3)   304
(49.8)   317
(63.3)   325
(63.9)   330
(71.1)   379*
(92.2)   379
(66.9)   399*
(82.8)

Algebra I
(n=204)   Geometry
(n=360)   Algebra II
(n=264)   Summative Math
(n=239)

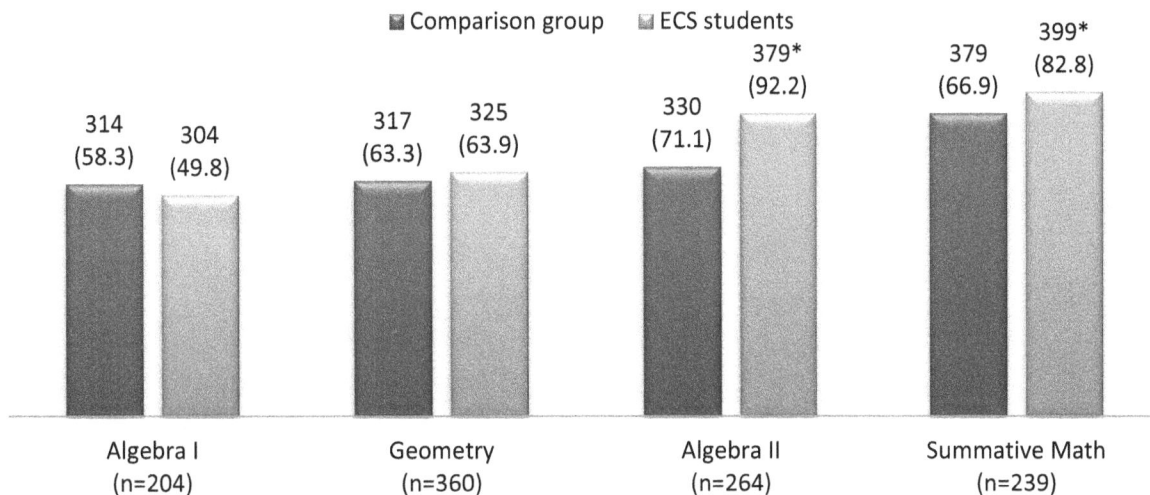

Figure 3. CST scores for ECS students and comparison group by CST math test, all years and schools

Table 2. CST mean scores for ECS students and comparison group by grade and math test, all years and schools

Grade	Algebra I		Geometry		Algebra II		Summative Math	
	Non-ECS	ECS	Non-ECS	ECS	Non-ECS	ECS	Non-ECS	ECS
11	298 (s.d.=54.9) n=12	*264 (s.d.=17.2) n=3 (p.=.33)*	307 (s.d.=70.3) n=36	277 (s.d.=35.9) n=31 (p.=.04)	300 (s.d.=58.0) n=52	305 (s.d.=42.4) n=54 (p.=.62)	**372 (s.d.=60.6) n=73**	**385 (s.d.=81.9) n=112** (p.=.25)
10	294 (s.d.=51.8) n=36	*270 (s.d.=27.1) n=7 (p.=.24)*	303 (s.d.=56.1) n=78	316 (s.d.=56.6) n=63 (p.=.18)	**347 (s.d.=67.7) n=47**	**371 (s.d.=71.5) n=31** (p.=.16)	402 (s.d.=86.6) n=18	439 (s.d.=66.3) n=26 (p.=.13)
9	323 (s.d.=58.9) n=110	314 (s.d.=50.7) n=37 (p.=.36)	**343 (s.d.=60.8) n=57**	**347 (s.d.=65.6) n=96 (p.=.72)**	377 (s.d.=80.5) n=16	444 (s.d.=83.1) n=65 (p.<.01)	402 (s.d.=66.7) n=4	*482 (s.d.=58.2) n=7 (p.=.10)*

5.4 Scores by Math Placement

California's content standards recommend that students take Algebra I in 8th grade, Geometry in 9th, Algebra II in 10th, and the Summative Math test in 11th grade [11]. Table 2 categorizes CST math scores by test subject and student grade level when taken, thus allowing students to be grouped relative to this recommendation and (by implication) their affinity for math.

Students following the recommended sequence are highlighted in the table and represent 45% of ECS and 33% of non-ECS students. Students in the lower right of the table are following an accelerated math sequence and comprise 18% of ECS and 7% of non-ECS students. However, many of the state's students do not begin Algebra I until 9th grade or later. They are those in the upper left, and represent 37% of ECS and 60% of non-ECS students.

The data shown in a light italic font for 10th and 11th grade Algebra I and for 9th grade Summative Math is inconclusive due to very small samples sizes of ECS students, invalidating any meaningful comparisons in those subgroups.

Students who do well in math typically also do well in computer science. Since students self-select ECS as an elective, one might suspect that ECS students are mostly those that excel in math. Indeed, the table indicates that fewer ECS students began Algebra I late and more of them follow an accelerated math sequence compared to their peers.

ECS students who had higher CST math scores than non-ECS students tend toward the lower right of the table, indicating that the strongest relationship was observed for accelerated math students who participated in ECS early in their high school career.

The table also shows, however, that other ECS students also experience gains.

Multiple linear regression results demonstrate that when controlling for students' relative placement in math courses (e.g. standard vs. accelerated), ECS participation is associated with increased student's math CST score by 18 points ($p < .01$).

5.5 Scores by Gender

Differences in CST scores were also assessed by categorizing data by gender to assess whether participation in ECS influences males and females differently. Across all project years , male ECS students' mean CST score was 362 (s.d.=85.3) while males in the comparison group scored 330 (s.d.=70.2) on average. on average. Female ECS students scored an average of 347 (s.d.=80.3) and non-ECS females scored 330 *s.d.=66.2) Both differences were statistically significant ($p < .01$ for males and $p < .03$ for females).. No significant difference in CST scores for males vs. females related to participation in ECS was evident ($p = .13$).

6. SUMMARY

Overall, the data indicates an encouraging correlation between ECS participation, attendance rates and academic achievement as measured by performance on the CST math test:

- **Attendance:** In the last year of the study, ECS students' attendance was higher than overall attendance for eight out of nine schools, which may have indirectly contributed to an increase in ECS students' CST math scores.

- **CST Math Overall:** ECS students at all schools had higher CST math scores than non-ECS students across all years of the study. These differences were statistically significant in five of the ten schools, and approached significance in four.

- **CST Math by Grade Level:** ECS students had statistically significantly higher CST scores at each grade level, with 9th graders having the greatest difference.

- **CST Math by Gender:** Observed differences in CST math scores do not appear to differ significantly by gender.

- **CST Math by Subject:** ECS student scores were statistically significantly higher in Algebra II and Summative Math and approached significance in Geometry. No difference in Algebra I scores was observed, but this result is inconclusive due to the small number of ECS students in the sample.

- **CST Math by Placement:** The strongest correlation seems to exist between accelerated math students who participated in ECS early in their high school career.

The large number of factors affecting the data makes it impossible to claim causation, yet we believe that our results do confirm a synergistic effect between computer science and mathematics as described by Rich et al [5]. Further research should attempt to collect pre- and post-test data from experimental and comparison groups to assess whether baseline abilities of experimental and comparison groups are statistically significantly different. In addition, tracking students over time to compare students who have never taken ECS to those who are taking a course would be beneficial. Finally, since the number of students in ECS was relatively low compared to non-ECS students, increasing the size of the ECS group will also improve the power of the analyses conducted by correcting for unmet statistical assumptions.

7. ACKNOWLEDGEMENTS

This material is partially based upon work supported by the National Science Foundation under Grant Numbers CNS-1019217 and DGE-1045434. Any opinions, findings, and conclusions or recommendations expressed in this material are those of the author(s) and do not necessarily reflect the views of the National Science Foundation.

8. REFERENCES

[1] Clements, D. H., & Battista, M. T. (1989). Learning of geometric concepts in a Logo environment. *Journal for Research in Mathematics Education*, 450-467.

[2] Goode, J. and Chapman, G. (2013). Exploring Computer Science, v5.0. Retrieved August 19, 2014 from http://www.exploringcs.org/wp-content/uploads/2014/02/ExploringComputerScience-v5.0.pdf

[3] Milner, Stuart. (1973). The Effects of Computer Programming on Performance in Mathematics. Presented at the annual meeting of the American Educational Research Association, New Orleans, Louisiana, February 25 – March 1, 1973.

[4] Noss, R. (1987). Children's learning of geometrical concepts through Logo. *Journal for Research in Mathematics Education*, 343-362.

[5] Rich, P. J., Leatham, K. R., & Wright, G. A. (2013). Convergent cognition. *Instructional Science*, *41*(2), 431-453.

[6] Schanzer, E., Fisler, K., & Krishnamurthi, S. (2013). Bootstrap: Going beyond programming in after-school computer science. In *SPLASH Education Symposium*.

[7] Tracy, D. M., Luera, G. R., Killu, K., & O'Hagan, J. (2003). Linking Math, Science, and Inquiry-based Learning: An Example From a Mini-Unit on Volume. *School Science and Mathematics*, *103*(4), 194-207.

[8] Wright, G., Rich, P., & Lee, R. (2013, March). The Influence of Teaching Programming on Learning Mathematics. In *Society for Information Technology & Teacher Education International Conference* (Vol. 2013, No. 1, pp. 4612-4615).

[9] CS Education Statistics – Exploring Computer Science. Comparing California and National AP Computer Science and LAUSD ECS Participation Rates (2011-12). Retrieved August 19, 2014 from http://www.exploringcs.org/resources/cs-statistics

[10] Principled Assessment of Computational Thinking. Retrieved August 31, 2014 from http://pact.sri.com

[11] Understanding California's Standardized Testing and Reporting (STAR) Program. Retrieved September 3, 2014 from https://www.ed-data.k12.ca.us/Pages/Understanding-the-STAR.aspx

Enhancing Robot Programming with Visual Feedback and Augmented Reality

Stéphane Magnenat
Disney Research Zurich,
Switzerland
stephane@magnenat.net

Morderchai Ben-Ari
Dept. of Science Teaching
Weizmann Inst. Sci., Israel
moti.ben-ari@weizmann.ac.il

Severin Klinger
Computer Graphics Lab.
ETH Zurich, Switzerland
severin.klingler@inf.ethz.ch

Robert W. Sumner
Disney Research Zurich,
ETH Zurich, Switzerland
sumner@disneyresearch.com

ABSTRACT

In our previous research, we showed that students using the educational robot Thymio and its visual programming environment were able to learn the important computer-science concept of event-handling. This paper extends that work by integrating *augmented reality (*AR*)* into the activities. Students used a tablet that displays in real time the event executed on the robot. The event is overlaid on the tablet over the image from a camera, which shows the location of the robot when the event was executed. In addition, visual feedback (FB) was implemented in the software. We developed a novel video questionnaire to investigate the performance of the students on robotics tasks. Data were collected comparing four groups: AR+FB, AR+non-FB, non-AR+FB, non-AR+non-FB. The results showed that students receiving feedback made significantly fewer errors on the tasks. Those using AR made fewer errors, but this improvement was not significant, although their performance improved. Technical problems with the AR hardware and software showed where improvements are needed.

Categories and Subject Descriptors

K.3.2 [**Computers & Education**]: Computer and Information Science Education - *Computer Science Education*; I.2.9 [**Robotics**]

General Terms

Human Factors

Keywords

robotics in education; Thymio; Aseba; VPL; augmented reality; event-actions pair

ITiCSE'15, July 04–08, 2014, Vilnius, Lithuania.
Copyright is held by the owner/author(s). Publication rights licensed to ACM.
ACM 978-1-4503-3440-2/15/07 ...$15.00.
http://dx.doi.org/10.1145/2729094.2742585 .

1. INTRODUCTION

Robotics activities are widely used to introduce students to *science, mathematics, engineering, technology (*STEM*)* in general and to *computer science* in particular [6]. Robotics activities are exciting and fun, but we are also interested in investigating if the activities lead to learning of STEM subjects. In a previous paper [9], we described research conducted during an outreach program using the *Thymio II* education robot and its *Visual Programming Language* (VPL). We showed that students successfully learned the important computer-science concept of event-handling.

However, while students were able to comprehend behaviors consisting of independent events, they had trouble with sequences of events. This paper explores two independent ways of improving their understanding of robotics programming: *visual feedback* (FB) that shows which event handler is currently being executed and *augmented reality* (AR) (as originally suggested by the first author [7]).

The research methodology was improved. In [9], learning was measured by administering a textual questionnaire containing exercises about VPL programs and the behaviors of the robot that could be observed when the programs were run. We observed that some young students found the textual questionnaire difficult to understand. Therefore, we implemented a new type of research instrument—a video questionnaire—where the students were given a multiple-choice among several short video clips.

The performance of the students was measured in a 2×2 experimental setup: treatment groups that used AR compared with control groups that did not, and treatment groups that received FB compared with those that did not.

Section 2 describes the robot and the software environment, while Section 3 discusses previous work on AR in education and the AR system that we developed. The research methodology and the design of the video questionnaire are presented in Section 4. The results of the analysis, the discussion and the limitations of the research appear in Sections 5–7. Section 8 describes our plans for the future.

2. THYMIO II AND ASEBA

The Thymio II robot [11] (Figure 1) and its Aseba software were created at the Swiss Federal Institute of Technology

Figure 1: The Thymio II robot with a top image for tracking by the camera of the tablet.

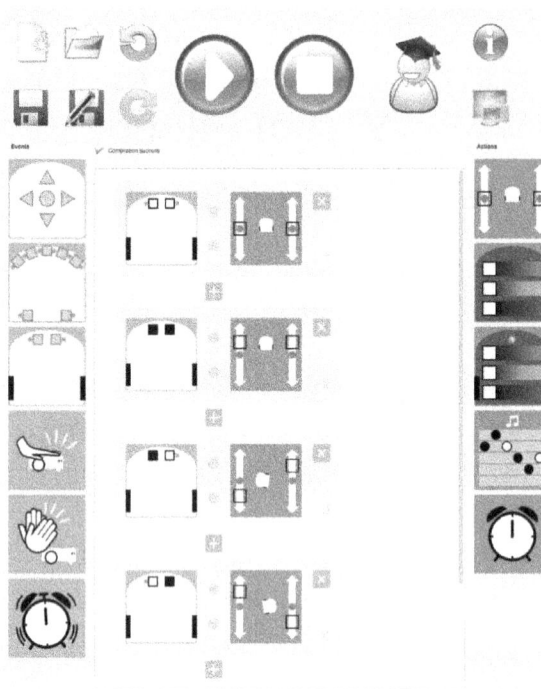

Figure 2: The Aseba/VPL environment

(EPFL and ETHZ) and ECAL (University of Arts and Design). Both the hardware design and the software are open-source.

The robot is small ($11 \times 11 \times 5\,\mathrm{cm}$), self-contained and robust with two independently-driven wheels for differential drive. It has five proximity sensors on the front and two on the back, and two sensors on the bottom. There are five buttons on the top, a three-axis accelerometer, a microphone, an infrared sensor for receiving signals from a remote control and a thermometer. For output, there are RGB LEDs at the top and bottom of the robot, as well as mono-colored LEDs next to the sensors, and a sound synthesizer. A printed image was attached to the top of the robot so that the camera could recognize the robot when AR was used (Figure 1).

The Aseba programming environment [8] uses the construct **onevent** to create event handlers for the sensors. VPL is a component of Aseba for visual programming.[1] Figure 2 shows a VPL program for following a line of black tape on a white floor. On the left is a column of *event blocks* and on the right is a column of *action blocks*. By dragging and dropping one event block and one or more action blocks to the center pane, an *event-actions pair* is created. Both event and action blocks are parametrized, enabling the user to create many programs from a small number of blocks.

The robotic activities reported here used a development version of VPL; the most important improvement is that several actions can be attached to a single event.[2]

Visual feedback is implemented by causing an event-actions pair to blink whenever it is executed. This facilitates understanding the temporal relation between the pairs and the spatial relation between the robot and its environment.

3. AUGMENTED REALITY

3.1 Background

Visual programming languages have been used extensively [1] and event-based programming is claimed to be an effective approach for teaching introductory programming [5]. However, we found that the asynchronous nature of visual event-based programming renders the understanding and tracing of their execution difficult [9]. Nevertheless, when a visual language is used, we can perceive a relation between the spatiotemporal location of the robot and the execution of the program. Building on the neurological evidence on grounded cognition [3], we propose to make this relation explicit and available to the student. Our hypothesis is that this will allow the students to understand better what their program is doing and to lead them to learn faster. We propose to use a tablet to provide a "window" into the "live mind" of the robot, localizing the robot using AR. The resulting live inspection system uses both the spatiality and the temporality of event execution to help students understand what their program is doing.

Previous work on AR in education [2, 13] has highlighted that AR systems have a cost in term of weight and bulkiness; furthermore, little quantitative comparison of their effectiveness against non-AR solutions for the same problem has been conducted [13]. Moreover, there has been little use of AR in computer-science education. Some work has explored how to input programs using physical artifacts [4], but none has used AR to provide facilities for tracing and debugging.

3.2 The augmented reality system

The AR system consists of an Android or iOS application, which runs on a tablet and connects to the computer running VPL. The application finds the position of the tablet by detecting a ground image using the tablet's camera (Figure 3), and the position of the robot by detecting the printed image on its top (Figure 1). The camera's image is shown on the screen of the tablet and is overlaid with the event-actions pairs at the physical locations they were executed by the robot (Figure 4). At the bottom of the tablet screen, the execution times of these events are shown on a local time line that can be scrolled and zoomed using drag and pinch gestures. Augmented pairs can be selected by touching them on screen, and the corresponding time in the local timeline will be highlighted. A global timeline indicates which part of the total recording the local timeline shows.

---

[1] A reference manual and a tutorial are available at http://aseba.wikidot.com/en:thymioprogram.

[2] This is the reason we now use the term event-action*s* pair.

Figure 3: The concept of the VPL AR App

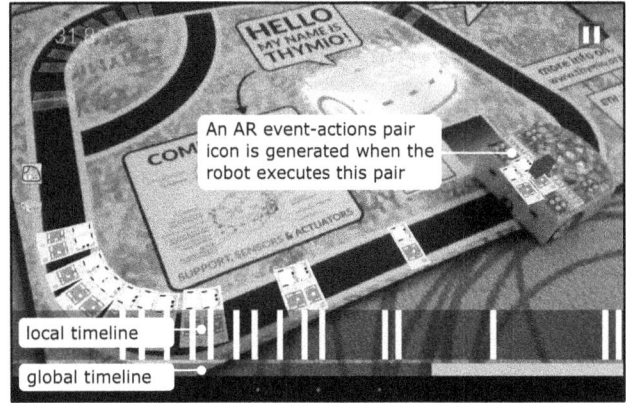

An AR event-actions pair icon is generated when the robot executes this pair

local timeline

global timeline

Figure 4: The GUI of the VPL AR App

The AR system was implemented using the Vuforia library[3] for tracking the image of the ground and the top of the robot, and its plugin for the Unity framework.[4] It communicates with VPL through TCP/IP.

4. RESEARCH METHODOLOGY

4.1 Population

The workshops consisted of 14 sessions of 75 minutes. Two sessions were run in parallel. The workshops took place in Lugano, Switzerland on October 16–17 2014.

There were 10–18 high-school students per session from high schools in the Swiss canton of Ticino. The median age of the students was 16 (low/high quartiles: 16/17). Consent forms were required and participants were allowed to opt out of the study.

There was one robot and tablet per 2 or 3 students. Various models of iOS and Android tablets (7 10 ") were used.

There were four teaching assistants, two per room, who were students at USI (Università della Svizzera italiana). The same two assistants were always paired together. After every two sessions, the assistants exchanged rooms to prevent bias due to a specific pair of assistants.

4.2 Experimental setup

There were two independent variables in our research:

- Augmented reality: AR was used by the students in room 1, while in room 2 VPL was used without AR.

- Visual feedback: The first session in each room used FB from VPL and the AR system, whereas FB was not used during the second session.

The first 15 minutes of each session were devoted to introducing the robot and its built-in behaviors. During the next 15 minutes, the students learned about VPL; this was followed by 30 minutes devoted to solving increasingly challenging tasks.[5] During the final 15 minutes the students answered the video questionnaire.

We collected usage data from the VPL editor: addition and deletion of blocks, change of parameters, and clicks on buttons. For the AR system, we collected usage data from the tablet: its position in 3D, the position of the robot in 2D, and the state of the application.[6]

4.3 The questionnaire

In our previous research [9], the questions consisted of an image of a VPL program, together with multiple-choice responses that were textual descriptions of the behavior of the robot when executing the program.[7] The students were asked to choose the description that correctly described the behavior. We found that some students had difficulty understanding the textual descriptions.

For the current research we used a novel type of questionnaire based upon video clips.[8] There were eight questions, four each of the following types:

- The student is shown a video of the behavior of a robot and then asked to select a program (one out of four) that causes the behavior.

- The student is shown a program and four videos and then be asked to select the video that demonstrates the behavior of the robot running the program.

The questionnaire was constructed using the Forms facility of Google Drive. In Forms, you can include videos by uploading the videos to YouTube and providing the URL.

The questionnaire in [9] was constructed using the taxonomy in [10] that combines the Bloom and SOLO taxonomies. For this research, we limited the questions to those at the *applying* level of the taxonomy, because a student who is able to track the execution of a program can be assumed to understand what the individual instructions do and how they work together, whereas at the *understanding* level, rote learning might be sufficient to select a correct answer. Evaluating higher cognitive levels such as *creating* will be done in later phases of the research. In VPL, every program has both

---

[3] http://www.qualcomm.com/products/vuforia
[4] http://www.unity3d.com
[5] The tasks were the same as those used in [9]. Some tasks were very simple like changing colors when a button is

pressed; others were more difficult like following a track or navigating a labyrinth.
[6] The raw data is available at https://aseba.wikidot.com/en:thymiopaper-vpl-iticse2015.
[7] http://thymio.org/en:thymiopaper-vpl-iticse2014
[8] http://thymio.org/en:thymiopaper-vpl-iticse2015

	treatment	control	p-value
Feedback	0.81 (n = 47)	1.74 (n = 34)	0.003
Augm. Reality	1.00 (n = 41)	1.40 (n = 40)	0.10

Table 1: The mean mistake count and the p-value of Pearson's chi-square test for different conditions.

	Q1	Q2	Q3	Q4	Q5	Q6	Q7	Q8
AF	0.0	0.0	4.0	32.0	4.0	24.0	0.0	4.0
AN	18.8	0.0	0.0	37.5	18.8	25.0	18.8	31.2
NF	0.0	0.0	0.0	22.7	18.2	18.2	18.2	18.2
NN	16.7	5.6	5.6	38.9	16.7	44.4	33.3	33.3

Table 2: The error rate (%) of the questionnaire answers. n = AF:25, AN:16, NF:22, NN:18

an event and an action, so we did not make the unistructural / multistructural distinction from the SOLO taxonomy.

5. RESULTS

5.1 The questionnaire

To compare the treatment vs. the control groups, we counted the number of mistakes for every participant. Table 1 shows the mean mistake count and the p-value of Pearson's chi-square test of its histograms, for the null hypothesis of no effect. We used Laplace smoothing (adding 1 to each bin) to apply the chi-square test even when the control group has 0 entries for a given mistake count. We see that using FB decreases the mistake count significantly, while using AR is not significant.

Table 2 shows the error rate of the answers for the four setups in the experiment: AF = AR and FB, AN = AR with no FB, NF = no AR but with FB, NN = neither AR nor FB. We see that some questions were answered correctly by almost all students, while other questions were more difficult and more than 30 % of the students gave the wrong answers. We also see that the error rate depends on the setup.

We see from Table 3 that the error rate is always lower with FB than without, and that this difference is significant for Q1 and Q8, and borderline significant for Q7.

Q1 showed a video of the robot turning right when presented with an object in front of its left sensor. The students had to select one of four programs, which differed in inverting the left/right sensors and the direction of movement. The correct program was:

	Q1	Q2	Q3	Q4	Q5	Q6	Q7	Q8
F	0.0	0.0	2.1	27.7	10.6	21.3	8.5	10.6
N	17.6	2.9	2.9	38.2	17.6	35.3	26.5	32.4
p	0.01	0.87	0.62	0.44	0.56	0.25	0.06	0.03

Table 3: The error rate (%) for fb/non-fb; p-values of Pearson's chi-square test. n = F:47, N:34

	Q1	Q2	Q3	Q4	Q5	Q6	Q7	Q8
A	7.3	0.0	2.4	34.1	9.8	24.4	7.3	14.6
N	7.5	2.5	2.5	30.0	17.5	30.0	25.0	25.0
p	0.69	0.99	0.48	0.87	0.49	0.75	0.06	0.37

Table 4: The error rate (%) for AR/non-AR; p-values of Pearson's chi-square test. n = A:41, N:40

Q8 showed the following program:

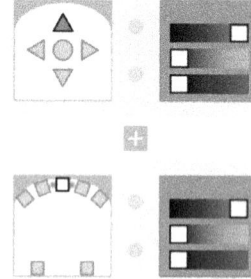

The students had to select one of four video clips that varied in the condition that could cause the robot's LEDs to become red. The correct video showed red when *either* the front button was pressed *or* an obstacle was placed in front of the robot. Although these questions are relatively simple, the students must reason on the spatial and logical relations between sensing and acting. The significant improvement when using FB probably indicates that the FB caused the students to become more aware of these relations while experimenting with the robot.

Table 4 shows that the error rate is generally lower with AR than without, but the difference is not significant except for Q7 whose significance is borderline. In Q7, the students had to select one of four video clips that varied in the behavior of the robot when an object was placed in front of its sensors. The program caused the robot to turn right or left when an object was detected in front of the left or right sensors, respectively; when the object was detected by the center sensor, the robot moved forward.[9] This question required understanding the relation between two event-actions pairs in sequence and the specific sensor events. We believe that seeing the execution of the event-actions pairs in context improved the understanding of these relations.

5.2 The usage data

To better understand the differences between treatment and control groups for the different conditions we investigated the usage data that we collected during the study. Figure 5 compares the median time between consecutive clicks on the run button in the VPL environment with the median number of actions between two consecutive runs, when using AR or not and when using FB or not. For AR, there is a significant difference between the treatment group and the control group. With AR, there were significantly fewer actions between the runs and significantly less time between clicks (Mann-Whitney U test, $p < 0.001$). When FB is given, there is no significant difference in the usage data of the treatment and control groups.

---

[9]The program and videos can be examined at http://thymio.org/en:thymiopaper-vpl-iticse2015.

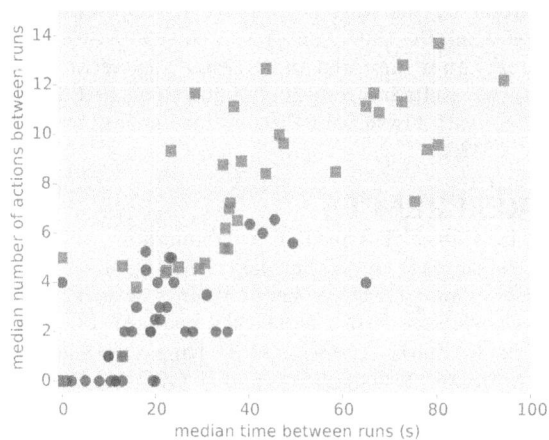

Figure 5: Comparison of usage behavior of students using AR (circles) or not (squares).

	treatment	control	p-value
Time between runs (s)			
Feedback	23.5 (n = 47)	24.8 (n = 34)	0.39
Augm. Reality	19.0 (n = 41)	36.0 (n = 40)	< 0.001
Action count between runs			
Feedback	4.0 (n = 47)	4.8 (n = 34)	0.45
Augm. Reality	2.0 (n = 41)	7.9 (n = 40)	< 0.001

Table 5: Median statistics of usage behavior and the p-value of Mann-Whitney U test.

A possible explanation for this difference is that using AR enabled students to identify possible errors in their programs quicker and more precisely, so they had a better understanding of the necessary steps and were addressing smaller problems at a time. Therefore, the more advanced learning environment led to the reduced reaction times and fewer actions between runs. Conversely, this difference could be interpreted as follows: the additional complexity introduced by the AR system caused stress for the students and prevented them from focusing on the programming task. In turn, this could have led to a trial-and-error behavior where the students tested different programs at random without understanding the underlying concepts. Further research is necessary to show which of these two hypotheses is correct, or find another reason.

5.3 The observations

In this section we present some issues that we observed during the sessions.

5.3.1 Design and implementation of the AR

- The groups with AR required intensive support because AR significantly increased the complexity of the setup. By intensive support we mean that students had more than two questions per hour in average and answering these questions required more than one minute.

- Some students found using the tablet as a debugger to be unintuitive.

- Several students tended to keep the tablet too close to the robot and therefore the tablet did not see the ground image.

- The use of the tablet was not uniform: some students did not use the tablet at all, while others seemed lost in contemplating reality through the tablet.

- The students did not always realize whether the tablet was tracking the ground or not.

- The software did not work uniformly well on different devices, especially those with different screen sizes.

- Energy consumption was a problem.

- The current setup of a computer running VPL while a separate tablet runs the AR is cumbersome.

- Some tablets have poor focusing abilities and sometimes stayed out of focus for several minutes.

- The AR system sometimes lost track of the robot.

These problems point out the technical and pedagogical difficulties of deploying AR in an educational context. Several technological difficulties can be solved by investing more effort in development. For example, VPL should run on the tablet so a computer is not needed, energy-saving algorithms should be implemented, as should algorithms for robust localization [12, Chapter 5]. The pedagogical difficulties point to the need for careful instruction on how to use AR and how to debug programs.

5.3.2 Implementation of the questionnaire

Feedback from colleagues and observations from a pilot use of the questionnaire led us to re-do the video clips. The original clips were taken with the robot *facing* the user and the camera. This makes it easy to see the horizontal proximity sensors, which were widely used in the questionnaire's programs, but it required mental effort to interpret the directions "right" and "left" when they referred to the body of the robot. The video clips were photographed again, this time from the back of the robot. The advantage is that there is no need to mentally translate the directions; the disadvantage is that the sensors cannot be seen.

We found Google Forms easy to use, but there were two disadvantages: there is little flexibility in the format of the questions, and YouTube shows unrelated videos after each clip, which proved to be distracting to some students.

6. DISCUSSION

For all the questions in the questionnaire, students who received FB achieved lower errors rates than those who did not receive FB. Similarly, students who used AR achieved lower error rates in seven out of the eight questions. However, the improved performance was only significant in a few cases. The results are therefore more encouraging than conclusive. They do seem to indicate that visualization such as that provided both by FB and AR can improve students' spatial and temporal understanding of programs in the context of robotics.

The observations in Section 5.3 show that implementing AR is a difficult technical challenge. One has to take into account physical aspects such as the weight and position of the tablet, as well as algorithmic aspects such as the localization, and interaction design aspects such as the user interface. It is also not surprising that intensive support and explicit instruction is needed if students are to obtain the maximum benefit from a sophisticated technology like AR.

We found the video-based questionnaire to be very successful; it allowed the students to answer the questionnaire in less time than with the textual questionnaire of [9]. A video questionnaire is more appropriate when studying young children as it does not require a high level of linguistic capabilities. Even when language is not a problem, we believe that video questionnaires should be used when asking about the physical behavior of robots. Free and easily available tools—Google Forms and YouTube—enabled us to quickly construct an adequate questionnaire, although more flexible software support is needed for an optimal experience.

7. LIMITATIONS OF THE RESEARCH

The large population ensures that the results are reliable, but the experiment was carried out in one location, at one time and using a specific robot and AR system, so it may not be generalizable.

While the technical difficulties described in Section 5.3 were not surprising in a first attempt to use AR in this context, they did cause the activities to be sub-optimal and possibly prevented AR from realizing its full potential.

The limitation of the questions to those at the analyzing level of the Bloom taxonomy means that the research focused on only one form of learning.

8. CONCLUSIONS

We carried out a quantitative study of the effect of visual FB and AR on the learning of a CS concept using a mobile robot. Visual FB had a significant positive effect on some questions, while AR had a positive effect but the improvement was not significant, although it did improve the students' performance. Together with our previous study [9], this research supports the claim that robotics activities are effective for teaching introductory CS at the K-12 level.

We described a new research tool—the video-based questionnaire—that is appropriate for investigating learning in young students.

We believe that this paper is the first report of a study of using AR to improve learning in CS education, and one of the small number of quantitative study on the use of AR in education in general [13]. We described some of the difficulties of using AR in the context of educational robotics activities. As next step, the AR hardware and software need to be made more robust and easy to use, and learning materials designed for AR must be developed. Then further research is needed to accurately characterize when FB and AR improve learning.

9. ACKNOWLEDGEMENTS

We thank Alessia Marra, Maurizio Nitti, Maria Beltran and Manon Briod for their artistic contributions to VPL and its augmented reality version. We also thank Prof. Matthias Hauswirth for allowing us to run the USI workshop, and Elisa Larghi for her help in organizing it. We thank the assistants of the USI workshop: Christian Vuerich, Matteo Morisoli, Gabriele Cerfoglio, Filippo Ferrario for their dedication running the workshops. We thank the students attending the workshops for their cooperation. Finally, we thank the anonymous reviewers who provided useful feedback that improved the article. The research leading to these results has received funding from the European Union's Seventh Framework Programme under grant agreement n° 603662.

10. REFERENCES

[1] A. L. Ambler, T. Green, T. D. Kumura, A. Repenning, and T. Smedley. 1997 visual programming challenge summary. In *Proceedings IEEE Symposium on Visual Languages*, pages 11–18, 1997.

[2] T. N. Arvanitis, A. Petrou, J. F. Knight, S. Savas, S. Sotiriou, M. Gargalakos, and E. Gialouri. Human factors and qualitative pedagogical evaluation of a mobile augmented reality system for science education used by learners with physical disabilities. *Personal and Ubiquitous Computing*, 13(3):243–250, 2009.

[3] L. W. Barsalou. Grounded cognition. *Annual Review of Psychology*, 59(1):617–645, 2008.

[4] M. U. Bers, L. Flannery, E. R. Kazakoff, and A. Sullivan. Computational thinking and tinkering: Exploration of an early childhood robotics curriculum. *Computers & Education*, 72:145–157, 2014.

[5] K. Bruce, A. Danyluk, and M. Thomas. *Java: An Eventful Approach*. Prentice Hall, 2006.

[6] K. P. King and M. Gura, editors. *Classroom Robotics: Case Stories of 21st Century Instruction for Millennial Students*. Information Age Publishing, Charlotte, NC, 2007.

[7] S. Magnenat and F. Mondada. Improving the Thymio Visual Programming Language experience through augmented reality. Technical Report EPFL-200462, ETH Zürich and EPFL, March 2014. http://infoscience.epfl.ch/record/200462 (last accessed 16 November 2014).

[8] S. Magnenat, P. Rétornaz, M. Bonani, V. Longchamp, and F. Mondada. ASEBA: A Modular Architecture for Event-Based Control of Complex Robots. *IEEE/ASME Transactions on Mechatronics*, PP(99):1–9, 2010.

[9] S. Magnenat, J. Shin, F. Riedo, R. Siegwart, and M. Ben-Ari. Teaching a core CS concept through robotics. In *Proceedings of the Nineteenth Annual Conference on Innovation & Technology in Computer Science Education*, pages 315–320, Uppsala, Sweden, 2014.

[10] O. Meerbaum-Salant, M. Armoni, and M. Ben-Ari. Learning computer science concepts with Scratch. *Computer Science Education*, 23(3):239–264, 2013.

[11] F. Riedo, M. Chevalier, S. Magnenat, and F. Mondada. Thymio II, a robot that grows wiser with children. In *IEEE Workshop on Advanced Robotics and its Social Impacts (ARSO)*, 2013.

[12] R. Siegwart, I. R. Nourbakhsh, and D. Scaramuzza. *Introduction to Autonomous Mobile Robots (Second Edition)*. MIT Press, Cambridge, MA, 2011.

[13] P. Sommerauer and O. Müller. Augmented reality in informal learning environments: A field experiment in a mathematics exhibition. *Computers & Education*, 79:59–68, 2014.

A Comparison of Preschool and Elementary School Children Learning Computer Science Concepts through a Multilanguage Robot Programming Platform

Cecilia Martínez
Facultad de Filosofía y
Humanidades
Universidad Nacional de
Córdoba/CONICET
Córdoba, Argentina
cecimart@gmail.com

Marcos J. Gómez
FAMAF, Universidad Nacional
de Córdoba
Córdoba, Argentina
mgomez4@
famaf.unc.edu.ar

Luciana Benotti
Logic, Interaction and
Intelligent Systems Group
FAMAF, Universidad Nacional
de Córdoba/CONICET
Córdoba, Argentina
benotti@famaf.unc.edu.ar

ABSTRACT

This paper describes a school intervention to teach fundamental Computer Science (CS) concepts to 3-11 year old students with a multilanguage robot programming platform (using drag and drop, Python and C++ languages) in Argentina. We analyze students' performance and learning process based on multiple choice test and classroom observations. Data show that all students can intuitively learn sequence, conditional, loops and parameters and that girls performed slightly better than boys. Older students can easily combine these concepts to write a program. The multilanguage platform promotes student spontaneous exploration of more sophisticated CS concepts and languages. These findings imply that introducing CS in mandatory schooling from an inquiry based approach is both achievable and beneficial.

Categories and Subject Descriptors

K.3.2 [**Computer and Information Science Education**]: Computer science education

General Terms

Education

Keywords

Computer science K-7 outreach, robots, experimental evaluation, iconic programming language

1. INTRODUCTION

There has been a lot of debate on whether preschool and elementary school children should use computers or are developmentally ready to learn programming [2]. On one side, children are using computers much earlier each decade [14].

On the other side, this intensive use that many children have of computers may not be contributing to early access of Computer Science as a discipline (CS) which includes notions of creating and developing technology, programming, designing, and automatizing actions. We could argue that children become software consumers very early but they do not learn some basics of how this technology works. Bergen [1] points out that re-programmable toys such as robots, give children the possibility of creating, imagining, programming and exploring rather than developing procedural digital competences.

Previous research suggests [2] that early introduction of some basic CS concepts benefits both children cognitive development and learning about CS. Nevertheless, we still are debating what kind of CS concepts should be taught in preschool and elementary school [15]. Some countries such as Estonia and the UK have recently introduced CS in these levels [5], but most others—including ours—are still deliberating when would it be appropriate to introduce CS in schools and what content is most suitable for the general basic education. While research on teaching CS in different educational levels is vast, and colleagues have proposed curricular designs [9, 3], comparisons among different age groups performance that inform curriculum selection and scope is not as common [5, 11].

With the purpose of both investigating how children learn basic CS concepts in schools using programmable toys and contributing to a CS curriculum selection and scope; we designed an exploratory study to compare how preschool children (ages 3 and 5), and elementary school children (ages 8 to 11) learn some basics CS concepts. We piloted CS lessons in a real school setting focusing on loops, variables, conditionals, sequence, and parameters; and their application to robot programming. We analyzed children' learning of CS using a multilanguage robot programming platform and compared boys and girls performance. The main contributions of this paper are: 1) Analyzing how different age group of children learn fundamental CS concepts. 2) Introducing a multilanguage robot programming platform that permits students to discover new CS concepts on their own, growing with the platform. 3) Evaluating gender and age differences in the acquisition of CS concepts in preschool and elementary school.

We begin the paper summarizing previous work. Then, we describe a multilanguage robot programming platform and its rationale. We address the study design followed by our findings. We close this paper with conclusions and implications for teaching CS in preschool and elementary school.

2. PREVIOUS WORK

Starting preschool, children can create, run and debug simple computer programs using specific platforms that are both challenging and attainable for most children [2, 10, 8]. The effects and implications of learning CS at such an early age have also been analyzed. According to Clements [2], children who use computer assisted programs have the opportunity to analyze a situation and reflect on the properties of objects they have to manipulate.

While exploring how to teach CS to little children some researchers have found that the difficulties in children programming laid in their immature motor skills and on syntax problems [12, 8]. Thus, there has been a vast development on specific programming platforms to address the developmental traits of preschool children (such as Toon Talk, Scratch Jr, CHERPS, etc). In this context, programming robots has been an interesting line of work to teach CS to little children.

Flannery and Berns [7] showed that as a result of robot programming in preschool, children imagine, plan its action, and construct a robot. In their study, the authors found that all 4-6 year old students program short challenges and explore robot's capabilities.

Although most interventions to teach programming with robots achieve high student engagement and task completion, we still need to understand more how the use of these platforms promotes learning specific CS concepts. Morgado and Kahn [12] have documented how preschool children learn competences and concepts such as syntax, parameter passing, compound procedures, parallelism and concurrency, communication channel, input and client and servers using Toon Talk platform. We also need to learn more about what CS concepts children can understand in different developmental stages to establish a school curricula content and scope. We found only a handful of studies that compare different age groups performance on similar CS teaching activities. Magnenat and his colleagues (2014) [11] taught CS with robot programming to different age groups of children using event handler language to program a robot action in different events. Comparing the groups performance with the same task, they found that most children understood and solved simple tasks such as moving a robot upon a touch of a button or identifying robot's instructions. However, older children performed better on complex programming that required several conditions or events. Dagiene et al [5] compared students from Finland, Sweden and Lithuania ages 7 to 12 performing similar algorithmic thinking tasks exercises. Using multiple choice questions, they evaluated concepts such as graphs, search algorithms, data structures, and executing sequences. They found no strong difference across age groups, but rather among countries. The authors suggest that educational context, academic quality and in particular, reading ability promoted by each school system may be strongly related to learning CS concepts. Thus, we want to highlight the value of conducting exploratory studies in pur-posely selected geographical context that may be transferable to similar places, to contribute to CS curriculum design appropriate for each region. In this paper we compare different age groups performance on robot programming tasks and analyze students learning of basic CS concepts in a real school context in Argentina.

3. A ROBOT PROGRAMMING LANGUAGE

The UNC++Duino programming environment is an extension of blocklyDuino[1], a platform based in blockly, for programming Arduino[2] boards supporting Grove System. Code org uses Blockly in their Hour of Code initiative [16]. We extended blocklyDuino to adapt it to a multiplo N6[3], an educational robot platform created in Argentina and selected for our pilot study (illustrated in Figure 1). UNC++Duino includes a drag and drop language, that allows students to focus in solving CS problems without thinking about syntax. The platform can also be programmed in other full programming languages such as Python and C++ with different levels of language difficulties and expressiveness. The simplest one is the iconic language, but the student can switch into a more complex one, being C++ the hardest and most expressive. Our iconic programming language, with no natural language, allows kindergartners to sixth graders to easily program the N6 robot. Each block represents an executable robot action. A set of arrows enables the robot to move forward (20 cm), turn 90 degrees left or right. We also created blocks for control structures such as loops, conditionals, parameters, among others. The program has a musical block (represented by a saxophone), allowing kids to choose different songs for the robot to play. Two images, one showing the robot in front of an object, and the other one with nothing in front of the robot, represent conditional (Figure 1e). We programmed the platform to translate each iconic block automatically into Python and C++ encouraging children to explore into the different languages, seek other robot functions and grow out of the iconic interface

Figure 1: The N6 robot

Figure (1a), shows a program that allows children to move the robot 60 cm. Simply selecting arrows make it easy for all students to code. In contrast, coding with blocklyDuino (1b), requires working with numbers, time delay, engine like objects and calculating the relation between the defined speed and time to advance 60 cm. If we wanted the robot turn 90 degrees to the left, on UNC++Duino, students simply select the Turn left arrow block (1c). Image (1e) shows

[1] https://github.com/gasolin/BlocklyDuino
[2] http://www.arduino.cc/
[3] http://www.robotgroup.com.ar/index.php/productos/131-robot-n6#especificaciones

160

	UNC++Duino	BlocklyDuino
Advance	(a)	(b)
Turn left	(c)	(d)
Conditional	(e)	(f)

Table 1: Comparison between UNC++Duino and blockly-Duino.

how students can program their own Object detector robot selecting the pictures representing the conditions (1f).

4. STUDY DESIGN

We describe the school context where we conducted the study outlining the different interventions in preschool and elementary school.

4.1 The Setting for the Study

We made the intervention in a privately run school receiving state public and students' tuition funds. There are no children below the poverty line and most children have middle class, professional parents. The school follows an experience based pedagogy and organizes its curriculum on problem, case and project based learning. The institution has strong links with the School of Education at Cordoba National University, and constantly organizes professional development events for their teachers. We decided that this context provided a unique opportunity to pilot discovery based CS teaching experiences. Our team provided materials and expertise on teaching CS and the school provided expertise on reaching elementary and preschool children.

4.2 The Preschool Intervention

University professors and preschool teachers designed an academic unit to program a robot following three stages. During the first stage, students acted as the robots who followed their peers commands. Teachers designed a floor game that consisted on a 5 by 5 square grid with obstacles and targets randomly sprawled in the grid. Children chose a sequence of arrows that took the robot (i.e., the child) to the matching target. There were three types of arrows: straight, turn right and turn left. Students made one to one correspondence (one arrow followed by one movement) to

play this game. Also, children placed arrows in the specific square where the robot had to move making spatial correspondence as well.

The second stage consisted in replicating the floor game into a board game using a table size cardboard and toy robots. Similar to the floor game, children made one to one spatial and movement correspondence but moving a toy robot instead of their bodies. This was the first step to detaching their bodies from the robot's actions.

In the third stage children programmed the N6 robot in a computer with the described platform UNC++Duino. Children programed the robot to run on the floor squared grid using notions of *sequence* and *parameter*. Then, children programmed the robot to avoid objects using *conditionals* working freely on the floor without the grid. Finally, 5 year-old students learned *Loop*. The task required advancing the robot many times using only two lines of code.

4.3 The Elementary School Intervention

From May to December 2014 a university professor in CS and member of our research team taught CS lessons to 8-11 years old children for one hour a week. Before the professor took over, students have learned a mix of offimatics and LOGO. However, upon recalling previous knowledge, students remembered almost no CS concepts. Similar to the preschool experience, there were three different stages.

During the first stage, children worked with Code.org [16] tutorials using concepts such as *sequence*, *conditionals* and *loops*. In the second stage, students developed their own animations using the platform Alice [4, 6]. In the final stage, students programed the N6 robots with the *UNC++Duino* platform focusing on *sequence*, *conditionals*, *parameters*, and loops.

4.4 Data Collection and Analysis

In all, 190 students participated in this exploratory study. Table 2 describe participants' distribution.

School level	Pre	Pre	Elem	Elem
Number of students participating	25	30	70	65
Number of students tested	17	26	42	43
Student's age	3-4	5-6	8-9	10-11

Table 2: Participants Distribution(some students were absent on the test day).

All students programmed the robot employing sequences, parameters, conditionals, and loops in different tasks. Tasks required either using one concept (e.g. sequence), a combination of concepts (e.g. sequence and conditional) or applying concepts to two different programming situations (e.g. using the same program the robot must run in two different labyrinth). After each lesson, children took the same multiple choice test to assess how different age groups understood each CS concept. The test included 7 different multiple choice programming tasks. A "simple" task required applying one or two concepts (such as combining sequence and conditional to make an obstacle dodger robot). A "complex tasks" required combining concepts and selecting a program to solve two different problems. Thus, a higher level of abstraction.

We also conducted lesson observations during all of the robot programming classes. Observations allowed us to gather data on student engagement with programming and on transferring concepts learned with other platforms. In this paper, we only report on the robot programming stage to compare how preschool and elementary school children learned basic CS concepts and applied them to robotic programming. We do not present data on students learning other CS concepts with code.org or Alice.

Because the focus of this paper is understanding how different age group of children understand basic CS, we compared results of both preschool and elementary school interventions. We analyzed test results with descriptive statistics. We crossed preschool and elementary school data and compared gender differences in elementary school. We triangulated these results with qualitative data from observations that provided further indicators of emerging themes.

5. RESULTS

In this section we present age and gender differences in learning CS concepts at preschool and elementary school. Figure 2 summarizes the multiple choice test results showing performance by age group. Because of organizational issues, not all age groups were tested on all concepts.

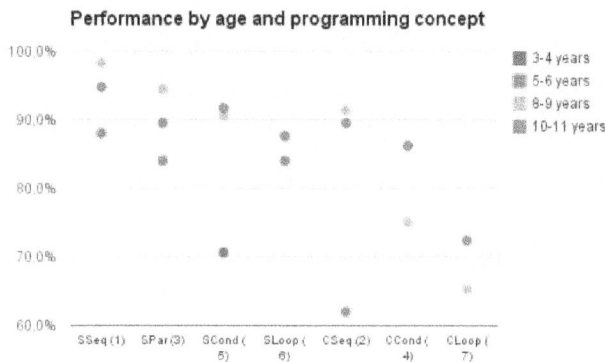

Figure 2: Percentage of correct test results per age group and CS concept (Capital S, stands for Simple y Capital C stands for Complex).

5.1 Learning Sequences

23 out of 26 preschool children selected the right sequence of instructions. Lesson observations indicated that most preschool children could provide a series a sequential instructions including both straight arrows interleaved with turn arrows. By the time children played the board game and programmed a robot on the computer they could clearly indicate the amount and orientations of arrows needed to make the robot get to target. Divergent thinking was also present as children suggested different paths for the robot to get to target. However, systematically, 3-4 years old placed one arrow only when the robot had to turn instead of selecting both an straight and turning arrow. This last group of preschool students also had difficulties realizing that robots run the sequence code written on the computer. Linking the virtual world of the screen with the concrete spatial movements of the robots was not a problem for 5 years old.

Most elementary school students performed high on both the simple and complex sequence multiple choice test. Observations showed that students solved the sequence challenge in five minutes and quickly moved into discovering other types of commands and robot functions. Only 2 groups of students took longer to program the robot because instead of reading the task they simply wrote the sequence they wanted the robot to run. Based on observation data, both simple and complex sequence were not challenging for elementary school students. However, most importantly we observed that the activity of programming a robot seemed to encourage exploration of other CS concepts. Elementary school children of all age groups immediately designed new robot challenges. For example, one observations in 4th grade (9 to 10 years old) indicated:

"Because the proposed challenge is to simple, students create their own circuit. The loudest and more 'active' group of the class, is the one thinking the most complex challenge where the robot has to run under a chair made tunnel. They walk the circuit with their bodies and go back and forth from the circuit to the computer to decide each line of code. Only 2 out of 30 children did not complete the task. One group wants the robot to run in circles, another is experimenting how the robot run into things. From this exploration children demand learning about sensors and turning upon an obstacle. One student asks how a proximity sensor is activated."

Excerpt such as this one showed that, thirsty for more, students started asking how to control speed, wheels and other functions. Children spontaneously opened the different UNC++Duino interfaces and made changes on the C++ lines of codes that was automatically generated from their first iconic program.

5.2 Learning Conditionals

In Preschool, children approached the concept of conditional creating their obstacle dodger robot. Classroom observations noted that the teacher simply asked them "What would it happen if a box is in the way of the robot?" Spontaneously and unanimously children replied "The robot has to turn". We showed students the block 1e that would allow them to create their own obstacle dodger robot. 3-5 year old children worked in groups of 5 to 6 children and each group programmed the robot using conditional. Upon showing them the block representing conditional all of them placed the turn arrow command when the block showed an obstacle, and an straight arrow command when the block showed no obstacles. While 5-6 years old read the code and predicted robot's actions, 3-4 years old could not realized that the robot would performed actions written in the computer.

12 of 17 preschool students solved the conditional multiple choice test correctly. The 5 students who responded incorrectly argued that they wanted the robot to crash into the box. When we asked: "Why did you chose this answer" they replied "because I want the robot to crash". Thus, we inferred that the wrong answers is not related to children' understanding of conditional, but rather of student's will.

Similar to the preschool children, elementary students applied conditional creating their obstacle dodger robot. Observations notes showed that one group of 10-11 years old students spontaneously called the conditional "decisions" and compared this function with the robot music block. Thus, students immediately transferred the notion of conditional learned with Hour of Code and Alice platforms. Learning to program an obstacle dodger robot was intuitively and fairly easy for students. However, while 8 to 11 year old children have similar performance on simple conditional, 10 to 11 years old students have better results on complex conditional. We believe that tasks that require combining different fundamental concepts such as sequence, loops and conditional demands deeper understanding and levels of abstraction.

5.3 Learning Loops

Because understanding loops requires some minimal comprehension of counting and multiplying, we only taught loops to 5-6 year old preschoolers. We simply told the students that the new block allowed writing the many times we wanted the robot to move forward instead of placing the amount of arrows we would need. Checking for understanding we asked:"So, if I write here 4 times what would happen?" Students responded "It will advance 4 times. We won't get tired of writing so many arrows" (excerpt from observation notes). Children' expressions are evidence that there is some understanding of loops as a repeated action that provides economy in programming. Moreover, each of the groups that programmed a loop selected different numbers of repetitions. One boy wanted the robot to move forward 10 times, so he selected a loop of 5 times and place 2 arrows inside. When we asked what would the robot do with that code, without hesitation he answered that the robot will move 10 times as it will advance 5 times each of the 2 arrows.

In elementary school, observation data showed that a group of students spontaneously asked the teacher where was the "repeat" instruction when they had to write a simple sequence code. Thus, children correctly "assumed" that the robot program had the loop function, transferring what they have learned with Alice and Hour of Code. Results on the loops multiple choice test showed the same performance pattern that we noted for sequence and conditional evaluation. All students, regardless of age and gender, effectively applied the concept of loop on simple tasks. However, when the task required combining concepts such as conditional and loops, older children performed better.

5.4 Learning Parameters

In order to introduce parameters in preschool, we asked students that upon completing the sequence they programmed, the robot must sing a song that matched the target. Within the block that allowed students to program the robot to sing, they had three options: sing any of two popular songs, or remain silent. All of the students were able to add the singing block at the end of the sequence selecting the appropriate song and they were extremely enthusiastic with the "singing" robot. In addition, about 85% of the students pick a song that matched a given picture in the test.

Elementary school students easily transferred notions of parameter previously introduced in Alice. They also enjoyed the idea of a singing robot, and added the song block every time they programmed. But in contrast to preschool children, because the platform allowed to see the code both in blockly and in C++, children spontaneously switched to the C++ or python interface, without having previous experience on them. Upon programming the robot, children soon wanted to change the robot speed and avoid the pause between each movement. They had two possibilities: up-

loading the block-code into the robot directly from the platform or they could use the arduino translator and copy the code into the arduino interface IDE and uploaded from it. They decided to read the arduino code, without any previous knowledge about it, and modify it to change speed. First, they observed that inside the loop function, there were tabs for the advance method. Upon this discovery, their first intention was to add a numerical argument to modify speed. When compiling the code, they observed an error, so they started to read the whole code and discovered the $avanzar()$ method, without knowing what a method was. They also learned that in the body of avanzar(), there were many instructions such as $motor0.setSpeed(50), motor1.setSpeed(50)$ and $delay(1000)$. They realized if they changed the argument of the $setSpeed()$ of both engines they could change the robot speed and they did it. But the robot still was moving for only 1 second. So they came back to the arduino code, and noticed that the instruction $delay(1000)$, was responsible of engine movement time. They erased the delays and the $setSpeed(0)$ instructions, making the robot advance quickly and for a longer time. They continued playing with the arguments of the instructions, making the robot move backward or in circles, actions that would not be possible with the initial version of block code.

5.5 Gender Gaps in CS in Elementary School?

We analyzed test results by gender and identified that while both boys and girls have similar performance applying simple concepts, girls did systematically better on complex concepts (Figure 3). About 12% more of the girls were better at choosing options where loops, conditional and sequence were applied. In addition, the teacher noted that at the beginning of the lesson girls were not enthusiastic with programming a robot because they assumed it was similar to playing with toy cars. However, when noting that the robot responded to their orders or commands, they became progressively more interested. Boys enthusiasm remained constant One hypothesis explaining the different achievement is that girls are generally more focused on academic tasks while boys at this age are very playful. Previous work shows that female students have considerable lower marks in the first year of university than male students. Redmond et al (2013) [13] argues that their lower marks correlates with the fact that they have less exposure to computers and thus, lower confidence with CS. Based on our data, we suspect that the gap between boys and girls may occurs later during their teenage years.

6. CONCLUSIONS

Through a school intervention focusing on fundamental CS concepts we found that all children, regardless of their age group, could intuitively learn sequence, loops, parameters, and conditional, and were capable of applying these notions into robot programming. However, as expected, older children could combine these concepts to create a new program. As obvious as these results may seem, we still need strong empirical evidence about what CS concepts different age group can learn to inform the design of a CS school curricula. We also identified that 3-4 year old students could not correspond the written code in the computer with the robot actions. Girls did a slightly better than boys combining CS on robot programming suggesting that the "gender gap" may occur later in the teenage years. Students

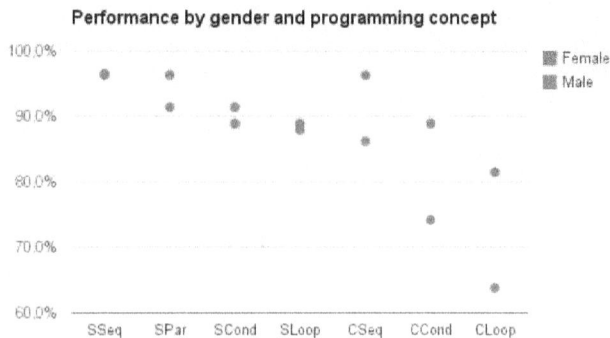

Figure 3: Percentage of correct test results per gender and programming concept

showed high engagement with robots and most importantly, our multilanguage platform triggered students exploration of other CS concepts and allowed children to easily switch from simple to complex languages focusing on concepts rather than on syntax. There are several implication of these findings. 1) Based on our research we suggest that it is not only possible to teach CS in K to 12 mandatory schooling but it is also beneficial in terms of developing CS literacy. 2) Programming robots, while it is costly, highly engage our students. 3) Inquiry based developmentally appropriate teaching strategies proved valuable because they allowed students to build intuitively on concepts, explore with their bodies and apply these concepts to multiple situations, platforms or environments (such as animations, games, board games, etc); and then transfer these ideas into robot programming. This is an important contribution to the field of CS education since we are still debating about pedagogical approaches to introduce CS in schools. 4) Our multilanguage platform designed for k to 12 students was a great tool to expand children exploration and knowledge on CS concepts. In general children grow out of computer platforms designed for a particular age group very quickly. Our platform encourage students to grow with it and because of it. We acknowledge that further research is necessary with multilanguage platforms, but this could be one direction to encourage children growth in CS.

7. ACKNOWLEDGMENTS

The authors wish to thank Science and Technology Secretary at Universidad Nacional de Cordoba, Google for Education, and Manuel Sadosky Foundation at the Argentinean Ministry of Science, Technology and Productive Innovation.

8. REFERENCES

[1] D. Bergen. Technology in the classroom: Learning in the robotic world: Active or reactive? *Childhood Education*, 77(4):249–250, 2001.

[2] D. H. Clements and J. Sarama. Teaching with computers in early childhood education: Strategies and professional development. *Journal of Early Childhood Teacher Education*, 23(3):215–226, 2002.

[3] Computing at School Working Group. *Computer Science: A Curriculum for Schools*. Computing at School Working Group, 2012.

[4] S. Cooper, W. Dann, and R. Pausch. Teaching objects-first in introductory computer science. In *Proceedings of the 34th SIGCSE Technical Symposium on Computer Science Education*, pages 191–195, 2003.

[5] V. Dagiene, L. Mannila, T. Poranen, L. Rolandsson, and P. Söderhjelm. Students' performance on programming-related tasks in an informatics contest in finland, sweden and lithuania. In *Proceedings of the 2014 Conference on Innovation; Technology in Computer Science Education*, ITiCSE '14, pages 153–158, New York, NY, USA, 2014. ACM.

[6] W. Dann, S. Cooper, and D. Slater. Alice 3.1 (abstract only). In *Proceeding of the 44th ACM Technical Symposium on Computer Science Education*, pages 757–757, 2013.

[7] L. P. Flannery and M. U. Bers. Let's dance the "robot hokey-pokey!" children's programming approaches and achievement throughout early cognitive development. *Journal of Research on Technology in Education*, 46(1):81–101, 2013.

[8] L. P. Flannery, B. Silverman, E. R. Kazakoff, M. U. Bers, P. Bontá, and M. Resnick. Designing scratchjr: support for early childhood learning through computer programming. In *Proceedings of the 12th International Conference on Interaction Design and Children*, pages 1–10. ACM, 2013.

[9] J. Goode, G. Chapman, and J. Margolis. Beyond curriculum: The exploring computer science program. *ACM Inroads*, 3(2):47–53, June 2012.

[10] E. Kazakoff, A. Sullivan, and M. Bers. The effect of a classroom-based intensive robotics and programming workshop on sequencing ability in early childhood. *Early Childhood Education Journal*, 41(4):245–255, 2013.

[11] S. Magnenat, J. Shin, F. Riedo, R. Siegwart, and M. Ben-Ari. Teaching a core cs concept through robotics. In *Proceedings of the 2014 Conference on Innovation and Technology in Computer Science Education*, ITiCSE '14, pages 315–320, New York, NY, USA, 2014. ACM.

[12] L. Morgado, M. Cruz, and K. Kahn. Preschool cookbook of computer programming topics. *Australasian Journal of Educational Technology*, 26(3):309–326, 2010.

[13] K. Redmond, S. Evans, and M. Sahami. A large-scale quantitative study of women in computer science at stanford university. In *Proceeding of the 44th ACM Technical Symposium on Computer Science Education*, SIGCSE, pages 439–444, New York, NY, USA, 2013.

[14] V. Rideout. Zero to eight: Children's media use in america 2013. *Pridobljeno*, 11(1):2014, 2013.

[15] A. Tucker. A model curriculum for k–12 computer science: Final report of the acm k–12 task force curriculum committee. Technical report, New York, NY, USA, 2003. ACM Order No.: 104043.

[16] C. Wilson. Hour of code: We can solve the diversity problem in computer science. *ACM Inroads*, 5(4):22–22, Dec. 2014.

Using Learning Analytics to Visualise Computer Science Teamwork

Harmid Tarmazdi, Rebecca Vivian, Claudia Szabo, Katrina Falkner and Nickolas Falkner

The School of Computer Science

The University of Adelaide

South Australia, Australia, 5005

firstname.lastname@adelaide.edu.au

ABSTRACT

Industry has called upon academia to better prepare Computer Science graduates for teamwork, especially in developing the soft skills necessary for collaborative work. However, the teaching and assessment of teamwork is not easy, with instructors being pressed for time and a lack of tools available to efficiently analyse student teamwork, where large cohorts are involved.

We have developed a teamwork dashboard, founded on learning analytics, learning theory and teamwork models that analyses students' online teamwork discussion data and visualises the team mood, role distribution and emotional climate. This tool allows educators to easily monitor teams in real-time. Educators may use the tool to provide students with feedback about team interactions as well as to identify problematic teams. We present a case study, trialing the dashboard on one university Computer Science course and include reflections from the course lecturer to determine its utility in monitoring online student teamwork.

Categories and Subject Descriptors

K.3.1 [**Computer Uses in Education**]: Collaborative learning

General Terms

Data visualisation, teamwork, groupwork, learning analytics, problem based learning, assessment.

Keywords

Learning analytics, Computer Science Education, Collaboration.

1. INTRODUCTION

As the complexity of software projects has grown over the years and teamwork has become an integral part of software industry, the ability for Computer Science (CS) graduates to participate effectively in face-to-face and online professional teamwork has become crucial [1, 17]. To better prepare students for industry, academics have integrated team projects into CS curriculum.

ITICSE '15, July 04 - 08, 2015, Vilnius, Lithuania

Copyright 2015 ACM 978-1-4503-3440-2/15/07... $15.00

http://dx.doi.org/10.1145/2729094.2742613

Despite the presence of teamwork in university curricula, industry still express concern with graduates' abilities to work in teams effectively [18].

Although teamwork is fundamental to software development, many CS students express a dislike for teamwork and group projects because of conflicts and tensions that arise when some peers are perceived to not be performing [5, 24]. Instructors can assist student teams in overcoming some difficulties, however, they may not be aware of all team issues that arise [7]. To effectively monitor student teams and provide meaningful feedback, academics require information about the activity of individual team members and the team as a whole. This information is usually unavailable to academics as teamwork is often undertaken outside of the classroom, in face-to-face contexts or using personal technologies and tools; making it difficult for lecturers to know how students are performing. Where teamwork is online, the development of learning tools that visualise teamwork activity and climate may provide crucial key to support academics in monitoring and assessing online teamwork.

Early work in learning analytics tools has focused on the visualisation of detailed, individual student data, and the development of teamwork analysis tools remains a crucial issue for the advancement of education practices in this topic. Current tools only offer metrics such as frequency of student contributions and access frequency: these metrics, while useful, cannot inform educators in the teaching of teamwork [19].

This paper provides a review of existing learning analytics techniques and tools and presents a teamwork dashboard developed to support educators in monitoring online teamwork for CS students in problem-solving, team projects. We trial our dashboard on a final year CS class and invite the lecturer to respond about their experience with using the dashboard to monitor student teamwork during the course.

2. LITERATURE

In university courses, the assessment of team projects usually focuses on 'the product' and application of knowledge, rather than on teamwork processes [11]. Efforts to provide feedback on peer contribution have usually considered only peer or self-assessment methods. However, students may not necessarily be accurate in their own assessment and peer-assessment may be affected by social pressure [26]. These post-evaluation methods, however, do not assist educators in identifying teams that are encountering issues or conflicts as it is often too late to resolve team conflict or for advice to be useful [7]. As a result, there are missed opportunities for the early-identification of teams that are at-risk of failing or are not functioning well.

Although online teamwork illuminates some conversations, it may be difficult for teachers to traverse the large amount of activity when managing multiple classes and to know how to use student dialogue assess team functioning. There is a clear demand for tools in education to assist academics in effectively and efficiently interpreting student teamwork. Automated tools will allow academics to direct time and effort toward providing timely and useful feedback to teams or the early identification of team issues. In the following subsection, we explore the field of learning analytics and describe techniques within this field that have guided the development of our teamwork dashboard.

2.1 Learning Analytics

Learning analytics is the field associated with taking large sets of student-related data and using analysis techniques to decipher trends and patterns to advance and personalize education [12]. The *Horizon Report* [12] describes early work in learning analytics as focusing on the identification of at-risk learners to improve retention, with more recent work extending to include the development of software to guide students toward more productive study behaviours. In this section, we move on to present a number of techniques and examples of tools that visualise learner data in online environments.

A number of software systems have focused on collecting and visualising student access and activity data. These tools focus on how human and non-human entities interact with one another. Such tools collect data about user access to course materials, the time spent viewing material as well as fine grained logging of user activity during quizzes, frequency of contributions in online discussion forums. There are a number of tools available but some examples of learning dashboards include that by Santos *et al* [19] in which the authors have worked on the visualisation of student activity data between learners and Learning Management Systems (LMSs), incorporating weekly activity graphs and categorisation of activity type. Schmitz *et al* [20] and Govaerts *et al* [6] have also worked on visualising individual student data, but with the ability to select specific time periods or activity types. Govaerts *et al* also move somewhat from the individual to the group by incorporating basic statistics indicating average student behaviour. These tools are usually available as plugins for learning management systems (LMS) such as Moodle (www.moodle.org) or as stand-alone applications. However, a challenge of LMS plugins is they are not useful when students are collaborating outside the LMS environment.

Social Network Analysis (SNA) examines the existing strength of relationships between various actors (i.e. learners) in a network. In a learning context, SNA tools take message data and present the links between learners in a visual graph. "SNAPP" [2] is an example of an SNA tool that provides real-time analysis and visualisation of social networks between collaborators. The SNAPP tool has potential to be used early on in team projects for the early identification of an isolated team member, prompting educators to respond. However, SNA tools, such as SNAP, are primarily used for post reflection of teamwork and assessment of relationships within the team and/or the instructor.

To better understand online teamwork, Computer-Supported Collaborative Learning (CSCL) researchers have developed frameworks for examining online activities and knowledge construction in online problem-solving tasks [9]. In their work, the researchers present a chronology of group dynamics, over a period of time, using linear visualisations to assist with the identification of behavioural patterns. Although the visualisations are thorough and detailed, one criticism is that they are too complex to be useful for educators [7]. To make the information more accessible, Gweon *et al* [7] developed visualisations identified as being relevant to educators. Such information

included learning goals, group and individual processes and contributions toward the team product. The visualisations display activities at the group level, as well as at an individual level using a team 'evidence wheel' to represent contributions. However, a limitation of the measurement used is the focus on contribution quantity rather than type of contribution. Another area of work has been to apply manual content analysis to identify team role behaviours evident in team online discussion text [23]. However, a limitation of this work is that manual content analysis is time consuming and such methods are not feasible for educators wishing to provide timely support to students or to teams undergoing conflict.

A tool that takes elements of Human Computer Interaction (HCI) analysis, SNA and CSCL mapping is "Cohere" [13]. The authors use argument-mapping techniques to collect and analyse discourse where the users are required to provide metadata with their message. For example, a message post, in addition to the content, will include information on the message target and the underlying nature, which can be used to map learner interactions. This approach provides the opportunity to create a semantic network from otherwise temporal sequence of text messages.

Another technique of interest in CS education has been to examine the sentiment expressed by students in their reflections of learning activities. Sentiment analysis is the field of study that analyses people's opinions, sentiments, evaluations, attitudes and emotions in written text using natural language processing (NLP) and text analysis [14]. Sentiment analysis has primarily been used within the domains of business and social sciences and very limited research has investigated its use within education contexts. Some of the work that has been done in education has been to explore sentiment expressed by students in diaries [16]. The researchers extended sentiment analysis work to also extract and identify expressions that aligned with eight fundamental emotions of anger, trust, surprise, sadness, joy, fear, disgust and anticipation. These emotions in the text were tracked and visualised using spider graphs. Sentiment analysis can be useful in identifying students who display extreme cases of negative emotions and may be applied to other texts within learning contexts to identify positivity and negativity and as a means to provide insight to the emotional state of students or groups.

There is potential for CS education researchers to also apply learning analytics techniques, such as these mentioned, to explore and monitor team performance. However, researchers suggest a crucial part of developing tools with learning analytics, is the ability to present this information to educators meaningfully and through automated processes [8]. Further, some of the tools and techniques described in this paper so far may be across multiple tools, requiring more effort and time to process data. Thus, automated and flexible tools that can be used across platforms may be particularly useful for academics.

3. MOTIVATION

A challenge identified in the field of learning analytics is that there is often little mention of pedagogy, learning or teaching [21]. Authors attribute this cause to learning analytics as having roots in business intelligence and argue that it will become crucial that tools based on learning analytics will require a strong pedagogical foundation and hold academic and ethical integrity. Particularly for cases in which student data is collected as a by-product (discussion data, access to materials) as oppose to intentionally (e.g. quizzes, essays). Moreover, Vartrapu *et al.* [22] recommend a need for researchers in this field to extend learning analytics towards real-time monitoring and feedback, to provide "computational as well as methodological" support for educators.

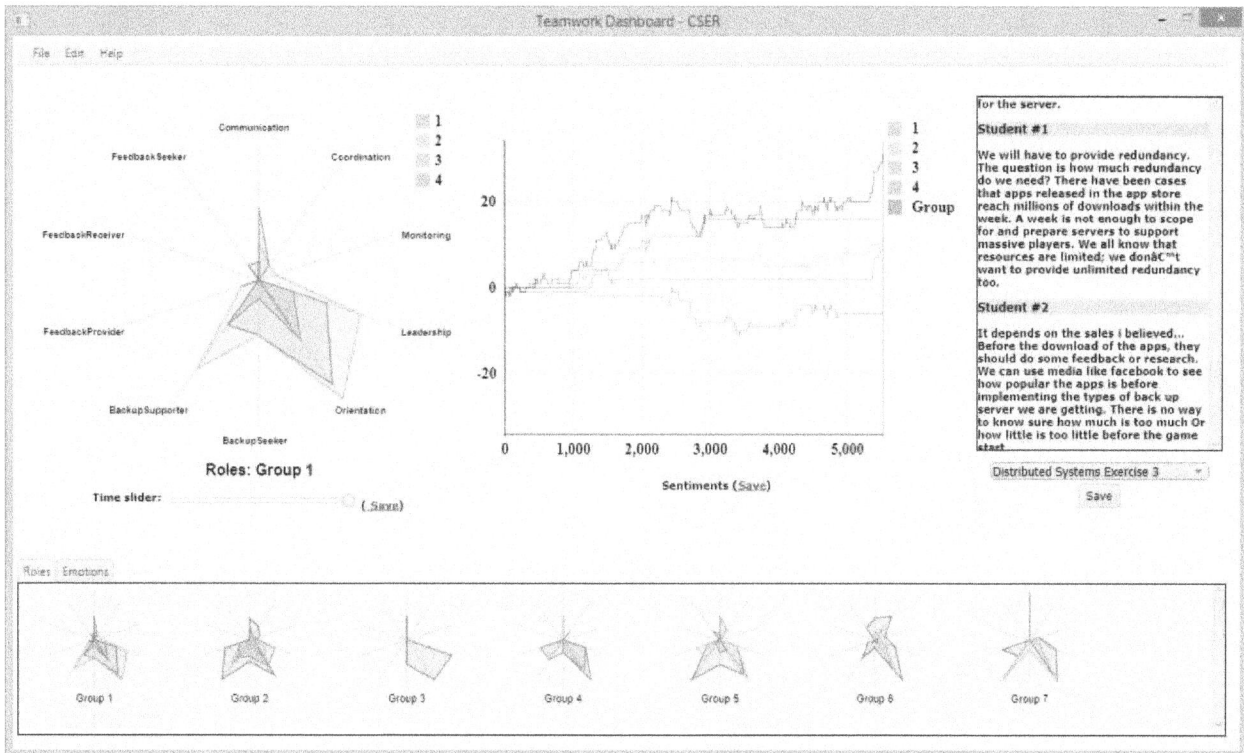

Figure 1: The Teamwork Dashboard

To support academics with monitoring online student teamwork in discussion forums, we have developed a teamwork dashboard. The dashboard is founded on learning theory, elements of learning analytics and teamwork models. In this paper, we present the functions of the dashboard and follow with a test of the dashboard on a third-year Distributed Systems course. We present the lecturer's reflection and experience with using the dashboard and discuss how this informs future work.

4. THE TEAMWORK DASHBOARD

The teamwork dashboard presents a visualisation of collaboration showing detected roles for each participant, and discussion sentiment for the group as a whole. The dashboard analyses a text-based transcript of the collaboration, and has been constructed to operate over on-line collaboration transcripts from systems such as Piazza (www.Piazza.com). To import the data into the tool, a script is run regularly (daily) that converts Piazza messages into input data. This method of import can be adapted for other LMS discussion boards.

The user can interact with the dashboard by selecting teams to explore by clicking on elements on the screen. Figure 1 illustrates a snapshot of the teamwork dashboard, illustrating one team's team-role classification in focus, along with sentiment analysis graphs. The dashboard features a summary of all teams at the bottom of the screen, where the educator may select between a summary of all teams and their sentiment analysis or the team's role adoption. To investigate a team in more detail, the user clicks on the particular team of interest, which presents a larger graph and the team's sentiment chart.

Our approaches build upon extensive prior manual analysis [23], devised from the work of Dickinson and McIntryre's teamwork model [4] and educational psychology. We have employed a combination of NLP and information retrieval techniques to aid automated identification of team roles, and the

use of sentiment analysis techniques to identify emotion within online student collaborations.

Dickinson and McIntyre's teamwork model [4] was selected because the model focuses on practical roles of self-organising teams. Dickinson and McIntyre classified seven core components of teamwork: Team Leadership, Team Orientation, Monitoring, Coordination, Communication, Feedback and Backup Behaviour and provided with their model a guide to measure performance. The authors recommend three formats for constructing teamwork measures: a behavioural observation scale, behavioural summary scale, and behavioural event. While the model is focused on practical use and assessment, the measurement relies on how teams respond to critical events according to numbered scales, rather than the explicit identification of behaviours. More information about the manual classification of this model is available in a previous paper [22].

The teamwork dashboard provides analysis and monitoring with a focus on teamwork roles adapted by learners in the discussion. Figure 2 illustrates the team role identification for a single team. Each point on the spider graph represents a role and the frequencies of utterances for that particular role, captured in discussion data. A different number and colour represents each team member and a user can see the frequency of occurrence for each role for each individual member. Learners' roles are visualized through spider graphs showing behavior frequencies (the longer the line, the greater the frequency). This is generated from executing search queries on the discussion data. The "time slider" may be selected and shifted from left to right, which displays the time-evolution of roles for all members as the team progresses through their task (according to total word frequency).

The evolution of emotions [16] is also extracted and visualized, both as an overall positive/negative sentiment graph and through the identification of individual, commonly expressed emotions. Figure 3 illustrates the visualisation of emotions established via sentiment analysis techniques, demonstrating the overall group sentiment over time, along with the sentiment attributed to each individual, displayed as a spider graph (Figure 4). Like the spider graph for team roles, each point on the graph represents the frequency of occurrences for each emotion, captured in the discussion data. Each colour represents a team member and, once again, the "time slider" can be moved to show the evolution of emotions over time (according to word count). The sentiment and emotions are extracted from discussions using a lexicon based sentiment analysis method [10], with POS tagging to reduce ambiguity [25]. To classify the discussion posts for team roles, we implemented "classification by standing queries". In this method, a technical expert develops hand crafted rule sets that are written as regular expressions and used for classification of the documents. Although rules can be difficult to develop and maintain, this method is comparable or better than machine learning methods [15].

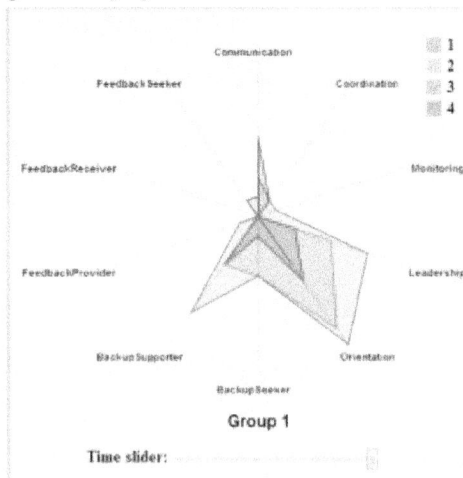

Figure 2: Spider Graph Illustrating Team Role Identification for a Single Team.

The data presented in the visualisation has been automatically generated using NLP and information retrieval algorithms that searched the discussion text for phrases of "common combinations or patterns" based on the coding framework established in our previous work [23]. Our automated analysis framework is specialised to the field of CS, through the inclusion of *stopword* lists (words to be ignored in discussion) that incorporate common CS technical terms.

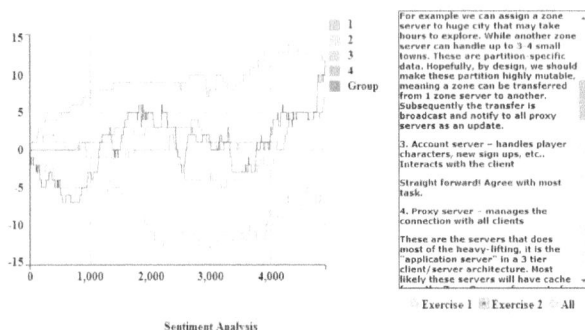

Figure 3: Sentiment Analysis for a Team's Collaboration.

In our initial work, the validation of the teamwork dashboard was performed by comparing the manual classification of the teamwork roles across 52 teamwork exercises, each consisting of

3-5 students within CS courses, against the results of the automated analysis within our dashboard, with high levels of agreement. However, our teamwork dashboard had not been used within a live course to inform ongoing teaching and assessment. In this study, we extend our validation with a live case study of the use of the dashboard as a teaching tool by a lecturer as the group-based project is taking place.

5. METHOD

We have undertaken a pilot qualitative study gathering lecturer perspectives on the utility and suitability of the tool in assisting lecturer interventions in online collaborations. We have applied a case study approach to test the dashboard on the dataset of a final year Distributed Systems course at the University of Adelaide with 15 teams, and in excess of 2,500 individual discussion contributions. An instrumental case study approach was adopted as it involved the use of a particular case to test the dashboard and incorporate the lecturer's experience with using it [3]. The benefit of case study methods is that of allowing for the in-depth assessment of particular topics.

5.1 Context

The dashboard was employed on an online Piazza group discussion as part of an assignment for a third year distributed systems course. The assessment for the course comprises of three assignments, worth a total of 30% of the final mark, and an exam worth 70%. The group-based assignment required the students to choose a large-scale distributed system and discuss how the system addresses the challenges of heterogeneity, scalability, transparency and openness. The 49 students were split into self-selected teams of 2-4 students, and once these teams were formed (there were 15 teams in total) the lecturer created Piazza groups on which the discussion would take place. This ensured that not only students conducted research about a particular distributed system, but that they also had a medium of written discussion about various aspects of the system under study. The capability of discussing about research issues in a written form is an important graduate attribute that is otherwise difficult to assess.

The assignment had two deadlines. The first deadline required the students to decide which distributed system to discuss. A list of systems was provided as guidance, but students could select their own. The second final deadline was four weeks later and comprised of the submission of a report (as a Piazza note) addressing the above challenges. The assignment was worth 10% of the final mark. The assignment marks were equally distributed among clear discussions about how the system addresses the above challenges (20% each, awarded to the entire team) and on continuous and consistent online activity in Piazza (20%, individual mark). The students were briefed on the purpose of the exercise, on how to use Piazza for discussions, and on the requirements for consistent online activity. Specifically, constructive discussions on whether a particular distributed system met the challenges and how, and on how team members wrote about them were required as part of the online activity.

5.2 Research Question

In this case study, we explored two aspects of the teamwork dashboard, by testing it on a live course and inviting the lecturer to reflect upon the tool's usefulness, to answer the following:

1) Does the dashboard work on datasets outside that which it was developed on?

2) To what extent does the developed teamwork dashboard provide a lecturer with useful support and information about students' teamwork during the course of their assessment?

We present the results of the teamwork analysis on the new cohort's discussion data. Following, we include the lecturer's reflection on how the teamwork dashboard was used to monitor the students' teamwork and how useful it was to the lecturer.

6. LECTURER EXPERIENCE

The lecturer employed the dashboard regularly, roughly every three-four days. The lecturer used the dashboard for two main purposes. In the first stages of the assignment, that is, before the first deadline, the dashboard was used to identify groups that were not engaged with the assignment. In this stage, the lecturer expected to see a large number of groups with orientation and coordination behaviours. Groups not exhibiting these roles were contacted by lecturer and asked about difficulties. In the second stage of the assignment, the dashboard was used for observation purposes. The lecturer observed both the progression of roles within each team, but also the progression of emotions as the assignment unfolded. These observations allowed the lecturer to more effectively focus on teams that required attention. For example, in the initial stages of the assignment, in one group there was a single student that was contributing. The student was showing *frustration* and *anger* in the dashboard emotion tab, but was not discussing this directly with the lecturer, who, without the use of the dashboard, would have risked not seeing this (on that particular day, the lecturer had received 150 Piazza emails about the assignment). Emotions of *surprise* allowed the lecturer to identify some issues with the Piazza forum; *trust* emotions showed that students were confident about their knowledge and existing resources about their selected distributed system; whereas feelings of *anticipation* or in some cases *joy* showed that students were discovering how well the distributed system met particular challenges (through the use of words such as "great", "good", "cool" etc.) as shown in Figure 4, with the corresponding discussion in Figure 5.

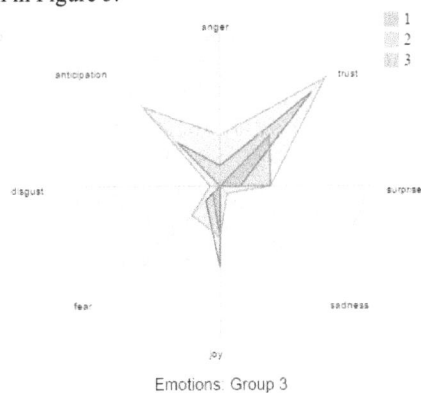

Figure 4 Anticipation and Joy Emotions.

The role analysis within the dashboard allowed the lecturer to identify teams that were on the right track (that is, those teams where constructive feedback and discussions on the topic were taking place), as shown in Figure 6. The role analysis also allowed the lecturer to identify teams that required attention, where members posted content but where no feedback was given nor requested. In these cases, the lecturer intervened either on the Piazza forum, or discussing with the teams offline, by highlighting the constructs necessary both for requesting feedback and for providing it. The use of the role analysis allowed the lecturer to identify valuable educational opportunities that would have been missed otherwise.

The dashboard was extremely useful both for observing the teams' progress, but also for assessment, as the progression of both team and student activity could be visualised over time. This informed a more detailed analysis of each user's posting activity, which is facilitated by Piazza. Piazza has the option of notifying the lecturers anytime a post is updated. However, continuously keeping track of these emails was not scalable as this assignment generated 2,503 Piazza emails, for a reasonably small cohort.

Figure 5 Discussions Showing Anticipation and Joy.

7. DISCUSSION

The use of our teamwork dashboard to inform the teaching of teamwork in CS shows its potential but also highlights avenues of future research. The lecturer who employed the tool was able to identify students and teams that needed attention, both with respect to how the teams engaged with the work, but also with how the work was carried out. The nature of the assignment limited the possible interventions that the lecturer could perform: because this was a fairly large, written, research-focused discussion, the lecturer could comment on the tone used, on how feedback should be requested and given, and on how some team members needed to participate more.

Moreover, the delegation of tasks and the team organization was, for some teams, straightforward, in that a team member was chosen to be responsible for a challenge; the team member did the research and communicated its outcomes, receiving feedback from his peers. A more complicated teamwork scenario would have students continuously allocated tasks and to discuss various outcomes. We envisage that our tool will be even more useful in this scenario.

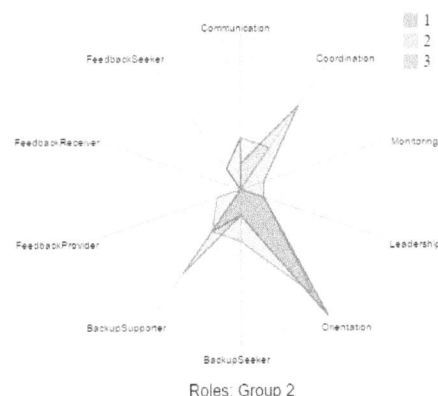

Figure 6 Snapshot of Team Roles.

The live use of our tool also highlighted several avenues of improvement. For example, particular roles could be associated with the assignment timeline (e.g., teams should show "orientation" roles at the beginning of their work on a particular tasks) and automated warnings could be raised once the teams do not meet this expectation. Similarly, automated warnings could be raised when specific sentiments are detected. This would allow for even a more timely intervention as the lecturer could be alerted immediately about current issues.

A limitation of this study is that we have based the use of the tool on one lecturer's experience in one single case study. Future work aims to explore the use of the dashboard and usability with lecturers of different subjects and with different teamwork discussions, to improve its features and effectiveness. Further work could also explore the impact of the use of the tool on assessment and students' experiences of teamwork.

8. CONCLUSION

Often group work is undertaken with the submission of a 'product', without any indication about the process that led to the product and without giving the lecturer the opportunity to address issues. As shown in this paper, the use of our teamwork dashboard during the completion of a group work assignment is beneficial for the lecturer as it allows for the tracking of the evolution of team roles across each team, and of the identification of various sentiments within each team. This allows the lecturer to assess and monitor teamwork processes, without having to traverse a large discussion forum. It also makes educators aware when particular teams are behaving differently to the majority, so that appropriate interventions can be made if necessary. The use of the dashboard may also provide guidance for educators wanting to construct collaborative learning activities where students are scaffolded in the adoption and transfer of roles.

9. REFERENCES

[1] Archer, W. et al. 2008. Graduate employability: what do employers think and want?, CIHE, Available, http://www.voced.edu.au/content/ngv25673

[2] Bakharia, A. and Dawson, S. 2011. SNAPP: A bird's-eye view of temporal participant interaction. LAK11, Banf, Alberta, 168–173.

[3] Crowe, S. et al. 2011. The case study approach. BMC Medical Research Methodology. 11, 1, 100.

[4] Dickinson, T.L. and McIntyre, R.M. 1997. A conceptual framework for teamwork measurement. Team performance assessment and measurement: Theory, methods, and applications. M.T. Brannick et al., eds. Lawrence Erlbaum Associates Publishers. 19–43.

[5] Falkner, K. et al. 2013. Collaborative learning and anxiety: A phenomenographic study of collaborative learning activities. Proceeding of the ACM Technical Symposium on Computer Science Education, Denver, USA, 227–232.

[6] Govaerts, S. et al. 2010. Visualizing activities for self-reflection and awareness. Advances in Web-Based Learning. X. Luo et al., eds. Springer Berlin Heidelberg. 91–100.

[7] Gweon, G. et al. 2011. A framework for assessment of student project groups on-line and off-line. Analyzing Interactions in CSCL. S. Puntambekar et al., eds. Springer US. 293–317.

[8] Haig, T. et al. 2013. Visualisation of learning management system usage for detecting student behaviour patterns. Proceedings of the Australasian Computing Education Conference, Sydney, Australia, 107–115.

[9] Hmelo-Silver, C.E. 2003. Analyzing collaborative knowledge construction: multiple methods for integrated understanding. Computers & Education. 41, 4, 397–420.

[10] Hu, M. and Liu, B. 2004. Mining and summarizing customer reviews. Proceedings of the ACM SIGKDD International Conference on Knowledge Discovery and Data Mining, Seattle, Washington, 168–177.

[11] Hughes, R.L. and Jones, S.K. 2011. Developing and assessing college student teamwork skills. New Directions for Institutional Research. 2011, 149, 53–64.

[12] Johnson, L. et al. 2013. The NMC Horizon Report: 2013 Higher Education Edition.

[13] De Liddo, A. et al. 2011. Discourse-centric Learning Analytics. LAK11, Banf, Alberta, 2011, 23–33.

[14] Liu, B. 2012. Sentiment analysis and opinion mining. Synthesis Lectures on Human Language Technologies. 5, 1, 1–167.

[15] Manning, C.D. et al. 2008. Text classification & Naive Bayes. Introduction to Information Retrieval. Cambridge University Press. 253–287.

[16] Munezero, M. et al. 2013. Exploiting sentiment analysis to track emotions in students' learning diaries. Proceedings of Koli Calling, Finland, 145–152.

[17] Robles, M. 2012. Executive perceptions of the top 10 soft skills needed in today's workplace. Business Communication Quarterly.

[18] Ruff, S. and Carter, M. 2009. Communication learning outcomes from software engineering professionals: a basis for teaching communication in the engineering curriculum. Frontiers in Education Conference, San Antonio, TX, 1–6.

[19] Santos Odriozola, J.L. et al. 2011. Visualizing PLE usage, EFEPLE11, La Clusaz, France, 34-38.

[20] Schmitz, H.C. et al. 2009. CAMera for PLE. Lecture Notes in Computer Science, vol. 5794, 2009, 507–520.

[21] Shum, S.B. and Ferguson, R. 2012. Social learning analytics. Educational Technology & Society. 15, 3, 3–26.

[22] Vatrapu, R. et al. 2011. Towards visual analytics for teachers' dynamic diagnostic pedagogical decision-making. LAK11, Banf, Alberta, 93–98.

[23] Vivian, R. and Falkner, K. 2013. Analysing computer science students' teamwork role adoption in an online self-organised teamwork activity. Koli Calling, Finland, 105–114.

[24] Wiggberg, M. 2010. Computer science project courses: contrasting students' experiences with teachers' expectations. Available, http://uu.diva-portal.org/smash/get/diva2:302515/FULLTEXT01.pdf

[25] Wilks, Y. and Stevenson, M. 1997. The grammar of sense: Using part-of-speech tags as a first step in semantic disambiguation, Natural Language Engineering, 1, 1, 1-13.

[26] Willcoxson, L.E. 2006. "It's not fair!": Assessing the Dynamics and Resourcing of Teamwork. Journal of Management Education. 30, 6, 798–808.

Question-Posing Strategies Used by Students for Exploring Data Structures

Shitanshu Mishra
Inter-Disciplinary Program in Educational Technology
Indian Institute of Technology Bombay
Mumbai, India
shitanshu@iitb.ac.in

Sridhar Iyer
Department of Computer Science and Engineering
Indian Institute of Technology Bombay
Mumbai, India
sri@iitb.ac.in

ABSTRACT
Question posing by students is a valuable mechanism for learning. In this paper we demonstrate how student generated questions can result in unfolding of knowledge. We conducted field studies in Data Structures courses, where we provided a semi-structured question-posing situation to students. We analyzed the questions generated by students using inductive qualitative data analysis. We found that students pose exploratory questions and unfold knowledge using seven strategies, viz., *Apply, Organize, Probe, Compare, Connect, Vary, and Implement*. These strategies were validated within the data structures domain and were also found to be valid in another CS application domain (Artificial Intelligence). The content analysis of the questions has shown that students tend to unfold more conceptual knowledge than procedural knowledge.

Categories and Subject Descriptors
K.3.2 Computer Science Education.

Keywords
Question-posing; Data Structures; Knowledge unfolding; Inductive qualitative analysis; Question-posing strategies

1. INTRODUCTION
Learning science requires that students ask the right questions and get the right answers. It has been argued that asking questions is both harder and more important [24]. Asking question enables students to seek information to address their knowledge deficit and is a way to promote the independence in learning. We refer to Question Posing (QP) as the generation of a new question or a problem by a student based on the given situation [12]. The situation could be a given classroom room lecture, a piece of text, a video lecture, etc. We have employed a semi-structured [26] QP situation in which, the generated questions are neither very unfocused nor are they confined to only a single question, unlike the free and structured situations [26], respectively. The semi-structured situation comprised a short 10-15 minutes seed instruction followed by question posing, so that knowledge unfolding happens around the seed knowledge. **"Seed**

ITiCSE'15, July 4–8, 2015, Vilnius, Lithuania.
Copyright © 2015 ACM 978-1-4503-3440-2/15/07$15.00.
DOI: http://dx.doi.org/10.1145/2729094.2742635

knowledge"**, as used in this paper, refers to the knowledge delivered by the instructor explicitly during the lecture.

We conducted three question posing sessions and generated a corpus of 104 questions. We performed inductive qualitative analysis of this corpus to answer our first research question (RQ1): "How do students integrate prior knowledge and seed knowledge to arrive at a question during question posing?" Here **"prior knowledge"** refers to the all past knowledge and experiences of the student *except* those which were explicitly contained in the seed knowledge. Further we performed content analysis of the generated questions to answer our second research question (RQ2): "What type of knowledge do the generated questions unfold?". Here the term **"unfolded knowledge"** is the knowledge which constitutes the answer to a student generated question. Unfolded knowledge is new to the student and not part of either prior knowledge or seed knowledge.

Finally, we validated the evolved strategies within data structures (DS) course and artificial intelligence course. We found that students pose questions using eight strategies: *Apply, Organize, Probe, Compare, Connect, Vary, Procedurize* and *clarify*. The first seven strategies (not *clarify*) are exploratory and found to result in the unfolding of knowledge. These strategies are generalizable to CS application courses, as the strategies identified in the Data Structures (DS) course questions are also applicable to the Artificial Intelligence (AI) questions. It was found that students were able to unfold new topics/ concepts through QP activities.

2. BACKGROUND AND RELATED WORK
In this section we describe the theoretical motivation behind our research in question posing. We also discuss how existing question categorization schemes fail to come up with successful strategies of unfolding new knowledge based on the prior and current knowledge.

2.1 Question Posing
The notion of QP that we are interested in is question posing involving the generation of new questions (questions/ issues) around a given situation. We want student to pose questions, such that students use the QP activity as a way to unfold new knowledge, around conceptually preceding and/or related seed knowledge, in any given domain. We want that the QP situation should not restrict the posed questions around a specific problem solving task, as in [6]. At the same time we also want the posed questions to be within the scope of a course, or a domain. This QP situation is described as a "semi-structured" [26] QP situation, as opposed to the "free" and "structured" QP situations [26]. It

enables divergent thinking, and it is driven by students intrinsic motivation and therefore positively affects question posing [17].

2.2 How do students pose questions

Graesser et al. (1992) identified four different psychological mechanisms that underlie the asking of questions. The mechanisms [11] are: (i) *Correction of knowledge deficits* (ii) *Establishing Common grounds* (iii) *Social coordination of actions* (iv) *Conversational Control*. Out of these four psychological mechanisms, only the first one i.e., "correction of knowledge deficits", is directly useful for learning, and prevalent in academic settings, where students pose questions in order to scaffold learning by identifying gaps in understanding. It describes the natural QP strategy that is followed by a learner. Based on this motivation, many researchers have devised a number of question posing strategies. Some of the frequently used QP strategies in literature are as follows: (i) "Modifying givens" - It is a QP strategy where questions are generated by modifying the conditions in a given problem statement [7]. (ii) *"What if not"* – As described in [16], in this strategy new questions are posed by negating any data, objects, operations or any other component of another question. (iii) "What if Strategy" - In this strategy [25] components of a given question are changed to generate new questions. (iv) *"Imitation strategy"* - It was presented by Kojima et al. [15], where the learner generates questions by reproducing the QP strategy demonstrated by examples of questions and their generation processes [15]. Cruz Remirez (2006) proposed a strategy consisting of six non sequentially dependent steps – searching, selection, transformation, classification, association and posing. [5]

2.3 Question Analysis Schemes

There have been a variety of question analysis schemes proposed by researchers. Graesser et al. (1992) proposed a scheme [11] in which 18 question categories are defined based on the content of the information requested. They also presented a dimension called degree of specification (low, medium high) which describes how specific or vague the information requested by the question is. [11].

Nielsen, et al. presented another scheme of question categorization based on the content of the information requested, and proposed 5 broad question categories, viz., Description Questions, Method Questions, Explanation Questions, Comparison Questions, and Preference Questions [22]. Olney, et al. proposed three categories of specificity of questions (high, medium low), based on whether information sought by a question is vaguely or explicitly marked [23]. Many of the researchers use revised Blooms Taxonomy [1] to categorize questions based on cognitive levels and/ or knowledge type of the information requested.

Most of the question analysis schemes cater to questions posed in general situations, and do not talk specifically about questions generated in semi-structured [26] QP situations. Moreover, none of the schemes were based of reflecting on how a question utilizes prior knowledge and the knowledge presented in the current QP situation, to arrive at a question. To fill this gap, in this paper we have developed a question classification scheme using grounded theory based inductive qualitative analysis of a question corpus generated in a semi-structured situation.

3. IMPLEMENTATION AND RESEARCH METHODOLOGY

In this section we describe the QP sessions, in which we collected questions generated by students, and the research method followed in our study.

3.1 The Question Posing Sessions and Data Collection

Each QP session described below was implemented in two phases 1) Instruction Phase, and 2) Question posing phase. The instruction phase was used as a semi-structure QP situation [26], which was characterized by an initial lecture (seed), and was light (less in content), and short (of short time), to ensure that student assimilates [20] most of the contents of it.

In the second phase, students were asked to pose questions based the content they studied in seed. Students were explicitly told that they can generate questions for two purposes – (a) when they want to clarify any muddy point (doubts) related to the seed or any previous lecture, and (b) when they want to discover more knowledge related to, or based upon, the contents of the seed instruction.

3.1.1 Data Structure Sessions

We administered a QP session in a 4th semester engineering classroom of 60 students. The instruction phase was executed for 15 minutes. Topics covered in the seed lecture were "Node Structure" and "Linking two nodes". The learning objective of the seed instruction was: "By the end of the seed instruction, student should be able to define, declare, construct, and access their own nodes and linkages between nodes using Java."

The QP phase continued for 10 – 15 minutes. Students were told to write their questions on paper slips and submit to the TAs. We collected all the generated questions (corpus 2) and after discarding the redundant and irrelevant questions, we were left with a corpus of 56 distinct questions.

Another set of questions were collected (corpus 3) from three other similar QP sessions which were administered in Data Structures course with 12 third semester engineering undergrads respectively.

3.1.2 AI Sessions

Similar to the data structure session, we administered two QP sessions in a 7th semester engineering classroom of 35 students in the Artificial Intelligence course. The first phase or the seed instruction phases were of 15 minutes each. The topic covered in the seed lecture of the first AI session was *"Comparison of Attributes of Intelligence in Utility based, Goal Based, and Simple Reflex agents"*. The learning objective for the first session of the seed instruction was: *"By the end of the seed instruction student should be able to identify differences between simple-reflex, goal-based, and utility-based agents, with respect to the level and attributes of intelligence."*

Topic covered in the seed lecture of the second AI session was *"The architecture of learning agents."* Learning objective for this session of the seed instruction was: "By the end of the seed instruction student should be able to identify the attributes of intelligence present in the learning agents".

The QP phases in the both sessions continued for 10 minutes. Here also students wrote their questions on paper slips and submitted to the TAs. Students were explicitly told about the types – clarification and exploratory – of questions, similar to the Data Structures sessions. We collected 25 distinct questions in the first session and 23 distinct questions in the second session (corpus 1).

3.2 Research Design

We wanted to conduct an in-depth study of student question statements and our research question was broad. The grounded theory [21, 27] based approach is appropriate for this kind of study since "the grounded theory approach is a qualitative research tool that enables the researchers to seek out and conceptualize the latent social patterns and structures of the area of interest" [19]. We adapted grounded theory and performed inductive qualitative research. Grounded theory traditionally requires that data collection and analysis be intertwinned. However this was not possible in our case as the entire question set was collected at once and hence interleaving of data collection and analysis was not possible.

After the question set collection, we followed the first two coding procedures prescribed in the grounded theory to further investigate patterns in the questions. We did the data analysis for both AI and the DS questions separately. The first two coding procedures, i.e., open coding and axial coding, were carried out **separately** for each of the question sets (corpus 1 and 2). This helped in testing if the results of the axial coding are valid across the Computer Applications domains (DS and AI). Coding procedures, along with their results are presented in the next section. In addition to this we validated the results of our axial codding using corpus 3 to see if the results are applicable for another instance of QP activity in DS.

4. DATA ANALYSIS AND RESULTS

In this section we explain the two coding procedures [4] – open coding and axial coding, and present the incidents, the strategies and the core strategies emerged for the analysis. We also present results of the content analysis done and present an account of knowledge unfolding.

4.1 Open coding to generate incidents

The goal of the open coding was to explore the question data and identify incidents, i.e., units of analysis to code for meanings, feelings, actions, events and so on [21]. We started reviewing the question set (Corpus 1 and 2) with the research question "How do students arrive at questions in our semi-structured QP situation?" We did not predefine any rubric or predetermine any concepts to aid the qualitative conceptualization of the data. This was done to ensure that we do not get biased to any of the possible answer to the broad research question. We adopted the method of constant comparison [4], i.e., the emerging incidents were compared, merged, modified, and renamed. When we identified any new incident, we reviewed the dataset back and forth to compare the new incident with the older ones. If the new incident came to be similar, then it was merged and modified, and renamed with the older ones. There were two researchers working together, therefore the inter-rater reliability was not calculated.

Both researchers analyzed each question within the question corpus while working together. They start with reading the question, reading the focused research question, discussing the possible observable strategy of question posing, and coded the potential incident(s). For example: the question (from 2nd QP session in AI) - "Can we use neural network and fuzzy logic to create an agent?" yielded following two possible incidents to start with: "Applied prior known concepts."; "Making a richer understanding of the seed concept." After some iterations of constant comparison these two incidents were modified to "Use of concept(s) from prior knowledge to develop a richer understanding about the seed knowledge."

At the end there were a total 15 different incidents identified for the Data Structure question set, and 13 different incidents in the Artificial Intelligence question set. These are given in figure 1.

Common incidents identified in the DS and AI question sets
• Identifying an application of a knowledge component(s) in the seed from real life. (P1)
• Use of concept(s) from prior knowledge to develop a richer understanding about the seed knowledge. (P3)
• Variation on some attribute of the seed knowledge. (P6)
• Using prior procedural knowledge, create an operation that can be done on the seed concepts. (P7)
• Using prior knowledge about an operation transform the state of the seed concept(s). (P7)
• Clarifying a concept in the seed knowledge. (P8)
• Requesting reiteration of a concept from previous lectures. (P8)

Additional incidents identified in the DS question set	Additional incidents identified in the AI question set
• Identifying an application of a knowledge component(s) in the seed from the same domain. (P1)	• Examining how to apply SK in a known context. (P1)
• Identifying an application of a knowledge component(s) in the seed from other domain. (P1)	• Use of alternate conceptions from prior knowledge to develop a richer understanding about the seed knowledge. (P3)
• Reorganize components of SK to create a new structure of the SK. (P2)	• Comparing SK with prior knowledge from real life. (P4)
• Comparing the SK procedural knowledge with prior procedural knowledge. (P4)	• Making an analogy between prior knowledge and seed knowledge. (P5)
• Comparing SK with prior knowledge from other domain. (P4)	• Associating SK with prior knowledge from other domain. (P5)
• Associating prior knowledge from same domain with SK. (P5)	• Associating experiences from real world with the seed. (P5)
• Creating a procedure using prior knowledge to perform a target operation on the seed. (P7)	
• Resolving a conflict about the seed knowledge. (P8)	

Figure 1. List of different incidents identified in the DS and AI question set after open coding. Strategies are given in *( )*.

4.2 Axial coding to generate QP Strategies

Axial coding, as stated by Strauss & Corbin [27] is done to reorganize the incidents obtained from the open coding on the basis of connections between the incidents. During the axial coding, the incidents obtained from the open coding were grouped into subcategories and core categories. Final categories and sub categories were identified using a group review process [8], which was operationalized using a series of meetings between researchers. The researchers continued working together in this manner to group related incidents together until consensus was reached. In some cases, incidents seem to be relevant in more than one category. For example, "Comparing the seed procedural knowledge with some procedural prior knowledge." fit in both "Operate", and "Associate" categories. In these situations, we either re-reviewed the questions, or if needed we re-specified the definitions of different categories. We call these categories as Question Posing Strategies, as these categories reflect different ways in which students arrived at a question in the semi-structured QP situation. We arrived at 4 core-strategies, and 8 strategies at the end of the iterations.

4.2.1 Question Posing Strategies

The axial coding of the incidents obtained from the open coding revealed 8 different QP strategies. It was evident that students make use of seed (and/or prior) knowledge in various ways to arrive at questions. In the subsequent section we describe all these 8 categories with examples. The examples used in the next subsections come predominantly from the question set collected from Data Structures QP-session.

Strategy 1 (P1): Apply

In this strategy, student employ the concept(s) from the seed knowledge to create a 'known application' from prior knowledge. These prior known applications are either from 1) the same domain, or 2) a different domain. The different domain could either be 2a) a different academic domain, or 2b) some real life experience. We note that the explicit identification of prior known application is mandatory in this strategy. Examples:

"Can trees be made using nodes?"
Here application ("tree") comes from same domain i.e. Data Structures.

"We can create groups?"
Here application ("groups") comes from different domain, i.e., Discrete mathematics.

"social network graph, is it possible?"
Here application ("social network graph") comes from real life experiences.

Strategy 2 (P2): Organize

In this strategy, student pose question to unfold an arrangement of the seed knowledge by organizing multiple instances of the seed concept to obtain a structural arrangement (which comes from prior experience). Example:

"Cyclic list of nodes possible?"
Here multiple instances of the concept (from seed) node, i.e., large number of nodes are proposed to be organized in a cyclic manner to unfold a variant of the seed (i.e. circular linked list).

Strategy 3 (P3): Probe

In this strategy, students pose question to associate prior knowledge to the seed knowledge with an objective to add more understanding to the latter. Here prior knowledge is NOT the prior known application, as in P1. The review of questions shows that these associations use prior knowledge as a basis to make a richer enquiry into the seed knowledge.

Example: *"address (next) is relative or direct?"*
Here concepts from prior knowledge ("relative/direct addressing") has been used to make a richer understanding of the construct "next", which is a part of seed.

Strategy 4 (P4): Compare

In this strategy, question is posed to unfold associations between prior knowledge and seed knowledge with an objective to compare or contrast some concepts in the seed knowledge with some concepts from prior knowledge.

Example: *"chain of nodes vs. array?"*
In this question the prior knowledge (*array*) is contrasted with seed concept (*chain of nodes*).

Strategy 5 (P5): Connect

In this strategy, student associates the seed knowledge to some prior knowledge from same domain, from other domains, or from real life. This strategy can lead to learning of additional knowledge (distinct from prioir or seed knowledge) rather than enriching the understanding of the seed. Making analogy between some prior knowledge with seed knowledge can come into this strategy. Contrasting or comparing the seed with some prior knowledge does NOT come under this strategy.

Example: *"Can we use neural network and fuzzy logic to create an agent?"*
In this question the prior concept of neural netwobe rk and fuzzy logic is connected with the context (*agent*) of seed knowledge.

Strategy 6 (P6): Vary

In this strategy the objective of the question is to modify/vary a component(s), attribute(s), or part(s) of the seed to unfold the variants of the seed concepts. These questions may or may not give rise to some application of the seed, but applications are not explicitly identified as in P1. Example:

"Can we have 'previous' node in addition to 'next'?"
In this question, instead of having just one pointer/reference to another node, the idea of having two reference/ pointer variables in the node structure, is proposed. In this way a variant of singly-linking (i.e. a doubly linking) is unfolded.

Strategy 7 (P7): Implement

In this QP strategy the objective of questioning is to inquire about operations/procedures that can be performed on the seed knowledge to achieve a goal state related to the seed. It should be noted that prior knowledge, in the form of an operation/procedure, is explicitly evident from the question statement. Example:

"How to perform inheritance from a node possible to give "multi-nodes"?"
Here the operation inheritance has been explicitly identified, and question is about how to implement that operation on the seed concept (nodes).

Strategy 8 (P8): Clarify

The analyses revealed that students ask question to clarify their doubts. All the questions which need reiteration of the content that has been explicitly been taught in the seed lecture are categorized under this strategy. It should be noted that *Clarify* questions do not unfold any new knowledge. Example:

"What is the use of 'this' method?"
The use of "this" operator was explicitly taught in the seed.

Some observations from an examination of the incidents and categories are:

i. Students have used a range of question posing strategies;
ii. During question posing students use different types of prior knowledge;
iii. Students use prior knowledge from same and/or different domains;
iv. Student may employ more than one strategy for generating a single question.

Typically axial coding is followed by selective coding, which is performed to identify a "story line" that emerges out of linkages between categories from axial coding. In our case, our research objectives are fulfilled with axial coding.

4.2.2 Further grouping of the QP strategies

Figure 2 shows the core-strategies and their underlying subcategories. We can see that the two broad purposes of QP are to explore/ unfold unknown knowledge and to clarify the muddy points from the given lesson. The Exploratory QP can further be grouped into three core categories: 1) *Employ*, where the concepts from seed knowledge are used to create some goal 'application' or 'arrangement'. 2) *Associate*, where concepts from seed and prior knowledge interact with each other to give insight about the seed knowledge or about some new knowledge. 3) Operate, where the question posing aims at exploring the operation(s) required for achieving a goal state or modification related to the seed concepts.

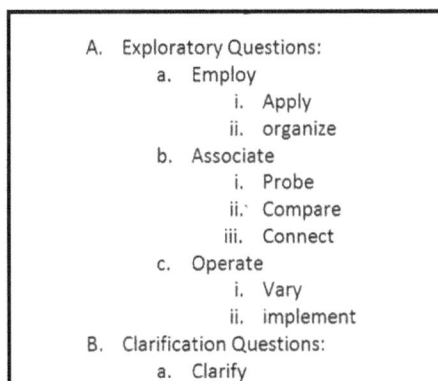

```
A. Exploratory Questions:
    a. Employ
        i. Apply
        ii. organize
    b. Associate
        i. Probe
        ii. Compare
        iii. Connect
    c. Operate
        i. Vary
        ii. implement
B. Clarification Questions:
    a. Clarify
```

Figure 2. Question Types and categorization of QP strategies

4.3 Validation

We did a qualitative analysis of the corpus 3 (data structures) and tested if any question can be categorized as per the descriptions of one or more of the eight QP strategies. We found that each of the 25 questions satisfied at least one category of the identified QP strategies.

4.4 Content analysis to study unfolded knowledge

We have used the taxonomy of knowledge types proposed in the revised Bloom's 2-D taxonomy [1] and analyzed the corpus 1 and 2 for types of prior knowledge and unfolded knowledge associated with the generated questions. Table 1 shows the normalized frequency of knowledge types of the unfolded knowledge by in 104 questions (corpus 1 & 2). The frequencies do not sum to 1 because there are few problems which may have used more than one unit of prior knowledge.

Table 1. Frequency of types of knowledge requested (unfolded) by the 104 questions (corpus 1 & 2)

Knowledge Type	Normalized Frequencies (N= 104)	
	Prior knowledge	Unfolded Knowledge
Factual	0.04	0.19
Conceptual	0.58	0.43
Procedural	0.17	0.19
Meta -Cognitive	0.09	0.00

5. DISCUSSION & CONCLUSION

We have employed grounded theory based qualitative data analysis on the question set generated in a semi-structured QP situation. We identified 16 incidents, 8 sub-categories (strategies) and 4 core-strategies, from the two coding procedures – open and axial coding. Descriptions of the different strategies in the section 4.2 bring out how the prior knowledge and the seed knowledge are used to pose any question. (RQ1). Out of eight strategies, we found seven strategies, under "employ", "associate", and "operate" core-strategies, result in knowledge unfolding. (RQ2), whereas the "clarification" strategy was used to request the reiteration of information which was delivered explicitly during the seed lecture. Thus we discovered a total of seven strategies which generate exploratory-questions and one strategy that generates clarification questions. From the dimension of knowledge type, we found that the question posing activities resulted in the unfolding of the three types of knowledge - Factual, Conceptual, and Procedural, out of which the conceptual knowledge was predominant (RQ2).

We performed open coding and axial coding separately for AI and DS datasets (corpus 1 and 2 respectively). However we observed that while there were few different (but similar) incidents present in both the AI and DS datasets, results of the axial coding were same from both of the datasets. Therefore, it is important to note that the QP strategies that have emerged from the data are generalizable for CS Application domains. The analysis of the corpus 3 validates the results within DS domain. Yet we need more data to claim saturation of the strategies. Most of the existing QP strategies in literature deal with QP in a structured QP situation. Moreover no strategies exist which explicitly are based on how students use prior and seed knowledge to arrive at any questions in a semi-structured PP. This research can be an initiative to develop a new taxonomy of question posing strategies in Computer Science Applications domain.

While QP has the obvious benefit of addressing muddy points (doubts), it supports knowledge unfolding through generation of exploratory questions. Moreover, the seven QP strategies show the seven different ways by which students were found to integrate their prior knowledge and the seed knowledge. This shows that question posing by students initiates the knowledge integration process. We are now studying how student QP activities based on these question prompts influence their knowledge integration performance [18].

It is desirable to have teaching–learning activities that can elicit exploratory questions from students. In order to operationalize the emerged QP strategies as teaching–learning activities we have translated them into question prompts, as shown in (fig 3). These prompts can be used to scaffold QP activities (as in [14]).

Strategy	QP Prompts
Organize	Can we apply the concept_X to create structure_Y?
Compare	How is concept_X is compared to concept_Y?
Implement	How can we do procedure_Y on X to achieve something?

Note. Red colored text (with X) can be replaced by knowledge piece from the seed lecture. Blue colored text (with Y) can be replaced by a concept or idea from prior knowledge or experience.

Figure 3. Snippet of three QP prompts used in an ongoing study

6. REFERENCES

[1] Anderson, L. W., Krathwohl, D. R., and Bloom, B. S. 2001. A taxonomy for learning, teaching, and assessing: A revision of Bloom's taxonomy of educational objectives. Allyn and Bacon.

[2] Bairac, R. 2005. Some methods for composing mathematical problems. International Journal for Mathematics Teaching and Learning.

[3] Beal, C. R., and Cohen, P. R. 2012. Teach Ourselves: Technology to Support Problem Posing in the STEM Classroom. Creative Education, 3, 4(2012), 513.

[4] Cohen, L., Manion, L., and Morrison, K. 2013. Research methods in education. Routledge, London.

[5] Cruz Ramirez, M. 2006. A mathematical formulating strategy. International Journal for Mathematics Teaching and Learning, ISSM1473-0111, December.

[6] Dillon, J. T. 1982. Problem Finding and Solving*. The journal of creative behavior, 16, 2(1982), 97-111.

[7] El Sayed, R. A. E. 2002. Effectiveness of problem posing strategies on prospective mathematics teachers' problem solving performance. Journal of science and mathematics education in Southeast Asia, 25, 1(2002), 56-69.

[8] Fitzgerald, S., Simon, B., and Thomas, L. 2005. Strategies that students use to trace code: an analysis based in grounded theory. In Proceedings of the first international workshop on Computing education research, ACM, 69-80.

[9] Ghasempour, Z., Bakar, M. N., and Jahanshahloo, G. R. 2013. Innovation in Teaching and Learning through Problem Posing Tasks and Metacognitive Strategies. Int. J. Ped. Inn, 1, 1(2013), 57-66.

[10] Good, T. L., Slavings, R. L., Harel, K. H., and Emerson, H. 1987. Student passivity: A study of question asking in K–12 classrooms. Sociology of Education.

[11] Graesser, A. C., and Person, N. K. 1994. Question asking during tutoring. American educational research journal, 31,1 (1994), 104-137.

[12] Graesser, A. et al. 2009. Guidelines for Question Generation Shared Task Evaluation Campaigns. Chapter 1. QGSTEC Workshop Report 2009.

[13] Kilpatrick, J. 1987. Problem formulating: Where do good problems come from? In A. H. Schoenfeld (Ed.), Cognitive science and mathematics education, Hillsdale: Lawrence Erlbaum Associates, 123- 147.

[14] King, A. 1994. Guiding knowledge construction in the classroom: Effects of teaching children how to question and how to explain. American educational research journal, 31, 2(2009), 338-368.

[15] Kojima, K., Miwa, K., and Matsui, T. 2009. Study on support of learning from examples in problem posing as a production task. In Proceedings of the 17th International Conference on Computers in Education. Hong Kong: Asia-Pacific Society for Computers in Education.

[16] Lavy, I., and Bershadsky, I. 2003. Problem posing via "what if not?" strategy in solid geometry—a case study. The Journal of Mathematical Behavior, 22,4(2003), 369-387.

[17] Lee, H., and Cho, Y. 2007. Factors affecting problem finding depending on degree of structure of problem situation. The Journal of Educational Research, 101, 2(2007), 113-123.

[18] Liu, O. L., Lee, H. S., Hofstetter, C., and Linn, M. C. 2008. Assessing knowledge integration in science: Construct, measures, and evidence. Educational Assessment, 13,1(2008), 33-55.

[19] Martin, P. Y., and Turner, B. A. 1986. Grounded theory and organizational research. The Journal of Applied Behavioral Science, 22, 2(1986), 141-157.

[20] Mayer, R. E., and Moreno, R. 2003. Nine ways to reduce cognitive load in multimedia learning. Educational psychologist, 38,1(2003), 43-52.

[21] Niederman, F. 2009. Using grounded theory to generate indigenous MIS theory. In Proceedings of the 15th Americas Conference on Information Systems, San Francisco, CA, August 6-9, 2009.

[22] Nielsen, R.D., Buckingham, J., Knoll, G., Marsh, B., and Palen, L. 2008. A taxonomy of questions for question generation. In Proceedings of the workshop on the Question Generation Shared Task and Evaluation Challenge, Arlington, Virginia, September 25-26, 2008.

[23] Olney, A. M., Graesser, A. C., & Person, N. K. 2012. Question Generation from Concept Maps, 3,2 (2012), 75–99. doi:0.5087/dad.2012.204.

[24] Orr, H.A., 1999. An evolutionary dead end? Science, 285, 343 - 344.

[25] Pintér, K. 2012. On Teaching Mathematical Problem- Solving and Problem Posing. Doctoral Thesis, Doctoral School in Mathematics and Computer Science, University of Szeged.

[26] Stoyanova, E., and Ellerton, N. F. 1996. A framework for research into students' problem posing in school mathematics. Technology in mathematics education. Mel bourne: Mathematics Education Research Group of Australia.

[27] Strauss, A., and Corbin, J. 1990. Basics of Qualitative Research: Grounded Theory, Procedures, and Techniques. Newbury Park, CA: Sage Publications, Inc.

Enhancements to Support Functions of Distributed Pair Programming Based on Action Analysis

Tomoyuki Urai
x0t1511@students.chiba-u.jp

Takeshi Umezawa
ume@chiba-u.jp

Noritaka Osawa
n.osawa@faculty.chiba-u.jp

Graduate School of Advanced Integration Science, Chiba University, Japan

ABSTRACT

Pair programming is a practice of software development where two programmers work together to create programs. It is important for students to understand and learn effective pair programming in software engineering. A pair of programmers at distributed sites can program in pairs by using a support system including text chats or synchronized editors. It is important to enable effective communication in distributed pair programming as well as in collocated human dialogue.

We conducted experiments to collect information about students' activities, communications, and answers to questionnaires. These collected data were analyzed to clarify functions that enhanced distributed pair programming. The analysis revealed that it is important for support systems to facilitate easy communication in pairs and for them to have functions that enable appropriate partner changes and role switching.

Categories and Subject Descriptors

D.2.2 [Software Engineering]: Design Tools and Techniques; K.3.1 [Computers and Education]: Computer Uses in Education

General Terms

Performance, Human Factors, Verification

Kcywords

Pair Programming, Communication Method, Collaborative work, Action analysis.

1. INTRODUCTION

Extreme programming (XP), which was proposed by Beck, is a software development methodology [2]. Pair programming is a practice in XP where two programmers work together to write codes. There are two roles in pair programming. The first is that of a driver who writes codes. The second is that of a navigator who reviews codes written by the driver, checks for errors, and verifies designs. The driver and navigator generally switch roles in a pair and also change partners in pairs. They are able to write better codes more quickly in paired programming than in non-paired programming as will be explained in what follows. The study by Williams *et al.* demonstrated improved accuracy in codes of 15%, and the time to produce codes was reduced to 20–40% through pair programming [15]. Further, their study also revealed a 15–60% increase in programming efficiency that was measured in terms of total programmer hours. This indicated that pair programming is one of the most important practices that students need to understand and learn to achieve effective software development.

We carried out experiments on collocated pair and distributed pair programming. We collected subjects' operation logs and videos/audios to record their activities and the communications between them. Moreover, we administered a questionnaire on pair programming. We then analyzed the logs and videos/audios to find features that could enhance distributed pair programming. The results revealed important functions and features for efficient distributed pair programming. Our study suggested functions that automatically detect and remind pairs of role switching may be able to facilitate more efficient pair programming.

2. RELATED WORK

2.1 Distributed Pair Programming

Distributed pair programming can facilitate effective and cooperative programming because students can perform pair programming even if they are at different locations. A pair of students at distributed sites can carry out pair programming using a support system. The system usually includes functions of text chats and synchronized editors. It allows a pair to share data, codes, and ideas between distributed sites.

There have been studies that have compared productivity of collocated pair programming with that of distributed pair programming. If distributed pair programming is less productive than collocated pair programming, the value of carrying out distributed pair programming is reduced. Baheti *et al.* collected data when programmers performed pair programming in four work environments to investigate the efficiency of distributed pair programming in software development [1]. Their results indicated that productivity and quality in distributed pair programming were equivalent to those in collocated pair programming.

It is important to enable communication that is as close as possible to collocated human dialogue [4] to make distributed pair programming effective. Previous studies have proposed functions to support communications, but characteristic usage of the systems and inherent functions in pair programming have not been fully analyzed. In other words, functions to enhance distributed pair programming have not been completely clarified. Moreover, it would be possible for computer-mediated

ITiCSE'15, July 6–8, 2015, Vilnius, Lithuania.
Copyright © 2015 ACM 978-1-4503-3440-2/15/07...$15.00.
DOI: http://dx.doi.org/10.1145/2729094.2742616

communications with intelligent functions in distributed programming to enhance pair programming more than that in face-to-face communication in collocated pair programming by using only one computer at one site.

2.2 Support System

Productivity gains from distributed pair programming can be increased by using appropriately distributed pair programming support functions. Dou *et al.* discussed a conversation model for pair programming based on language and action theory [5]. Their study clarified four essential functions in distributed pair programming from a survey of existing support systems of distributed pair programming.

- A synchronized editor to share codes in real time.

- A repository to share files and to control versions of the files.

- Partner change support to help form an appropriate pair.

- Communication support for conversation and negotiation regarding designs and algorithms.

Furthermore, Canfora *et al.* conducted experiments where pairs of subjects performed collocated pair programming and distributed pair programming [4]. Their results revealed functions that were required in distributed pair programming. They are supporting functions which enable communication as close as possible to the collocated human dialogue, e.g., a voice call to communicate with one's partner and a blackboard to transmit algorithmic drafts and design diagrams.

There have been support systems for distributed pair programming. Functions in those systems are summarized in Table 1.

Table 1: Functions of systems

System's name	Synchronized editor	Repository	Partner change support	Support for simple conversation
COPPER [10]	■			■
RIPPLE [3]	■	■		■
COLLECE[6]	■	■		■
Sangam [7]	■			■
Saros [11]	■	■	■	■

Previous studies did not fully take differences into consideration between collocated and distributed communications and actions. Programmers in distributed pair programming may take different actions from those in collocated pair programming because they cannot see their partners' facial expressions or directly indicate their intents. Moreover, if their partners are at different locations, the ways that they can communicate are limited. Therefore, we investigated how individual actions influenced communication in a pair, and what actions were taken in distributed programming instead of actions that were taken in collocated programming. We will discuss functions, such as pointing and annotations, that enable us to more effectively carry out collocated and distributed pair programming using the results obtained from action analysis and questionnaires.

2.3 Differences in Abilities

Performance in pair programming is expected to be changed significantly due to pair decisions. Jensen [8] reported that pair programming was best performed when a pair's abilities were different. However, Stephens and Rosenberg reported that pair programming exhibited the best effect when the pair's abilities were almost the same [12]. Lui and Chan found that the gains in productivity were greater in novice pairs than those in expert pairs [9].

Toll *et al.* compared two cases where a pair's abilities were different in one case and nearly equal in another case on the basis of Jensen [8] and Stephens and Rosenberg [12] to evaluate the usefulness of pair programming in a classroom setting [13]. The study claimed that pair programming was more effective for students to learn programming languages than reading books individually if there were minimal differences between a pair's abilities. The study also claimed that subjects were able to concentrate and work on tasks while feeling "pair pressure" [14]. "Pair pressure" is a positive form of peer pressure [15]. It makes students concentrate, and improves their performance when working on tasks. According to these studies, a student who has no or slight differences from his/her peer's abilities can feel "pair pressure", but a student who has excessive differences from his/her peer's abilities cannot feel this. The study by Toll *et al.* [13] had five subjects who formed four pairs in collocated pair programming, but it did not have a sufficient number of subjects to analyze relationships between differences in abilities and "pair pressure". Therefore, we conducted experiments that had more subjects to collect additional experimental data.

3. OBJECTIVES

More data on relationships between differences in abilities and those in actions are needed to design a support system for distributed pair programming. The two main objectives of this research were to clarify functions that were important to enhance distributed pair programming. The first objective was to investigate characteristic actions that were related to communication in pair programming. The second objective was to investigate the influence of differences between the abilities of partners in pairs. Here, we propose functions to facilitate distributed pair programming on the basis of our results.

4. METHOD

We carried out experiments on collocated pair programming and distributed pair programming. Each subject worked as a member of a pair working on a single task using Java programming language. We collected subjects' operation logs, videos, and audios, by using a USB camera (320-by-240 resolution at 30 fps) and software to record voice and capture the screens (640-by-520 resolution at 6–10 fps) for action analysis. We also asked the subjects to answer questionnaires and collected the answers.

4.1 Pre-experimental survey

We asked the subjects to answer pre-experimental questionnaires about the extent of their programming experience before the experiment. This pre-experimental survey was conducted to collect information about subjects' programming experience, self-evaluation of their abilities, and frequency of programming. These results were used to find what influence a pair's differences in abilities had on programming. The questionnaire used a five-point Likert scale (5: strongly agree, 4: agree, 3: neutral, 2: disagree, 1: strongly disagree). Figure 1 provides subjects' answers regarding "How good are you at programming using Java language". The figure also shows the years of experience subjects had in Java programming and the frequency per week they used Java language.

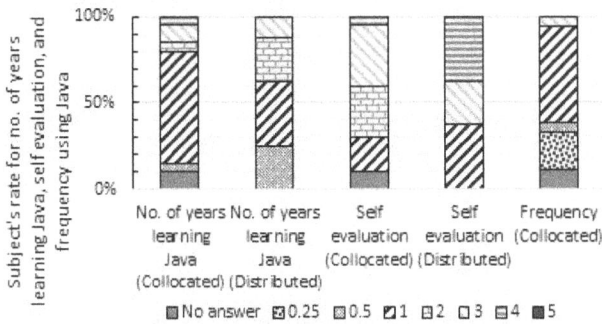

Figure 1: No. of years of experience with Java, self-evaluation of Java programming abilities, and frequency of use of Java per week.

4.2 Collocated Pair Programming

Twenty undergraduate students (12 males and 8 females aged 20–22 whose nationality was Japanese) took part in the collocated programming experiment. Ten pairs were formed. The pairs were given one assignment on fraction computation, which was divided into three problems. These problems were designed for students to create a function to display fractions, functions to perform four arithmetic operations, and a function to convert a fraction into a decimal. We designed the difficulty of the three problems in which many pairs could write code by sharing much information with the partner. The assignment had a time limit of 60 min for all three problems. The pairs could solve these problems in any order.

Roles in a pair were fixed during each problem and the roles were switched every time they finished a problem. Pairs were formed on the basis of subjects' preferences.

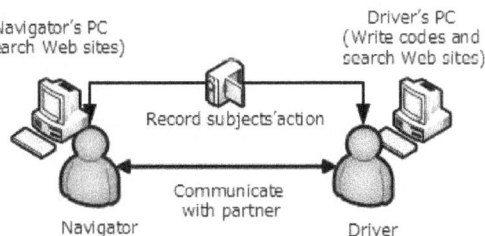

Figure 2: Environment for collocated pair programming

Figure 2 outlines a collocated pair programming environment. One pair used two PCs in the experiment. One PC was used by a driver to write codes and search references or information. The other PC was used by a navigator to search for references or information. Eclipse (version.3.6 Helios) was used as the programming environment.

After the subjects had finished the assignment, we collected the subjects' opinions on effective pair programming and subjective evaluations on the ease of communication.

4.3 Distributed Pair Programming

Six undergraduate students and two graduate students participated in the distributed pair programming experiment (eight males aged 22–23 whose nationality was Japanese). Four pairs were formed. Three problems were assigned to the pairs. The first problem was to code a program that outputs the maximum amount of input data. The second problem was to code a program for a game called "Hit and Blow". The last problem was to code a program for the game of "rock-paper-scissors". Each problem had a time limit of 30 min.

The roles in a pair were fixed during the first and second problems. By fixing roles in a pair, we could observe how a navigator helped a driver when the driver became confused. We analyzed these cases to find ways of supporting the navigator and of preventing the driver from becoming confused. The subjects might have switched roles in solving the third problem. After the subjects had finished the three problems, we collected the subjects' suggestions on effective pair programming, and subjective evaluations on the ease of communication.

Figure 3 is a schematic of a distributed pair programming environment. Saros (an Eclipse version.4.3 Kepler plug-in for distributed party programming) [11] and Skype (a voice call tool for communication with a partner) were used in the programming environment.

Figure 3: Environment for distributed pair programming

5. RESULTS

5.1 Method of Communication

We analyzed actions in collocated and distributed pair programming. Figure 4 lists characteristic actions we found and the number of occurrences of the actions and average number of these actions per person. Many subjects undertook characteristic actions while they discussed the problem with their partner. Three actions were observed in collocated pair programming: looking at their partner's window, communicating by pointing, and searching for references. Two actions were taken by subjects in distributed pair programming to explain their intents simply: characteristic actions such as using text chats, and comments in codes as annotations.

Subjects in collocated and distributed programming also searched references when they did not understand what to do next or how to design an algorithm. However, actions to share references were different for each situation. Nineteen subjects searched references in collocated programming and five subjects did so in distributed programming when they did not understand how to design algorithms. Each subject searched references an average of nearly five times in collocated programming and six in distributed programming. Subjects in collocated programming explained references to their partners by pointing or using gestures, and they confirmed references by looking at the navigator's screen. However, subjects in distributed programming explained references to their partners with text chats. Text chats were used to explain important parts or the URLs of references.

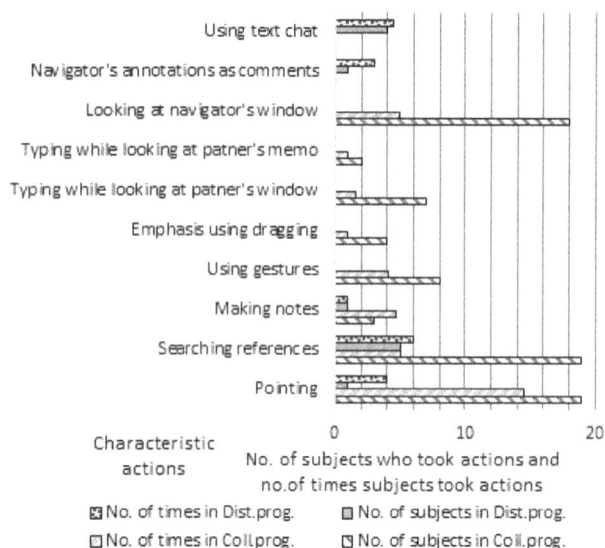

Figure 4: Characteristic actions

Moreover, subjects not only looked at navigator's windows to observe references but also to check what their partners were doing. Seven subjects typed codes while looking at navigator's windows to confirm references that their partner had searched. However, subjects in distributed programming used voice calls to check what their partner had done because they could not directly see their partner's facial expressions or windows. Some of the subjects occasionally continued to unilaterally explain matters to their partner because they could not confirm their partner's state.

Furthermore, handwritten notes and gestures were used in collocated programming when subjects discussed problems with their partners. Three subjects took handwritten notes of their ideas and algorithms. Eight subjects also used gestures. However, no pairs used both note taking and gestures. One subject in distributed programming left comments in source codes instead of handwritten notes.

Pointing was used by 19 subjects in collocated programming not only to explain references but also to directly indicate the intended position. One subject in distributed programming also used comments in source codes as annotations instead of pointing. Figure 5 has an example of annotations used as a navigator's comments.

```
Scanner sc=new Scanner(System.in);    //ここに警告
while(sc.hasNext()){
    int[]in=new int[5];|              This means "Caution"
    boolean[]rsp=new boolean[3];
    in[0]=sc.nextInt()-1;             //ここ大丈夫？
                              This means "Is this OK?"
```

Figure 5: Annotations as comments to indicate navigator's intent (rectangles enclose comments and balloons have their meanings)

5.2 Progress

Six pairs executed programs many times in collocated programming. After they had created a program that could run properly, they changed roles with their partner, and they got to solve the next problem. If their program did not run properly,

they investigated errors and discussed the errors with their partner. All pairs in distributed pair programming executed their programs many times. They acted as well as subjects in collocated programming, i.e., they executed programs, and then investigated and discussed errors, or changed roles and solved the next problem. On the other hand, all subjects in distributed programming needed to use much time to share their conditions and to confirm whether programs were running properly or not because the output's displays of programs were not shared with their partner. Therefore, the output of programs should be shared in distributed pair programming.

Moreover, three pairs in collocated programming did not execute programs. One pair could not solve any problems because they did not have sufficient programming skills in Java. Other pairs did not confirm whether programs could run properly or not. They gave priority to finish programming of all problems and did not test programs very frequently.. After all, all the algorithms for the programs created by the three pairs were incorrect, so they could not solve any problems properly. Therefore, if they did not execute programs within a specific period of time, the system could automatically present some remainders to switch roles or change partners.

5.3 Subjective Evaluation

Subjects answered post-experimental questionnaires using a five-point Likert scale (5: strongly agree, 4: agree, 3: neutral, 2: disagree, 1: strongly disagree). Figure 6 presents subjects' answers to "Could you communicate better with your partner when you were a driver or a navigator?" More than 70 percent of subjects in distributed pair programming answered the question positively in both of the two roles. However, A lower ratio of subjects answered the question positively in collocated pair programming than in distributed programming.

Moreover, two pairs who used gestures many times in collocated pair programming felt that they could explain their intent to partners well in either role, which was established from activity logs and answers to questionnaires. However, two subjects who did not use either pointing or gestures very much felt that they could not explain their intent to their partners well when their role was a navigator. We also did not find significant relationships between actions that they took and evaluation of Figure 6 in distributed pair programming from activity logs and answers to questionnaires.

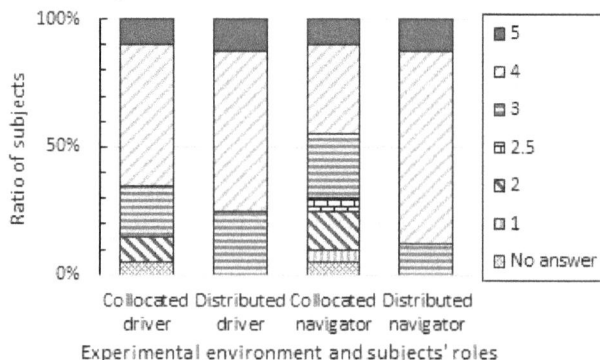

Figure 6: Ease of communication

5.4 Differences in Abilities

We analyzed the influence of differences in the abilities of partners in a pair, and compared our results with those of Toll *et al.* [13]. Eight pairs in collocated programming were similar to those in Toll *et al.* [13]. Six of the eight pairs had no or slight differences in abilities in a pair, and seven of the 12 subjects had opinions about efficiency similar to those in Toll *et al*. Other subjects felt dissatisfaction, difficulty, or worries about communication with their partners.

Moreover, we found two new cases (Cases X and Y) in which different behaviors in a pair were observed from the viewpoint of differences in the abilities in a pair. Figure 7 shows the pre-experiment survey results as abilities of members in both cases.

Subject A in Case X had inferior abilities to Subject B. Subject A as a navigator could not keep up with his driver and when he could not do anything to fix the situation, he gradually lost motivation and did totally irrelevant things with pair programming, such adjusting the microphone that was recording their voices. Subject A said "I never want to perform pair programming again" in responses to the questionnaire, and he also said "I felt that I could not help my partner" during operations. However, Subject B did not feel frustrated in either role. This was different from that in Toll *et al.*'s study [13] in terms of the emotions that subjects who had higher levels of ability felt.

One pair in Subsection 5.2 who did not execute any programs could barely solve any problems in Case Y because they could barely understand basic parts of Java although there were few difference in their abilities. Subject C could not support or talk to Subject D and Subject D felt frustrated because he could not solve problems. This indicated that pair programming was not effective when the abilities of both partners in a pair were substandard.

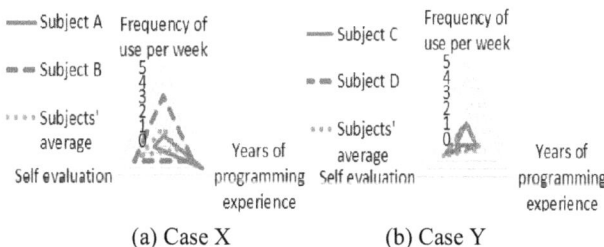

(a) Case X   (b) Case Y

Figure 7: Subject' answers to questionnaire on pairs' abilities.

6. DISCUSSION

We will discuss support functions that should enable programmers to perform distributed pair programming more effectively.

6.1 Method of communication

Some characteristic actions were taken to explain subjects' intents simply. Actions were influenced by the locations of partners in a pair. The major difference in actions between collocated and distributed programming was dependent on whether subjects could directly indicate their intents or not.

Subjects in collocated environments communicated with their partners face-to-face, and indicated their intended position directly by pointing. However, subjects could not convey their ideas directly in a distributed environment. One subject in such an environment used comments in a program as annotations instead of pointing, but other subjects did not do this. Subjects in the distributed setting also used their time to share their

contexts and outputs from the development tool. Moreover, video data revealed that subjects restated explanations many times because they could not easily use demonstrativeness and their partners could not understand their intents. Furthermore, one subject tried to use the "Saros Whiteboard" [11]. However, he gave up on using it because he experienced difficulties in drawing various diagrams. He took too long to explain his ideas through only vocal communication without the use of diagrams.

More than 80 percent of subjects used various actions such as using gestures and pointing in addition to vocal communication in collocated pair programming. This suggests that systems for distributed pair programming need to have functions instead of these actions. Example functions include video calls to display memos, diagrams on pieces of paper, and a remote annotation tool to share comments and diagrams. Figure 8 shows an example of a remote annotation tool to draw diagrams and typed textual annotations. We also think that support systems for distributed environments should have a function where a pair can simply and easily share contexts and outputs.

According to Canfora *et al.* [4], video calls are sometimes regarded as noise in distributed pair programming. Therefore, it is necessary to evaluate and compare video calls and remote annotation tools. We plan to comparatively evaluate these two functions.

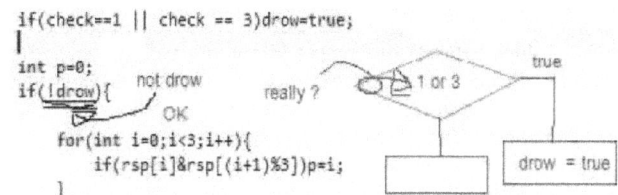

Figure 8: Example of proposed tool to draw diagrams and add comments

6.2 Pair Change Based Actions/Conversations

As was described in Subsection 5.2, some pairs did not frequently execute programs for testing. Tests by executing programs are important for subjects to confirm whether programs are running properly or not, and to find incorrect codes. It is common for subjects in agile development to carry out Test first and Test-driven development. Therefore, we think that the frequency of test execution is a useful indicator to find pairs who cannot advance development and who are worried about coding.

Subsection 5.4 explained that subjects in Cases X and Y could not perform pair programming very well. We think that these cases were caused by the pair's abilities. Pair abilities influenced the actions and motivation of subjects.

Subjects pointed an average number of 14.5 times in collocated pair programming (c.f. Figure 4). In other words, an average occurrence of pointing per pair was 29. The pair in Case X only used pointing once. Moreover, they did not use other actions, such as gestures and handwritten notes. We think that the frequencies of characteristic actions can indicate how well a navigator can catch up with a driver.

However, pair programming in Case X was effective when a driver had lower levels of ability. He actually answered that he could explain his intent to his navigator well in the questionnaire, and his self-evaluation was level four, i.e., relatively high (c.f. Figure 6). The other pair in Case Y used pointing 34 times and handwritten notes. However, they could not write codes very well because they did not understand Java programming very well. We think that the efficiency of pair programming was not only influenced by the frequencies of characteristic actions but also a pair's abilities.

Therefore, we propose a function that suggests the timing of role switching for a pair, when the system detects that the volume of newly written and changed codes is small, even if they have communicated well as a pair. Moreover, it is possible to have a function to automatically detect a delayed or stagnated pair by measuring the frequency of test execution, and a function of reminders to change pairs. Furthermore, if a navigator has been left behind, it is important for the system to remind his/her driver of this. The system can detect whether the navigator has been left behind by measuring the frequency of pointing. We intend to conduct experiments in the future to evaluate these proposed functions.

7. CONCLUSION

We conducted experiments in both collocated and distributed environments, and analyzed actions in collocated and distributed pair programming. We focused attention on actions regarding communication in a pair. We also focused attention on the relationships between differences in abilities and characteristic actions. Characteristic actions, such as pointing, handwritten notes, and gestures were observed in collocated pair programming. Characteristic actions, such as text chats and annotations, were observed in distributed pair programming.

We discussed functions that would be effective in distributed pair programming. Our study revealed that it is important for a system that supports distributed pair programming to have functions to enable easy communication and appropriate partner change. Moreover, this study clarified that two items need to be evaluated to accomplish effective functions for distributed pair programming.

- Comparative studies on the effectiveness of video calls and remote annotations.

- Evaluation of algorithms to detect timing for partner changes and role switching.

We intend to evaluate the proposed functions in distributed project-based learning. We also plan to build a total support system in the near future after carrying out this evaluation.

8. REFERENCES

[1] Baheti, P., Gehiringer, E., and Scotts, D. 2002. Exploring the Efficacy of Distributed Pair Programming. In Programming and Agile Methods – XP/Agile Universe 2002, Chicago, IL, USA, pp. 208–220.

[2] Beck, K. 1999. Extreme Programming Explained: Embrace Change, Addison-Wesley Professional. Boston, MA, USA.

[3] Boyer, K. E., Dwight, A. A., Fordren, R. T., Vouk, M. A., and Lester J. C. 2008. A development environment for distributed synchronous collaborative programming. In Proceedings of the 13th Annual SIGCSE Conference on Innovation and Technology in Computer Science Education, pp. 158–162.

[4] Canfora, G., Cimitile, A., and Visaggio, C. A. 2003. Lessons learned about distributed pair programming: what are the knowledge needs to address? In Twelfth International Workshop on Enabling Technologies: Infrastructure for Collaborative Enterprises, Los Alamitos, CA, USA. IEEE Computer Society, pp. 314–319.

[5] Dou, W., Hong, K., and He, W. 2010. A Conversation Model of Collaborative Pair Programming Based on Language/Action Theory. Proceedings of the 2010 14th International Conference on Computer Supported Cooperative Work in Design, pp. 7–12.

[6] Duque, R. and Bravo, C. 2008. Analyzing Work Productivity and Program Quality in Collaborative Programming. The 3rd International Conference on Software Engineering Advances, pp. 270–276.

[7] Ho, C. W., Raha, S., Gehringer, E., and William, L. 2004. Sangam: a distributed pair programming plug-in for eclipse. In Proceedings of the 2004 OOPSLA workshop on eclipse technology eXchange, pp. 73–77.

[8] Jensen, R. W. 2003. A Pair Programming Experience. The Journal of Defense Software Engineering, Vol. 16, No. 3 (March, 2003), pp. 22–24.

[9] Lui, K. M. and Chan, K. C. C. 2006. Pair programming productivity: Novice-novice vs. expert-expert. International. Journal of Human-Computer Studies Vol. 64, No. 9 (September, 2006), pp. 915–925.

[10] Natsu, H., Fravela, J., Moran, A. L., Decouchant, D., and Martinez-Enriquez, A. M. 2003. Distributed pair programming on the Web. In Proceedings of the 4th Mexican International Conference on Computer Science, pp. 81–88.

[11] Salinger, S., Oezbek, C., Beecher, K., and Schenk, J. 2010. Saros: An Eclipse Plug-in for Distributed Party Programming. CHASE 2010'10 (May, 2010), pp. 48–55.

[12] Stephens, M. and Rosenberg, D. 2003. Extreme Programming Refactored: The Case Against XP. Apress 2002, Berkeley, CA, USA.

[13] Toll III, T. V., Lee R. and Ahlswede, T. 2007. Evaluating the Usefulness of Pair Programming in a Classroom Setting. International Conference on Computer and Information Science, pp. 302–308.

[14] Williams, L. A. and Kessler, R. R. Experimenting with Industry's "Pair-Programming" Model in the Computer Science Classroom. http://classes.soe.ucsc.edu/cmpe012/Winter08/handouts/PairedProgrammingforCS.pdf

[15] Williams, L., Kessler, R. R., Cunningham, W., and Jeffries, R. 2000. Strengthening the Case for Pair Programming. IEEE Computer Society, pp. 19–25.

Using the Readiness Assurance Process and Metacognition in an Operating Systems Course

Michael S. Kirkpatrick
Department of Computer Science
James Madison University
kirkpams@jmu.edu

Samantha Prins
Department of Mathematics and Statistics
James Madison University
prinssc@jmu.edu

Categories and Subject Descriptors

K.3.2 [**Computing Milieux**]: Computer and Information Science Education—*Computer science education*

General Terms

Human Factors

Keywords

active learning, education, pedagogy, metacognition

ABSTRACT

There is significant evidence that active learning techniques facilitate superior learning outcomes when compared to traditional lecture-based techniques. However, adopting an entirely new pedagogy is a time-consuming endeavor that requires considerable effort. In this work, we describe simple transitional steps that we used to increase the amount of active learning in our Operating Systems (OS) course. After introducing these techniques in the Fall 2013 offering of this course, we observed dramatic improvements in a variety of measures of student outcomes, including withdraw-D-failure (WDF) rates and final exam performance. We also observed marked improvement in project completion rates. Our results suggest that adopting components of active learning pedagogies can contribute to positive outcomes with modest investments in time and effort.

1. INTRODUCTION

The body of evidence supporting active learning methodologies is significant and continues to grow [4, 6, 15, 5]. Several papers (*e.g.,* [14, 8, 7, 9, 10, 2, 3]), have documented the success of these approaches in computer science specifically. It is becoming increasingly clear that courses that rely on lecture alone are less effective in terms of concept retention and transfer when compared to courses that incorporate in-class activities that provide opportunities for formative assessment. The challenge now is *how* to make the

change to active learning. Adopting a new pedagogy is a time-consuming process that can require a significant effort by the instructor, and wary instructors frequently express concerns about the impact of the techniques on coverage of material. In contrast to previous work on new pedagogies, the focus of this paper is to describe our experience with a transitional step of integrating two techniques into our existing interactive lecture[1] course structure, rather than adopting a completely new pedagogy.

Our first technique is based on the Readiness Assurance Process (RAP) as used in Team-Based Learning (TBL) [12].[2] The RAP consists of four components: an individual Readiness Assessment Test (iRAT), a team Readiness Assessment Test (tRAT), Appeals, and Corrective Instruction. In the iRAT and tRAT phases, students take a quiz first as individuals then again as a team; the questions are identical in both cases. The iRAT holds individuals accountable for doing preparation work on their own; failure to prepare will impact their course grade. The tRAT provides a valuable opportunity to discuss concepts with peers, which leads to improved understanding by the group, even if none of the students originally knew the correct answer [16]. During the Appeals phase, teams can submit a written appeal for additional points if they can provide evidence for why their answer should also be considered correct. During the Corrective Instruction phase, the instructor clarifies material based on feedback from the iRAT and tRAT phases.

Our second technique is a variant on two metacognitive Classroom Assessment Techniques (CATs) known as the $RSQC^2$ and muddiest points [1]. (Note that the ^{2} is an exponent and does not indicate a footnote; we use the name as it was used in [1] for consistency.) The $RSQC^2$ stands for *recall, summarize, question, connect, comment*. Students are asked to *recall* and *summarize* the most important point, then craft a precise *question* that they would like answered; students are then asked to *connect* the concepts to previous material in the course or the discipline and then *comment* on their learning process. This activity provides an opportunity to bring metacognition into the course, which is beneficial

---

[1]Note that *interactive lecturing* is distinct from the *traditional lecturing* that has been criticized by studies such as [5]. The former technique involves the deliberate integration of in-class activities, such as think-pair-share, that are designed to avoid many of the problems of the latter.

[2]While we adopted elements of TBL beyond just the RAP, it would be an overstatement to classify our Fall 2013 offering as a TBL course. We are currently redesigning this course to use TBL, and this paper focuses on a transitional step in that direction.

	Sat./Sun.	Mon.	Tue.	Wed.	Thu.	Fri.
In class:		tRAT, muddiest points		interactive lecture		interactive lecture
Out of class:	readings, iRAT					RSQC^2

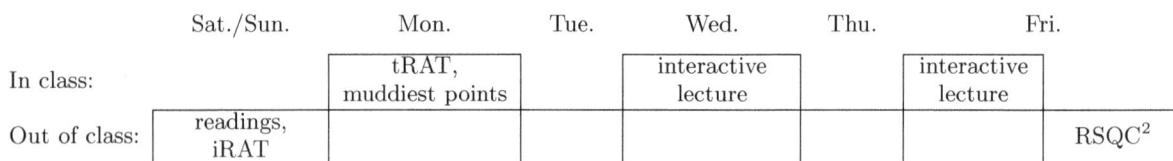

Figure 1: Castle-top diagram illustrating timing of interventions

for both students and instructors [11]. In our approach, which we describe in the next section, we combined RSQC^2 with the muddiest points activity, where students identify the topic that they found the most confusing.

We introduced these activities into our Fall 2013 offering of our Operating Systems (OS) course (CS 450). We compared the outcomes of this offering (two sections with 52 students total) with our Fall 2012 offering (two sections with 49 students total). Despite demographic similarities in the two offerings, we observed dramatic improvements in student performance, specifically in terms of the withdraw-D-failure (WDF) rate, final exam performance, and course project completion. We performed a number of statistical tests on these factors and found statistically signifcant improvements in the intervention group.

While programming project completion rates also increased in Fall 2013, building a predictive model for completion rates proved difficult. From 2012 to 2013, the students had a statistically significant increase in self-reported C programming experience. As the projects involve modifications to the Pintos kernel [13] and are written exclusively in C, it seems intuitive that the increased experience would contribute to success on these projects. Interestingly, though, we found that C experience had no significant impact on project success once the significant intervention factor was considered. However, statistical tests indicated that the model was weak.

Based on our results, we find compelling evidence that these techniques, which require a very modest effort on the part of the instructor, can play a part in improving student learning outcomes. Informally, we observed that classes after the intervention were more interactive and successful. Statistical analysis supported our observations, as we found significant improvements in the intervention group, while controlling for a variety of demographic factors. The use of an online learning management service, such as Canvas (which we use) or Blackboard, and Immediate Feedback - Assessment Techniques (IF-ATs) can further alleviate the overhead of accommodating these techniques. The result of this combination is a low-cost and effective transitional step toward active learning.

2. IMPLEMENTATION

This section describes our specific versions of the interventions in the Fall 2013 offering. Figure 1 shows a *castle-top diagram* that illustrates the timing of these activities during the week. This illustration does not show homework and project work, which students completed on their own outside of class according to their own schedules.

2.1 RSQC^2 technique

In the traditional approach to the RSQC^2, students answer the questions during class time and are given approximately 10 minutes to respond. We found this time commit-

ment to be burdensome, given that our sections were only 50 minutes long. As such, we used a Canvas quiz to conduct the RSQC^2. Students had until Friday evening each week to complete the quiz. Furthermore, we modified the phrasing of the questions as follows (the term in brackets was not part of the question given to students and is only intended to map to RSQC^2 and metacognition):

1. What one idea from this week did you find most interesting and why? [recall]

2. Explain one concept that you understand more now than you did a week ago. [summarize]

3. What helped you to learn the most this week? [comment, metacognition]

4. Identify one thing from this week that you are confused about in some way. This could be a concept from the lectures and/or book, a requirement of the current project, the relevance of this material, course policies, etc. In addition, try to *explain what you don't understand or why it is confusing.* [question, muddiest point, connect, metacognition]

5. What can *you* do to overcome the confusion you just identified? [metacognition]

6. Is there anything else you would like to add? [comment]

2.2 RAP technique

In TBL, the RAP is designed to ensure students have completed required readings prior to class and are prepared to engage in more advanced activities. This activity includes the iRAT and tRAT, both of which are to be conducted during class. In a true TBL course, both of these activities are in-class and graded to ensure accountability for both the individual and the team. In our variation, we moved the iRAT to before class as a weekly online Canvas quiz due each Sunday night. Students could take the iRAT up to 3 times. Immediately after each attempt, students were given their score but Canvas provided no indication of which questions were correct and which were not; consequently, retaking the quiz required students to re-evaluate all of their answers independently. Only the highest score of the 3 attempts was used for grading. Figure 2 shows sample questions that were used on the iRAT/tRAT.

On each Monday, students would retake the quiz as an ungraded tRAT. In the early part of the semester, students reported their responses with a show of hands. The advantage of this approach was that, if different groups came to different conclusions, students had the opportunity to debate and discuss the correct answer. Later in the course, we introduced IF-AT forms, which are pre-printed scratch-off cards. Scratching off the correct response reveals a star,

| One technique for speeding up thread creation is to automatically create several threads when the process starts. What is the term for this technique? (a) thread pools (b) implicit threading (c) many-to-many model (d) lightweight processes | On the command-line, if I type `ls \| head`, the output produced by running the "`ls`" program is redirected as the input to the "`head`" program. What type of IPC is this? (a) shared memory (b) message passing (c) pipe (d) socket | Which of the following describes the notion of a safe state? (a) Enough resources are available to satisfy the next request (b) All resources can be granted in any order and deadlock is impossible (c) Resources can be granted in some particular order that makes deadlock impossible (d) The system is currently not deadlocked |

Figure 2: Sample iRAT/tRAT (individual/team Readiness Assessment Test) questions

while the others are blank. The advantage of the IF-AT approach is that students can discuss the questions in their small groups; this allows students who are reticent to participate in large-group discussions to voice their opinions in a more comfortable setting. However, even with the IF-AT approach, most classes included a large-group discussion to clarify questions at the end of the tRAT.

After completing the tRAT, we then began a discussion of the most common responses to question 4 from the RSQC^2. This is similar to the standard TBL approach, which often includes a muddiest point discussion as part of the Clarifying Instruction after the tRAT. The key distinction is that, in standard TBL muddiest point discussions, the instructor can respond to points of confusion that arise during the tRAT, whereas our approach involved collecting this information before class time. The disadvantage of the TBL approach is that fewer voices may be heard (*e.g.*, if some students are shy), and it is difficult to discern larger trends at the time. In our approach, the instructor was able to analyze the questions (which are asked on Friday) to identify fundamental misunderstandings that may be influencing the muddiest points. On the other hand, the disadvantage of our approach is that the students may come up with new questions during the iRAT and tRAT that get missed.

2.3 Grading procedures

Grading the iRATs involved no work, as this task was handled automatically by Canvas. For the RSQC^2, we graded each submission on a 10-point scale with two points per question (question 6 was ungraded). If the student provided a good faith effort to respond, they would receive full credit. If the student responded to the question with an inadequate response (*e.g.*, providing a nonsense response such as "blargh"), they would receive one point. This low-stakes approach allowed students to respond freely without concern about providing the "correct" answer. The iRATs and RSQC^2 activities accounted for 5% each of the total grade for the course.

2.4 Additional activities

The primary teaching style for this course consists of interactive lecturing. That is, material is presented in a lecture format that is punctuated with informal application activities, such as in-class exercises, worksheets, and discussions. This style was used in both offerings considered in this paper, so there was no overt attempt to introduce a new pedagogy other than the previously described activities. However, it is our observation that introducing these new techniques made more class time available for in-class activities, as we had to spend less time covering foundational

concepts. That is, incorporating the RAP and RSQC^2 allowed us to devote more class time to active learning without making a radical change to our pedagogy.

3. ANALYSIS

To analyze the possible impact of our intervention on this course, we compared the demographics and outcomes for the Fall 2012 ($N = 49$) and 2013 ($N = 52$) offerings with a number of statistical tests. Note that, due to incomplete questionnaire responses, the histograms and linear regression that we report are based on a subset of this data ($N = 44$ and $N = 43$ for Fall 2012 and 2013, respectively).

3.1 Demographics

In our analysis, we identified three demographic factors that required careful consideration. The first difference was an increase in the amount of self-reported C programming experience, which was a consequence of a change made in the prerequisite course. This was measured on a 4-point Likert scale (1 = "No experience," 2 = "Very limited experience," 3 = "Written several small programs (less than 100 lines)," and 4 = "Written large programs"). Figure 3 shows the distribution of responses. For reasons we will describe in Section 3.3, we combined the 1 and 2 responses, as well as the 3 and 4 responses. After combining the groups, a χ^2 test showed that there was a significant difference in C programming experience between the two offerings ($p = 0.001214$).

Next, there was a significant difference in the number of students who completed the prerequisite (CS 350) as a community college equivalent. The number of students who took the equivalent course decreased from 17 in Fall 2012 to 8 in 2013. A χ^2 test yielded $p = 0.04374$.

The third demographic factor that we considered was the students' self-reported[3] grades (based on a 4.0 GPA scale) in the prerequisite. While teaching the course, we felt that the students were fairly comparable and neither group was clearly better than the other. To validate this intuition, we compared the proportions of students who earned either As or Bs in the prerequisite. In Fall 2012, this ratio was 23/44 whereas the ratio for Fall 2013 was 29/43. A χ^2 test yielded $p = 0.221$, indicating no significant difference between the overall quality of students in the two offerings.

3.2 Impact on course grades

Despite having performed similarly in the CS 350 prerequisite, the students in the intervention group (Fall 2013)

---

[3]The decision to use self-reported grades, rather than accessing student records, was made after consultation with our Institutional Review Board (IRB).

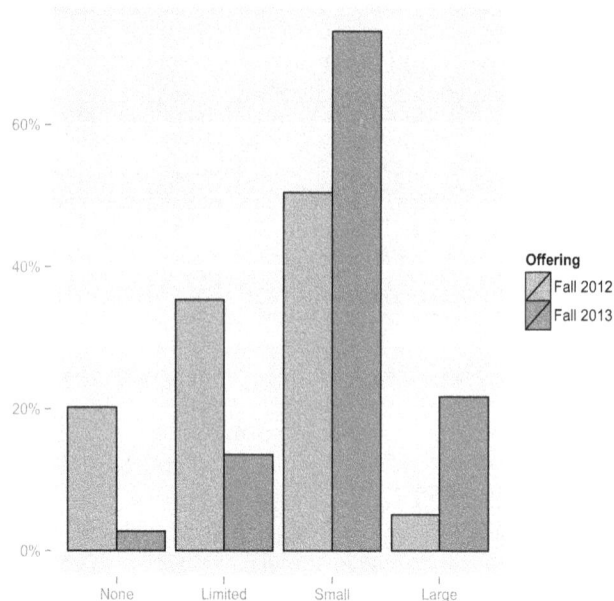

Figure 3: Self-reported C programming experience

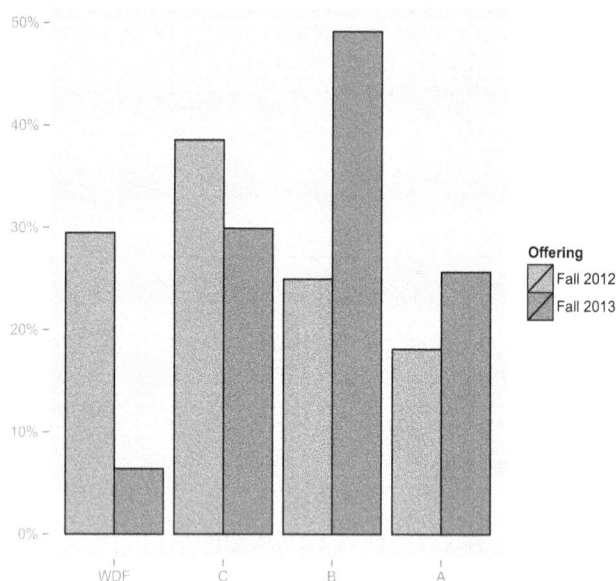

Figure 4: Fall 2012 vs. Fall 2013 CS 450 grade distribution

performed significantly better in CS 450 than those in the control group. Figure 4 shows the grade distributions for the two offerings. The WDF rate improved from 13/49 in Fall 2012 to 3/52 in Fall 2013; a one-sided χ^2 test yielded $p = 0.004893$, indicating significance. Similarly, if we look at the students who did well in CS 450 (those earning As and Bs, and only considering the subset of students who responded), we see that the ratio of As and Bs improved from 17/44 in Fall 2012 to 35/43 in Fall 2013, which yields $p = 0.0000596$ in a one-sided χ^2 test. Thus, the intervention group showed a significant improvement in course grades.

In addition to overall course grades, we also observed a significant improvement on programming projects. For instance, both offerings were required to complete (working in groups) portions of the Pintos OS projects [13]. In these courses, the `userprog` project was completed at the end of the semester. The average number of test cases (only a subset were required) that the teams passed increased from 28/50 to 40/50. A t test yields $p = 0.02391$, thus indicating significance. As these were team projects, we attempted to perform a linear regression that modeled the number of test cases passed as a function of the team's average C programming experience and the intervention. The only factor found to be significant was the intervention ($p = 0.0678$), but the adjusted R^2 value was 0.1535 (overall $p = 0.09181$ for the model), indicating the model produced by the regression is rather weak. However, what is interesting about this regression is that teams' average C programming experience is **not** a significant predictor of test case success, regardless of whether or not the intervention was present. This finding is counterintuitive, as the Pintos projects are all written in C, but it is welcome: *It suggests that teams with less C experience in both groups were able to catch up with those with more experience by the end of the semester.*

3.3 Impact on final exam performance

As noted above, our intervention group (Fall 2013) demonstrated significant improvements in the WDF rate, overall course grade, and programming projects. We also observed

that students performed better on the exams, as well. To analyze exam performance in more detail, we performed a multiple linear regression analysis aimed at describing final exam scores as a function of demographics (C programming experience, community college equivalency of the prerequisite, and prerequisite grade) and our intervention. Linear relationships between final exam scores and each of the demographic and intervention variables were reasonable, and residual diagnostics for the final model (described below) revealed no issues with model form or assumptions. We found the community college equivalency factor to be insignificant with the other factors present, and removed it based on ANOVA results ($p = 0.4958$).

Recall that the C programming factor was self-reported Likert-scale data. While we initially considered all four Likert responses as factors in the regression, we found the increase to the third level, "Written several small programs," relative to having "No experience," to be the only significant factor ($p = 0.0551$). Consequently, we found it appropriate to group the responses into two categories: those with limited or no experience, versus those with at least some experience with C programming.

Table 1 shows our model, which is significant with an overall $p = 1.153 * 10^{-12}$ and $R^2 = 0.5114$, indicating that this model captures the behavior well. According to this model, the y-intercept for students in the intervention group was 24 points higher on the final exam when all other factors are held constant. Furthermore, there was a significant interaction between the prerequisite grade and the intervention, which changes the slope of the line for that class. The result is that the weakest students (those who scored a D in the prerequisite) in the intervention group benefited the most. At the same time, though, the strongest students in the intervention group *also* benefited but to a lesser extent.

Figure 5 illustrates the model in graphical form. In this figure, the dotted lines indicate the model for the students who had limited or no C programming experience, whereas the solid lines indicate those who came into CS 450 with prior C experience. In all cases, holding prerequisite grade

Factor	Estimate	$Pr(>|t|)$
(Intercept)	37.530	$1.6 * 10^{-12}$
C programming	8.562	0.000961
Prerequisite grade	7.658	$2.9 * 10^{-7}$
Intervention	24.228	0.001015
Prerequisite grade:Intervention	-4.301	0.076666

Table 1: Final linear regression model of final exam scores in two offerings of CS 450

and C experience constant, students in the intervention group did significantly better than those in the control.

We emphasize that this analysis should be taken as illustration, rather than generalizable quantitative evidence. There were differences between the exams that our statistical analysis does not consider. For instance, there were some questions asked on the Fall 2012 final that appeared on the Fall 2013 midterm instead. Similarly, some questions from the Fall 2012 midterm were added to the Fall 2013 final. Consequently, our exam cannot be considered a valid instrument and we acknowledge the possibility that the exam differences were responsible for some of the improvement. To counter this objection, we observed improved performance on the parts of the exam that were similar, and students also did better on the midterm, as well. Thus, we find enough corroborating evidence that suggests our regression model is consistent with student performance, and students in the intervention group did significantly better than the control.

3.4 Limitation of interpretations

To be clear, our analysis presented here shows that students in our intervention group performed better in a variety of measurements even while considering the impact of certain demographic factors. There are many other factors that could have played a role that were not considered. For instance, our analysis did not consider the possible effect of having different instructors for CS 350. Also, the Fall 2013 students may have selected either into or out of our sections of CS 450 based on what they heard from the Fall 2012 students. This selection bias could have included differences in motivations between the groups. As another example, the increased number of students who completed the prerequisite in our department may have led to a shared cultural identity that helped the Fall 2013 students to work together more effectively. Our statistical model does not capture either of these affective characteristics. Thus, we do not assert a causal link between these techniques and the improved outcomes. Rather, we reiterate the point that these techniques allowed us to increase active learning opportunities in the classroom, and the statistical findings corroborate our personal observations that the collective whole of the Fall 2013 experience led to improve outcomes.

4. DISCUSSION

Overall, we feel that there is a significant amount of anecdotal evidence and empirical results to suggest that these techniques were beneficial and contributed to improved student outcomes in the Fall 2013 offering. In this section, we will discuss additional points to consider when implementing these techniques in future courses.

On the $RSQC^2$ variation, questions 4 and 5 proved problematic and we abandoned this structure in later courses,

returning to a more traditional $RSQC^2$ format. The problem with question 4 was its attempt to serve multiple purposes. Some students responded with specific questions (*i.e.,* muddiest points) while others focused on how the material related to other topics (*i.e.,* connection). Question 5 was designed to complement in-class discussions of metacogniition that introduced students to the idea of reflecting on how they learn. In class, they were provided guidance to think about what other resources (*e.g.,* Wikipedia) they would consider using. Despite this guidance, we found student responses to this question quite varied and unhelpful, and we have omitted it in subsequent courses.

In more recent semesters, we have also changed the grading system used for the $RSQC^2$. Rather than awarding two points per question, we now award a single point for each, regardless of the quality of the students' responses. We had initially feared that this approach, which rewards insightful comments and gibberish equally, would lead to a reduction in the quality of responses. In practice, we have no evidence that this fear is warranted and the overall quality of students' responses has stayed at the same level as previously.

Responses to the $RSQC^2$ questions provide valuable feedback to the instructor regarding student progress. However, in a subsequent course[4], we moved the muddiest point discussion from class time to the class discussion forum on Canvas, and we shifted the responsibility of answering the questions to the students. In this approach, we enumerated the questions, paraphrasing as necessary, in a weekly discussion forum post that was published on Saturdays. Students then collectively provided answers in the style of a Wiki, with the stipulation that each student could only provide the initial answer for a single question; once a question was answered, anyone could edit. The advantage of this approach is that it provides students with a valuable opportunity for peer teaching and formative assessment by allowing them to answer a question with no grade repercussions. In almost all cases, students were able to come up with a correct answer with minimal feedback from the instructor. This variation also reduced the instructional overhead, as we no longer needed to prepare specific responses.

While we observed significant improvements in measurable student outcomes, these techniques also produced a number of intangible improvements, as well. The introduction of the RAP and muddiest points, in particular, had an influence on the flow of classroom activities. By reducing the need to cover basic definitions and fundamental concepts in class, more time was available to devote to the exercises and in-depth discussions. Furthermore, by starting the class with an activitiy that required discussion, students were primed to be engaged with the class that day. We hypothesize that this engagement may have had more influence than the actual pre-class preparation, but we made no attempt to distinguish between the preparation and the engagement components, and we do not see an easy way to do so. However, we do not see a need to at this point, as the primary goal was to find a way to bring active learning into our systems courses.

---

[4]Our analysis and results sections focus on the outcomes in the Fall 2013 OS course. We introduced this additional variation in Spring 2014 in a different course, so our analysis does not consider its impact on student outcomes. Anecdotally, we found this variation beneficial and include it here for other instructors to consider as they see fit.

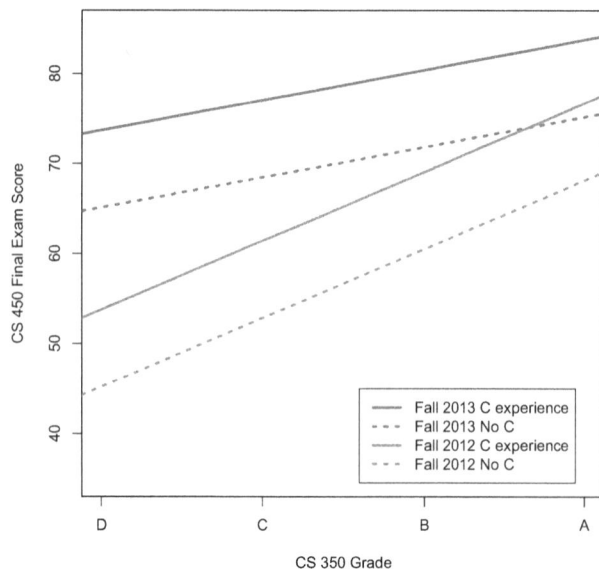

Figure 5: Visual representation of the linear regression model of final exam score

Finally, we also need to address a commonly cited concern about switching to active learning techniques: its impact on coverage. That is, instructors often worry that adopting a new pedagogy will interfere with their ability to cover all required material. In this instance, we do not feel that such a concern is warranted. After doing an informal retrospective mapping to the ACM 2013 curriculum recommendations, we found no differences between coverage of Core Tier-1 and Core Tier-2 topics. Any differences between coverage of Elective topics was negligible. Consequently, we find that adopting these techniques will not have any measurable impact on coverage.

5. CONCLUSION AND FUTURE WORK

In Fall 2013, we introduced two new techniques into our OS course in an attempt to increase the amount of active learning that happened in the classroom. These two techniques, the RAP and the RSQC^2, require a very modest amount of effort on the part of the instructor, but initial evidence indicates that they can be powerful first steps toward improving student learning. Our statistical analysis, which compares the Fall 2012 and Fall 2013 offerings of OS, shows that there were statistically significant improvements in a variety of measurements, even when demographic differences were considered. Thus, for any instructor contemplating a switch to an active learning pedagogy, we recommend these two techniques as a low-cost transitional step.

6. REFERENCES

[1] T. A. Angelo and K. P. Cross. *Classroom Assessment Techniques: A Handbook for Faculty.* Jossey-Bass, San Francisco, CA, 1993.

[2] J. Campbell, D. Horton, M. Craig, and P. Gries. Evaluating an inverted CS1. In *Proceedings of the 45th ACM Technical Symposium on Computer Science Education*, SIGCSE '14, pages 307–312, New York, NY, USA, 2014. ACM.

[3] J. Davis. Experiences with just-in-time teaching in systems and design courses. In *Proceedings of the 40th*

[4] R. M. Felder and R. Brent. Active learning: An introduction. *ASQ Higher Education Brief*, 2(4), August 2009.

[5] S. Freeman, S. L. Eddy, M. McDonough, M. K. Smith, N. Okoroafor, H. Jordt, and M. P. Wenderoth. Active learning increases student performance in science, engineering, and mathematics. *Proceedings of the National Academy of Sciences*, 2014.

[6] R. R. Hake. Interactive-engagement vs. traditional methods: A six-thousand-student survey of mechanics test data for introductory physics courses. *American Journal of Physics*, 66(1):64–74, 1998.

[7] S. Horwitz, S. H. Rodger, M. Biggers, D. Binkley, C. K. Frantz, D. Gundermann, S. Hambrusch, S. Huss-Lederman, E. Munson, B. Ryder, and M. Sweat. Using peer-led team learning to increase participation and success of under-represented groups in introductory computer science. In *Proceedings of the 40th ACM Technical Symposium on Computer Science Education*, SIGCSE '09, pages 163–167, New York, NY, USA, 2009. ACM.

[8] H. H. Hu and T. D. Shepherd. Using POGIL to help students learn to program. *Trans. Comput. Educ.*, 13(3):13:1–13:23, Aug. 2013.

[9] P. Lasserre and C. Szostak. Effects of team-based learning on a CS1 course. In *Proceedings of the 16th Annual Joint Conference on Innovation and Technology in Computer Science Education*, ITiCSE '11, pages 133–137, New York, NY, USA, 2011. ACM.

[10] C. B. Lee, S. Garcia, and L. Porter. Can peer instruction be effective in upper-division computer science courses? *Trans. Comput. Educ.*, 13(3):12:1–12:22, Aug. 2013.

[11] M. Mani and Q. Mazumder. Incorporating metacognition into learning. In *Proceeding of the 44th ACM Technical Symposium on Computer Science Education*, SIGCSE '13, pages 53–58, New York, NY, USA, 2013. ACM.

[12] L. K. Michaelsen, A. B. Knight, and L. D. Fink. *Team-Based Learning: A Transformative Use of Small Groups in College Teaching.* Stylus Publishing, Sterling, VA, 2002.

[13] B. Pfaff, A. Romano, and G. Back. The Pintos instructional operating system kernel. In *Proceedings of the 40th ACM Technical Symposium on Computer Science Education*, SIGCSE '09, pages 453–457, New York, NY, USA, 2009. ACM.

[14] L. Porter, C. Bailey Lee, and B. Simon. Halving fail rates using peer instruction: A study of four computer science courses. In *Proceeding of the 44th ACM Technical Symposium on Computer Science Education*, SIGCSE '13, pages 177–182, New York, 2013. ACM.

[15] M. Prince. Does active learning work? a review of the research. *Journal of Engineering Education*, 93(3), July 2004.

[16] M. K. Smith, W. B. Wood, W. K. Adams, C. Wieman, J. K. Knight, N. Guild, and T. T. Su. Why peer discussion improves student performance on in-class concept questions. *Science*, 323, January 2009.

Combining Challenge-Based Learning and Scrum Framework for Mobile Application Development

Alan R. Santos
PUCRS
Porto Alegre, RS, Brazil
alan.santos@pucrs.br

Afonso Sales
PUCRS
Porto Alegre, RS, Brazil
afonso.sales@pucrs.br

Paulo Fernandes
PUCRS
Porto Alegre, RS, Brazil
paulo.fernandes@pucrs.br

Mark Nichols
The Challenge Institute
Chandler, AZ, USA
marknichols@mac.com

ABSTRACT

The market for mobile applications has been growing dramatically, as has the complexity of the applications and the speed of the development process. These changes require a rethinking of the development process and of how developers are trained. In order to better prepare faculty and students for the emerging mobile application market, this study presents a new learning and software development framework that combines Agile methodologies with the Challenge-Based Learning (CBL) framework. CBL provides a student-centered learning framework that mirrors the modern workplace. Agile methodologies address the changing landscape of mobile development environments. A combination of the CBL learning framework and Agile methodologies can better prepare students for the development market. This paper presents an empirical study applying CBL and Scrum in a mobile application development course evaluated through a series of post surveys. The results indicate that a teaching and learning environment based on practical experience combining the CBL framework with the Scrum process is an effective model to promptly teach undergraduates how to be successful mobile application developers.

Categories and Subject Descriptors

K.3.2 [**Computing Milieux**]: Computers and Education— *Computer and Information Science Education*

Keywords

CBL, Scrum, Mobile Application Development

1. INTRODUCTION

In recent years, the growth in both the development and use of mobile applications has presented new challenges to the software engineering field. The adoption of features such as cameras, sensors, touch and GPS in mobile platforms has rapidly expanded the possibilities for mobile applications. These applications have become more complex and mission critical [10] due to the sudden wave of mobile device use. Simultaneously, speed of deployment has become a key factor due to developers' possibility of submitting apps directly to the market. These changes make it is necessary to identify new ways to prepare developers, and new ways to develop as well. The popularity of mobile application development and the easy access to the market has resulted in more people dedicating themselves to the field of computing who have not been trained as either computer scientists or software engineers. This points to another reason to explore new ways to train future mobile application developers.

Challenge-Based Learning (CBL) [5] is an active, student-directed instructional strategy in which skills are gained through working on real-world problems. At the center of CBL is a call to action that requires students to develop solutions and implement them in authentic environments [7].

The contribution of this paper is an empirical study that combines CBL and Scrum, enabling structured reasoning and decision-making on teaching mobile application development. Although both methodologies/frameworks are commonly used, to our knowledge there is no existing resource that illustrates how the two methods may be combined in a mobile application course.

2. BACKGROUND

Mobile Application Development is a process in which applications are developed for small handheld devices, being either pre-installed on devices during manufacture or downloaded from application stores or other software distribution platforms [3]. In a report from the 2013 ICSE 1st International Workshop on Engineering Mobile, Lewis *et al.* [10] argued that mobile applications are becoming an increasingly important part of enterprise and mission critical systems. According to Wasserman [16], *"using a mobile device is different from working with a desktop or laptop computer. While gestures, sensors, and location data may be used in game consoles and traditional computers, they play a dominant role in many mobile applications"*. The challenge is to understand how to best prepare students to operate in this emerging market [11]. The combination of the Scrum and

CBL frameworks may be an option for a mobile application development environment.

2.1 Scrum Framework

Scrum is an iterative and incremental agile software development approach, presented by Ken Schwaber on a paper describing the Scrum Methodology in 1995 [15]. Hasnain [4] performed a literature review of agile methods and demonstrated that the number of Scrum studies has been increasing each year. Tore and Torgeir [2] performed a literature review of empirical studies of agile software development and found that agile methods like Scrum deserve further attention.

The Scrum workflow is a sequence of iterations, named *Sprints*, which have a duration between one and four weeks. The team is guided by the work foundation as part of a product backlog which is a list of requirements and priorities. Each Sprint has daily meetings where each team member presents what has been done on the previous day, what is going to be done until the next day, and whether there is any roadblock to move forward on development activities. At the end of each Sprint there is a product demo or *Sprint Review*, and following each Sprint Review there is a lessons learned session or *Sprint Retrospective* [14].

Harleen and Swati [3] performed a review and analysis of agile methodologies in mobile development contexts and found that the agile approach is effective in mobile application development [4]. Kajeel and Harishankar [8] studied agile and Scrum practices in the context of android software development, confirming that Agile and Scrum processes are effective in project development scenarios with requirements changing frequently and fast.

In the context of studies conducted to evaluate the effectiveness of agile practices in classroom settings, Scharff and Verma worked with Scrum in a classroom setting at Pace University [14]. They report that mobile applications can be developed in a short time, that Scrum was the main reason for the success of the project when time was a constraint, and that throughout the project, mobile application development content was learned just-in-time.

2.2 Challenge-Based Learning

Experiential learning is based on the idea that students learn best when actively involved in open-ended activities rather than as passive participants in staged activities. The foundations of experiential learning can be found within the history of most cultures, but were formally organized and presented by David Kolb [9], drawing heavily on the works of John Dewey [1] and Jean Piaget [13]. The overarching ideas of experiential learning have spawned a wide variety of learning frameworks, including Problem-Based Learning, Project-Based Learning, and Expeditionary Learning, among others. We reviewed these existing learning frameworks and they place the student at the center and focus on students working together to discover or uncover knowledge, rather than acquiring knowledge through traditional direct instruction from a professor. These learning approaches have recently been advocated as a better way to prepare students for a fluid and dynamic modern work environment.

Challenge-Based Learning (CBL)[1] is a learning framework pioneered by educators working with Apple Inc. which has

been implemented in a wide variety of educational and corporate settings [5]. CBL has roots within experiential learning, in which students actively acquire knowledge through work on open-ended problems.

CBL has the following characteristics: i) the professor, students and stakeholders work as active collaborators in the learning process; ii) the inclusion of both technical and workplace skills [6]; iii) a focus not only on the final product, but on the process developed through ongoing reflection and publishing of perspectives about what was learned; and iv) more time allocated to incorporating divergent and creative thinking.

The CBL white paper [5] defines the Challenge-Based Learning as a process that begins with a big idea, moves to an actionable challenge, and eventually to the implementation of a carefully considered solution. Details of each phase are presented in Table 1.

Table 1: Challenge-Based Learning stages

Name	Description
Big Idea	A broad concept that can be explored in multiple ways, is engaging, and has importance to students and the broader society.
Essential Question	A process of personalizing and pinpointing the important concepts within the big idea.
Challenge	A call to action designed by professors and students to create a solution that can result in concrete action.
Guiding Questions	A series of questions developed by the learning community, identifying and representing the knowledge and skills needed in order to develop a successful solution.
Guiding Activities and Resources	The activities and resources that learners identify, participate in and utilize to answer the guiding questions.
Analysis	A process for exploring the answers to the guiding questions and identifying overarching themes and concepts. This sets the foundation for solutions.
Solution	A concrete, actionable and clearly articulated idea to solve the challenge. Complicated challenges will often have multiple solutions.
Implementation	This is when the solutions are put into action with an authentic audience.
Evaluation	Learners evaluate their process through the results of the implementation and refine their solution.

Studies of experiential approaches to learning have demonstrated that students acquire more solid workplace skills than when taught with traditional methods such as lecture [6]. Timothy *et al.* [12] presented a comparison of Lecture-Based Learning and Challenge-Based Learning in a workplace setting. The study found that participants in the challenge-based group scored significantly better in post-test items requiring integration [12].

---

[1]Details and samples about CBL are also available at http://www.challengebasedlearning.org

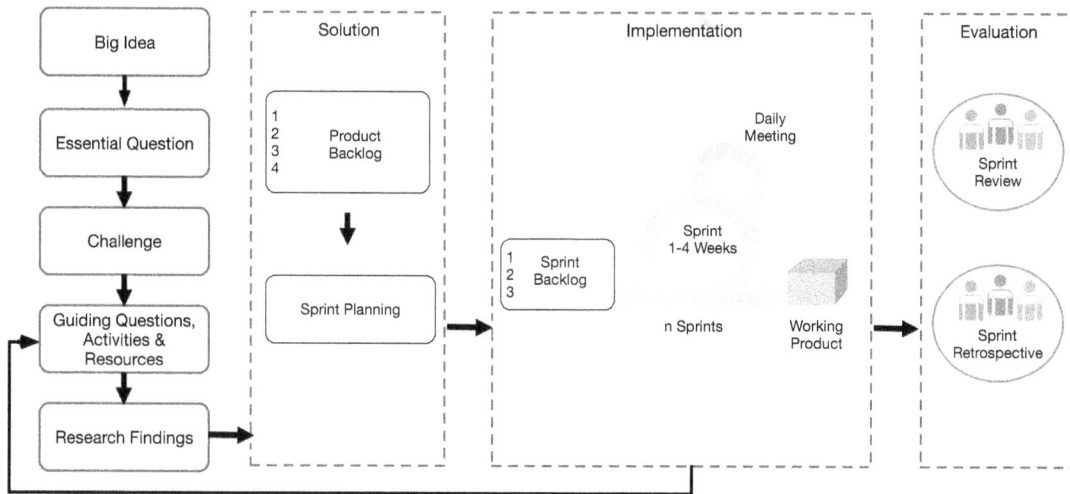

Figure 1: Combining CBL and Scrum

3. THE COURSE

The course focus of this research was a six month iOS development course with 94 undergraduate students. The format of the course involved learning mobile applications programming concepts through completing challenge-based learning assignments. The course was taught in a unique learning space configured to provide a variety of working environments. Each student had his/her own equipment to use as part of class meetings and projects. The course curriculum included the following: Object-Oriented Programming, UI components, Model View Controller, Datasources, Navigation, Animations and Frameworks.

Instead of following a linear content coverage model using direct instruction, the CBL framework and process guided the content, timing and delivery of the curriculum. The faculty and students worked together to identify and acquire the knowledge and skills necessary to solve a variety of real world development challenges. Through this process they covered the specific learning objectives in the course syllabus.

Most of the participants in the course are from an IT related field: 34% from Computer Science, 41% from Information Systems, 8% from Computer Engineering and the remaining students were from other types of undergraduate courses. In this context, 21% of the students were in the 3rd semester, 31% were in the 4th semester, 11% in the 5th semester, 15% in the 6th semester, and the others in different semesters. Another profile information from students is that 35% of the students had already had previous software development courses using Java and C#. In this context, 68% had up to 3 years of experience in development, 18% had between 3 and 5 years of experience, and 14% had more than 5 years software development experience. Most of this previous experience is from other courses, as well as from the industry.

The course was facilitated by 6 instructors. They had knowledge of iOS development, academic and project management background, and four of these instructors had more than five years of experience as software developers.

4. COMBINING CBL AND SCRUM

During course planning, CBL and Scrum were considered as elements separate from the class. CBL was the teaching methodology, while Scrum was to be a development methodology taught to the students. It immediately became apparent that the two approaches overlapped and complemented each other.

An important step in combining CBL and Scrum was setting a timeline with due dates for the Big Idea, Essential Question, Challenge, Guiding Questions, Resources and Activities (GRA), prototype, alpha/beta versions and the final application. In the course, each Challenge began with the students identifying a big idea that was of interest to them. Working together with the faculty, they contextualized this idea through a questioning process that led to a challenge involving the development of a mobile application. The students then used the Guiding Questions, Resources, and Activities to organize and to document their work. This is a critical step in the learning and development process, as it provides time to deeply and widely think about the challenge before developing a solution and starting to code. This step is critical and must be performed before starting the Scrum integration stage, as it ensures that a solution has been thoroughly conceptualized. The combination of CBL and Scrum is presented in Figure 1.

Students may not move to the solution stage until they have answered their core guiding questions, analyzed the results and can support their solution. The professors must also work with students in order to recognize that the iterative process of CBL leads to ongoing guiding questions and the continuing need for activities to answer them. The transition from the challenge to the solution is a critical element in the CBL process, and is often difficult for students who may want to move directly to solutions [5].

After finishing GRA, students present their research findings and analysis. The research findings from GRA are used to build the product backlog sorted by priorities.

The CBL solution stage is when the Scrum product backlog and sprint planning definitions occur, and it repeats as needed through sprints in order to address the scope of work. The mobile development and testing activities are executed as part of each Sprint during the implementation stage. The evaluation stage is when the Sprint Review assesses the incremental product developed, and also when the Sprint Retrospective is performed to verify what the team should start/continue doing and what the team should stop doing in order to promote continuous improvement and learning. At the end of each sprint, the stage of evaluation repeats as long as there are product reviews and lessons learned sessions to be conducted.

In this context, the integration between CBL and Scrum starts at the Solution gate and ends at the Evaluation gate. In order to allow for continued improvement, the stages of Solution, Implementation and Evaluation repeat according to the number of sprints required to address the scope of work. Throughout this process, guiding questions emerge and are answered, deepening the student's understanding of the solution. We have performed an empirical study in order to assess the combination proposed on this research, as follows.

5. EMPIRICAL STUDY

In order to validate the proposed approach, we performed an empirical study between November 2013 and May 2014, organized in three challenges.

5.1 Implementation of the first challenge

Students had two months of mobile software development technical content, CBL methodology introduction and Scrum framework introduction. They were distributed in 25 Scrum teams of two to five (part-time) students each. The first challenge duration was three weeks. One week was dedicated to work on Big Idea, Essential Question, Guiding questions resources and activities. Time was also allocated to build the product backlog. The next two weeks served as sprints to work on the challenge solution, implementation and evaluation. Daily scrum meetings were held every day in order to track what had been done on the previous day, what was going to be done that day and whether there were any impediments or roadblocks. At the end of the solution gate and the implementation gate, sprint reviews and sprint retrospectives were promoted as part of the CBL evaluation process. As a result, 24 teams were able to finish their own mobile applications, while one group was unable to finish their first mobile application version. The scope of the apps delivered as part of this first challenge covers the following areas: social charity, urban mobility, law, productivity, HR, gastronomy, health care, politics, finance and tourism.

Based on the daily meeting status tracking, it was possible to detect the reasons why one group did not achieve the end result: i) the group did not organize a product backlog; ii) the group did not perform a sprint planning; iii) lack of communication among team members and lack of engagement from part of the team.

5.2 Implementation of the second challenge

After the implementation of the first challenge, students had one more month of mobile software development technical content and a review on CBL methodology and Scrum framework. They were distributed in 25 Scrum teams of two to five (part-time) students each. The second challenge duration and Scrum practices were the same as the first challenge. As a result, 24 teams were able to finish a mobile application version and one group was unable to finish their

mobile application project. The scope of the apps delivered as part of this second challenge covers the entertainment and games area. Based also on the daily meeting status tracking, it was possible to detect the reasons why one group did not achieve the end result: i) lack of configuration management which caused several issues on code merge; ii) design solution issues; iii) lack of commitment from part of the team.

5.3 Implementation of the third challenge

After the implementation of the second challenge, students had one more month of mobile software development technical content. They were distributed in 29 Scrum teams of two to four (part-time) students each. The third challenge duration and Scrum practices were also the same as those of the first and second challenges. As a result, all teams were able to finish a mobile application version, with seven teams doing incremental work from previous challenges and 22 teams building brand new applications. The scope of the apps delivered as part of this third challenge covers the following areas: nutrition, sales, sustainability, accessibility, entertainment, psychology, education, beauty services, social networks, urban mobility, security, productivity, services, health care and pets.

5.4 Surveys

Surveys were conducted after the end of each challenge project in order to measure variables related to Mobile Application Development, Challenge-Based Learning and Scrum.

Survey Protocol:

The goal of the surveys conducted in this study was to identify initial student perceptions of the combination method and its impact on mobile application development. The sample population was composed of undergraduate students in a mobile application development program, who were chosen using the convenience criteria due to the fact that participants were selected for their availability. The sample population size was defined using the higher number of available people to participate (94 students).

The questionnaires used the following structure: demographic questions; questions about CBL in order to evaluate aspects such as learning improvement, work control, performance, flexibility and ease to use; questions about Scrum to evaluate aspects such as productivity, effectiveness and utility.

5.5 Results

5.5.1 First challenge results

After ending the first challenge project, the first survey was applied. The survey received 78 responses out of 94 participants. In this sense, 86% of students stated that CBL is very helpful to build better requirements.

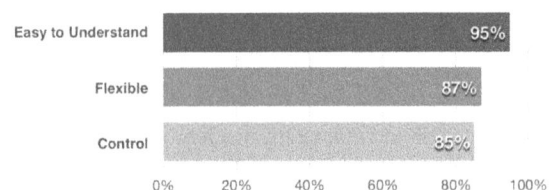

Figure 2: CBL First Challenge results

Moreover, 95% of the students stated that CBL is easy to understand; 87% confirm that CBL is flexible due to the fact that various contents can be practiced when using it; and 85% confirm that by using CBL they have more control over educational activities related to the course.

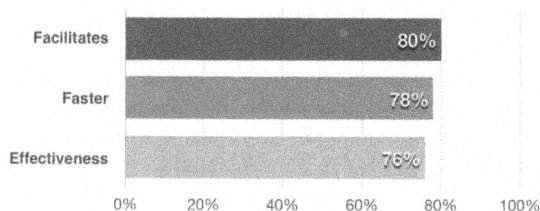

Figure 3: Scrum First Challenge results

In the context of the use of Scrum in the first challenge, 76% confirm that by using Scrum they have improved effectiveness in conducting challenge activities; 78% confirm that Scrum led to faster performance of activities related to the challenges; and 80% confirm that Scrum facilitates mobile applications development organization.

5.5.2 Second challenge results

After ending the second challenge implementation, another survey was applied to collect students input about the use of CBL integrated to the Scrum framework. The survey received 83 responses out of 94 participants.

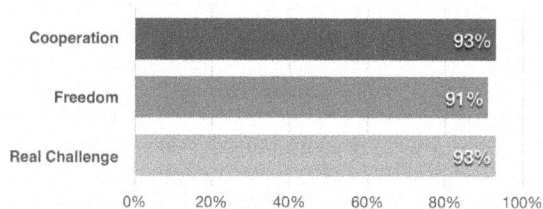

Figure 4: CBL Second Challenge results

In regards to the use of CBL in the second challenge, 93% confirm that with CBL they have real world challenges that demand instructors and students to work on complex solutions; 91% confirm that CBL provides an environment where students have freedom to learn and to teach; and 93% confirm that by using CBL they work in cooperation with instructors and teammates.

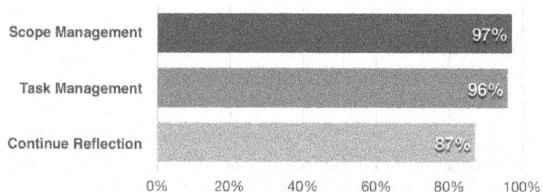

Figure 5: Scrum Second Challenge results

In the context of the use of Scrum in the second challenge, 87% confirm that using daily meetings makes them continually reflect on the CBL solution implementation; 96% confirm that by using Scrum they organize the tasks to be developed during the sprint, which facilitates the development process organization; and 97% confirm that by using Scrum they apply the product backlog artifact, facilitating the CBL solution scope management. In this second challenge, when asked if they would like to share any other opinion about the learning and development process using CBL and Scrum on challenges, it was possible to confirm the effectiveness of CBL and Scrum based on the answers: *"The process is becoming more structured, speeding development"*; *"The purpose of the CBL has become clearer in the second challenge due to the experience gained in the first challenge"*; *"The use of both methods helps to have a greater perception of the size of the project scope, resources and tools. This allows for a better management of the project, since it helps to ensure that tasks are completed"*.

5.5.3 Third challenge results

After ending the third challenge, a final survey was applied in order to collect students' impressions on the use of CBL integrated to the Scrum framework. The survey received 80 responses out of 94 participants.

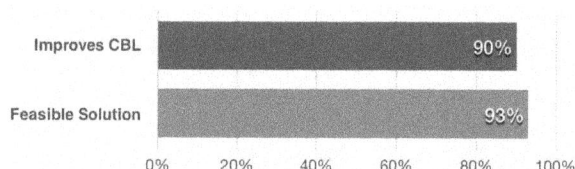

Figure 6: CBL and Scrum Third Challenge results

In regards to CBL and Scrum, 90% confirm that the use of Scrum improves the CBL framework for mobile application development, and 93% confirm that CBL is a feasible solution for a mobile learning development environment.

Based on the open question about how using Scrum improves CBL to develop mobile applications, some interesting results were found: *"Scrum is to assist the development of the app, especially team communication and project documentation. Scrum keeps the team at an appropriate pace with no impact on application development"*; *"By organizing backlog, prioritization and ownership of the activities you can keep development scope under control"*; *"With Scrum, we always know where we are and where we should go in developing the app, avoiding waste of time"*.

When asked about the factors that make the CBL a feasible solution for a mobile development learning environment, answers included: *"The CBL reminds students to look for more knowledge and not to be limited, thus making it a more effective learning"*; *"Possibility of changes over work, division of tasks and clarification of what is required or not for the project"*. When asked about their knowledge on mobile application development before the course using a scale from 0 to 10, the average value was 2.75. When asked about their knowledge on mobile application development after the course using the same scale, the average value was 8.03. This indicates that our course actually represented a change on the knowledge of the majority of the students.

6. DISCUSSION

As far as we know, this is the first documented empirical study examining the use of Challenge-Based Learning and

Scrum with undergraduate students learning mobile application development. This work contributes to two important discussions: how to educate developers of mobile applications and effective models for the development of mobile applications.

None of the participants had contact with Challenge-Based Learning before the course, and for 68% of the participants it was their first contact with Scrum. For 85% of participants it was their first contact with mobile application development. For the majority of the students, it was their first contact with CBL methodology, Scrum framework and mobile application development.

According to the results of students' perceptions, we found that a teaching and learning environment based on practical experience, combining the Challenge-Based Learning framework with the Scrum process, was an effective model for undergraduate students to learn in a short time to be effective mobile application developers. We were able to obtain important information on mobile application development environments, demonstrating that a majority of participants agree and completely agree that Scrum helps to efficiently perform activities related to challenges, and that CBL enhances the use of Scrum concerning the quality of the solutions due to the big idea, essential question, challenge and research stages. We were able to confirm that CBL is effective in technology-rich learning environments [6], and we confirmed that ongoing student and professor reflection and publishing improves the learning process.

7. FINAL REMARKS

The main objective of this study was to empirically explore processes and practices aimed at integrating the Challenge-Based Learning framework and Scrum methodologies. Based on the findings of this study, we reach the following conclusions: Challenge-Based Learning is a successful framework for mobile software development. The results also demonstrate that Scrum can be successfully integrated with CBL for mobile application development. The results also revealed that the mobile application development projects require a documented process where agile processes such as Scrum can help.

Our research also contributes to the dialogue on new methodologies for application development learning. Combining CBL with Scrum not only improved the learning process, but also resulted in a new approach that was effective in the rapid development of high quality mobile applications.

The research strategy applied to conduct this study presents potential limitations due to the research method selected. In future studies examining CBL and agile integration, more empirical studies and surveys will be applied in order to collect other aspects related to the proposed integration approach.

8. ACKNOWLEDGMENTS

Afonso Sales is funded by CNPq-Brazil (Universal 470096/2013-6) and Paulo Fernandes is also funded by CNPq-Brazil (PQ 307602/2013-3).

9. REFERENCES

[1] J. Dewey. *Experience and Education*. Kappa Delta Pi., New York, NY, 1938.

[2] T. Dybå and T. Dingsøyr. Empirical studies of agile software development: A systematic review. *Information and Software Technology*, 50(9-10):833–859, 2008.

[3] D. S. V. C. Harleen K. Flora. A review and analysis on mobile application development processes using agile methodologies. *International Journal of Research in Computer Science*, 3(4):9–18, 2013.

[4] E. Hasnain. An overview of published agile studies: A systematic literature review. In *Proceedings of the 2010 National Software Engineering Conference*, NSEC '10, pages 3:1–3:6, Rawalpindi, Pakistan, 2010.

[5] A. Inc. Challenge based learning: A classroom guide. Technical report, Apple Inc., Cupertino, CA, 2012.

[6] L. Johnson and S. Adams. Challenge based learning: The report from the implementation project. Technical report, The New Media Consortium, Austin, TX, 2011.

[7] L. F. Johnson, R. S. Smith, J. Smythe, and R. K. Varon. Challenge-based learning: An approach for our time. Technical report, The New Media Consortium, Austin, TX, 2009.

[8] S. B. Kaleel and S. Harishankar. Applying agile methodology in mobile software engineering: Android application development and its challenges. Technical report, Department of Computer Science, Ryerson University, 2013.

[9] D. Kolb and R. Fry. *Toward an Applied Theory of Experiential Learning*. C. Cooper (ed.). Theories of Group Process, London: John Wiley., London, 1975.

[10] G. A. Lewis, N. Nagappan, J. Gray, D. Rosenblum, H. Muccini, and E. Shihab. Report of the 2013 icse 1st international workshop on engineering mobile-enabled systems (mobs 2013): 12. *SIGSOFT Software Engineering Notes*, 38(5):55–58, Aug. 2013.

[11] L. Naismith, P. Lonsdale, G. Vavoula, and M. Sharples. Literature review in mobile technologies and learning. Technical report, University of Birmingham, 2013.

[12] T. K. O'Mahony, N. J. Vye, J. D. Bransford, E. A. Sanders, R. Stevens, R. D. Stephens, M. C. Richey, K. Y. Lin, and M. K. Soleiman. A comparison of lecture-based and challenge-based learning in a workplace setting: Course designs, patterns of interactivity, and learning outcomes. *Journal of the Learning Sciences*, 21(1):182–206, 2012.

[13] Routledge and K. Paul. *The construction of reality in the child*. Basic Books Inc., New York, NY, 1954.

[14] C. Scharff and R. Verma. Scrum to support mobile application development projects in a just-in-time learning context. *Proceedings of the 32nd ICSE*, pages 25–31, 2010.

[15] K. Schwaber. SCRUM Development Process. In J. Sutherland, C. Casanave, J. Miller, P. Patel, and G. Hollowell, editors, *Business Object Design and Implementation (OOPSLA'95 Workshop Proceedings, Austin, Texas)*, pages 117–134. Springer London, 1997.

[16] A. I. Wasserman. Software engineering issues for mobile application development. In *Proceedings of the FSE/SDP Workshop on Future of Software Engineering Research*, FoSER '10, pages 397–400, Santa Fe, New Mexico, USA, 2010. ACM.

Teaching Pervasive Computing to CS Freshmen:
A Multidisciplinary Approach

Natalia Silvis-Cividjian
Department of Computer Science
VU University
Amsterdam, The Netherlands
n.silvis-cividjian@vu.nl

ABSTRACT

Pervasive Computing is a growing area in research and commercial reality. Despite this extensive growth, there is no clear consensus on how and when to teach it to students. We report on an innovative attempt to teach this subject to first year Computer Science students. Our course combines computer science, engineering and social disciplines, such as: data acquisition, signal processing, control theory, machine learning, quality control and ethics. This unusual mix of disciplines is induced by a project-based learning approach. The project challenges the students to develop an assistive pervasive computing system that infers its context by using pattern recognition. This course is yearly taught to approximately 200 freshmen, and receives positive evaluations. Its main strength is that it motivates both non CS major strugglers, as well as top students. This paper describes the course design and its teaching artifacts, and shares our teaching experiences. We are confident that this teaching formula can be applied to other target groups, such as computer engineering, or even liberal arts.

Categories and Subject Descriptors

K.3.2 [**Computers and Education**]: Computer and Information Science Education – *Computer Science education.*

H.1.2 [**Information systems**]: Models and Principles-*User/Machine Systems.*

I.5.4 [**Pattern recognition**]: Applications–*Signal processing.*

Keywords

undergraduate CS education; pervasive computing; project-based learning; differentiation; assistive intelligent systems; Lego® Mindstorms NXT; Matlab®.

1. INTRODUCTION

Pervasive Computing, also known as Internet of Things or Ubiquitous Computing, is an emerging trend of seamlessly integrating computing in everyday objects.

It assumes a number of interconnected devices that interact both with users and with the environment, and deliver customized services in a context-aware manner [24]. We believe that students studying Computer Science (CS) should be exposed to the opportunities and challenges of this exciting field as early as possible in the curriculum.

However, teaching Pervasive Computing this early is not easy, for at least two reasons. First, teaching such a multidisciplinary field risks to overwhelm students with many, loosely-related topics, such as: embedded architectures, mobile devices, operating systems, sensor networks, context awareness, tagging, wearable computing, user interfaces, augmented reality, artificial intelligence, privacy, security, and so on [1, 12, 18, 25]. Second, there is a common belief that incoming freshmen first need to learn skills and how to *use* technology, before being able to *make* technology. As a result, Pervasive Computing is usually taught in more advanced, senior undergraduate or graduate-level courses.

The undergraduate CS curriculum at the VU University in Amsterdam, the Netherlands, features a Pervasive Computing course in the first semester of the first year. As educators we had to deal with two challenges. First, we had to mitigate the risk of overwhelming students with rich factual information that is hardly applicable in practice. Second, we had to target a large group of approximately 200 students, with a wide range of computing background, abilities and career interests, studying computer science, business informatics and lifestyle informatics. After having experimented for a few years, we have found a successful formula to teach Pervasive Computing to these freshmen. Our main goal was to give students the feeling that they can build realistic pervasive computing applications even before they learn how to program properly. The key decision to lead us to success was to drastically reduce the number of addressed topics. The result is a homogenous, multidisciplinary course, that motivates the entire targeted cohort. New teaching material to support this course has been developed, consisting of a syllabus, a set of practical tutorials and a collection of worked-out project examples.

In this paper, we will detail the course design strategy and the teaching artifacts we developed, and we will share our teaching experiences. The remainder of the paper is organized as follows. Our thoughts and choices prior to the course development will be outlined in Section 2, and we will describe the course in its final shape in Section 3. In Section 4 we will share our teaching experiences. Section 5 will discuss the contributions that inspired us in designing this course, and finally, we will outline our future plans in Section 6.

2. COURSE DESIGN

2.1 Course requirements

We started to design this course with the following requirements in mind: (1) The course should convey interesting and in-depth knowledge from the pervasive computing field. (2) Each student should feel comfortable with his/her level of prior computing knowledge (here we target especially non-major CS students) and at the same time, feel encouraged to learn more (here we target especially the top CS students). (3) Even after the course conclusion, the students should be eager to discover how surrounding computing systems work, and even dare to imagine novel solutions. We will use student questionnaires to evaluate our course by its completion, and assess whether we fulfilled the requirements specified at this stage.

2.2 Teaching approach

In this subsection we outline the ideas that eventually led to the actual course structure. Students join a university because they expect to develop useful knowledge and skills that empower them for the future. Traditional teaching tries to achieve this through lectures conveying theory, followed by assignments, to assess whether students assimilated the explained theory. Alternative teaching approaches have been proposed in the last decades, aiming to keep students better motivated and stimulate their active learning. Of these, we decided to use the project-based learning (PBL) approach that organizes teaching around a classroom project. The reason was the evidence of PBL effectiveness for long-term retention, skill development, and satisfaction of students and teachers [21]. We believe that an attractive project should be anchored in reality and appeal the entire targeted cohort. Therefore, we decided on a project that challenges students to design a pervasive system that improves the quality of life. We deliberately do not completely specify the project assignment, to encourage differentiation and give students the chance to brainstorm in small collaborative teams to generate a project idea. A part of the knowledge they need to implement this idea will be conveyed through lectures, mainly teaching principles that hardly change from one technology to the next. Practical lab sessions, tutored by a teaching assistant (TA) supplement these lectures, and offer an experimental ground. The students' freedom level is gradually increased throughout the course, by letting them discover the remaining knowledge through independent exploration driven by the project. During the project the students have to build and program a mockup of their product. We hope that these tangible results within a context will trigger their motivation [6]. At the project completion, the students report on their project, present and demonstrate their products in class, and reflect on their teamwork and learning process. Moreover, the students will realize while working on the project how complex it is to build a real, working pervasive system. This is the right moment to organize a community of learners by inviting a few guest speakers from industry and research to highlight their challenges and solutions in similar projects.

2.3 The scope

The essence of pervasive computing is that we are surrounded by hundreds of different types of intelligent systems. We hypothesized that addressing only a reduced subset of these systems can be the key to a successful course. Based on this speculation, we organized our teaching around one single theme, addressing only assistive pervasive systems that infer their context through pattern recognition. Examples from this category

are: intelligent vehicles, multi-modal wheelchairs, robotic social companions, and smart homes. For example, an intelligent car can prevent accidents by recognizing distraction patterns in a driver's brain activity. In a more extreme case of a driver-less car, the embedded computer system can recognize traffic signs, traffic lights or pedestrians, and notify, take control and act in critical situations. A multi-modal wheelchair can be controlled by recognizing brain activity patterns specific to certain mobility wishes of its disabled user (drive, turn left, turn right, slow down, speed up), or by recognizing spoken commands. A robotic companion offers comfort to its socially isolated users, but additionally infers mood and emotions by analyzing their body language. A smart home monitors the users' well-being, detects abnormalities in their behavior pattern, such as high blood pressure, insomnia, forgetfulness or fall incidents, and notifies caretakers and medical staff.

All these systems have some common features. They consist of the same building blocks: (1) a sensing module, that acquires a physical signal from the environment (video, audio, electroencephalogram (EEG), or acceleration), (2) a software agent, that reasons based on the sensed data and takes a decision, and (3) an actuation module, that executes this decision by activating/breaking the wheels, notifying the caretakers or generating an alarm. The software agent uses pattern recognition techniques to generate a decision. Moreover, these systems interact with people, and therefore raise ethical, privacy and safety challenges.

As a consequence, the topics we decided to cover are: signal acquisition and processing, sensors, actuators, control theory, classification, quality control and ethics. Guided by the principle "less is more", we discarded typical Pervasive Computing teaching topics such as: embedded architectures, sensor networks, tagging, user interfaces, security, which will be treated in other CS major courses. The drawback of this approach could be a lack of completeness, which we hope to compensate with a gain in course clarity, homogeneity and depth.

2.4 Learning outcomes

We expect that by the end of this course, students will be able to:

- Design a realistic pervasive computing system with a significant potential to benefit human lives. The system should acquire raw sensor data from the environment (video, audio, acceleration or EEG), process it, and use pattern recognition to take a decision and affect the environment accordingly.

- Build a mock-up demo and program a software agent to model this system.

- Identify safety and ethical problems related to their design.

- Work in a collaborative team and communicate the project progress through reports, presentations, in class demos and reflections on the learning process.

2.5 Lab infrastructure

As specified in subsection 2.4, the project challenges the students to design a pervasive computing system and to demonstrate a small part of its functionality in an as realistic as possible way. For this demonstration the students need to build a simplified, sensor-actuator system that simulates the real-world situation, and program a suitable software agent for it. All this happens in a lab. This subsection elaborates on the hardware and software choices made to provide this lab infrastructure.

2.5.1 Hardware

We decided to use the Lego Mindstorms NXT 2.0 robotic toolkit [16] to build the sensor-actuator system hardware. This is a widely used, robust, easy-to-program and not too expensive microcontroller-based system, featuring a standard set of sensors (light, color, sound, distance, touch) and a few actuators (servomotors, LEDS, loudspeakers). Blessed with mobility, scalability and versatility, this toolkit seemed perfect to model popular intelligent systems, such as cars, wheelchairs, wheeled robots, and other smart homes appliances.

especially among students who wanted and could write larger programs. In these circumstances, an attractive alternative became Mathworks Matlab [15], a relatively easy-to-learn scientific programming environment. A short analysis of its features revealed that: (1) it is possible to program Lego Mindstorms NXT systems with Matlab [19], (2) Matlab features powerful toolboxes for image/sound acquisition and processing, pattern recognition and machine learning, and (3) Matlab can be used to acquire raw data from a Neurosky brain headset, as reported in a recent BSc project in our group [11]. These facts promoted Matlab to a perfect programming environment for our lab.

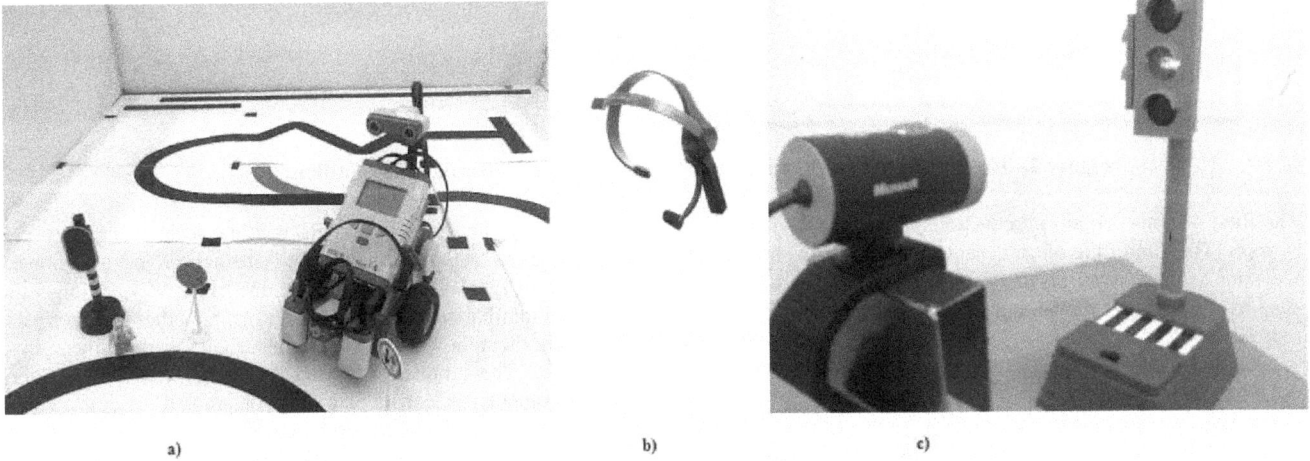

Figure 1. Examples of lab equipment used in this course: a) a Lego Mindstorms NXT vehicle in its mini-world, b) a Neurosky MindWave brain headset, c) a webcam positioned in front of a traffic light.

Nevertheless, we discovered that Mindstorms NXT platform alone has a limited capability to acquire raw sensor data and therefore could not completely satisfy our course goals. We overcame this shortcoming by purchasing Microsoft LifeCinema webcams with embedded microphones, for a high-quality image and sound acquisition, HiTechnic [13] accelerometers for activity and gesture recognition, and Neurosky Mindwave brain headsets to develop simple, but robust brain-computer interfaces [17]. Additionally, we built miniature physical worlds, featuring vertical walls and a floor marked with black lines, in which the vehicles can navigate. These mini-worlds can be populated with different objects, such as miniature traffic-lights and traffic signs, obstacles of different shape and colour, and Lego people. Figure 1 shows some examples of the equipement used in this lab.

2.5.2 Software

Next, we needed a suitable programming environment to control this sensor-actuator system. As many students couldn't program yet, we ruled out third party firmware based on a high-level Java or C programming languages, such as Lejos and RobotC. We also ruled out visual tools, such as Lego NXT-G visual programming environment. The reason was that although they reduce the hesitation of novice users to start programming robots, we experienced that this is only beneficial for small programming tasks. More specifically, icons wiring and a limited memory capacity of the Lego intelligent brick generated frustration,

3. COURSE IMPLEMENTATION

This section describes the course in its final shape. The course is given for a period of seven weeks, and consists of a series of lectures and practical labs, both driven by a project.

3.1 Lectures

In accordance to PBL principle, we inferred our lectures' content from a few running examples. Let us consider for demonstration a widely used example of an autonomous, driver-less car, and particularly its functionality to recognize traffic lights. This functionality is realized by an embedded computer system, whose behavior can be modelled by a reactive software agent, as illustrated in Figure 2. Basically, the sensor is a video camera that acquires an image of the road scene. This image is first interpreted by the software agent, and the status of the traffic light is classified. Consequently, the software agent takes a decision based on a combination of this status and a set of rules. The two rules used to take the decision in our example are: (1) "stop" the car when the spotlight is at the TOP and RED, and (2) "drive" when the spotlight is at the BOTTOM and GREEN. The decision is then translated into an action for the wheels actuators, that break or accelerate the car accordingly. The lectured topics cover all components featured in Figure 2 and are detailed in a syllabus we wrote specifically for this course.

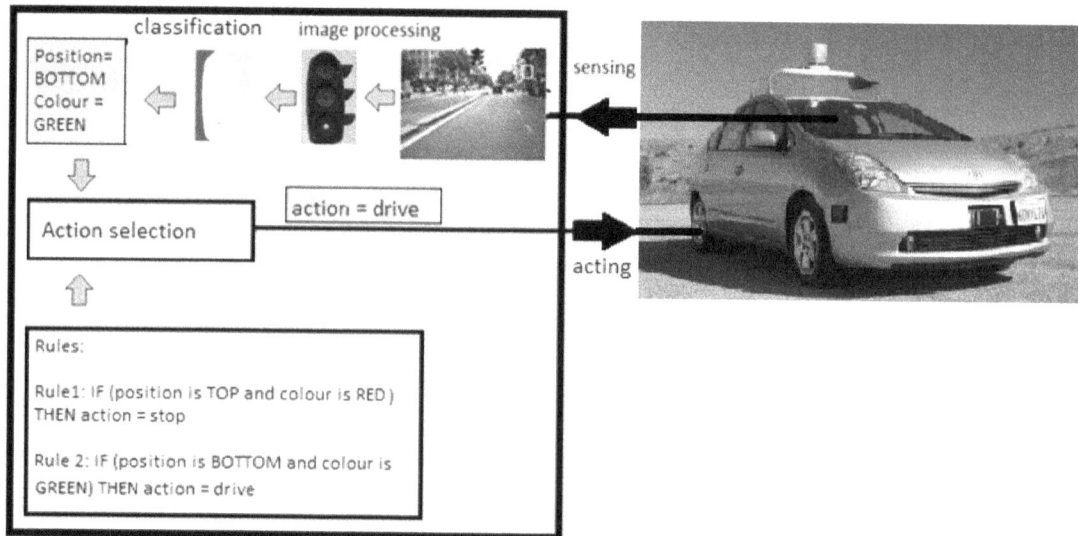

Figure 2. The architecture of a reactive software agent for traffic light recognition.

The first chapter is an introduction to pervasive computing systems. The aim of the second chapter **Signals,** is twofold. First, we want to emphasize the mapping between real-world signals, such as a 2D image of the street scene, and their mathematical representation in the computer, such as a numerical array. Second, we aimed to treat signal acquisition, necessary for example to obtain a road scene image in Figure 2. Chapter 3 treats **Image processing**, necessary in our example to improve the street scene image quality, and eventually identify the Binary Large OBject (BLOB) corresponding to the active traffic spotlight. For this object of interest, we have to determine its state, given by two features: its position (TOP, MIDDLE, BOTTOM) and colour (RED, YELLOW or GREEN). This means **Classification,** treated in the following chapter. To learn how to stop or to drive according to some rules and sensory input requires a chapter on **Control Theory.** Other types of pervasive computing applications use voice recognition, and this is why we included a separate chapter on **Audio processing.** Moreover, we describe a few techniques to assess whether this system functions as expected by its users. Finally, we ask the students to critically think whether building a driver-less car that recognizes a traffic light is indeed such a good idea. We identify the ethical implications of this gadget, like who is legally and morally responsible in case of a failure, if the traffic spotlight was red and the car did not stop in front of a pedestrian? This is the domain of **Quality control** and **Ethics.** The final chapter combines all these topics in an example of **Building a pervasive computing system.** The course ends up with a few guest lectures, given by researchers on pattern recognition, both from academia and industry.

3.2 Practical lab sessions

Students are encouraged from day one to think about their project. However, we consider it our duty to guide them during their first small investigating experiments. This is the reason why we first scheduled four practical lab sessions, labeled with Lab1 to Lab4. Here the students work in small groups, guided by a tutorial. Each tutorial begins with some short examples, followed by graded exercises.

In this way the students acquire confidence in technology and algorithms so that they can later estimate their project ambitions. The aim of **Lab1** is twofold. On the one hand, we want to get the students familiarized with Matlab, and on the other hand we want to teach them how to acquire signals and handle them in a computer. The rationale is based on our observation that very often, computer scientists take data for granted. In other words, the moment a computer scientist gets on stage, the data are "already there". This is probably because raw data acquisition from sensors is often regarded as a highly technical, typical engineering topic. However, we consider this topic essential for understanding and building a real pervasive computing system.

Lab2 teaches students how to program a Matlab controller (or software agent) to make the Lego robot follow a line, wander in a restricted are, and avoid or track an obstacle.

Lab3 treats video and audio processing. Students learn how to count similar objects on an image, and how to calculate the Fourier frequency spectrum and the spectrogram of different synthetized or acquired audio signals.

Lab4 is dealing with classification. Students use a simple rule-based classifier and experiment with different image and sound features. All lab sessions make intensive use of Matlab toolboxes for data acquisition, image and audio processing, pattern recognition and a third party toolbox for Lego Mindstorms control [20].

3.3 Project

After having completed their lab sessions, the students should be sufficiently prepared and informed to start with their project. As already mentioned, their challenge is to design a pervasive computing system that improves the quality of life, be it an existing system, such a voice-controlled wheelchair, or a novel one. The only constraint they have is to infer context through pattern recognition. We provide some simple worked-out classification solutions, such as traffic-light recognition in a simplified setup, shown in Fig. 1c). In this setup, the camera is fixed in front of a miniature traffic light. In this way, the traffic light in the acquired image always has the same size, making the recognition process easier. The project is very flexible and enables differentiation. Students are allowed to reuse our solutions, but also have the freedom to extend them, encouraged by the "The sky is the limit" principle. For example, they could think of mounting a camera on the driving Lego robot, and deal with the more complex case where the traffic light in the image varies in size. Or they could extend our example, by designing a car that recognizes traffic signs, instead of traffic lights. Moreover, they could improve their classification with a better algorithm, such as a neural network. According to our plans, outlined in subsection 2.2, we stimulate active learning by lecturing only on video and audio signals. In this way, students have the possibility to explore new types of sensors and signals, like for example EEG or acceleration. In any case, we advise students to plan realistically, and make use of best practice software engineering concepts, such as requirements prioritization, time management and planning, risk analysis, safety-driven design, testing and project postmortem analysis. The project ends with a report, a presentation and a demo.

4. EVALUATION AND REFLECTION

We implemented an introductory course on Pervasive Computing following the design strategy described in the previous section, and we have been teaching it for three years now. The evaluation forms filled in by students at the end of the course show that the requirements aimed in section 2.1 are met. Around 85% of the respondents found the course interesting, instructive and commensurate with their novice skills.

Table 1. Excerpt from the 2014 student evaluations

	--	-	+/-	+	++
Rate your interest in pervasive computing systems at the beginning of the course	4	11	28	13	6
Rate your interest in pervasive computing systems at the completion of this course	1	2	13	30	16
It was fun building realistic systems that work	1	2	7	19	33

Table 1 shows that the large majority of students experienced fun in building realistic systems that work. Moreover, a large increase in students' interest in pervasive computing systems was achieved. The positive evaluations we received are, in our opinion, not a result of one single silver bullet, but rather of a mix of decisions, summarized as follows: (1) reduce the number of covered topics, (2) adopt a project-based approach, (3) enable differentiation, (4) use an easy-to-learn and powerful mathematical software, such as Matlab, (5) use an easy-to-program robust robotic toolkit, such as Lego Mindstorms NXT, and (6) invest in additional, high-performance sensors, such as cameras, microphones, accelerometers, and EEG headsets.

From the teacher's perspective, we noticed that engineering topics, such as data acquisition, control theory, spectral analysis and safety analysis are quite unfamiliar for CS students, but nevertheless interesting. The students are motivated to dive into these topics, as soon as they realize that this will lead to tangible results.

Matlab and its powerful toolboxes proved to be an excellent choice for our course. However, care should be taken when using its out-of-the-box functions. For instance, it is extremely easy to get erroneous frequency calculations, caused by a wrong interpretation of the Fast Fourier Transform (FFT) function output.

We also noticed that some students experienced difficulties in mapping a real-world case into a simplified mock-up. Therefore, we emphasize that the steering role of the teacher and its TAs is paramount, especially at the start of the project.

Despite our worries that reducing the area of application to only pattern recognition based systems could lead to a limited number of applications, we were pleasantly surprised that this was not the case. The theme turned out to be broad and challenging enough for a seven weeks course and 65 collaborative groups. This is demonstrated by the diverse and well-working project products, such as a voice-controlled vehicle, an optical handwritten character recognizer, a brain-controlled assistant for immobilized patients, and a robot that accurately sorts balls of different color.

5. RELATED WORK

A few previously published teaching experiences inspired us during the course design process. Dan Chalmers describes a Pervasive Computing course, taught to 3rd year and master level students at the University of Sussex, UK [7]. This author also decided to teach a reduced number of topics (mobile and ad-hoc networks, sensors and data processing), but uses Phidgets as hardware platform for the practical assignments. Project-based learning has been used recently in teaching robotics, as reported for example in [19]. The Lego Mindstorms NXT platform has been extensively used in the last decade in teaching undergraduate courses on different computer science and engineering topics, such as programming, robotics, control theory, data acquisition, and intelligent systems [2, 3, 8, 9, 10, 22]. The combination Matlab - Lego Mindstorms has been experimented at the University in Aachen, for teaching engineering courses [4]. The toolbox they developed there has been extensively and successfully used in our course. Controlling Lego robots with a Neurosky brain headset has been explored by Vourvopoulos and Liarokapis in [22]. However, these authors used the Neurosky's proprietary software, and did not have direct access to the raw data of brain activity. Ethics concerns in pervasive computing and in particularly in robotics have been highlighted in [5, 14].

Although the ideas expressed in these references partially overlap with our vision, we believe that the course we developed combines a unique mix of disciplines, approaches and lab infrastructure.

6. CONCLUSION AND FUTURE WORK

We succeeded in successfully teaching Pervasive Computing to first year CS major and non-major students. We achieved this by designing a project-driven multidisciplinary course, that covers data acquisition, signal processing, control theory, machine learning, quality control and ethics. The novelty resides in combining these disciplines to address assistive pervasive systems that infer context through pattern recognition. As a result, these disciplines don't seem to be randomly chosen, but fit in a natural and logical way into a homogenous, clearly structured course. Matlab and its toolboxes proved to be a perfect programming environment for this course. However, we believe that Lego Mindstorms NXT robotic toolkit alone is hardly suitable to model pervasive computing systems. The platform has to be extended with better quality sensors, such as cameras, microphones, accelerometers and EEG headsets, in order to offer a versatile and performant solution.

Moreover, we believe that students should become aware that the Internet of Things is not equivalent to solely solving technical problems. A successful course on Pervasive Computing should create a balance between technical and user-related issues.

This course serves as cornerstone for future courses and graduation projects in our curriculum. We believe that this formula can be used to teach other target groups, such as computer engineering or even liberal arts.

In the future, we think about new sensing solutions, and we would also like to more actively engage the students in ethical discussions related to pervasive computing systems. Moreover, we believe that testing of assistive robotic agents is an interesting, though underestimated teaching topic, and therefore we intend to extend its presence in our course.

7. ACKNOWLEDGEMENTS

The author would like to thank Herbert Bos and Wan Fokkink for their encouragement and comments, and to Michel Klein for his idea to address ethical issues in this course.

8. REFERENCES

[1] Adelstein, F., Gupta, S.K.S., Richard III, G., and Schwiebert, L. 2004. *Fundamentals of Mobile and Pervasive computing*. McGraw-Hill Professional.

[2] Aufderheide, D., Krybus, W., Witkowski, U. 2012. Experiences with LEGO MINDSTORMS as an embedded and Robotics Platform within the Undergraduate Curriculum. In *Advances in Autonomous Robotics, Springer Lecture notes in Computer Science*, 7429, (2012), 185-196. DOI= 10.1007/978-3-642-32527-4_17.

[3] Barnes, D.J. 2002. Teaching introductory Java through LEGO MINDSTORMS models. In *Proceedings of the 33rd SIGCSE technical symposium on Computer science education.*(2002), 147-151. DOI= http://doi.acm.org/10.1145/563340.563397.

[4] Behrens, A., et al. 2010. MATLAB Meets LEGO Mindstorms - A Freshman Introduction Course Into Practical Engineering, *IEEE Transactions on Education,* 53(2), 306-317. DOI= 10.1109/TE.2009.2017272.

[5] Bohn, J., Coroama, V., Langheinrich, M., Mattern, Friedemann, Rohs, M. 2005. Social, economic, and ethical implications of ambient intelligence and ubiquitous computing. In *Ambient intelligence.* Springer, Berlin Heidelberg. DOI= 10.1007/3-540-27139-2_2.

[6] Carter, J., et al. 2011. Motivating all our students? In *Proceedings of the 16th ACM annual conference reports on Innovation and technology in computer science education – working group reports*, 1-18. DOI = http://doi.acm.org/10.1145/2078856.2078858.

[7] Chalmers, D. 2011. *Sensing and systems in pervasive computing*, Springer.

[8] Cruz-Martín A., et al. 2012. A LEGO Mindstorms NXT approach for teaching at Data Acquisition, Control Systems Engineering and Real-Time Systems undergraduate courses, *Computers & Education*, 59 (3), (2012), 974-988. DOI=10.1016/j.compedu.2012.03.026.

[9] Cuéllar, M. P. and Pegalajar, M. C. 2014. Design and implementation of intelligent systems with LEGO Mindstorms for undergraduate computer engineers. *Computer Applications in Engineering and Education,* 22, (2014), 153–166. DOI= 10.1002/cae.20541.

[10] Ferri, B.H., et al. 2009. Signal processing experiments with the LEGO MINDSTORMS NXT kit for use in signals and systems courses. In *Proceedings of the 2009 conference on American Control Conference*, 3787—3792.

[11] Fliert, C.R. van de, Brain controlled computer systems, BSc thesis, Computer Science Department, VU University Amsterdam, 2012.

[12] Genco A., Sorce S. 2010. *Pervasive systems and ubiquitous computing*, WITpress.

[13] "Hitechnic", *Online:* https://www.hitechnic.com

[14] Lin P., Abney K. and Bekey, George A., eds. 2012. *The Ethical and Social Implications of Robotics.* MIT Press.

[15] Matlab, the language of technical computing, *Online:* http://www.mathworks.nl/products/matlab/

[16] Mindstorms NXT Hardware Developer Kit, *Online:* http://mindstorms.lego.comhttp://www.mindstorms.lego.com

[17] "Neurosky", *Online:* https://www.neurosky.com

[18] Poslad, S. 2009. *Ubiquitous Computing: Smart Devices, Environments and Interactions*, Wiley.

[19] Qidwai, U. 2011. Fun to learn: project-based learning in robotics for computer engineers. *ACM Inroads* 2, 1, 42-45. DOI=http://doi.acm.org/10.1145/1929887.1929904.

[20] *RWTH* - Mindstorms NXT Toolbox for *MATLAB®, Online:* http://www.mindstorms.rwth-aachen.de/

[21] Strobel, J., van Barneveld, A. 2009. When is PBL More Effective? A Meta-synthesis of Meta-analyses Comparing PBL to Conventional Classrooms. *Interdisciplinary Journal of Problem-based Learning*, 3(1), 4.

[22] Tsang, E., Gavan, C., Anderson M. 2014. The practical application of LEGO® MINDSTORMS® robotics kits: does it enhance undergraduate computing students' engagement in learning the Java programming language?. In *Proceedings of the 15th ACM Annual Conference on Information technology education.* 121-126. DOI=http://doi.acm.org/10.1145/2656450.2656454.

[23] Vourvopoulos, A., Liarokapis, F. 2011. Brain-Controlled NXT Robot: Tele-operating a Robot Through Brain Electrical Activity. In *Proceedings of the 2011 Third International Conference on Games and Virtual Worlds for Serious Applications*, IEEE Computer Society, 140-143. DOI= 10.1109/VS-GAMES.2011.27.

[24] Weiser, M. 1991. The computer for the 21st century, *Scientific American*, 265, 66-75. DOI= 10.1038/scientificamerican0991-94.

[25] Yan, L. 2007. On Teaching Ubiquitous Computing, *IEEE Distributed Systems Online*, 8 (7), 4-. DOI=10.1109/MDSO.2007.45.

A Quantitative Study of the Relative Difficulty for Novices of Writing Seven Different Types of SQL Queries

Alireza Ahadi, Julia Prior, Vahid Behbood and Raymond Lister

University of Technology, Sydney, Australia

{Alireza.Ahadi, Julia.Prior, Vahid.Behbood, Raymond.Lister}@uts.edu.au

ABSTRACT

This paper presents a quantitative analysis of data collected by an online testing system for SQL "select" queries. The data was collected from almost one thousand students, over eight years. We examine which types of queries our students found harder to write. The seven types of SQL queries studied are: simple queries on one table; grouping, both with and without "having"; natural joins; simple and correlated sub-queries; and self-joins. The order of queries in the preceding sentence reflects the order of student difficulty we see in our data.

Categories and Subject Descriptors

H.2.3 [**Database Management**]: Languages – query languages.

General Terms

Management, Measurement, Human Factors.

Keywords

Online assessment; databases; SQL queries.

1. INTRODUCTION

The chief executive officer of edX, Anant Agarwal, has been quoted as saying that Massive Open Online Courses (MOOCs) will be the "*particle accelerator for learning*" (Stokes, 2013). A similar sentiment was expressed 30 years earlier. In her study of the usability of database query languages, Reisner (1981) asked rhetorically, "*Why experiment at all?*" before answering:

> ... *should not just using one's own judgment, or the judgment of some expert, suffice? ... Unfortunately, the computer scientist is not necessarily a good judge of the abilities of* [students]; *there are no experts whose opinions would be generally accepted, and if there were, they might not agree. ... A more cogent reason to forego judgment by peers or by an expert is that such judgment is not quantitative.*

With the same spirit as Agarwal and Reisner, in this paper we use data collected over eight years, from 986 students, to study quantitatively the relative difficulty our students had with completing seven different types of SQL queries.

ITiCSE'15, July 4–8, 2015, Vilnius, Lithuania.
Copyright © 2015 ACM 978-1-4503-3440-2/15/07…$15.00.
http://dx.doi.org/10.1145/2729094.2742620

2. BACKGROUND

Many reports have been published about online SQL tutoring/assessment tools. However, most of these reports focus on the functionality of the tool itself, or on how the system supports a certain pedagogical model (e.g. Brusilovsky *et al.*, 2008 & 2010; Mitrovic, 1998 & 2003; Prior *et al.*, 2004 & 2014). Those reports do not analyze the data collected by those systems to determine the difficulties students have with SQL queries.

From the literature, we identified only Reisner (1981) as a published systematic study of student difficulties with SQL queries. She found that the subjects in her study had difficulty recognizing when they should use "group by", but her subjects could successfully use "group by" when explicitly told to do so. Reisner's focus was on comparing SQL with three other query tools that were then seen as competitors to SQL. Thus, the "group by" case was her only discussion of an aspect of SQL that was troublesome for novices. Over 30 years later, we believe a new study is warranted that focuses on SQL and looks at multiple aspects of SQL.

We also found some papers in which the authors mentioned their intuitions about student difficulties, based upon their teaching experiences. These intuitions were mentioned briefly in the introductory/motivation sections of the authors' papers, before those authors went on to describe the architecture of their tutoring/assessment system. Kearns *et al.* (1997) and also Mitrovic (1998) mentioned "group by" as a problem, especially aggregate functions and the use of "having". They also mentioned as a problem the complete specification of all necessary "where" conditions when joining multiple tables. Sadiq *et al.* (2004) nominated the declarative nature of SQL as a problem for students as it "*requires learners to think sets rather than steps*" (p. 224).

3. ASSESQL

We collected our data in a purpose-built online assessment system, AsseSQL. It is therefore necessary to describe some aspects of how AsseSQL works, so that readers can assess for themselves the validity of our data. In this paper, we provide the briefest possible description of the system. Further details of AsseSQL, and how we used it to test our students, can be found in prior publications (Prior *et al.*, 2004 & 2014). The students in this study were all undergraduates at our university, studying Bachelor degrees in Information Technology or Software Engineering.

In the online test, students were allowed 50 minutes to attempt seven SQL questions. On their first test page in AsseSQL, students see all seven questions, and they may attempt the questions in any order. All seven questions refer to a database that is familiar to the students prior to their test.

Each question is expressed in English, and might begin, "*Write an SQL query that …*" A student's answer is in the form of a complete SQL "select" statement.

When a student submits a "select" statement for any of the seven questions, the student is told immediately whether their answer is right or wrong. If the student's answer is wrong, the system presents both the desired table and the actual table produced by the student's query. The student is then free to provide another "select" statement, and may repeatedly do so until they either answer the question correctly, run out of time, or choose to move on to a different question. If a student moves to a new question, the student may return to this question later.

The grading of the answers is binary – the student's attempt is either correct or incorrect. As there may be more than one correct SQL statement for a specific question, a student's SQL statement is considered to be correct when the table produced by the student's "select" statement matches the desired table. (Some simple 'sanity checks' are made to ensure that a student doesn't fudge an answer with a brute force selection of all required rows.)

Prior to taking a test, the students are familiarized with both AsseSQL and the database scenario that will be used in the test. About a week before the test, students receive the Entity Relationship Diagram (ERD) and the "create" statements for the scenario database. Note, however, that students are not provided with the data that will fill those tables, nor are they provided with sample questions for that database scenario. Several weeks before the actual test, students are provided with access to a 'practice test' in AsseSQL, which has a different scenario database from the scenario database used in the actual test.

4. A SCENARIO DATABASE: BICYCLE

One of the scenario databases that we use in the online SQL test is called "Bicycle", based on a database from Post (2001). This is the database from which most of the results described in this paper are generated. The Bicycle database is composed of four tables, as shown in the Entity Relationship Diagram (ERD) of Figure 1. A bicycle is made up of many components; each component can be installed in many bicycles. Each installed component on a bicycle is called a 'bikepart'. Just one manufacturer supplies each component, but one manufacturer may supply many components to the store, so there is a 1:M relationship between Manufacturer and Component. There is a self-referencing relationship in Component, as one component may be made up of many other components.

5. PRELIMINARIES TO RESULTS

5.1 A Wrong Answer versus No Attempt

Suppose for a given question, one third of students answered the question correctly, one third attempted the question but never answered it correctly, and one third never attempted the question – what should we consider the success rate to be? There are two options:

- 33%, if non-attempts are treated as incorrect answers.
- 50%, if non-attempts are ignored.

In the results presented below, we have supplied both options when reporting success rates for one of the seven types of questions. In cases where we are comparing two different types of questions, the issue arises as to whether a student did not attempt one of the two questions because the student knew they could not do it, or because they ran out of time. For that reason, when comparing performance between question types, we have applied the option where non-attempts are ignored.

5.2 Differences in a Pool of Variations

In the online test, students are presented with seven questions. Each question requires a different type of SQL "select" statement (e.g. a "group by", a natural join, etc). Each of the seven questions presented to a specific student is chosen at random from a small pool. In this paper, to avoid confusion between the actual questions presented to a student, and the questions in a pool, we henceforth refer to the questions in a pool as "variations".

In this section we discuss differences in success rates among variations within a single pool. To make the discussion more clear, we will focus on a concrete example – the four "group by" variations of the Bicycle Database. We chose this example as these four "group by" variations exhibited the greatest differences in success rate of any pool. The performance of each of these "group by" variations is shown in Figure 2.

In Figure 2, the line beginning "Baseline" provides the aggregate statistics when the data from all four variations are combined. That baseline row shows that a total of 986 students were assigned one of these four variations. Of those 986 students, 742 students successfully provided a correct answer, which is 75% of the total number of students. While 986 students is a large sample, if we collected data from another set of students, of similar ability, the success rate for that new sample is likely to be at least a little different. Equally, Figure 2 shows that the success rate for Variation 1 is 87% and 70% for Variation 2, but if we collected data from more students, how likely is it that the success rate for Variation 1 would drop below the success rate for Variation 2? To address those sorts of issues, we assumed a normal distribution of student abilities and estimated a 95% confidence interval for the success rate of the baseline and each of the four variations, using a well known statistical technique – the offset to the upper and lower bounds of the confidence interval is 1.65 × Standard Eror (SE), where the SE is estimated as:

$$ SE = \sqrt{\frac{Success\ Rate(1 - Success\ Rate)}{Total}} $$

For instance, the lower and upper bounds of the Success Rate for the baseline shown in Figure 2 are 72% and 78% respectively (i.e. the offset was estimated as being 3%). That confidence interval and the confidence intervals for all four variations are also represented graphically in Figure 2. The colors in the confidence intervals of the variations show the proportion of those confidence intervals that are outside the baseline confidence interval.

In Figure 2, the column headed "p-value" indicates the probability that the difference in the success rate of a variation from the baseline is due to the existing sample being atypical. Those p-values indicate that the success rates of variations 1 and 3 are likely to remain higher than the baseline, and variation 4 remain lower, if another sample of data was collected from an equivalent group of students. The column headed "improvement" shows the difference in success rate between each variation and the baseline. The 95% confidence interval shown in that "improvement" column was calculated the same way as above.

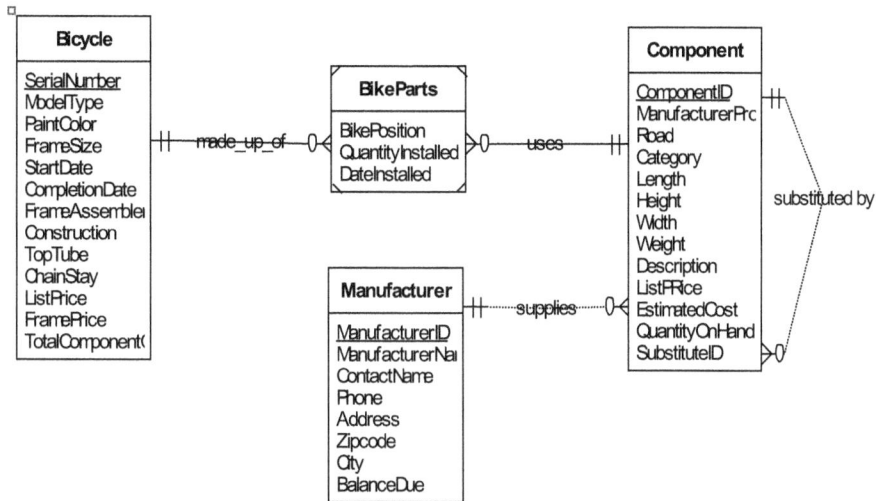

Figure 1. Bicycle Database ERD.

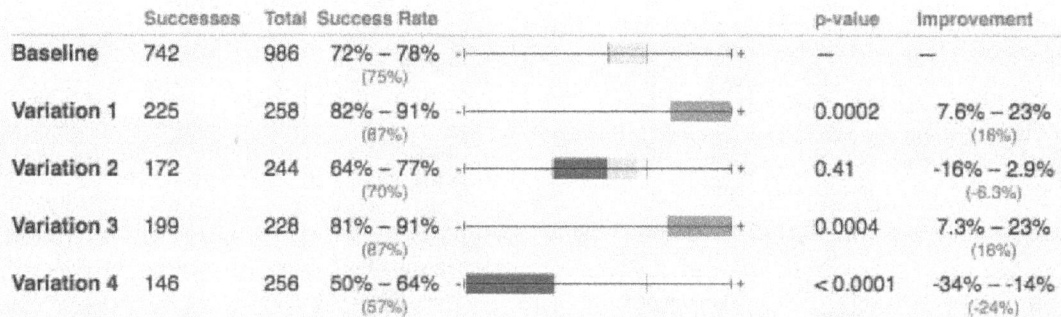

Figure 2. Variation in Success Rate for the "group by" pool.

The analysis illustrated in Figure 2 indicates that, even among questions considered to be variations that test the same fundamental SQL concept (i.e. "group by"), the success rates of the variations can be quite different. (Recall, however, that the "group by" example illustrated here manifested the greatest differences of any set of pool variations.) The reason for those differences is an issue we will return to in the "Results" section.

6. RESULTS

Table 1 summarizes the performance of students on the Bicycle database. In AsseSQL, the order in which the seven questions are presented on the computer screen to the students is fixed. (Recall, however, that students may attempt the questions in any order.) That same ordering is used in Table 1. Our choice of this ordering reflects our *a priori* intuition (i.e. when AsseSQL was built), of the relative difficulty of the seven query types.

As a general rule of thumb, based upon the estimation of the 95% confidence interval described in the previous section, the success rate percentages in Table 1 that differ by more than 5% can be considered to be significantly different. Table 1 shows that, in general, our intuition was correct – the success rate tends to fall from question type 1 to 7. Our intuition proved to be incorrect at the bottom of the table, as students were substantially less successful on self-joins then they were on correlated sub-queries.

Table 1. Query Success rates for various types of queries on the Bicycle database.

	Type of "Select" statement required in answer	No. of question variations	Success Rate: non-attempts wrong	Success Rate: non-attempts ignored	Non-attempts
1	Simple, one table	6	89%	90%	1%
2	"group by"	4	74%	75%	2%
3	"group by" with "Having"	4	58%	61%	5%
4	Natural Join	3	57%	61%	6%
5	Simple subquery	4	53%	58%	9%
6	Self-join	3	18%	24%	23%
7	Correlated subquery	6	39%	46%	16%

6.1 Simple Queries on a Single Table

We begin a more detailed analysis by considering the simplest queries in the system: queries made on a single table, using only the reserved words "select", "from", "where" and "and". Table 1 summarizes student performance on these queries for the Bicycle database (see row 1). For that particular database, there are six variations. AsseSQL randomly assigned one of these six queries to each student.

As Table 1 shows, 90% of the students were able to provide a correct query. That students did so well is not surprising, given the simplicity of this type of query, but it does establish that at least 90% of the students were able to understand the English-language instructions given by AsseSQL (which could not be taken for granted, since many of our students have English as a second language) and that 90% of the students are competent users of AsseSQL.

6.2 "Group By"

Table 1 shows that around 75% of students were able to answer a question that required "group by". However, as described in the method section, the "group by" pool exhibited the greatest differences in success rate of any set of variations.

One possible explanation for the difference in the success rate is the linguistic complexity of the four variations, since English is the second language of many of our students. However, Table 2 shows that there is no clear relationship between success rate and linguistic complexity, when linguistic complexity is estimated by the number of words in each variation. In fact, the variation with the lowest success rate also has the lowest word count.

Table 2. Success rates for the "group by" variations.

Variation	Success Rate: non-attempts considered wrong	Word count	Signal words
1	87%	17	"average"
2	70%	24	"average total"
3	87%	19	"average"
4	57%	16	"number of"

On inspection of the text of the four questions represented in Figure 2, another explanation suggests itself as to why variation 4 was substantially harder. This explanation is consistent with Reisner's (1981) observation that the subjects in her study had difficulty knowing when to use "group by", but they could successfully use "group by" when explicitly told to do so. With the exception of variation 4, all the variations use the word "average", which is a clear signal to the student that the aggregate function "avg" is required, and hence "group by" is probably required. In contrast, the use of "number of" in variation 4 does not transparently signal that a specific aggregate function is required. In variation 2 the use of "average total" may have confused students, as those words signal two possible aggregate functions, which perhaps explains that variation's middling success rate.

This analysis of differences in the success rates of the "group by" variations demonstrates the pedagogical value of looking at the data collected by our "particle accelerator" (i.e. AsseSQL). Because of this analysis, our teaching team was led to discuss exactly what it is that we are looking to test when we ask a "group by" question. Is our goal to (1) test whether a student recognizes

that "group by" is required, or (2) merely test whether a student can actually write such a query when they know that "group by" is required? If our goal includes the former, then variations 1-3 need to be reworded or replaced. If the latter is our goal, then variation 4 needs to be replaced.

6.3 "Group By" Queries with "Having"

Table 3 compares the performance of students on two types of "group by" queries – queries with "having" and queries without "having" (i.e. the queries in rows 2 and 3 of Table 1). Table 3 shows that these two types of queries are significantly correlated (p < 0.0001), but only moderately so (phi = 0.49). The 19% in the top right of Table 3 may understate how much difficulty students have with "having", as that is a percentage of all 986 students represented by the entire table. When the 186 in the top right cell is expressed as a percentage of the 742 in the top row, the figure is 25%. That is, a quarter of all students who could provide a correct "group by" without a "having" could not provide a correct "group by" that required a "having".

Table 3. Comparison of "group by" with and without "having". (N =986; phi correlation 0.49; χ2 test p < 0.0001)

	with "having" right	with "having" wrong
"group by" right	556 (56%)	186 (19%)
"group by" wrong	49 (5%)	197 (20%)

6.4 Natural Join and Self-join

Table 4 shows that the correlation between natural joins and self-joins is a moderate 0.41. The 38% in the top right of Table 4 is a percentage of all 986 students represented by that table. When the 371 in that top right cell is expressed as a percentage of the 599 students in the top row, the figure is 62%. That is, 62% of all students who could answer a natural join could not provide a correct self-join.

Table 4. Comparison of natural join and self-join. (N = 599; phi correlation 0.41; χ2 test p < 0.0001)

	self-join right	self-join wrong
natural join right	228 (23%)	371 (38%)
natural join wrong	9 (1%)	380 (38%)

Table 5. Comparison of simple and correlated sub-queries. (N =986; phi correlation 0.49; χ2 test p < 0.0001)

	Correlated right	Correlated wrong
Simple right	387 (39%)	189 (19%)
Simple wrong	71 (7%)	341 (35%)

6.5 Simple and Correlated Sub-queries

Table 5 shows, perhaps unsurprisingly, that the correlation between simple and correlated sub-queries is a moderate 0.49. The 189 (19%) in the top right of Table 5 is a percentage of all 986 students represented by that table. Expressed as a percentage of the 576 students in the top row, this figure is 33%. That is, one third of all students who could provide a correct simple sub-query could not provide a correct correlated sub-query.

6.6 Generalizing to Other Databases

We also collected data from students for two other databases, of similar complexity to the Bicycle database. Figure 3 compares the success rates for each query type in the Bicycle database with the success rates for those other two databases. (The numbers on the horizontal axis refer to the row numbers in Table 1.) All three databases show approximately the same pattern. The success rate for self-joins (point 6 on the horizontal axis) is the lowest success rate for all three databases. The only major difference between the three databases is that the "having" questions (point 3 on the horizontal axis) were especially difficult in "Bicycle2".

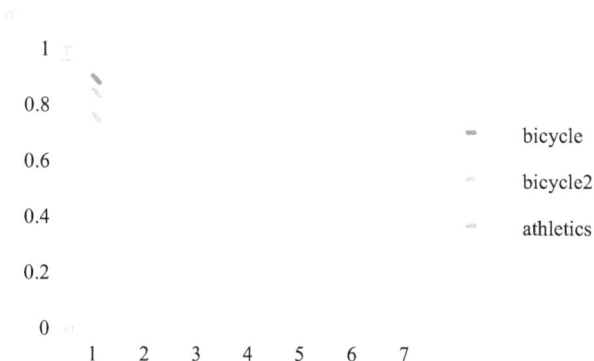

Figure 3. Success rates of the Bicycle database compared with two other databases.

6.7 Number of Attempts

In the "real world", nobody knows the desired result table before they write their query. In that sense, AsseSQL and most other online SQL testing systems are unnatural environments, as these systems provide the student with the desired table. We have therefore wondered whether a large portion of students may have answered questions correctly, particularly the easier questions, by brute force – that is, by making many attempts at the question, with quasi-random changes.

Analysis shows that this does not appear to be the case. For all three databases, the correlation (Pearson) between the median number of attempts at a question and that question's success rate is between -0.6 and -0.7, which is a strong negative correlation. The average number of attempts also exhibited a strong negative correlation between -0.6 and -0.7 for all three databases.

For the Bicycle database, this negative correlation is illustrated in Figure 4. The middle plot in that figure indicates the median number of attempts by the students who eventually provide a correct answer. A surprising aspect of Figure 4 is that students required relatively few attempts for the correlated sub-query. Note, however, that in this figure (and throughout this section of the paper) we are only considering students who eventually provide a correct answer. Thus, the figure merely shows that 39% of students (as shown in Table 1) who did provide a correct correlated sub-query were able to do so in relatively few attempts. The speed of those students on correlated sub-queries further emphasizes the difficulty of self-joins, since only 18% of the students could provide a correct self-join, half of whom needed 9 or more attempts, with a quarter requiring 16 or more attempts.

Figure 5 compares the median number of attempts needed to answer questions correctly in each of the three databases. All three databases show approximately the same pattern. There are two major differences across the three databases: (1) the number

of attempts for simple sub-queries (i.e. point 5 on the horizontal axis) is relatively low in the "Bicycle2" and "athletics" databases, and (2) the number of attempts for self-joins (i.e. point 6 on the horizontal axis) is relatively low in the "athletics" database.

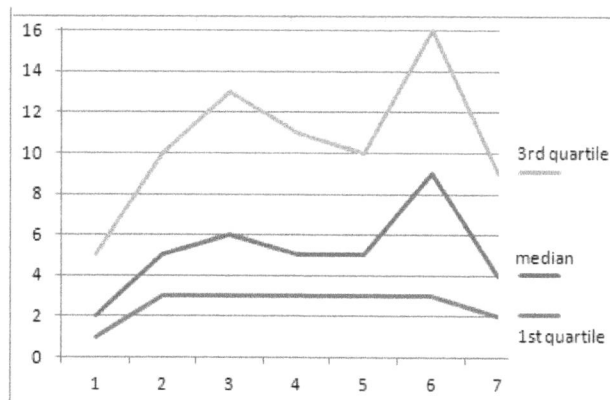

Figure 4. The distribution of number of attempts needed to answer each question type correctly in the Bicycle database.

In AsseSQL, we do not distinguish between attempts that are wrong because of a syntactic error, and attempts that are syntactically correct but return an incorrect table. It would be interesting to study data where that distinction is made.

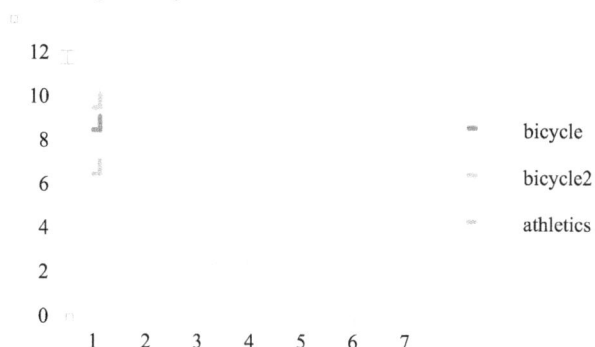

Figure 5. The median number of attempts needed to answer questions correctly in each of the three databases.

7. DISCUSSION

Many of our quantitative results are probably consistent with the intuitions of experienced database educators. It is important, however, that intuitions are tested. (After all, to return to Agarwal's metaphor quoted in the introduction, the Large Hadron Collider was expected to find the Higgs' Boson).

Perhaps our most surprising result – it was certainly a surprise to the authors of this paper – is that students found self-joins to be the most difficult of the query types we tested. Our intuition from many years of teaching databases was that correlated sub-queries were the most difficult type of query. Furthermore, we were surprised that our students found self-joins to be far harder than simple sub-queries, when these two types of queries can often be used interchangeably. A slightly surprising result was the extent of the difficulty of "having". While we suspected from experience that "having" troubled many students, we were surprised that a quarter of our students who could answer a "group by" that did not require "having" could not also correctly use "having".

Why are self-joins and (to a lesser extent) "having" troublesome for so many students? Our students have an equal opportunity to practice all the query types, so we are less inclined to believe that the trouble lies with insufficient practice. (But the prevalence in the database education literature of online tutoring systems may imply that the many educators believe that the problem is a lack of practice.) We are more inclined to believe that self-joins and "having" expose a conceptual problem for students. In the traditional teaching of SQL queries, the early emphasis is on the concept of a table. This leads to students thinking of operations on database tables as being much like the "real world" tables, such as spreadsheets. But self-joins and "having" have no common "real world" analog, so those operations are troublesome for many students. Reisner (1981) hypothesized a similar explanation, specifically about "group by". She wrote "*We suspect that ...* [students] *... adopt an "operations-on-tables" strategy ...* [which] *... does not work for the "group by" function, which requires users to think in terms of partitioning a table into subgroups*". As many database educators know, the foundational data structure for databases is the row, not the table, and database educators need to communicate that knowledge explicitly to their students. Furthermore, while we agree with Sadiq *et al.* (2004) that the declarative nature of SQL is a problem for some students, we suspect that it is especially a problem in the very early stages of learning SQL, and after students have begun to acquire that declarative understanding on simpler SQL queries, they are then taught "having", self-joins and correlated sub-queries, which do require a procedural grasp of SQL.

Part of the contribution of our work is the establishment of a method for studying the difficulties students have with SQL queries. Our principal methodological contribution is our focus on the relative difficulties students have with SQL queries. For example, of our students who could provide a correct simple sub-query, one third could not provide a correct correlated sub-query, but it would be absurd to claim that this same ratio (i.e. one third) is universal. Clearly, that ratio will vary from database to database, from institution to institution, and even semester to semester within an institution. What we are claiming is that, when a cohort of students manifests significantly different success rates at (for example) simple and correlated sub-queries, then it will be the correlated sub-query that exhibits the lower success rate. (And likewise for other pairs of query types.) Note that our claim is not negated by cohorts that do not display any difference in success rates on simple and correlated queries. Clearly, an immature or low achieving cohort will find both simple and correlated sub-queries to be difficult, while a mature or high achieving cohort will find both simple and correlated sub-queries to be easy. What our quantitative results suggest are developmental stages in learning SQL – for example, competence at simple sub-queries precedes competence at correlated sub-queries. (And likewise for other pairs of query types.)

As another methodological issue, we advocate that prior to studying the relative difficulty of two different query types, a third query type be used as a screening test. In our study, a simple select on a single table (i.e. row 1 of Table 1) served that purpose. The purpose of the screening test is to establish that students have an interesting minimum level of knowledge. In our case, since 90% of our students met the minimum requirement, and since students in AsseSQL can answer questions in any order, we elected not to remove that 10% from our analysis. However, in future studies, it may be useful to conduct the screening test as a pre-test, and remove from the data those students who fail the screening test, especially when the percentage of students who fail the screening test is much greater than 10%.

Our analysis of the four variations in the "group by" pool points to one interesting future research direction. In that pool, three of the four variations clearly signaled that a "group by" was required, while the fourth variation did not. It would be interesting to verify and extend upon Reisner's (1981) observation, that her subjects had difficulty recognizing when they should use "group by", but they could successfully use "group by" when explicitly told to do so – does that observation hold for any other query types?

8. CONCLUSION

At the back end of many internet applications there is a database. However, the prevalence and importance of databases is not reflected in the computing education literature. There certainly is education literature on databases, but nothing like the literature on (for example) learning to program. Furthermore, most of the existing database education literature focuses on the architecture of online tutorial and assessment systems. There is very little literature on what students find difficult about writing database queries. This paper is the first published quantitative study of the relative difficulty for novices of different types of SQL queries. This paper provides a quantitative and methodological foundation upon which further studies may be built.

9. REFERENCES

Brusilovsky, P., Sosnovsky, S., Lee, D., Yudelson, M., Zadorozhny, V., and Zhou, X. (2008) *An open integrated exploratorium for database courses*. ITiCSE '08. pp. 22-26. http://doi.acm.org/10.1145/1384271.1384280

Brusilovsky, P., Sosnovsky, S., Yudelson, M. V., Lee, D. H., Zadorozhny, V., and Zhou, X. (2010) Learning SQL Programming with Interactive Tools: From Integration to Personalization. *Trans. Comput. Educ.* 9, 4, Article 19 (January 2010). http://doi.acm.org/10.1145/1656255.1656257

Kearns, R., Shead, S. and Fekete, A. (1997) *A teaching system for SQL*. ACSE '97. pp. 224-231. http://doi.acm.org/10.1145/299359.299391

Mitrovic, A. (1998). *Learning SQL with a computerized tutor*. SIGCSE '98, pp. 307-311. http://doi.acm.org/10.1145/273133.274318

Mitrovic, A. (2003) *An Intelligent SQL Tutor on the Web*. Int. J. Artif. Intell. Ed. 13, 2-4 (April 2003), pp. 173-197.

Post, G.V. (2001) *Database management systems: designing and building business applications*. McGraw-Hill.

Prior, J., and Lister, R. (2004) *The Backwash Effect on SQL Skills Grading*. ITiCSE 2004, Leeds, UK. pp. 32-36. http://doi.acm.org/10.1145/1007996.1008008

Prior, J. (2014) *AsseSQL: an online, browser-based SQL skills assessment tool*. ITiCSE 2014. pp. 327-327. http://doi.acm.org/10.1145/2591708.2602682

Reisner, P. (1981) *Human Factors Studies of Database Query Languages: A Survey and Assessment*. ACM Comput. Surv. 13, 1 (March), pp. 13-31. doi.acm.org/10.1145/356835.356837

Sadiq, S., Orlowska, M., Sadiq, W., and Lin, J. (2004) *SQLator: an online SQL learning workbench*. ITiCSE '04. pp. 223-227. http://doi.acm.org/10.1145/1007996.1008055

Stokes, P. (2013) *The Particle Accelerator of Learning*. Inside Higher Ed. https://www.insidehighered.com/views/2013/02/22/look-inside-edxs-learning-laboratory-essay

Tangible Media Approaches to Introductory Computer Science

Evan Barba
Georgetown University
Washington, DC
evan.barba@georgetown.edu

Stevie Chancellor
Georgia Institute of Technology
Atlanta, GA
schancellor3@gatech.edu

ABSTRACT

Computing is an increasingly important component of many jobs and demand for computing skills is far outpacing the number of computationally literate workers available. Non-majors, adult learners, and other non-traditional students can potentially fill some of these positions. However, traditional CS education pathways do not currently address the unique needs of these students. New approaches to CS education that fit with the goals and lifestyles of non-traditional CS students are needed. In line with Computational Media approaches known to be successful with non-majors, we designed and implemented two graduate-level courses, one using a Pixelsense and the other using Arduino, to teach computational thinking, programming, and design skills. We compare findings from these two courses with specific focus on non-major graduate students, but including topics relevant for traditional CS educators, such as, the importance of choice of platform, structure of assignments, maintaining student motivation, and the impact of self-guided final projects.

Categories and Subject Descriptors

K.3.2 [Computer and Information Science Education]

General Terms

Design, Experimentation, Human Factors, Management

Keywords

Tangible Media, Non-majors, Computational Media, Late Bloomers, Physical Computing, Introductory Computer Science

1. INTRODUCTION

The need for computer science (CS) literacy in the workforce has grown rapidly and does not show any signs of abating. The U.S. Bureau of Labor Statistics projects that, by the year 2020, half of all Science, Technology, Engineering and Math (STEM) jobs will be in computing-related fields. Many of these new job opportunities incorporate computing into the work practices of previously unrelated fields. Journalists, public relations analysts, lawyers, advertisers, educators, and many others are expected to

ITICSE '15, July 04 - 08, 2015, Vilnius, Lithuania Copyright is held by the owner/author(s). Publication rights licensed to ACM. ACM 978-1-4503-3440-2/15/07 $15.00
http://dx.doi.org/10.1145/2729094.2742612

create computational artifacts and use computational tools for data analysis, information visualization, simulation, and more. Students in these disciplines are looking for introductory computing courses that authentically reflect the way computing is being adopted in those professions [3]. Moreover, workers already in those fields are finding that they need introductory computing courses to advance in their careers. These non-major and non-traditional "late blooming" CS students are a growing demographic in CS education that warrants our attention.

We describe two experimental approaches to teaching concepts in computer hardware, software engineering, and interaction design to graduate and undergraduate students in an interdisciplinary educational context. We designed and taught two courses. The first was "Tangible and Embodied Computing" (TEC), a course that introduces computer programming topics and user interface design in the context of a Microsoft Surface v1 (Pixelsense) tabletop computer. The second was "Interaction Design Electronics and Semantics" (IDEAS), a course using a physical computing approach that included Arduino and electronics in addition to programming and design instruction. We consider both of these courses to fall in the category of "Tangible Media" [6,7]. Our courses represent the extremes of Tangible Media. The experiences in TEC couple everyday non-computational objects to processes and entities in the virtual world and therefore heavily emphasize the virtual. IDEAS, in contrast, emphasized the physical by embedding digital sensors and actuators into physical artifacts. Both TEC and IDEAS used a constructionist learning approach in which students combined physical objects and software to create interactive artifacts. We compare the effectiveness of these approaches for learning basic concepts in computational thinking for a small sample population.

We found that students were able to acquire programming and design skills and responded favorably to each course. Students in both courses also demonstrated soft skills associated with communication and problem solving. Each course had its own benefits and drawbacks for students. TEC was more difficult with its expectation of coding and programming, but students reported that they had more insight into computing as a professional practice. IDEAS was received better by the students but provided students less marketable skills despite learning some of the same core principles of computational thinking. Our discussion includes insights into student motivations, different learning styles, the effectiveness of tutorials, and teaching "code as a component" of larger multifaceted project. In addition to findings that are generally relevant to introductory CS courses, we identified a number of factors that make the population of adult learners we observed in our studies unique and suggest areas of future research relevant to this demographic.

2. BACKGROUND AND RELATED WORK

The majority of research in introductory CS courses focuses on undergraduate education and address issues of pedagogy, language selection, and course assignments [11]. The target of most of these courses is undergraduate CS majors, students who are expected to continue building the foundations of computational literacy well into their undergraduate careers. Notable exceptions are courses created explicitly for non-majors that take a "Media Computation" approach to introductory CS [2]. That research shows that introducing computing as new media is effective for non-majors and promotes more engagement and learning. We hypothesized that adult learners might also benefit from a Media Computation approach that is specifically focused on Tangible Media. This focus on Tangible Media as a subset of Computational Media came directly from polls of student interest conducted by our department, which showed that learning technologies associated with "Making" and the "Internet of Things" were highly desired by our incoming students.

The interdisciplinary graduate program where our courses were taught is one example of a growing number of programs that offer students the opportunity to do interdisciplinary graduate work around the production and consumption of technology. Our program caters to students with backgrounds in the humanities and social sciences that want to integrate the use of information communications technologies into their existing skillsets. Typically this is done to improve their career outlook by making them more competitive applicants for jobs and doctoral programs. Most of our students begin with little to no experience in programming but are sophisticated and critical consumers of digital technologies. Although they are more highly educated and often have more work experience than undergraduate students, they are similar to undergraduate non-majors in terms of their level of hands-on experience in CS. Classes in this department are small (enrollment is capped at 15 students) and the department often attracts advanced undergraduate students from other areas. For these reasons we chose to base our course designs in a Media Computation approach that leveraged students' expressed interest in working with Tangible Media.

Tangible Media as an introductory approach to CS has been discussed before. However, these efforts either focus on primary and secondary CS education [4], on informal settings [8], or on learning topics outside of CS [5,10]. The most typical approach is one in which computer code is physically embodied in some modular object and then combined and recombined to create different behaviors. This is an elegant and effective approach for elementary school and young adults, although some evidence suggests that they can introduce problems around knowledge transfer to more traditional domains [1,9]. The graduate students we work with have demonstrated the capacity to learn more sophisticated techniques and are specifically asking for skills and knowledge that is directly transferrable to workforce skills; therefore, more simplistic approaches that reduce the complexity of computational concepts are not appropriate for our context. Still, there is much that is applicable. Namely, that students' intuitive understanding of the physical world is an effective gateway to a more sophisticated understanding of the digital virtual world. This supposition proved true in both TEC and IDEAS.

Some of the key concepts of the Computational Media approach noted in [2] are listed below, summarized in our own language:

- authenticity and relevance: how closely the classroom experience matches real world practices

- creativity: how well the class supports the creation of personally expressive and meaningful artifacts
- tailoring: how closely the course matches individual student needs and wants
- motivation: whatever it is that keeps students engaged for the duration of the course

We hypothesized that these broad concepts would also apply to our students, and we designed our specific learning objectives (bolded below) for each of these courses to reflect these concepts. We forced students to **learn to ask effective questions** with authentic sources of information like classmates, instructors, online forums, or search engines. We gave students **relevant and authentic technology** in the Arduino and Pixelsense. Both syllabi emphasized the importance of **learning generalizable skills and concepts** that could extend to other domains. We gave them the opportunity to be creative by designing their own projects and insisted that they **become comfortable with an iterative design methodology** that is commonly employed in software engineering and other design-related work. Students filled out a pre-class survey (TEC) or a blog post (IDEAS) detailing prior experience with design and programming for purposes of later assessment, but which also asked them to provide their own goals for the class and we referred to and assessed these goals frequently during our one-to-one interactions with individual students. By fostering an attitude of ownership over their projects, we hoped that students would remain motivated to learn essential concepts and practices in CS that could transfer to their career goals later.

The courses were taught by the same instructor and teaching assistant (instructors hereafter) and combined focused tutorials and homework assignments with longer, student-driven projects. Tutorials were started in-class under supervision and were finished after class as homework. Students proposed ideas for their final projects and the instructors helped scale and develop timelines for each. Those who demonstrated a better grasp of the material in their tutorials were encouraged to develop more robust final projects. Evaluation of students' performance in both classes was also done similarly. Smaller programming and design projects came with a list of criteria needed to receive high marks. Final projects were demonstrated to the class. We gathered data about student experiences in both courses for purposes of formative assessment. Learning progress toward the stated goals was evaluated through course blog posts, interactions with the instructors, recorded conversations, and grading of the projects. Students were required to submit documentation alongside their programs. TEC also had a post-course focus group conducted by an independent external evaluator.

3. COURSE OVERVIEWS AND RESULTS
3.1 TEC

TEC was taught in Fall 2013 to eight students, one undergraduate and seven graduate students, five men and three women. Only the undergraduate had any previous programming experience. The structure for TEC consisted of six short tutorials to guide the students through programming tasks specific to the Pixelsense environment, three homework assignments that extended these tutorials to more complex problems including a four-function calculator, and a final project defined by the student and approved by the instructor.

3.1.1 Pixelsense Platform

There were several reasons we chose to use the Pixelsense table. First, it is an "authentic" real-world device that is not a sandbox for beginners. Furthermore, the touch and gesture recognition capabilities are now familiar to most users and common across mobile and tablet platforms, while the large size, tabletop orientation, and object tracking capabilities are unique enough to be cutting-edge. The biggest downside to the Pixelsense table is its lack of online developer resources. We did not anticipate this in our design phase because of the availability of Microsoft's own documentation and community forums; unfortunately, these were often incomplete and not appropriate for beginners. To compensate, we created a course blog as a repository of knowledge for our class. Although students used the blog to ask a few questions, instructors almost always gave the answers.

3.1.2 Assignments

TEC's tutorials included topics in basic programming (syntax, control flow, etc.), object-oriented and event-driven design principles (encapsulation, polymorphism, event listening), user interface design (affordances, visual hierarchies), and API and library management. The first three tutorials focused on XAML and the remaining tutorials focused on C#. Each tutorial took an incremental approach with detailed descriptions of programming concepts, screenshots of expected output, and code snippets. We designed the progression so that students would learn how to create simple interface elements through XAML and carry this knowledge with them into the development of C# "backcode."

Students completed tutorials in class after a 45-60 minute lecture on the topic, giving them around 90 minutes of class time for each. Unfinished tutorials were assigned as homework to allow slower students to catch up, and faster students often used this time to add flourishes to their projects, suggesting that they were engaged and motivated with the work. For example, some students added additional components and functions to the calculator project and added design and interaction components (like 3D printed objects) to their final projects.

The similarity of XAML to HTML and XML make it both familiar to beginning students and relevant beyond the class. Nearly all the students were able to complete the first two tutorials in class, and even those who struggled were able to complete them as homework with some assistance given during office hours. However, the early burst of confidence in programming in XAML lulled students into a false sense of security; specifically, students believed that C# would be as simple or as quick to write as XAML. One student described the transition between XAML and C# as "a brick wall a month in."

The use of the common and powerful C# programming language was clearly relevant outside the course and students were excited to know that what they were learning could be applied across any Microsoft platform. But the relationship between XAML and C# also proved to be a major stumbling block. The concept of "binding" interface elements to C# was troublesome for all students. Students had difficulty abstracting behavior away from the visible interface elements and into C# program logic. As one student noted, "I felt like everything that could do something should be on the screen." Despite integrating the two languages incrementally in the tutorials and the homeworks, most students initially could not see how the two were related. Although most students were eventually able to grasp this abstraction, a few did not, and this was a continued source of frustration as they tried to move forward.

Each student was responsible for two short homework projects that directly extended the skills taught in the tutorial by asking them to reimplement the design patterns used in the tutorial in a different context. The majority (5 of 8) of the students completed these with few problems. However, most had a superficial understanding of the concepts and techniques involved and when they were required to transfer these concepts onto different programming elements (from a button in the tutorial to a slider in the homework, for example) some students struggled despite having successfully completed the tutorial. We came to understand that this was because students were unable to see the larger pattern. They were daunted by the idea that a slider behaved differently than a button, even though both are implemented in the exact same way (only a change of name and one additional variable was needed).

The last homework was a small project designed to integrate the six tutorials and related concepts together by programming a digital four-function calculator. This is where we saw a clear divergence in student aptitude. Some completed the calculator in a timely matter, some completed it with sloppy results and errors, and two students were unable to complete it for many weeks. Once the class moved on to final projects, these students had to split their attention and became overwhelmed with the amount of work left for them. One student asked for an incomplete in the course so that they could finish the work over the next semester.

Another interesting finding was how different aspects of programming confused students. For some, syntax was difficult but overall programming structure, including object-oriented concepts and event handling, were intuitive. Still others were fine with syntax, control flow, and structure but struggled with softer skills such how to iterate and improve code incrementally or ask effective questions. Success in one of these skills could not be predicted by early success with homework or the midterm project. Students who submitted homework assignments early and showed strong aptitude for programming syntax and language were just as likely to struggle later in the semester as lagging students. One student completed all of the homeworks rapidly and even became a resource for others but could not decompose their final project into manageable pieces and struggled for the latter half of the semester. These individual differences are often hidden in larger classes where everyone proceeds in lock step. Identifying these individual differences in learning specific topics and developing tailored techniques match is an area we have identified as having tremendous value to CS education at all levels.

In an attempt to let students manage their workload with their own schedules and give students agency in their learning, we allowed students to work at their own pace while completing assignments. Deadlines were strongly suggested, but flexible. The majority of our students were graduate students, and we expected them to have the maturity to manage their time. This approach met with mixed results. Students that were engaged made appropriate progress on their homework and mini-projects and submitted assignments at the recommended deadlines. These students received quick feedback on their work that they could then apply to future work. However, struggling students could put off the discomfort of working through difficult concepts until it was far too late for instructor feedback to be incorporated into their work. Rather than creating a relaxed atmosphere for cooperative work between students with different skillsets, this approach allowed students to diverge onto their own paths and rarely interact students outside their skill level.

3.1.3 Final Projects

In the last eight weeks, the pedagogical style of the course shifted to a studio model to give students the time and support needed to work on their final projects. Final projects included a "whack-amole" game, a fantasy football draft application, and an application integrating geo-tagged Twitter posts with a map and physical objects. TEC students reported that they enjoyed the process of planning, designing, and coding the final project. One student said, "Getting 'sent in' to just accomplish our projects and do it ourselves - it's been very hands on - this is DEFINITELY the way to do this!" Another said, "After this class, although it was super tough, I feel more confident in my abilities to accomplish things, especially in technology." These statements suggest that what was learned was not programming content but softer skills and a deeper understanding of what is involved in CS.

Overall, five of the eight students were able to produce completed final projects. Of those five, three were at a level that would be expected of high-quality introductory CS students. However, these successes were hard-fought and took a significant toll on the instructors as well as the students. Each student's project was individually defined and scoped and each student had their own distinctive areas of difficulty. The emerging instructional style was a continuous loop of creating ad-hoc individualized scaffolds appropriate for each student. As students reached an unsolvable problem, they would approach one of the instructors who would need to context shift into the project, identify the reason for the difficulty, and devise and explain a solution for the student. Sometimes this was straightforward, like incorrect syntax or scope, and other times it required real debugging that a novice programmer could not be expected to perform on their own. Even when students tried to find solutions online to their problems, results were so scattered for the Pixelsense table that students could not proceed. By the time every project had been troubleshot, the students would present a new round of problems. This close mentoring was exhausting both for instructor and student and would be difficult to scale to larger class sizes. Furthermore, it privileged making progress toward the final goal over a student's self-discovery of a solution, and possibly hampered learning.

3.2 IDEAS

IDEAS was offered in Spring 2014 to fifteen students, two undergraduate and thirteen graduate, seven women and eight men. Three students from TEC enrolled in IDEAS. None of the students in IDEAS had experience with electronics or prototyping but four had previous programming experience. With nearly twice the enrollment, it was obvious from the beginning that something about IDEAS was more attractive to this population of students.

3.2.1 Assignments

IDEAS took a physical computing approach that taught both electronics and programming through two progressions of tutorials and projects. As with TEC, students completed tutorials in class after a 45-60 minute lecture and unfinished tutorials were completed as homeworks. The first progression of three tutorials reinforced the basics of electronics and prototyping. Topics included how to use a multimeter to test components, how to draw a circuit diagram, and how to assemble parts on a breadboard. Students found these straightforward and interesting and were engaged throughout, but also showed great apprehension about working with electricity. Most of the students completed these tutorials easily.

The first group of tutorials culminated in a longer project where the students assembled an Atari Punk Console (APC).[1] The APC is a beginner electronics project that produces sounds similar to an

Atari 2600 gaming system. Students were also required to prototype an external housing for their APC that made it a suitable intervention for a particular task or environment. Completed projects included a series of flex resistors in a box to make the APC act as a windchime, adding a thermistor to make a boiling water alarm, and attaching the APC to the back of cardboard character for use at sporting events.

Despite having successfully completed the tutorials and reporting comprehension of the lecture material, almost every student had tremendous difficulty with the APC project. This is because students could not comprehend the wiring diagrams. While the tutorials had them assemble components in a stepwise manner with diagrams, the jump to a more complex diagram and lack of incremental instructions increased the difficulty too quickly. Although students could eventually assemble the APC it took twice as long as expected. They did, however, do excellent design work, creating interesting and functional external housings using a range of materials.

Whereas the lack of tutorials for the Pixelsense required us to create them from scratch for TEC, electronics tutorials are plentiful and we hoped that having a variety of explanations and perspectives would aid in student learning. We directed students to tutorials from Instructables[2] and similar sites for the initial electronics projects and the tutorials supplied on the Arduino website for six Arduino programming tutorials, but students were encouraged to use whatever they could find on their own. Every student was given an Arduino Uno prototyping platform to use for the class, and we supplied them with additional electronic components as needed. Despite these tutorials being more thoroughly vetted than the ones we created in TEC, students had similar difficulty seeing the broader patterns being introduced. Although they did get a sense of what the Arduino was capable of, and exposure to programming concepts like variables and loops, they also showed little ability to transfer this knowledge into new contexts. We had to continually refer them back to relevant tutorials and in many cases had to explain why it was relevant to the current situation.

After completing the tutorials, students defined a final project in consultation with the instructors. Students could work in teams to develop a new project or working individually to iterate on their APC project. Our choice to allow groups to form was a direct consequence of our experience in TEC, where we ended up tutoring students on individual projects. IDEAS had more students; requiring individual projects would have made the same level of assistance impossible. IDEAS had the same number of projects as TEC, but the workload was less taxing on the instructors and less frustrating for the students. This was partly a reflection of the number of people working on a project but was also due to the amount and quality of the online assistance. Students had many examples to draw from and it was likely that someone had already encountered problems similar to their own and posted solutions on an online forum. In the end, the students completed projects of equal complexity with far less assistance.

The availability of online sources introduced one complication that we did not foresee, but also provided an authentic learning opportunity. By relying on tutorials, we implicitly suggested that following a tutorial was an acceptable final project rather than creating something new and innovative. Three student groups

---

[1] http://en.wikipedia.org/wiki/Atari_Punk_Console

[2] http://www.instructables.com

took this approach, and we allowed it because creativity and originality were not stated as grading criteria. Students who chose this path still had difficulties and it led to some interesting observations. Parts do not always match completely, code is not always updated and maintained, pictures and descriptions are not always accurate. Although they were not working on projects they defined themselves they encountered the same problems that teams working on original projects did. Interestingly, they did not appear any less motivated. This suggests that motivation is not necessarily tied to creativity and ownership over a project and the idea of "measuring up" is a powerful motivator as well. These students were motivated by not wanting to feel a sense of inadequacy. The only real problem with this approach was that students ignored solutions that deviated from the prescribed steps. One student tried to install a software MIDI converter used in the project tutorial and became so preoccupied with making it work that they didn't think to try another converter until the instructors urged them do so. Students who reproduced projects they saw online still learned how to troubleshoot electronics and debug code. In fact, because they did not start from scratch with their own idea they learned a valuable and authentic skill. Many jobs require new employees to enter a project that has been ongoing for years or to adapt existing work to suit new purposes.

Students who designed their own artifacts went through the entire design process and we believe generally learned more in the course regardless of the quality of their final projects. One group's project integrated pressure sensors into a seat cushion to alert sitters when they had been sitting for too long by playing an alarm. Although this product exists already, the students prototyped everything themselves in multiple iterations, found relevant code snippets and additional hardware, and were able to integrate and patch together the code to produce the logic they wanted.

In general students in IDEAS remained motivated throughout the semester, largely because they felt the projects were producing polished artifacts that they could show their friends. They felt great pride in showing their creativity. Gaining social capital through presenting polished artifacts proved to be a powerful motivator.

4. COMPARISON

IDEAS was the more popular course from the start. Nearly twice the number of students in TEC enrolled in IDEAS. Students cited various reasons why they were more interested in the class. The perceived accessibility of the subject matter, "design" versus "computing," appealed to more students even though students learn design skills and computing skills in both classes. Students also reported that IDEAS seemed like an easier class. Several of the students in IDEAS told us they had considered taking TEC, but the topic seemed too hard and out of reach for them. With its focus on building artifacts, IDEAS was thought to be easier because it appeared more like "arts and crafts."

Although they were aware that C# is a widely used programming language, TEC students' initial enthusiasm waned when they realized it would take more than a single class to become proficient. Combined with the physical immobility of the Pixelsense table, students were left feeling like the technologies involved were specialized and inaccessible, a feeling that was reinforced by the lack of prominent online resources. In contrast, there are sites that offer technical assistance and discussion of electronics projects. These projects appear in places that are not dedicated solely to these technologies (Instructables covers topics outside of electronics), so these skills appeared more broadly

supported and relevant outside a niche audience. The design and prototyping skills in the IDEAS curriculum are attractive to students because they are trending as part of a national discussion surrounding "innovation" and "Making," and students felt like they were learning things relevant to possible future careers that were more creative and enjoyable. The skills learned in TEC were perceived as more constrained and device-specific despite being more relevant to the workforce.

Still, despite the perceived inflexibility of the TEC coursework, students also recognized that they had an authentic programming experience, learned to become conversant with programmers, and got a better understanding of, and respect for, professional programmers. Increasing general awareness of how authentic computing is done in the real world was actually quite a useful skill, as many of these students were expected to communicate with more technical personnel in their jobs. One student told this story, "At work the other day, one of the designers, I saw them working with code and programs, and I thought - I know what you're doing! I could look at what you're working on, and probably understand it!" This is the essence of computational literacy.

4.1.1 Code as a Component

One of the major differences between the technologies used in TEC and IDEAS is the role of code. In TEC, code is central. The end product is a computer program that includes physical components that have specific meanings in the context of the program. One student used playing cards, another used spoons, and another created a 3D print of targeting reticle as an interface. These helped bridge the divide between physical and virtual; however the projects were still perceived as "computing projects," and, to their dismay, the students felt more like programmers than designers.

In IDEAS this was largely reversed. Students' projects ended up as physically distinct forms with unique characteristics and the code was hidden away as one of the components that make the object behave. This helped take some of the pressure off of the students to learn programming. Objects could behave somewhat erratically as they debugged the code but still appeared "finished" because they had a physical manifestation. Students could take them home, talk about them, and point to the various components as evidence of their work and ingenuity even if it didn't function. When Pixelsense programs crashed, students were dismayed that the overall impression was of a non-working artifact with little visible evidence of their efforts.

The major advantage to IDEAS, however, was in students' ability to reason about how to achieve the behaviors they wanted. Students were better at identifying the logic of physical interactions than the logic of their more abstract tabletop applications. For example, the alerting seat cushion required integration with additional software for data-logging, timing, and audio playback, which were more complex than many of the tabletop applications created in TEC. These students independently arrived at the notion that their artifact needed to have different "states" to handle the different combinations of sensor input and audio output. The logical flow of the program followed the logical flow of their physical interaction and they could repeatedly perform these actions in the physical world to think through the different conditions that would arise in the use of their artifact. There was real learning of computational thinking, abstraction specifically, that is arguably more valuable than understanding the intricacies of C#.

4.1.2 Soft Skills

The most relevant soft skill that students learned was how to properly ask for help, from both the instructors and from online sources. There was marked improvement throughout both courses in the vocabularies students used to describe the problems they encountered. These improvements were more pronounced in TEC. Programmers build up a sense of how to ask a good question and identify a relevant answer over time. Even knowing how to properly search to get relevant results took considerable time to master. At first, students would use vague and unspecific language. For example, referring to variables as "numbers" instead of "ints" or "floats." As they realized these differences carried meanings, they paid more attention to their language and would use the more specific name. Developing these softer skills are a part of CS literacy that is often overlooked and is particularly salient for students in this demographic who are often asked to be liaisons between programmers and clients.

4.2 Learning from Tutorials

We have already mentioned the similar results in the two classes regarding the effectiveness of tutorials, and we find this point indicative of a larger problem that needs more study. Our observations around the effectiveness of tutorials have led us to suggest the following: tutorials are best treated as a kind of scaffolding rather than a primary source and, when used, should not be scaffolded any further. This untested hypothesis needs deeper investigation, but it raises an issue of critical importance to both online and classroom settings beyond CS education alone.

When students develop projects on their own, there is no known pre-existing solution. This forces them to synthesize information into a solution of their own devising. Scaffolding this process of design with multiple tutorials that reveal parts of the solution is a useful pedagogical tool in this case. Students are still learning to identify problems, search out, sort, and map possible solutions, and integrate knowledge. Tutorials serve to support learning specific techniques when students have independently decided they need that support. Projects in which students had an original idea, and assembled a new artifact without a roadmap often used tutorials this way and were the most successful. In these cases students were able to decompose a problem into sub-problems and locate tutorials on how to solve these sub-problems. The student who made a boiling water alarm first followed tutorials on how to connect thermistors to the Arduino. She then had to program it to respond at the correct temperature ranges by assembling code from different tutorials, such as those on reading the Analog-to-Digital Converter and playing tones. These were sub-problems that she identified and solved herself.

Contrarily, when tutorials presented a stepwise recipe that defined both problem and solution, it was difficult for students to generalize these to other situations. Solutions to problems and questions encountered during the completion of the tutorials *should not be scaffolded*. Students must learn to seek out these answers themselves in order to transfer this knowledge to other contexts. This was a major problem that both courses encountered. Students would ask the instructor for "clarification" of what the problematic step was and to explain the concept they were missing. This process resulted in a completed tutorial, but little actual learning. The answers came too easily. Although many of the tutorials were also accompanied by an exercise that asked students to stretch and apply their knowledge, they were not effective at engraining any knowledge.

Tutorials seem to be most effective at showing students *how* to do something when they are already aware of *why* they need to do it, but the important step of being able to identify when a technique shown in a tutorial could be applied was crucially missing..

5. CONCLUSIONS

Through our work designing and implementing TEC and IDEAS, we found that students respond favorably to Tangible Media as computational and pedagogical tools. Many of our findings align with what is known about Media Computation approaches more generally. For CS1 instructors looking to engage their students, we think several of the themes from these courses could be implemented into undergraduate classes. Finally, two questions, "How do we use tutorials to facilitate knowledge transfer?" and "What are the most effective techniques for addressing the unique needs of late-blooming CS students?" come to the forefront as areas for future research.

6. REFERENCES

[1] Barba, E., Xu, Y., MacIntyre, B., and Tseng, T. Lessons from a class on handheld augmented reality game design. *Proceedings of the 4th international conference on foundations of digital games.* ACM Press (2009), 2–9.

[2] Guzdial, M.Exploring hypotheses about media computation. Proceedings of the ninth annual international ACM conference on International computing education research - ICER '13, ACM Press (2013), 19.

[3] Hewner, M. and Guzdial, M.Attitudes about computing in postsecondary graduates. *Proceeding of the fourth international workshop on Computing education research ICER 08 293*, 5527 (2008), 71–78.

[4] Horn, M.S. and Jacob, R.J.K.Tangible programming in the classroom with tern. *Proceedings of ACM CHI 2007 Conference on Human Factors in Computing Systems*, (2007), 1965–1970.

[5] Horn, M.S., Solovey, E.T., Crouser, R.J., and Jacob, R.J.K.Comparing the use of tangible and graphical programming languages for informal science education. *Proceedings of the 27th international conference on Human factors in computing systems CHI 09 32*, (2009), 975.

[6] Hornecker, E. and Buur, J.Getting a Grip on Tangible Interaction : A Framework on Physical Space and Social Interaction. *Clavier*, (2006).

[7] Ishii, H.The tangible user interface and its evolution. *Communications of the ACM 51*, 6 (2008), 32–36.

[8] Lovell, E. and Buechley, L.An e-sewing tutorial for DIY learning. *Proceedings of the 9th International Conference on Interaction Design and Children - IDC '10*, ACM Press (2010), 230.

[9] Owen, S. and Disalvo, B.Graphical Qualities of Educational Technology. (2014), 14–17.

[10] Parkes, A.J., Raffle, H.S., and Ishii, H.Topobo in the wild: longitudinal evaluations of educators appropriating a tangible interface. *Proceeding of the twenty-sixth annual SIGCHI conference on Human factors in computing systems*, ACM (2008), 1129–1138.

[11] Pears, a, Seidman, S., Malmi, L., et al.A survey of literature on the teaching of introductory programming. *SIGCSE Bulletin 39*, 4 (2007), 204–223.

Teaching Software Engineering with LEGO Serious Play

Stan Kurkovsky
Central Connecticut State University
kurkovsky@ccsu.edu

ABSTRACT

LEGO Serious Play (LSP) is a methodology that helps people brainstorm and discuss complex ideas through storytelling and metaphors. LSP has been successfully applied in higher education as a mechanism for team building and promoting creativity. In this paper, we discuss using LSP to teach several core software engineering topics through hands-on case studies. Initial results suggest that LSP has a positive impact on student learning, while also improving student engagement with the course material. This paper describes the details of two LSP-based case studies along with many practical aspects of using LSP to teach software engineering.

Categories and Subject Descriptors

D.2.0 [**Software Engineering**]: General.
K.3.2 [**Computing Milieux**]: Computer and Information Science Education – *Computer science education.*

General Terms

Management, Design, Human Factors

Keywords

Software Engineering; case studies; LEGO Serious Play

1. INTRODUCTION

Software engineering courses often serve as an integrative experience where students apply programming skills together with their knowledge of many Computer Science areas. However, studying software engineering must be more than just participating in a capstone course where existing knowledge and skills are put to practice. There are many important principles and concepts that are central to the practice of modern software engineering, which usually are not covered in other courses forming the traditional computing curriculum. These include requirements engineering, emergent properties, socio-technical systems, etc. Given the engineering nature of the discipline, one of the best ways to learn these principles is usually to apply them in a practical context, such as a course project or a case study.

This paper discusses the application of LEGO Serious Play (LSP) to studying software engineering concepts through hands-on case studies. While there are no published reports concerning the use of LSP in software engineering education (except as a team-building method), LEGO bricks are being successfully used to introduce agile software methods [11,18]. Most notably, LEGO Mindstorms have become a popular learning tool in engineering and computing classrooms and provided a strong positive impact on student learning over the last 15 years [5]. LSP is a highly

participative facilitated methodology that helps people brainstorm and discuss complex ideas through storytelling that revolves around the metaphors represented through LEGO models. In LSP, LEGO models only act as a starting point for discussion. Students open up and start brainstorming ideas together, explore and often find unexpected solutions to the presented problems. LSP has a very strong theoretical background rooted in constructionist learning theory, as described in Section 2. Many LSP practitioners refer to this methodology as a 'programming language,' using which it is possible to build a solution for the given problem. Practical rules of LSP described in Section 3 are based on the 'build-share-reflect' sequence, where the facilitator poses a question or a challenge related to the problem at hand, in response to which the participants build LEGO models, share stories about them, and reflect on their understanding of the problem.

The author has developed and tested a number of LSP-based case studies to teach software engineering concepts, such as architectural patterns, requirements engineering, and software dependability. Section 4 lays out this approach, which leverages intentional emergence to combine the fragmented knowledge of each individual student in a way that would help the team gain a deeper and fuller understanding of the given concept. The effects of these case studies on student learning are discussed in Section 5. Section 6 describes the lessons learned and practical implications of using LSP in the classroom.

2. SERIOUS PLAY AND LEGO

Rieber et al [20] define *serious play* as "an intensive and voluntary learning interaction consisting of both cognitive and physical elements. Serious play is purposeful, or goal oriented, with the person able to modify goals as desired or needed. Most importantly, the individual views the experience of serious play as satisfying and rewarding in and of itself and considers the play experience as important as any outcomes that are produced as a result of it." Serious play is an example of an optimal life experience or *flow* proposed by Csíkszentmihályi [4]. Flow is a state of concentration when the person is completely immersed and is "carried by the flow" of the activity, often ignoring the passage of time. The key aspect of serious play is in experiencing flow due to the satisfaction of understanding something complex, confusing, or previously unknown.

Theoretical foundations of LEGO Serious Play were developed by Roos and Victor as a novel methodology to harness creativity and imagination for business strategy development [22]. This approach is grounded in Jean Piaget's *constructivism* theory stating that children develop their knowledge based on their hands-on experiences of the surrounding world. Seymour Papert later extended Piaget's theory. Papert's concept of *constructionism* rests on the idea that learning occurs when we build something external to ourselves that is related to the studied subject. One might say that constructivism explains how we build knowledge in our heads, while constructionism explains how creating tangible objects solidifies that knowledge. Constructivism and constructionism helped us move away from traditional lectures to actively engage students in hands-on experiences that help them make sense of the real world.

The central idea behind the LSP methodology is that "when you build in the world, you build in your mind" [19]. This refers to our own mental models that we use to make sense of the world, whether they represent our work environment, computer programming concepts, or personal beliefs. Using one's hands is the key concept of constructionism. Official LSP training manual suggests that touching, manipulating, and constructing physical objects with our hands activates a richer kind of learning. Extending the constructionist concept of "thinking with object," LSP can be viewed as a language for articulating complex and tacit knowledge [9]. Instead of LEGO bricks, one could use modeling clay, construction paper, sticky notes, or some other kind of medium. Many serious play practitioners agree, however, that LEGO bricks are the preferred choice because they are much easier to work with, require no special skills, or a cleanup after playing. It is important to point out that the richness of LSP is not in the medium used to construct models, but rather in what these models represent [15]. The modularity of LEGO bricks allows the participants to continuously modify their models and elaborate on their stories. At the same time, participants are usually quick to understand that none of their models will look very realistic and will have little meaning without providing their own stories. This observation helps the participants stop worrying about their artistic abilities and encourages them to build models with rich metaphorical meaning [6].

LSP uses special sets of bricks that are designed to "inspire the use of metaphors and story-making" [19], such as minifigures, animals, money, etc. The facilitator poses a question or a challenge, e.g. "Build a model of a nightmare professor," in response to which participants build their individual models and then explain their model and its meaning to everyone. The etiquette of LSP ensures that everyone gets to express their ideas without being influenced by others. When a question is posed, everyone starts with building their models, and only after that the story-telling begins. This approach significantly helps students who otherwise might be shy and hesitant to engage in a classroom discussion. At the same time, this helps to quiet down those students who are always eager to jump into a discussion and/or have an answer to every question. This democratic process and the level playing field created by the universal language of LEGO bricks not only gives everyone an equal opportunity to participate, but also creates a playful and positive shared experience of discussing and making sense of a complex problem.

3. THE PRACTICE OF LSP
LSP has been developed for use in facilitator-led workshops consisting of 6-10 participants. Workshops can range in duration from 1.5 hours to two days. During each workshop, participants build a series of models with the goal of team building, gaining a deeper understanding of a complex problem, or developing a strategy. The process of building a model includes four steps:

1. Facilitator poses a question/challenge;
2. Participants build models;
3. Participants explain their models by sharing stories; and
4. Participants reflect on their understanding of the models and their meanings.

There are several fundamental ethical principles that guide LSP and help each workshop stay focused and productive. Each participant owns his or her model and only that participant can

change it or give it a meaning. All discussions are focused on the models only and not on their owners.

Each LSP workshop begins with a skill-building exercise aimed to stimulate different types of imagination described in [22]. This warm-up exercise guides the participants through basic LEGO construction skills, building representations and metaphors, and explaining them through story telling. Upon completing this exercise, participants should be comfortable enough with LSP to begin working on the tasks directly related to the specific objectives of the workshop.

LSP methodology defines seven Application Techniques [10]:

AT-1. Building individual models and stories;
AT-2. Building shared models and stories;
AT-3. Creating a landscape;
AT-4. Making connections;
AT-5. Building a system;
AT-6. Playing emergence and decisions; and
AT-7. Extracting simple guiding principles.

Depending on the goals and the context, an LSP workshop can include any combination of the application techniques, but it always starts with building individual models and stories (AT-1). We illustrate this principle in detail in Sections 4.2 and 4.3.

4. LSP AND SOFTWARE ENGINEERING
The value of serious play in education has long been recognized [21]. Despite the fact that LSP is fundamentally based on several educational theories, there are just a handful of reports on using LSP in the context of education. LSP has been applied in a few higher education areas: reflecting on their learning process by creative arts students [7], fostering creativity of students studying management information systems [17], team building in a graduate information technology program [23] and engineering [1], developing assessment strategies by students in a post-secondary teacher education program [16], and leadership development in an industrial engineering program [8]. The majority of these reports do not indicate that LSP was used to teach students the 'core' topics of the corresponding courses or programs. On the contrary, our approach uses LSP to create a series of hands-on case studies that help students master the major topics in a software engineering course along with building better teamwork skills and promoting creativity.

LSP has a proven track of success in professional software engineering. Requirements elicitation in human-computer interaction has been studied [2] and later formulated as a formal LSP-based technique called "User Requirements with LEGO" (URL) [3]. As a custom designed workshop focusing on web-based projects, URL guides the participants through identifying their roles, types and expectations of the users, modeling the content and key functionality of the website, connecting stakeholders with website content, features, and users, and identifying any possible shortcomings (e.g. website functionality that no users need, or a feature demanded by a large population of users that does not have an adequate level of support).

Teamwork is central to software engineering. Effective teams need to possess an ability to communicate effectively, develop shared mental models, and remain motivated while working together to achieve the project objectives [13]. The concept of a *shared mental model* refers to the team's mutual understanding of their tasks and objectives, the workflow process, and their teamwork strategy to reach the goals [12]. Although originally

developed as a strategy-making tool, LSP is also an effective team-building methodology, which encourages participants to share their assumptions and ideas [1,24]. Using LSP can help the team build a shared mental model through continuously expressing individual ideas by building and explaining the models to the team. As illustrated in the case studies below, shared models (AT-2) help the team build a consensus by integrating the ideas of each team member, while landscape models (AT-3) enable forming a shared understanding constructed out of individual and sometimes different perspectives.

Mabogunje et al describe the phenomenon of *intentional emergence* in the context of product development process [14]. Emergence may be viewed as the ability of a complex system to produce behaviors or properties as a result of interactions among its components, which by themselves cannot produce such behaviors or properties. LSP is used as a mechanism that can make emergence intentional. Our approach leverages intentional emergence by combining individual and often partial knowledge of a certain software engineering concept and the background of each student in a way that would help the team gain a deeper and fuller understanding of that concept. We use LSP in a number of hands-on case studies that are aimed to reinforce student understanding of a particular software engineering concept, such as requirements engineering, software design patterns, or software dependability. A lecture on the given topic precedes the case study. Each participating student brings in their current understanding of the topic supplemented by any relevant experience with it they may have accumulated from other courses or practical experience. During an LSP-based case study, students build models and tell stories explaining their views and understanding of the topic. The overarching goal of all LSP-based case studies is to leverage the combined knowledge, experience, and backgrounds of all participating students. Throughout the case study, students are guided to form a shared understanding of the given concept that combines all correct and relevant elements of the topic in the focus of the case study, which would ultimately reinforce and deepen their mastery of the course material.

4.1 LSP-based Case Studies in the Classroom

Below we describe the experience of using LSP in a senior software engineering course with 20 students, which met twice a week for 75 minutes. A typical LSP experience begins with the skill-building exercise, to which the author dedicated an entire 75-minute block.

The introductory skill-building exercise consisted of the following three challenges. The *building challenge* requires student to build a simple structure (a tower) in order to (re)acquaint students with the LEGO bricks. No two resulting structures are ever the same, which serves as a learning point: we all have our own perspectives and our models are unique. The *metaphor challenge* requires students to build a model from Imaginopedia, a brochure included with the LSP Starter Kit. The students are then asked to modify their creations, if necessary, so that the model would illustrate the concept of being a CS student, a software engineer, or an IT professional. Then, students were asked to explain the meaning of their models. This challenge helps students see their models in an entirely different way: not as a scale model of a real-world object, but as a metaphor that can be used to tell a story. In the *story-making challenge* students were asked to build a model from scratch that would represent a nightmare assignment, a project, or a 'professor from hell,' and then tell a story explaining their model. Expert LSP facilitators agree that it is always easier to begin by building models illustrating some extreme qualities of

something that is very familiar to all participants. During this challenge, students are encouraged to ask each other to explain specific details of their models, which eases them to focus on their models while communicating the elements of complex concepts.

For all subsequent case studies, the class was split into two groups that met in separate classrooms and worked on the same assignment: one group using LSP and building LEGO models, and the other group using a whiteboard as a medium to support their discussion. The use of LSP alternated between the groups so that all students would receive a comparable exposure to this methodology. All students were graded based on the worksheets that they completed while working on a case study. Each student working in the LSP group used a single LSP Starter Kit, which costs about $37.

All LSP-based case studies went beyond building individual models and included building either a shared or a landscape model, both of which promote team building and creating of shared understanding. These two kinds of models force students to compare their thoughts and views on the same concept, which helps each student correct any possible misconceptions and crystallize their understanding of that concept.

The author piloted a total of five LSP-based case studies:

1. Requirements engineering: formulate and refine use cases of a software system;
2. Software architecture: identify architectural components of a system and choose a suitable architectural style;
3. Design patterns: choose a software design pattern best suited to implement a software component;
4. Socio-technical systems: study emergent properties and behaviors in a complex socio-technical system; and
5. Dimensions of dependability: identify, analyze, and mitigate the risks to dependability of a complex system.

Each case study is structured as a typical LSP workshop, in which instructor poses a challenge relevant to the corresponding software engineering topic, and students build and explain their models. Students reflected on their understanding of that topic both through discussions and by completing a worksheet, which was later graded using a rubric consisting of 8-10 criteria.

4.2 Case Study: Requirements Engineering

The objective of this case study was to identify, analyze, and refine the use cases of a software system. This case study was about a hypothetical software system called Programming Assignment Submission System (PASS). The objective of PASS is to help multiple CS instructors by automating the process of managing programming assignments in their courses. The core functionality of PASS is described as follows: for instructors – post the assignments and suggested solutions, review and grade the work submitted by students; for students – submit their solutions, get email reminders when an assignment is almost due and when it is overdue; and for teaching assistants – view the assignments and submitted student work. Using their worksheets, students were required to draw a UML use case diagram for PASS paying a special attention to using <<include>> and <<extend>> relationships, and to write a description of one non-trivial use case using the table format, a sample of which was provided. The description of system functionality given to the students was intentionally somewhat ambiguous and open to interpretation in order to promote student discussion.

The room was arranged so that each student had an individual building table. Students were asked to place and discuss their models at a separate discussion table. Each student used one LSP Starter Kit.

The students were first asked to identify the actors in PASS and build their models. The models were brought to the discussion table and placed on small platforms so that all models representing the same actor would be on the same platform. The most obvious actors are a student, an instructor, and a teaching assistant, but other possibilities also included a system administrator and a secretary.

Then, each student was asked to build one individual model of a use case for PASS (AT-1). Each student built his or her own individual model and the discussion did not commence until after everyone was done building. This ensured that the reasoning of each student was not affected by others and that everybody's voice was heard. The models of use cases were then brought to the discussion table where each student told the story of how their use case plays out in PASS. Models of similar or duplicating use cases were grouped together and their owners were asked to build a single shared model upon which all of them must agree (AT-2). In order to do this, students identified the most crucial component (typically consisting of several bricks) in their individual model

and then constructed a shared model out of these components. Most importantly, the owners of the shared model came up with a unified story explaining how their new model represented the corresponding element of PASS's functionality. This ensures that each student has some ownership of the use case on which they worked and that their views and opinions are taken into account. The process of building use case models can be repeated if one or more use cases have not yet been identified and if the time allows. A collection of shared use case models now represented a landscape model (AT-3), which portrayed different aspects of the system's functionality. When the previously built actors were connected with the models of use cases using the special LEGO elements, the result represented a connection model of PASS (AT-4), which by now resembled a UML diagram. Students were asked to discuss the role of each use case within the system so that any candidates for using the UML <<extend>> or <<include>> relationship could be identified and properly reconnected. Now that a complete model was built, students drew the resulting UML use case diagram on their worksheet and wrote a detailed description of one non-trivial use case of their choice. A subset of the resulting LEGO models and a fragment of the corresponding UML use case diagram are shown in Figure 1.

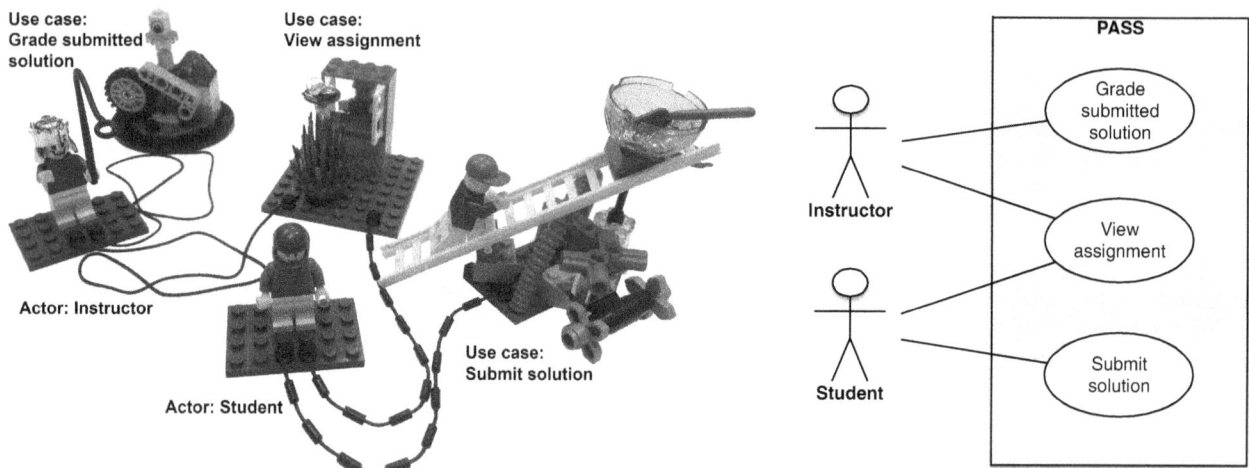

Figure 1. A subset of LEGO models of actors and use cases in PASS and the corresponding UML use case diagram.

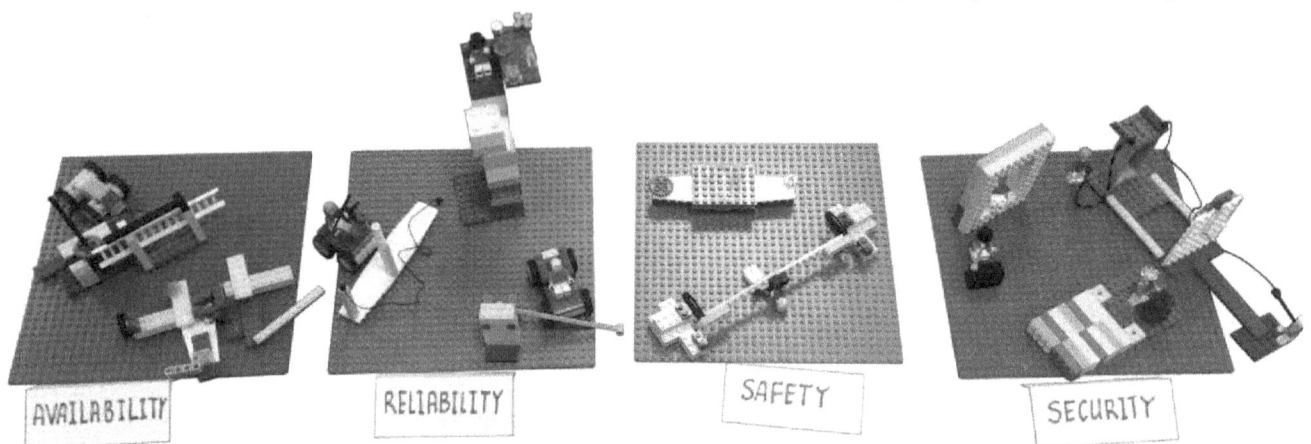

Figure 2. LEGO models of four dimensions of system dependability.

4.3 Case Study: Dimensions of Dependability

The objective of this case study was to identify, analyze, and mitigate the risks to dependability of a complex socio-technical system. In particular, this case study explored four different dimensions of dependability: availability, reliability, safety, and security. It is important to note that system dependability also includes other properties, such as survivability, maintainability, integrity, etc. These four properties were examined in the context

of four different systems: an automatic parking garage gate, a smartphone, a digital picture frame, and a traffic light control system. We used two decks of cards to create random combinations, e.g. reliability of a parking garage gate or security of a digital picture frame. Each card in one deck was labeled with one dimension of dependability, while the other deck included different systems. Each student picked a random card from each of the decks. Given these selections, students were asked to build a model and come up with an event/scenario illustrating the corresponding risk to dependability in the given system.

Once the individual models were built (AT-1), students explained their models grouped by the dependability feature, e.g. reliability. After all stories related to system reliability were shared, all corresponding models were grouped together into a landscape model (AT-3) and the students were asked to reflect upon them: does each model create a good scenario illustrating a risk to the system's reliability? Students were asked to pick the best or the most relevant scenario, improve upon it, if necessary, and briefly describe that scenario in their worksheets. This process was repeated for the models related to each of the remaining dimensions of dependability.

Once all models were discussed and the landscape models were built (Figure 2), students performed a risk-based analysis of their models, given the system/scenario combinations. Students were asked to identify and describe the specific risk factors, analyze and assess that risk based on its severity/probability, decompose the risk to identify its root cause, and reduce the risk by choosing an appropriate risk mitigation strategy to improve system dependability (risk avoidance, risk detection and removal, or risk tolerance). Students were asked to explain their reasoning to the team based on the models they've built and to write down the key points in their worksheets.

5. EFFECTS ON STUDENT LEARNING

During each case study, students completed a graded worksheet consisting of 8-10 questions gauging the level of student skills in the cognitive domain of Bloom's taxonomy, as shown in Table 1 (not all case studies included questions aimed at assessing evaluation skills, and none had questions related to the synthesis skills). During each case study, the test group used LSP, while the control group solved the same problem without using metaphors and LEGO models. Students in the test and control groups alternated to ensure a more equal exposure to the LSP techniques by the entire class. Individual student work in each case study was scored on the scale of 0 to 5. The sample size n indicates the number of questions testing the given skill level multiplied by the size of the student pool; there were 10 students in the test and 10 students in the control group. The difference between student grades in the test and control groups was assessed using a one-tailed t-test to determine the effect of using LSP on student learning. As shown in Table 1, students who used LSP attained a higher level of skills (statistically significant, $p<0.05$) in the areas of comprehension, application, and analysis. The level of evaluation skills was also higher for students who used LSP, but with a weaker statistical significance ($p<0.1$).

At the end of the semester, students were asked to reflect whether LSP-based case studies helped them learn the course material:

I believe that the concepts learned with LEGO go deep in my mind. I will remember them because I played. I explained my design to my teammates. When I build with LEGO, it creates more meaning to the concepts from each lecture.

I tend to think verbally and conceptually, but forcing me to visualize added an extra dimension to my learning.

I recall many of the LSP case studies better than the whiteboard sessions. The requirements engineering case study in particular was made very clear by constructing representations of system components, actors, etc.

Both types of case studies were useful, but using LEGO made it easier to understand the systems being discussed. It also made it easier to explain the details to other students because I could show them using my LEGO designs.

Table 1. Comparative analysis of student learning with LSP.

Characteristic	Group	Mean	SD	n	Δ	t	p
Comprehension	test	4.68	0.90	110	0.34	2.772	0.007
	control	4.35	1.09				
Application	test	4.66	0.69	150	0.17	2.006	0.047
	control	4.49	0.99				
Analysis	test	4.61	0.98	130	0.22	2.044	0.043
	control	4.39	1.04				
Evaluation	test	4.45	0.87	60	0.28	1.886	0.064
	control	4.17	1.14				

6. CHALLENGES AND LESSONS LEARNED

The author's experience shows that some faculty are apprehensive about using LEGO bricks in a university classroom. A common perception is that this is a just a toy and it cannot be used for anything other than developing spatial reasoning skills in first-year engineering students. Some can be persuaded by the global track record of LSP, but a few will always believe that it is just a corporate training technique and a waste of time in the classroom.

Timing considerations are extremely important when planning an LSP activity that is supposed to fit a single class period. All LSP case studies described here were designed for 75-minute blocks. Building and reflecting must be carefully timed because a properly designed serious play activity will put both students (and professors too!) in the state of flow when they can be easily carried away and keep on tinkering with their models and discussing them. It is sufficient to allow 3-5 minutes for building (nobody gets bored if they finish building quickly) and, based on the team size, 5-15 minutes for discussion/reflection.

Given the timing considerations, a detailed script of the case study must be developed beforehand. It should include full details of all building steps and all instructions that will be given to the students. Ideally, each script should be given a trial run to test whether the instructions are sufficient, the tasks have the appropriate level of difficulty, and the timing is realistic. The script should also include any other elements that must be planned in advance, e.g. table arrangement, additional materials, etc.

A short debriefing session is always useful at the end of every LSP activity to help reinforce the key concepts and learning points. This also gives students an opportunity to provide feedback about what went well and what did not. The author's experience shows that it is immensely important for the facilitator to write down their own reflection so that the activity can be improved the next time it is offered.

From the outset, a few students were hesitant about using LEGO in what they perceived as a very serious course. Most of them changed their mind during the LSP skill-building exercise, but a couple remained skeptical throughout the entire course. It is important to identify such students soon enough after introducing LEGO and LSP to attempt changing their minds.

Finally, it is crucial to point out the importance and necessity of professional LSP certification that provided the author with the vital background, insight, and skills for developing LSP activities.

7. CONCLUSIONS

The analysis of quantitative and qualitative data suggests that LSP had a positive impact on student learning in a senior software engineering course. Compared to a traditional method of running case studies, LSP-based activities resulted in students reaching higher skills in many levels of Bloom's taxonomy. Formal data along with written and informal feedback from students suggests that LSP helped improve soft skills, such as teamwork and oral communication. Students indicated that LSP increased their motivation, promoted creativity, and improved retention by actively engaging students into the coursework.

Focusing on LEGO models helped students open up and start discussing complex software engineering concepts with their team. Some students reported that having their models in front of them made them feel more relaxed, which, in turn, helped alleviate their fear of public speaking. Students very frequently took pictures of their models and shared them on social media networks, which not only helped them to extend their reflection of the models, but also indicated that they enjoyed LSP case studies and were proud of their work.

Running LSP activities is always fun and helps break up the routine. LSP helps foster a creative, playful, and imaginative classroom atmosphere; consequently, many students reported looking forward to more LSP-based case studies.

8. ACKNOWLEDGMENTS

The author is thankful to Robert Rasmussen, LSP's main architect, for showing and teaching the *serious* side of LEGO.

9. REFERENCES

[1] Bulmer, L. 2011. The Use of LEGO Serious Play in the Engineering Design Classroom. *Proceedings of the Canadian Engineering Education Association.*

[2] Cantoni, L., Botturi, L., Faré, M., and Bolchini, D. 2009. Playful Holistic Support to HCI Requirements Using LEGO Bricks. In *Human Centered Design*, 844-853. Springer.

[3] Cantoni, L., Faré, M., and Frick, E. 2011. *URL: User Requirements with Lego. Ver. 1.0.* May 2011. http://www.webatelier.net/url-user-requirements-with-lego

[4] Csíkszentmihályi, M. 1991. *Flow: The psychology of optimal experience.* Harper & Row.

[5] Danahy, E., Wang, E., Brockman, J., Carberry, A., Shapiro, B., and Rogers, C. B. 2014. LEGO-based Robotics in Higher Education: 15 Years of Student Creativity. *Int. J. Adv. Robot Syst., 11*, 27.

[6] Gauntlett, D. 2007. *Creative explorations: New approaches to identities and audiences.* Routledge.

[7] James, A. R. 2013. Lego Serious Play: a three-dimensional approach to learning development. *J. Learning Development in Higher Education*, (6).

[8] Jentsch, D., Riedel, R., and Mueller, E. 2013. Flow and Physical Objects in Experiential Learning for Industrial Engineering Education. In *Advances in Production Management Systems. Competitive Manufacturing for Innovative Products and Services*, 566-573.

[9] Kristiansen, P., Hansen, P. H. K., and Nielsen, L. M. 2009. Articulation of tacit and complex knowledge. In *13th International Workshop of the IFIP WG 5.7 SIG*, 77-86.

[10] Kristiansen, P. and Rasmussen, R. 2014. *Building a Better Business Using the Lego Serious Play Method.* John Wiley & Sons.

[11] Krivitsky, A. 2011. *Scrum Simulation with LEGO Bricks.* http://www.lego4scrum.com.

[12] Landy, F. J. and Conte, J. M. 2010. *Work in the 21st century: An introduction to industrial and organizational psychology.* John Wiley & Sons.

[13] Leonard, H. S. and Freedman, A. M. 2000. From scientific management through fun and games to high performing teams: A historical perspective on consulting to team-based organizations. *Consulting Psychology Journal: Practice and Research, 52*(1), 3-19.

[14] Mabogunje, A., Hansen, P. K., Eris, O. and Leifer, L. 2008. Product Design and Intentional Emergence facilitated by Serious Play. *Proc. of NordDesign 2008 Conf.*

[15] McCusker, S. 2014. Lego, Seriously: Thinking through building. *Intl. J. Knowledge, Innovation and Entrepreneurship, 2*(1), 27-37.

[16] Nerantzi, C. and Despard, C. S. 2014. Do LEGO Models Aid Reflection in Learning and Teaching Practice?. *J. Perspectives in Applied Academic Practice, 2*(2), 31-36.

[17] Oberer, B. 2013. Integrating Creative Learning Elements in Higher Education Shown in the Example of a Management Information Systems Courses. *Education, 3*(6), 319-324.

[18] Paasivaara, M., Heikkilä, V., Lassenius, C. and Toivola, T. 2014. Teaching students Scrum using LEGO blocks. In *Proc 36th Intl. Conf. on Software Engineering*, 382-391.

[19] Rasmussen, R. 2006. When You Build in the World, You Build in Your Mind. *Design Management Review, 17*(3), 56-63.

[20] Rieber, L. P. and Matzko, M. J. 2001. Serious design of serious play in physics. *Educational Technology, 41*(1), 14-24.

[21] Rieber, L. P., Smith, L. and Noah, D. 1998. The value of serious play. *Educational Technology, 38*(6), 29-37.

[22] Roos, J. and Victor, B. 1999. Towards a new model of strategy-making as serious play. *European Management J., 17*(4), 348-355.

[23] Scharlau, B.A. 2013. Games for teaching software development. In *Proc 18th ACM Conf. on Innovation and technology in computer science education*, 303-308.

[24] Schulz, K.-P., and Geithner, S. 2011. The development of shared understandings and innovation through metaphorical methods such as LEGO Serious Play. *Intl. Conf. on Organizational Learning, Knowledge and Capabilities.*

A TUI-based Programming Tool for Children

Danli Wang[1,2]   Lan Zhang[2]   Yunfeng Qi[2]   Fang Sun[3]

1. State Key Laboratory of Computer Sciences, Institute of Software, Chinese Academy of Sciences. Beijing, China.
2. Beijing Key Lab of Human-Computer Interaction, Institute of Software, Chinese Academy of Sciences. Beijing, China.
3. School of Computer and Information Technology, Liaoning Normal University, Dalian, Liaoning, China.
{danliwang2009, zhanglans.ac, qiyunfeng123}@gmail.com, sf8552@126.com

ABSTRACT

TanPro-Kit 2.0 is a programming tool for children aged 6 to 8, which is based on tangible user interface (TUI). It consists of programming blocks and a LED pad. The pad presents visual and audible feedback according to the arrangement of programming blocks with which children construct programs to play a maze game. Based on TanPro-Kit, we expanded three important programming concepts: parameters, Boolean logic and branch, and improved the system to support two-dimensional connection, which aims to make the program structure clearer. To realize these new features, we added three kinds of programming blocks accordingly, improved the process of block sequence in Arduino, and modified the infrared and wireless communications of the Single-Chip Microcomputer (SCM). A lab-based user study with 15 children was conducted, and the results show that the children can use the system to complete tasks easily and have a basic understanding of the related programming concepts.

Categories and Subject Descriptors

K.3.1 [Computers and Education]: Computer Uses in Education; H.5.2 [Information Interfaces and Presentation]: User Interfaces

General Terms

Design, Experimentation, Human Factors

Keywords

Tangible User Interfaces; Children; Programming Languages; Learning;

1. INTRODUCTION

At present, children's life is heavily influenced by computing, and many of them will work in fields that involve computing. They must begin to work with algorithmic problem solving and computational methods and tools in k-12 [1]. As programming usually involves solving problems, designing systems, and understanding human behavior, Wing describes computational thinking as a fundamental skill for everyone, not just for computer scientists [14]. Research has shown that programming education can have a positive and measurable effect on children's achievement, not only in areas such as math and science, but also in language skills, creativity, and social emotional interaction [4].

However, children face barriers in learning programming. Most existing programming languages are based on texts and symbols which are difficult for children to understand [6, 9]. New designs are needed to help children learn programming.

Tangible user interfaces (TUIs) have created new opportunities for learning programming languages [5]. TUIs, as an interaction method that embraces the richness of human interaction with the physical world [6], can enhance learning [7] and easily involve children in programming [8]. Research has shown that children can understand programming concepts when they are as young as four years old with the help of TUIs [3]. Sapounidis et al. [10] present that TUIs has advantages for younger children learning programming. Tangible programming languages have the potential to facilitate learning of complicated syntax, to improve collaboration, and to facilitate teachers or parents to maintain a positive learning environment [5].

Many studies [5, 13] have explored using the metaphors by blocks to support children's understanding of programming sequence and basic logic. And the study by Baytak and Land [2] found that 5th grade students use more complicated programming concepts most frequently with Scratch, including Boolean expression, conditions, and loops. However few studies focus on how well younger children understand these programming concepts.

In this paper, we present *TanPro-Kit 2.0* (Figure 1) based on *TanPro-Kit* [13]. We integrated three programming concepts in the tool (parameters, Boolean logic and branch) and improved the rules of arranging blocks as two-dimension connections to make the program structure clearer. Besides, a user study was conducted to evaluate children's performance.

2. RELATED WORK

Using modular tangible tokens to express programming concepts is an established idea, and there are much relevant research, which inspired us a lot.

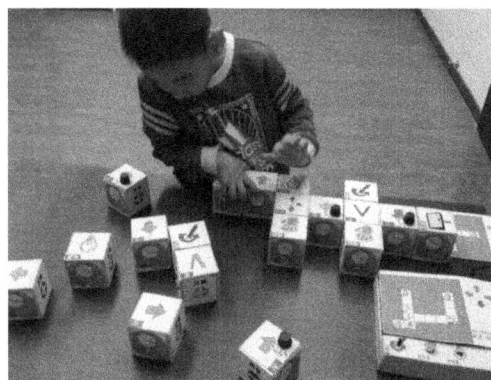

Figure 1. Children with TanPro-Kit 2.0

Tern [5] is a tangible programming tool, with which children could control a real walking robot. The programs written by *Tern* contain rich programming concepts: conditional branches, loops and subroutines. However, the computer vision technology used in the tool was limited by illumination, and children need to manually capture the image of the block sequence with a camera after writing a program, which is difficult for younger children.

Tangible Programming Bricks [8] is built with PIC microprocessor in each physical programming brick. This work is highly functional, with rich programming concepts, such as parameters and branch. Children can set parameters by put number bricks into the slot. The programming method of conditional statement in the system is well structured, including both "If" and "End If". However, there is no mechanism, such as real-time feedback, to help children find out potential errors in time.

Tangicons 3.0 [11] is an educational game allowing children to solve problems together by manipulating physical objects to move virtual characters on a map on the computer screen. It has a modification cube which can modify the next cube to perform desired steps. In this way, children can perform multiple steps at a time, which can convey parameter concepts to children. It uses a computer screen as output and its programming blocks are built based on Sifteo cubes, which increase the cost of the tool.

Electronic Blocks [15] are physical *Lego* blocks designed to allow young children (aged 3-8) to create *Lego* forms with interesting behaviors. It provides three types of blocks: sensor blocks, logic blocks and action blocks. Children can build block towers that flash when they talk or cars that move when a flashlight shines on them. But the system offers little real-time feedback, which make the tool difficult for younger children debugging.

roBlocks [12] uses modular building block units to construct a physical robot. It contains actuator blocks, sensor blocks and logic blocks similarly. Logic blocks can be arranged between sensor blocks and actuator blocks, which are used to process logical operation of data sensors detected. The blocks are in different colors, but with no visual semantic tips, which is not straightforward, especially for novices and children.

TanPro-Kit [13] is a tangible programming tool for children aged 5 to 8, and includes two major components: *programming blocks* including *start/end blocks*, *direction blocks* and *sensor blocks*, and a *LED pad*. By assembling programming blocks, children can build a command sequence to control each step getting out of a maze displayed on the LED pad where animation and real-time feedback are also provided. With technologies like LED, RFID, wireless and infrared, TanPro-Kit can be widely used in different environments, such as at school or home. The previous user study proved TanPro-Kit is attractive to children and easy to learn and use. The programming concepts integrated in TanPro-Kit are acceptable for the young children.

Inspired by above works, we implemented TanPro-Kit 2.0 based on TanPro-Kit, trying to introduce programming concepts such as parameters, Boolean logic and branch to younger children aged 6-8. We improved the rules of arranging blocks as two-dimension connections to make the program structure clearer. We also conducted a user study to evaluate whether children can easily use the programming function of TanPro-Kit 2.0.

Figure 2. TanPro-Kit 2.0 is composed by (a) LED Pad, (b) Maze Maps, (c) Start /End Block, (d) Direction Blocks, (e) Direction blocks with parameters, (f) Sensor Blocks, and (g) Logic Blocks & Branch Block

3. TANPRO-KIT 2.0
3.1 Overview
TanPro-Kit 2.0 is a tangible programming tool for children, composed of two parts: a LED pad and programming blocks (Figure 2). Three kinds of programming concepts (parameters, Boolean logic and branch) were integrated by adding *direction blocks with parameters*, *logic blocks* and *branch blocks* accordingly. Besides, we modified the process of block sequence in Arduino and improved the infrared and wireless communication in SCM to support two-dimension connections. While playing the game, there are two successive stages: programming stage and running stage, corresponding to the programming and execution of a traditional program.

In programming stage, the main task of children is constructing a command sequence by arranging programming blocks, which defines a routing path getting out of current maze displayed on the LED pad. The LED pad can detect the program sequence and provide real-time feedback. For example, if a block is placed correctly, the LED pad will lighten a maze cell accordingly, otherwise it will flicker a cross to inform children there is an error.

In running stage, the LED pad will execute the commands and display an animation of a light spot moving along according to the commands. The light spot would stop at sensor cells and logical-sensor cells, waiting for children to trigger the corresponding sensors on the LED pad. When the light spot reaches the end cell in the map, the running is over with a piece of music, and the LED pad displays a green "check" as a reward.

3.2 Implementation
3.2.1 LED Pad
The LED pad is composed of Maze Maps and a LED Box (see Figure 3), displaying animations and providing feedback.

In TanPro-Kit [13], there are three kinds of cells on the Maze Map, including a start cell and an end cell which represent the entry and the exit of the maze, blank cells which are related with direction blocks, and sensor cells relevant to three kinds of sensors on the LED pad. In TanPro-Kit 2.0, we added new kinds of cells on the Maze Map according to the new programming concepts (parameters, Boolean logic and branch), including successive blank cells, logical-sensor cells and IF cell (Figure 4).

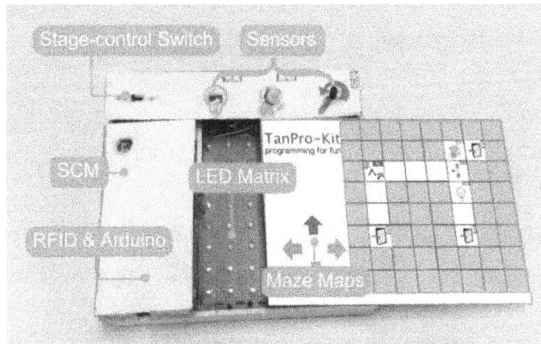

Figure 3. LED pad

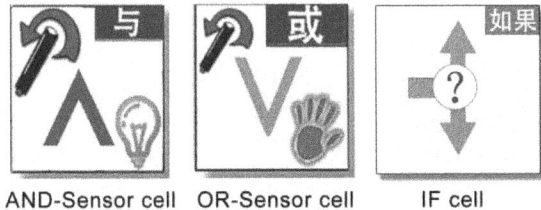

AND-Sensor cell   OR-Sensor cell   IF cell

Figure 4. New cells on Maze Map

Each logical-sensor cell is constituted by symbols of two sensors and a logic operator (AND or OR). And in the IF cell, there is a branch shaped symbol. Beside the IF cell, there are separately two adjacent sensor cells, indicating two different conditions and leading to two subsequent branches. All the symbols, except those of logic operators, are quasi-physical which are straightforward for children. We chose the standard symbols in mathematical logic representing logic operator, which are not straightforward enough, but have the advantage to introduce formalized symbols. In order to enhance the mapping between the symbols and concepts, as well as to help children recognize the symbols, we added text prompts on the top right corner.

LED Box is 19 cm long, 21 cm wide and 4 cm high. The stage control switch is used to toggle between programming stage and running stage. Inside the LED Box, there is a wireless communication module, which receives wireless information from programming blocks and updates the command sequence, and an Arduino serving as a controller of the LED pad. All the mazes that correspond to the maps are pre-stored here. And the maze maps can be detected by the RFID. The Arduino handles data received from the wireless communication module while programming and controls all the animations and interactions while executing programs. There are three kinds of sensors, button sensor, light sensor and rotary sensor, which act as input during running stage. And we improved the implementation, so they could be triggered according to new programming concepts, such as Boolean logic semantic and branch structures.

In programming stage, when the Arduino receives the digital codes of the block sequence from the wireless communication module, it translates the information into command and store it in different branches based on the branch information and ID. Then it will match digital codes of the block sequence with the Maze Map information to decide whether it is right or wrong and give real-time feedback. We have improved this process to support new programming concepts and connection rules.

In running stage, LED pad moves the light spots one by one according to the command sequence, and detects the sensors when

encounters a sensor cell or a logical-cell. It flicker the LED spot until the right sensors are triggered. If it is an IF block, LED pad will first lighten the IF cell for a few seconds, then flicker the sensor cells next to it and listening the trigger events until either of the two sensors has been triggered. Then lighten the branch following the sensor triggered.

3.2.2 Programming Blocks

TanPro-Kit 2.0 totally contains six kinds of programming blocks: *start/end block*, *direction blocks*, *sensor blocks*, *direction blocks with parameters*, *logic blocks*, and *branch blocks* (Figure 2).

Start/end block, *direction blocks* and *sensor blocks* were inherited from TanPro-Kit and we made some improvements. *Start block* and *end block* represent the beginning and the end of a program respectively. Four kinds of *direction blocks* are involved, indicating four different directions. *Sensor blocks* act as conditions to pass some maze cells, and we improved the implementation so they could be combined with the new added *logic blocks* and *branch blocks* to form Boolean logic semantic and branch structures. In these cases, children shall trigger specific sensors in running stage to make the conditions true, so the light spot can move along.

Direction blocks with parameters were designed to introduce the concept of parameters to children. There are four *direction blocks with parameters*, and each of them is a conventional *direction block* with an extra knob on the upper surface which could be rotated into different values. The parameters of these blocks indicate how many steps the light spot will go towards a specific direction. Programs can be built with fewer blocks by properly using *direction blocks with parameters* when there are successive blank cells on the map. Some previous works [e.g. 8, 10] supported the concept of parameters too by providing an individual block to represent parameter. This manner is flexible as the parameter blocks could be reused with different actions. For younger children, however, the extra parameter blocks might course confusion and be used in wrong conditions as there are little physical constraints about how to connect them. We combined the adjustable parameter with an action in one block, so the parameter is clearly for the block itself rather than the block next to it.

Logic blocks, including *AND Block* and *OR Block*, aim to introduce Boolean logic. The *Logic blocks* can connect two *sensor blocks* in two-dimensional way (Figure 5), which means *sensor blocks* could be connected on the front side and the back side of *logic blocks*, together forming logic semantic such as "*Light AND Button*". The two-dimensional arrangement rules were designed to stress the integrality of the logic semantic and to make the structure of the whole program clearer. When it comes to a logic block while running, children need to trigger proper sensors to make the logic condition true. Only if the two related sensors are triggered at the same time, the light spot could pass an AND-sensor cell. As for the OR-sensor cell, triggering either sensors or the both can make it pass.

Branch block, which is also named *IF block* here, was designed to introduce the concept of branch, which is an important program structure. *IF block* can connect two *sensor blocks* in two-dimensional way too. The *sensor blocks* represent two different conditions, and can be followed by other programming blocks to compose two branches (Figure 6). In programming stage, when there is a branch on the Maze Map, children need to build a

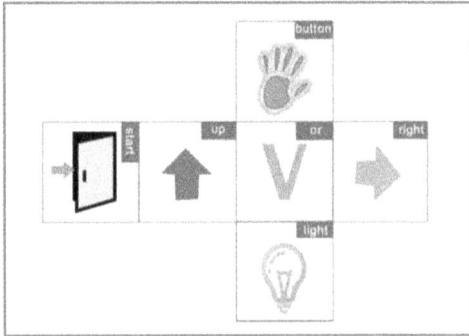

Figure 5. Top view of the connection between logic block and sensor block in 2-D way

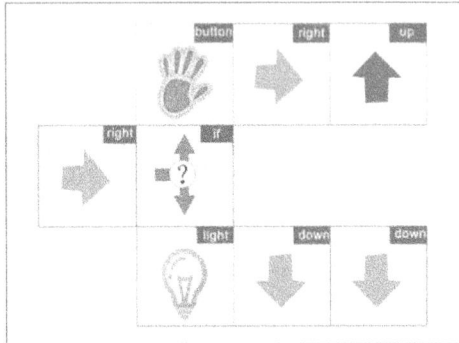

Figure 6. Top view of the connection between IF block and sensor blocks

branch structure accordingly. And when it comes to the *IF cell* in running stage, children could decide which branch to take by triggering one sensor to make that condition true.

The symbols on the programming blocks are identical with those on the maze cells, which helps children realize the connection between programming blocks and maze maps.

Inside each programming block, there is a SCM, integrated with Infrared transmitters, Infrared receivers and a wireless module (Figure 7). In programming stage, the infrared transmitter inside the start block keeps sending infrared signal. Once a programming block is added in the block sequence, it can be activated by the previous one via Infrared communication. Every active block keeps sending infrared signals too, so that a sequence of active blocks can be built. In order to make the controller (Arduino) recognize the program structure, each active block except the Start Block would transmit its own ID and the ID of the previous one wirelessly to the LED pad.

3.3 Example of the game
Each maze game has two stages, programming stage and running stage. Here we present a typical example of the game with the maze map in Figure 3.

3.3.1 Programming Stage
To start programming, the stage-control switch must be turned to the left, indicating programming stage. Then, put a maze map on the surface of the pad to activate a game. The LED pad will first lighten the LED beneath start cell. The programming sequence starts by start block, then put a *direction blocks with parameter*, setting parameter to 2, which can make the light spot go up for two cells (Figure 8). As a feedback, two lights in the LED matrix are lightened. Then the passable path encounters the *AND-sensor*

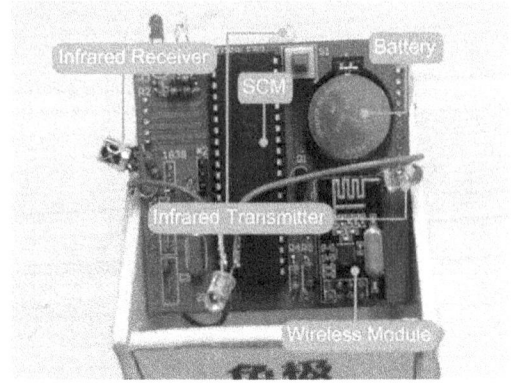

Figure 7. The hardware inside logic block

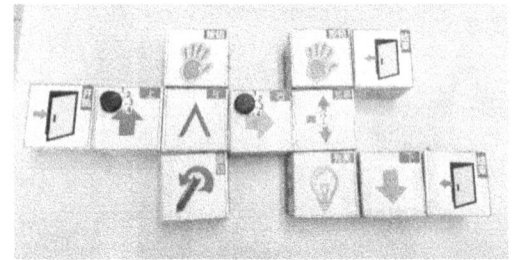

Figure 8. Programming Sequence

cell. Put *AND block*, then put *button sensor block* and *rotation sensor block* on the back and front face of *AND block*. Only if the three blocks are all arranged rightly will the LED of the cell be lightened. Then put a *right direction block with parameter* whose parameter is set to 3，the LED path will goes to *IF cell*. After arrange the *IF block*, there will be two paths. Children can put *button block* on the back side of *IF block*, then *end block* right of *button block*. As for the path conduct by the *light sensor block*, its arrangement is similar. The order of the two paths' arrangement is facultative. Not until the paths come to the two end cells will the LED pad play a piece of music, which means it's ready to run.

3.3.2 Running Stage
After programming, turn the stage-control switch to the running stage and the program will be executed. In the LED matrix, the light spot of the start cell flashes once. Then, the lights beneath the cells which correspond to the block sequence flash in turn, forming an animation of a light spot "moving" along a path. When the light spot comes to the AND-sensor cell, it will stop moving until children make the result of AND operation true by triggering the button sensor and rotation sensor at the same time. Next, it goes right for three cells and comes to IF cell. After the IF cell, LED pad lightens button sensor cell and light sensor cell, and flicker in the two cells. Children can choose either path by triggering the relevant sensor. If children trigger light sensor, the light spot will goes along the way down first and then the end. If children trigger button sensor, it will go along another way. Then it will lighten a check mark and play a piece of music.

4. USER STUDY
4.1 Study Setting
We were concerned about the difficulties children met and how they solved while using TanPro-Kit 2.0. Besides, we paid special attention on whether children could correctly use TanPro-Kit 2.0 to complete tasks based on the involved programming concepts.

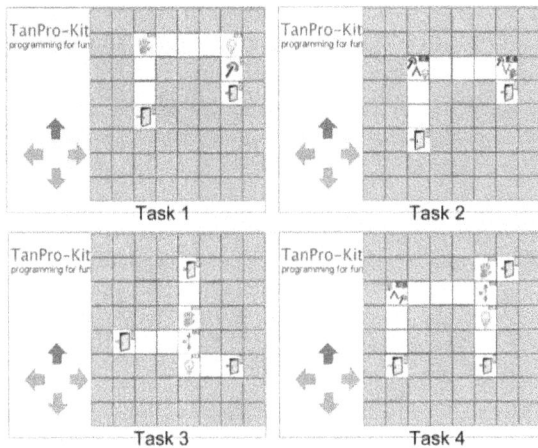

Figure 9. The Four Tasks

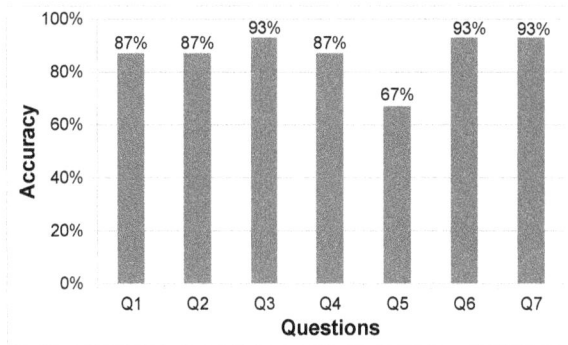

Figure 10. Scores of 7 questions in the interview

Fifteen children (6 females and 9 males) aged 6 to 8 with the average age of 7.07 were involved. We set up a video recorder to capture children's behaviors and voice during the whole experiment, which provided us with a lot of useful details.

We designed four tasks in total (Figure 9). The first three tasks serve as practices and respectively focus on one of the programming concepts: parameters, Boolean logic (AND/OR) and branch. In detailed, the first task has three blank cells successively, which encourages children to use the Direction blocks with parameters. The second task contains two Logical Sensor cells, which request children to arrange logic blocks and trigger sensors correctly. The third task contains an IF cell, so children need to build a branch structure in the programming stage and choose one in the running stage. And the fourth task integrates all three concepts mentioned above.

We began the user study by demonstrating how to use TanPro-Kit 2.0, including choosing a specific game, arranging different kinds of programming blocks, turning the stage-control switch, and interacting with the three sensors on the LED pad. Then children were asked to play the four tasks one by one. After they completed all the tasks, they were interviewed by our researchers.

During the interview, we asked seven questions about interaction with TanPro-Kit 2.0 under some specific circumstances. As well as oral response, children were allowed to give some demonstrations with the blocks as their answers, but no real-time feedback was provided on the LED pad, which could avoid children's trial and error. In this case, we still encouraged children to give their own explanations of the demonstrations, which represented some fundamental thought of programming concepts.

4.2 Results

We analyzed the data collected from observation, video, questionnaires and interview. And the results are as follow.

As for the completeness, after practicing in the first three tasks, all children could finish the fourth task successfully. They correctly arranged the programming blocks, adjusted the parameter of the *direction blocks with parameters*, used *AND block*, *OR block* and *IF block*, and entered the running stage to give appropriate sensor inputs on the LED pad.

To get more information of children's completeness and knowledge, we analyzed the results of the seven questions (Figure 10) and performance of children during the tasks.

Q_1, which is about parameters, asks children to give two solutions of arranging blocks to pass three consecutive blank cells. 87% of children successfully gave two solutions. All children could give us a demonstration, using one *direction block with parameter* and set the parameter to three. And 13 of them successfully figure out another solution by involving conventional *direction blocks*. During the tasks, we found that children preferred using the *direction blocks with parameters* and seldom use the *Direction blocks*. They thought *direction blocks with parameters* were interesting due to the real-time feedback when rotating the knob and it can save blocks. This may result in the rest 2 children forget using the *direction blocks* when answering Q_1.

The Q_2 and Q_4, which ask children the arrangement rule of And-sensor and Or-sensor cell, have the same accuracy (87%). Children use blocks to demonstrate their answers. All children knew that they should place the three blocks together but some of them still met difficulties remembering the arrangement rules. During tasks, all children complete correctly for the real-time feedback assists them in arranging the blocks. Children will keep trying to correct the mistakes until the 'Cross' symbol disappear. In the interview, the lack of real-time feedback made it a little difficult to realize their mistakes, which makes the accuracy lower than we had observed during the tasks.

Q_3 asks children how to pass an And-sensor cell in the running stage. And Q_5 asks them how to pass an Or-sensor cell. For Q_3, 93% of the children gave a correct answer. One child said, "Wait for it, and push the two spots at the same time", and some other children triggered the two sensors physically as their answer. From the video, we found the feedback help children with triggering the sensors of AND-sensor cell. However, for Q_5, only 67% of the children gave a correct answer, such as "Either one is OK, both are also OK". Other children considered Or meant "Trigger one of the sensors" and didn't figure out that it's also right to trigger both. Based on observation, we find Logical Or is indeed difficult than Logical And with TanPro-Kit 2.0. For Logic And, there is only one correct way to trigger sensors, which is triggering both sensors. However, there are two ways to trigger sensors with logical Or (trigger either sensor or trigger the both). Once a child has chosen one way, the light spot will go on, and then he or she may continue this trigger way in next tasks and doesn't explore new ways. In the future, we would improve our design to better practice the Logical-Or concepts.

Q_6 is concerned with the arrangement rule of *IF block*. Most children gave the right answer verbally or practically arrange the blocks. Q_7 is that if the LED spot twinkles at the two sensor cells nearby the If cell, what actions could be taken, and how you understand this action. The two questions have high accuracy (93%). All children gave the right answer and expressed their understanding for IF sensor interaction, such as, "Push one of them to choose one road" and "IF has two choices". And children expressed their preference of IF blocks for it allows children to choose. A boy gave his explanation, "I can choose one path, as if I was a commander, driving a train at the cross road".

The user study results showed that children understand the interaction rules in TanPro-Kit 2.0, which represent the corresponding programming concepts. The real-time feedback helped children overcome difficulties and confusion they met in the tasks. In addition, children enjoyed the new programming concepts and features in the tool. They thought TanPro-Kit 2.0 was interesting and they wanted to participant further study with it. Some of the children also expressed that they thought programming was interesting and wanted to take some programming courses after school.

5. SUMMARY AND FUTURE WORK

TanPro-Kit 2.0 is a tangible programming tool for children aged 6 to 8. It consists of programming blocks and a LED pad which can be placed anywhere at the kindergarten or homes. With TanPro-Kit 2.0, children can play maze games by assembling the tangible blocks to construct passable paths through the mazes. It delivered three main programming concepts (parameters, Boolean logic and branch) to children. We conducted a lab-based user study with 15 children, and the results show that children can use the tool to explore all programming features of TanPro-Kit 2.0 in a short time and they were attracted by the new concepts such as IF.

In the future, the work can be improved in several ways. First, we will extend programming concepts to make the system more efficient when conveying children about programming concepts. Second, we hope to improve the design of representation of programming concepts to make it easier for children to understand and remember. Furthermore, we will enhance the technology in LED pad to better represent feedback. In addition, we will design and conducted a stricter user study to investigate the learning outcome with a long period of course.

6. ACKNOWLEDGMENTS

We would like to thank the participants in the user study, and acknowledge the financial support from the Major State Basic Research Development Program of China under Grant No.2013CB328805, the National Natural Science Foundation of China under Grant No. 61272325, 60970090 and 61232013.

7. REFERENCES

[1] Barr, V. and Stephenson, C. 2011. Bringing computational thinking to K-12: what is Involved and what is the role of the computer science education community?. *ACM Inroads.* 2, 1 (March. 2011), 48-54.

[2] Baytak, A. and Land, S. M. 2011. Advancing elementary-school girls' programming through game design. *International Journal of Gender, Science, and Technology.* 3, 1 (2011), 243-253.

[3] Bers, M. U. 2008. *Blocks to robots: learning with technology in the early childhood classroom.* Teachers College Press, New York, NY, USA.

[4] Clements, D. H. 1999. The future of educational computing research: the case of computer programming. *Information Technology in Childhood Education Annual. 1999,* 1 (1999), 147-179.

[5] Horn, M. S., Solovey, E. T., Crouser, R. J., and Jacob, R. J. 2009. Comparing the use of tangible and graphical programming interfaces for informal science education. In *Proceedings of the SIGCHI Conference on Human Factors in Computing Systems* (Boston, USA, April 04-09, 2009). CHI '09. ACM, New York, NY, 975-984.

[6] Ishii, H., Ullmer, B. 1997. Tangible bits: towards seamless interfaces between people, bits and atoms. In *Proceedings of the SIGCHI Conference on Human Factors in Computing Systems* (Atlanta, Georgia, USA, March 22-27, 1997). CHI '97. ACM, New York, NY, 234-241.

[7] Manches, A., O'Malley, C. 2012. Tangibles for learning: a representational analysis of physical manipulation. *Personal and Ubiquitous Computing.* 16, 4 (April, 2012), 405-419.

[8] McNerney, T. 2004. From turtles to tangible programming bricks: explorations in physical language design. *Personal and Ubiquitous Computing.* 8, 5 (September, 2004), 326-337.

[9] Revelle, G., Zuckerman, O., Druin, A. and Bolas, M. 2005. Tangible User Interfaces for Children. In *CHI '05 Extended Abstracts on Human Factors in Computing Systems* (Portland, Oregon, USA, April 02-07, 2005). CHI '05 EA. ACM, New York, NY, 2051-2052.

[10] Sapounidis, T., Demetriadis, S. and Stamelos, I. 2015. Evaluating children performance with graphical and tangible robot programming tools. *Personal and Ubiquitous Computing.* 19, 1 (January, 2015), 225-237.

[11] Scharf, F., Winkler, T., Hahn, C., Wolters, C. and Herczeg, M. 2012. Tangicons 3.0: An Educational Non-Competitive Collaborative Game. In *Proceedings of the International Conference on Interaction Design and Children* (Bremen, Germany, June 12-15, 2012). IDC '12. ACM, New York, NY, 144-151.

[12] Schweikardt, E. and Gross, M. 2008. The Robot is the Program: Interacting with roBlocks. In *Proceedings of the 2nd International Conference on Tangible and Embedded Interaction* (Bonn, Germany, February 18-20, 2008).TEI '08. ACM, New York, NY, 167-168.

[13] Wang, D., Qi, Y., Zhang, Y. and Wang, T. 2013. TanPro-kit: a tangible programming tool for children. In *Proceedings of the 12th International Conference on Interaction Design and Children* (New York, USA, June 24-27, 2013). IDC '13. ACM, New York, NY, 344-347.

[14] Wing, J. M. 2006. Computational thinking. *Communications of the ACM.* 49, 3 (2006), 33-35.

[15] Wyeth, P. 2008. How Young Children Learn to Program With Sensor, Action, and Logic Blocks. *Journal of the Learning Sciences.* 17, 4 (Oct 2008), 517-550.

Reflections on Teaching Refactoring: A Tale of Two Projects

Shamsa Abid
Computer Science Department
SBA School of Science and Engg.
Lahore Uni. Of Mgmt. Sciences
(0092) 42 3560 8194
shamsaabid123@gmail.com

Hamid Abdul Basit
Computer Science Department
SBA School of Science and Engg.
Lahore Uni. Of Mgmt. Sciences
(0092) 42 3560 8194
hamidb@lums.edu.pk

Naveed Arshad
Computer Science Department
SBA School of Science and Engg.
Lahore Uni. Of Mgmt. Sciences
(0092) 42 3560 8194
naveedarshad@lums.edu.pk

ABSTRACT

Teaching refactoring effectively while making students realize the importance and benefits of refactoring is a challenge. In this direction, an experiment was carried out while conducting the course project for the Refactoring and Design Patterns course. This paper discusses the results of the experiment that involved two different project schemes to carry out refactoring activities on the same code base. One scheme was *post-enhancement refactoring* and the other was *pre-enhancement refactoring*. The aim of the experiment was to decide which scheme was beneficial in terms of better understanding, appreciation, and implementation of refactoring.

Categories and Subject Descriptors

D.2.7 [**Software Engineering**]: Distribution, Maintenance, and Enhancement - *restructuring, reverse engineering, and reengineering.* K.3.2 [**Computer Science Education**] Computer and Information Science Education – *computer science education, curriculum.* K.6.1 [**Management of Computing and Information Systems**]: Project and People Management - *life cycle*, Software Management – *software development, software maintenance.*

General Terms

Management, Measurement, Design, Experimentation, Human Factors

Keywords

Software refactoring, teaching refactoring, refactoring course project, student survey

1. INTRODUCTION

Refactoring is the process of transforming the internal structure of existing code, while keeping its functionality intact. It improves the design of code and makes it easier to maintain and understand [4]. Software refactoring is a highly desirable activity for good quality maintainable software [5], and for increased developers' productivity [6]. In the past few years, software development has shifted from traditional software processes to agile software development. According to recent industry surveys[12], agile methodologies are being used in almost three quarters of software development projects now. Since agile development stresses on working software and shorter release cycles with less upfront design, refactoring is a cornerstone of these methodologies. To this end, it is important to cultivate the realization of the importance and benefits of refactoring in aspiring but novice developers. This responsibility of nurturing developers with the right principles and practices falls on the academia; wherein lies the challenge of figuring out the best approach to teach refactoring, which enhances students' understanding and appreciation of refactoring.

In this regard, an experiment was conducted to compare two schemes of carrying out the course project for the Refactoring and Design Patterns course, offered to Computer Science graduate and senior undergraduate students at Lahore University of Management Sciences. The Refactoring and Design Patterns course includes the teaching of software design patterns, design principles, and refactoring practices, which are then applied on the course project by the students. The course project is a crucial and practical part of the course. It comprises of refactoring a given code base, with the intent of improving the structure and design of the code with respect to its readability, maintainability, and changeability.

The experiment was conducted on two groups of students (23 in all) who were required to work on one of the two different project schemes. In the first scheme, which we call *post-enhancement refactoring*, the students were asked to first perform a series of functional enhancements on the provided code. After that, they were required to perform an analysis of code quality metrics and code smells on the resultant code, and follow it up by refactoring the identified code smells. *Code smells* are a metaphor to describe code patterns that are generally associated with bad design and bad programming practices, and indicate that refactoring can be applied [4][9]. In the second project scheme, which we call *pre-enhancement refactoring*, the students were asked to first analyze the code quality metrics and code smells, and refactor those smells. After that, they were asked to perform a series of functional enhancements on the refactored code. Both project schemes had a final phase of application of design patterns, after the enhancement and refactoring phases had been completed. The two project schemes are illustrated in Figure 1. The two schemes vary only in terms of ordering of project phases; whether refactoring is done prior to, or after the enhancement phase.

ITICSE'15, July 4–8, 2015, Vilnius, Lithuania.
© 2015 ACM ISBN 978-1-4503-3440-2/15/07…$15.00
DOI: http://dx.doi.org/10.1145/2729094.2742617

---

[1] https://www.planbox.com/blog/agile/scrum/research/2013-Study-reveals-Statistics-on-Agile-Market-Share.html

[2] http://www.versionone.com/pdf/2013-state-of-agile-survey.pdf

The objective of the experiment was to evaluate the performance and feedback of the students working on the two different project schemes. By evaluating the performance and feedback of the students, we were able to make conclusions as to which project scheme resulted in a better performance of students; in terms of better quality refactorings, better quality of resulting code, better understandability, and better appreciation of refactoring.

In this paper, we address the following research questions:

RQ1: What is the better scheme to teach refactoring? Should students perform refactoring first or enhancement first?

We compare the teaching effectiveness of the two project schemes with respect to understanding and appreciation of refactoring. We draw conclusions after detailed analysis of students' performance and evaluation of their project deliverables.

RQ2: How to make students realize the benefit of refactoring?

We investigate which project scheme was better able to highlight the benefits of refactoring. The answer is found through the feedback obtained from the surveys conducted.

RQ3: Which student group is more satisfied?

To answer this, we analyze which project scheme is personally favored by students, by analyzing students' feedback.

The remainder of this paper is organized as follows. Section 2 describes the related work. In Section 3, we discuss the experimental setup for our research methodology. We give details on how the course project was carried out, and how the data was collected. In Section 4, we present the results of our analysis and discuss the threats to validity. Section 5 concludes the paper and mentions future work.

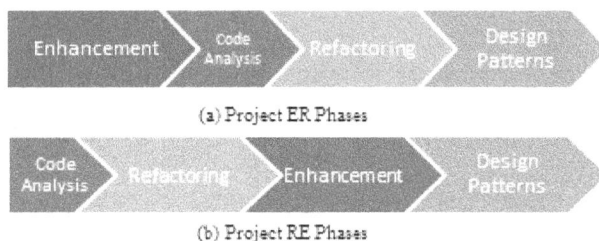

(a) Project ER Phases

(b) Project RE Phases

Figure 1. A comparison of two project schemes

2. RELATED WORK

To the best of our knowledge, our study is the first of its kind to compare two approaches to conducting a refactoring course project, with the intent of enabling better understanding, appreciation, and implementation of refactoring techniques among students.

Work has been done in the domain of teaching refactoring with innovative techniques. One such technique by Smith et. al., [1] recommends structuring the lesson plans in a way that every lesson plan would cover a few refactorings, which would be performed as a hands-on activity incrementally as the lessons proceed. In our course, the students are expected to perform refactorings studied in class on their project as the lectures proceed. They are not restricted to a certain set of refactorings, and depending on the code smells, they are free to perform relevant refactorings. The students working on enhancements are free to perform opportunistic refactoring wherever the need arises. Students are given the flexibility to choose to refactor while working on enhancements. Their technique also contrasts with

ours in the use of enhancement activity to make the students realize the need for the refactored code.

Dibble and Getswicki [2] advocates the need for dual analysis using automated and manual methods. We also require students to first perform a full fledge analysis of code smells using automated and manual inspection techniques, and then perform refactoring on the problem areas detected.

Murphy-Hill and Parnin [7] have observed that refactoring is often interleaved with changes to a project's functionality. Their observation was that refactoring was seldom done exclusively; rather it was mostly performed in conjunction with other code changes. In view of this observation, it was expected that our students working on the *pre-enhancement refactoring* scheme would write refactored code while working on the enhancements. However, the deadlines forced them to abandon refactoring entirely during enhancement.

It was observed by DeMeyer et. al. [1] that having a good example to teach refactoring is important, and they used a LAN Simulation example to work on, using a variety of refactoring tools. They propose using that example as a benchmark and common example for students and researchers, suggesting its benefits of being small enough to be easily understood, yet representative of real-world tasks. El_Ramly [3] has shared similar experiences in teaching a software re-engineering course, and emphasized the need for real industrial examples for better understanding and appreciation of re-engineering concepts among students. From the students' feedback, we have also felt that students need to work on a real industrial project to better understand the implications of changing an unknown legacy code. Our approach also gives the students exposure to a real industrial example to work on. The use of a real life industrial example served the purpose of better appreciation of refactoring techniques among students.

3. EXPERIMENTAL SETUP AND EXECUTION
3.1 Course Project Details
3.1.1 Project Domain
To conduct this course project, we used a real-life software from the industry - with appropriate permissions. It is a smart phone application implementing a Goods Collection System. The same code was provided to all the students. It was confirmed that the code had enough refactoring opportunities by the Teaching Assistant (TA) of the course, who was among the developers of the application.

3.1.2 Two Project Schemes
The experiment involved the execution of two different project schemes: Project ER was done with the *enhancement followed by refactoring* scheme (post-enhancement refactoring), whereas Project RE followed the *refactoring followed by enhancement* scheme (pre-enhancement refactoring). One group of student teams worked on Project ER, while the other worked on Project RE. The students formed their own teams and were randomly assigned a project scheme. Each team had two to three members each. Each team worked independently on their projects. The functional enhancements required in Project ER were different from those of Project RE; however, they were of the same difficulty level.

3.1.3 Weekly Meetings

Weekly assessment meetings were held not only to assist the students with their problems but also to monitor their progress actively. It was felt very useful to talk to the students during their projects to know what kind of issues they were facing, and how well their work was progressing.

3.2 Project Phases and Milestones

The phases of each project scheme were clearly defined and distributed across a fixed timeline. During the execution of the projects, some deadlines had to be extended according to students' demand. Following is a breakdown of the work carried out across the major phases, and the project evaluation activities.

3.2.1 Pre-Project Survey

On the very first day of the course, a survey was conducted to assess the technical skills of the students, and their industrial and academic background. It was important to see if all the students were sufficiently equipped with the programming skills to be able to work on the course project. Also, an initial opinion of the students' perception of the importance of refactoring was obtained, and it was found that everyone agreed on its importance at the very start of the course.

3.2.2 Project Setup and Transfer of Domain Knowledge

The TA transferred the domain knowledge through a demo and a tutorial at the start of the project. The running application was shown during the demo, and functional specifications for Project ER enhancement requirements were shared and discussed. Students not familiar with *Eclipse IDE*[3] and *Android SDK*[4] were given a startup tutorial on important topics like setting up these platforms, running the emulator, and debugging etc. The structure of the code was discussed and some important code files were explained in more detail to enable the students to get a better feel of the code. Since almost everyone was familiar with Java, it was assumed that the technology hurdle could be overcome by providing minimal assistance in the enhancement phase.

3.2.3 Project ER (Post-Enhancement Refactoring)
Enhancement (3 weeks)

In this phase, the students doing Project ER were provided with a set of enhancement features to be implemented in the current application. Screenshots of desired screens and use case descriptions were provided for understanding the new requirements. They were supposed to meet the deadline, and were left free to code as they like. It was expected that they would code quick and dirty, and that was what actually happened.

Code smells and statistics (10 days)

In this phase, the students were asked to inspect their code for smells, using both automated and manual detection techniques. They were also asked to compute some of the major code metrics like LOC, complexity, depth, number of classes, number of calls, coupling, statements per method etc. This was meant to serve as a baseline for comparison with their post refactoring code status. Some of the tools used for identifying code smells and code metrics were Sonar Qube[5], SourceMonitor[6], FindBugs[7] and

PMD[8]. A UML class diagram of the code was also required, which would enable them to study the associations and level of coupling between the classes.

Refactoring and code statistics (4 weeks)

In this phase, the entire project code had to be properly refactored. The students were asked to refactor the problems identified in the previous phase, using either Eclipse's built-in automated refactoring capability, or some other refactoring tool, or manually. At the end of the phase, they were asked to compare their resulting code metrics with the ones taken earlier to quantify the improvements.

Design Patterns (3 weeks)

In this phase, the students were asked to redesign and reorganize the code, keeping in mind the design principles and design patterns taught in the class. They were asked to identify the problem areas in the existing code which could be improved with the application of suitable design patterns, and then modify the code accordingly.

Final report (4 days)

The students were asked to submit a detailed consolidated project report, documenting work done in all the project phases along with the enhanced, redesigned, refactored, and fully functional code. The reports evaluated the variations in code metrics and code smells after each phase was completed, and conclusions were drawn by observing changes in code metrics across all phases. The students were asked to justify how their new design was more reusable, flexible, and extendable after refactoring.

3.2.4 Project RE (Pre-Enhancement Refactoring)

The phases of Project RE were identical to that of Project ER, only the sequence of refactoring and enhancement phases was interchanged.

Code smells and statistics (1 week)
Refactoring and code statistics (4 weeks)
Enhancement (3 weeks and 5 days)
Design Patterns (3 weeks)
Final Report (4 days)

The students working on Project RE were encouraged to write clean code during their enhancement phase. Furthermore, they were asked to report if they felt their refactoring proved useful to write new enhancements easily. It was expected that some of them would code quick and dirty, and some would perform opportunistic refactoring, and almost all would need to perform a final round of refactoring on the entire code. A final code metrics analysis would reveal if their enhanced code was better or worse than their refactored code.

After culmination all phases of both projects, a comparison was made on the refactorings performed by the two groups.

3.2.5 Pre Refactoring Survey

A survey was conducted a week after the project initiation (while one group was working on their enhancement phase while the other had just completed their code smells detection and metrics analysis phase). This survey questioned students on their opinion on conducting refactoring before or after enhancement, considering a real-life scenario at their workplace. It was asked on

---

[3] https://eclipse.org
[4] http://www.android.com/
[5] http://www.sonarqube.org/
[6] http://www.campwoodsw.com/sourcemonitor.html

[7] http://findbugs.sourceforge.net/
[8] http://pmd.sourceforge.net/

which factors the decision to refactor first would depend. Their opinion on their value perception towards refactoring for ease of maintenance was also taken. In the end, they were asked to provide the lessons they learnt, and the challenges they faced during their current phase.

3.2.6 Post Refactoring Survey

The third survey was conducted after both groups had finished their refactoring phases. The students were again asked which project scheme they thought was better. Their opinion about the benefits of each scheme was also taken. As a self-assessment of the work performed, they were asked to rate the quality and amount of refactoring they had performed on their project. They were also asked whether the course had motivated them to start refactoring at their workplace, and whether it increased their value perception toward refactoring. In the end, open-ended suggestions and feedback regarding the project were recorded.

3.2.7 Final Presentation

The students delivered a final presentation, detailing the work done throughout the project lifecycle. Together with the course instructor and the TA, an external guest with 5 years of industrial software development experience was also invited as an unbiased evaluator to give feedback regarding the work done by the students. The projects were evaluated on the basis of identification of problems in code, and quality of refactorings performed. It was assessed whether the refactorings contributed significantly to the improvement in code metrics, reduction in code smells, understandability, and ease of maintenance. It was also gauged by the way the students communicated their work, how well the students understood the benefits and application of refactoring techniques.

4. ANALYSIS AND DISCUSSION

To understand and decide which project scheme was better, we analyzed the results of our surveys, performed quantitative analysis of students' code and submitted reports, and used analytical feedback from the industry expert to draw conclusions.

4.1 Pre-Project Survey Results

In the first survey, it was observed that: all of the 23 students were graduate students and had previously taken object oriented programming courses, 16 had medium to high Java proficiency, all of the students had worked on Eclipse, 14 had worked on Android, all of them rated the importance of refactoring as high (even those who were not familiar with the theory and principles of refactoring had a preconceived notion of its importance), 12 claimed to be slightly familiar with the concepts of refactoring and code smells whereas the rest were not familiar, 9 had less than a year industry experience, 6 had 1 to 3 years industry experience, and 7 had 4 to 6 years experience working in the industry. These results ensured that all the experimental subjects had the required level of expertise to enable us to conduct the experiment, without posing a major threat to its validity in terms of outliers.

4.2 Pre Refactoring Survey Results

This survey questioned students on their opinion on conducting refactoring before or after enhancement in a real-life scenario at their workplace. In response, 36% said that they would enhance with refactoring in parallel, and end with full fledge refactoring. The top two factors that affect their decision to refactor turned out to be the project deadline, and whether the code is self-written or not. 91% rated refactoring as highly important. 81% agreed that

refactoring improved readability. Surprisingly, the number of students voting for *pre-enhancement refactoring* scheme was *equal* to the number of students voting for *post-enhancement refactoring* scheme. 64% selected that refactoring first gives you a chance to improve code so that smells are not accumulated. 64% selected that enhancement first gives you a chance to understand existing code. 73% agreed that refactoring first would take longer, but it would enable quicker enhancement. 82% thought it was easier to enhance after refactoring, and 55% thought it was easier to refactor after enhancing. In reply to when they would perform refactoring at their workplace, 45% said they would refactor as a personal principle.

Some of the student responses in favor of refactoring first are as follows:

"If you know what you are going to code next, you can keep it in mind while refactoring"

"If everything is clean already, new enhancements are not likely to create mess and it is easier to know where to add which type of code. So, it saves time."

Some of the student responses describing the benefits of doing enhancement first are as follows:

"By wrestling with bad code and then looking at the refactored version we can imagine how easy it (enhancement) could have been."

"There isn't any overhead of doing refactoring again."

4.3 Post Refactoring Survey Results

The third survey was conducted after both groups had finished their refactoring phase. The students were again asked which project scheme they thought was better. Table 1 indicates that Project ER was favored slightly more that Project RE.

Table 1. Students' votes in favor of referred project scheme

	Project ER	Project RE
Total number of students	13	9
Number of responses	10	9
Number of votes in favor	11	8

From Table 1, we were able to derive the answer to *RQ3: Which student group is more satisfied?* By noting that four students from Project RE were in favor of Project ER, whereas three students from Project ER were in favor of Project RE, we can say that Project ER students were more satisfied with their scheme of work.

When asked about the benefits of each scheme, students of Project ER in favor of Project ER scheme expressed their views as follows:

"Doing enhancement first helps in gaining the domain knowledge and code review while we are learning different code smells. We can get to know the code flow, coding conventions, project domain. Once enhancement is completed, we can easily refactor it later."

"It helped me to understand the flow of code first and give me the idea that what are the required refactoring to improve this code."

"My major reason is that in the case of this project, making enhancements in the code gave me a chance to get familiar with the domain and technology of the project which later made it easier for me to perform refactoring."

Following are the comments of Project RE students in favor of Project ER:

"Because when you do enhancement you actually understand code by debugging. After complete understanding of code one can easily refactor. Moreover, in Project RE you have to do refactoring again after enhancement. Project RE approach works if the code is yours, or you understand code to refactor it without any danger of code/functionality loss."

"If we do enhancements first that will make sure better understanding of code and its work flow. During refactoring we mostly tried to follow rules with lesser familiarity with code."

"Since the domain was new to me, writing a code would have given more familiarity to the domain rather than reading it, and/or refactoring it."

Some other findings from the third survey are: 15% respondents were highly satisfied with the quality and amount of refactoring done on their projects while 80% were satisfied on a medium scale, 95% affirmed that the course had motivated them to start refactoring at their workplace, and everyone agreed that it had increased their value perception toward refactoring. The students' unanimous agreement on becoming familiar with the advantages and benefits of refactoring answered *RQ2. How to make students realize the benefit of refactoring?* It was seen that both project schemes were equally effective in making students realize and appreciate the benefits of refactoring.

4.4 Quantitative and Qualitative Analysis

Our quantitative analysis is based on counting the number of big refactorings performed by students in each project scheme. Refactorings that consists of multiple smaller refactorings, and solve a bigger architecture or design level problem, are considering as big refactorings. The code smells indicating the need for big refactorings were instances of *god classes, divergent change, shotgun surgery, feature envy, inappropriate intimacy* and *middleman*. Some of the big refactorings performed were *Extract Hierarchy, Separate Domain from Presentation,* and using the *MVC Pattern.*

We compared the average number of big refactorings performed by students working on Project ER to those working on Project RE. It was seen that students of Project ER performed 70% more big refactorings than students of Project RE. Therefore, we deduce that the Project ER scheme results in better quality refactoring.

A qualitative analysis of our work through interviews and meetings with students and general observations by the course instructor, teaching assistant and external evaluator reveals that the primary reason Project ER students had a better understanding of the project was their ability to comprehend the structure of the code during the enhancement phase before moving on to code refactoring. Their better quality of work was entirely due to the opportunity to enhance existing code whereas the Project RE students were seen to gain little understanding by only conducting code analysis using tools or manually. It can be inferred that the best manual analysis is only possible while actually working on enhancing given code. The Project ER students gained more experience by working on the code whereas the Project RE students had to rely on basic code metrics for guiding their refactoring efforts. Since the Project ER provided the opportunity for students to better understand the code, therefore, they were able to produce better results by performing better quality of refactoring. Responses from students from the ER group were indicative of higher satisfaction after refactoring and they were better able to analyze their code for the possibility and

opportunities of using relevant design patterns. On the other hand, the efforts by students to apply design patterns were forceful rather than intuitive. Overall, the main reason why Project ER is a better scheme to enhance students learning and makes them perform better quality refactoring is that it helps them gain insight into the core architecture of the project by enhancing first, thereby gaining experience of the issues and code smells.

4.5 Industry Expert's Analysis

As mentioned earlier, an expert from the software industry was invited during the presentations of the students work. It was overall noted by the expert that the Project ER groups performed better than the Project RE groups; 80% students from Project ER were rated above average as compared to only 25% students from Project RE who got this rating. It was also observed by the expert that the Project ER group members had a better understanding of the problems in their code, and they performed refactorings that had a stronger impact. This observation corroborates with the quantitative analysis of results from students' code submissions.

The chart in Figure 2 shows the marks obtained in the final evaluation by the student groups working on the two different project schemes, as assigned by the external evaluator. The observation from this chart is that the students working on Project ER have outperformed those working on Project RE. This answers *RQ1: What is the better scheme to teach refactoring? Should students perform refactoring first or enhancement first?* Since the performance of students working on Project ER is better, we can say with confidence that the better approach to teaching refactoring would be to make the students perform enhancements before refactoring activities.

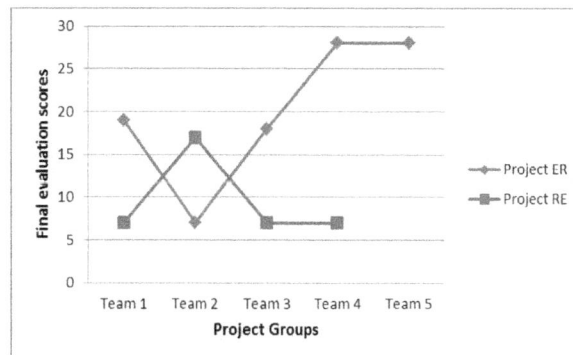

Figure 2. Final evaluation scores of student groups

4.6 Surprises

For the students who were working on Project RE (*pre-enhancement refactoring* scheme), it was assumed or expected that they would write clean code during their enhancement phase after having refactored their code, however, that was not the case. Similarly, 73% students thought that if you refactor before enhancement, the refactoring will take longer, but the enhancement will take less time. However, it turned out that refactoring did not decrease code enhancement time.

4.7 Summary of Results

In short, we found the following answers to our research questions from this experiment:

RQ1. What is the better scheme to teach refactoring? Should students perform refactoring first or enhancement first?

The students who performed enhancement first were better able to understand the structure of code, and it was easier for them to detect potential areas to refactor. Students who refactored before enhancement performed mostly superficial refactorings like *renaming*, *removing comments*, *removing dead code* etc., and the code enhancement phase was not made much easier. Also, the overall performance of students working on *post-enhancement refactoring* scheme was better, as measured in the final evaluations. Therefore, *post-enhancement refactoring* is the better scheme to teach refactoring effectively.

RQ2. How to make students realize the benefit of refactoring?

Both the schemes to carry out refactoring were equally effective in increasing the value perception towards refactoring. However, the *post-enhancement refactoring* scheme resulted in better quality refactorings.

RQ3. Which student group is more satisfied?

Project ER students were slightly more satisfied with their scheme of work because they found it easier to analyze and refactor code after performing enhancement.

4.8 Threats to Validity

4.8.1 Internal Threats
Our claim regarding the success of the Project ER scheme to enable students to better understand the need, application and benefits of refactoring is measured only through their performance in the project and their feedback. It is possible that some confounding factors may have promoted to the success of Project ER scheme, including the previous experience and expertise of the students. The results of the survey may not be totally accurate because a few students were unable to respond. It is also noteworthy that three out of four teams in Project RE were comprised of two members only, whereas two out of five teams in Project ER were comprised of two members. Although the evaluation was done keeping the size of the teams in mind, however, we cannot ignore the possibility of team size affecting the students' performance in the project. Even though the project started out with an equal number of teams in both the project schemes, and an equal number of students in each team, however, when some students opted out of the course once the project started, it was too late to change the grouping structure to balance the number of students in each project scheme. The sample size of our experiment is 23 students only, which might affect the validity of our results.

4.8.2 External Threats
We think that our experiment might produce different results and different user feedback if the project domain and technology platform are changed. It is possible that switching a real life industrial example with an open source project having a familiar domain or with a project that the students have already worked upon in the past would produce different results. Other factors such as the timespan given to refactor code, the quality of lectures, and the students' technical skills might affect the validity of our results.

5. CONCLUSIONS AND FUTURE WORK
In the end, we can conclude that both project schemes were comparable in terms of increasing the students' value perception towards refactoring, however, the *post-enhancement refactoring*

resulted in an overall better quality of refactorings performed and better final code structure. It was concluded that the student groups who performed *post-enhancement refactoring* performed better in project assessments, because of their better understanding of the problems in code. It was also deduced that self-written code is better refactored than foreign code.

In terms of the quality of refactorings done, we can say that those who followed *post-enhancement refactoring* scheme performed better quality of refactorings, and their analysis of problems in code was also better. Therefore, we can safely conclude that they had a better learning experience by performing more important and relevant refactorings than the other group. On the other hand, it was observed that the refactoring performed by students on Project RE were superficial, and theirs was a different set of refactorings compared to the other group who knew where the problems were in their own enhancement.

For better statistical results we plan to re-execute the same experiment with more participants. We propose future research directions on conducting refactoring course projects by investigating another project scheme that would involve multiple enhancements and refactoring phases, one after the other, so that the overall effect of refactoring in parallel with enhancement is gained. In future, we might use a project that has a simpler domain, and give flexibility for variation in technology.

6. ACKNOWLEDGEMENTS
We would like to thank Techlogix Pvt. Ltd. for providing us with the source code and Saima Mushtaq for being the evaluator.

7. REFERENCES
[1] Demeyer, S., Van Rysselberghe, F., Girba, T., Ratzinger, J., Marinescu, R., Mens, T., & El-Ramly, M. (2005, September). The LAN-simulation: a refactoring teaching example. In Principles of Software Evolution, Eighth International Workshop on (pp. 123-131). IEEE.

[2] Dibble II, C., & Gestwicki, P. (2014). Refactoring code to increase readability and maintainability: a case study. *Journal of Computing Sciences in Colleges*,30(1), 41-51.

[3] El-Ramly, M. (2006, May). Experience in teaching a software reengineering course. In *Proceedings of the 28th international conference on Software engineering* (pp. 699-702). ACM.

[4] Fowler. M. *Refactoring: Improving the Design of Existing Code*. Addison-Wesley, 1999.

[5] Kim, M., Zimmermann, T., & Nagappan, N. (2012, November). A field study of refactoring challenges and benefits. In Proceedings of the ACM SIGSOFT 20th International Symposium on the Foundations of Software Engineering (p. 50). ACM.

[6] Moser, R., Abrahamsson, P., Pedrycz, W., Sillitti, A., & Succi, G. (2008). A case study on the impact of refactoring on quality and productivity in an agile team. In *Balancing Agility and Formalism in Software Engineering* (pp. 252-266). Springer Berlin Heidelberg.

[7] Murphy-Hill, E., Parnin, C., & Black, A. P. (2012). How we refactor, and how we know it. *Software Engineering, IEEE Transactions on*, 38(1), 5-18.

[8] Smith, S., Stoecklin, S., and Serino, C. "An innovative approach to teaching refactoring." *ACM SIGCSE Bulletin* 38.1 (2006): 349-353.

[9] Van Emden, E., & Moonen, L. (2002). Java quality assurance by detecting code smells. In *Reverse Engineering, 2002. Proceedings. Ninth Working Conference on* (pp. 97-106). IEEE.

Teacher Perspectives on Web Design Instruction

Hauwa Muibi
Univ. of Nebraska at Omaha
6001 Dodge St
Omaha, NE 68182
hmuibi@unomaha.edu

Brian Dorn
Univ. of Nebraska at Omaha
6001 Dodge St
Omaha, NE 68182
bdorn@unomaha.edu

Thomas H. Park
Drexel University
3534 South 108th St
Philadelphia, PA 19104
park@drexel.edu

ABSTRACT

Web development is an inherently interdisciplinary field that offers a unique introductory path to computing prior to more traditional programming courses. While significant earlier work has investigated the challenges that novice web developers encounter, little research is available about teaching while coping with the field's considerable breadth. This paper reports findings from interviews with practicing web design instructors in secondary and post-secondary teaching environments. We present emergent themes related to recruitment strategies, student expectations, teaching techniques, and common challenges. We find significant effort is needed to cope with mismatches between students' expectations of what web design is and the HTML/CSS syntax-oriented view of the discipline often emphasized by teachers. We conclude with implications for new teaching tools that would help better sustain student motivation while equipping them with fundamental skills in web development.

Categories and Subject Descriptors

K.3.2 [**Computers and Education**]: Computer and Information Science Education—*computer science education*

Keywords

Web design, Web development, K-12 teaching

1. INTRODUCTION

Web design is often discussed as an area that allows people to explore basic computational literacy skills while also connecting them to other areas such as art and graphics, e-business, marketing, etc [4, 9]. This inherent interdisciplinarity attracts a wide variety of people with diverse backgrounds to the subfield, including those who might not otherwise be interested in traditional aspects of computer science [4]. In fact, 2013–2014 enrollment data collected across one US state showed that the number of secondary school students taking intro web design exceeded the number of students in all available programming courses combined [5].

At the same time, data from the US Bureau of Labor Statistics places web design and development careers at or near the top of the list of the most rapidly growing occupations. Their data projects the addition of 28,500 jobs during the 2012-2022 decade.

To meet these job demands it will be necessary for students to explore web design and development as part of their formal educational environments, especially given increased complexity of modern web-based systems. Put simply, learning web development is no longer a matter of a weekend crash course in HTML markup. Indeed, competitive would-be developers need to be able to simultaneously grapple with markup, stylesheets, front-end scripting, and server-side languages. In addition they likely need to be familiar with basic information assurance to prevent common exploits, usability and user experience design to build functional sites, and potentially limitless other areas including advertising, e-commerce, and web analytics.

Looking through just about any course catalog reveals that web design is regularly taught in contexts ranging from even early secondary school, to 2 year college, to 4-year undergraduate programs. However, we know very little about the experiences of the teachers who offer these courses at the various levels, including their broad curricular goals, their recruitment strategies, their teaching methods, and the challenges they regularly face. In this paper, we explore these issues through an interview study of 13 practicing web design educators teaching both secondary and post-secondary students.

In conducting the interviews for this study we sought to explore the following research questions:

1. What are the pedagogical goals teachers of web design have and what strategies are employed to attract and retain students for these classes?
2. How do teachers describe the students who typically take web design classes, and how do these traits influence their overall attitudes about the class?
3. What significant challenges do instructors face while teaching a web design class?

The remainder of the paper is organized as follows: Section 2 reviews previous research on the teaching and learning of web design, along with challenges faced by novices. Section 3 describes our study methods for data collection, analysis and interpretation. Section 4 details our qualitative thematic analysis results, while section 5 synthesizes these results by drawing out implications for future educational efforts. Finally, Section 6 concludes by elaborating on the implications of the findings and the next steps to be taken.

2. RELATED WORK

Prior research has examined web development from both the perspective of the learner and the teacher. Analyzing the issues students sought help for in a web development course, Park and Wiedenbeck [9] identified a wide range of barriers they encountered, including those caused by tool configuration and ongoing difficulties related to authoring and communicating about code. The literature also reveals that the challenges novice web developers face are not limited to the classroom. For instance, Rosson et al. [11] interviewed web developers who did not possess formal training but maintained websites as part of their daily activities; due to the context in which they practiced web development, they attained only "pockets of expertise" as they encountered and learned to resolve specific problems. Through interviews with professional web developers, Dorn and Guzdial [4] found that although participants recognized the value of having a more systematic understanding of computing, mismatches between CS course offerings and what appealed to them about web development led few to take these courses.

Nonetheless, numerous teachers have reported on their individual experiences teaching web development as part of a CS curriculum [1, 6, 7, 8, 10, 13, 14, 15, 16]. In discussing their approaches to designing and delivering web development courses, two major considerations emerge. First, teachers note a tension between web development as a broad and complex activity involving many different topics, and the time limitations of a single course. Second, the tools and techniques of web development advance rapidly, compelling teachers to constantly update their courses if they wish to keep pace with the state of the art.

Our study continues this work investigating teacher perspectives on teaching web design, building on it in two principal ways. Rather than focusing on the self-reported experiences of an individual instructor of a single course, we conduct semi-structured interviews with multiple instructors, analyzing their responses to our prompts to uncover common themes. Additionally, we broaden the population under study. While prior research has primarily offered the perspectives of CS faculty using web development as a motivating context for programming, we include a diverse sample of teachers from both secondary and post-secondary education. We expect that these differences will lead to new findings that contribute to our understanding of current practices and inform how we might improve on them.

3. STUDY METHOD

3.1 Data Collection

In the Spring of 2014, we recruited participants for the study through email using the CSTA (Computer Science Teachers Association) mailing list and contacts gleaned from school websites and college and university directories. The participants were teachers of web design in settings ranging from secondary schools to two-year colleges and four-year universities in the United States. While there are clearly significant differences across these teaching environments, a broad sampling of instructional contexts was appropriate since we were intentionally seeking to explore the general commonalities teachers share based on the nature of the course content in web design/development.

Local participants were interviewed in person, and remote participants were interviewed via telephone or video conferencing software. Each participant was asked to send an electronic copy of their syllabi prior to being interviewed. We then conducted a 30–45 minute semi-structured interview with participants regarding their experience in teaching web

Table 1: Participant Background and Courses

#	School Type	Education	Classes Taught
P1	Secondary school	Math Ed Degree, Some Comp. Engr.	CS classes, Web Design, Math
P2	Secondary school	Math Ed. Degree	Physical Science, Math, CS, Hardware, Web Design
P3	Secondary School	Business Ed. Degree	Info Tech, Web Design, Personal Finance, Business Law
P4	4-yr Univ	CS Degree, Former Developer	Into to Web Design, Advanced Web design
P5	Secondary School (All Girls School)	CS Degree, 1 Web Design class, Former programmer	Web Design, Comp. Animation, Intro to CS
P6	Secondary School	Industrial Eng. Degree	Spanish, Web 1, Web 2
P7	4-yr Univ	Math Degree, PhD in CS.	Web Design, Web Programming
P8	Secondary School	Business & Marketing Degree, 12 years experience in business.	Web Design (Business), Database Mgt., Accounting, Career Development, Intro to Dreamweaver
P9	Secondary School	Tech. & Engr. Ed. Degree	Intro to Engineering, CS, Software Engr.
P10	2 Year College	Journalism Degree	Web Design, News Editing, Media Law, Publication Layout Design.
P11	Secondary School	Ed M.S. in Info Learning & Tech. Degree, Former graphic designer	Technology, Physics, Chemistry, Engr., Math
P12	Secondary School	Teaching Cert.	AP in CS, Programming, Web Design
P13	2 Year College	A.S. Web Support Specialist B.S. E-Business	Mobile App Development, Intro to Web design, Dreamweaver, Info Tech.

design, the teaching methods and tools employed, and the challenges they encounter.

After completion of the interviews, audio recordings of the interviews were transcribed by the first author, and any personally identifying information was redacted or otherwise anonymized. We used Nvivo for qualitative data analysis, performing an iterative process of thematic analysis where we sought to identify the emergent themes in the data collected. Thematic analysis is a method used in analyzing qualitative data to identify and elaborate on patterns discovered in data collected [2]. It is important to note that in the thematic analysis approach, the number of participants who repeated a particular theme is not the only criteria for determining its relevance to the study.

In conducting our analysis, we initially created high level codes for the transcripts using a top-down approach with initial categories related to the questions we sought to explore in this study (tools, techniques employed, types of students etc.). We then conducted an iterative process of refining these codes into sub-codes which helped us identify more emergent themes present in the initial categories. In the section below, we illustrate the themes identified by using representative quotations from participants. In presenting these transcript excerpts, we have edited direct quotations to protect the identity of participants and for brevity.

3.2 Demographics and Teacher Background

Table 1 provides details about participants' educational background as well as the classes they have taught and were presently teaching. A total of 13 teachers were interviewed,

9 of whom were secondary school teachers, 2 were instructors at 2-year associates-granting colleges, and 2 were faculty members at bachelors-granting colleges/universities. Our participants had a wide variety of backgrounds including some who had a few formal CS classes and others who had taken a course in web design. Our participants spoke passionately about teaching web design classes having, found a field that provides an opportunity to attract students from various educational backgrounds. However, only two of the participants had some formal training in web design, with one having attained an Associates degree in Web Support and then earned a Bachelors in E-Business, while the other took a web design course as an elective towards completing the requirement for a Bachelors in CS. All but two of twelve participants taught different subjects including Journalism courses, Intro to IT, Accounting, Intro to programming, Intro to Engineering, Mathematics and Chemistry. As might have been expected, secondary school and 2-year college faculty taught a much wider range of course topics than those at 4-year universities. However, only one participant taught an advanced web development class designed for final year CS undergraduate students.

4. RESULTS

In this section, we present the results of our thematic analysis. The most prevalent themes expressed related to patterns in recruitment strategies employed to attract students to these classes; the expectations students have alongside their motivation; the similarities in techniques to maintain engagement; and finally the major challenges encountered including student morale. The following four sub-sections elaborate on each of these themes.

4.1 Recruitment & Class Objectives

Participants identified methods they employed in recruiting students who approached them or to boost morale and motivation for students who were already registered in the class. About half of the participants mentioned that they simply talked about the possible job opportunities that stem from having a fundamental understanding of how to create web pages. For example:

I always tell them that this is one of those developing technologies that you see a lot of demand for it everywhere regardless of what you're going into. If they are thinking of going into business or really anything, having the fundamental understanding of how to create any content across the web is something in demand. Usually what I talk about more is additional skills they can put into their resume, it makes them more employable. (P10)

I would talk about current opportunities and describe skill sets I think that would be needed for a web designer or developer based on my understanding or a combination. (P13)

Although this recruitment strategy was mentioned to have yielded good results by the educators at the post-secondary level, one-fourth of the secondary school teachers also used this approach in advising students to take web design classes. One participant went as far as promising to help get students jobs on campus if they showed promise in the class.

Participants also spoke about the shift in attitude by students when they are told of the possibilities of using web design skills in terms of removing restrictions. For example, a participant explained the capabilities of WordPress,

an open source content management system, and stated that at a certain point, there will be limitations. However, with knowledge of the fundamentals and applications of HTML and CSS, lies an opportunity to go further than a developed blogging tool.

Another strategy employed was explaining the sense of fulfillment that comes with complete ownership of one's work which is almost impossible with the professional content management systems in use today.

The best part about web design is that you get to make your own creations, the project that we do. I may give you a scenario that you are creating a business or say I want you to teach me about something and you get to make it yourself and you get to choose within the confines of the overall perimeter. You get to choose the topic, book report, movie etc. There is a lot of freedom, creativity and this is a skill understanding how web pages are designed and this is a huge skill no matter what career you go into. (P5)

The easy answer is everybody has a website, now well a lot of people think I have got Facebook or Tumblr or WordPress blog which is great but in all those instances you are constrained by what those services have to offer. So, if you use Tumblr you can still mess with the themes or whatever but you are still at somebody else's mercy as to how you can polish your information in WordPress and stuff like that. So what I would say is: you can understand how to build your own website and present yourself in your best way possible. What best represents you? Those sites, those services can give you a great window to the world, that's why they are so popular. But if you crave more control over your data and how you present things... Yea... it's all about power; controlling the message. (P4)

In contradiction to these recruitment strategies, a few participants discussed the following general class objectives:

I don't really expect them to be gurus upon graduation; some do go off and do that. What I really want is for them to get just an overall sense of the process you know how you would prepare a content. I also want them to get the essence or the potential of the technology and what it could help them do in the future. (P9)

I would say my main goal is for students to have a better understanding of what the web is and where it is going. I would also hope that they keep an open mind and that sort of changing practices because that's something you sort of have to embrace if you are going to get into any sort of CS field nowadays. (P10)

There was a consensus in that the end goal is not necessarily for students to become professional web designers but to understand the possibilities of computing and develop an appreciation of the web and its capabilities. Only a few participants spoke passionately about the hope that students would try to go further, especially the students who did exceedingly well, to pursue being a professional web developer:

I hope that they decide to take it further, we only have one class that they really get to work with web design alone but that might give them a start to see well can I use this to help myself out in another career field. (P12)

4.2 Student Traits and Expectations

The participants taught a diverse group of students with a range of interests in art, computer science, journalism and mass communication. High school teachers mentioned that students were often more fascinated with the graphics aspect of the class. Three participants explicitly mentioned that many students registering for web design classes were mostly interested in arts and graphics, and this led to the misconception that web design and graphic design were one and the same. For example:

I get a lot of students who like art; also kids who think graphic design and web design are the same thing. (P5)

I have some students who are really interested in web design because they've taken a lot of art classes and so they are kind of looking at it from a graphic perspective. (P8)

We note that this is not necessarily a disadvantage, but it likely affects student motivation since some elements of web design involve more logical thinking and coding in addition to the creative design and aesthetic aspects. Participants mentioned that this certainly frustrates some students, especially the ones who decided to enroll in a web design course to design an artistic artifact using graphical tools. More than half of the participants mentioned that most of their students were on the creative side, and some indicated that there were some students who simply took the class in order to learn how to build an online portfolio to show off another skill such as drawing, painting, etc.

Highlighting a slightly different but related goal, one of the 2 Year college teachers reported that students often took the class to improve skills for future job opportunities, to look more attractive to potential employers, or to gain web design skills for a personal business.

The expectations that these students bring into a course pose a number of challenges. In particular, the common goal of being able to build a fully functional website to showcase a personal skill (e.g., through a personal portfolio) or to demonstrate Web development abilities to a third party (e.g., for a business client) may be unrealistic with respect to typical skills taught and tools used in beginning classes. Four participants explicitly discussed that they have to spend a good deal of time managing student expectations.

4.3 Teaching Techniques

4.3.1 Methods

All participants mentioned that they believed in live coding and demonstrating how to solve problems in class. More than half of the teachers mentioned that that a typical day in class started with a brief overview of the agenda for the class period and the rest of the class was spent showing students how to solve a particular problem. In the remaining time, students were assigned an in-class guided activity with individual help provided by the teacher. A fundamental aspect of demonstrating in-class involved participants showing students how previous students or other sources had tried to solve a particular problem or the end goal of an in-class problem and then showing students that there are multiple ways of solving it. The challenge that arose with this style of technique was the time it took to get all the students on the same page when a particular student got stuck.

Another technique mentioned was connecting the classes to an issue that was personally important to the student with the goal of building class morale. Most students were encouraged to build websites about something they liked. Participants who mentioned this also stated that students became more enthused and eager to learn the code when projects were more open-ended and students were allowed

to choose a topic of their interest therefore allowing them showcase their personal skills.

...first and foremost I say try to relate it to their interests, I tried to leave projects very open ended, um. I don't really restrict what the site is going to be on or what page it's going to be of. I noticed that really helped because let's stay a student likes horseback riding, I mean they could be doing school work but while they were doing it they are typing their own opinions and gathering facts and it's also a very open kind of environment. (P9)

Another concern was the need to build critical thinking skills with the use of the tools available to teach web design. In other words, students were encouraged to reason as a professional web developer would, particularly in terms of usability, aesthetic design choices and other aspects to which a non-programmer might not attend. For example:

As a programmer you always need to be thinking about the user. What is it that the user will expect? (P2)

I identify and try to find answers to why. Like why choose a font or color over the other etc. Therefore I introduced them to a rationale behind making those decisions, that they now form a technical standpoint they can make very easily but they don't have the guide because again it's in the CS department and no one really thought of the design aspect of it... (P6)

4.3.2 Assessments and Projects

As mentioned in the previous section, the nature of the projects assigned to students was most commonly described in ways that connected to students' personal interests. The types of projects described involved construction of a complete website that incorporated all that was taught through the semester. Therefore students were assessed based on a comprehensive understanding of the class materials, with the final product serving as a manifestation of their knowledge.

They spend the first half of the semester doing HTML and then over the course of seven or eight assignments we continually add things to a three page website that they build about themselves (P4)

By reviewing participants' syllabi, we found that about half of the teachers used grading schemes heavily weighted to hands-on projects. On average, a class was 70% dependent on in-class guided activities, group projects and individual projects while the remaining 30% was for tests and exams.

4.4 Challenges

4.4.1 Expectation Management

Many participants articulated the challenge of redefining students' expectations. As mentioned earlier many students perceive web design and graphic design as the same and this in turn hinders morale. Additionally teachers perceived that those students who take the course with the goal of immediately building a fully-functional website often get frustrated half way through the course due to the pace of the class. Participants explained that a lot of time is spent "deprogramming" students to understand that learning the fundamentals of web design is essential before aiming for a professional website.

Along with managing student expectations, teachers discussed student misconceptions of professional web design tools. They described that some students were reluctant to learn the fundamentals of HTML and CSS because they were already exposed to the functionality of professional blogging tools and content management systems:

They look at professional websites or professional programs and that's not what they are making. They are making very rudimentary programs and it feels like there's a disconnection in what I want to play or look at and what I can actually achieve and so that sort of readjusting their expectations with what they can do. (P1)

Some students come in thinking that because they took a class on Code Academy and built an app, that they know everything. So you spend some time with a few students trying to deprogram them and let them understand that they need to learn the fundamentals of web designing. Using WordPress doesn't mean you know how to do web programming. (P4)

In these cases, professional web authoring environments and students' exposure to them prior to enrolling in class was viewed as an obstacle necessitating the need to convince students about the value of "the fundamentals".

4.4.2 Connecting the Dots

Another challenge mentioned by participants was how to explain the connection between HTML and CSS. Students were usually asked to tackle HTML-specific problems and then after a couple of lessons they were introduced to CSS. This is a problem for a lot of students as they find it difficult to understand how CSS applies to HTML. This sets the class back as the teachers try to correlate the two conceptually and demonstrate their relationship using a variety of separate tools (ie. code editors, web browsers):

A vast majority would do that and a few won't and sometimes like if you run a CSS rule and apply it back in the HTML page, sometimes there's a little bit of a disconnect. It takes a long time for some of them to understand that connection. For example, you know between what a CSS file does and the effect it might have on a page. (P10)

When you teach CSS it really doesn't make sense until you attach it to that web page and then you're like oh now I understand... (P3)

When they look at the HTML, it's hard for the students to visualize what it's going to look like and normally in the process in the way I teach, you have to save it as an HTML file and then go open it in the browser separately and refresh.(P5)

4.4.3 Student Morale

Lastly, the issue of morale generally was mentioned as a challenge teachers had to tackle all semester. Although participants mentioned ways in which they tried to get students interested through personal projects, real world exercises, or fun topics, it was still difficult to get some students genuinely interested in web design as soon as they saw it involved coding. Some participants spoke quite passionately about this challenge and how they strive to keep students motivated:

Many times, especially girls, they are resistant to coding and writing code and I do tell them that this is in the CS department because we are the ones that are well aware of the technology that is available because this could very well be an art class. Yes, there is the technical aspect of it, but there's a lot of art, aesthetics involved and the code part is really the easy part. Deciding proportion and colors and fonts and deciding all those things are really important aspects of web designing. (P6)

5. DISCUSSION

Here we examine the results presented in the previous section by highlighting some of their relationships and implications for teaching.

5.1 Dealing with Interdisciplinarity

The educators in this study had one thing in common: a passion for teaching web design. Given the diversity of their expertise/backgrounds which ranged from business to journalism to math, it was surprising that only one participant mentioned her disciplinary background as a challenge. She stated that as a person with a CS background, she felt that there was a disservice to students who might want to learn the business side of web designing such as presenting a webpage in a form that would attract an employer:

One would be that because there is a desire to have more of a business side and I don't know business that well, it might be better if I knew more but I can collaborate with the business department a lot and ask for their input and you can't know everything. (P12)

This comment recognizes how diverse web design is along with the way that a teacher's own background colors the educational experiences. That is, teachers may tend to focus on what they know and are comfortable with, rather than seeking out a more integrated and truly interdisciplinary experience. While there are obvious content limitations due to the introductory nature of all of these courses, a teacher's emphasis placed of the set of "fundamentals" with which she has expertise can be discouraging for students whose interests lie elsewhere—a sentiment expressed by many of our participants at various points. It seems important for teachers with different backgrounds and perspectives towards web design to share their approaches to present a more well-rounded view of the field.

5.2 Competing Authenticities

Shafer and Resnick introduced a multifaceted view of the concept of "authenticity" wherein educational experiences can be examined along four different spectra: personal authenticity to the students' interests, real world authenticity, disciplinary authenticity with respect to the tools and techniques used, and assessment authenticity in how students are evaluated [12]. Here we saw unique examples of when these different forms of authenticity can be in direct conflict with one another.

In general, educators in this study described courses that strived for a high degree of authenticity by tying flexible projects to students' personal interests, making use of actual tools/languages used by professional web developers as they understood them (namely, HTML and CSS), and assessing students largely based on a comprehensive understanding of the course (e.g., emphasizing hands-on project work) rather than artificially testing students on the idiosyncrasies of syntax. However, competing views of what constitutes a "professional tool"—content management systems vs. raw HTML—leads to a conundrum that is difficult to resolve. In truth most professional web sites do make use of CMSes to manage the complexity and volume of content, while enabling a unified look and feel across a large site. These systems allow for a range of professional roles in the web authoring process including copy editors, graphic designers, as well as developers who write the necessary front and back-end code to customize and extend the CMS beyond its default functionality. Put simply, students' lived experience with the web is one that is richly interactive, visually appealing and highly reliant on use of third party APIs [3], but the artifacts they are able to construct with just basic knowledge of HTML and CSS do not reflect their view of the "real world" both in terms of the final product and in terms of the tools they know are widely available. In many cases, students have already used such tools prior to enrolling in the class.

Thus if the primary goal of teachers in this elective course was to ensure that students have a positive experience while introducing them to some basic computational principles and tools, it appears necessary to explore new tools that more readily strike a balance between student expectations and instructional goals of code-oriented learning objectives. Rather than fight to redefine student expectations, as was so often mentioned by our participants, perhaps it is better to embrace those expectations as important motivators and find ways to bridge the gap.

As computing educators we are not advocating for a course centered on building WYSIWYG content in an out-of-the-box CMS, but rather we are highlighting a need for pedagogical development tools for web design that take both of these considerations seriously in a similar way to pedagogical programming environments (like AppInventor, Scratch, and Calico) that balance the authenticity of working in an IDE on personally meaningful projects with the need to scaffold learners and focus their attention on particular concerns of import. Further as educators it may be time to rethink what it means to practice and teach web design/development by incorporating tools, languages, and frameworks of increasing levels of abstraction.

6. CONCLUSION

In this study, we interviewed educators to identify themes that give us a broader insight on the experiences of teachers as they introduce web design to novice students. We acknowledge some limitations in this work that suggest multiple follow-up lines of investigation. First, our recruitment approach (e.g., using the Computer Science Teachers Association mailing list) may have attracted volunteers more interested in code-oriented views of web design than would be typical in the general population. This, coupled with the limited number of teachers interviewed, constrains the generalizability of our claims. In future work, we hope to complement this work by surveying a larger and more representative sample of teachers to explore the prevalence of the themes identified here. Direct interviews with students would also help corroborate teachers' perceptions of students' goals for taking these courses.

Even so, our work here contributes to the CS education literature by providing an objective examination of modern web design instruction across multiple instructors and contexts. Our themes provide additional evidence and alternative explanations for the challenges reported in earlier work. These results underscore the need to teach web courses in multiple phases and/or from multiple perspectives to fully articulate the vast nature of web development. Further, new educational environments that approximate the affordances of CMS systems while engaging students with basic syntax and semantics of markup and stylesheets may be valuable tools to balance the objectives of both students and teachers.

ACKNOWLEDGMENTS

This work is funded by the National Science Foundation under grant CNS-1339344. Any opinions, findings, and conclusions or recommendations expressed in this material are those of the authors and do not necessarily reflect the views of the NSF.

References

[1] D. R. Adams. Integration early: A new approach to teaching web application development. *Journal of Computing Sciences in Colleges*, 23(1):97–104, 2007.

[2] V. Braun and V. Clarke. Using thematic analysis in psychology. *Qualitative research in psychology*, 3(2): 77–101, 2006.

[3] R. W. Connolly. Awakening Rip Van Winkle: Modernizing the computer science web curriculum. In *Proc of ITiCSE '11*, pages 18–22, 2011.

[4] B. Dorn and M. Guzdial. Discovering computing: Perspectives of web designers. In *Proc of ICER '10*, pages 23–30, 2010.

[5] B. Dorn, D. Babb, D. M. Nizzi, and C. M. Epler. Computing on the silicon prairie: The state of CS in Nebraska public schools. In *Proc. of SIGCSE '15*, pages 296–301, 2015.

[6] A. H. Lee. A manageable web software architecture: searching for simplicity. In *Proc. of SIGCSE'03*, pages 229–233, 2003.

[7] B. B. L. Lim. Teaching web development technologies in CI/IS curricula. In *Proc. of SIGCSE'98*, pages 107–111, 1998.

[8] R. Mercuri, N. Herrmann, and J. Popyack. Using HTML and JavaScript in introductory programming courses. In *Proc of SIGCSE '98*, pages 176–180, 1998.

[9] T. H. Park and S. Wiedenbeck. Learning web development: Challenges at an earlier stage of computing education. In *Proc of ICER '11*, pages 125–132, 2011.

[10] D. Reed. Rethinking CS0 with JavaScript. In *Proc. of SIGCSE'01*, pages 100–104, 2001.

[11] M. B. Rosson, J. F. Ballin, and H. Nash. Everyday programming: Challenges and opportunities for informal web development. In *Proc. of VL/HCC'04*, pages 123–130, 2004.

[12] D. W. Shaffer and M. Resnick. "Thick" authenticity: New media and authentic learning. *Journal of interactive learning research*, 10(2):195–215, 1999.

[13] K. Sridharan. A course on web languages and web-based applications. *IEEE Transactions on Education*, 47(2):254–260, 2004.

[14] M. Stepp, J. Miller, and V. Kirst. A CS 1.5 introduction to web programming. In *Proc. of SIGCSE'09*, pages 121–125. ACM, Mar. 2009.

[15] K. Treu. To teach the unteachable class: An experimental course in web-based application design. In *Proc of SIGCSE '02*, pages 201–205, 2002.

[16] E. L. Walker and L. Browne. Teaching web development with limited resources. In *Proc. of SIGCSE'99*, pages 12–16, 1999.

Academic Integrity and Professional Integrity in Computing Education

Simon
University of Newcastle, Australia
simon@newcastle.edu.au

Judy Sheard
Monash University, Australia
judy.sheard@monash.edu

ABSTRACT

Certain practices, such as unauthorised collaboration with other students and unreferenced copying from external sources, are generally considered in the educational context to be breaches of academic integrity. This paper explores whether there are differences between the perceptions of the acceptability of these practices in the academic context and in the professional context.

From focus groups of computing academics and students, and an online survey, we find that there are indeed differences in perceptions: that many practices considered unacceptable in the academic context are considered significantly more acceptable in the professional context.

This raises questions concerning the roles of summative assessment and the possibilities of authentic assessment. The paper concludes that in much of programming education there is an unbreachable rift between the goal of authentic assessment, which necessarily entails collaborative work, and the need for summative assessment of individual effort, which typically requires work in isolation.

The findings of our research have implications for computing education programs, particularly in regard to preparation of students for the workforce.

Categories and Subject Descriptors

K3.2 [**Computers and education**]: Computer and Information Science Education – *computer science education*

Keywords

Academic integrity, professional integrity, computing education

1. INTRODUCTION

A core aim of work in academic integrity is to ensure that work submitted by students for assessment is indeed their own work. Recent research on academic integrity in computing focuses on staff and student perceptions of the issues, why students breach

academic integrity, and how such breaches are detected and dealt with.

In this paper we go further to consider the purpose and validity of academic integrity in computing education. Academic integrity is integrally related to assessment rather than to learning. Assessment has a number of functions, often separated into formative, which assist students in the learning process, and summative, which serve to measure the extent of the students' learning.

Authenticity is a further consideration in assessment, with the suggestion that assessment is better and more valid if it is conducted in an environment and a manner that reflect those in which the equivalent real-world task would be carried out.

The goal of this paper is to explore these three notions of academic integrity, the distinct roles of assessment, and authentic assessment, and consider whether they can all be consistently applied in programming education.

2. BACKGROUND

Because this paper draws together the three distinct threads of academic integrity, authentic assessment, and the summative and formative purposes of assessment, it is appropriate to begin by briefly considering the background of each of these threads.

2.1 Academic integrity

Questions of academic integrity have been considered by a number of computing education researchers [5-8, 10-13, 15, 16]. Evidence from these papers suggests that academic integrity is an important issue in computing education; that the incidence of various forms of cheating is unacceptably high and is typically underestimated; and that the issues are not as straightforward in regard to computing assessments as they are in regard to essays.

One clear finding from the literature is that many students and academics see no problem with students reusing code that they have written for another project [6, 10, 16], although outside computing education this is called self-plagiarism and is considered academically inappropriate [3].

There is also a widely held view that there is nothing wrong with students working together on individual assignments, or copying much of another student's assignment, so long as the student submitting the assignment does a reasonable amount of the work [6, 10, 16]. Again, in the broader world of academic integrity these practices are considered inappropriate, and are generally called collusion [3].

2.2 Authentic assessment

Herrington and Herrington [9] suggest that assessment is most likely to be authentic if its context reflects the conditions under which the performance will occur; if it requires students to craft polished products; and if it requires significant student time and effort in collaboration with others.

In the computing education literature most mentions of authentic assessment appear to leave the advantages of such assessment implicit. For example, Cajander et al [2] observe that "forms of assessment that are seen as authentic, meaningful and understandable by the students, teaching staff and curriculum developers are of utmost importance if professional skills are to be accepted and included in the formal curriculum" (p145). Authentic assessment is most often mentioned in the context of capstone projects.

In the context of academic integrity, Carter et al [4] propose that "providing situationally authentic assessment tasks could … reduce the likelihood of cheating. For example, online programming examinations or open book examinations may provide a more realistic assessment of programming skills and are closer in nature to the actual work the students have already done and will potentially need in their future employment" (p118).

In general, it appears that authentic assessment is understood to be desirable, but with little explicit indication of the reasons for this. Our own interpretation is that authenticity in assessment is valued because it helps to ensure that what is being assessed is the skill that is required in the normal working environment: if a task is normally performed in one way but is assessed in another way, there must be some doubt about the validity of the assessment.

2.3 Summative and formative assessment

The terms summative assessment and formative assessment are widely used in the literature of education, often as though they were general knowledge. It is perhaps important to consider their origins. According to Wiliam and Black [20], "Bloom et al [1] were the first to extend the usage to its generally accepted current meaning. They defined as summative … those assessments … which are designed to judge the extent of students' learning of the material in a course, for the purpose of grading, certification, evaluation of progress or even for researching the effectiveness of a curriculum" (p537). By contrast, formative assessment is designed to provide students with feedback that they can use as part of their learning.

The grading aspect of assessment is probably the aspect most often considered by academics undertaking summative assessment. As explained by Sheard et al [14], "a final examination … the ultimate in summative assessment … typically provides the final evidence for the judgments that teachers make about their students' grades and progression" (p141). Nevertheless, we must not overlook the certification aspect, which is one of what Taras [19] calls the social roles of summative assessment. In a sense, prospective employers rely upon the grades of graduates as evidence of the skills and capabilities that they seek in their employees. In an ideal word employers might conduct their own comprehensive tests on all candidates for a position, but in the real world the academic grades of the graduates are often taken as a surrogate for such directed testing. Rightly or wrongly, the educational assessment process is used to certify the fitness of graduates for particular professional roles and their proficiency with certain skills.

It would appear to follow that when the certification function of summative assessment is considered, there is a role for authentic assessment: if we assess students in circumstances unlike those that they will meet in their professional lives, the assessment will be of limited value in certifying their fitness for those professional lives.

3. RESEARCH APPROACH

In a broad survey of computing students and academics [16], we presented a number of scenarios and asked respondents both whether they constituted plagiarism or collusion and whether they were academically acceptable practices. In other parts of the survey we asked respondents to rank some possible sources from which students might copy code, then posed a number of scenarios and asked respondents whether they considered them acceptable, first in the context of academic study and then in the context of professional practice.

Prior to the survey we conducted some focus groups of computing students and of computing academics, to pilot and refine the questions that we intended to ask in the survey.

4. FINDINGS

Three focus groups were held with 18 computing academics, and three focus groups with 12 computing students. The subsequent survey was conducted online, and drew responses from 70 computing academics and 486 computing students. In the remainder of this section we analyse those responses, supplementing them with observations from the focus groups.

4.1 Sources of Academic Copying

To estimate how common various sources of plagiarism or collusion might be, survey respondents were asked to rank six possible sources from the most common (1) to the least common (6).

There are a number of methods of finding an aggregate ranking from a question such as this. One common approach is to average the response rates for each question weighted by the ranking number. For a particular source, if $p1\%$ of respondents rank it 1, $p2\%$ rank it 2, etc, its weighted average will be $p1 + 2p2 + 3p3 + 4p4 + 5p5 + 6p6$. These weighted averages are then used to determine an aggregate rank for each option.

Table 1 shows the six listed sources and their aggregate rankings by the students and by the academics. For both groups there was a clear gap between the first and second rankings, with the third ranking very closely following the second.

The difference between the first and second rankings is interesting: the students think that the internet is the principal

Table 1: students' and academics' rankings of sources of plagiarism/collusion, most common (1) to least common (6), with the weighted averages in parentheses

Source of plagiarism/collusion	Students	Academics
Copying from the internet	1 (35%)	2 (44%)
Copying from another student's work	3 (51%)	3 (44%)
Copying from a published source	5 (72%)	5 (75%)
Having another person undertake the work on the student's behalf	6 (76%)	4 (66%)
Working with other students but presenting the result as the work of one student	2 (51%)	1 (41%)
Substantially reusing work that the student has submitted for another assignment	4 (61%)	6 (78%)

source of student plagiarism or collusion, whereas the academics think that working with other students is the biggest issue. These positions are reversed for the second rank, and both groups see copying from other students as the third most common problem.

These issues are further addressed in the remainder of the survey, in which respondents were presented with a number of scenarios and asked whether they were acceptable in the academic context and whether they were acceptable in the professional context.

4.2 Using Code from External Sources

Is it acceptable to use code from external sources, such as the web, when writing a program? The general feeling from the focus groups is of broad acceptability, so long as the student still contributes substantially to the work.

> "I just Google and I implement and … because I had to implement it … and make it work within my code and add things to it, it becomes mine. Whereas if it was like the variables were set and I just copied a chunk, pasted a chunk and then left it, it would be closer to plagiarism."

> "In essays it's the same when you're in uni … as when you go out in the real world. Basically if you're stealing someone else's essay and reselling it or something it's plagiarism. But in the real world in IT … there's different rulings based on different things which makes them a bit more complex."

> "…when you're just getting chunks of code, you're not really copying, you're just getting concepts behind it and interpreting it to yourself."

The survey had two questions on the use of code form external sources. In one the external source was referenced, while in the other it was not. The answers of the survey respondents are shown in Table 2. For both scenarios, both the students and the academics consider the practice more acceptable in the professional setting than in the academic setting. There are many academics who do not consider it academically acceptable even when the external source is referenced; but almost all consider it professionally acceptable. The students, on the other hand, offer similar responses for the academic and professional contexts.

When the external source is not referenced, the acceptability is substantially lower, but the same pattern applies: the academics find the practice highly unacceptable in the academic context and more acceptable in the professional context, and both student acceptability rates are bracketed between these extremes.

Where possible, the differences between responses have been tested for significance using the *difference in proportion* test.

Table 2: using code from external sources

Basing a computer program on code that is freely available on the web, and referencing the source			
Students (p<0.05)		Academics (not binom)	
Academically acceptable	Professionally acceptable	Academically acceptable	Professionally acceptable
73%	80%	58%	94%
Basing a computer program on code that is freely available on the web, without referencing the source			
Students (p<0.01)		Academics (not binom)	
Academically acceptable	Professionally acceptable	Academically acceptable	Professionally acceptable
10%	16%	3%	19%

This is possible only when the sample size n and the proportion p satisfy the standard binomial requirement that both $np>5$ and $n(1-p)>5$. For the 70 academic respondents this requirement is not met when either of the proportions is below 8% or above 92%. In this and subsequent tables, a pair of proportions is marked $p<0.01$ or $p<0.05$ if the difference is significant at the specified level, and *not binom* if either proportion fails to meet the requirement.

Computer programming is largely a component assembly task, where the components are also known as plans [18] or design patterns [17]. Reuse of existing components is encouraged by some academics and practised by many professionals. Programmers are expected to recognise what components are required for the solution to a given problem and to assemble those components appropriately. If any of the components is not readily available it must of course be built, but where there are available components the programmer is expected to incorporate them into the emerging structure, adapting them if necessary.

Viewed in this light, it is surely essential that programmers use and adapt code from external sources, and it is therefore baffling that a handful of academics find it professionally unacceptable to incorporate external code even when referencing it. We suggest that the question of referencing externally sourced code has not yet been resolved either in the realm of professional computing or in the realm of computing education, although some have attempted to resolve it [8]; but clearly most of our respondents believe that if externally sourced code can be used, it must be referenced.

4.3 Getting Help to Debug Troublesome Code

Software developers and programming students alike recognise that debugging is often much easier if somebody else is helping. This recognition is built into most programming courses, with lab sessions and consultation times in which students can seek help from academics or from more advanced students.

The general feeling from the student focus groups was that it is appropriate and necessary to seek help from others.

> "I don't understand collusion myself, because basically collusion is working together, right? And 99% of the world is made up of people working together to get things done. So in my eyes I'm not really for rules against."

> "If you're stuck on code or something, and you just don't know how to fix it, if you don't seek help you can't finish the assignment. You're going to have to get help."

The feeling was less consensual in the academic focus groups, but was still expressed by some of the academics.

> "I was trying to think of a model where we didn't make it illegal for them to work together, because as far as I'm concerned if four of them work together and they turn in a good assignment, well, they've learnt something. It doesn't worry me."

Three of the survey questions concerned the acceptability of various ways of seeking assistance with troublesome code. The questions and their responses are shown in Table 3.

Each of these practices was considered academically acceptable by about half the academics and professionally acceptable by nearly all of them; once again, the student assessments of acceptability fell between these extremes, but still increased significantly from the academic context to the professional

Table 3: getting help from others

Posting troublesome code on a message board and asking for help			
Students (p<0.05)		Academics (p<0.01)	
Academically acceptable 52%	Professionally acceptable 60%	Academically acceptable 41%	Professionally acceptable 81%
Discussing the detail of one's code with colleagues			
Students (p<0.01)		Academics (p<0.01)	
Academically acceptable 57%	Professionally acceptable 78%	Academically acceptable 56%	Professionally acceptable 91%
Asking colleagues to help when code is not working as intended			
Students (p<0.01)		Academics (not binom)	
Academically acceptable 69%	Professionally acceptable 83%	Academically acceptable 57%	Professionally acceptable 93%

context. It is clear that practices involving getting help from others, which are considered acceptable in the professional context, are not considered acceptable in the academic context.

4.4 Reusing one's own Code

Is it acceptable to take code that one has written for one project and reuse it in another project, without explicitly acknowledging the reuse? This question was not discussed in the focus groups. Most survey respondents do not believe it to be acceptable (Table 4), with the only acceptability rate over 50% being from the academic respondents in the professional context.

This finding again seems at odds with the component nature of the programing task. If one has already written a component that seems appropriate for the current task, it arguably makes sense to reuse that component rather than to design and write it again. In the academic context it is presumably considered necessary to acknowledge the source of components that one has written in previous work, but it is not clear why such an acknowledgement would be required in professional practice.

4.5 Paying for Code

Is it acceptable to pay for code, either as a complete program or for incorporation into one's own programs? This question was not discussed in the focus groups. On the survey (Table 5), no academics and very few students found this acceptable in the academic context. The acceptability rates were substantially higher in the professional context, but still not as high as might be expected.

Outsourcing is generally considered a legitimate option in the world of professional computing, but more than half of the respondents do not consider it acceptable in that setting. Do

Table 4: reusing one's own code

Reusing code that one wrote for another project without acknowledging this			
Students (p<0.01)		Academics (p<0.01)	
Academically acceptable 22%	Professionally acceptable 37%	Academically acceptable 9%	Professionally acceptable 53%

Table 5: paying for code

Purchasing code written by others to incorporate into one's own programs			
Students (p<0.01)		Academics (not binom)	
Academically acceptable 4%	Professionally acceptable 37%	Academically acceptable 0%	Professionally acceptable 47%
Paying somebody else to write the whole program			
Students (p<0.01)		Academics (not binom)	
Academically acceptable 2%	Professionally acceptable 19%	Academically acceptable 0%	Professionally acceptable 36%

these respondents not acknowledge that it is an acceptable practice? Or did they perhaps understand the question in the sense of an employee who is paid to write code subcontracting that task without the employer's approval?

4.7 The Non-Binomial Differences

As discussed in the context of Table 2, a number of the differences in academics could not be tested for significance because one of the proportions was too low (less than 8%) or too high (more than 92%). Nevertheless, all of those differences look substantial, so an informal test was carried out as follows: proportions less than 8% were replaced with 8%; proportions more than 92% were replaced with 92%; and the test was reapplied. In every case, a significant difference was then found at the 0.01 level. That is, if more of the academics had found the practice academically acceptable, or fewer had found it professionally acceptable, the difference, while smaller, would have been found significant. Combining these informal measures of significance with the formal measures where these applied, for every scenario both students and academics found the practice significantly more acceptable in the professional context than in the academic context.

5. DISCUSSION

We have surveyed computing students and academics on eight different practices, and have found substantial differences between the acceptability of those practices in the academic and the professional contexts. Every practice is considered acceptable by substantially more respondents in the professional context than in the academic context.

A clear inference from this finding is that in a substantial range of computing courses, assessments are not authentic. When assessing students for summative purposes, we often require them to work in a way that is different from the accepted professional practice, by imposing restrictions on them that would not apply in the professional context.

To make the assessments more authentic we would need to apply them in a setting more like that of the computing professional: we would need to accept the appropriate reuse of the student's own code and the code of others; we would need to accept that programmers encountering problems will discuss those problems with others and be helped towards the solution; we might even be tempted to permit the use of outsourcing.

The problem with all of this is the mismatch between the formative function of assessment and the summative function, especially in its social role of certification. If we want students to learn to program as professional programmers program, we should permit them all the latitude that goes with professional programming. However, if we intend to take seriously the certification role of summative assessment, we require confidence in our assessment of each individual student. This in turn means that we must conduct some of our assessment in an environment that rejects the collaborative nature of professional computing and instead requires each student to perform in isolation.

If we wish to have some confidence that we are assessing the capabilities of the individual, it is clear that we must sometimes assess inauthentically, accepting that there is often no way to reliably conduct an authentic assessment of the individual student in what is inherently a collaborative and social skill.

Further to this mismatch between authentic assessment and individual summative assessment, the learning process itself is subject to a similar mismatch. For somebody who is good at programming, using the code of other people and getting help from others are powerful learning experiences; whereas for somebody who is not good at programming, using the code of others and getting help from others can be substitutes for learning, and potentially block their learning. Nevertheless, in the learning process we do expect students to use the code of others and to seek help from others, because it is not clear that there is any other way. But when it comes to assessing what the students have learnt, what skills they have acquired, we remove the opportunity for them to use the code of others and to seek help from others, because otherwise we have no way of knowing and assessing just how much of the work is their own.

The findings of our research have clear implications for computing education programs. The differences between the students' and the academics' perceptions of the acceptability of various coding practices indicate a need for instruction in how to use and attribute code from other sources. Furthermore, the lack of clarity in regard to professional practices suggests a strong need to focus on this question in order to better prepare students for the workforce.

6. ACKNOWLEDGEMENTS

Support for this project has been provided by the Australian Government Office for Learning and Teaching, grant SP12-2312. The views expressed in this publication do not necessarily reflect those of the Australian Government Office for Learning and Teaching.

The authors gratefully acknowldege the contribution of the other members of the project team.

7. REFERENCES

[1] Bloom, B.S., J.T. Hastings, G.F. Madaus (Eds) (1971). Handbook on the Formative and Summative Evaluation of Student Learning. New York, McGraw-Hill.

[2] Cajander, Å., M. Daniels, R. McDermott, B.R. von Konsky (2011). Assessing professional skills in engineering education. 13th Australasian Computing Education Conference (ACE 2011), 145-154.

[3] Carroll, J. (2002). A Handbook for Deterring Plagiarism in Higher Education. Oxford Centre for Staff and Learning Development, Oxford, UK.

[4] Carter, J, K. Ala-Mutka, U. Fuller, M. Dick, J. English, W. Fone, J. Sheard (2003). How shall we assess this?. SIGCSE Bulletin 35(4), 107-123.

[5] Chuda, D., P. Navrat, B. Kovacova and P. Humay (2012). The issue of (software) plagiarism: a student view. IEEE Transactions on Education 55(1): 22-28.

[6] Cosma, G. and M. Joy (2008). Towards a Definition of Source-Code Plagiarism. IEEE Transactions on Education 51(2): 195-200.

[7] Dennis, L. (2004). Student attitudes to plagiarism and collusion within computer science. International Plagiarism Conference 2004. www.plagiarismadvice.org/research-papers/category/2004, accessed 9 Jan 2015.

[8] Gibson, J.P. (2009). Software reuse and plagiarism: a code of practice. 14th Annual SIGCSE Conference on Innovation and Technology in Computer Science Education (ITiCSE'09), 55-59.

[9] Herrington, J., A. Herrington (1998). Authentic assessment and multimedia: how university students respond to a model of authentic assessment. Higher Education Research & Development, 17(3), 305-322

[10] Joy, M.S., J.E. Sinclair, R. Boyatt, J.Y.-K. Uau, and G. Cosma (2013). Student perspectives on source-code plagiarism. International Journal for Educational Integrity, 9(1), 3-19.

[11] Riedesel, C.P., A.L. Clear, G.W. Cross, J.M. Hughes, Simon, H.M. Walker (2012). Academic integrity policies in a computing education context. Proceedings of the final reports on Innovation and Technology in Computer Science Education 2012 Working Groups, 1-15.

[12] Sheard, J., M. Dick (2011). Computing student practices of cheating and plagiarism: a decade of change. 16th Annual SIGCSE Conference on Innovation and Technology in Computer Science Education (ITiCSE'11), 233-237.

[13] Sheard, J., S. Markham, M. Dick (2003). Investigating differences in cheating behaviours of IT undergraduate and graduate students: The maturity and motivation factors, Journal of Higher Education Research and Development 22, 91-108.

[14] Sheard, J., Simon, A. Carbone, D. D'Souza, M. Hamilton (2013). Assessment of programming: pedagogical foundations of exams. 18th Annual SIGCSE Conference on Innovation and Technology in Computer Science Education (ITiCSE'13), 141-146.

[15] Simon, B. Cook, J. Sheard, A. Carbone, C. Johnson (2013). Academic integrity: differences between computing assessments and essays. 13th International Conference on Computing Education Research (Koli Calling 2013), 23-32.

[16] Simon, B. Cook, J. Sheard, A. Carbone, C. Johnson (2014). Student perceptions of the acceptability of various code-writing practices. 19th Annual SIGCSE Conference on Innovation and Technology in Computer Science Education (ITiCSE'14), 105-110.

[17] Shalloway, A., J.R. Trott, (2001). Design patterns explained, a new perspective on object-oriented design. Addison-Wesley.

[18] Soloway, E. (1986). Learning to program = learning to construct mechanisms and explanations. Communications of the ACM, 29(9), 850-858.

[19] Taras, M. (2005). Assessment – summative and formative – some theoretical reflections. British Journal of Educational Studies, 53(4), 466-478.

[20] Wiliam, D., Black, P. (1996). Meanings and consequences: a basis for distinguishing formative and summative functions of assessment? British Educational Research Journal, 22 (5), 537-548.

Measures of Student Engagement in Computer Science

Jane Sinclair
Department of Computer Science
University of Warwick, Coventry, CV4 7AL, UK
+44 2476 523986
j.e.sinclair@warwick.ac.uk

Matthew Butler
Faculty of Information Technology
Monash University, Caulfield East, VIC, Australia
+61 3 9903 1911
matthew.butler@monash.edu

Michael Morgan
Faculty of Information Technology
Monash University, Berwick Campus, VIC, Australia
+61 3 990 47155
michael.morgan@monash.edu

Sara Kalvala
Department of Computer Science
University of Warwick, Coventry, CV4 7AL, UK
+44 2476 523179
sara.kalvala@warwick.ac.uk

ABSTRACT

Data relating to university students' engagement is collected internationally via several large-scale student surveys such as the North American National Survey of Student Engagement. The instruments employed measure the extent to which students put their efforts into activities associated with effective learning. It is claimed that these process measures act as a reliable proxy for student attainment, and there appears to be some evidence to support this. So far, there has been little work done to investigate engagement instruments and the data they generate from a subject perspective. This paper brings together data relating to Computer Science (CS) across the range of major engagement surveys. The results of this meta-analysis appear to indicate that CS rates lower than average on many of the major engagement benchmarks and in some cases, considerably so. Particular benchmark areas giving cause for concern are identified prompting questions as to how these results should be interpreted and used in the context of a particular learning domain. We also critique aspects of the surveys themselves, suggesting that further research is needed to better understand their appropriateness for individual subjects or for groups of subjects with shared traits. The paper argues that more qualitative data is required and that other measures (such as student expectation and some subject-specific measures) are needed for a greater understanding of the CS student experience.

Categories and Subject Descriptors

K.3.2 [**Computer Science Education**]: Computer and Information Science Education

General Terms

Human Factors

Keywords

Student experience, CS, international measures

ITICSE '15, July 04 - 08, 2015, Vilnius, Lithuania
Copyright 2015 ACM 978-1-4503-3440-2/15/07...$15.00
http://dx.doi.org/10.1145/2729094.2742586

1. INTRODUCTION

For many years universities have conducted in-house surveys to discover students' opinion of the subjects they take and of the teaching and resources provided. Such exercises gather valuable feedback often local (sometimes to individual departments or degree programs) and focused on students' experience of the teaching and learning facilities. High profile national surveys such as the UK's National Student Survey [1] have again focused on student experience in areas such as timeliness of feedback and present of teaching sessions. In 2000, a North American National Survey of Student Engagement (NSSE) was introduced [2]. The concept of engagement relates to students' activities and the amount of effort expended on "high impact" learning activities. As stated by Kuh [3]: "NSSE annually assesses the extent to which students are participating in educational practices that are strongly associated with high levels of learning and personal development". Gathering feedback on both student experience and engagement provides valuable information on students' views regarding their overall learning experience. Proponents of engagement surveys go further in claiming that engagement measurements act as a reliable predictor for student learning and that such surveys represent an easy-to-implement means of assessing the quality of educational experience provided [4].

Use of NSSE has grown in North America and Canada and a variety of research studies have been undertaken which attest to the validity of the instrument. Such studies provide evidence of a significant relationship between survey results and a variety of educational targets including developing critical thinking and moral development, and institutional outcomes such as retention and graduation rates [5,6,7]. Engagement surveys are now being used or piloted at a national level in a number of countries including Australia, China, New Zealand and the UK. For example, the Australian Government has recently introduced the University Experience Survey (UES), to "provide a nationwide architecture for collecting feedback on key facets of the higher education experience, that are measurable, linked with learning and development outcomes, and for which institutions can reasonably be assumed to have responsibility." [11].

Aggregated NSSE and UES results are widely disseminated [2, 10] and institutional data is being actively used by universities in North America to direct the development of student services [6]. It is also apparent that the uses to which this data will be put are likely to spread beyond the stated intentions of the survey creators. It is therefore important that the implications of survey data are well-understood so that it can be used to best effect for specific groups but also to scrutinise the data collection instruments to ensure that they best capture the student experience of current students.

As yet, little work has been carried out to explore these surveys or investigate implications of engagement data for specific subject groups. Available aggregated data shows that different subjects have different mean values across the range of questions, but there is little understanding of subject profiles, of why variations occur or of what the appropriate action should be. This paper focuses on data collected from students majoring in CS. The main surveys currently in use are briefly reviewed, showing the factors assessed and the benchmarks used. Data relating to CS students is used to provide a meta-analysis of the profile for this subject group. The distinctive patterns of mean scores raise questions concerning the survey instruments and the way in which teaching and learning in CS programs is conducted.

2. CURRENT STUDENT ENGAGEMENT INSTRUMENTS

The following surveys are all used at a national level either with optional or mandatory institutional participation. NSSE is the longest-standing instrument, with other surveys developing from this to represent more tailored national instruments.

2.1 NSSE

NSSE has been delivered annually in North America and Canada for the past 15 years with the 2013 run reporting participation from 371,284 students representing 621 institutions. The survey, having 10 pages of multiple choice questions, is administered in the second half of the academic year to undergraduates of all subjects and levels of study. Questions include basic descriptive and demographic information. Engagement measures are grouped into 5 benchmarks of student behaviour evidenced by key indicators:

- Academic Challenge (17 questions) covers reflective and integrated learning; higher order learning; quantitative reasoning; and learning strategies.

- Learning with Peers (8 questions) covering collaborative learning; and discussions with diverse others.

- Experiences with Faculty (9 questions) examines student-faculty interaction; and effective teaching practices;

- Campus Environment (13 questions) covers quality of interactions; and supportive environment.

Most NSSE engagement questions use a 4 point Likert scale, with little qualitative data. Public search tools support result queries by question or according to the benchmarks. The benchmarks are assessed by different numbers of questions so a standardised measure (out of 60) is calculated for each contributing indicator, and an average for the indicators is reported. The full survey, together with access to query tools and links to supporting information can be found at the NSSE website [2].

2.2 UES

In 2011, the Australian Government commissioned a nationwide University Experience Survey (UES) [10]. The UES was originally intended for use as a means of allocating performance-based funds, but late in the development of this project, this was abandoned [13]. The UES has been in use since 2012, when it replaced the Australasian Survey of Student Engagement (AUSSE) [8] as the Australian instrument of choice. The UES was informed, in part, by the AUSSE survey (which itself has formative links with the NSSE) and as such some of the core ideas found in the NSSE are present in the UES, although it places less focus on specific academic activity to derive benchmark results. All 40 Australian universities are required to administer the survey on behalf of the Australian Government and Graduate Careers Australia (GCA).

In 2013, all 40 Australian universities administered the survey, with just over 100,000 completed surveys received. While there are significant ties to the NSSE survey, the UES identifies five different benchmarks for student engagement:

- Skills Development (8 questions) rates development of general skills such as critical thinking, ability to work with others, communication skills, and knowledge of the field.

- Learner Engagement (7 questions) covers a number of engagement areas, such as belonging to the university, participation, and interactions with other students.

- Teaching Quality (11 questions) focuses on rating overall educational experience quality, as well as expected aspects such as quality of in class experiences and feedback.

- Student Support (14 questions) relates primarily to the university services provided.

- Learning Resources (7 questions) rates a wide range of physical and virtual academic resources.

Responses are on a five-point Likert scale and are used to calculate an overall figure for each benchmark. There is also a noticeable lack of qualitative questions. Some results are made public through the Australian Government "MyUniversity" website [12], which provides a variety of information for prospective students.

2.3 SES

In the UK the Higher Education Academy began trialing a pilot student engagement survey in 2013 [9]. The pilot used a subset of 14 NSSE questions with data gathered from nine participating universities. This is referred to as the Student Engagement Survey (SES). Both the survey and number of participating institutions was extended for 2014. The pilot aims to investigate suitability and reliability of the survey in the UK context and to "support the participating institutions in using engagement data for enhancement" [9]. The NSSE-based nature of the survey allows direct comparison to the North American data. A report of the pilot gives overall outcomes [9] but detailed results are made available to participating institutions only. The expectation is that they will interpret and act on the data to enhance their teaching.

3. HOW COMPUTER SCIENCE FARES

Unfortunately, on face value, Computer Science (CS) does not fare well in the NSSE, UES or SES surveys. Although there are some differences in the method of administration and the nature of some questions, overall responses do not paint a promising picture. Note that the term Computer Science (CS) will be used to broadly represent ICT study, given the term's prevalence in North America and the UK.

3.1 NSSE

Table 1 shows data from the most recent available NSSE survey.

Table 1. Summary of NSSE 2013 benchmark indicator scores (max. 60 for each indicator, higher is better)

Subject Area	CS	Phys. Sci. (not CS)	Eng	Overall
Higher Order Learning	38	40	39	39
Reflective Learning	32	34	33	39
Learning Strategies	34	39	36	41
Quantitative Reasoning	28	38	37	29
Collaborative Learning	32	36	40	32
Discussions with Diverse Others	38	41	41	41
Student Faculty Interaction	20	28	23	24
Effective Teaching Practice	37	41	38	41
Quality of interactions	42	43	41	43
Supportive environment	31	34	32	33

As shown in Table 1, CS scores are below the overall average for all categories except Collaborative Learning on which it is equal. On several indicators, CS is only 1 or 2 points (out of 60) behind, but in Reflective Learning and Learning Strategies in particular, the gap is wider. In both those indicators, as well as Learning Strategies, Discussion with Diverse Others and Effective Teaching Practices, the Physical Sciences and Engineering are generally low-scoring and might be regarded as close subject comparisons for CS. These subject groupings are therefore included in Table 1. CS has the lowest scores in all but one indicator. Surprisingly, on the one indicator in which STEM subjects generally score well, Quantitative Reasoning, CS is a long way behind its STEM counterparts and is even slightly lower than the overall average. CS is also lower than other STEM subjects on Collaborative Learning, another aspect of STEM strength in general.

Each indicator is constructed from several questions so it is also instructive to consider how CS fares on particular questions. At this level, results are reported according to the 4-point Likert scale provided to respondents. For comparison, a score for each question is calculated by assigning a value of 0 to 3 to each answer and finding the average. A total of 34 questions form the first eight indicators listed in the table (the ninth uses a different scale and the tenth is less subject-specific). Of these 34 questions, CS is below average on all but six. In ten cases CS is 10-20% below the average, including two quantitative reasoning questions and one on interaction with staff. On no question did CS score 10% or more above average.

Challenge is explored directly by the additional key question "to what extent have your courses challenged you to do your best work?" which uses a response scale from 1 (not at all) to 7 (very much). The NSSE report refers to responses of 6 or 7 as

indicating a "highly challenging" course. Only 50% of CS students rate their course as highly challenging compared to 62% of students overall (61% for Physical Sciences apart from CS, 61% for Engineering).

Another point of comparison is the difference between 1st year students and seniors. Table 2 shows benchmark data for these groups for CS compared to the general average. Overall for the general average, in all but one case (Supportive Environment) scores remain the same or increase. As students progress through their degree they generally improve with respect to the engagement benchmarks. This seems desirable as an indication of learning development. However CS results decrease for six of the ten indicators (marked by *). How to interpret this or what action needs to be taken is unclear, but it is worrying that, for example, CS students appear to spend less time engaged in reflective learning as they progress through their studies.

Table 2. NSSE 2013 benchmark indicator scores for year of study (max. 60 for each indicator).

Subject Area	CS 1st Year	CS Senior	Overall 1st Year	Overall Senior
Higher Order Learning	38	38	39	39
Reflective Learning	33	32*	36	39
Learning Strategies	36	34*	40	41
Quantitative Reasoning	28	28	26	29
Collaborative Learning	31	32	32	32
Discussions with Diverse Others	40	38*	41	41
Student Faculty Interaction	18	20	20	24
Effective Teaching Practice	40	37*	40	41
Quality of interactions	43	42*	42	43
Supportive environment	36	31*	37	33*

Similar poor results are observed in the 2010 AUSSE data. CS is ranked lowest in the categories of: Levels of Engagement, Academic Challenge, Group and Practicum Activity, General Development, Learning Outcomes and, especially disappointingly, Higher Order Thinking. AUSSE has similar questions to NSSE so, although it is no longer the primary Australian survey, it is worth noting these results alongside the NSSE data as similar concerns are raised.

3.2 UES

The UES is now the significant Australian student survey instrument and in it, fortunately, CS performs more creditably. In 2013, approximately 3200 responses were received in CS (labeled IT in the UES). The UES analysis report delivered by Graduate Careers Australia [11] breaks subject areas down into 11 broad fields (of which CS is one) and 45 specific subject areas (of which CS is only represented by one, labeled "Computing and Information Systems"). Table 3 gives a summary of UES results. Of the general categories in the UES, CS performs poorly in two: equal second lowest in Skills Development in comparison within the 45 specific subject areas; and tenth lowest in Teaching Quality. Other categories show IT in a better light, being one above average for Learner Engagement and also Student Support, and just two below average for Learning Resources.

Table 3. UES 2013 Summary (max. 100 for each indicator).

Subject Area	Skills Dev	Learner Engage-ment	Teach. Quality	Learning Resource	Student Support
CS	72	58	74	81	54
Overall	79	57	79	83	53

As with NSSE, there is an inherent difficulty in understanding what a difference of 7 points means in the context of low Skills Development rating. Since the benchmark comprises 8 questions, more granularity is needed to understand if concerns with CS are confined to just a few elements, or if problems are widespread across the whole Skills Development area. Unfortunately access to this data is difficult, and appears limited on an institutional basis. Of the specific questions for which data has been publicly reported, two key ones relating to Teaching Quality appear problematic for CS: Quality of Educational Experience rated 75 (avg 79) and Quality of Teaching scoring 72 (avg 79). These two areas of reported concern suggest a need for further investigation.

3.3 SES

The UK pilot survey does not make data publicly available, however, the general report [9] does list some key differences between subject groups. Mathematics and Computer Science (MCS) is used as the reporting category so such results are not directly comparable to those noted above for CS alone. We might still view these as indicators of areas of interest to be investigated further. There are marked differences in response between disciplines in a number of areas. One of particular note is that only around 36% of MCS respondents reported that they had spent "very much" or "quite a bit" of time evaluating their own or others' work compared to 80% and more in some other subjects. In comparison with surveys from other countries, MCS respondents from SES notably spent more time discussing course issues and academic progress with staff, but less time talking about their career plans. In SES, students of STEM subjects reported spending significantly less time on evaluation and synthesis, but were more engaged with application of information than their counterparts from arts, humanities and social sciences.

4. ISSUES FOR COMPUTING EDUCATION

The pattern emerging for CS is a somewhat surprising one. It might be expected that, when comparing any one subject to the whole cohort, students from the subject group would display strengths in some areas and weaknesses in others. However, in NSSE in particular, CS students are below average in most indicators, and are no better than average in aspects such as quantitative reasoning where they might be expected to have an advantage. It is also surprising that, whereas students in general will improve their learning skills and their approach to studying

will develop and mature, CS students show a decline in most indicators of engagement as they progress through their degree. This section highlights some of the main areas of concern.

4.1 Academic Challenge

For NSSE indicators of "Academic Challenge", CS averages 33 (out of 60) compared to the average across all subjects of 37. Further questions relating to challenge reinforce this. This is unexpected, seeming at odds with the generally acknowledged view that CS, particularly the study of programming, is difficult [15]. High levels of attrition in CS are often cited as evidence of this [16]. Why then are students assessing CS as low in questions to do with academic challenge? Why do only 50% feel that their course is highly challenging? For example, one of the contributing NSSE questions asks how much the student's work has emphasised "evaluating a point of view, decision or information source". Only 49% of CS students claim to do this "quite a bit" or "very much" compared to 73% overall. It may be that CS students are not encouraged to evaluate their work in this way or it may not be interpreted by CS students as referring to the activities they generally undertake. STEM teaching methods were observed to be particularly lacking in pedagogy to support integrative and reflective learning. Also there are indications that CS staff in the US are doing much less than non-STEM faculty to incorporate deep learning experiences into the curriculum [17]. These results are disturbing and warrant further investigation. It would also be useful to investigate the suitability of the measures across different subjects and possible differences in interpretation between students from different disciplines.

4.2 The Impact of Teaching Innovation

Many CS departments strive to develop and improve their teaching and to introduce new and innovative approaches and pedagogies to help support and engage their students. Given the poor survey results it is appropriate to question the effectiveness of the myriad teaching innovations being undertaken since they do not appear to be having a widespread impact on student engagement as measured by the NSSE across the discipline. It may be that these innovations in teaching methods are being evaluated against other measures (although it is common to see reports of interventions or new learning technologies introduced with little indication of evaluation). However, it would be interesting to regard proposed innovations from the perspective of student engagement measures and to determine their effect, particularly on measures in which CS needs to improve

4.3 Skills Development

Another key area for concern is in the acquisition of so-called "soft skills", or those that are not directly related to the CS discipline. These skills include aspects such as professional writing, presentation skills, research skills, and those that are supportive to CS professionals (and indeed all university graduates). The skills development theme of the UES has a heavy focus on such skills, and poor CS ratings may suggest that too much focus is currently placed on specific CS (and technical) skills at the expense of more generalised skills. Emphasis of soft skills in survey instruments reflects increasing awareness of their importance to all graduates. A lack of such skills will disadvantage CS graduates in the employment market. The low level of quantitative reasoning skills uncovered by NSSE is another (and rather surprising) example of low CS skills achievement.

5. IMPROVING DATA COLLECTION

The survey instruments discussed are designed to provide generic measures of student engagement and satisfaction. Given their widespread use and the public release of summarised data, they are also considered an important mechanism to provide prospective students with an insight into specific courses and universities. The amount of information available varies, for example NSSE data for individual institutions is currently released to the institution only, whereas NSSE satisfaction scores are publicly published by institution and course [14]. Even where data is not automatically made public, some universities deem it a measure of transparency to publish their results. It seems likely that, whatever the intended purpose, pressure will increase for institutions to publish results or else it may appear they have something to hide.

NSSE developers stress that the aim of the survey is to provide individual institutions with data to inform development of their teaching, learning and support provision. In contrast, UES was initially intended as a tool for allocating performance based funds, with other functions such as public reporting regarded as secondary [13]. The Australian government later abandoned the funding link and the survey now continues to provide institutional information. However, the possibility of linking results to national funding indicates how seriously engagement surveys are taken and the acceptance at a high level that engagement measures are a valid proxy for high quality education. With surveys portraying CS in a negative light, deeper understanding is needed of the meaning of the results, and also of the instrument design and whether certain disciplines are likely to receive accurate results.

5.1 Appropriateness for CS Students

The disappointing results for CS in the various international student surveys warrant questions to be raised concerning both current teaching and the survey instruments. Each formulates different benchmarks. Also, instruments may produce differing results regardless of similarities in questions or data collection methodology. However, there are issues between the instruments and their results that highlight some key questions. One key difference between NSSE and UES is in questions relating to Higher Order Learning in NSSE and Skill Development and Teaching Quality in UES. While the UES has questions of a general nature that are applicable to all disciplines, NSSE asks specifically: "During the current school year, about how many papers, reports or other writing tasks of the following length have you been assigned", with students asked to rate for tasks up to 5 pages, between 6-10 pages, and 11 pages or more. For CS this question poses two potential difficulties. Firstly, the nature of CS study (relative to many other disciplines) does not lend itself to so many lengthy writing challenges so responses from CS students are destined to be much lower than many other areas of study. Secondly, for students who extrapolate the question to relate to coding exercises, design specifications, or other CS related tasks, responses would vary wildly, rendering this question unreliable.

The UES is not without its concerns in this area but in the area of Skill Development only two of the eight contributing questions relate to discipline specific knowledge, whereas the remaining six ask students about the extent to which their course has developed general skills. In the UES, these are more general academic abilities that there would be a reasonable expectation that all university students would develop. This may be one of the reasons for better CS achievement in the UES compared to NSSE.

Overall, the suitability of the survey instruments to accurately capture levels of academic engagement in the CS context should be examined. While there is no question that many of the skills examined in both NSSE and UES are those considered to be key graduate attributes of any discipline, there needs to be a better understanding of how engagement is evidenced within specific disciplines. It should not be biased towards some disciplines nor should it focus on factors crucial to a particular discipline.

5.2 Reliability of Results

Concerns have been raised over the reliability of self-reporting and the interpretation of questions that are presented in a relative form. For example, some NSSE questions ask whether students perform a certain activity "very often", "often" and so on. These scales may be interpreted in a variety of ways. Terms used in the survey may also give rise to a variety of interpretations. The approach relies on students self-reporting and questions are not repeated in different ways. This has led to claims that such surveys lack the basic requirements for validity and reliability [18]. This has been met with robust response from survey proponents [19] however, although various studies have been conducted to refute the suggested deficiencies, very little work has been done to establish the appropriateness and validity of the instruments across different subjects or to explore the possibility of different interpretations of questions by different groups of students.

A further concern is the significance of points of difference, for example, how should we regard a 32 in relation to a 34? As benchmarks, the figures can be taken by institutions to map their own progress by longitudinal study of successive surveys and to identify areas to be enhanced to improve aspects significant for the particular context. However, this inevitably involves questions about sector comparability in order to make decisions on interventions. Since many interventions occur at a subject or faculty level, it also requires an understanding of what the indicators mean and what should be targeted at a subject level.

Given the importance of the results of such international surveys both for understanding our students and for public perception, it is important to understand the extent to which CS courses are falling short (and in what ways) or if in some cases there might be more appropriate measures of student experience.

5.3 Understanding the Issues Raised

In order to utilise the survey results effectively at a departmental level, it is important to understand what they really represent and how best they are to be used to suggest effective interventions. The SES report notes, "there were marked differences between disciplines, likely to be due to different pedagogies and expectations." [9]. However, there has been no work to confirm the reasons or to establish the implications of such differences. Nelson Laird et al [20] provide a statistical analysis to show the relationship of discipline traits (such as hard/soft, pure/applied) to engagement scores but this provides little interpretation or guidance to direct practice. Further, differences within the groups of subjects sharing traits are not explored and hence it does not provide explanation for a pattern of results within a single subject, which differs from the norm for subjects with shared traits.

Ultimately, while the surveys discussed highlight poor engagement levels, they do little to provide insight into meaningful reasons for disappointing results. Reporting is mainly focused on quantitative representations of academic engagement.

Consequently there is no explanation of the way CS students report their engagement with general skills development, reflective learning, learning strategy and the like. Inclusion of more qualitative questions would enable educators to understand more deeply the issues at hand and institute programs to address them. Similarly, questions that more broadly encompass the total university experience could paint a more balanced picture of "experience". The surveys discussed arose from a desire to quantify student experience for comparison between disciplines, institutions, and for ease of reporting. However if such huge effort is being undertaken to obtain insight for students across North America, Europe, and Australia, then the opportunity should be taken to obtain a richer and more complete understanding of student experience.

6. Further Work

This paper has considered widely used student engagement instruments and noted the consistently low scores recorded for CS students. Areas exhibiting a particularly large gap include level of academic challenge, reflective and integrative learning, learning strategies and effective teaching practices. Levels of transferable skills also appear to be low for CS students. These all need further investigation to understand the meaning, implications and appropriate action to be taken (if any). For example, it is unlikely that CS degrees should be altered to include multiple assessments involving extended essays simply because this is an "engagement measure". Other measures for CS may be more appropriate. However, if writing skills are genuinely lacking then appropriate ways to address the problem in the CS curriculum are needed. There is also a need to study further the surprising and worryingly low score relating to quantitative reasoning.

Student engagement surveys provide just one source of information about students' experience, activity and learning. To understand areas of low performance it is necessary to bring together different perspectives. Beaubouf & Mason [16] point to a number of factors in CS attrition, including misconceptions about what CS involves, poor information and advice when choosing CS, poor teaching, lack of feedback and lack of study skills. Some of this (for example, poor study skills) reinforces the survey findings. However, other aspects of CS student experience need to be examined further to see what our students think and why their survey responses are as they are. The issue of expectation and of how students' views change over their first year is of particular interest here and further work is planned to gain a better insight.

There is also a need for further work to deal with the data now available, to determine statistical significance of results and to compare additional data from other countries with different approaches. As noted by the UES 2011 Development Report [13]: "the availability of a student ID number provides incredible potential for tracking students over time and … requires an 'information model' to be established to support statistical analysis" (p.67). The divergence of different national instruments intended for similar purposes raises the question of how (and if) results can be compared internationally.

7. REFERENCES

[1] NSS survey http://www.thestudentsurvey.com/content/ nss2012_questionnaire_english.pdf

[2] National Survey of Student Engagement, http://nsse.iub.edu/

[3] Kuh, G. D. (2001). The national survey of student engagement: Conceptual framework and overview of psychometric properties. Bloomington: Indiana University Center for Postsecondary Research.

[4] Gibbs, G. (2012). Implications of 'Dimensions of quality' in a market environment (York, Higher Education Academy).

[5] Kuh, G.D., Kinzie, J., Cruce, T., Shoup, R., & Gonyea, R. M. (2006). Connecting the dots: Multi-faceted analyses of the relationships between student engagement results from the NSSE, and the institutional practices and conditions that foster student success. Indiana University, Center for Postsecondary Research.

[6] Pascarella, E. T., Seifert, T. A., & Blaich, C. (2010). How effective are the NSSE benchmarks in predicting important educational outcomes?. Change: The Magazine of Higher Learning, 42(1), 16-22.

[7] Pike, G.R. (2012). NSSE Benchmarks and Institutional Outcomes: a Note on the Importance of Considering the Intended Uses of a Measure in Validity Studies. Research in Higher Education, 54:149-170.

[8] Australasian Survey of Student Engagement, http://www.acer.edu.au/ausse

[9] Buckley, A. (2013). Engagement for enhancement: Report of a UK survey pilot. Higher Education Academy, UK.

[10] University Experience Survey, http://www.ues.edu.au/

[11] Graduate Careers Australia and the Social Research Centre (2014), "2013 University Experience Survey National Report", https://education.gov.au/university-experience-survey

[12] MyUniversity, Australian Government, myuniversity.gov.au

[13] Radloff, A., Coates, H., James, R. and Krause, K. (2011). "Report on the Development of the University Experience Survey". http://research.acer.edu.au/higher_education/30

[14] Unistats: the official website for comparing UK higher education course data, https://unistats.direct.gov.uk

[15] Jenkins, T. (2002, August). On the difficulty of learning to program. In Proc. 3rd Annual Conf. of the LTSN Centre for Information and Computer Sciences (Vol. 4, pp. 53-58).

[16] Beaubouef, T., & Mason, J. (2005). Why the high attrition rate for computer science students: some thoughts and observations. ACM SIGCSE Bulletin, 37(2), 103-106.

[17] Nelson Laird, T. F., Sullivan, D. F., Zimmerman, C., & McCormick, A. C. (2011). STEM/Non-STEM differences in engagement at US institutions. Peer Review, 13(3), 23-26.

[18] Porter, S.R. (2011). Do college student surveys have any validity? The Review of Higher Education, 35 (1), 45-76.

[19] McCormick, A. C. & McClenney, K. (2012). Will these trees ever bear fruit? A response to the Special Issue on Student Engagement. Review of Higher Education, 35 (2), 307-333.

[20] Nelson Laird, T. F., R. Shoup, G. D. Kuh, and M. J. Schwarz. 2008. "The Effects of Discipline on Deep Approaches to Student Learning and College Outcomes." Research in Higher Education 49: 469–494.

Predicting Success in University First Year Computing Science Courses: The Role of Student Participation in Reflective Learning Activities and in I-clicker Activities

Diana Cukierman
Simon Fraser University
Burnaby, B.C.
Canada
diana@cs.sfu.ca

ABSTRACT

Educators find that many students have difficulty succeeding in first-year university Computing Science (CS) courses. Initiatives are pursued to address this challenge and to support students' academic success. Instructors and institutions have reported providing different forms of academic support with programs where learning strategies are discussed with students, such as the Academic Enhancement Program (AEP). The AEP is a student focused proactive intervention developed and run by the School of Computing Science and the Student Learning Commons at Simon Fraser University, providing opportunities for self-reflection and exposure to study strategies activities, incorporated within and tailored to selected first year CS university courses, since 2006. To further enhance the students' learning experience, instructors also incorporate novel activities in class, such as peer instruction and active learning aided with the use of audience response systems (i-clickers). Experimental studies to determine whether the incorporation of these activities in a course cause a variation in some outcome measures (such as final exam scores) may be not feasible to do. In this paper we present instead results from performing statistical studies on course evaluation data, which even if they cannot prove causality, they may allow to determine if these activities are statistically significant predictors of course success.

Categories and Subject Descriptors

K.3.2 [**Computer and Education**]: **Computer and Information Science Education** - *Computer Science Education*

General Terms

Human Factors, Experimentation.

Keywords

Predictors of course success; study strategies; class active participation; i-clickers; experience report; CS education research.
.

1. INTRODUCTION

Educators find that many students have difficulty succeeding in first-year university Computing Science (CS) courses, in our institution and worldwide (e.g. [2]). Many initiatives are pursued

ITICSE '15, July   04 - 08, 2015, Vilnius, Lithuania
© 2015 ACM. ISBN 978-1-4503-3440-2/15/07 $15.00
DOI: http://dx.doi.org/10.1145/2729094.2742623

to address this challenge and to support students' academic success. Instructors and institutions have reported providing different forms of academic support with programs where learning strategies are discussed with students, such as the Academic Enhancement Program (AEP), jointly developed and coordinated by the author and colleagues [7,8,9].

Recent studies have found that predictors of success in first-year CS courses include having good mathematical background, self-efficacy in the discipline, and self-attribution of success to luck [15,14,5,4]. These results in turn support the relevance of the AEP program objectives, and correspondingly the relevance of the topics addressed in the AEP to enhance student academic success. The AEP has also received encouraging feedback from students, instructors, and academic advisors regarding its benefits [9]. However, we have not conducted experiments to determine whether there is a causal connection between student AEP participation and some objective measure of course success, such as final exam scores. For the time being we have decided to not perform studies where different groups of students are assigned to different conditions with respect to participation in the AEP program. We believe that it is neither desirable nor ethical to not provide access to such program to selected students, especially in the same class and within a university setting, given the evidence we have collected on the program benefits and as it may affect their course grades. Hence, the interest of exploring whether AEP participation may be a statistically significant predictor of students' success in the course above and beyond other predictors, or whether it improves predictions of students success overall.

Independent of learning strategy programs, instructors also incorporate novel activities in class, such as active learning and peer instruction aided with the use of audience response systems (i-clickers) [17]. Educators have reported that i-clicker usage and peer instruction in class improve final grades in CS courses [10,13]. However, there are varied opinions about the appropriate way to measure accomplished learning and how to best utilize i-clickers in class [18]. Additionally, there are no unique ways to grade students based on i-clicker participation. As well, again in this case, it may be undesirable to allow some students to use i-clickers and not others. Still, as in the case of the AEP participation, it is feasible to study if the i-clicker participation is a statistically significant predictor of some measure of student course success.

In the remainder of this paper a statistical study utilizing ordinary multiple regression analysis is presented. The study was done based on data from a course taught by the author. The study aims to explore whether the participation of students in AEP activities and in the class i-clicker activities improve predictions of course success (measured as final exam scores), above and beyond midterm exam scores (an intuitively strong predictor). The next section briefly describes the AEP. Section 3 describes how the AEP and i-clicker activities were incorporated in the course. A method and results sections describe the regression study done in detail. A discussion and future work section conclude this paper.

2. ACADEMIC ENHANCEMENT PROGRAM (AEP)[1]

The AEP is a collaborative program between the School of Computing Science and the Student Learning Commons (SLC). The program is co-developed and co-coordinated by a teaching faculty member in the School of CS (the author of this paper) and a learning specialist from the SLC.

Our institution is a Canadian comprehensive university with a population of more than 30,000 students across three campuses. The School of Computing Science offers undergraduate, master's, and doctoral degrees and has more than 1,000 registered undergraduate majors. The SLC is an academic learning centre mandated to assist and support students in their academic pursuits, providing writing and learning support.

The AEP operates across all three of SFU's main campuses depending on the semester and the courses offered, and, to date, it has served more than 4,000 students spanning all semesters since the program began in 2006.

The AEP encourages students to gain self-awareness and self-confidence and to become active participants in their own learning. AEP activities are tailored to course topics and are an integral part of the courses, as a required component to all the students in the class, as approved by the department. We invite students to improve their self-management by maintaining a balanced dedication to studying and "life" and incorporating better time management and study practices into their routine. Our workshops are designed to elicit active, collaborative, and reflective participation from students. We develop the AEP activities acknowledging the various ways of learning and teaching that different individuals prefer, while encouraging an open mind about adapting to different realities. Fundamentally we seek to encourage students to apply appropriate study strategies for the discipline/course.

Other goals for the AEP are to increase the communication among students and between students and faculty to enhance learning and foster a sense of community and belonging. We also inform students about additional academic support available for them at the university offered by different units and including the SLC, to further enhance their sense of support and community.

2.1 AEP 101 workshop

A brief description of the AEP 101 workshop is presented here; for more details please see [9]. AEP 101 is a two hour workshop run by two co-facilitators, one a specialist in learning, and the other a CS faculty or CS grad student (who may or not be the course instructor) in a small group setting of up to 25 to 30 students. The workshop is tailored to the course contents; facilitators briefly present materials and guide highly participatory activities related to time management, self-management and using

appropriate study strategies for CS programming courses. We begin AEP 101 by presenting students the *Ladder to Success*, a framework to guide learners through five steps for successively addressing academic barriers: (1) *'Identification'* of barriers and attribution of problems to controllable factors. The next step in the Ladder to Success encourages study *'planning'*, in particular, adoption of time management strategies (2). The *'study strategies'* component focuses on strategies organized around a paradigm that we developed for the workshop called *Range of Complexity (ROC)*. The stages in this model were inspired by the revised version of Bloom's [3] taxonomy by Anderson et al. [1] who propose the categories Remember, Understand, Apply, Analyze, Evaluate, and Create. The model is also inspired by cognitive constructivist approaches to learning [e.g.11] and literature in mathematical problem solving [e.g.12]. We intend to introduce students to desirable series of processes for learning CS concepts, including reiterative problem solving. We also stress the variety and range of complexity in questions and skills that are part of the course learning outcomes and in general in the discipline, and correspondingly we encourage students to adopt a range of study strategies (3). The proactive *'Help seeking'* step invites students to dialogue and share ideas to solve concrete situations within the university context and identify other resources for help (4). The *'Reflection'* step (5) concludes the workshop, and invites students to visualize the whole *Ladder to Success* framework as adaptable to addressing challenges in general through successive iterations of the process.

For more details about the AEP including a description of other activities and developed workshops we refer the reader to [7,8,9] and the AEP website www.cs.sfu.ca/CC/AEP/.

3. INCORPORATION OF AEP ACTIVITIES AND OF I-CLICKERS IN THE COURSE

The course chosen to do the present study was an introductory CS course offered in the Fall 2013 semester, with 363 students, taught by the author of this paper. The AEP activities were a required part of the course, and students received 1.5% course points for this. AEP required activities for this course involved the students' participation in the AEP 101 workshop described above. Alternatively, in the case of scheduling conflicts with AEP 101 workshop sessions, students were encouraged to do an activity involving write-up of a reflective report describing some other workshop, a reading or a video related to CS learning topics as they relate to the course contents.

I-clickers were used in this course as a pilot trial, and as such it was announced to students. Students were not required to buy the remote devices, and rather a borrowing system was developed (thanks to the support of the i-clicker provider company). I-clickers were planned to be used during weeks 7 and 8 of the 13-week semester. Due to the highly successful dynamics developed in the classroom as the i-clickers were incorporated and the enthusiasm of both the students and the instructor, and also thanks to the possibility to extending the loan period, i-clickers were used from week #7 until the end of the semester.

The i-clickers points' participation provided 2% of the course points. The points were obtained by accumulating points every lecture that i-clickers were used. For each lecture a weighted formula was used: 1 point was provided if the student answered at least 75% of the questions, 1 point was provided if the student answered at least 50% of the questions and 1 point was provided if the student correctly responded at least 50% of the questions.

---

[1] This section includes a brief description of the AEP and in particular of the AEP 101 workshop, adapted from [7] and [9].

Each class was developed including lecturing and students would be invited to answer i-clicker questions, sometimes individually and sometimes allowing a brief discussion among peers. In several occasions the same question was asked first individually and again after discussion in groups. The improvement after the peer discussion was evident; these observations were shared with students. A general discussion and clarifications followed the showing of the students' replies. The time dedicated to the general discussion after an i-clicker question depended on the understanding reflected in the answers obtained. The number of questions per lecture would vary (as well as the moment when the question was presented during the lecture), from 4 to 9 questions in a lecture. The questions presented to students involved multiple choice answers, often requiring brief analysis of code or examples, referring to materials that were discussed in class in some previous lecture, some previous lab exercise, or to topics discussed earlier within the same lecture.

4. METHOD

Anonymized evaluation data from this CS introductory course was analyzed. No access to demographic data such as gender, intended major or prior Grade Point Average (GPA) was available for this study. Data from students who withdrew from the course officially, or who did not come to the final exam were eliminated (list-wise) from the data base, leaving a data sample size of 343.

The following variables were defined:

AEP: Participation in AEP activities. This is dichotomous predictor which indicates whether students participated (coded 1) or not (coded 0) in the AEP activities.

MID: Midterm scores. This is a continuous predictor, ranging from 0 to 100.

WIC: Weighted I-clicker participation. This is a continuous predictor measuring i-clicker participation ranging from 0 to 100 and calculated by accumulating points from all lectures when i-clickers were used. In such lectures, points were based on a weighted formula as described above, including participation and correct answering of i-clicker questions.

FIN: Final exam scores. This is the continuous criterion or outcome variable, which ranges from 0 to 100.

As described, data was taken from concrete values and not as the result of processing responses to items in surveys involving self-reporting or raters, therefore checking internal consistency of survey items and reliability of variables did not apply. Likewise, construct validity was not a concern as this study does not delve into the question of how well the final exam scores measure learning or not, nor does it attempt to look at whether the variables directly measure active participation in said activities. Since the values are unique for each student, course and semester, test-retest reliability was also inapplicable. The variable WIC could be studied for reliability and consistency by comparing it with other I-clicker measures (attendance to lectures only for example); however, this was not explored in the current study.

The main goal of this study was to establish whether the variables AEP, WIC, and MID are predictors of final exam scores (FIN), and whether any of the variables predicts the criterion (FIN) above and beyond the others, using OLS regression analysis.

Three Models were considered. Initially (Model 1) the OLS regression model included one predictor, MID, for the criterion

FIN. A second predictor, WIC, was added into the second block (Model 2). AEP was added into the third block (Model 3).

Extreme values on the predictors and criterion, and global and specific influential cases are reported for Model 3 (the final, multivariate model). For each model, assumptions were checked to test linear relationship, no omitted variables, and homoscedasticity. Independence of errors and normality of errors were also checked. The assumption of reliability of measures was met since scores that students obtained are exactly what is measured. For each model, it was tested and calculated if the model predicts the criterion or outcome variable (FIN) and the proportion of variance in FIN that is explained by the regression model using the predictors in the model. When there was a correlation with the criterion, it was tested whether each predictor separately accounted for more variance above and beyond the other predictors. In particular it was calculated the number of units of change (increase or decrease) in the criterion (FIN) for every unit increase in each predictor, controlling for the effect of the other predictors. Errors of type I and II were controlled.

5. RESULTS

The Statistical Package for the Social Sciences (SPSS) was used to conduct all the statistical analysis.

5.1 Descriptive analyses

The scores on MID ranged from 0 to 100, mean = 74.01, standard deviation, sd = 20.87, median = 75.93, skew = -.85 (95% confidence interval CI: [-1.11,-0.59]), kurtosis = .49 (95% CI: [-.02,1.01]). The scores of WIC ranged from 0 to 100, mean = 76.58, sd = 29.00, median = 88.79, skew = -1.46 (95% CI: [-1.72,-1.20]), kurtosis =1.10 (95% CI: [0.58,1.61]). The scores of FIN ranged from 6.34 to 98.59, mean = 67.57, sd = 17.47, median =70.42, skew = -.75 (95% CI:[-1.01,-0.49]), kurtosis =.44 (95% CI: [-0.08,0.95]). Fifty seven students did not participate in the AEP activities (16.60% of the sample). See Figure 1 for the continuous variables distributions; notice that the study (and hence the graph) did not include students who withdrew the course or did not come to the final exam. Intuitively, students performed quite well in the midterm, with a large number of students scoring more than 90%. Students obtained very good values in the weighted i-clicker points (the formula was, as intended, benevolent) and in the final exam one can observe results are more normally distributed, although negatively skewed.

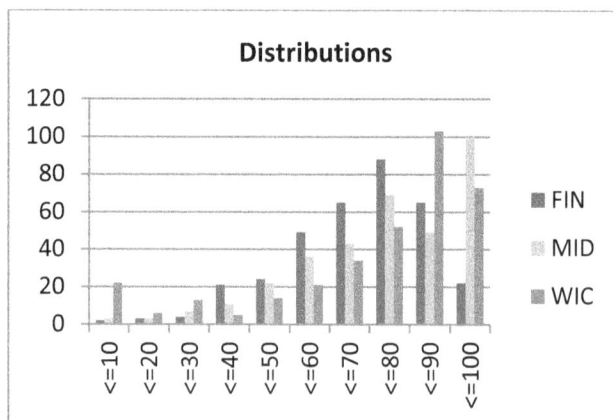

Figure 1. Distributions of FIN, MID and WIC. The graph does not include students who withdrew the course nor with FIN = 0

5.2 Hierarchical regression

Only diagnostics for Model 3 are reported (predictors: MID, WIC and AEP). Cases were considered to be extreme on MID if their centered leverage was greater than 0.0058 (2k/n; [6], p. 410). As a result, 72 (21%) cases were flagged. Looking at the MID and FIN scores for these cases it appears that they corresponded to the lowest midterm scores. Thus, it was considered that these extreme cases do not have to be eliminated from the study since low midterm scores are part of the course reality. Two cases were extreme on the criterion (or outcome variable). In these two cases MID and FIN scores are quite different (e.g., case #102 has (MID= 53.8, FIN= 9.86 (both out of 100)). Again, since this is part of the reality being modelled these cases are not excluded. Global influence was measured resulting in flagging 21 cases. Calculations were done to determine specific influence that the cases have on the estimates of the regression coefficients. Six percent (6%) cases were flagged as influencing B_0, 5.5% cases for B_{MID}, 5.8% cases for B_{WIC}, and 7.6% cases for B_{AEP}. Very few cases were flagged as influencing more than one coefficient. More analyses and interpretation need to be conducted in order to uncover the characteristics of the flagged cases; however, it was decided that outliers would not be excluded, since they are part of the course reality.

For each of the three models it was inferred that there are no assumption violations for the OLS regression after checking linear relationship, no omitted variables, homoscedasticity, and normality of errors. Observations and calculations also suggested that prediction would not be improved by incorporating higher order or interaction terms and it was inferred that there is no multicolinearity among the predictors. To control for type I error, α was set to .007 (.05/7), considering all the tests performed.

For each model, an F test was conducted to test whether the overall model squared multiple correlation coefficient (R^2) was equal to zero. Rejecting such hypothesis would allow to conclude that the model predicts the criterion (or outcome variable FIN); the correlation coefficient provides the proportion of variance in FIN that is explained by the regression model using the predictors in the model. When there was a correlation with the criterion, it was tested whether each predictor separately accounts for more variance above and beyond the other (using a t-test on the regression coefficients Bj). The coefficient magnitude determines the number of units of change (increase or decrease) in the criterion (FIN) for every unit increase in each predictor, controlling for the effect of the other predictors. For the second and third model an F-test on the change in the squared coefficient, (ΔR^2) compared to zero was also done. Estimated values and 95% confidence intervals (CI) of coefficients are reported next. Table 1 summarizes the Model 3 results.

Model 1 (predictor MID) was found to significantly predict the final scores, estimated R^2_{M1} = .487, (95% CI: [.4096,.5580]), F(1,341)= 323.498, p < .001). The statistically significantly proportion of variance in FIN that is explained by the regression Model 1 (using MID) is 48.7%. A one unit increase in MID significantly increases FIN by .52 to .65 points ($B_{MID,M1}$ = .584 (95% CI: [.520, .648]). The intercept $B_{0,M1}$, = 24.35; hence, when MID = 0, the final score is on average 24.35 (95% CI: [19.44, 29.26]). Adding WIC as a predictor (Model 2) does not significantly improve the prediction of FIN, ΔR^2_{M2} was not confirmed to be statistically significantly different than 0, (F(1,340) = 2.012, p =.157). Similarly, WIC was not confirmed to be a significant predictor of FIN (t(340) = 1.418, p =.157). WIC was still kept in the model as planned in the study. Adding AEP to

Model 2 (Model 3) resulted in a slight increase of the variance in prediction of FIN with respect to Model 2 (ΔR^2_{M3} = .017, 95% CI: [.00062,.0538]). This indicates that there can be up to 5.38 % variance increase predicted by AEP above and beyond the other predictors; ΔR^2 was confirmed to significantly differ from 0, (F(1,339) = 11.946, p =.001).

Table 1. Results from the OLS Hierarchical regression for Model 3. Sources: SPSS, and Confidence intervals of correlation coefficients calculated via Fisher transformations. N = 343

Coefficient	Estimated	95% Confidence intervals	F/t observed	sig
B_0	19.706	[13.979, 25.434]	t = 6.768	.000
B_{MID}	.564	[.500, .629]	t = 17.318	.000
B_{WIC}	.008	[-.040, .056]	t =.337	.736
B_{AEP}	6.548	[2.822, 10.274]	t = 3.456	.001
R^2	.507	[.429,.5776]	F= 116.309	.000
ΔR^2	.017	[.00062,.0538]	F = 11.946	.001

The overall model (Model 3) significantly predicts FIN, and accounts for 50.7% of the variance in FIN (R^2_{M3} = .507, 95% CI: [.429,.5776]), F(3,339)= 116.31 , p <.001). When MID, WIC and AEP are 0 (i.e., students who did not do the AEP activities and got 0 points in MID and WIC), the average FIN is 19.71 (= $B_{0,M3}$, 95% CI: [13.98,25.43]). MID is a statistically significant predictor of final exam scores while controlling for the effect of the other predictors, although the criterion (FIN) increases on average only 0.564 points out of 100 for every unit increase in MID, controlling for the effect of the other predictors (B $_{MID,M3}$ = .564 (95% CI:[.500,.629]), t(339) = 17.318, p<.001). WIC is not a significant predictor (t(339) = .337, p = .736); AEP is a significant predictor and separately accounts for more variance above and beyond the other predictors (t(339) = 3.456, p = .001). One unit increase in AEP (from no participation to participating in the AEP activities) increases the final exam score on average by 6.55 points (out of 100) and statistically significantly, with 95% confidence it increases the final exam scores between 2.82 to 10.27 points out of 100 (B $_{AEP,M3}$ = 6.55,95% CI [2.82 ,10.27]), controlling for the other predictors.

The power of the F test for R^2 =0 for the bivariate regression (Model1), also used for correlations diagnostics, and the F test for R^2 =0 in (Model3) were checked. With those correlation coefficients and α value, to obtain a .99 power a sample of size 35 (or 34) would be needed for those tests in respectively Model 1 and Model 3, and the sample size was 343, guaranteeing an adequate power.

6. DISCUSSION

This paper presents a regression study to statistically infer whether certain activities incorporated in a CS introductory university course are statistically significant predictors of course success, measured as points obtained in the course final exam. The variables that were investigated to be predictors are the midterm scores, the participation in the Academic Enhancement Program (AEP) activities associated to the course [7,8,9] and the usage of audience response systems (i-clickers) in class [17]. The literature in education and studies that we have done so far about the AEP provide evidence of the AEP being highly beneficial to students. Similarly active participation and peer instruction aided with i-clickers have been reported as very positive, and after trying out the i-clicker the instructor of said course was further convinced that these class participation and peer support activities are highly positive, in particular to engage students in the course. Anecdotally, it seems that students' questions and explorations became more sophisticated with respect to previous semesters when i-clickers had not been used; it would be interesting to explore in more detail if the usage of i-clickers encourage deeper learning and understanding.

An analysis of surveys done to students about their perception of these activities is not included here although it is part of current and future work. The core of this paper is an ordinary multiple regression analysis study, to investigate the predictive potential of these activities over course success. Three predictors were defined in the regression models: MID: the points obtained by students (which is an intuitively strong predictor of final exam results), WIC: i-clicker participation points calculated by accumulating points from all lectures when I-clickers were used, and AEP, indicating whether the student participated on not in the AEP activities. Overall the three predictors proposed in the OLS regression model explained on average 50.7% of the variance in the criterion, FIN, ranging from 43% to 58%, 95% confidence interval (CI), where all the regression analysis assumptions were valid. Interaction and higher order terms did not increase the criterion variance predicted, but future work could include expanding the model with other predictors aiming to obtain a more accurate model. For example, prior GPA, intended major, and discipline background were not available; these have been reported to be good predictors of course success in the CS Education literature; thus, future studies could include considering how to measure some of these and then test the influence of these predictors in final exam scores. Measures for self-efficacy and motivation should be interesting to explore as additional predictors.

While causality was certainly not proven, one strong result that follows from this study, is that considering the data base with only those students who took the final exam, students who attend the AEP activities have on average 6.55/100 (and 95% statistically significantly from 2.8/100 to 10.3/100) more points in the final exam than those who do not participate in the AEP activities, controlling for the other predictors (MID and WIC). Connected to this result, a study that would be interesting to pursue is investigating the predictive power of participation in the AEP activities with respect to abandonment of the course and or success in future courses.

Additionally to planning other regression studies, we are considering doing studies to explore causality, and investigate whether it is supported that AEP statically significantly improves some measure of course/learning success, such as final exam points or cumulative grade point average. For example, one could subdivide students in a course in different groups, where a group is required to participate in AEP activities and the other, acting as a control group, does not. While in theory such study (and especially if the groups are randomly selected) could potentially provide useful evidence, the AEP team believes that performing such kind of study may not be adequate or ethical, especially in the same class and within a university setting, as we would be negating the participation of randomly selected students in a program for which we have anecdotal and initial formal evidence that it is beneficial and may potentially positively affect the

students' grades. Yet, we are considering running such studies when a course is offered in different sections and so that important variables can be controlled. Furthermore, we believe that the benefits of participating in the AEP go beyond quantitative measurable improvements, and may become even more evident via qualitative studies. Thus, both further quantitative and qualitative studies are part of our current and future work.

The weighted i-clicker variable (WIC) was not found to be a significant predictor of final exam scores. This result is interpreted to follow from the weighted formula being too benevolent, as intended and as indicated by the high mean and negatively skewed distribution of WIC. However this does not provide any evidence in favour or against the benefit of using i-clickers and peer discussions in class towards improving final exam scores, as this result may again be caused by the way the formula was constructed. Arguably, and anecdotal data and self-perception surveys would suggest that using this (benevolent) formula is still useful to motivate class student participation, an issue that could be studied in the future, including measures about motivation. On the other hand, future studies could include investigating whether the raw i-clicker measures (such as attendance only or correct answering only) are significant predictors of final exam scores. Studies to investigate the long term impact of both AEP Participation and i-clicker activities on students' success and retention are also interesting future work that we aim to pursue.

7. ACKNOWLEDGMENTS

I would like to thank my colleague Donna McGee Thompson, Head of the Student Learning Commons at SFU for co-developing and co-coordinating the AEP program and our work together all these years. I would also like to thank Rachel Fouladi, faculty in the Psychology department at SFU and specialist in multivariate analysis for reading an earlier draft of this paper. The trial of the i-clickers in class was possible thanks to Shannon Frame and her company, Macmillan New Ventures, as they lent a number of remote devices for students to use as part of the i-clickers trial. I would also like to thank the AEP development team for our work through the years. Thank you also to the anonymous reviewers' constructive comments. Last but not least I would like to thank my students for their enthusiasm and feedback.

8. REFERENCES

[1] Anderson, L.W., Krathwohl, D.R., Airasian, P.W., Cruikshank, K.A., Mayer, R.E., Pintrich, P.R., Raths, J. and Wittrock, M.C., Eds. (2001). A taxonomy for learning and teaching and assessing: A revision of Bloom's taxonomy of educational objectives. Addison Wesley Longman, Inc.

[2] Biggers, M., & Brauer, A., & Yilmaz, T. (2008). Student perceptions of computer science: a retention study comparing graduating seniors with CS leavers. ACM SIGCSE Bulletin, 40(1), 402-406.

[3] Bloom B. S. (1956). Taxonomy of Educational Objectives, Handbook I: The Cognitive Domain. NY: D. McKay Co Inc.

[4] Byrne P., & Lyons G. (2001). The effect of Student Attributes on Success in Programming. Proceedings from ITICSE 2001: Innovation and Technology in Computer Science Education Conference, Canterbury, UK: ACM, 49-52

[5] Cantwell Wilson B., & Shrock S. (2001) Contributing to Success in an Introductory Computer Science Course: A

study of Twelve Factors. Proceedings from SIGCSE 2001: ACM Technical Symposium on Computer Science Education, Charlotte, NC, USA: ACM, 184-188

[6] Cohen , J.,Cohen, P., West, S.G., Aiken, L.S. (2003). Applied Multiple Regression/Correlation Analysis for the Behavioral Sciences, 3rd ed. Mahwah,NJ: Lawrence Erlbaum Associates.

[7] Cukierman D., & McGee Thompson D., & Guloy S., & Salimi F., & Karpilovsky M. (2014). Challenges students face in first-year university Computing Science and Engineering courses: Overview of a needs assessment and workshop. Proceedings of WCCCE 2014 Western Canadian Conference on Computing Science Education, Vancouver, Canada: ACM

[8] Cukierman, D., & McGee Thompson, D. (2009). "The Academic Enhancement Program: Encouraging Students to Learn about Learning as Part of their Computing Science Courses", ACM SIGCSE Bulletin, 41(3), 171-175, September 2009. Also Proceedings of and presentation at ITICSE 2009, 14th Annual Conference on Innovation and Technology in Computer Science Education, Paris, France, July 2009: ACM

[9] Egan R., & Cukierman D., & McGee Thompson D. (2011). The Academic Enhancement Program in Introductory CS: A Workshop Framework Description and Evaluation. Proceedings of Iticse 2011, 16th Annual Conference on Innovation and Technology in Computer Science Education, Darmstadt, Germany: ACM, 278-282.

[10] Mohr T., M. (2013). I-clickers and student performance. International Review of Economics Education, 14: Elsevier, 16-23.

[11] Piaget, J. (1985). *The equilibration of cognitive structures.* Chicago: University of Chicago Press.

[12] Polya G. "How to Solve It", 2nd ed., Princeton University Press, 1957.

[13] Porter L., & Bayley-Lee C., & Simon B (2013). Halving Fail Rates using Peer Instruction: A Study of Four Computer Science Courses. Proceedings from SIGCSE 2013: ACM Technical Symposium on Computer Science Education, Denver, CO, USA: ACM, 177-182

[14] Rountree N., & Rountree J., & Robins A., & Hanna R. (2004) Interacting Factors that Predict Success and Failure in a CS1 Course. INROADS, The SIGCSE Bulletin. 36(4): ACM, 101-104

[15] Simon, & Fincher S. & Robins A., & Baker B., & Box I., & Cutts Q., & de Raadt M., & Haden P., & Hamer J., & Hamilton M., & Lister R., & Petre M., & Sutton K., & Tolhurst D., & Tutty J. (2006) Predictors of Success in a First Programming Course. Proceedings of ACE 2006, Australasian Computing Education Conference, Conferences in Research and Practice in Information Technology, 52: Australian Computer Society, Inc.

[16] Simon B., & Cutts Q. (2012). Peer Instruction: A Teaching Method to Foster Deep Understanding. Communications of the ACM, 55(2): ACM

[17] Watkins J., & Mazur E. (2013). Retaining Students in Science, Technology, Engineering and Mathematics (STEM) Majors. Journal of College Science and Teaching 42(5), 2013, 36-41

[18] Zingaro D. (2014) Peer Instruction Contributes to Self-Efficacy in CS1. Proceedings from SIGCSE 2014: ACM Technical Symposium on Computer Science Education, Atlanta, GA, USA: ACM

Examining Classroom Interventions to Reduce Procrastination

Stephen H. Edwards, Joshua Martin, and Clifford A. Shaffer
Virginia Tech
2202 Kraft Drive
Blacksburg, VA 24060
+1 540-231-5723
edwards@cs.vt.edu, jdm522@vt.edu, shaffer@vt.edu

ABSTRACT

Procrastination is a common problem for students. Many believe procrastination may keep otherwise competent students from succeeding. However, the most effective interventions for procrastination are resource-intensive—providing supplemental training or courses in study skills and self-regulation. These techniques do not scale to large courses. This paper investigates three new classroom interventions designed to be low-cost and low-effort to implement. Reflective writing assignments ask students to reflect on how their time management choices affect their work. Project schedule sheets require students to plan out and schedule specific tasks on their projects. E-mail situational awareness alerts give students feedback on how their progress compares to others, and to expectations. 353 students over two semesters of a junior-level advanced data structures course participated in a study where these interventions were investigated. While neither reflective writing assignments nor schedule sheets produced any significant effect, e-mail alerts were associated with both significantly reduced rates of late program submissions, and increased rates of early program submissions. As a result, this intervention shows promise for further investigation as a potential strategy for reducing late submissions among students.

Categories and Subject Descriptors

K.3.2 [**Computers and Education**]: Computer and Information Science Education; K.3.1 [**Computers and Education**]: Computer Uses in Education

Keywords

procrastination, self-regulation, self-efficacy, scheduling, schedule sheets, e-mail alerts

1. INTRODUCTION

Procrastination is a pervasive problem that significantly affects students. Many computer science educators describe procrastination as one of the common problems that leads to non-success in courses. In this context, procrastination is "voluntarily delaying an intended course of action despite expecting to be worse off for the delay" [10]. It is theorized that procrastination has a particularly negative impact on student performance. According to a meta-analysis of a broad range of procrastination studies, between 70% and 95% of undergraduates procrastinate on coursework to a degree, while between 20% and 30% of undergraduates show signs of severe procrastination [10]. Such high rates of procrastination make it no surprise that students often use procrastination as an excuse for poor educational performance. More specifically, a "negative procrastinator" is one who procrastinates to the extent he or she experiences negative consequences from their delays. Negative procrastinators are more likely to turn in work late, receive lower scores both on assignments and exams, report greater stress, and have more health concerns than their peers [12].

The effects of procrastination in CS education are particularly acute. In a study examining the performance of 1,101 CS students over a five year period, a statistically significant correlation was found between when students started working on a project and their overall work quality [5]. At the same time, however, there was no statistically significant difference in the amount of time that students spent working—in fact, starting earlier was associated with finishing earlier rather than spending more time working.

While a number of interventions intended to address student procrastination have been investigated, the most effective seems to be some form of supplementary course or workshop on motivation and time management strategies [14]. While these approaches are effective, they are also costly in both time and manpower. While they are useful for targeted populations of students at risk, they do not scale to large classrooms. As a result, educators continue to search for practical methods to address procrastination that can be used across large numbers of students.

This paper reports on the preliminary investigation of three classroom interventions that are feasible for use with little additional class time or instructor effort: active reflection writing tasks, where students write a "minute paper" after each assignment on how their time management choices affected their work; schedule sheets that students fill out, requiring them to break down tasks and show how much time they plan to allocate for each piece, helping them to form, express, manage, and track smaller-scale deadlines; and situational awareness alerts based on a model of student progress that show each student how their current efforts compare to expectations for the class as a whole. All three interventions are grounded in temporal motivation theory, which explains why people procrastinate. The interventions were carried out in a junior-level advanced data structures course over two different semesters.

In this study, e-mail situational awareness alerts showed a significant reduction in the rate of late program submissions by students, while the other two interventions did not provide evidence of consistent impact. Section 2 describes previous work on procrastination in general and how it relates to this study. Section 3 describes the three interventions presented here in more detail. Section 4 describes the study method and Section 5 presents the results, while Section 6 discusses future work to build on the results presented here.

2. BACKGROUND

Despite being such a relevant issue to student performance, there is still a lack of understanding about procrastination. Steel published a meta-analysis of research into procrastination in 2007. He defines procrastination as a "prevalent and pernicious form of self-regulatory failure" [10]. Procrastination can be further defined as delaying a task one intends to perform, in spite of potential negative consequences. Some research indicates that an individual's level of procrastination tendency may be a personality trait [10]. A number of instruments have been developed to measure one's procrastination tendency [7][13].

Many potential causes for procrastination have been researched, including self-efficacy, self-esteem, self-regulation, fear of failure, task aversion, task rewards or punishments, neuroticism, and impulsiveness. Above all, procrastination is a failure of self-regulation, where one does not exercise influence over one's own behavior in the manner required [10]. In a study of 456 undergraduates, Klassen et al. found self-efficacy for self-regulation, or a person's view of their own ability to self-regulate, was a stronger predictor of procrastination. This includes other variables such as self-regulation itself, academic self-efficacy, and self-esteem [6]. Tuckman provides reasoning for this in the following statement:

> As one proceeds through school, the responsibility for control of one's own performance shifts progressively from parents and teachers to oneself, reaching a high point during the college years. The inability to overcome procrastination tendencies may be related to problems encountered by many college students, leading some researchers to be on the lookout for effective strategies that may be used to help such students regulate their own learning [13].

A more recent theory explaining procrastination is called temporal motivation theory (TMT). Proposed by Steel, TMT describes the utility (desirability) of a task in terms of four major variables: the expectancy (E) of success, the value (V) one places on the task, the delay (D) before a reward is received, and the individual's sensitivity towards delay (Γ) [10]. The formula for utility is:

$$Utility = \frac{EV}{\Gamma D}. \tag{1}$$

This theory incorporates the idea that students prefer tasks they can complete, will enjoy, and will see the benefits of sooner over others.

Previous attempts to combat procrastination have been targeted at smaller groups. In 2005, Tuckman described utilizing a "study skills" course to teach students psychological principles and various theories about procrastination. The course also teaches students which type of rationalization they use for procrastinating, and ways to overcome these issues to meet their deadlines. Tuckman reports that students who participate in this class typically see a 0.5 increase in GPA during the next semester [14]. While such techniques are clearly effective, it is difficult to provide such resources to all students in a university.

Alternatively, many instructors try lower cost interventions, including offering extra credit incentives for early assignment completion. While many instructors report anecdotal success, a previous study did not find any evidence that extra credit bonuses for early completion of programming assignments had a statistically significant effect on when students finished [1]. Further, there are ethical concerns with such bonuses, which may disproportionately favor academically strong students, further disadvantaging students who are struggling [11].

In studying the behaviors of successful students, we have collected data on student classroom performance from the first three programming courses at Virginia Tech for five years [5]. Students who consistently scored highly on all programming assignments within a course, as well as students who consistently performed poorly, were separated out for analysis, allowing a within-subjects comparison among the large remaining group of students who earned mixed results. Analysis of this data yielded several important results. First, on assignments where a given student received scores above 80% (A/B range), that student was more likely to have started earlier and finished earlier than on assignments where that same student received grades below 80% (C/D/F range). There also was no statistically significant difference in the amount of time that students spent on their work when starting earlier; instead, they simply finished earlier. Around two thirds of the time, when a student received an A or B-level score, that student began electronically submitting their work for checking over a day before the final deadline, while two thirds of the time when a student received a lower score, that student also started electronically submitting their work for checking on the assignment's due date or later.

3. INTERVENTIONS

3.1 Active Reflection

The first of the interventions we investigated is active reflection in the form of *reflective writing assignments*, an approach inspired by active learning techniques. The intent of these assignments is to engage students in reflection about their own time management behavior and how it affects their performance. This intervention was loosely inspired by the active learning technique called a "minute paper" [9][2]. After consulting with the instructors involved, the reflection activity was expanded to writing a brief reflective response to four prompts. Although conducting the activity in class is one option, in this study students completed their reflective writing activity outside of class, entering their responses in a one-page electronic form on-line. Students received a grade for completion of this activity, amounting to 1% for each reflective writing. Assignments were given around the time each programming assignment was given, asking students to reflect on their choices in completing the previous programming assignment in this (or an earlier) course. The writing activity was as follows:

This assignment involves writing one-paragraph responses to four questions regarding the last programming assignment you completed for this class, and should only take you about 15-20 minutes to complete.

Consider the following questions and answer each one in a separate paragraph.

1. *On the last software project you worked on for a class, consider when you began working on it, the way that you spent your time, and how you managed yourself as you worked to complete the project. Then describe the key elements of the plan or strategy you used to manage your time on that project.*

2. *Again considering the most recent software project you completed for a class, describe how your strategy for managing your time on the project affected the quality of your work or your ability to achieve your goals on the project.*

3. *Reflecting on your experience with past projects, describe the strategy or plan you intend to use for managing your time on the next software project that you will do for this class.*

4. *Again considering the most recent software project you completed for a class, a) describe your development strategy that you used to implement and test the program, b) describe how your development strategy affected the quality of your work or your ability to achieve your goals on the project, and c) describe any different strategy to implement and test your program that you will use for the next software project that you will do for this class.*

3.2 Schedule Sheets

The second intervention we investigated was the use of *schedule sheets*. For several years, instructors in our junior data structures course have been using "painless" schedule sheets [8]. Student survey data indicate that many students find them helpful for managing their projects, while others find them to be unhelpful. The purpose of schedule sheets is to encourage students to set a series of small, intermediate deadlines themselves, and to think about their progress on these tasks periodically. By helping students to form, express, manage, and track smaller-scale deadlines, this intervention aims to reduce procrastination.

To provide for effective schedule administration, an electronic schedule entry system was developed to allow students to submit schedules on-line. Students entered (or changed) their work breakdown structure in the form of a series of tasks–often, specific modules, classes, or identifiable pieces of required behavior. Each task had form fields for the student to enter the estimated number of hours of design time, coding time, and testing time, although students could optionally leave one or more of these blank if they were not applicable. In addition to estimating the number of hours

for each task, students were also required to enter their own personal target deadline for completing that task.

Student projects in the course used for this study lasted approximately four weeks on average. Students were required to fill out an initial schedule sheet showing their task breakdown and initial elements early in the process, typically within a week of when the assignment was given. As students progressed, they were required to turn in an intermediate schedule sheet approximately one week before the assignment was due. This intermediate sheet asked the student to report the number of hours actually spent on each task, as well as which tasks had been completed. Next, the student would have a chance to revise or update their previously entered schedule, entering revised estimates for time remaining to complete tasks and updating personal deadlines as necessary. When the assignment was due, students turned in a final schedule reporting the amount of time spent on completing tasks during the final week of work.

To promote more effective scheduling and to encourage students to plan their time effectively, students received immediate automated feedback as they entered their schedule information. A "check my work" button allowed students to get immediate feedback at any point while editing their schedule. The automated feedback included a large number of diagnostics on the consistency and appropriateness of time entries and deadlines on individual tasks and on the entire schedule as a whole. As a result, students were alerted to missing required elements, to over scheduling their own time, to creating schedules that were too coarse-grained or too fine-grained, and so on. A total of 23 different kinds of automated checks were performed to provide this feedback.

In addition to automated feedback, the scheduling system also permitted manual review of all schedules by the instructor and course staff. The instructor hand-checked all schedules that required attention and wrote additional feedback comments. For each programming assignment, students re-

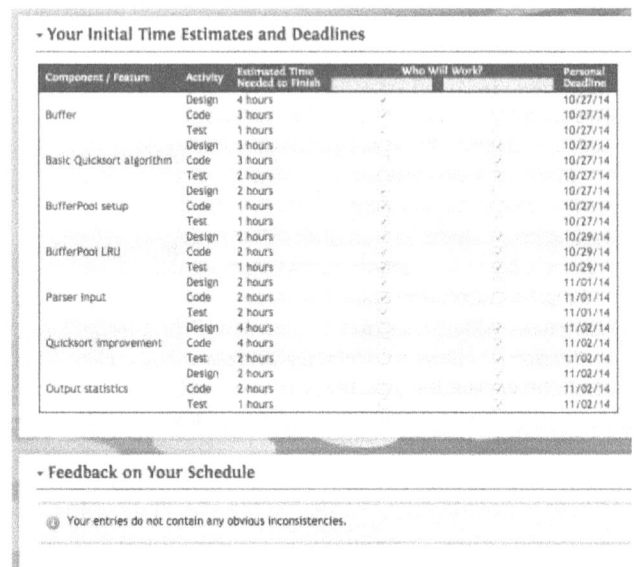

Figure 1: A screenshot of the schedule contents. Student names have been blocked out; checkboxes show which student is participating in which tasks.

ceived a grade corresponding to 1% of their semester grade, spread among the three schedule sheets for that assignment.

3.3 Situational Awareness Alerts

The final intervention we investigated was the use of automatically generated e-mail *situational awareness alerts*. These were periodic messages sent to students as they work on an assignment to raise their awareness of how their current level of effort compares to what others are doing. Because students had no concrete deliverables to turn in as part of this activity, they did not receive any grade for e-mail alerts. Instead, this group completed additional homework to earn the 1% grade credit allocated to other interventions.

While instructors routinely tell students to start programming projects early and spread the workload over time, admonishments alone appear to do little to affect student behavior. This intervention takes a different approach by providing alerts that are meaningful because they are individually relevant. Based in part on past student assignment data, we constructed a model of student progress that could be used to automatically assess a student's progress. In this study, students electronically submitted their program assignments using Web-CAT, an open-source automated grading system for programming assignments [3][4]. As part of this work, we built an automated alert system as a prototype extension to Web-CAT. By using data from the students' work-in-progress, in comparison with the model that we developed, it is possible to provide feedback about how well the student is doing compared to classroom expectations.

The e-mail alert treatment involved sending periodic e-mail messages to the students, beginning approximately one week before the assignment was due, then again at 4 days before and 2 days before the assignment deadline. Each e-mail alert was customized based on the work most recently submitted for electronic checking at that point. The student's work was classified along 4 dimensions: the amount of code written (relative to an approximate target size for the given assignment), the proportion of instructor-written reference tests passed (an approximation for functional correctness), the degree of testing performed (if the assignment requires students to write their own software tests), and the number of static analysis checks failed (measuring adherence to coding style guidelines, if required by the assignment). Along each dimension, the student's work so far was rated on a 4-point scale: Good, meaning the student's progress indicated advanced progress compared to the model for the amount of time remaining before the due date; Neutral, meaning the student's program was in line with the model for the amount of time remaining; Bad, meaning the student's progress was significantly behind the model; or Undefined, meaning there was insufficient information to assess the student's work.

A custom e-mail message was generated based on the four ratings. The subject line of the e-mail was phrased as "CS 3114: Your progress on Project 2". However, if the student's work indicated insufficient progress in one or more dimensions, the subject line would instead be "CS 3114: You may be at risk on Project 2", or even "CS 3114: You are at risk on Project 2". The body of the e-mail message contained a separate paragraph corresponding to each of the 4 dimensions on which the student's work was rated. As an example, here is an alert message that was automatically generated for one student:

This notification is to increase your awareness of your current progress on Project 4 compared to the rest of the class. Project 4 is due in 4 days.

Based on the work you have submitted to Web-CAT, it looks like you are making good progress towards a working solution for this assignment. Starting early is associated with a statistically significant increase in scores earned, compared to when the same student starts later. This increases your chances of success on the assignment.

Based on the tests you have submitted, it appears that you may be waiting until later to test your work, instead of testing it incrementally as you develop it. Typical students earn higher scores when they write tests incrementally with their code compared to when the same student waits to write tests until the code is substantially complete. This increases your risk of performing poorly on the assignment.

Based on the style checks on your assignment, it appears you are not formatting your code as expected when you write it, and may be intending to go back and correct the formatting later. Adjusting your code writing style so that you produce properly formatted and documented code as you write will increase your efficiency and reduce the time needed to clean up code later.

We wish you the best of luck as you work to complete this assignment.
– Web-CAT Situational Awareness Service

4. METHOD

We studied these three interventions in four separate sections of CS 3114: Data Structures and Algorithms, over two separate semesters. In Fall 2013, one section of this course had no treatment or intervention, serving as a control condition, while a second parallel section used the reflective writing assignment treatment. In Fall 2014, one section of this course used schedule sheets, while a second parallel section received e-mail situational awareness alerts. In each of the sections under study, students received the same treatment on all programming assignments in the course. In total, 362 students participated in the course as part of these four sections. All sections were taught by the same instructor using the same techniques and course materials. 353 of the students consented to the use of their data for educational research in this study (control: 71, reflective writing: 79, schedule sheets: 100, e-mail alerts: 103).

Students in all four sections completed a total of 4 separate programming assignments. Assignments ranged in difficulty and size, with solutions averaging from approximately 400-1800 non-commented/non-blank source lines of code. While the same assignments were not used in the two semesters, the assignments were comparable in complexity. In both semesters, the third assignment was the shortest, with the second and fourth assignments being hardest/longest. All assignments involved implementing one or more data structures, together with a simple command line interpreter modeled on entering, retrieving, and operating on real-world data to be inserted into the structure(s).

Students were required to write their own software tests to test their own work, and turned in both software and tests together using Web-CAT. Students received immediate feedback on correctness and programming style, and were encouraged to revise and resubmit their work frequently to maximize their scores. In all four sections, students were allowed to work in pairs on programming assignments, where they were encouraged to use pair programming [15], the extreme programming technique where two programmers work together with one playing the role of reviewer or "navigator" while the other actively writes as the "driver". However, since work on programming assignments was completed outside of class, no supervision of pair activities was available and the degree to which students adhered to pair programming practices is unclear. Students were also given the option to complete projects alone without a partner, although the majority of students chose to work together. Program assignments were then classified as "late" if they were submitted after the due date had passed.

In all programming assignments across both semesters, the insturctor offered students an extra credit bonus for completing the assignment at least one day early. This bonus was equivalent to 10% of the total project score. Since this bonus was consistent across all groups including the control group, and prior work did not show any evidence for its effectiveness, it does not appear to have affected the study.

5. RESULTS

Figure 2 shows the percentage of assignments turned in late after the due date for each treatment condition, together with the corresponding percentage of assignments completed at least one day early. Across all four assignments, 42.3% of programs were submitted late vs. 35.0% early in the control group, 38.6% late vs. 43.3% early in the reflective writing group, 38.1% late vs. 34.1% early in the schedule sheets group, and 32.4% late vs. 46.1% early in the e-mail alerts group. The data are suggestive, in that there were lower rates of late submissions for all interventions compared to the control, and higher rates of early submissions for two.

By using both the assignment and the treatment condition as independent variables, a multinomial logistic regression on whether programs were submitted late indicated that the null hypothesis that no differences were observed should be rejected ($DF = 6, \chi^2 = 44.2, p < 0.0001$). However, likelihood ratio test results did not indicate clear evidence for an effect from treatment condition alone ($DF = 3, \chi^2 = 6.9, p < 0.076$), while assignment differences were clearly significant ($DF = 3, \chi^2 = 38.0, p < 0.0001$). Instead, only the difference in late submissions between the e-mail situational awareness alerts and the control group were significant ($DF = 1, \chi^2 = 6.6, p = 0.01$).

From these results, it is also clear that the assignments themselves have an effect. Figure 3 shows the percentage of assignments turned in late for each assignment, grouped by treatment condition. While some instructors believe procrastination increases later in the semester, here this was not the case. Instead, the high point seems to be on the second programming project, which is one of the two harder and longer assignments. One possible explanation is that students who are struggling early in the course decide to drop out after that point, leaving only more persistent students who are more likely to complete work on time. Of course, other explanations are possible and it is likely that multiple factors are important.

Overall, however, these results are encouraging. First, it is notable that all four groups had comparable rates of late submissions on the first programming assignment, averaging near 40%. On the very first assignment, students had no previous exposure to the interventions being studied and were just trying them out for the first time. It is also worth

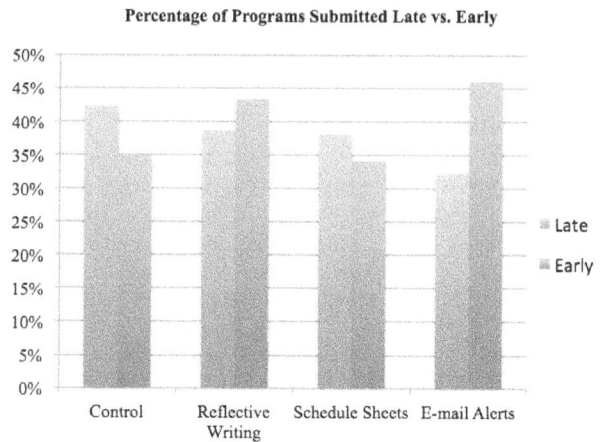

Figure 2: The proportion of assignments turned in late and early for each treatment condition.

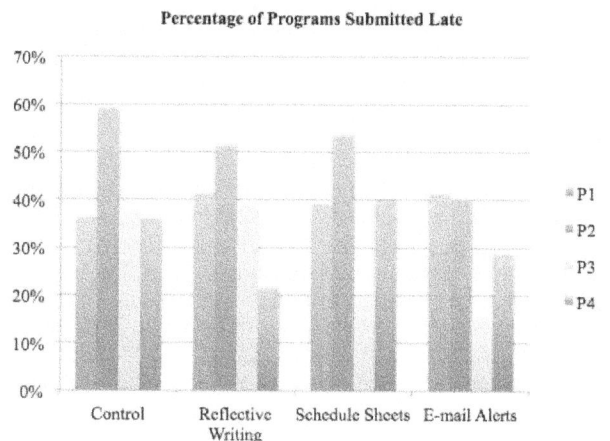

Figure 3: The proportion of assignments turned in late for assignments P1–P4, grouped by treatment condition.

noting that all assignments except for Project 2 had similar rates of late submissions throughout the semester in the control group—Projects 1, 3, and 4 were all between 36–38%. At the same time, however, all three interventions showed fewer late submissions on at least some later assignments, with the e-mail alert intervention showing consistently lower late submission rates on all assignments after the first.

Second, it appears the reflective writing intervention had minimal impact. A chi square test between just the reflective writing group and the control group does not reveal any difference ($\chi^2 = 0.75, p < 0.39$). While the number of late submissions was lower for Projects 2 and 4 compared to the control, the number was actually slightly higher for the other two projects. The schedule sheet intervention similarly had a questionable impact ($\chi^2 = 1.01, p < 0.32$), with two assignments having greater rates of late submissions.

In comparison, e-mail situational awareness alerts produced the only significant impact ($DF = 1, \chi^2 = 6.6, p =$

0.01). Students in this group saw a one third reduction in late submissions on the second assignment compared to the control group, a 58% reduction on the third assignment, and a 20% reduction in the final assignment. At the same time, as shown in Figure 2, the greatest proportion of students finished at least a day early with this intervention as well. This increased rate of early submissions was also significant ($DF = 1, \chi^2 = 7.1, p < 0.01$). However, while promising, it is important to keep in mind that differences between the assignments were also quite significant, and more research is necessary to strengthen evidence for this treatment.

6. CONCLUSIONS

This paper summarizes an investigation of three classroom interventions intended to address student procrastination in programming assignments. Of the interventions studied, the reflective writing assignments did not produce evidence for any significant impact on timeliness of student work. However, changes to the intervention, such as having students discuss their reflections, perhaps using a think-pair-share classroom activity or a peer learning activity, could improve its effectiveness. Similarly, schedule sheet assignments also did not produce consistent evidence for a significant impact.

This study does indicate that e-mail situational awareness alerts showed a statistically significant reduction in late submissions (23% fewer on average), as well as a statistically significant increase in early completion (31% more on average) compared to the control group. Because of the nature of studies such as this, however, there is a risk that other factors may also have played a role, such as differences in student populations, differences in assignments, or differences in competing class deadlines in other courses. Any of these factors could have contributed to the observed differences between the rate of late submissions between the groups.

To investigate further, we hope to conduct a future study using a randomized block design that will support within-subjects comparisons across treatments. Such a follow-on study may shed additional light on the scope of effect that may be achieved with interventions such as these. Also, it may be worthwhile to study them in combination—do they produce a bigger impact if they are used together?

At the same time, these interventions are only practical if instructors have access to the necessary tools. Both schedule sheets and e-mail alerts are only feasible with automation, since they would be prohibitively costly to employ manually. As a new form of intervention that is more data-driven, and that provides more immediate and more individual feedback, the personal nature of these interventions may be one part of why they have an impact. To this end, we have made the prototype tools used in this study available as part of the Web-CAT open source project. While the tools themselves are not ready for more generalized use by a wider audience, we hope that incorporating them into a more widely adopted project will make it easier for other educators and researchers who wish to explore these techniques.

7. ACKNOWLEDGMENTS

This work is supported in part by the National Science Foundation under grant DUE-1245334. Any opinions, findings, conclusions, or recommendations expressed in this material are those of the authors and do not necessarily reflect the views of the National Science Foundation.

8. REFERENCES

[1] A. Allevato and S. Edwards. Effects of extra credit opportunities on students' time management on programming assignments. In *Proceedings of the IEEE 43rd Annual Frontiers in Education Conference*, pages 1831–1836. IEEE, October 2013.

[2] C. Bonwell and J. Eison. *Active Learning: Creating Excitement in the Classroom*. School of Education and Human Development, George Washington University, 1991.

[3] S. H. Edwards. Using software testing to move students from trial-and-error to reflection-in-action. In *Proceedings of the 35th SIGCSE Technical Symposium on Computer Science Education*, SIGCSE '04, pages 26–30, New York, NY, USA, 2004. ACM.

[4] S. H. Edwards and M. A. Pérez-Quiñones. Experiences using test-driven development with an automated grader. *J. Comput. Sci. Coll.*, 22(3):44–50, Jan. 2007.

[5] S. H. Edwards, J. Snyder, M. A. Pérez-Quiñones, A. Allevato, D. Kim, and B. Tretola. Comparing effective and ineffective behaviors of student programmers. In *Proceedings of the Fifth International Workshop on Computing Education Research*, pages 3–14. ACM, 2009.

[6] R. M. Klassen, L. L. Krawchuk, and S. Rajani. Academic procrastination of undergraduates: Low self-efficacy to self-regulate predicts higher levels of procrastination. *Contemporary Educational Psychology*, 33(4):915 – 931, 2008.

[7] C. H. Lay. At last, my research article on procrastination. *Journal of Research in Personality*, 20(4):474–495, 1986.

[8] J. Spolsky. Painless software schedules. http://www.joelonsoftware.com/articles/fog0000000245.html. Accessed: 2015-01-11.

[9] D. Stead. A review of the one-minute paper. *Active Learning in Higher Education*, 6(2):118–131, July 2005.

[10] P. Steel. The nature of procrastination: a meta-analytic and theoretical review of quintessential self-regulatory failure. *Psychological Bulletin*, 133(1):65, 2007.

[11] J. Stodder. Experimental moralities: Ethics in classroom experiments. *The Journal of Economic Education*, 29(2):127–138, 1998.

[12] D. M. Tice and R. F. Baumeister. Longitudinal study of procrastination, performance, stress, and health: The costs and benefits of dawdling. *Psychological Science*, pages 454–458, 1997.

[13] B. W. Tuckman. The development and concurrent validity of the procrastination scale. *Educational and Psychological Measurement*, 51(2):473–480, 1991.

[14] B. W. Tuckman. Relations of academic procrastination, rationalizations, and performance in a web course with deadlines 1. *Psychological Reports*, 96(3c):1015–1021, 2005.

[15] L. Williams. Lessons learned from seven years of pair programming at North Carolina State University. *SIGCSE Bull.*, 39(4):79–83, Dec. 2007.

A Teaching System To Learn Programming: the Programmer's Learning Machine

Martin Quinson
Université de Lorraine, F-54506, France
Inria, F-54600, France
CNRS, LORIA, UMR 7503, F-54506, France
martin.quinson@loria.fr

Gérald Oster
Université de Lorraine, F-54506, France
Inria, F-54600, France
CNRS, LORIA, UMR 7503, F-54506, France
gerald.oster@loria.fr

ABSTRACT

The Programmer's Learning Machine (PLM) is an interactive exerciser for learning programming and algorithms. Using an integrated and graphical environment that provides a short feedback loop, it allows students to learn in a (semi)-autonomous way. This generic platform also enables teachers to create specific programming microworlds that match their teaching goals. This paper discusses our design goals and motivations, introduces the existing material and the proposed microworlds, and details the typical use cases from the student and teacher point of views.

1. INTRODUCTION

The Programmer's Learning Machine (PLM) is a free integrated educational software environment for learning and teaching programming. The main target audience is college and university students that learn programming in loosely tutored practical sessions, but it can be used by younger pupils. It comes with 200 exercises covering the basics of programming, sorting algorithms and recursion.

Figure 1a shows PLM's main window when discovering a new exercise. It is composed of two main panels: The left one presents the text of the mission, which provides any information needed by students to solve the exercise (ranging from the theoretical background and generic body of knowledge to practical details and hints) while the right panel displays a view of the current state of the exercise's world. Each world in PLM entails at least one active entity that executes the student code. A student can interact with the entity using the interactive controls which are located below the world view to perform some preliminary experiments in solving the exercise.

An effective way to understand the goals of an exercise is to switch to the second tab of the world view as depicted in Figure 1b. It displays the state of the world as it should be at the end of the exercise. Pressing the "demo" button starts an animation of the operations leading from the initial state

ITiCSE'15, July 6–8, 2015, Vilnius, Lithuania.
Copyright is held by the owner/author(s). Publication rights licensed to ACM.
ACM 978-1-4503-3440-2/15/07 ...$15.00.
DOI: http://dx.doi.org/10.1145/2729094.2742626.

to the expected one. The speed of this animation can be adjusted at will.

To pass an exercise, a student must type in the proper source code in the second tab of the left panel, as illustrated in Figure 1c. Any potential compilation or execution error is displayed in the console located at the bottom of the window. Then, the source code can be executed either continuously or step by step. At the end of the execution, if the world state does not match the final objective, an informative message explains the observed problem.

Exercises can be solved either in Java, Python or Scala, under the standard settings. The PLM uses the standard Java virtual machine in conjunction with either the standard Java or Scala compiler, or the standard Jython implementation of Python.

This short and graphical feedback loop improves the students' motivation and makes their learning more effective in practice. Moreover, the PLM makes it easy for teachers to adapt the provided teaching material to their teaching goals, or to create new original material.

This paper is organized as follows: Section 2 discusses the design goals and rationale of the project. Section 3 situates the PLM within the state of the art. Section 4 shows the effectiveness of our educational tool through the presentation of the teaching material developed on top of it. Section 5 presents how teachers and resources authors can adapt and create additional resources. Section 6 discusses some evidences of the tool usage. Finally, Section 7 concludes the paper and points out some future work.

2. DESIGN GOALS AND RATIONALE

The overall rationale of the PLM is that programming is a learn-by-doing activity. Given the major role of practice in the learning of programming, the PLM intends to be an automated exerciser allowing students to practice with the programming tasks. The PLM is geared toward three categories of users, each of them mandating specific goals.

2.1 Toward students

The PLM should facilitate autonomous learning and make programming engaging and satisfying. This main objective can be decomposed and detailed in several goals: Autonomous learning mandates *a consistent set of resources* with which the student can interact and experiment. Open-ended exercises enable free experimentation, but more guided exercises are precious to beginners that get easily paralyzed when facing choices. A *short feedback loop* provides a clear goal to the student's experimentation while an

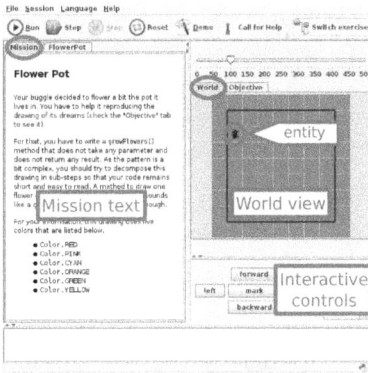

(a) Discovering a new exercise.

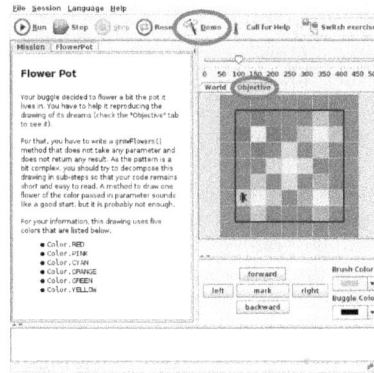

(b) Understanding the goal of an exercise through the use of the demo mode.

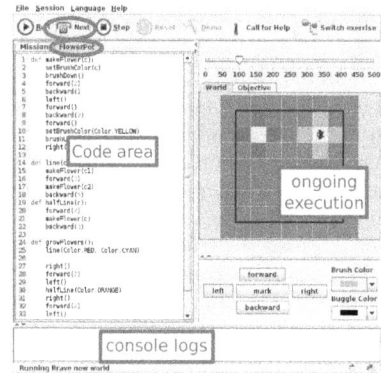

(c) Writing and executing code.

Figure 1: Basic use cases of the PLM.

automated evaluation leading to quick success experiences reinforces the student's motivation. A *visual feedback* allows to focus on algorithmic concepts through the program effects, reducing the importance of syntactic elements. Finally, the tool should be *intuitive, easy to use and available* on most systems to avoid that technical details hinder user experience. Along the same lines, the environment must be translated and adapted to be usable by non-native English learners. This is particularly true for younger pupils.

Another important design goal of the PLM is to ease the transition to other programming contexts through the use of standard tools and languages. *Several programming languages are proposed* in the environment, so that the user is free to choose. Generic purpose programming languages are however known to be less adapted to novice programmers [2]. Java programs must for example use **public static void main(String[] args)** as an entry point, exposing beginners to advanced notions on day one [13]. Even if this code can be provided to students, it induces an extra cognitive burden that can drown beginners. It is then preferable to *template the provided code and hide* the parts that are less relevant to the teachings.

2.2 Toward authors of resources

The PLM should provide technical support to ease the creation of innovative learning situations adapted to each context. In particular, it should be easy to build a new form of microworld providing a specific learning situation. Moreover, the environment should provide all non-functional code, for instance related to user interactions, code compilation or user sessions persistence. An integrated instrumentation infrastructure would allow to assess the efficiency of the developed pedagogical resources.

2.3 Toward teachers

The environment should provide convenient and ready to use tools without hindering the practitioner's pedagogical freedom. It is expected that most teachers will leverage existing resources. This is similar to the classical use of existing books that is common in most teachings. Nevertheless, it should be easy for teachers to adapt the existing resources and assemble them to build their own learning path on top of the existing resources.

3. CONTEXT AND STATE OF THE ART

The PLM builds upon the concept of Programming Microworld, introduced in the eighties through the LOGO programming language [10]. In such settings, the student controls an *entity* or actor that interacts with its *environment*. In the initial LOGO microworld, the entity is a robotic turtle that leaves trails on a sheet of paper as it walks. Many systems build upon this idea, such as LogoBlocks [1] or the LEGO Mindstorms System.

One drawback of the LOGO microworld is the scarce interactions between the entity and its environment: there is no way for the turtle to check the state of the sheet. Subsequent microworlds provide richer interactions. The most popular is certainly *Karel the robot* [11], where the actor, a robot named Karel, evolves in a world consisting of intersecting streets and avenues. It can pick and drop "beepers" (objects laying on the ground) but cannot pass the walls. This leads to richer interactions through predicates that can test the presence of walls and beepers. Kara [7] is another microworld where a ladybird picks leafs while avoiding trees. Many other similar microworlds have been proposed in the literature, as reviewed in [2].

In addition to such generic microworlds, specialized microworlds can introduce specific concepts. In [15], the authors leverage three microworlds: Most of the teaching are conducted with the *BuggleWorld*, a generic microworld with rich entity-environment interactions. Recursion is first introduced using the *PictureWorld* that allows the construction of complex quilt patterns by combining simple shapes with basic transformations. Recursion is then further exercised through the drawing of polygons, spirals and trees in a LOGO-inspired microworld. This idea is pushed further in [3] where each exercise leverages a specific microworld. The limit of this approach is that the microworlds of both projects are developed separately without any code reuse. The non-functional code then induces an important extra burden. By contrast, the PLM factorizes this code to ease the authoring of pedagogical resource.

Many other similar environments have been proposed in the literature. In the taxonomy of Kelleher and Pausch [8], the PLM is within the category *Teaching System/Mechanics of Programming*. It covers several sub-categories: Simplify Typing Code; Making New Models Accessible; Tracking Program Execution and Make Programming Concrete.

Scratch, Alice and Greenfoot are very renowned educational projects to teach and learn programming. Scratch [12] enables kids to develop interactive stories and animations. Since scripts are constituted of building blocks that are visually assembled, it is accessible to kids even before they master reading and writing. The Alice [5] environment teaches older pupils about object-oriented programming through the design of scripted 3D animations. Greenfoot [9] uses the standard Java language for a similar goal.

The main difference between the PLM and these projects consists in the ability to propose auto-evaluated resources. Scratch, Alice and Greenfoot can be considered as IDEs that are specifically tailored to learners. However, in the PLM, teachers can prepare specific exercises on which students work autonomously, at their own pace. Both approaches are complementary: learners could first start with guided resources on the PLM to learn the concepts they need, and then move to an educational IDE to build their own projects using these concepts.

4. EXISTING TEACHING MATERIAL

This section presents the teaching resources developed on top of the PLM and distributed with the environment itself. The main goal of this discussion is to demonstrate the effectiveness of the PLM as an educational environment. The presented resources are interesting per see, even if we have no formal evidence of their intrinsic effectiveness. Many of them were previously existing in the literature. The practical effectiveness of the PLM (and to some extend of these resources) is discussed in Section 6.

4.1 The PLM's Universes

Since the PLM entails several kind of microworlds, we refer to each family of microworlds as a *universe*. We now detail the existing universes, focusing on their pedagogical features and on their typical use in exercises.

The Buggles.

Originally, this generic universe was the only existing universe in the PLM. It relies on an original idea of Franklyn Turbak at Wellesley College [15]. It features *the buggles*, that are able of many interactions with their environment: they can pick and drop objects, paint the ground, read and write messages on the ground, hit walls, etc.

Thanks to its versatility, this universe is used in many proposed exercises.

Sorting Algorithms.

Several original universes are specifically tailored to teach sorting algorithms. The first one targets the exploration of sorting algorithms. The demo mode can be used at full speed to get a practical idea of the different complexity of algorithms, or to understand the specific behavior of an algorithm step by step.

Interestingly, it is not sufficient to sort the provided array of data to pass a typical sorting exercise, but the proposed solution must access the data exactly the same amount of time than the expected solution. This is enforced through adapted primitives that mediate and count any data access. Using `isSmaller(i,j)` to compare cells does account for two reads. Using `copy(i,j)` or `swap(i,j)` to modify the data accounts respectively for one read plus one write, or for

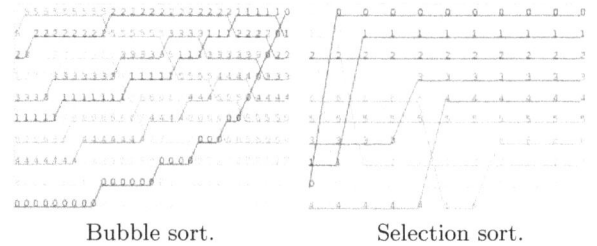

Bubble sort.   Selection sort.

Figure 2: Temporal view of the sorting world.

two reads plus two writes. This constraint on the amount of data accesses forces students to strictly implement the expected algorithm, which in turn requires a very good level of understanding of the presented algorithms.

When the amount of data accesses does not match, understanding the difference between the proposed code and the expected solution can be difficult. To ease this process, student can graphically explore the history of their sorting algorithm as shown in Figure 2. The time is represented as abscissa while ordinate represent the array cells. The lines represent the values in these cells; When two lines cross, this means that two values were swapped at this timestamp. This representation, introduced by A. Cortesi[1], is precious to understand the behavior of sorting algorithms.

The *Rainbow Baseball* is another PLM universe that applies the classical sorting algorithms in a funny and original setting. It builds upon the Pebble Motion Problem [4], where objects must be placed on the right vertex of a graph under several movement constraints. This problem is similar to the 15-puzzle problem. This engaging universe can be played by clicking on the pebbles to move them, but the provided lesson requires students to reimplement the major sorting algorithms. A temporal view allows to compare the proposed code with the expected one.

The *Pancakes Universe* builds upon the classical pancake problem [6], where a stack of pancake should be sorted only by flipping pancakes at the top of the stack. The corresponding lesson entails several existing algorithms to solve this problem, some of them being non-trivial.

The *Dutch Flag* universe is a simple universe whose solution is a linear sorting algorithm adapted to sort an array containing only three kinds of values.

Unit Testing.

This universe is very specific as it does not provide any graphical representation. Each exercise proposes a method prototype that the students must fill in. This method is then tested against a comprehensive test of parameter values. This universe, inspired from the work of Nick Parlante[2], is probably less motivating than graphical microworlds, but it is efficient to practice on a particular point. The introductory lesson provides for example short exercises on conditionals where the students must write simple boolean expressions matching the provided textual descriptions.

The LOGO Turtles.

This universe reimplements the classical LOGO microworld. It is used in two of the proposed lessons. In the

[1]http://corte.si/posts/code/visualisingsorting/
[2]http://codingbat.com/

recursive lesson, the students are asked to draw recursively polygons, spirals, trees and fractals. The "turtle art" lesson presents several classical LOGO drawings to inspire the students, that are expected to then play in creative mode where their solution is not checked against any objective.

Recursive Algorithms.

Recursive Lists are a classical data structure, even if vectors are more used in Java and Python. In Scala, the classical `List` datatype is used while a dedicated type is proposed in Python and Java. 17 classical exercises are proposed in this universe, such as computing the length or finding one element.

The *Hanoi Towers* problem is classically used to introduce recursive programming. In the PLM, 12 progressive exercises explore some less known variations of this problem to exercise the recursive decomposition abilities of the learners.

4.2 Proposed Learning Path

The exercises are not isolated in the PLM, but grouped by thematic lessons providing a coherent progression on each topic. This is particularly important to self-learners using the unmodified tool, even if most teachers will probably adapt this path to their settings.

Overall, more than 200 exercises are proposed in the PLM. Their corrections constitute a body of roughly 3000 lines of code (per programming language). The fastest students need around one week full-time to solve all the exercises.

4.2.1 Tactical Programming

The first lesson introduces the basic concepts of programming to absolute beginners. After a quick tour of the environment, the notion of instructions is presented through very simple Buggle exercises. The lesson then introduces conditionals and while loops. The concepts are presented as part of simple exercises and reinvested immediately in several application exercises that leverage the universes' versatility. An extra complexity comes from the fact that the pattern matching of Scala is more powerful than the switch-case construct of Java, while Python offers no switch construct. The mission text are then dynamically adapted to the chosen programming language so that the right concept and syntax are presented to the student.

Variables are the next introduced concept, before for loops and do-while loops. In python, we present the idiomatic way toward do-while loops since this construct does not exist in this language. 20 exercises are proposed for these notions, 15 of them being engaging and situated application exercises that follow uncluttered introduction exercises presenting the concepts. Some exercises induce more complex loop settings, with non-trivial loop conditions, limit cases and modeling task to identify the repeated instructions, as advised in [14].

Functions are then introduced, followed by methods and parameters. Functional decomposition is introduced through several exercises requesting to repeat a given pattern an increasing amount of time. About 15 exercises introduce and apply these concepts. Most of our students need 4 to 6 hours to reach the end of this unit.

About 40 unit testing exercises to practice with writing of simple conditionals take place at this point of the progression. They could theoretically be placed earlier, but our unit universe requires the student to know about meth-

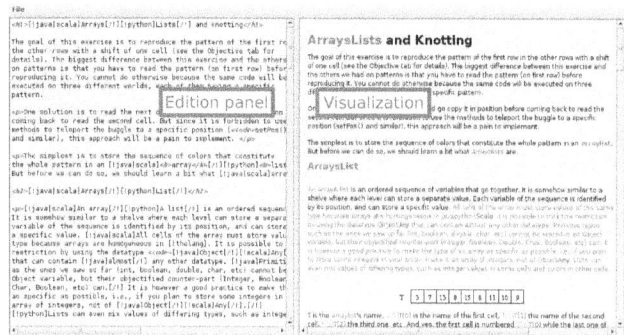

Figure 3: Mission text editor.

ods. Sequence of elements (arrays in Java and Scala, lists in Python) are then explored through 18 exercises.

This concludes the introductory lesson, that is usually completed by absolute beginners at university level in 10 to 20 hours. It can be followed by two application lessons: the first one quickly explores classical maze algorithms while the other introduces a simple form of cellular automaton called Langton's ant. This is easy to implement for the students, and leads to interesting drawings.

4.2.2 Algorithmic Basics

After the language syntax and basic constructs introduction, we move on to more algorithmic lessons. One lesson explores the classical sorting algorithm, while two other lessons situate these algorithms in the engaging microworlds presented in previous section. Another lesson explores recursion through recursive lists, Logo-based figures and variations of the Hanoi Towers problem.

5. EXTENDING THE PLM

Teachers can reuse the proposed material as-is, or they can adapt and extend it. One current limitation of the PLM is that such adaptation can only be done in Java for now, forcing teachers to have some notions of this language even if they teach Scala or Python.

5.1 Creating new lessons

The easiest PLM adaptation is to create a lesson that builds a new learning path from existing resources. This is trivially done by building a Java collection of the selected resources during the lesson's initialization. This could be further simplified in the future by using configuration files instead of Java code.

5.2 Creating new exercises

A typical exercise is composed of a mission text, the description of the initial environment's state, and a correction entity implementing the requested work.

The mission text is an HTML file, possibly with conditional inclusions to adapt the text to the selected programming language. Since such conditional texts tend to be intricate and burdensome to edit, the PLM provides an adapted text editor (Figure 3). The text is edited in the left panel and previewed in the right panel. A color code depicts graphically the parts that are specific to each programming language. The mission text can also entail optional *hints*, that are shown only on explicit student request.

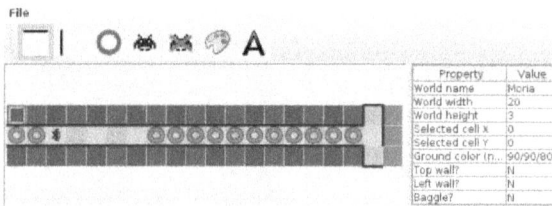

Figure 4: Buggle world map editor.

One way to build the initial state of the microworld is through a dedicated Java class whose complexity naturally depends on the world to instantiate. A graphical editor is provided for buggle worlds, that can become rather complex. This intuitive tool is depicted in Figure 4.

Most exercises test students' code on multiple instances of the problem to detect more errors. From the author perspective, this simply requires to attach several world instances to the exercise.

The correction entities have several roles: They are applied to the initial worlds to compute the objective worlds; They are executed when playing the demo, and they provide an hosting scaffold around the student's code chunk to produce valid files. This last usage requires to automatically edit the entity. To this end, the entity source code must be annotated as shown in Figure 5. When compiling the student's code, the section marked with BEGIN/{end template} is removed and replaced with the student code while the other parts are left unchanged. Once the BEGIN/{end solution} section is removed, the BEGIN/END TEMPLATE section is also used as initial content in the source code editor. Here, this mechanism preseeds the editor with the function's prototype that must be filled in by the student.

Since they are used as a scaffold around the student's code, it is necessary to write one correction entity in each programming language for each exercise.

5.3 Designing a New Microworld

Adding a radically new learning context to the PLM requires to extend the classes defining an universe: the *World* class contains the microworld state and data; the *Entity* class is the ancestor of all correction entities. This class is mainly responsible to adapt the World interface and provide to the user convenient primitives to alter the world. The

```
public class SlugTrackingEntity extends SimpleBuggle {
    // Some additional code adapted to this exercise
    /* BEGIN TEMPLATE */
    boolean isFacingTrail() {
        // Write your code here
        /* BEGIN SOLUTION */
        if (isFacingWall())
            return false;
        forward();
        boolean res = getGroundColor().equals(Color.green);
        backward();
        return res;
        /* END SOLUTION */
    }
    /* END TEMPLATE */
}
```

Figure 5: Example of annotated entity source code.

WorldView provides a graphical representation of a given World. Any universe should also be documented through an IITML following the same conventions than the mission texts of exercises. Finally, most universes should entail a *WorldPanel* class that provides the entities' interactive controls.

Universe	#lines	Universe	#lines
Buggle	1400	Panecake	500
Baseball	1000	Units	500
Sorting	900	Hanoi	500
Turtle	700	Dutch Flag	400

Table 1: Complexity of the main universes.

Table 1 presents the code complexity of each universe. The numbers remain surprisingly low despite the wealth of the proposed universes, proving the effectiveness of the code factorization enabled by the PLM.

6. TOOL ADOPTION

We use the PLM since seven years in our institution. Thanks to it, absolute beginners become quickly confident in the programming syntax, allowing to take on more advanced content in the same time than before its introduction. Although only spread by word of mouth so far, the environment is proposed as a complement to the regular teaching in a few institutions.

Figure 6 presents the feedback collected from our students after the semester. The evaluation was strictly anonymous; we received 53 responses from 100 enrolled students. Our Lickert scales did not propose any neutral choices to get more critical feedback. In response, some students did not provide any answer on controversial questions forcing us to consider the absence of answer as a neutral choice.

The perception of the educational value of the PLM is overwhelmingly positive, with only 3 students disagreeing and 34 students strongly agreeing with this statement. The entertaining value was also very appreciated although less strongly, with 31 students agreeing on this statement and only 16 strongly agreeing. The motivational aspect is also very well received as over 80% of the students agree or strongly agree that practical sessions are more motivating when using the PLM than with classical sessions. The actual educational value is more discussed as one third of the students report that they did not progress while using the PLM. This may be linked to the fact that some of the students that are requested to follow this teaching can already program beforehand. As noted previously, even these students find the PLM useful and entertaining to some extend.

After these questions on specific qualities, we evaluated the overall feeling of the students. Consistently with previous results, the vast majority would advice the environment to a friend. The last question was meant as a test of the students' objectivity. We asked whether they thought of the PLM as a good argument for potential candidates to our school. This statement is very arguable as the PLM is used only in very few teachings of the curriculum (even if students enrolled in the first year may oversee this fact). One third of the students disagreed with this statement, and one fourth skipped this question. This statement was thus very mildly agreed, reinforcing our confidence in the objectivity of this evaluation.

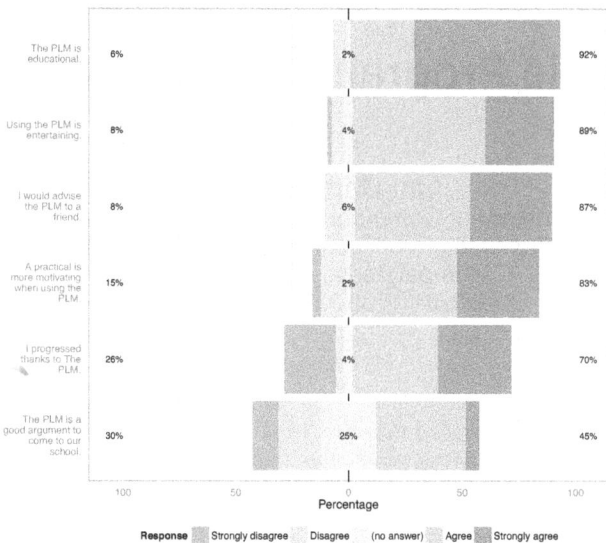

Figure 6: Anonymous Evaluation of the PLM by our Students (54 answers).

7. CONCLUSION AND FUTURE WORK

In this paper, we described the Programmer's Learning Machine, an integrated educational software dedicated to the learning and teaching of programming. It is designed for users with no or little programming experience and aims at providing practice in a friendly and attractive environment. An extensive but coherent set of exercises is presented to students, who can progress at their own pace. Several microworlds are leveraged, some of them specialized in specific programming concepts. The exercises can be solved using either the Java, Scala or Python programming language, using the standard compilers. The tool and all teaching materials are fully translated to English and French (and partially to Italian and Portuguese). The proposed lessons entail over 200 exercises, covering the imperative kernel (basic syntax and control structures), sorting algorithms and recursion.

The PLM is freely available from the project's web page[3], under an open-source license. It is also integrated to the Debian distribution of Linux. It is known to work on Windows, Linux and MacOS. We are now actively fostering the emergence of a user community.

Future work naturally entails the extension of the proposed teaching material and the addition of new microworlds to explore other concepts such as backtracking, dynamic programming, or classical data structures (heap, stacks, graphs). We are currently introducing an instrumentation infrastructure that could be used to quickly detect the students requiring the teacher's help. Such infrastructure could also be used to study the effectiveness of specific teaching strategies and approaches. This will enable formal studies of the apparatus efficiency that will in turn help improving further this educational environment.

---

[3]http://www.loria.fr/~quinson/Teaching/PLM/

8. REFERENCES

[1] Andrew Begel. Logoblocks: A graphical programming language for interacting with the world. Master's thesis, Massachusetts Institute of Technology, 1996.

[2] Peter Brusilovsky, Eduardo Calabrese, Jozef Hvorecky, and Philip Miller. Mini-languages: A way to learn programming principles. *Education and Information Technologies*, 2(1), 1997.

[3] Nadya Calderon, Jorge Villalobos, and Camilo Jimenez. Developing programming skills by using interactive learning objects. In *14th Annual Conference on Innovation and Technology in Computer Science Education (ITiCSE'09)*, Paris, France., July 2009. ACM.

[4] Gruia Calinescu, Adrian Dumitrescu, and Janos Pach. Reconfigurations in graphs and grids. In *LATIN 2006: Theoretical Informatics*, volume 3887 of *Lecture Notes in Computer Science*. Springer, 2006.

[5] Matthew Conway, Steve Audia, Tommy Burnette, Dennis Cosgrove, and Kevin Christiansen. Alice: lessons learned from building a 3d system for novices. In *CHI '00: Proceedings of the SIGCHI conference on Human factors in computing systems*, New York, NY, USA, 2000. ACM.

[6] William H. Gates and Christos H. Papadimitriou. Bounds for sorting by prefix reversal. *Discrete Mathematics*, 27(1), 1979.

[7] Werner Hartmann, Jurg Nievergelt, and Raimond Reichert. Kara, finite state machines, and the case for programming as part of general education. In *Proceedings of IEEE Symposium on Human-Centric Computing Languages and Environments*, Stresa, Italy, 2001. IEEE Computer Society.

[8] Caitlin Kelleher and Randy Pausch. Lowering the barriers to programming: A taxonomy of programming environments and languages for novice programmers. *ACM Comp. Survey*, 37(2), 2005.

[9] Michael Klling. The Greenfoot Programming Environment. *ACM Transactions on Computing Education (TOCE)*, 10(4), November 2010.

[10] Seymour Papert. *Mindstorms: Children, Computers, and Powerful Ideas*. Basic Books, 1980.

[11] Richard Pattis. *Karel the Robot: A Gentle Introduction to the Art of Programming with Pascal*. John Wiley and Sons, London, 1981.

[12] Mitchel Resnick, John Maloney, Andrés Monroy-Hernández, Natalie Rusk, Evelyn Eastmond, Karen Brennan, Amon Millner, Eric Rosenbaum, Jay Silver, Brian Silverman, and Yasmin Kafai. Scratch: Programming for all. *CACM*, 52(11), 2009.

[13] Eric Roberts, Kim Bruce, Kim Cutler, James Cross, Scott Grissom, Karl Klee, Susan Rodger, Fran Trees, Ian Utting, and Frank Yellin. The acm java task force project rationale. Technical report, ACM, 2006.

[14] Mara Saeli. *Teaching Programming for Secondary School: a Pedagogical Content Knowledge Based Approach*. PhD thesis, Technische Universiteit Eindhoven, 2012.

[15] Franklyn Turbak, Constance Royden, Jennifer Stephan, and Jean Herbst. Teaching recursion before iteration in CS1. *Journal of Computing in Small Colleges*, 14(4), may 1999.

Introducing Formal Methods via Program Derivation

Dipak L. Chaudhari
Department of Computer Science and Engg.
Indian Institute of Technology, Bombay
Mumbai, India, 400076
dipakc@cse.iitb.ac.in

Om Damani
Department of Computer Science and Engg.
Indian Institute of Technology, Bombay
Mumbai, India, 400076
damani@cse.iitb.ac.in

ABSTRACT

Existing attempts towards including formal methods in introductory programming courses focus on introducing program verification tools. When using the verification tools, there is no structured help available to the students in the actual task of implementing the program, except for the hints provided by the failed proof obligations. In contrast, in the correct-by-construction programming methodology, programs are incrementally derived from their specifications.

By restricting our attention to program derivation, we have identifed a small core of the formal method concepts that can easily be taught in the first two years of a computing curricula. Based on our learning from multiple years of paper and pencil based teaching, we have developed a programming assistant tool that addresses several of the issues faced by the students in the manual program derivation. The tool ensures that the most common students' error of performing incorrect proofs does not happen.

Categories and Subject Descriptors

K.3.2 [**Computers and Education**]: Computer and Information Science EducationComputer science education; D.2.4 [**Software Engineering**]: Software/Program Verification-Correctness Proofs, Formal Methods, Programming by Contract

General Terms

Algorithms, Verification, Human Factors

Keywords

Correct by Construction; Calculational Style; Teaching Formal Methods

1. INTRODUCTION

In its final report [1], the ITiCSE 2000 Working Group on Formal Methods Education aspired *to see the concepts*

of formal methods integrated seamlessly into the computing curriculum. Fifteen years later that aspiration still remains an aspiration. In our opinion, the major reason for this is the fact that the points of integration identified in the report, in Appendices C and E, come much later in the curriculum. By that time, the students are already used to the informal ways of developing programs and software and the old habits die hard. Ideally formal methods should be introduced as early as possible, particularly when students are just learning how to design programs [5].

Existing attempts in this direction focus on employing formal verification for teaching program correctness [13, 3, 7, 12]. The Implement-and-Verify program development methodology involves an implementation phase followed by a separate verification phase. Although the failed proof obligations provide some hint, there is no structured help available to the students in the actual task of implementing the programs. Students often rely on ad-hoc use cases and informal reasoning to guess the program constructs.

In contrast with this, in the *Calculational Style of Programming* (CSoP) [6, 10], programs are incrementally derived from their specifications. At every step in the derivation process, a partial program is transformed into a more refined form, by following certain transformation rules. The resulting programs are correct-by-construction since the correctness is implicit in the program transformations employed during the derivation. Since the students see the program transformation strategy that led to the introduction of a particular programming construct, they understand why a particular programming construct was introduced at a particular point in a program.

Based on the four offerings of the program derivation elective course to sophomores, we have identified a small core of the formal method concepts which is sufficient for teaching derivations of a large number of programs. We have also identified several difficulties faced by the students in using the method effectively (discussed in Section 4).

To address these difficulties, we have developed a tool called CAPS [4], for deriving sequential programs from their formal specifications. To the best of our knowledge, no comparable tool exists. As discussed before, existing tools [13, 3, 7] only ensure the correctness of the already implemented programs. Besides providing counter-examples, these tools provide limited help to the students in learning the program design techniques.

In CAPS, we have kept the derivation style and notation as close to the pen-and-paper style of derivation as possible. Our main emphasis has been on the usability in the class; in particular on being able to model and replay the ad-hoc interactions and iterations that usually occur during the manual program derivation by the students.

The organization of the rest of the paper is as follows. In Section 2, we discuss the core formal method concepts employed by us for teaching CSoP. In Section 3, we illustrate the methodology with a detailed example. In Section 4, we discuss our experiences from the years of teaching CSoP to sophomore students. In Section 5, the CAPS tool and the students experience with it is presented. Section 6 concludes the paper.

2. CORE IDEAS

The advantage of teaching formal methods via CSoP is that the students can quickly write programs to solve non-trivial problems after being exposed to a small set of concepts. After starting with the *sum of an array* and the *maximum element of an array*, we quickly move to the *binary search, fast exponentiation*, and the *maximum segment sum*. After that we cover various other optimal array segment and search problems, and other similar problems like *decomposing a number in a sum of two squares*. Then we move on to array rearrangement problems such as *array partitioning* and *sorting*. In one offering, we were able to cover even more advanced problems such as the *area of the largest square under a histogram*. We wish to emphasize that all of it can be done using a small set of formal method concepts. Besides propositional logic, and the concepts of assertions and loop invariants, we only need a formal concept of quantified expressions and the rules for manipulating them.

We employ the *Eindhoven* notation $(OP\,i : R.i : T.i)$ [10] for representing quantified expressions. Outside the formal methods community, this notation is typically used only for quantified terms in arithmetic $(\sum, \prod)$. Here OP (say, $\sum$ or MAX) is the quantified version of a symmetric, associative binary operator op (say, $+$ or max), i is a list of dummy/quantified variables, $R.i$ is the *Range* - a boolean expression restricting the possible values that the dummies can take, and $T.i$ is the *Term* - over which the underlying binary operator is repeatedly applied. For example, just the way $(\sum i : 0 \leq i < N \wedge A[i]\%2 = 0 : A[i] * A[i])$ represents the sum of the square of the even elements of the array A, $(MAX\,i : 0 \leq i < N \wedge A[i]\%2 = 1 : A[i] * A[i])$ represents the maximum of the square of the odd elements of the array A. Since all the quantified operators (including the logical operators $\forall$ and $\exists$) are represented using the same notation, we can use generalized calculational rules [10].

While a large number of quantified expression manipulation rules are known [11, 2, 10], we find that for our purpose only three rules suffice: Range Split, Empty Range and, One Point Rule. The Range Split rule is most commonly used to form an inductive hypothesis: to show that the loop body maintains the loop invariant. The Empty Range and the One Point rules are used to evaluate an expression when either zero or exactly one dummy satisfies the range condition. The entire expression is evaluated in an inductive fashion by applying the Range Split, and the Empty Range or the One Point rule. Due to the lack of space, we do not present a detailed discussion of these rules but only illustrate them with the help of an example.

Beside these rules, the only non-trivial concept from propositional logic that we use is that of Distributivity and its adaptation for the Quantifier Calculus. Just the way $*$ dis-

tributes over $+$: $x * (y + z) = x * y + x * z$, similarly $\wedge$ (logical *and*) and $\vee$ (logical *or*) distribute over each other: $(P \wedge (Q \vee R)) = (P \wedge Q) \vee (Q \wedge R))$, and $+$ distributes over max: $x + (y \max z) = (x + y)max(x + z)$. With this small set of core manipulation rules, we can teach derivation of a large number of problems.

Just the way ITiCSE Working Group on Formal Methods [1] viewed *formal methods as the "calculus" of software engineering*, we view rules for manipulation of Quantified Operators as the "calculus" of program derivation.

3. AN EXAMPLE DERIVATION

We now present a calculational derivation of the well-known Maximum Segment Sum problem. This derivation highlights the typical steps that are involved in a program derivation session. The natural language specification for this problem is:

Let $A[0..N]$ be an array of integers. Compute the maximum sum of the elements of all segments of A.

This problem is formally specified in a natural fashion as shown in Figure 1(a), where S is the required program with the desired postcondition R. To do inductive computation, we introduce a fresh variable n and rewrite postcondition R as $P_0 \wedge P_1 \wedge n = N$ where P_0 and P_1 are given in Figure 1(b).

We can take $P_0 \wedge P_1$ as the loop invariant and $\neg (n = N)$ as the loop condition. We observe that the assignment $r, n := 0, 0$ establishes the invariants P_0 and P_1 initially. Now, we arrive at the program shown in Figure 1(c).

We explore the inductive step $n := n+1$. Now, if we want the loop invariant P_0 to be true after the assignment, then we need the assertion $P_0(n := n + 1)$ before the assignment, where $P_0(n := n + 1)$ represents the formula obtained by replacing n with $n+1$ in the body of P_0. That is, if we want $\{r = (MAX p, q : 0 \leq p \leq q \leq n : Sum.p.q)\}$ to be true after $n := n + 1$ is executed then $\{r = (MAX p, q : 0 \leq p \leq q \leq n + 1 : Sum.p.q)\}$ must be true before the assignment is executed. This is called *necessary* (or *weakest*) *precondition* $np.(n := n + 1).P_0$ w.r.t. the assignment.

Now we expect to modify r to some r' before incrementing n, where r' is a metavariable. A metavariable is not a program variable - it just represents an unknown expression. Then, $np.(r := r').(np.(n := n + 1).P_0)$ is the necessary precondition for the assignment $r := r'$. To calculate r', we assume P_0, P_1, and $n \neq N$ and simplify the necessary precondition as shown in Figure 1(d). In calculational style, every step in a calculation is associated with a hint justifying the step.

In step 15 in Figure 1(d), the quantified expression is not easily computable or expressible in terms of the existing program variables. This motivates the introduction of a new variable s and the loop invariant $P_2 : s = (MAX p : 0 \leq p \leq n : Sum.p.n)$. P_2 can be established initially by $s := 0$, since the summation over an empty range equals 0. We now arrive at the program shown in Figure 1(e).

To establish $P_2(n := n+1)$ as a precondition of the assignment to r, we introduce an unknown program fragment S_1. To develop S_1, we introduce the assignment $s := s'$. Similar to the calculation of r', we calculate the value of s' to be $(s + A[n]) \max 0$. In computing s', once again we use the Empty Range rule that the summation over an empty range returns 0. The final program is presented in Figure 1(f). This completes our derivation. Note the small number of concepts that were needed to derive an elegant solution to a

con N: int $\{N \geq 0\}$; **var** A: array $[0..N)$ of int; **var** r: int; $\quad S$ $R : \{r = (MAXp, q : 0 \leq p \leq q \leq N : Sum.p.q)\}$ $Sum.p.q : (\sum i : p \leq i < q : A[i])$	$r, n := 0, 0;$ $\{ \ loop\,inv : P_0 \wedge P_1 \ \}$ **do** $n \neq N \rightarrow$ $\quad S_0$ **od**
(a)	(c)

$P_0 : \{r = (MAXp, q : 0 \leq p \leq q \leq n : Sum.p.q)\}$
$P_1 : \ 0 \leq n \leq N$
$P_2 : s = (MAXp : 0 \leq p \leq n : Sum.p.n)$

(b)

1		$np.(r := r').np.(n := n+1).(P_0)$
2	$\equiv$	$\{$ definition of P_0 $\}$
3		$np.(r := r').np.(n := n+1).(r = (MAXp, q : 0 \leq p \leq q \leq n : Sum.p.q))$
4	$\equiv$	$\{$ definition of np $\}$
5		$np.(r := r').(r = (MAXp, q : 0 \leq p \leq q \leq n+1 : Sum.p.q))$
6	$\equiv$	$\{$ definition of np $\}$
7		$r' = (MAXp, q : 0 \leq p \leq q \leq n+1 : Sum.p.q)$
8	$\equiv$	$\{ q \leq n+1 \equiv q \leq n \vee q = n+1 \}$
9		$r' = (MAXp, q : (0 \leq p \leq q \leq n) \vee (0 \leq p \leq q = n+1) : Sum.p.q)$
10	$\equiv$	$\{$ Range Split $\}$
11		$r' = \left(\begin{array}{l} (MAXp, q : 0 \leq p \leq q \leq n : Sum.p.q) \\ max \ (MAXp, q : 0 \leq p \leq q = n+1 : Sum.p.q) \end{array} \right)$
12	$\equiv$	$\{$definition of P_0 $\}$
13		$r' = r \ max \ (MAXp, q : 0 \leq p \leq q = n+1 : Sum.p.q)$
14	$\equiv$	$\{q = n+1 \}$
15		$r' = r \ max \ (MAXp : 0 \leq p \leq n+1 : Sum.p.(n+1))$
16	$\equiv$	$\{$let us introduce P_2; assume $P_2(n := n+1)\}$
17		$r' = r \ max \ s$

(d)

(e)	$r, n, s := 0, 0, 0;$ $\{ \ loop\,inv : \ P_0 \wedge P_1 \wedge P_2 \ \}$ **do** $n \neq N \rightarrow$ $\quad \{ P_2 \} \ S_1 \ \{ P_2(n := n+1) \};$ $\quad r := r \ max \ s;$ $\quad \{ P_0(n := n+1) \}$ $\quad n := n+1;$ **od**

$r, n, s := 0, 0, 0;$
$\{ \ loop\,inv : \ P_0 \wedge P_1 \wedge P_2 \ \}$
do $n \neq N \rightarrow$
$\quad s := (s + A[n]) \ max \ 0;$
$\quad \{ P_2(n := n+1) \}$
$\quad r := r \ max \ s;$
$\quad \{ P_0(n := n+1) \}$
$\quad n := n+1;$
od

(f)

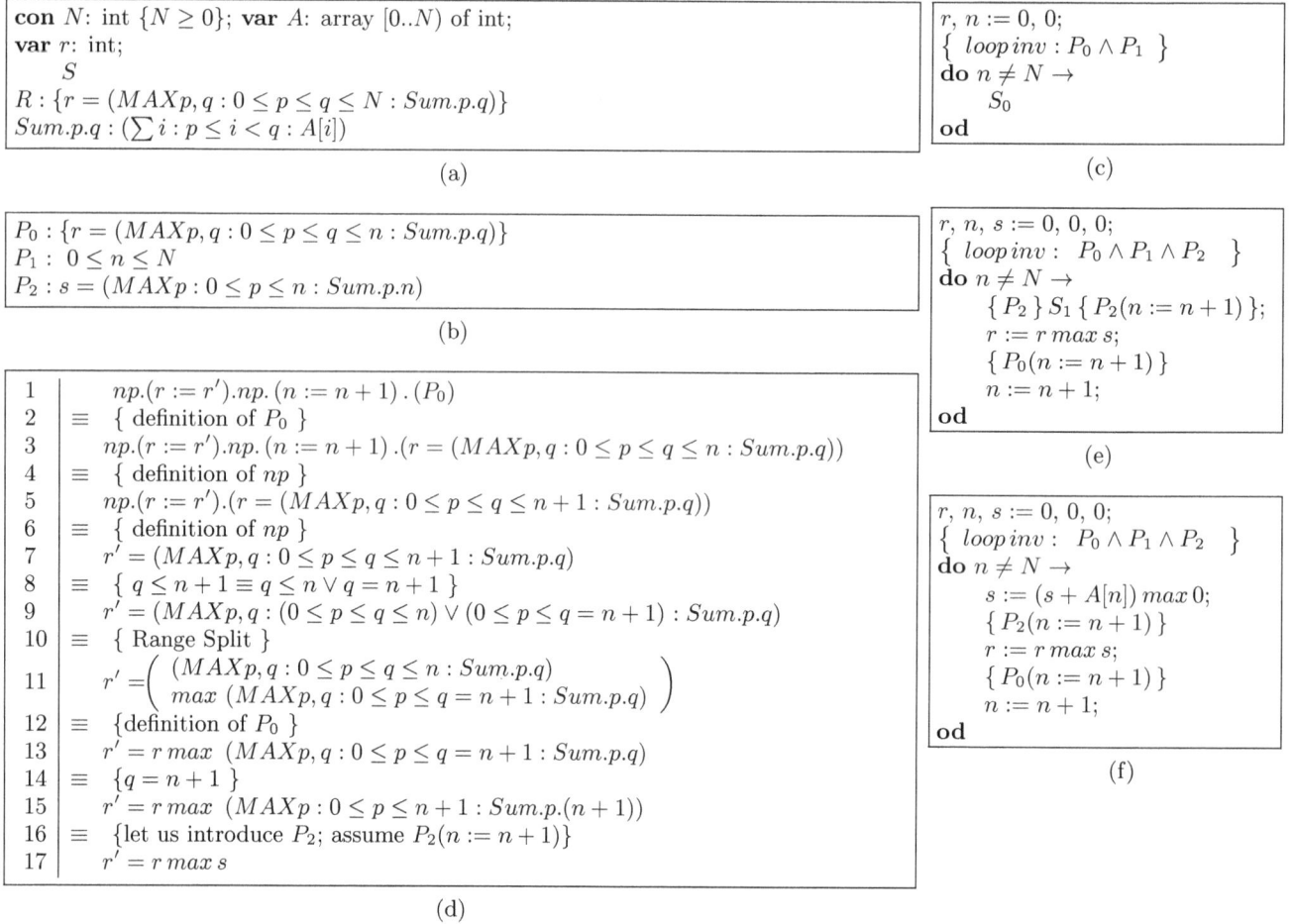

Figure 1: Selected stages in the derivation of the *Maximum Segment Sum* problem.

non-trivial problem. We next discuss our experience teaching this methodology.

4. COURSE FEEDBACK AND TOOL SUPPORT FOR CSOP

The students' interest in the methodology is reflected in the course feedback where we received 87% score in the last offering of the course. Following two comments exemplify the students' excitement: "*A quite different approach to programming, very innovating and interesting too. Some really great insights.*" and "*We learned many good things. I never thought that program could be derived. The experience was enriching.*" Despite the mostly positive feedback, we also realized that students were facing a number of difficulties in manually (without using any tool support) deriving the programs:

Common Difficulties:

(CD0) Difficulty in understanding formal logic: Used to informal reasoning, students make several mistakes in understanding and applying inference rules.

(CD1) Not checking transformation applicability conditions: Many of the program transformation rules have prerequisites that need to be checked. For example, + distributes over quantified MAX only if the range is non-empty. Students often forget to check such conditions.

(CD2) Long derivations: Compared to the guess and test approach, the calculational derivations are longer even for simple programs. Students get restless if the derivation runs too long, leading to more errors.

(CD3) Mistakes made during guessing: Manual derivations often involve small jumps where the unknown program expressions are simple enough to be guessed easily. Students often inadvertently take big steps during guessing, resulting in incorrect program expressions. For example, for program S_1 in Figure 1(e), many students make a jump and guess the value of s' to be $s + A[n]$.

(CD4) Forgetting to add bounds to the introduced variables: It is a general guideline to add bounds for a newly introduce variable, such as the bounds for n in the maximum segment sum problem. Students often forget to add such bounds, and later in the derivation, when the bound constraints are needed, they have to backtrack and take the corrective actions.

(CD5) Forgetting to prove proof obligations: With their focus on unraveling the unknown program fragments, students many times forget to prove some of the proof obligations.

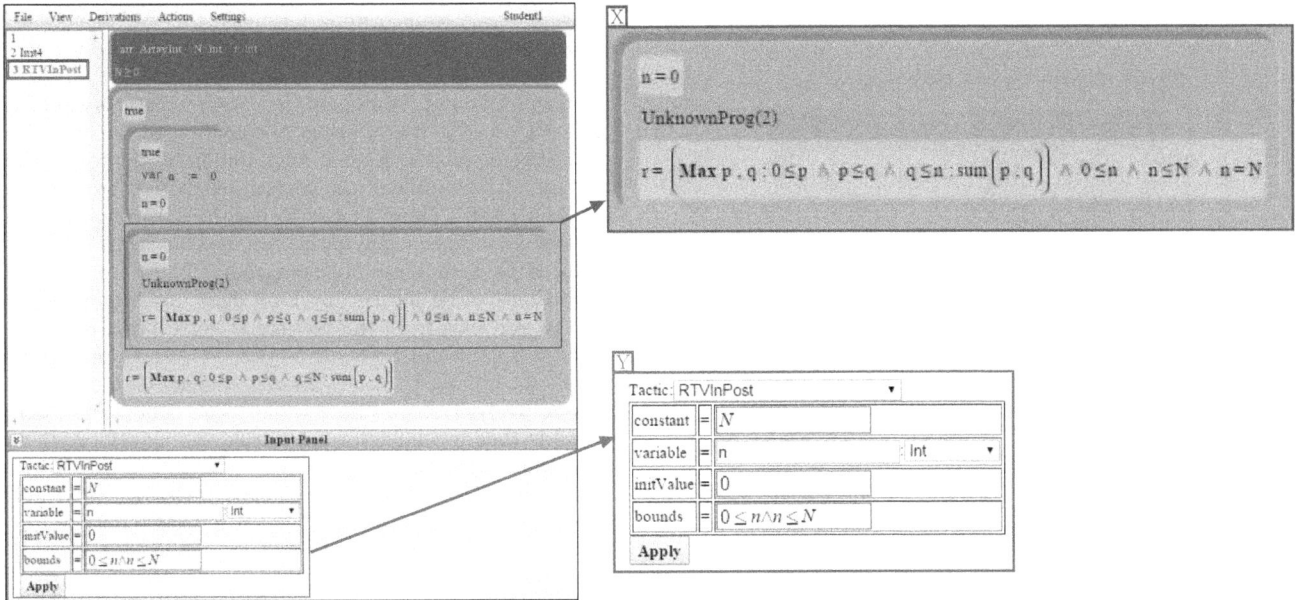

Figure 2: Graphical User Interface of the CAPS tool. The left panel is the *Tactics Panel*, the center panel is the *Content Panel* and the bottom panel is the *Input Panel*. Magnified area X shows an annotated unknown program along with its pre- and post- conditions whereas the magnified area Y highlights the form for entering the inputs of the "Replace term by variable"(*RTVInPost*) tactic.

(CD6) Problem with organizing derivation: The derivation process is not always linear; it involves multiple iterations involving failed derivation attempts. Students often fail organize the derivation in cases where they need to go back and make some corrective changes. Unorganized derivation often leads to some missing proofs of correctness.

Based on the errors experienced during the multiple course offerings, we decided to develop tool support for teaching this methodology. We next outline the required functionality for the desired tool support. First and foremost, we must ensure correctness of all the steps involved in the derivation. The manual derivation occasionally employs informal reasoning. For example, the Step 8 in the Figure 1(d) implicitly uses the rule that $\wedge$ distributes over $\vee$. To ensure correctness, we need to have a unified framework to manage both the program and the formula transformations. We must have a mechanism for dealing with the long derivations. In addition to automating the tasks involved, having the ability to organize the long proofs is vital. We also need to maintain history to provide backtracking and branching functionality. Finally, the user interface should allow seamless navigation across the derivation history.

5. CAPS TOOL

We now discuss the CAPS tool for the CSoP methodology. Its core components are implemented in the Scala language. The graphical user interface is implemented as a web application. The CAPS tool uses the Why3 [9] verification platform as an interface to various backend theorem provers. But the students need not concern themselves at all with how the theorem prover works. The implementation details of the tool have been published in [4] and here we concern ourselves only with the use of the tool in classroom teaching.

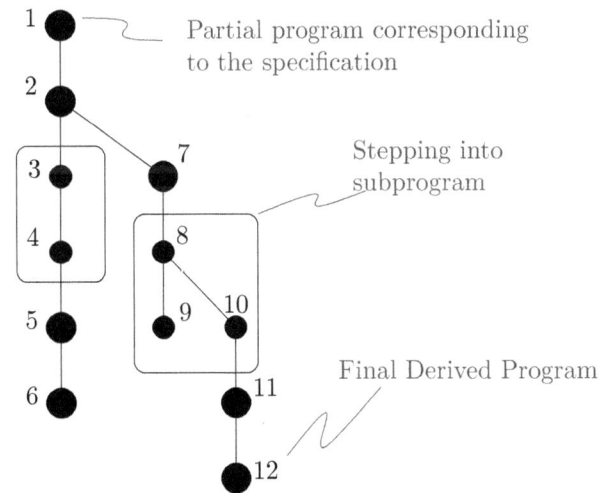

Figure 3: Schematic Derivation Tree.

5.1 Program Derivation Methodology

Students incrementally transform a formal specification into a fully derived program by applying predefined transformation rules called *Derivation Tactics*. For example, two of the tactics that we employed in derivation in Figure 1 are *Replace constant by a variable*, and *Range Split*. To apply a tactic, one needs to select a tactic from a list and provide the required input parameters, and the tool automatically performs the corresponding formula manipulations. By forcing students to enter the required parameters, errors such as

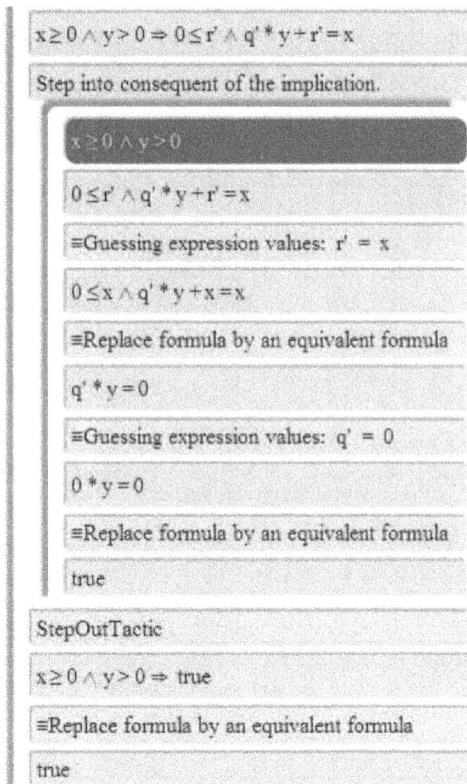

$$x \geq 0 \wedge y > 0 \Rightarrow 0 \leq r' \wedge q' * y + r' = x$$

Step into consequent of the implication.

$$x \geq 0 \wedge y > 0$$

$$0 \leq r' \wedge q' * y + r' = x$$

$\equiv$ Guessing expression values: $r' = x$

$$0 \leq x \wedge q' * y + x = x$$

$\equiv$ Replace formula by an equivalent formula

$$q' * y = 0$$

$\equiv$ Guessing expression values: $q' = 0$

$$0 * y = 0$$

$\equiv$ Replace formula by an equivalent formula

true

StepOutTactic

$$x \geq 0 \wedge y > 0 \Rightarrow \text{true}$$

$\equiv$ Replace formula by an equivalent formula

true

Figure 4: Calculation of initial assignment $(q, r := 0, x)$ **to establish invariant** $0 \leq r \wedge q * y + r = x$ **while deriving** *Integer Division* **program(Set** q, r **to the quotient & remainder of the division of** x **by** y **).**

$CD4$ are prevented. The tool ensures correctness after application of every tactic. The GUI of the tool is shown in Figure 2.

5.2 Derivation History and Backtracking

The CAPS tool maintains the entire derivation history in the form a derivation tree. The user can also branch off from any point in the derivation to explore different derivation strategies. This helps take care of the errors resulting from $CD4$ and $CD6$.

Figure 3 shows a schematic representation of a derivation tree. Node 1 is the starting node representing the specification and node 12 represents the final derived program. Node 6 and node 9 are the nodes where the user faces some difficulties with the derivation and decides not to carry out the derivation further and prefers to backtrack and branch out. The backtracking mechanism makes it easier for the user to try out different alternatives with least amount of rework. The user interface also makes it easy to navigate across different solutions.

5.3 Focusing on Subcomponents

At every stage in the derivation process, there exists a correct-by-construction program containing multiple unknown subprograms. The user may want to focus her attention on the development of one of these subprograms. Hence it is desirable that all the context information relevant for the derivation of the subprogram is extracted and presented.

Similarly, while transforming formulas, the user may want to focus on a subformula while ignoring the rest of the formula.

To focus on a subcomponent, the *StepIn* tactic is applied. Application of the tactic brings the context of the subcomponent under consideration in focus and hides the rest of the program. (The details of the context extraction process are described in [4].) After transforming the subcomponent to a desired form, users can apply the *StepOut* tactic to bring the focus back to the whole program. The *StepIn* tactic application can be nested any level deep. In Figure 3, the entry to and exit from the rectangles correspond to application of *StepIn* and *StepOut* tactics. Whenever user steps into a subcomponent, a new Frame is created to store the appropriate contextual information. The contextual information is then available for use during the transformations of the subcomponent.

Example: Figure 4 shows a calculation that uses the "Focusing on subformula" functionality. Contextual information (assumptions) for the inner frame are displayed at the top of the frame.

5.3.1 Automating Formula Transformations

In the manual calculations, all the steps are kept small enough to be manually verified by the user. This is the main reason why the program derivations are long even for simple problems, and formal methods are hated by several students. With a tool support, however, we can afford to take large steps, as long as the readability is maintained. In general, small steps are good for readability. However, there are situations where certain calculation is not important from the derivation point of view. We would like to automate such calculations. We employ a backend theorem prover to perform required proofs. This makes the program calculations flexible and reduces the derivation length. This helps with the observed errors $CD2$ and $CD5$.

Calculations not involving any metavariables should be automated to the extent possible. For example, in Fig. 1, we skipped the proof of preservation of the invariant $P_1 : 0 \leq n \leq N$. As no metavariable is involved this proof obligation, it is uninteresting from the derivation viewpoint. Students resent doing such proofs. We, however, still need to discharge them to ensure correctness. The proof obligation for P_1 can be directly transformed to *true* by applying a VerifiedTransformation tactic that uses the backend theorem prover. The introduction of this tactic takes care of the errors $CD1$ and $CD3$.

In case a proof obligation is not automatically discharged by the theorem provers, we have to carry out the detailed step-by-step proof. A failed calculational proof often provides clues about how to proceed further with the derivation.

Another example is the calculations involved in verifying the applicability conditions for some tactics. Consider the "Empty Range" tactic for the summation that transforms the formula $(\sum i : false : T.i)$ to 0. If a student wants to apply this tactic directly to $(\sum i : R.i : T.i)$, she first needs to show that $R.i \equiv false$ (which may take several steps) and then apply the tactic. Other way is to directly apply the Empty Range Tactic to $(\sum i : R.i : T.i)$ and the tool ensures that the $R.i$ is unsatisfiable.

Automated formula transformations take care of the most of the common logic related errors ($CD0$).

5.4 Evaluation

The tool became ready to be used by the students only towards the end of the last offering of our program derivation course. It received very enthusiastic response from the students. We did an anonymous survey to get specific feedback about the tool. There were a total of fourteen responses. Ten students felt that the use of the tool increased their confidence in the correctness of the derived program, while three did not feel so, and one student was unsure. Same pattern was observed for the question whether the tool simplifies or complicates the task of the derivation. To the question of how would they like to derive the programs in future, five said using the tool alone, six said that they would like to use the tool along with paper and pencil, and three students commented that they would not use the tool. Eight out of the fourteen students also felt that the tool should have been introduced right from the beginning of the semester, while three suggested introduction around the middle of the semester, and three students felt that the tool should not be introduced at all but they did not write any comments. Due to the anonymity of the survey, we are unable to determine why three students did not like the tool at all.

Overall, we are quite happy with the use of tool in the course. The biggest advantage was that the students could not submit incorrect derivation. They could only submit either correct or partially correct answers; since programs were correct-by-construction at all stages (although they may have been incomplete). We could look at the derivation history of partial submissions and identify the problems because of which they were stuck at a particular point. Students were happy about the fact that they knew that their solution was correct before making the submission. Note that this adds a completely new dimension to the concept of automatic grading of assignments [8]. We plan to use the tool right from the beginning of the next offering to understand its shortcomings in detail.

One unexpected downside of the introduction of the tool was the increase in ad-hocism in some of the derivations. In the class, we teach various derivation heuristics and the associated proof obligations, and students are supposed to follow them in the manual derivation. However, with the tool trying to automatically discharge proof obligations, some students make wild guesses about the required program constructs, resulting in very inelegant programs. For example, rather than deriving the value of s' in Figure 1(f), many students introduce several *if* statements enumerating different cases involving positive and negative values of s and $A[n]$. In comparison, *max* operator in our derivation can be implemented using a single *if*. Note that these programs were inelegant compared to what is possible with the derivation methodology, and not compared to what is achieved in the standard guess and test methodology. Essentially, these students use the tool as a program verification system and not as a program derivation system. This in some sense buttress the argument we made in the introduction section as to why the program derivation and not the program verification should be used to introduce formal methods.

6. CONCLUSION

Instead of program verification, we have been using program derivation as the vehicle for introducing formal methods in the introductory programming classes. This has been done employing only a small core of formal method concepts. Based on our experience in teaching this method to several batches, we have identified a list of common errors made by the students while deriving the programs manually, and have developed a programming assistant to take care of these problems. The preliminary student response to the tool has been very positive. Based on the learnings from the first offering of the tool, we plan to further enhance the tool and deploy it right from the beginning of the next offering of the course.

Acknowledgements.

The work of the first author was supported by the Tata Consultancy Services (TCS) Research Fellowship and a grant from the Ministry of Human Resource Development, Government of India.

7. REFERENCES

[1] V. L. Almstrum, C. N. Dean, D. Goelman, T. B. Hilburn, and J. Smith. Support for teaching formal methods. *SIGCSE Bull.*, 33(2):71–88, June 2001.

[2] R. Backhouse. *Program construction: calculating implementations from specifications.* Wiley, 2003.

[3] G. Caso, D. Garbervetsky, and D. Gorín. Integrated program verification tools in education. *Software: Practice and Experience*, 2012.

[4] D. Chaudhari and O. Damani. Automated theorem prover assisted program calculations. In *Proc. of the 11th International Conference on Integrated Formal Methods, iFM*, 2014.

[5] A. J. Cowling. Stages in teaching formal methods. In *23rd IEEE Conference on Software Engineering Education and Training*, 2010.

[6] E. W. Dijkstra and W. H. Feijen. *A Method of Programming.* Addison-Wesley Longman Publishing Co., Inc., Boston, MA, USA, 1988.

[7] I. Dony and B. Le Charlier. A tool for helping teach a programming method. In *Proc. of the 11th Annual SIGCSE Conference on Innovation and Technology in Computer Science Education, ITiCSE*, 2006.

[8] J. English and T. Rosenthal. Evaluating students' programs using automated assessment - a case study. In *Proc. of the Conference on Integrating Technology into Computer Science Education, ITiCSE*, 2009.

[9] J.-C. Filliâtre and A. Paskevich. Why3 – Where Programs Meet Provers. In *ESOP'13 22nd European Symposium on Programming*, volume 7792 of *LNCS*, Rome, Italie, Mar. 2013. Springer.

[10] A. Kaldewaij. *Programming: the derivation of algorithms.* Prentice-Hall, Inc., NJ, USA, 1990.

[11] D. G. Kourie and B. W. Watson. *Correctness-by-Construction Approach to Programming.* Springer, 2012.

[12] K.-K. Lau. A beginner's course on reasoning about imperative programs. In C. Dean and R. Boute, editors, *Teaching Formal Methods*, volume 3294 of *LNCS*. Springer Berlin Heidelberg, 2004.

[13] M. Sitaraman and B. Weide. Special session: "hands-on" tutorial: Teaching software correctness with resolve. In *SIGCSE 2014 - Proc. of the 45th ACM Technical Symposium on Computer Science Education*, 2014.

Task-Adapted Concept Map Scaffolding to Support Quizzes in an Online Environment

Thushari Atapattu, Katrina Falkner, Nickolas Falkner
School of Computer Science, University of Adelaide, Australia
{thushari.atapattu, katrina.falkner, nickolas.falkner}@adelaide.edu.au

ABSTRACT

This paper investigates the effect of different forms of concept maps as scaffolding techniques to support answering quizzes in an online learning environment. Concept maps which represent a course topic have being utilised as a scaffolding technique for learning the subject matters and problem solving. However, due to the typical amount of information presented in the topic concept maps, learners might feel overwhelmed, reducing their motivation and increasing the learners' disorientation. In order to overcome this issue, a study was conducted with 59 undergraduates of a Software Engineering course to measure the effect of different forms of concept maps on learning. The study obtained statistically significant results when using concept maps adapted to given quizzes (known as task-adapted concept maps). Students' reflections collected through a questionnaire were very positive towards task-adapted concept maps as a scaffolding technique.

Categories and Subject Descriptors

K.3.2 [**Computing Milieux**]: Computer Science Education – Computer and Information Science Education

General Terms

Human Factors

Keywords

Concept map, scaffolding, lecture slide, meaningful learning, quizzes

1. INTRODUCTION

Concept mapping is recognised as a valuable educational visualisation technique, which assists students in organising, sharing and representing knowledge. The use of concept maps as a way of supporting learning is well established [1]. According to the cognitive learning theory of Ausubel, which states "*learning takes place by the integration of new concepts and propositions into existing concept and propositional framework held by the learner*", there has been shown to be a significant increase in meaningful learning when using concept maps [2]. Concept maps

have been widely used in the educational context, particularly in supporting learners in adopting new concepts, and also in assisting learners to identify misconceptions and knowledge gaps through comparison with expert concept maps, and further gains in assisting knowledge organization, planning, and scaffolding purposes [1].

Concept maps are particularly well suited to Computer Science, due to the diverse and complex range of concepts covered within the curricula, which can be well supported through various concept map activities including drawing concept maps by students or utilising expert constructed maps for scaffolding. Berges and Hubwieser [3] explore the semi-automated extraction of concept maps from textbooks to assist in Introductory Object-oriented Programming course; Sanders et al. [4] explore the use of manually constructed concept maps within an Introductory Object-oriented Programming course; Calvo et al. [5] adopt concept maps within an intermediate Database Principles courses to facilitate collaboration and understanding; and Larraza-Mendiluze and Garay-Vitoria [6] explore an automatic comparison of manually generated concept maps within the area of Computer Architecture.

This research utilises concept maps generated from Computer Science lecture slides using a framework (known as *concept map mining framework*) developed by the authors for the purpose of scaffolding. The automated process of extracting concept-relation-concept triples to produce concept maps using Natural Language Processing (NLP) techniques and the evaluation of the framework with human experts has been broadly discussed in authors' previous works [7, 8]. The particular interest of this paper is to demonstrate the usage of auto-generated concept maps as a scaffolding technique to facilitate answering *quizzes* in an online environment. Quizzes in this context are similar to formative or summative questions provided through online learning environments (e.g. Learning Management Systems) to engage or motivate students, guide learning, provide opportunity for practice and self-assessment [9]. Scaffolding is the support given during the learning process with the intention of helping the student achieves his/her learning goals. The concept of 'scaffolding' was originally introduced in the context of adults assisting children in acquiring knowledge or solving problems in informal learning environments [10]. Scaffolding is grounded in the Social Constructivism Theory of Vygotsky [11] and his popular concept known as the *Zone of Proximal Development (ZPD)* [12].

Previous studies demonstrated that *concept mappers* who construct or utilise auto-generated concept maps possess significant improvements in problem solving, recall and conceptual knowledge [13, 14]. However, the existing approaches provide concept maps that represent a *domain* or *topic* (named *topic concept maps*) as scaffolding. Studies found that providing a topic concept map increases the risk of information overload which therefore rises the anxiety, stress, alienation and learning disorientation among learners [15, 16]. This research specifically focuses on providing the *most relevant information* to answer quizzes. More precisely, the concept maps utilised as scaffolding in this work will be adapted to the given quiz. This process is known as 'task-adapted knowledge organisation'. According to Novak and Canas [1], concept maps are more effective when they are produced to answer a question (known as a *focus question*) rather than using them to represent general knowledge in a domain or topic.

This research investigates following two research questions.

1. *Does task-adapted concept map as scaffolding improve learning gain over other forms of scaffolding?*

2. *What are the students' opinions of concept mapping and scaffolding?*

In this paper, we describe a randomised experiment to explore the effectiveness of different forms of concept map-based scaffolding in assisting learners in answering quizzes. In our study, we have found a statistically significant benefit when using task-adapted concept maps, in comparison to topic concept maps and lecture slides as scaffolding support. We undertook a further qualitative study on student reflections on their usage of various scaffolding techniques. Analysis of these qualitative reflections indicate a strong preference for task-adapted concept maps as a scaffolding technique, particularly for information- or theory-rich courses, but had no support for manual construction of said concept maps.

2. RELATED WORK

Concept map-based scaffolding can be provided in many ways, among them, learner model-based scaffolding is one of the widespread techniques to offer personalised learning experience according to learners' current knowledge and preferences. Recent research of concept map-based adaptive scaffolding can be found in the works of JSEM-HP [17], Chen et al. [18], and VLS-CCM [19].

Additionally, scaffolding can be provided based on a particular task or activity by emphasising the specific content knowledge required, reducing the information overload and increase learners' motivation. However, this approach is not adopted widely in literature due to the excess of manual workload involved. For instance, Bulu and Pedersen [20] investigated the effect of domain-general and domain-specific scaffolds on ill-structured problem solving. Domain-specific scaffolds include specific content knowledge to use during problem solving and domain-general scaffolds are otherwise. A total of 332 students were allocated into groups and provided scaffolds through domain-specific and domain-general with either continuous or faded support. The results showed that the continuous domain-specific scaffolds outperformed the other conditions on the post-tests. A similar study with 578 middle school students showed curricular scaffolds that focus on the content and task (context-specific) are significantly better than generic explanation scaffolds in terms of students' improvement and understanding of scientific content [21]. Eylon and Reif [22] suggested that "*higher levels of the hierarchy should preferentially contain information most important for the domain of tasks*". This hypothesis was tested by comparing the effectiveness of two hierarchical knowledge organisations that contained the same knowledge, with one of them adapted to a set of given tasks. The results demonstrated that the task-adapted information group performed significantly better than the control group in the performance tasks. However, according to Perkins and Salomon [23], domain-general and domain-specific knowledge is not viewed as a dichotomy, rather, both of them are important when performing reasoning tasks.

Thus, it is understood that content-based scaffolding has benefits to improve the learning experience, however, it is challenging when performed manually, and hence, this paper provides the first attempt, according to the authors' knowledge, that task-adaptation can be achievable through an automated approach.

3. METHODOLOGY

In this research, we undertook a mixed method of data collection, combining quantitative and qualitative techniques.

3.1 Experimental Design

In our randomised experimental design, 59 students, aged over 18 years, who were enrolled in an Introductory Software Engineering course in University of Adelaide, participated in a computer-based experimental study and a post-test. The Software Engineering course, a core Computer Science course, contains a large set of new concepts that students are required to assimilate in their second year of undergraduate studies. Software testing topic was selected for the experiments. In addition to the concept-wise importance of Software Engineering course, the concept maps generated from this course demonstrated strong positive correlation ($r_s = .83$) with human generated maps in a previous study of algorithm evaluation [8].

Ten multiple choice questions (MCQs) were constructed for the study which covered 68% of the important concepts in the 'software testing' topic. During the study, participants were expected to attempt 10 quizzes within 20 minutes through a web-based prototype. If attempted answer was incorrect, students were given an option to get 'help' through the scaffolding system (see Figure 1).

The help was specific to the each group. The control group received lecture slides (LS) as a PDF file. This file had fewer slides than the original slide set. A subset of the original slide set which was related to each quiz was extracted manually. This process reduced the disadvantage faced by the control group having more content than the treatments. Treatment group 1 received the topic concept maps generated from lecture slides (CMap – Figure 3(a)). Treatment group 2 received the same concept maps as group 1; however, in their maps, the context to answer the quiz is highlighted (HLCMap – Figure 2). The highlighting process was performed manually using the IHMC CMap tools [24]. The aim of introducing the HLCMap group is to measure whether there is any effect of having scaffolding in between topic concept maps and task-adapted concept maps. Treatment group 3 received task-adapted concept maps (TSKCMap – Figure 3(b)) extracted from task-adapted scaffolding framework [25]. All the scaffolding resources were stored as image files or as PDF files.

Once the participants completed the required learning through scaffolding, they were expected to go back to the initial question for which they requested help. However, the answers were shuffled at this stage to reduce guessing. This process could be repeated any number of times until the required study task is completed.

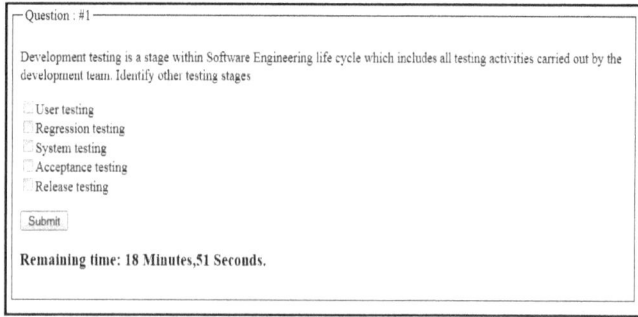

Figure 1: Screen shot of a quiz using web-based prototype

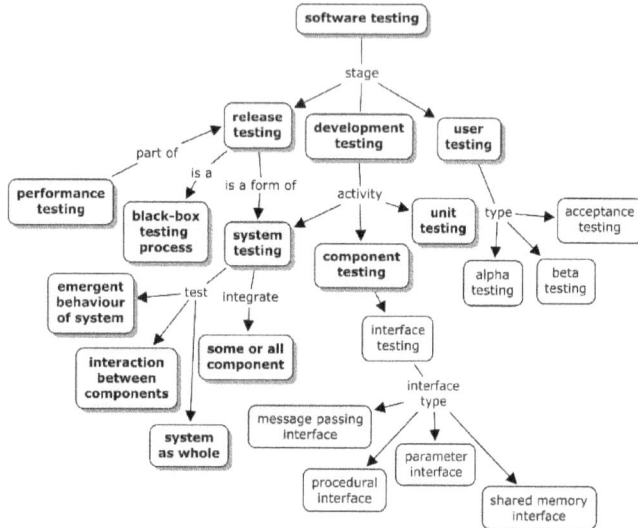

Figure 2: A subset of HLCMap for the question 'Compare and contrast system testing and release testing'

After the main study, students were requested to complete a questionnaire reflecting their issues, if any, they encountered, their opinion about the system, new features they wanted to see and their willingness to use the system for future studies. The questionnaire contained 10 questions with a combination of 5-point Likert scale (ranging from 'strongly disagree' to 'strongly agree') and open-ended questions. Students in the control groups who have not seen concept maps received a slightly different version of the original questionnaire.

Participants who were involved in the first stage of the experiments were invited to participate in the post-tests with a two week gap. The paper-based, ten post-test questions included combinations of MCQs, fill-in-the-blanks and open-ended questions to minimize the opportunity to guess, allowing the actual learning gain between pre- and post-tests. Post-test included new questions as well as similar questions as experimental study, but they were rephrased and shuffled to reduce the possibility of memorisation.

3.2 Task-adapted Scaffolding Framework

In order to provide concept map-based scaffolding, our work developed a framework with the use of NLP techniques. Each question was processed through a question analyser to identify the question type (e.g. descriptive, comparison) and an annotator to extract noun-verb-noun triples (question triples), in order to extract task-adapted concept maps using the topic concept maps as a basis. The framework is broadly discussed in authors'

previous work [25]. The process of extracting task-adapted concept maps is shown in Figure 3.

Question: *Identify the <u>interface types</u> in <u>component testing</u>*

Question triples: (component testing, interface types, ?)

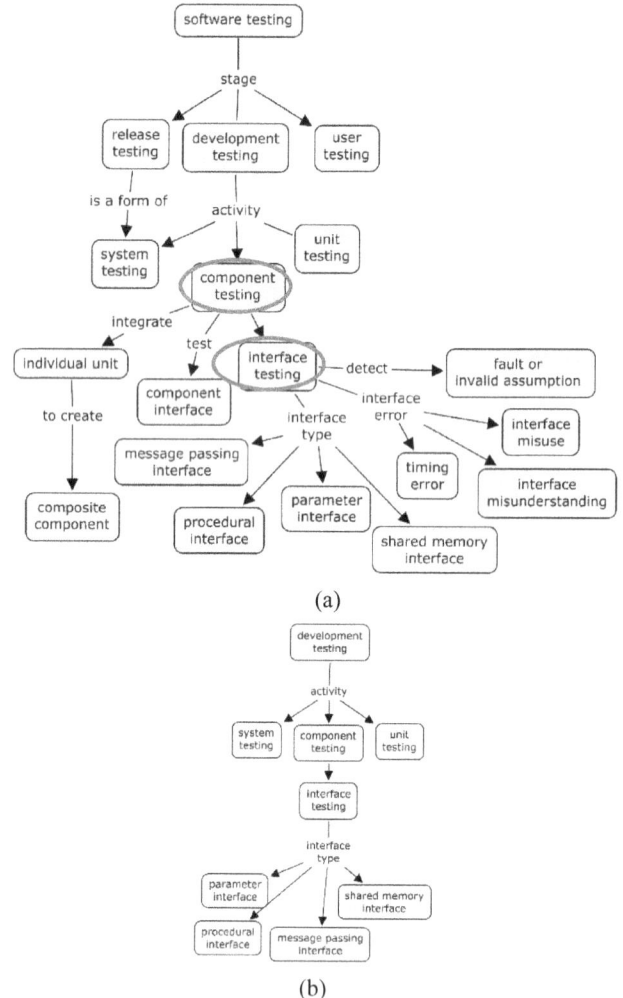

(a)

(b)

Figure 3: The task-adapted concept map scaffolding process (a) sub-set of a topic concept map (CMap) (b) task-adapted concept map (TSKCMap)

3.3 Quantitative Analysis

In order to answer the first research question '*Does task-adapted concept map as scaffolding improve learning gain over other forms of scaffolding?*', we conducted one-way ANOVA by comparing pre- and post-test scores. The response to the first attempt of each question was recorded as students' prior knowledge on the topic (i.e. pre-test). Even though 59 students participated for the main study, only 30 students were able to participate to the post-tests. The descriptive statistics of students' learning gain across different scaffolding groups are shown in Table 1. The scaffolding groups are indicated as LS – lecture slide, CMap – topic concept map, HLCMap – concept maps with context to answer the quiz is highlighted, and TSKCMap – task-adapted concept map in Table 1.

Table 1. Descriptive statistics of learning gain

Group	Mean	Median	Standard deviation	n
LS	2.5	2.0	.755	7
CMap	3.2	1.4	.532	7
HLCMap	3.6	2.0	.777	7
TSKCMap	5.0	1.5	.496	9
Total	4.0	1.9	.351	30

According to the results, TSKCMap group had the numerically highest mean ($M = 5.0$, $SD = 1.5$, $n = 9$) while the control group (LS) had the smallest mean ($M = 2.5$, $SD = 2.0$, $n = 7$).

The three assumptions of ANOVA – test of homogeneity of variances, normal distribution of dependent variable, and independence of observation were not violated. Table 2 illustrates the results of mean comparison within and between groups.

Table 2. Summary results of ANOVA

	Sum of Squares	df	Mean square	F	Sig.
Between Groups	28.292	3	9.431	3.103	.044
Within Groups	79.008	26	3.039		
Total	107.300	29			

Results of the one-way ANOVA indicated that the means between groups are significant; $F(3,26) = 3.103$, $p = .044$ ($< .05$), $\eta^2 = .263$. The results of the post-hoc test indicated that the students in the task-adapted concept map scaffolding group demonstrated statistically significant learning gain compared to the students who received lecture slides or topic concept maps as scaffolding. However, the results were not statistically significant between TSKCMap and HLCMap groups [25].

3.4 Qualitative Analysis

A comprehensive qualitative study was conducted to investigate the students' reflections on the research. Prior to collecting the opinions, statistics about students' prior experience on knowledge organisation techniques were collected (Table 3).

Table 3. Students' prior experience on knowledge organization techniques

Prior experience	Technique	Number of students
No prior experience		10
Have heard, but not used		11
Previously used	Concept maps	11
	Mind maps like inspiration	21
	Semantic networks	1
	Simple brainstorming ideas	1
Currently using	Concept maps	3
	Mind maps like popplet	10
	Knowledge maps	1

According to the statistics, 62% of participants had previously used or are currently using, some form of knowledge organisation techniques.

1. *What do you think about concept maps/lecture slides used in this study to answer questions?*

According to the statistics, students in the treatment groups were very positive about having concept maps as scaffolding. Among the treatment groups, 77%, 86% and 73% stated it was either 'helpful' or 'very helpful' while 30% of control group (LS) mentioned that it was difficult to utilise lecture slides to answer quizzes.

2. *Which form of resources do you prefer if our system made available through CS Forums (Learning Management System) in future?*

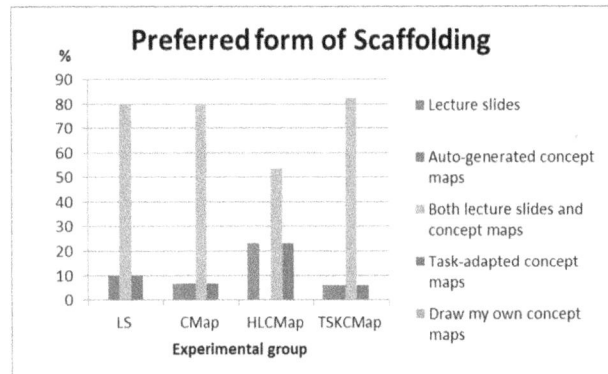

Figure 4. Students' preferred form of scaffolding

The results showed that the students are extremely receptive to the use of concept maps and lecture slides including 80%, 80%, 54% and 82% in the LS, CMap, HLCMap and TSKCMap groups respectively. It appears students believe utilising concept maps generated from lecture slides would be useful as a supplement to traditional learning approaches. In addition, none of the participants out 55 who answered this question were interested in constructing the concept maps manually. This feedback can be used to support the rationale of providing students with auto-generated concept maps as scaffolding for learning.

3. *Would you like a tool which can extract partial concept maps to assist answering questions?*

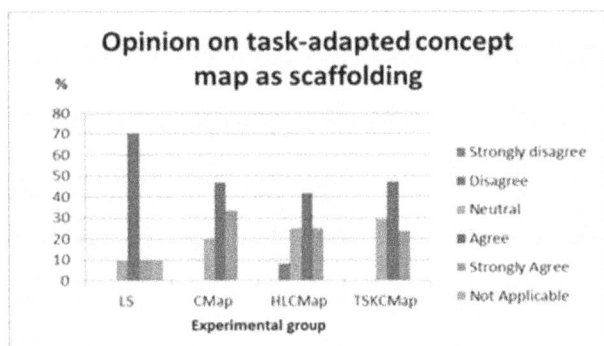

Figure 5: Students' opinion on task-adapted concept maps as scaffolding to answer questions

The results indicated that the majority of the students in each group either agreed or strongly agreed to incorporate task-adapted concept maps including 80%, 80%, 67% and 71% in the LS, CMap, HLCMap and TSKCMap groups respectively.

4. *Which type of courses do you think this kind of tool will be more useful?*

Statistics showed that majority of the participants in the LS group (89%) and the CMap group (83%) preferred to have concept maps for courses with less programming components or almost every course. In addition, 90% participants in the HLCMap group preferred to have concept maps for courses like Software Engineering and Operating Systems and 79% in the TSKCMap group chosen to have concept maps for every course. Some participants mentioned that they would like to see concept maps for the courses with more facts or heavy theory or concepts, emphasising "*based around memory information courses, courses with heavy theory/concepts which interconnects with each other*". The feedback provides evidence that it would be beneficial for students to have concept maps generated from lecture slides to see the interconnections between concepts. Previous studies provided evidence that the knowledge organisation techniques are more effective than sequentially-arranged lecture slides [26, 27].

5. *Write down any issues you had while interacting with concept maps*

Table 4: Pros and cons about concept maps as scaffolding

Group	Feedback (Pros and cons)
CMap	***Too much information*** *in concept map*
	Some questions had no correct answer in the concept map
	Problems I had with the concept maps were that they were **kind of bland**. *As more and more information is added to a concept map, it can be difficult to navigate*
HLCMap	***Larger maps are more difficult to read***
	Some questions required more information than showing
	Concept maps were **useful for hints**
TSKCMap	*Some maps did not easily show the information needed to answer the question*
	Question 10's concept map was basically useless with help answering the question
	Not enough information provided *in the concept tree*

According to the students' comments, it is correct that some concept maps did not have adequate information to answer all questions. The particular concepts and their relationships to learn the specific skills were included, but not the direct answer. In contrast, participants in the first two treatment groups (CMap and HLCMap) criticised about excess of information in topic concept maps.

6. *What are the features you would like to suggest to improve our tool?*

Table 5: Suggestions for improvements of the system

Group	Suggestions for improvement
CMap	*Removing timer or making optional, gives more time to think and* **less pressure**
	Use **colour** *for help identifying important sections*
	Improve appearance by providing **partial concept maps** *that applies to topic*
	Perhaps be able to view the concept maps before answering the question
	Need colours and switches
	Less concepts
	The concept map can be improved more to have **zoom in/out** *to smaller or larger sections*
	Perhaps a way to **toggle between maps** *of higher and lower*

	densities of information
	Colour code *hierarchies or* **smaller maps**
	In order to fix the problem of difficulty in navigating larger concept map, suggest to **use colour to differentiate** *different components and branches*
HLCMap	*Ability to* **search** *within the concept map, this would allow it to be useful for specific information or question rather than the full overview*
	More easier to **search**
	A feature in which you can **click on a concept to retrieve more information**
	Add extra notes
	More details in relation labels
TSKCMap	*Allow viewing the concept map at any time, not just when answering the question*
	More explanations in concept maps
	It was quite good
	Being able to select on elements and have connected or related information *and their paths highlighted*
	Click on a specific concept or relations could bring up more details *on that specific section*

From the feedback collected from the CMap and HLCMap groups, it is evident that there should be a mechanism to differentiate concepts that are more relevant to the context. Since, these two groups had no idea about task-adapted concept maps, they repeatedly mentioned the requirement of colour codes, 'search' option, zoom in/out or *smaller/partial maps* that focus on the *more relevant information* to learning (see highlighted comments in Table 5). In addition, all the groups were interested to have more details on specific concepts or relations by clicking them.

4. CONCLUSIONS

This paper presented an approach to adopting the different forms of auto-generated concept maps as scaffolding to facilitate answering quizzes in an online environment. Several previous studies explored similar approaches of adopting domain-specific or domain-general scaffolds to improve the learning experience. However, the widespread adoption of content-based scaffolding is hindered by the high workload required to construct scaffolds corresponds to given tasks. As a solution, this paper proposed an automated approach. The concept maps generated from this work was compared with other forms of concept maps (topic concept maps or topic concept maps with the context required to answer the quiz is highlighted) and lecture slides (control) and the results illustrated a statistically significant difference between topic concept maps and lecture slides on the post-tests. In addition, students were extremely receptive on utilising concept maps as scaffolding as a supplementary to lecture slides, emphasising the ability to perceive inter-connections between concepts. The students who received topic concept maps expressed the importance of having less information in their maps or mechanism to differentiate most important information for context using colour codes.

As a future work, current study can be expanded using a larger student cohort and multiple CS courses. As per the suggestions of students' through the questionnaire, an alternative form of task-adapted concept map can be introduced as a future work, in order to embed resources to concepts including underlying lecture slides or external resources such as multimedia. Additionally, there is a motivation to explore the effect of student-constructed task-adapted concept maps using an auto-generated topic concept maps as a basis. Within this study, we expect to investigate whether students can identify the parts of a topic concept map that would be associated with a specific question.

5. REFERENCES

1. Novak, J. D. and Canas, A. J. The Theory underlying Concept maps and How to construct and use them. Florida Institute for Human and Machine Cognition, Pensacola FI, 2006.
2. Ausubel, D., Educational Psychology: A Cognitive View. Halt, Rinehart and Winston, New York and Toronto, 1968
3. Berges, M. and Hubwieser, P., Concept specification maps: displaying content structures. in Proceedings of the 18th ACM conference on Innovation and technology in computer science education, (Canterbury, UK, 2013), 291-296.
4. Sanders, K., et al., Student understanding of object-oriented programming as expressed in concept maps. in Proceedings of the 39th SIGCSE technical symposium on Computer science education, (Portland, Oregon, USA, 2008), 332-336.
5. Calvo, I., et al., The use of concept maps in Computer Engineering education to promote meaningful learning, creativity and collaboration. in Frontiers in Education Conference (FIE), (Rapid City, SD, 2011), IEEE.
6. Larraza-Mendiluze, E. and Garay-Vitoria, N., Use of concept maps to analyze students' understanding of the I/O subsystem. in Proceedings of the 13th Koli Calling International Conference on Computing Education Research, (Finland, 2013), 67-76.
7. Atapattu, T., Falkner, K. and Falkner, N., Acquistion of Triples of Knowledge from Lecture Notes: A Natural Langauge Processing Approach. in The 7th International Conference on Educational Data Mining, (London, UK, 2014), 193-196.
8. Atapattu, T., Falkner, K. and Falkner, N., Evaluation of Concept Importance in Concept Maps Mined from Lecture Notes: Computer vs Human. in The 6th International Conference on Computer Supported Education, (Barcelona, Spain, 2014)
9. Dillon, J. T. Questioning and Teaching: A manual of practice. Teachers College Press, New York, 1988.
10. Wood, D., Bruner, J. S. and Ross, G. The role of tutoring in problem solving. *Journal of Child Psychology and Psychiatry, 17*(2), 89-100.
11. Vygotsky, L. S. Mind in society: the development of higher psychological process. *Harvard University Press*, Cambridge, MA, 1978.
12. Beed, P. L., Hawkins, E. M. and Roller, C. M. Moving Learners toward Independence: The Power of Scaffolded Instruction. *The Reading Teacher, 44*(9), 1991, 648-655.
13. Okebukola, P. A. Can Good Concept Mappers be Good Problem Solvers in Science? *Educational Psychology, 12*(2), 1992, 113-129.
14. Valerio, A. and Leake, D. B., Using Automatically Generated Concept Maps for Document Understanding: A Human Subjects Experiment. in Fifth International Conference on Concept Mapping, (Valletta, Malta, 2012).
15. Dias, P. and Sousa, A. P. Understanding navigation and disorientation in hypermedia learning environments. *Journal of Educational Multimedia and Hypermedia, 6*(2), 1997, 173-185.
16. Edmunds, A. and Morris, A. The problem of information overload in business organisations: a review of the literature. *International Journal of Information Management, 20*(1), 2000, 17-28.
17. Molina-Ortiz, F., Medina-Medina, N. and García-Cabrera, L., Applying a Semantic Hypermedia Model to Adaptive Concept Maps in Education. in Proceedings of the 11th International conference on Computer-aided Systems theory, (Las Palmas de Gran Canaria, Spain, 2007), 384-391.
18. Chih-Ming, C., Chi-Jui, P. and Jer-Yeu, S., Ontology-based concept map for planning personalized learning path. in IEEE conference on Cybernetics and Intelligent Systems, (Chengdu, 2008), 1337-1342.
19. Xu, N., et al., The Colored Concept Map and Its Application in Learning Assistance Program, in Proceedings of the 5th International conference on Hybrid Learning, (Guangzhou, China, 2012), 198-209.
20. Bulu, S. and Pedersen, S. Scaffolding middle school students' content knowledge and ill-structured problem solving in a problem-based hypermedia learning environment. *Educational Technology Research and Development, 58*(5), 2010, 507-529.
21. McNeill, K. L. and Krajcik, J., Supporting Students' Construction of Scientific Expalnation through Generic versus Context-Specific Written Scaffolds. in Annual meeting of the American Educational Research Association, (San Francisco, 2006).
22. Eylon, B.-S. and Reif, F. Effects of Knowledge Organization on Task Performance. *Cognition and Instruction, 1*(1), 1984, 5-44.
23. Perkins, D. and Salomon, G. Are Cognitive Skills Context-Bound? *Educational Researcher, 18*(1), 1989, 16-25.
24. Canas, A. J., et al., CmapTools: A knowledge modeling and sharing environment. in First International Conference on Concept Mapping, (Pamplona, Spain, 2004).
25. Atapattu, T., Falkner, K. and Falkner, N., Educational Question Answering motivated by Question-Specific Concept Maps. in 17th International Conference on Artificial Intelligence in Education (AIED 2015), (Madrid, Spain, 2015).
26. Hall, R. H. and O'Donnell, A. M. Cognitive and Affective Outcomes of Learning from Knowledge Maps. *Contemporary Educational Psychology, 21*(1), 1996, 94-101.
27. Kinchin, I. M., Chadha, D. and Kokotailo, P. Using PowerPoint as a lens to focus on linearity in teaching. *Journal of Further and Higher Education, 32*(4), 2008, 333-346.

A New Approach To Teaching Red Black Trees

Franceska Xhakaj
Department of Computer Science
Lafayette College
Easton, Pennsylvania 18042
xhakajf@lafayette.edu

Chun Wai Liew
Department of Computer Science
Lafayette College
Easton, Pennsylvania 18042
liewc@lafayette.edu

ABSTRACT

Red black trees are considered an important data structure and students can find it to be challenging and difficult to learn. Many approaches to teaching red black trees have been tried but not very successfully. This paper describes our new approach, the granularity approach, to teaching the top-down insertion algorithm for red black trees. Past approaches have focused on teaching the mechanics of applying the rules (color flip, single rotation and double rotation). The new approach is based on the hypothesis that students have more difficulty selecting the correct rule than in applying a selected rule. Our approach focuses on helping students learn how to correctly select the rules to be applied We supplement classroom lectures with an intelligent tutoring system that incorporates our approach. The approach and the tutoring system were used and evaluated in a small data structures class in the fall semester of 2014. The early results indicate that our approach and tutoring system are effective at helping students learn the top-down insertion algorithm.

Categories and Subject Descriptors

K.3.1 [**Computer Uses in Education**]: Computer science education; E.1 [**Data Structures**]

Keywords

Balanced trees, red black trees

1. INTRODUCTION

In a computer science curriculum data structures provides students with the knowledge and skills that are fundamental in later parts of the curriculum, such as in databases, networks, architecture, algorithms, etc [3]. Data structures are part of the programming fundamentals and core topics in a computer science curriculum [1]. Red black trees (and all balanced trees) are an important data structure with many applications. Learning the red black tree algorithms can

be quite challenging and difficult for the students for many reasons. Many approaches to teaching red black trees have been tried but they have not been very successful. These approaches have focused on teaching students the mechanics of applying the transformations (color flip, single rotation, double rotation) associated with red black trees. This paper describes a new approach for teaching the **top-down insertion algorithm** for constructing and maintaining red black trees. The new approach focuses on the recognition of the applicability of the transformations based on the hypothesis that students have more difficulty determining when to apply a transformation rather than how to apply it. We tested and evaluated our approach in a data structures class in the fall semester of 2014. The early experimental results validate our hypothesis and indicate that the approach is successful in helping students learn the top-down insertion algorithm for red black trees.

2. RED BLACK TREES

A red black tree is a self balancing binary search tree data structure, that has the following properties [9]:

1. The nodes of the tree are colored either red or black.

2. The root of the tree is always black.

3. A red node cannot have any red children.

4. Every path from the root to a null link contains the same number of black nodes.

A red black tree must display all of the properties listed above. In addition, every operation performed on a red black tree such as insertion or deletion, should preserve these properties resulting in a changed, but still correct red black tree.

The top-down insertion algorithm described in [9] starts at the root of the tree and in a single iterative pass, modifies the tree by applying one or more of the insertion rules described below and eventually adds a new item to the tree. A new item is always inserted in a leaf position in the tree, and it is colored red.

Just as with a binary search tree, during the top down traversal the algorithm selects the next node to examine based on a comparison of values at the current node and the value to be inserted. In addition, the algorithm uses the *current node* reference to keep track of its position in the tree and also to determine which rules (see description below) are applicable at the current node. The *current node* is marked with an X in each of the rules shown in Figure 1.

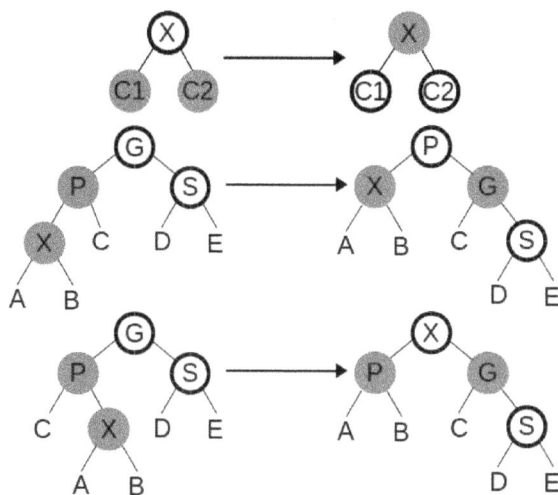

Figure 1: Top-Down insertion rules (top to bottom): color flip, single rotation, double rotation. X is the current node and relative to X, C1, C2, P, S, and G are the left child, right child, parent, sibling and grandparent. A, B, C, D and E are other nodes which may or may not be present.

Figure 1 shows the rules for top-down insertion in red black trees [9]. Starting from the top we have *color flip*, *single rotation*, and *double rotation*. In addition, we consider as a fourth rule *simple insertion*, insertion of a leaf node into the tree. There is also a fifth rule *color root black*, which is applied at the end of every insertion operation to ensure that the root of the tree is always black, as specified by the second red black tree property. The first rule (color flip) is to minimize the transformations arising from inserting a new leaf node that is colored red. The second (single rotation) and third rules (double rotation) are used to correct any violations (two red nodes in sequence) that arise from either applying rule 1 or by inserting a new node (simple insertion). The rules together ensure that only a single traversal from the root of the tree to a leaf is required to insert a new node and still maintain the red black tree properties.

The rules described above are not always applicable and applicability (preconditions of the rules) is determined by the color and structural relationships of other nodes in relation to the current node. For example, for a color flip (rule 1) to be applicable the current node must be black and its two children must be red (For further details, please see [9]). Rule 1 is always applied first (if applicable) and if this results in two red nodes in sequence, either rule 2 or 3 is applied to correct the problem. Similarly after applying rule 4 to insert a new node, rules 2 and 3 are applied to correct any problems. To determine what rules are applicable at a node, we have to find (1) the links of the current node, i.e., identify the nodes that are the children, parent and siblings of the current node, and (2) the color of each of these nodes.

3. TEACHING RED BLACK TREES

Typically, students are first introduced to the properties of red black trees and then taught the algorithm for insertion and later, deletion. A standard way of evaluating whether students have learned the insertion algorithm is for the in-

structor to provide an input sequence of data and have the student construct the equivalent red black tree while (optionally) showing all the steps taken to arrive at the solution. This evaluation can be performed either electronically (online) or on paper. In our experience, students have generally not performed well on these questions. Red black tree algorithms have always been problematic for students to learn. Past approaches to teaching red black trees (or other balanced trees such as the AVL tree) and the associated algorithms have assumed that the students had difficulty applying these rules and have focused on the mechanics of applying the rules, specifically the single and double rotation rules. These approaches have included:

- textbook exercises to learn how to apply a rule (e.g., [9, 4]),

- visualizations to show how the rules are applied. This approach has been used with many data structures including balanced trees [6, 5], and

- animations to show the steps of the application of the rules [8, 7].

Our experience is that even with the aid of these approaches, students still have difficulty with solving the standard problem, i.e., creating a red black tree from a series of input values. Extensive classroom discussions with students along with analyses of exam questions indicate that the students successfully learn the mechanics of applying the rules (color flip, single and double rotation, simple insertion) but have difficulty in determining when each should be applied. This has led us to identify the following problems:

1. *identification of the current node* when iteratively traversing the tree and applying the rules (Figure 1),

2. *selection of the rule* to be applied at the current node, and

3. *application of the rule* correctly, depicted by the left to right transitions for each of the trees in Figure 1.

Based on this list, we developed a new approach for teaching top-down insertion in red black trees. The earlier approaches focused on the specific mechanics of the color flip, single and double rotation operations. Our approach focuses on (1) the recognition of when each of these rules is valid, i.e., the recognition of the localized context at each step, and (2) the sequence of steps that must be executed to apply one or more rules on the tree.

3.1 A New Approach: The Granularity Approach

In contrast to previous approaches, our approach which we call the *granularity* approach (1) breaks down the algorithm and the accompanying insertion exercises into a combination of smaller exercises so that students need to follow explicit steps to (1) identify the current node, (2) select the rule to be applied, and (3) apply the identified rule at the current node. This explicitly separates out the identification of the current node and selection of the applicable rule from the the application of the rule itself.

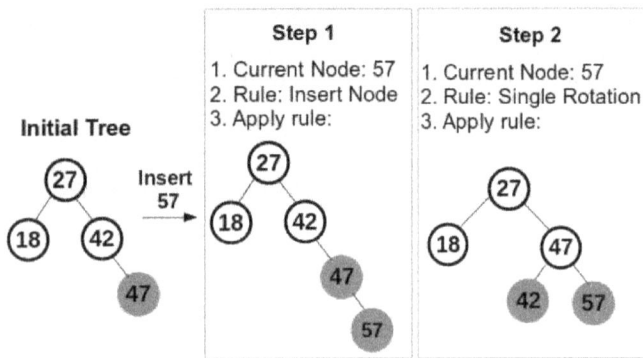

Figure 2: An Exercise Using The Granularity Approach: insertion of 57 into the tree in 2 steps.

3.1.1 An Example Exercise Using The Granularity Approach

An exercise using the granularity approach is shown in Figure 2. To simplify the discussion, we assume that the values stored in the nodes of the tree are integers ranging from 1-100. Students are provided with a red black tree and are then asked to apply the top-down insertion algorithm to add a single number (*57*). They are required to show all the steps of their work to reach a solution, with each step representing one single change to the tree from the previous step. In the example in Figure 2, to insert number *57* in the tree, students have to go through two steps to reach the solution. First, they have to apply a *simple insertion* on the *Initial Tree*, that results in the tree in *Step 1*. Secondly, they have to correct the tree from *Step 1* by applying the *single rotation* rule, as shown in *Step 2*, thus arriving at the final correct solution.

We developed granularity based exercises to provide practice for the use of the five rules of top-down insertion, namely color flip, single rotation, double rotation, simple insertion and color the root black. The exercises varied in the context for the selection of each rule. For example, we created exercises where students could apply the color flip rule with the current node being (1) the root of the tree, (2) the left child of the root, and finally (3) the right child of the root. Similarly, we designed exercises for the other rules of top-down insertion.

3.2 Teaching The Granularity Approach With A Tutoring System

We implemented our approach both in the classroom (lecture) and in laboratory exercises. This section describes how the students use the laboratory exercises. The laboratory exercises were provided through an intelligent tutoring system (RedBlackTree Tutor) that we developed using the Cognitive Tutor Authoring Tools (CTAT) [2]. The RedBlackTree Tutor is a web based tutor that students can use to work through the exercises.

Figure 3 shows a sample problem from the RedBlackTree Tutor. In the left part of the figure students are given an initial tree and a single value (a number) to insert. The right part shows an empty tree that allows for many possible transformations (both correct and incorrect). The student now has to provide the answer for the step, and the answer requires that she identify the current node by inserting its

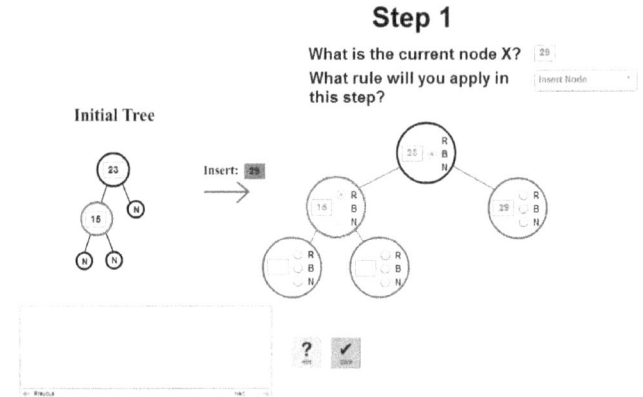

Figure 3: The RedBlackTree Tutor: Left to Right - (1) the problem, (2) solving the problem (simple insertion)

value in the textbox next to "What is the current node X?" question. In addition, the student is asked to select the rule to be applied in that step by choosing one of the five rules from the drop-down menu next to the "What rule will you apply in this step?" question. Lastly, the student is asked to apply the rule by filling in the empty tree. The student can input the appropriate value of the nodes by filling in the textboxes inside each node, and they can specify the color of the node by clicking the 'R', 'B' and 'N' radio buttons which stand respectively for 'Red', 'Black' and 'Null'.

The tutor provides feedback by color highlighting whatever the student enters in a textbox, or selects from a radio button or a drop-down menu. A green color indicates that the student answer is correct, while a purple color signals that the answer is incorrect. In addition, if the student is having difficulties in identifying the current node or rule at a particular step, the student can ask for hints from the tutor.

The RedBlackTree Tutor imposes ordering restrictions on the problem solving path of the student. The first restriction requires the student to provide the correct answer for the current step before moving to the next step. The second restriction is imposed within a particular step, and requires students to answer the two questions at the top, namely identify the current node and select a rule, before going on to applying the rule. The tutor will not allow the student to work on the application of the rule before completing the identification questions correctly. The order restrictions make the students follow the granularity approach, while separating (1) steps from each other, and (2) the identification and selection parts of the problem from the application part.

4. EXPERIMENT DESIGN

We evaluated the granularity approach on the students in our data structures class during the fall semester of 2014. Students are introduced to red black trees during week 8, after they have covered binary trees and binary search trees.

This is the first balanced tree data structure that they will have seen. There were sixteen students in the class, mostly computer science and computer engineering majors and all the students participated in the study. We only analyzed the results for 12 of the students because 4 students had worked and practiced on additional problems on their own in the period between steps 2 and 3 of the evaluation process described below. Their results were discarded from the overall evaluation because we could not disambiguate between the effects of using the RedBlackTree Tutor and the work that they did on their own.

The evaluation process followed the following steps:

1. one week of lecture to cover red black trees,

2. in the following week, a pre-test of 25 mins followed by,

3. a 1 hr session with the RedBlackTree Tutor, and

4. two days later, a 25 min post-test.

4.1 Step 1: Lecture

At the beginning, the class had one week of lecture time (2.5 hours) where red black trees were covered. Students were expected to read the description of the algorithm outside the class time and any misunderstanding or confusion was addressed and discussed in class. During this time the applicability requirements for each rule were described and discussed. In the second half of the week, the students were divided into groups of 3-4 students and were asked to apply the insertion algorithm to a list of 16 values and create the corresponding red black tree showing the tree after every iteration. Each group presented their answers to the class and they compared their solutions. Differences between solutions were discussed and resolved in class.

4.2 Step 2: Pre-Test

In the following week, the students took a 25 min pre-test. Students were asked to show all the steps of their work, and for each step, to identify the current node, select the applicable rule and apply the rule. The pre-test had 4 granularity based exercises that separately tested the students ability to select and apply a double rotation, color flip, single rotation and simple insertion rule respectively. There was a fifth question that tested the students ability to solve problems that required the selection and application of a combination of rules. For this question the students were asked to create a red black tree and sequentially insert the given numbers in the tree.

4.3 Step 3: Working With The RedBlackTree Tutor

We developed 20 granularity based exercises for use with the RedBlackTree Tutor. The exercises were divided into two problem sets that were identical in the rules that were required for each exercise but differed in the numbers used in the initial trees and the numbers to be inserted. In each set there were 3 exercises where students could perform a simple insertion, 3 exercises where they could perform a color flip, 2 for single rotation and 2 for double rotation. In the first problem set, the types of exercises were presented in the order listed above, while in the second problem set, the exercises were mixed so that there was no particular order to their appearance.

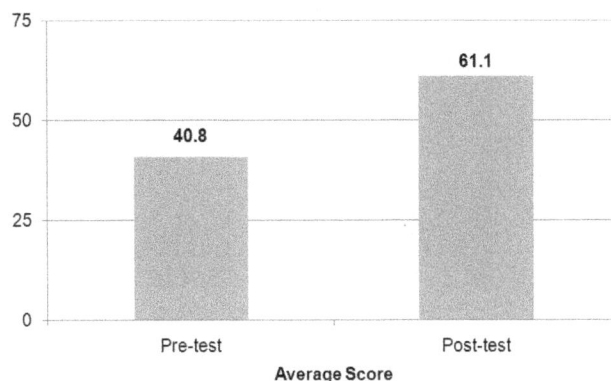

Figure 4: Class performance in pre-test and post-test

4.4 Step 4: Post-Test

Two days later the students had a 25 minute post-test. The exercises for the pre-test and post-test were the same, except that they differed in the numbers used for the initial red black trees and the numbers used for insertion.

5. EXPERIMENTAL RESULTS

The pre-tests and post-tests were graded and scored based on the correctness of each part of each step. We broke down each step in the exercises into 3 parts - identification of the current node, selection of the applicable rule, application of the rule - and graded the answers accordingly. As much as possible, we graded the parts independently. For example if a student started with an incorrect tree from a previous tree but then correctly identified the current node, applicable rule and applied the rule she would be given full credit for all the parts. A part is considered missing when there is no information, e.g., the student does not identify the current node or rule or skips the application of a rule. A missing part, or a missing step can mean (1) the student knows how to fill in the part/step but they did not write it down, or (2) the student does not know how to fill in the part and leaves it blank.

The average score in the pre-test was 40.8 (out of 75) and it improved to 61.1 in the post-test (Figure 4). All 12 students improved their score in the post-test with 8 students having an improvement of 30.0% or more. The maximum percentage increase from the pre-test to the post-test was 169.2% while the standard deviation dropped from 12.2 in the pre-test to 10.2 in the post-test. Overall the average class score increased by 49.6% from the pre-test to the post-test.

The improvement in average scores between the pre-test and post-test is explained by a an overall decrease in the number of incorrect and missing parts, and an increase in the number of correct parts. The number of incorrect parts decreased from 11.67 in the pre-test to 3.92 in the post-test (Figure 5) while the number of missing parts dropped from 22.5 to 10.0 and the number of correct steps increased from 40.83 to 61.08.

We analyzed the scores of the students in (1) identifying the current node at a particular step, (2) selecting the rule, and (3) applying the rule, between the pre-test and post-test. Figure 6 shows that the scores for node identification improved from 10.5 to 18.83 while the scores for rule selec-

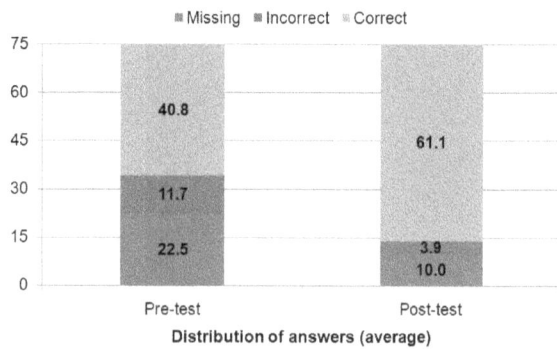

Figure 5: Distribution of the answers for each part in the pre-test and post-test

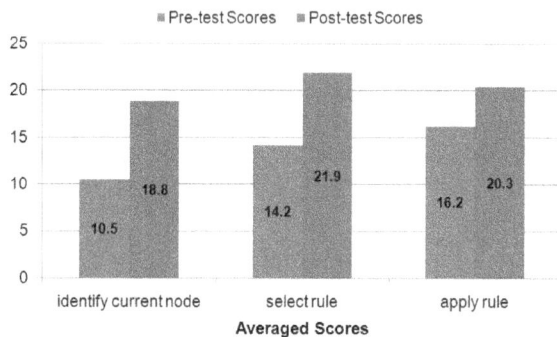

Figure 6: Scores for each part from pre test to post test

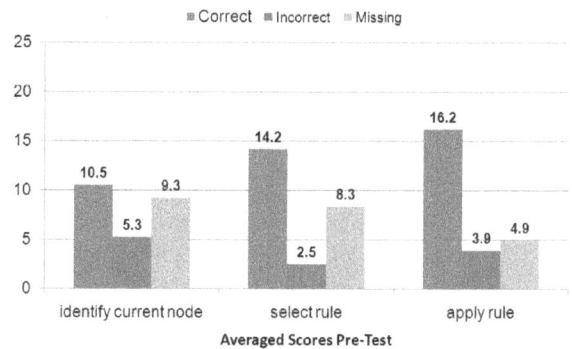

Figure 7: Pre-test scores for each part broken down by correct, incorrect and missing categories

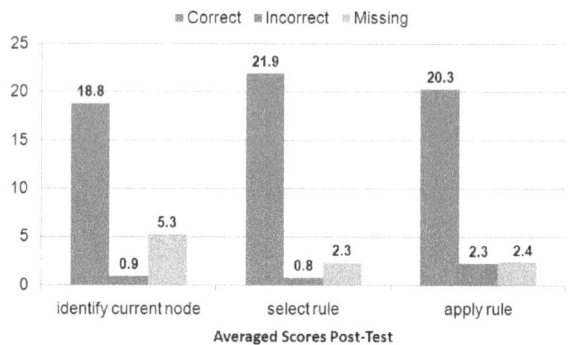

Figure 8: Post-test scores for each part broken down by correct, incorrect and missing categories

tion improved from 14.17 to 21.92 and the scores for rule application improved from 16.2 to 20.3. Thus the scores for node identification increased by 79.33%, rule selection increased by 54.7% and rule application improved by 25.73%.

The data from the pre-test and post-test allowed us to determine the main issues students face when learning the top-down insertion algorithm for red black trees. Figure 7 shows a breakdown of the scores in the pre-test in the areas of identifying the current node, selecting a rule and applying the identified rule correctly. The maximum score for each part is 25. The pre-test shows that following the week of lecture time, the students are best at rule application, followed by rule selection. They are weakest at identifying the current node where the answers have the highest number of missing and incorrect parts. These results support our hypothesis that students have the most difficulty in identifying the current node when learning top-down insertion in red black trees. The data also supports our hypothesis that students have more difficulty in selecting the applicable rule than in applying a selected rule.

Figure 8 shows a similar analysis of the post-test data with 25 being the maximum possible score for each part. The scores in all three parts (node identification, rule selection, rule application) showed substantial improvement from the pre-test so that they show similar values and the answers are mostly correct. The improvement in node identification comes from a drop in the number of incorrect parts and a corresponding increase in correct parts. The data shows that the RedBlackTree tutor has helped students learn how

to correctly (1) identify the current node, (2) select the applicable rule and (3) apply the selected rule.

5.1 Discussion

The pre-test data shows that the students had difficulty in applying the top-down insertion algorithm even after a week of lectures that included examples and group work on practice problems. We believe that this is one of those instances where learning the process effectively requires a significant amount of practice. The data shows that after a week of lectures the students had learned the process of applying the rules far more effectively than they learned the process of selecting a rule. The students were able to correctly identify the current node in approximately 40% of the cases while they were able to correctly apply the rule in 65% of the cases.

The data we have collected shows that we may have been incorrectly approaching how we teach red black trees, and perhaps all balanced trees. It will take more experimentation and analysis before we can determine the cause of the problems, but in the meantime the granularity approach has been shown to effective at solving the problems.

6. CONCLUSION AND FUTURE WORK

This paper has described a new approach for teaching students about insertion in red black trees. We have described its implementation in an intelligent tutoring system, Red-BlackTree Tutor and evaluation in a data structures course in the fall semester of 2014. The initial analysis of the data collected in the pre-tests and post-tests of this first iteration showed that students had significant learning gains of 49.6% in performance. The data showed an overall performance improvement, individually and in the class overall. We also noticed a significant decrease in the number of incorrect and missing parts from the pre-test to the post-test and a corresponding increase in the number of correct parts.

The data we collected provides insights as to the source of the difficulties for students learning insertion in red black trees. The data indicated that the main problems students face are in correctly identifying the current node and selecting the applicable rule, rather than in applying a selected rule. We intend to extend our approach to include deletion in red black trees and also to carry out a similar evaluation in the spring semester of 2015.

7. REFERENCES

[1] ACM/IEEE-CS Joint Task Force on Computing Curricula. ACM/IEEE Computing Curricula 2001 Final Report. http://www.acm.org/sigcse/cc2001, 2001.

[2] V. Aleven, B. M. Mclaren, J. Sewall, and K. R. Koedinger. A new paradigm for intelligent tutoring systems: Example-tracing tutors. *International Journal of Artificial Intelligence in Education*, 19(2):105–154, 2009.

[3] D. Chinn, P. Prins, and J. Tenenberg. The role of the data structures course in the computing curriculum. In *Proceedings in The Journal of Computing Sciences in Colleges*, volume v19 #2, 2003.

[4] W. J. Collins. *Data Structures and the Java Collections Framework*. McGraw-Hill, 3rd edition, 2011.

[5] D. Galles. Data structure visualizations. http://www.cs.usfca.edu/~galles/visualization.

[6] S. Ha. VisuAlgo. http://www.comp.nus.edu.sg/~stevenha/visualization.

[7] J. Kloss. Animated data structures. http://www.cs.jhu.edu/~goodrich/dsa/trees.

[8] W. C. Pierson and S. H. Rodger. Web-based animation of data structures using jawaa. *ACM SIGCSE Bulletin*, 1998.

[9] M. A. Weiss. *Data Structures & Problem Solving Using Java*. Pearson Education Inc., 3rd edition, 2011.

Enriching a Course with Web Resources: A Case Study

Herman Koppelman
Human-Media Interaction
University of Twente
PO Box 217
7500 AE Enschede, The Netherlands
+31534322894
H.Koppelman@utwente.nl

ABSTRACT

The web offers a lot of resources that might be useful in higher education. This paper describes the experiences with a course that offers a lot of links to web resources. These resources are meant as enriching existing content and are announced as optional. The context is distance education. Through a survey we gained insight into the actual use of the web resources and in the appreciation of the different types of resources. Findings indicate that students differed greatly in their actual use of resources and also in their preferences. Many students preferred resources that could make them study efficiently, such as videos with summaries of subject matter or explanations of hard topics. Students benefitted from links to web resources that go together with relevant information about the resource, in order to be able to make sensible decisions whether to access a resource or not.

Categories and Subject Descriptors

K.3.1 [**Computers and Education**]: Computer Uses in Education – *distance learning*; K.3.2 [**Computers and Education**]: Computer and Information Science Education – *computer science education, information systems education.*

General Terms

Measurement, Human Factors.

Keywords

Web resources, Distance learning, Open Educational Resources (OER), Massive Open Online Course (MOOC)

1. INTRODUCTION

The number of resources on the web available and suitable for teaching and learning has been growing enormously during the last decade. Numerous universities publish course materials, there are TED-talks, Khan Videos, websites of publishers, and so on. Recent developments are the emergence of MOOCs (Massive Open Online Courses) and the OER (Open Educational Resources) movement.

As a result there are a huge number of very diverse learning opportunities. One can find websites and papers with suitable

content, primary sources, applications and examples, monologues, discussions between experts, video lectures, how-to videos, and so on.

Several questions arise: Which functions can online resources have in higher education? What are the potential benefits to student learning? Will students actually use these resources? Which resources do they prefer, and why? Which factors stimulate or discourage lecturers to incorporate web resources in their teaching?

For distance education another question is relevant. What might be the impact of the use of web resources on the motivation of students? Many distance education students are confronted with motivational problems. They feel more isolated and less a member of a group, compared to students in face-to-face classes. Can enriching courses with suitable web resources, videos in the first place, help in making courses more motivating and inspiring?

This paper focuses on the students' perspective of the use of such resources in the context of distance education. One of our courses refers to a lot of web resources. We asked students of this course how they used and rated them.

Our main questions were:

- To what extent do students actually use web resources?

- How do they rate the different types of resources?

- How do they rate the way the links to resources are incorporated in the course?

It was our intention to enrich an existing course, but also to preserve its characteristics. We did not opt for major changes in the content or the pedagogical approach. Therefore, we selected only resources that we could easily integrate into the existing pedagogical approach. For reasons of efficiency, we also strived for resources that we could use integrally; we selected only resources that needed no adaptations.

This approach is in line with findings in literature. Recker et al. [12] found that teachers are more likely to use learning resources that need little or no modification, and can easily be incorporated into planned instructional activities. Harley [3] found in an extensive study of humanities and social sciences faculty that use of digital materials created by other institutions was rather low. The foremost reason for not using such resources was that they simply did not support faculty's teaching approaches.

The web resources in our course are optional, in the sense that they do not add to the mandatory content. The subject matter to be assessed is fully covered by printed materials (except for some small exceptions). The web resources are meant to enrich the course, for example by giving introductions, summaries, additional explanations, or illustrations of mandatory topics.

Section 2 describes the content and the pedagogical setting of the course. We also discuss some useful experiences with enriching resources in higher education as found in literature. Section 3 describes the results of the survey. Section 4 discusses the results.

2. COURSE

Web Culture is a mandatory course in the bachelor programs Computer Science and Information Science. The context is distance education. Our students usually study part-time, combining study and work.

The printed course book is the core of the course materials. The main communication medium for the students is the Blackboard site, with its discussion groups. This course offers no face-to-face or online classes.

2.1 Content

The course analyses the way the web influences everyday life, and discusses the changes in communication between people, new ways of conduct and the emergence of new sub cultures. Key topics are:

- Hofstede's cultural dimensions theory, applied to web cultures
- models of communication, for example, the models of Shannon and Weaver, and De Saussure
- media theory, for example, the theories of Manuel Castells, Marshall McLuhan and Howard Rheingold
- semiotics
- usability and web design.

A typical feature is that the course book gives links to all kinds of resources on the web. These links refer, among other things, to:

- web sites that illustrate subject matter; the course invites students to surf on the web and to analyse phenomena such as social media, games, and Art on the Web
- primary sources, as articles of Marshall McLuhan, Tim Berners-Lee and Don Norman
- several kinds of videos, among them:
  - videos with short lectures introducing subject matter, for example, semiotics and usability
  - experts presenting interesting topics, for example Sherry Turkle on Alone Together, Nicholas Carr with Is Google making us stupid?, and Tim Berners-Lee about the future of the world wide web
  - some episodes of the BBC documentary The Virtual Revolution.

The course offers more than 150 links to resources on the web. These are explicitly announced as enriching the course and optional, except for a very few mandatory videos.

2.2 Pedagogical setting

2.2.1 Integration of links into the course
Several studies stress the effect of the way supplementary and enriching resources are offered. Kirkwood [8, 9] discusses the use of enrichment materials by students in the context of e-learning. He suggests that students' use of web resources is more closely

related to the pedagogic design of courses, than to the availability of information sources per se. Just providing a list of resources without integrating them in the other course materials acted in his study as a disincentive: students perceived them as completely optional and mostly ignored them. Therefore, resources should form an integral part of the course activities and assignments. Lillis and Murton [11] found that just providing a list of resources did not work well. Resources at the beginning of the list were accessed more frequently that those at the bottom of the list. Resources after the fourth resource were hardly accessed at all.

Jonas and Norman [6] studied the use of supplementary resources as offered by publishers of textbooks. Examples of such resources are PowerPoint slides, quizzes, additional readings, and links to papers. According to Jonas the usage of these resources is low. Faculty encouragement is seen as an essential factor for student usage of these resources. Jonas suggests that these resources should be mandatory or highly integrated into the course.

From these studies we learn that it is the integration of the resources into an overall pedagogical approach that can make the difference, not the resources on their own. Therefore, in our course links to resources are integrated into rest of the course materials. Each link is given and explained in the context of the subject matter it is related to.

2.2.2 Videos
During the last decade the use of videos (also called podcasts) in educational contexts has grown rapidly. As a consequence, several reports with guidelines and best practices can be found. An issue relevant for our course is the length of videos. Face-to-face lectures usually last at least 45 minutes, but review studies (for example Heilesen [4]) show that that is much too long for e-learning. Guo et al. [2] focus upon the importance of videos in the context of MOOCs. Their paper discusses the results of an extensive empirical study of how video production decisions affect student engagement in educational videos. The study analyses four courses on the edX MOOC platform, with hundreds of videos and millions of student watching sessions, supplemented with qualitative insights from six edX staff. Video length was by far the most significant indicator of student engagement. Based upon their analysis they recommend segmenting videos into short chunks, ideally shorter than 6 minutes. The tentative explanation for the preference for short videos is that it takes meticulous planning to explain a concept succinctly, so shorter videos are engaging not only due to length but also because they are better planned.

In our course every link to a video informed the student about its the length. Moreover, we gave preference to short videos.

3. RESULTS

To learn the opinions of our students we distributed a survey. The survey consisted of closed questions, with the possibility to write comments in text fields. We announced the survey to students who had (almost) completed the course. 45 respondents (about half of the alerted students) filled out the survey. Respondents were students of the bachelor programs Computer Science and Information Science, and students who were interested in this particular course, without following any program.

3.1 Usage and usefulness of resources
The course offers a lot of web resources. To what extent did the students actually use them? Figure 1 shows that the use of web resources varied considerably among the students. About half of

them used at least about half of the resources; the other half used the resources much less or not at all.

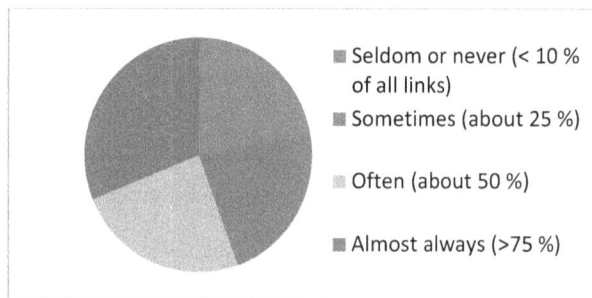

Figure 1. To what extent did you use the web links?

The comments suggest that a main reason for not using them was that students wanted to spend their study time economically. Typical comments were:

- *I only read the book, I have a minimal amount of time because I am doing another study as well.*

- *The course book is clear enough.*

- *Resources might be relevant, but usually I study in a room without access to the web, to avoid distraction.*

- *Having a look at web resources is too much.*

- *It is a waste of time to access optional course materials.*

Some comments from students using web resources are:

- *I especially like web links to video's. For me, pictures work better than words.*

- *I absorb stuff better when somebody tells and shows it in a video.*

- *Resources are clarifying and give a useful explanation of the content of the course.*

The next question was: to what extent did the students perceive the web resources as useful? We asked this question for all resources, and also for videos in particular. Tables 1 and 2 give the results, in percentages. They show that the students were mostly positive about the resources, especially the videos.

Table 1. The resources I accessed proved to be useful (1 = seldom, 5 = often)

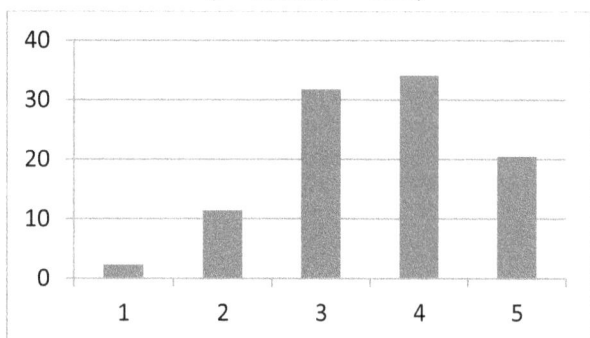

Table 2. The videos I watched proved to be useful (1 = seldom, 5 = often)

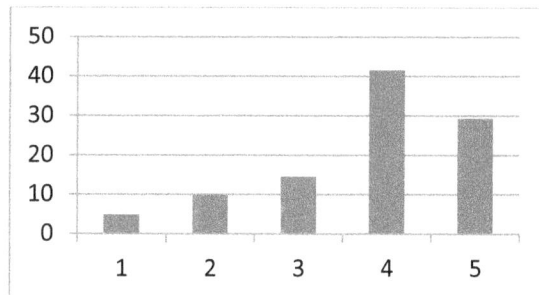

Several students commented that the usefulness was high, because they had enough information to be selective in accessing resources. For them the information in the course book about the resources was crucial. Typical comments were:

- *Success rate was high, because I only consulted resources that seemed to be useful or nice, based upon the information provided by the course book.*

- *The information in the course book determines whether I access a resource or not.*

- *I especially liked videos and interactive sites.*

Sometimes one regrets afterwards the time spent surfing on the web. Did students have such experiences with the web resources of the course? Table 3 gives the results in percentages. It shows that 'waste of time' experiences did not occur often, but they occasionally did, according to comments:

- *Positive: alternation; negative: I am inclined to continue surfing.*

- *Links are useful, but often I lose a lot of time because I continue 'clicking'.*

Table 3. Consulting resources proved to be a waste of time (1 = seldom, 5 = often)

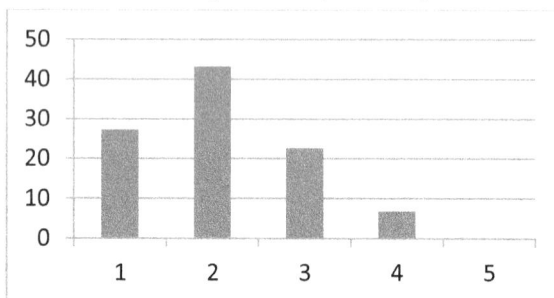

We provided links to resources with a context, as discussed in section 2.2.1. But some students asked for more information. One student commented:

- *Maybe rating the relevance with 1 to 5 stars would help. An indication of the size is also relevant.*

3.2 Preferences: number and kind of resources

Is there an optimum in the number of web links to provide? Is it possible that too large a number is overwhelming? Is it better to provide students with a restricted number of carefully selected resources? We asked the students about the preferred number of web links. The answer possibilities were:

- I don't care, I don't use them, but they don't bother me.
- Please no web links, they distract me and add to study load.
- I prefer a limited number of carefully selected links.
- I prefer as many links as possible that have a relation to the course.

Figure 2 shows the responses. A vast majority preferred to have a restricted number of web links.

Comments show why:

- *If there are too many links, you stop following them*
- *Links are useful, but only a limited number, otherwise there is hardly a difference with Google.*
- *There should be a balance between useful and study load.*

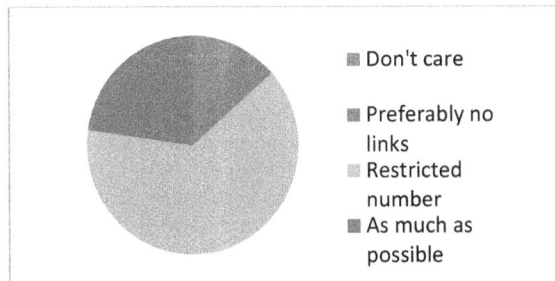

Figure 2. Preferred number of links to web resources

There were also a substantial number of students who preferred as much relevant links as possible. Several comments explain this position:

- *Many links is better, because the students have different preferences. It doesn't take much time to see if links are interesting.*
- *It is a good idea to give the relevance of the links, so that you can decide yourself.*
- *Maybe the topics are optional, but then you know where to find information in the future.*
- *It does not take much time to decide whether a resource is useful or not.*

The next question focused upon videos. Videos can have several functions in distance education. For example, resources can summarize parts of the subject matter, give additional examples, explain hard topics, or show discussions between experts. We asked the students about their appreciation of several possible functions, based upon their experiences. Those experiences might have been gained in the course Web Culture, but we also included types of video they experienced in other courses in the answer options. Examples are recordings of online Elluminate classes (which many courses offer, but the course Web Culture does not) and videos summarizing or introducing topics. Table 4 gives the (ranked) means and standard deviations of the students' ratings, on a 10-point scale.

Table 4. Ranked student mean ratings for videos (10-pt scale)

	Type of video	Mean (sd)
1	Summary of content	7.9 (2.3)
2	Additional explanation of hard topics	7.9 (1.8)
3	Illustrations and examples	6.8 (2.3)
4	'Guest speakers', for example famous experts	6.6 (2.6)
5	Recorded online classes	6.5 (2.4)
6	'How to do' instructions (tool use, give presentation, ..)	6.5 (2.7)
7	Motivation why topics are important	6.3 (2.7)
8	Optional topics	6.1 (2.3)
9	Discussions between experts	6.1 (2.5)
10	Recorded face-to-face classes	5.7 (2.7)

Table 4 shows two distinct favorites: 'Summaries' and 'Additional explanations of hard topics'. Also noteworthy are the large standard deviations, indicating a lot of variation in the answers. For example, 'Discussion between experts' scored a rather low mean of 6.1. But almost 40 % of the respondents scored '8' or higher, which means they highly appreciated such resources. 'Guest speakers' had a mean score of 6.6, but even more than 50 % of the respondents scored '8' or higher.

Several students commented that videos should be short. Typical comments were:

- *If relevancy and quality compensates for the time needed to watch, then I like videos. But I will avoid a 30 minutes presentation of something I can read in 20 minutes.*
- *Videos should be short; I don't like watching long monologues.*

3.3 Problems with resources

We asked the students about possible problems they had experienced with links to web resources. The students could choose from:

- Links were dead.
- Information on the site differed from what I expected.
- Site offered too much information.
- Mismatch between the site and the course content.

Table 5 shows the means of the responses.

We also asked about problems they had experienced with videos on the web. The students could choose from:

- Could not play the video.
- Videos were too long.
- Audio/video quality was bad.
- Relation between video and course content was unclear.

Table 6 shows the means of the responses.

Table 5. Problems with links to resources
(1 = seldom, 5 = often)

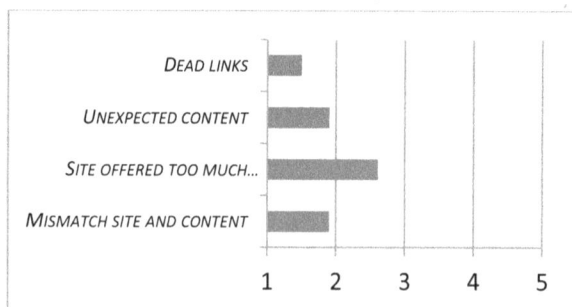

Table 6. Problems with links to videos
(1 = seldom, 5 = often)

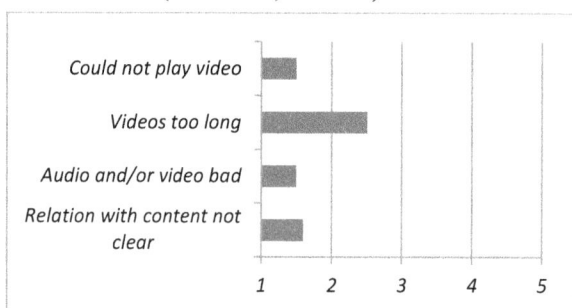

From Tables 5 and 6 we can conclude that no serious problems were reported. Sometimes sites offered too much information (Table 5) and sometimes videos were perceived as too long (Table 6).

An interesting comment that several students made was that it was much harder for them to assess the relevance of videos than the relevance of texts:

- *Drawback of videos is their fixed pace. Text you can read fast or slow, or you can skip parts. With videos you have to sit it out until the end.*
- *The problem with videos is that it takes a lot of time before you know whether they are interesting enough to keep watching.*
- *Videos take more time than text, because it takes time before you know whether they are relevant. You can't 'scan' them in the way you scan texts.*

4. DISCUSSION

4.1 Actual use of web resources

A main finding is that our students were very different with respect to the actual use of web resources. Figure 1 and the comments of the students suggest different types of students:

- Some students do not, or only very seldom, use web resources. These students tend to use only mandatory resources, because they feel other demands imposed upon them (employment, family) and try to study as economically as possible. They don't follow web links, but on the other hand Figure 2 shows that there are no signs that web links annoy them very much.

- Other students use web resources selectively. These students also want to study effectively and efficiently. But if resources look promising to better learn the material or to save time, they are inclined to use them.

- Yet another group of students feels less time pressure. If they think a resource is interesting, they access it, whether doing so might save time or not.

For a large number of our students study efficiency was important. This is in line with the findings of Jonas and Norman [6], that students constantly juggled the many demands imposed upon them from school, employment and family. They tended to only use enriching resources if they were convinced of their usefulness, for example, because the resources helped them learn the material and helped them prepare for examinations, or helped them save time. In a study about the usefulness of videos in distance education Fernandez et al. [1] found that one of the most important ways that videos helped their (distance education) students was by allowing them to efficiently manage their time. The videos gave them the feeling that the concepts of the course were easier to assimilate.

Many studies suggest that students are not inclined to use course materials that are not directly linked to assessment. In an empirical study Kirkwood [8] found that providing links to resources that were perceived as optional acted as a disincentive. Kirkwood [9] concludes: "Optional or enrichment activities and materials tend to be underutilised if they do not contribute directly to assessment outcomes. As far as e-learning activities are concerned, those aspects that are not perceived by students as being linked to assessment will receive little or no attention." Lillis and Murton [11] mention the broadly supported 'what is assessed is what will drive what is learned' premise.

Almost all of the offered web resources in our course were presented as optional, in the sense that they did not cover mandatory subject matter that is not covered by other (mainly written) materials. Students knew that no direct link to assessment exists: they would be able to get the highest mark without using them. As a consequence, some of our students simply skipped all (optional) web resources. But our study also shows that many students behaved critically and selectively with regard to web resources. They were inclined to access resources that support understanding and did not add (too much) to study load. It seems they realized that different kinds of relations might exist between the content of the web resources and the mandatory subject matter. Some resources offer additional, optional subject matter, for example topics that deepen or broaden mandatory topics. Other resources do not offer new content, but support the understanding and processing of the mandatory content. Such resources have the promise that you might 'earn back' the time spent at them. Clear examples are videos that summarize or introduce subject matter, or offer additional explanations of hard topics.

4.2 Students' preferences

Most students preferred the course developers to select a restricted set of highly relevant resources. This fits within the picture of the student who strives for efficiency. A restricted number of highly relevant links has the promise of having maximal effect with minimal efforts; too many resources works counterproductively. Only a very small minority preferred no web resources at all, because of the danger of being distracted from studying efficiently.

What type of resources did the students prefer? Based upon Table 4 and several comments of the students we have two observations

- Students were not only very different in the actual use of web resources (as we noted in the former section), but also in which kind of web resources they preferred. What exactly was liked depended on personal preferences. This is reflected in the large standard deviations of the scores in Table 4.

- On the other hand there was a clear overall tendency that students preferred videos that were short, to-the-point, and directly related to the subject matter they had to study. This held for the top-2 of the list in Table 4: Summary of content and Additional explanation of hard topics. These types of resources give direct support to improve understanding or even to save time. In contrast, recorded classes and discussion between experts (two other types of resources mentioned in Table 4) are much less focused, in the sense that you can expect a combination of useful and less useful sections. The efficiency-driven student might have to distil the useful parts from much more information. In a preliminary study about student wishes for the content of videos (in a different context with different students), we found much the same preferences [10]. Juban et al [7] found also similar preferences in a study about textbook reading behaviors. Students perceived a chapter summary to be a significantly more useful supplement than other supplements.

4.3 Support for optimal use

Section 2.2.1 explains that links to resources should be integrated into the (primary) course materials. But many students asked for more. They made deliberate choices whether to access web resources or not. Enough data about every resource should be available to base these choices upon. First of all, the relation between the content referring to the web resource and the resource itself should be clear. Which topic exactly does the resource support and in what way? Does it offer additional content? Is it an introduction to the content, or a summary of it?

Maybe a rating system might help the students. Instructors could, for example, rate every resource with 1 to 5 stars, depending on its relevancy. It is also thinkable to give the students the opportunity to 'Like/Dislike' resources, or to review them.

The 'size' of the resource is also important: how many pages or words does it have, how much time does it take (for videos)?

The information is important for videos in the first place. We are accustomed to 'scan' long texts, to get an impression of its usefulness, and to read details only if needed. But 'scanning' is much more difficult for videos.

Some students remarked that they would like to have had the opportunity to control the playback speed of videos.

5. WHAT WE LEARNED

We enriched the course Web Culture with web resources that were announced as optional. The actual use of these resources varied considerably among the students. Some hardly accessed any resource at all, primarily because they skipped all optional course materials for efficiency reasons. But we also had students who accessed almost all of the resources. Many students were selective: they made deliberate choices which resources to access.

The appreciation for the different types of resources also varied substantially among the respondents. Each type we distinguished was appreciated highly by some of them. The fact remains that there was a general trend. Many students preferred resources, videos in the first place, that did not give new information, but directly supported them to understand the course materials. Examples of popular resources were videos with summaries of mandatory subject matter and additional explanations of hard topics. It should be noted that exactly that type of tailor-made videos might not be easy to find on the web.

Links to web resources work best if they are embedded in the (mandatory) course materials. Links should go together with information about the resources: what exactly is the nature of the resource, how does it relate to the content, what is the size of it (amount of time or text). In this way students can make a sensible decision to access resources or not. This is especially the case for videos, which are hard to scan for interesting episodes.

6. REFERENCES

[1] Fernandez, V., Simo, P., and Sallan, J. M. 2009. Podcasting: A new technological tool to facilitate good practice in higher education. *Computers & Education*, 53(2), 385–392.

[2] Guo, P. J., Kim, J., and Rubin, R. 2014. How video production affects student engagement: An empirical study of MOOC videos. In *Proceedings of the first ACM conference on Learning@ scale conference*, 41-50.

[3] Harley, D. 2007. Use and users of digital resources. *Educause Quarterly*, 30(4), 12-20.

[4] Heilesen, S. B. 2010. What is the academic efficacy of podcasting? *Computers & Education*, 55(3), 1063–1068. doi:10.1016/j.compedu.2010.05.002.

[5] Jeong, H. and Hmelo-Silver, C.E. 2010. Productive use of learning resources in an online problem-based learning environment. *Comput. Hum. Behav.* 26, 1 (January 2010), 84-99. doi:10.1016/j.chb.2009.08.001

[6] Jonas, G.A. and Norman, C.S. 2011. Textbook websites: User technology acceptance behaviour. *Behaviour & Information Technology*, 30(2), 147-159.

[7] Juban, R. L. and Lopez, T. B. 2013. An exploration of textbook reading behaviors. *Journal of Education for Business*, 88(6), 325-331.

[8] Kirkwood, A. 2008. Getting it from the Web: Why and how online resources are used by independent undergraduate learners. *Journal of Computer Assisted Learning*, 24(5), 372-382.

[9] Kirkwood, A. 2009. E-learning: you don't always get what you hope for. *Technology, Pedagogy and Education*, 18(2), 107–121.

[10] Koppelman, H. 2013. Using Podcasts in Distance Education. In: *Proceedings of the International IADIS Conference E-Learning 2013*, 303-308.

[11] Lillis, S. and Murton, S. 2012. Does the order of presentation and number of online resources affect the frequency of access by learners? *J. Prim. Health Care*, 4(3), 213-216.

[12] Recker, M., Dorward, J., and Nelson, L. M. 2004. Discovery and use of online learning resources: Case study findings. *Educational Technology & Society*, 7(2), 93-104.

Classroom Versus Screencast for Native Language Learners: Effect of Medium of Instruction on Knowledge of Programming

Yogendra Pal
Inter-Disciplinary Program in Educational Technology
Indian Institute of Technology Bombay
Mumbai, India
yogendra.pal3@gmail.com

Sridhar Iyer
Department of Computer Science and Engineering
Indian Institute of Technology Bombay
Mumbai, India
sri@iitb.ac.in

ABSTRACT

Students, who study in their native language in K-12 and go on to do their undergraduate education in English, have difficulty in acquiring programming knowledge. Solutions targeted towards improving their English proficiency take time, while those that continue with native language in the classroom limit the students' ability to compete in a global market.

Another solution could be the use of video-based instructional material to empower a student for self-paced learning. In this paper, we present a comparative study of classroom instruction versus self-paced screencasts for native language learners' acquisition of programming concepts. We conducted four introductory programming workshops, each of six days duration. Two workshops were classroom based, one having Hindi (native language) as the medium of instruction and other in English. Two other workshops were screencast based, again one in Hindi and one in English.

We measured differences between the groups using a post-test, across different content types such as fact, concepts and process. We found that when medium of instruction is different from language of K-12 instruction, there is an adverse impact on learning. However, when self-paced screencast is used instead of classroom environment, there is a statistically significant improvement in performance. Our work informs the choice of MoI and choice of environment for native language learners.

Categories and Subject Descriptors

K.3.2 [**Computers and Education**]: Computer and Information Science Education - *computer science education*.

Keywords

Computer programming education; screencast; native language instruction

1. INTRODUCTION

Students who study in their native language in K-12 and go on to do their undergraduate education in English, have significant difficulty due to the language barrier [1], leading to high drop-out rates[2].

ITICSE '15, July 04 - 08, 2015, Vilnius, Lithuania
© 2015 ACM. ISBN 978-1-4503-3440-2/15/07…$15.00
DOI: http://dx.doi.org/10.1145/2729094.2742618

Attempts to overcome this barrier by either (i) improving English proficiency, or (ii) continuing with native language instruction, have limited success. This is because acquiring English proficiency takes time [3], while continuing with native language limits their social context of choice [4].

Another solution to this difficulty is the use of video-based instructional material that empowers the student for self-paced learning. With present day technology, creation of such videos has become easy and affordable. Videos can be created in several ways, for example, classroom lecture video, talking head and screencast [5]. However there are not many studies that examine the effectiveness of video-based material in the context of native language learners, few studies are reported in [1].

In this paper, we present a comparative study of classroom instruction versus self-paced screencasts for native language learners' acquisition of programming concepts. While there is work on the use of native language for classroom teaching of programming [10] and computer science subjects[6][8][9], there is no experimental data that compares the impact of classroom versus screencast, as well as the effect of medium of instruction (MoI), on student achievement. Towards this end, we conducted the following study.

We created four introductory programming workshops (W1-W4), each of six days duration. W1 was classroom based and had Hindi (native language) as the MoI. W2 was also classroom based but had English as the MoI. W3 was screencast based with Hindi as the MoI. W4 was also screencast based but had English as the MoI. Our sample consisted of first year undergraduate engineering students, some of whom had K-12 instruction in English while others had K-12 in Hindi. They were divided into groups, as shown in Table 1. The topics were taken from ACM CS curriculum [10], as shown in Table 2.

Table 1. Detail of participating groups

Environment	Work-shop	Medium in K-12	MoI of workshop	Name of Group	N
Classroom	W1	Hindi	Hindi	HHc	35
	W2	Hindi	English	HEc	35
		English	English	EEc	35
Screencast	W3	Hindi	Hindi	HHs	35
	W4	Hindi	English	HEs	35
		English	English	EEs	35

Table 2. Topics of each day screencasts

Topic number	Subtopics of each day (comma separated)	Day
T1	Introduction to programming, program, development process	1
T2	Identifiers, data type, memory representation, integer, use of variable.	2
T3	Arithmetic instructions, operators, operators precedence	3
T4	printf, scanf	3
T5	Relational operators, equality operators, branching statement, if, if-else	4
T6	Functions, Function call, pass by value, return types	5
T7	Recursion	6

We measured differences between the groups using a post-test of 59 items, across different content types such as fact, concepts and process. For classroom environment, we found that the difference between the experimental group (HHc) and control group (HEc) was statistically significant with moderate effect size, thereby confirming that when MoI is different from language of K-12 instruction, there is an adverse impact on learning. On the other hand, the difference between experimental group (HHc) and baseline group (EEc) was not significant. This shows that when the MoI is the same language as in K-12 instruction, there is no adverse impact on the learning, in classroom environment.

For classroom versus screencast, we found that the difference between the control group (HEc) and experimental group (HEs) was statistically significant, with moderate effect size. We also found that the difference between HHc versus HHs, as well as difference between EEc versus EEs, were not significant. This implies that when MoI is different from the language of K-12 instruction, the use of self-paced screencast is desirable. Thus our work informs the choice of MoI and choice of environment for native language learners.

In Section II we present the related work on teaching programming through native language instruction. In Sections III and IV, we give the details of our research questions and methodology, respectively. The results are in Section V, followed by discussion in Section VI.

2. RELATED WORK

Benefits of native language instructions in mathematics [11] and physics [12] are reported in the studies. In a work [6] authors suggested a bilingual model for teaching programming in China, but it is still being implemented and no experimental data is available.

Screencast have several benefits over traditional classroom including low cost and high availability [14]. Students in a traditional classroom are unable to concentrate after 20 minutes [15]. Screencast enables self-paced learning so students can maintain their level of concentration by breaking the lecture into smaller chunks [16]. Students can rewind and replay the screencast if they miss any part of the material [16]. Also, sometimes in classroom, the distance from instructor makes it difficult for students to focus and creates distractions. While self-paced screencasts create the impression that a learner is sitting quite close to the lecturer [16]. In traditional classroom students tend to focus on taking notes for later use, while in screencast they do not focus on note-taking but on understanding concepts [16]. Also, the classroom environment is more difficult for learners who are studying in a foreign language, as they have to understand the content and language at the same time [18].

In a pilot study conducted by Simpson [16], students self-reported that they prefer screencasts over traditional classroom environment. Students who were part of the study also found video player controls acting as a scaffold for better learning. One study on statistics [13] found that students watching screencast took less time to study and performed better than those who were receiving text-based instructions.

While students and teachers agree that screencasts should be created in native languages [19], there is no work on the effect of native language screencasts on student achievement, in the context of programming. Moreover, there is no study that compares the performance of students in classroom versus screencast in the native language. In this paper we address these gaps. We study the effect of medium of instruction on acquisition of programming knowledge by native language learners, in both classroom and screencast settings.

3. RESEARCH QUESTION

We use the term "medium" to denote the medium of instruction in K-12 years of schooling. In our experiment, the medium could be the same as the native language (Hindi) or different (English). We use the term "MoI" to denote the medium of instruction in the treatment. In our study, the MoI for the screencast or classroom is either English or Hindi.

By using screencast in classroom we want to say use screencast in classroom rather than live lecture or screencast at home.

We are answering three major questions. First major question is: What is the impact of the MoI on the programming abilities of native language learners in classroom? This is operationalized into the following specific question:

Do undergraduate Hindi medium students learning introductory programming in classroom in Hindi perform better than similar students who learn programming in Classroom in English?

Second major question is: How does moving from classroom to screencast affect the performance of students? This is operationalized in the following question:

Do undergraduate Hindi medium students learning introductory programming by watching Hindi screencast perform better than similar students who learn programming in Hindi in Classroom environment?

Our third major question: How does medium of instruction affect the performance of native language students, for both classroom and screencast?

Do undergraduate Hindi medium students learning introductory programming by watching English screencast perform better than similar students who learn programming in English in Classroom environment?

4. METHODOLOGY

4.1. Sample

The sample consisted of 210 engineering 1st year undergraduate students of North India. The sample was divided into 6 groups according to their prior medium of instruction, medium of instructions in the treatment (MoI) and treatment environment (classroom or screencast), as shown in Table 1.

We included only those learners who are studying programming in their current semester. Moreover we used purposive sampling, i.e., participation was made voluntary thereby excluding students who are not interested in learning programming. Further, we selected only those students who had no or little prior knowledge of programming. We ensured equivalence of the groups on prior academic achievement.

4.2. Instruments and Data Collection

To measure programming ability, performance scores on a post-test were collected. To determine prior knowledge of programming a 10-item pre-test was conducted. To determine prior academic achievement levels, overall percentage of marks in 12th grade final examination were collected.

We used a 3-item survey to collect data about students' background. The items for each student were: (i) MoI in 12th standard (English or Hindi), (ii) Overall percentage of marks in 12th standard, and (iii) Whether they have prior knowledge of programming (yes or no). We verified their self-reported knowledge of programming using the pre-test.

We used paper-based post-test every day after workshop. We looked for a concept inventory for programming but found that the standardization of assessment instruments for programming ability is still ongoing [20]. So we created the post-test based on questions that typically appear in the University exams and those given in standard textbooks. We included only those questions that directly mapped to the learning objectives in our screencasts. There were 59 items in the post-test, 44 multiple choice, 7 short answer questions, 3 write a program and 5 matching type questions. Also, 22 of the 59 items were on factual knowledge, 31 on conceptual knowledge and 6 were on knowledge of process. One sample post-test question from each category is given in Table 3.

Table 3. Sample post-test questions from each category

Checking knowledge of	Sample Question
Fact	**Q4. \n & \t are** a. Keywords b. Escape Sequence c. Format Specifier d. None of the above
Process	**Q1e. What will be the control flow of given program?** a. 9, 10, 11, 3, 4, 5, 6, 11, 12 b. 3, 4, 5, 6, 7, 9, 10, 11, 12, 13 c. 9, 10, 11, 12, 13, 3, 4, 5, 6 d. Other please write ....
Concept	**Q11. Value of L if?** **L = 6 != 5** a. 6 b. 5 c. 1 d. 0 e. Other please write ....

4.3. Procedure

Survey: We first conducted the survey and then divided the students into 6 groups, based on the medium of their 12th Std, as shown in Table 1. We compared the means of the 12th Std marks for the groups and found them to be equivalent. We did ANOVA to confirm the equivalence. We also conducted a pre-test after survey with the selected students. We removed all students who got more than 40% marks in pre-test because we wanted to include only those who had either no or little knowledge of programming.

Arrangement for screencast based treatment: We arranged separate computer lab for the three groups. In lab each computer was equipped with headphone and media player was installed on each computer in advance.

Arragement for classroom based treatment: We arranged two different classes. MoI of one class was English which was conducted for HEc and EEc groups. MoI of other class was Hindi which was attended by HHc group.

Treatment for screencast: Each student was alloted one computer. Each student watched screencast on the alloted computer in computer lab. Each computer was equipped with headphone so that students can not hear outside noise. Students were allowed to watch screencast for 45 continuous minutes. They were free to use video player controls according to their need. Shortest screencast is 22:00 minutes in length and longest is 45:00 minutes. There were no additional tutorials or laboratory exercises. The topics of the screencast of each day are listed in Table 2.

Treatment for classroom: The class that was conducted in English was attended by HEc and EEc groups. Both groups were sitting in different rows. HHc group attended the classroom that was in Hindi. There were no additional tutorials or laboratory exercises. The topics of the classroom of each day were same as screencast and listed in Table 2.

Slides and live coding [21] was used in screencast as well as in classroom. We used digital pen in both environment so that teacher can draw diagrams, symbols and other necessary things on screen. Figure 1 shows an example of using digital pen with live-coding method. Slides were completely in English for all six groups. The explanation was in Hindi for HHc and HHs groups and English for EEc, EEs, HEc and HEs groups. Screencasts and classrooms in two languages were identical in terms of explanation, source-code, examples and analogy. Sample screenshots of the material are given in Figure 1 and Figure 2 Note that only the vocal explanation is in Hindi for the HHc and HHs groups.

Figure 1. A screenshot that shows use of digital pen-tablet.

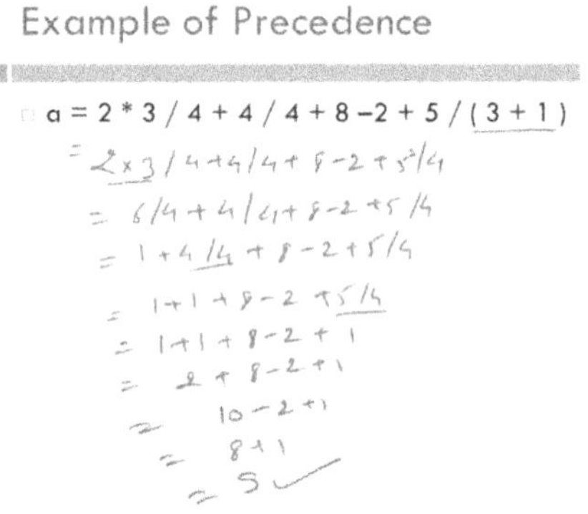

Figure 2. Screenshot showing a source code with result

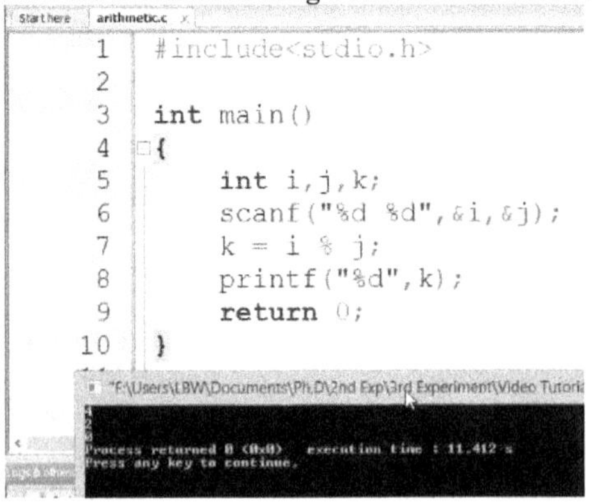

Screencast and classroom of each day for each group addressed the same Learning Objectives (LOs). The list of LOs is given below in Table 4.

Table 4. Learning objectives of screencasts

LO number	Learning Objective
LO1	Analyze and explain the behavior of simple programs involving the fundamental programming constructs covered by this unit.
LO2	Identify and describe uses of primitive data types.
LO3	Write programs that use each of the primitive data types.
LO4	Modify and expand short programs that use standard conditional structures and functions.
LO5	Design, implement, test, and debug a program that uses each of the following fundamental programming constructs: basic computation, simple I/O, and standard conditional, the definition of functions, and parameter passing.
LO6	Choose appropriate conditional constructs for a given programming task.
LO7	Describe the concept of recursion and give examples of its use.
LO8	Identify the base case and the general case of a recursively-defined problem.
LO9	Identify and describe the use of standard conditional structures and functions.

Posttest: To investigate the effect of the MoI on achievement scores, we conducted a post-test everyday after the treatment using the instrument we had designed earlier. Each student had to attempt the posttest individually, within a time limit of fifteen minutes. There was no negative marking.

Analysis: We performed quantitative analysis of the post-test scores for the different groups and question categories. We computed the means for each group. We used one-way ANOVA to compare groups to determine which means are statically significantly different from one another.

5. Result Analysis

The mean of post-test scores (out of 59) for the six groups (HHs, HEs, EEs, HHc, HEc and EEc) are shown in Table 5.

Table 5. Mean of post-test scores for all groups

Group	N	Mean	Std. Deviation	Std. Error of Mean
HHs	35	45.00	7.472	1.263
HEs	35	37.57	5.937	1.004
EEs	35	42.51	5.511	.932
HHc	35	43.14	7.781	1.315
HEc	35	27.86	8.229	1.391
EEc	35	42.00	8.578	1.450

Mean of scores for HHc group and the EEc group is higher than the HEc group, and the mean of scores for the HHs and EEs group is higher than the HEs group (see Table 5). This indicates that for both environments Hindi medium students who get the treatment in English performed lower than other students. HHc, HEc and EEc group perform lower than HHs, HEc and HEc respectively (see Table 5). This indicates that students who study in self-paced

screencast based environment perform better than those who study in classroom based environment.

The distribution of percentage of post-test scores for all three categories of questions, fact, process and concept is presented in Figure 3, Figure 4 and Figure 5 respectively.

Figure 3. Percentage of post-test scores of fact type questions

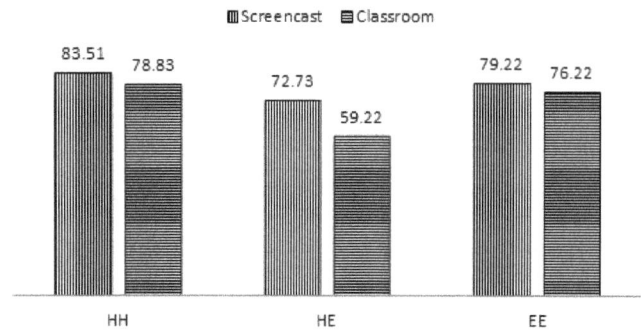

Figure 4. Percentage of post-test scores of process questions

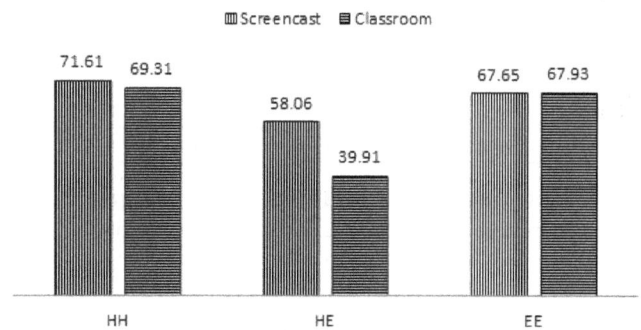

Figure 5. Percentage of post-test scores of concept questions

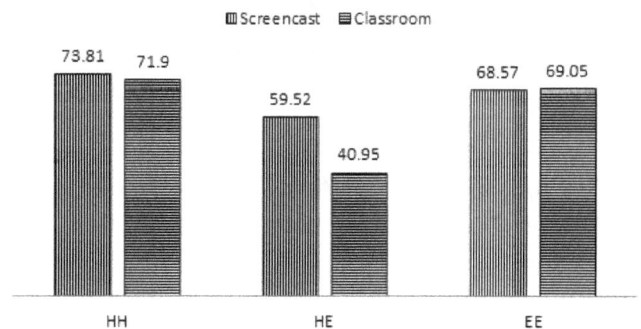

5.1. Comparison of HHc and HHs groups

We performed one-way ANOVA [23] to compare HHc and HHs groups and found no significant difference in total score as well as in all three question categories, as shown in Table 6.

Table 6. One way ANOVA for HHc and HHs groups

		Sum of Squares	df	Mean Square	F	Sig.
Fact	Between Groups	18.514	1	18.514	2.656	.108
Process	Between Groups	.229	1	.229	.111	.740
Concept	Between Groups	8.929	1	8.929	.471	.495
Total	Between Groups	60.357	1	60.357	1.037	.312

5.2. Comparison of EEc and EEs groups

We performed one-way ANOVA [23] to compare EEc and EEs groups and found no significant difference in total score as well as in all three question categories, as shown in Table 7.

Table 7. One-Way ANOVA for EEc and EEs groups

		Sum of Squares	Df	Mean Square	F	Sig.
Fact	Between Groups	6.914	1	6.91	.822	.368
Process	Between Groups	.014	1	.014	.009	.923
Concept	Between Groups	.129	1	.129	.007	.934
Total	Between Groups	4.629	1	4.63	.089	.766

5.3. Comparison of HEc and HEs groups

We compare HEc and HEs groups by performing one-way ANOVA [23] and found statistically significant difference in total score (effect size 0.56) as well as in all three question categories, as shown in Table 8.

Table 8. One-Way ANOVA of HEc and HEs groups

		Sum of Squares	df	Mean Square	F	Sig.
Fact	Between Groups	154.514	1	154.51	18.60	.000
Process	Between Groups	21.729	1	21.73	12.82	.001
Concept	Between Groups	554.414	1	554.41	34.52	.000
Total	Between Groups	1651.429	1	1651.43	32.08	.000

5.4. Comparison of HHc and EEc groups

We performed one-way ANOVA [23] on post-test scores of HHc and EEc groups and found no significant difference in total score as well as in all three question categories, as shown in Table 9.

Table 9. One-Way ANOVA of HHc and EEc groups

		Sum of Squares	df	Mean Square	F	Sig.
Fact	Between Groups	5.157	1	5.16	.650	.423
Process	Between Groups	.514	1	.514	.274	.603
Concept	Between Groups	3.214	1	3.214	.153	.697
Total	Between Groups	22.86	1	22.86	.341	.561

5.5. Comparison of HHc and HEc groups

We performed one-way ANOVA [23] on post-test scores of HHc and HEc groups and found significant difference in total score (effect size 0.69) as well as in all three question categories, as shown in Table 10.

Table 10. One-Way ANOVA of HHc and HEc groups

		Sum of Squares	df	Mean Square	F	Sig.
Fact	Between Groups	325.73	1	325.73	43.53	.000
Process	Between Groups	60.36	1	60.36	31.04	.000
Concept	Between Groups	1453.73	1	1453.73	69.47	.000
Total	Between Groups	4088.93	1	4088.93	63.76	.000

6. DISCUSSION AND CONCLUSION

From Figures 3-5, we observe that the performance of HEc group is the lowest among all the groups, while HHs group is the highest, for all categories of questions. This reconfirms the fact that classroom based instruction in English is not suitable for native language learners. On the other hand, while classroom based instruction in native language is suitable, self-paced screencasts in native language lead to maximum performance.

Within a classroom environment, the difference between HHc and EEc is not statistically significant (Table 9), showing that the language of instruction does not matter when MoI is matched with medium of K-12. This also confirms that the classroom lectures in both languages were equivalent. The difference between HHc and HEc groups is statistically significant with effect size 0.69 (Table 10), showing that native language learners are at a disadvantage when MoI is not matched with their medium of K-12.

Within a screencast environment, in a previous experiment [24], we found that the difference between HHs and EEs was not statistically significant, while the difference between HHs and HEs was significant. Thus, in both settings (classroom as well as screencast), we conclude that native language learners perform comparable to English medium learners, when they continue to learn in their native language, but are unable to do so when forced to learn in the secondary language.

When we compare groups within the same medium of instruction, we find that the difference between HHc and HHs groups is not statistically significant (Table 6), and the difference between EEc and EEs is also not significant (Table 7). This leads to the conclusion that the environment (classroom versus screencast) does not play a role in performance if MoI and medium in K-12 are the same. On the other hand, the difference between HEc and HEs groups is statistically significant (effect size 0.56) for total post-test score as well as all categories of questions (Table 8). This indicates that when MoI is different from medium of K-12 instruction, the environment plays a role in the performance. Thus we conclude that if MoI is mis-matched for native language learners, then it is better to use self-paced screencast rather than a classroom setting.

One limitation of our study is that our sample was from cities where standard of education is higher than towns and villages. Conducting the same experiments on sample from small towns and villages is required to further generalize our results.

7. REFERENCES

[1] Probyn, M. (2001). "Teachers Voices: Teachers Reflections on Learning and Teaching through the Medium of English as an Additional Language in South Africa." International Journal of Bilingual Education and Bilingualism 4(4): 249-266.

[2] Bhardwaj, B. K. and S. Pal (2012). "Data Mining: A prediction for performance improvement using classification." arXiv preprint arXiv:1201.3418.

[3] Guerrero, M. D. (2004). "Acquiring Academic English in One Year An Unlikely Proposition for English Language Learners." Urban Education 39(2): 172-199.

[4] McConnell, B. (1980). "Does Bilingual Education Work?" Bilingual Resources 3(2): 23-27.

[5] Guo, P. J., J. Kim and R. Rubin (2014). How video production affects student engagement: an empirical study of MOOC videos. Proceedings of the first ACM conference on Learning @ scale conference. Atlanta, Georgia, USA, ACM: 41-50.

[6] Hanjing, L., W. Kuanquan and W. Yuying (2009). A Bilingual Teaching Modal in a Programing Language Course. Education Technology and Training, 2009. ETT '09. Second International Conference on.

[7] Leo Gomez, David Freeman and Yvonne Freeman. Dual Language Education: A promising 50-50 model. Bilingual Research Journal, volume 29, Issue 1, 2005. pages 145-164

[8] Jinshu Han (2010). Bilingual Teaching Practice of Undergraduate Computer Graphics. Second International Workshop on Educational Technology and Computer Science. Pages 441-444.

[9] Shuang Liu, Xizuo Li and Li Zuo (2011). Adopting communicative teaching method in computer major bilingual teaching. Theory and Practice in language studies, vol 1, no 2, pp. 187-190, February 2011

[10] Joint Task Force on Computing Curricula, A. f. C. M. and I. C. Society (2013). Computer Science Curricula 2013: Curriculum Guidelines for Undergraduate Degree Programs in Computer Science, ACM.

[11] Dong-Joong Kim, Joan Ferrini-Mundy, Anna Sfard (2012), How does language impact the learning of mathematics? Comparison of English and Korean speaking university students' discourses on infinity", International Journal of Educational Research. Feb. 2012.

[12] D. Venkatesan, Dr. RM Chandrasekaran and Dr. A. Velangani Joseph (2010), "Significance of Medium of Instruction and Personality in Designing Adaptive e-Learning Systems.", In the International Journal of Computer Applications, Oct. 2010, pp. 25-28.

[13] Lloyd, S. A. and C. L. Robertson (2012). "Screencast Tutorials Enhance Student Learning of Statistics." Teaching of Psychology 39(1): 67-71.

[14] Kathleen Barnes, John Bowers, Julie H. Dent (2009), "Video Tutorials: A Sustainable Method for Campus Technology Training", In EDUCASE Quarterly (EQ), 2009 Vol. 32, No. 3.

[15] Middendorf, J. K., A. (1996). "The 'Change-Up' in Lectures." National Teaching and Forum 5(2).

[16] Ellis, C. (2008). 'You Can't Do That in a Classroom!': How Distributed Learning Can Assist in the Widespread Adoption of Hybrid Learning Strategies. Hybrid Learning and Education. J. Fong, R. Kwan and F. Wang, Springer Berlin Heidelberg. 5169: 1-16.

[17] Simpson, N. (2006). "Asynchronous access to conventional course delivery: a pilot project." British Journal of Educational Technology 37(4): 527-537.

[18] John L. FaLconer, J. d., J. Will Medlin, and Michael P. Holmberg (2009). "Using ScreenCasts in ChE Courses." 43(4).

[19] J. Ravi, H.J. Jani (2011), "A Critical Study of NPTEL", In International conference on Technology for Education (T4E), Aug. 2011, pp. 35-42

[20] Allison Elliott Tew and Mark Guzdial (2011). The FCS1: A Language Independent Assessment of CS1 Knowledge." SIGCSE, Mar. 2011, pp. 111-116.

[21] Gaspar, A. and S. Langevin (2007). Restoring "coding with intention" in introductory programming courses. Proceedings of the 8th ACM SIGITE conference on Information technology education. Destin, Florida, USA, ACM: 91-98.

[22] https://www.youtube.com/watch?v=m4zqbaiUj4sM as seen on 28 nov. 2012

[23] Glass, G. V. and K. D. Hopkins (1996). Statistical methods in education and psychology (3rd ed.). Needham Heights, MA, US: Allyn & Bacon. pp. 295, 387-388

[24] Pal, Y., & Iyer, S. (2015). "Effect of medium of instruction on programming ability acquired through screencast." In International Conference on Learning and Teaching in Computing and Engineering (LaTiCE), 2015, pp. 17-21.

Supporting Diverse Novice Programming Cohorts through Flexible and Incremental Visual Constructivist Pathways

Charles Thevathayan
RMIT University
GPO Box 2476, Victoria 3001, Australia
613 999259604
charles.thevathayan@rmit.edu.au

Margaret Hamilton
RMIT University
GPO Box 2476, Victoria 3001, Australia
613 999252939
margaret.hamilton@rmit.edu.au

ABSTRACT

Novice programmers rely mainly on formative assignments to develop their problem solving skills. Such assignments can be made more engaging by structuring them into visual tasks with instant feedback. Constructivist theory however, suggests such tasks can facilitate learning only if they are designed considering student mental models. Designing such tasks is difficult given the diversity of students in introductory programming courses. This paper presents a flexible and incremental visual constructivist model that enables different pathways for individual students. Formative and summative evaluations based on assignment tasks suggest such an approach can help improve learning outcomes and student satisfaction significantly even when students have varying cognitive abilities.

Categories and Subject Descriptors

K.3.2 [**Computers and education**]: Computer and information science education – *computer science education*

General Terms

Assessment Design, Novice Programming.

Keywords

Motivation, Diversity in the classroom, Learning Programming. Visualisation, Constructivism

1. INTRODUCTION

Multi-national teams of investigators have found that many students who have completed one or two programming courses performed much worse than anticipated in coding standard computer science problems, with a significant number of students described as "clueless" [17, 6]. Poor performance and high attrition in introductory programming courses can be partially attributed to the wide range of student backgrounds and aptitudes. Students in our introductory programming course come from a number of different disciplines such as software engineering, games development, IT and computer science with varying

cognitive abilities and motivational levels. Students with good cognitive abilities learn new concepts easily while others may require regular feedback and instructor intervention. Failing to correct student misconceptions early exacerbate learning difficulties and lead to poor performance in programming assessments. Alleviating these problems requires a new approach to designing formative assessments.

Novice programmers react in different ways when given challenging tasks requiring much abstract reasoning. At one extreme, some become active and engrossed while some others become completely disengaged through frustration [9]. Such disparate groups can be effectively catered if multiple pathways are provided towards the same final goal. Students unfamiliar with abstract reasoning may choose longer pathways where initial concrete tasks may require little or no cognitive skills.

Invalid mental models of basic constructs are also a major reason for poor performance in programming tasks [14]. Students relying on passive learning alone often form invalid mental models. Constructivism is a learning theory that suggests students actively construct their own mental models from sensory data inputs and existing beliefs, instead of passively receiving knowledge [3]. Learners construct their own meanings to programming concepts combining their past knowledge with the information and feedback they receive [11].

Visualization tools using a notional machine have been used since the early 1970s to promote understanding of programming constructs [15]. However, having to learn another tool can introduce additional barriers for novice programmers. A concept specific metaphor can avoid any additional cognitive load [20], especially if the metaphor is close to a known real-world system [24]. Graphical feedback in visual metaphors can aid a constructivist approach if visual tasks are designed with cognitive conflicts that foster expansion of student mental models. If such tasks are to cater to a mixed cohort, alternative pathways may be necessary. Some students may require pathways with small cognitive increments that permit a more gradual increase in mental models. Our research questions were therefore:

- Can visual assignments be structured to meet the cognitive needs of diverse student cohorts?

- Does such an approach improve student satisfaction and performance?

The visual scenario where a robot object is required to perform increasingly complex tasks, allowed a gradual expansion of student mental models and abstract reasoning skills. Student feedback and assignment results show visual constructivist pathways can promote student engagement, satisfaction and completion rates. Exam performance of average students also showed small but significant gains in topics covered by the

ITICSE '15,July 04 - 08, 2015, Vilnius, Lithuania
© 2015 ACM. ISBN 978-1-4503-3440-2/15/07…$15.00
DOI: http://dx.doi.org/10.1145/2729094.2742609

incremental visual constructivist assignment. The remainder of this paper is organized as follows. Section 2 reviews some of the relevant literature that attempts to overcome the barriers faced by introductory programming students. Section 3 describes the rationale for the design decisions of the visualization tool. Section 4 presents an evaluation of our approach which is followed by discussion and conclusion in Sections 5 and 6.

2. RELATED WORK WITH NOVICE PROGRAMMERS

Visualization aids novice programmers by reducing the level of abstraction necessary [2]. Alice, a common visualization tool used in introductory programming courses allows virtual objects in 3D worlds to be manipulated through calls to pre-created methods [22]. Though effective in promoting engagement using a trial and error approach, lack of state variables in Alice limits its ability to foster abstract reasoning skills. Reliance on trial-and-error is also known to stifle development of reasoning skills necessary for problem solving [2]. Ideally visual tools for introductory programming courses should be structured to make it increasingly difficult to rely on trial-and-error as students move from concrete tasks to more abstract ones. In the past many visual tools allowed only a passive involvement, where a student simply watches an animation of an algorithm, such as sorting or searching. Active visualization requires varying both the data and the algorithm. These involvement levels have since been classified into more fine grained categories: no viewing, viewing, responding, changing, constructing and presenting [25]. Learning gains were significantly higher for active involvement (83%) when compared with passive ones (33%) [19].

Teaching programming courses is difficult as it requires imparting abstract reasoning skills necessary for problem solving [26]. Constructivist theory suggests better learning outcomes require tasks that permit gradual expansion of student mental models [3, 14]. Students should have developed a good mental model of variables and loops before handling arrays as any misconception get propagated [7]. Misconceptions occur when students with inadequate understanding of a concept, construct their own rules. Misconceptions can also occur when familiar terms are used in an unfamiliar context. For example, in the statement "wait while I am talking on the phone" a continual testing is implied, unlike in the while construct where testing happens only once per iteration [4]. Visualization can help correct misconceptions as they commonly occur when outcomes are not readily visible [23].

Learning programming requires developing skills such as discipline, critical thinking and problem solving [26]. Such learning takes place when properly organized tasks set in motion various developmental tasks [12]. Advanced tasks could be designed to facilitate critical thinking by rewarding optimal or near optimal solutions as they cause students to reflect on their strategies. Moreover, publishing optimal benchmark figures for different configuration may promote greater interaction about possible strategies thus leading to a form of social constructivism that promotes higher levels of learning [12].

3. DESIGN OF LEARNING TASKS

This section describes the design of learning tasks for an introductory programming course common to a number of disciplines including computer science, software engineering, IT, and games development. Java is used as the vehicle for teaching control structures, algorithms and object oriented programming. Assessments include class tests (20%), two assignments (40%) and a final exam. Section 3.1 presents some of the challenges we

face when setting assignments and how we address them. Section 3.2 presents a brief overview of our robot tool. Sections 3.3 to 3.6 present the design of assignment tasks in greater details.

3.1 Flexible Assessment Structure

Declining enter-scores for IT and computer science (CS) make it necessary to cater for a wide range of student abilities. Early programming courses often cater to students from non-CS disciplines some of whom may lack any motivation to learn programming. For our mixed cohort, the average mark in the first class test was 5.96 out of 10, with a standard deviation of 2.31. Such diversity makes it necessary to structure our first assignment covering data-types, variables, operators, control structures, arrays and algorithms. Our overall design strategy had been to start with simple concrete tasks requiring little reasoning before advancing to tasks demanding more cognitive skills, as shown in Table 1.

Table 1. Flexible Assignment Tasks and Marking Criteria

Task	Required Competency	Marks
Initial	Variables, Constant loops	Up to 2 marks
Intermediate	Variable loops and Nested loops, Arrays, Simple Algorithms	Up to 5 marks
Advanced 1	Manipulating Arrays, More complex algorithms	Up to 8 marks
Advanced 2	Efficient Algorithms using control structures and arrays	Up to 10 marks

Though the tasks T1...T4 are made progressively more difficult students are free to choose any of the 8 different pathways (T1,T2,T3, T4), (T1,T3,T4) , (T2,T3,T4), ... (T4). A student who starts with a higher level task but unable to make progress is also free to move to a less abstract task. Such an approach allows students the flexibility to choose pathways that best suit them.

3.2 Our Robot Tool

Our tool uses a robot based scenario, as a familiar metaphor is known to lower the cognitive load [20, 24]. Moreover, robot tasks can be easily varied from year to year. The scenario is made up of a 3-armed robot, a stack of blocks and a set of bars forming obstacles as shown in Figure 1. The robot methods provided the means to develop and measure the learning outcomes desired: the first arm up() and down(); the second horizontal arm extend() and contract(); the third arm lower(), raise(), pick() and drop(). Figure-1 shows a snapshot of our 3-armed robot while attempting to move 6 blocks of varying heights (colour coded yellow for odd heights and red for even) over obstacle bars (colour coded black) also of variable heights. The robot arms are currently of size 10, 8 and 0, and are colour-coded pink. Note the target destination of a block is determined based on whether the block size is odd or even.

The initial configuration can be varied by specifying the number and heights of bars and blocks respectively, in the command line. For example, inputting *672183 231212* in the command line creates the initial configuration shown in Figure 1. These values are then passed as arrays to the *control* method of the *RobotControl* class, which students are required to complete. The robot tool also displays specific diagnostic messages when students test their code, as they help sustain interest of novice programmers [20]. Explicit messages specify the method causing the error such as "Error in call to pick()" and the cause such as "can pick only from the top of column 10" as shown Figure 2.

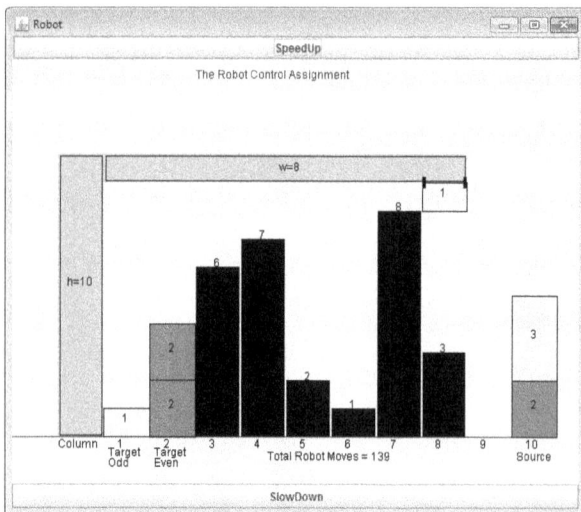

Figure 1: Scenario consisting of a 3-armed robot with Bar Heights (6,7,2,1,8,3) Block Heights (2,3,1,2,1,2)

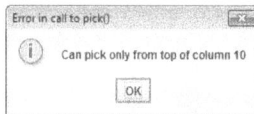

Figure 2: An explicit diagnostic message

3.3   Initial Task: Mental Model for Loops

The initial task avoids any complex expressions involving logical and relational operators, which have contributed to loop learning difficulties [21]. The task also explicitly specifies any repetitive code should be replaced before final demonstration. Figure 3 presents the result of running the program with no command line arguments, where the default values are set to 666666 and 222, resulting in 6 bars all of height 6 and 3 blocks all of height 2. Fixed bar and block heights eliminate the need to access any array elements. Moving a single block requires exercising all three arms of the robot. Though initially a student may call a robot method repetitively, they soon learn to use simple fixed size loops aided by visual feedback and diagnostic messages [13].

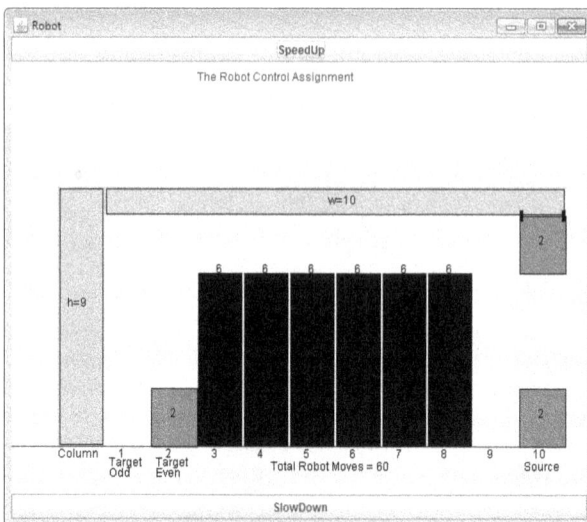

Figure 3: Initial Task: Fixed Bar (6) and Blocks Heights (2)

This task also fosters a problem solving mindset as the main task naturally decomposes into subtasks of moving one block at a time.

Visualization aids a divide-and-conquer strategy by allowing partial solutions to be tested. Successful partial completion in turn provided the necessary stimulus to complete all remaining tasks. Tutors reported 98% of students successfully complete this task in their first lab session itself using loops. Code size varied between 20 – 80 lines with shorter versions using nested loops.

3.4   Intermediate Task: Array Mental Model

Visually depicting array elements was shown to be effective in correcting invalid mental models, common among novice programmers [14, 5]. The intermediate task therefore introduces a visual scenario which facilitates creation of mental models for arrays and variable sized loops by allowing the heights of bars to be specified in the command line. The scenario in Figure 4 shows the results of specifying *687234*. Input values stored in the array *barHeights* are depicted as a series of bars, creating a mental model of an array as a construct for storing one or more values. This task ensures a valid solution is possible only after students become competent in the use of arrays and variable loops.

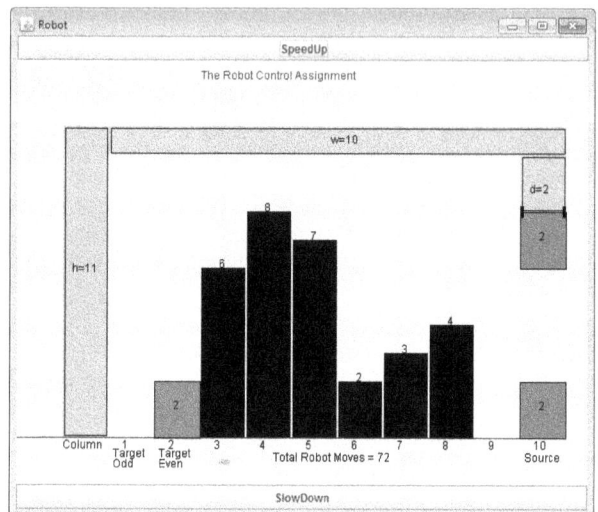

Figure 4:   Intermediate Task – Variable Bar Heights (6,8,7,2,3,4) but Fixed Block Heights (2)

This task of moving the blocks over variable sized bars requires students to modify the constant loops used in the initial task. For example, moving the current block in Figure 4, requires the height of arm 2 to be raised to at least 11, to avoid any collision. The students are thus led to extend their mental model of fixed sized loops to one that allow variable number of iterations. At this point students are presented with two problems, first to access the variable bar heights and second to compute the tallest bar. The first problem leads them to access the elements of the array *barHeights,* passed as an argument. The second problem leads them to write an algorithm to find the maximum value stored in that array. Initial attempts often lead to collisions with abnormal program termination. Diagnostic messages highlight the need to move from concrete solutions to more abstract strategies. Student results show this task involving arrays and variable loops was completed successfully by 95% of students.

3.5   Advanced Task 1: Problem Solving

Problem solving skills require much more than having a valid mental model of basic constructs [16]. Imparting such generic problem solving skills requires a more constructivist project oriented model where students are required to design and construct artifacts [10]. In this section visualization is used primarily to analyze whether the student artifact is abstract enough to handle different configurations. The desired learning outcome was therefore measured based on the percentage of students with such valid abstract algorithms.

The more complex and varied task in this section is a natural progression from the previous one. It allows both bar and block heights to be input. Figure 1 shows the results of typing *672183 2311* in the command line. The varying configurations make students realize the need for abstract strategies using additional variables such as *clearance, sourceHeight, targetHeight*, etc. This additional requirement also necessitates substantial changes. Firstly, the target column for the current block should be determined dynamically based on its size. The extent of robot moves had to be expressed in terms of variables representing current heights of source, target and current blocks.

Though the advanced task requires much more abstract reasoning, visualization helps students understand why a particular student strategy may not work for a specific configuration. For example, a strategy which works when the tallest bar is higher than the sum of all source blocks may not work when the reverse is true. This approach also allows students to develop increasingly complex algorithms incrementally by relaxing some of the requirements. Input values may be restricted initially to bars and blocks of the same height. Such an incremental strategy combined with visual feedback of algorithm allows students to progress at different rates. Despite a steep rise in complexity over 95% attempted this advanced task with over 82% getting it completely correct by devising abstract algorithms that work with any valid configuration. However, the time taken to complete the task varied significantly between students, ranging from 2 to 15 hours.

3.6 Advanced Task 2: Algorithm Efficiency

Introducing efficiency criteria in early programming courses develops better awareness of performance issues. Unlike passively comparing existing algorithms, active hands-on involvement helps to enhance critical thinking skills [8]. Novice programmers developing analytical ability can be aided by animation and visualization techniques [1]. This task therefore required students to analyze and optimize their code assisted by the total-moves-counter as shown in Figure 1. Even above average students found it challenging to aim for optimal performance, which often required devising a new strategy. Even though only 25% of students got the optimal solutions for all test cases, nearly 80% of students managed to get near optimal solutions. Moreover, nearly 40% of the discussion board items were related to strategies for better performance and best benchmark figures. Tasks promoting such discussions about optimal strategies helped to introduce algorithm efficiency and analysis in an informal way.

4. LEARNING OUTCOMES EVALUATION

Measuring effectiveness of visual tools require both formative and summative evaluations [18]. We relied on anonymous survey for formative evaluation. For summative evaluation, we compared the exam performance in topics covered by this visual assignment with topics covered by the non-visual assignment.

4.1 Formative Evaluation

The anonymous survey for formative evaluation consisted of 12 statements using Likert scale: Strongly disagree (SD), Disagree (D), Neutral (N), Agree (A) and Strongly agree (SA), students as shown in Table 2. In addition, students were presented with 3 open-ended questions, as shown in Tables 3 - 5. Out of the 47 students in the class, 66% responded by filling the survey.

Table 2. Responses to Formative Evaluation Statements

Statement	SD	D	N	A	SA
I found the visualization of robot based scenario enjoyable.	1	2	5	13	10
Diagnostic error messages helped me correct logical errors.	0	4	4	13	10
It was easy to program the 3-armed robot using move(), extend() etc.	0	2	2	13	14
The scenario made it easy to grasp control structures and arrays.	1	0	3	20	7
The initial task was easy	1	1	2	8	19
The first task provided the impetus and means to learn and test loops.	0	1	5	15	10
The second task provided the impetus and means to learn arrays.	1	1	11	13	5
The advanced part required me to come up with my own strategy.	1	0	3	11	16
I was able to improve my code after visualizing the robot moves.	0	3	3	14	11
I found the efficiency requirements for minimum-moves challenging.	1	1	5	16	8
Current number of moves helped to improve the algorithm efficiency	0	3	3	15	10
Incrementally complex visual tasks can assist in learning introductory programming and problem solving.	0	1	6	14	10

Majority of the students doing the survey found incremental visual constructivist approach beneficial for learning. The assignment also appears to be effective in challenging students through advanced tasks while making the initial tasks easy. Relatively poor response to question 7, however, suggests the second task did not provide adequate practice for arrays or that the metaphor used for arrays is not effective.

Table 3. Feedback on Assignment Learning Experience

> *"It was an enjoyable assignment and motivated me to find the best/most optimal solution."*
>
> *"I found the arrays storing the block sizes a bit confusing at first as I didn't know how to access them"*
>
> *"I found it rewarding going through each increment. Once I finished each part I felt a great sense of pride."*
>
> *"I liked visual feedback divided into more difficult parts."*
>
> *"Excellent assignment, helped me to understand importance of loops and not repeating code."*
>
> *"Good introduction to loops and arrays, it also provided useful visual feedback while learning to problem solve"*
>
> *"I liked the instant feedback through visual means."*
>
> *"I attempted the last part directly; I liked the flexibility."*
>
> *"It made me to keep working at it."*
>
> *"The robot provided good feedback when something was wrong. Visualization made it easier to reason and optimize."*

Table 4. What did you like about the Robot Assignment?

"It's great to see visual results for our own coding"
"The robot provided good error messages when something wrong was attempted.".
"The visuals really helped"
"Easy, fun, to understand if/else, array and stuff"
"The GUI , the logic behind it and trying to make it work"
"Helped me visualize my own code"
"Tests understanding of loops and arrays"
"Interesting you can have visual feedback on the code"
"Getting instant feedback through visual means"
"It was challenging but not completely impossible"

Table 5. What are the things that can be Improved?

"Perhaps naming conventions, the similarity 'blocks' and 'bars' may be confusing to some"
"I had trouble with arrays initially"
"More emphasis on arrays would be good"

The written feedback was very positive overall and our diverse groups of students appear to have benefitted from different aspects; above average students liked the flexibility to bypass simpler tasks and the way visualization aids with optimization, while others benefitted from greater engagement through visual tasks and the sense of achievement from completing individual tasks. Such tasks also appear to impact pass rates; over 95% of the students passed the visual assignment as opposed to only 72% for the subsequent non-visual assignment. However, the improved results cannot be attributed to the type of assignment alone as the second assignment covered more abstract concepts. It is therefore necessary to design and test whether incremental visual constructivist tasks covering more abstract concepts also significantly improve student engagement and performance.

4.2 Summative Evaluation

For summative evaluation we used objective questions based on Bloom's taxonomy, which defines six learning levels including knowledge, comprehension, application, analysis, synthesis and evaluation. Questions were limited to first four levels as questions at synthesis and evaluation levels are difficult to set. For application level, we used the selecting-the-missing-code type, similar to the skeleton-code questions [27]. Our analysis level questions required students to analyze a given piece of code. We evaluated student performances in five questions each, from topics covered in first (visual) and second (non-visual) assignments. The non-visual assignment required students to demonstrate competency in classes, inheritance, polymorphism, exceptions and files using a simple text based car-rental system.

For evaluation, we used an approach similar to earlier work [18], where the effects on mental models of novice programmers were measured separately for above average and normal students. The Table 6 shows the average marks of students for these groups.

Table 6. Average marks for Topics Covered by Visual and Non-Visual Assignments

Criteria	Student Nos.	Non-Visual Assign.	Visual Assign.	% Improve
marks >= 80	16	4.38	4.44	1.4%
marks <80	31	2.26	2.77	22.6%

For students scoring 80 and more in the final exam, there is no significant difference in performance in questions related to visual and non-visual assignments either in absolute or percentage terms. However, for average and below average students a noticeable improvement can be seen in questions related to the visual constructivist assignment. These differences however, may not be solely due to the type of assignment as there are a number of other factors which must be considered. Firstly, the questions related to second assignment are generally more abstract and therefore only students with better cognitive abilities perform better. Secondly, average students who generally need longer period to grasp new concepts may perform better in concepts taught earlier in the course. More work need to carried-out to determine how these different factors influence the final exam results.

5. DISCUSSION AND FUTURE WORK

The proposed approach uses a visual scenario with multiple objects to provide an environment for incremental constructivist tasks. The proposed methodology differs from tools such as Alice in that it allows state of objects to be captured, thus allowing development of complex algorithms incorporating state variables. Each individual object is chosen as a metaphor for teaching a particular concept; robot to allow loops and nested loops, bars and blocks to depict the array values, and target columns to exercise selection based on current block size. Together, these objects visually animate the algorithm devised by the student. The initial simple configuration can be made incrementally more complex by passing initial values for various objects. This approach can also be extended to teach other more abstract concepts such as recursion and synchronization. For example, students can be asked to develop recursion based solution for Towers of Hanoi problems. Similarly, multiple collaborating robots running in separate synchronized threads can be made to share the work.

Summative evaluation of student learning outcomes shows incremental visual constructivist tasks can help narrow the learning gap of diverse student cohorts. Student written feedbacks and survey responses also suggest improved performance and engagement can at least be partially be attributed to incremental visual tasks that reflect the expanding mental models. The main benefit of the proposed approach is the number of different pathways it provides. Students are free to choose their own pathways towards the final goal by progressing at their own pace. Students needing more cognitive support can choose pathways with tasks that provide greater level of visual feedback and diagnostic support. Depending on the composition of student cohort the instructor may vary the number and type of incremental tasks. The number of pathways (p) can be expressed as a function of the number incremental tasks (n) as in $p = 2^{(n-1)}$.

Currently our approach limits the order in which concepts can be learnt. For example, before attempting the first task involving selection students must be familiar with repetition and arrays. A more flexible approach would give students the choice to learn basic constructs in isolation and in any order (selection before repletion or vice-versa). This requires learning tasks to be organized using an inverted tree structure resulting in even greater number of learning pathways.

6. CONCLUSION

We have proposed a model that addresses the learning needs of diverse novice programming groups by enabling flexible and incremental visual constructivist pathways. In the initial stage, assignment specifications are decomposed into incremental visual tasks that map to expanding student mental models. The number of pathways in the model is of $O(2^n)$ where n is the number of incremental tasks. The model allows greater guidance and reinforcement in the early stages through increased diagnostic support for low level concrete tasks. Such a flexible approach allows students to choose an appropriate pathway that match their own learning needs. Over 85% of students' surveyed felt the visual robot based scenario made it easy to grasp control structures and arrays. About 80% of students' surveyed also felt incremental visual tasks can assist in learning introductory programming courses. Though initial results are promising more work need to be carried out to verify whether such an approach can help reduce the learning gap in diverse student cohorts.

7. REFERENCES

[1] R. Baecker, *Sorting Out Sorting: A Case Study of Software Visualization for Teaching Computer Science*, MIT Press, 1998.

[2] M. Ben-Ari, *Bricolage forever*, *Eleventh Psychology of Programming Interest Group Workshop*, 1999, pp. 53-57.

[3] M. Ben-Ari, *Constructivism in Computer Science Education*, Journal of Computers in Mathematics and Science Teaching, 20 (2001), pp. 45-73.

[4] J. Bonar and E. Soloway, *Preprogramming knowledge: A major source of misconceptions in novice programmers*, Lawrence Erlbaum Associates, 1989.

[5] N. B. Dale, *Most Difficult Topics in CS1:Results of an Online Survey of Educators*, ACM SIGCSE Bulletin 38 (2006), pp. 49-53.

[6] M. De_Raadt, M. Hamilton, R. Lister, J. Tutty, B. Baker, Q. Cutts, J. Hamer, M. Petre, Simon, I. Box, S. Fincher, P. Haden, A. Robins and K. Sutton, *Approaches to learning in computer programming students and their effect on success.*, *Annual International Conference of the Higher Education Research and Development Society of Australasia*, Sydney, Australia, 2005.

[7] A. Eckerdal, R. Mccartney, J. E. Mostr¨Om, M. Ratcliffe, K. Sanders and C. Zander, *Putting Threshold Concepts into Context in Computer Science Education*, in ACM, ed., *ITiCSE'06*, 2006.

[8] J. Gal-Ezer, T. Vilner and E. Zur, *Teaching Algorithm Efficiency at CS1 Level: A Different Approach*, Computer Science Education, 14 (2004), pp. 235-248.

[9] S. Hansen and E. Eddy, *Engagement and Frustration in Programming Projects*, *38th SIGCSE technical symposium on Computer science education*, ACM, Covington, 2007.

[10] L. Hohmann, M. Guzdial and E. Soloway, *SODA: A computer-aided design environment for the doing and learning of software design*, *Computer Assisted Learning 4th International Conference*, Nova Scotia, Canada, 1992, pp. 307-319.

[11] A. Koohang, L. Riley and T. Smith, *E-Learning and Constructivism: From Theory to Application*, Interdisciplinary Journal of E-Learning and Learning Objects, 5 (2009).

[12] A. Kozulin, B. Gindis, V. S. Ageyev and S. M. Miller, *Vygotsky's Educational Theory In Cultural Context*, Cambridge University Press, 2003.

[13] C. Lewis and G. M. Olson, *Can Principles of Cognition Lower the Barriers to Programming?*, *Empirical Studies of Programmers: Second Workshop*, Ablex, Norwood, NJ, 1987, pp. 248-263.

[14] L. Ma, J. Ferguson, M. Roper and M. Wood, *Investigating and improving the models of programming concepts held by novice programmers* Computer Science Education, 21 (2011), pp. 57-80.

[15] R. E. Mayer, *Different problem-solving competencies established in learning computer programming with and without meaningful models*, Journal of Educational Psychology, 67 (1975), pp. 725-734.

[16] R. E. Mayer, *The psychology of how novices learn computer programming*, ACM Computing Surveys, 3 (1981), pp. 121-141.

[17] M. Mccracken, Y. Kolikant, V. Almstrum, C. Laxer, D. Diaz, L. Thomas, M. Guzdial, I. Utting, D. Hagan and T. Wilusz, *A multi-national, multi-instititional study of assessemnt of programming skills of first-year CS students.*, ACM SIGCSE Bulletin, 33 (2001), pp. 125-140.

[18] T. Naps, G. Rößling, J. Anderson, U. W. Oshkosh, S. Cooper, B. Koldehofe, C. Leska, J. Rantakokko, W. Dann, A. Korhonen, L. Malmi, R. J. Ross, M. Kuittinen and M. Mcnally, *Evaluating the Educational Impact of Visualization* ACM SIGCSE Bulletin 35 (2003), pp. 124-136.

[19] T. L. Naps, Et Al., *Exploring the Role of Visualization and Engagement in Computer Science Education*, ACM SIGCSE Bulletin, 35 (2002), pp. 131-152.

[20] J. F. Pane and B. A. Myers, *Usability Issues in the Design of Novice Programming Systems*, Carnegie Mellon University, 1996.

[21] J. F. Pane, C. A. Ratanamahatana and B. A. Myers, *Studying the Language and Structure in Non-Programmers' Solutions to Programming Problems*, International Journal of Human-Computer Studies, 54 (2001), pp. 237-264.

[22] K. Powers, S. Ecott and L. Hirsgfield, *Through the Looking Glass: Teaching CS0 with Alice*, ACM SIGCSE Bulletin 39 (2007), pp. 2007.

[23] T. Sirkia and J. Sorva, *Exploring Programming Misconceptions An Analysis of Student Mistakes in Visual Program Simulation Exercises*, *12th Koli Calling International Conference on Computing Education Research* ACM, Koli, 2012.

[24] D. C. Smith, A. Cypher and J. Spohrer, *KidSim: Programming Agents Without a Programming Language*, Comm. of the ACM, 37 (1994), pp. 54-67.

[25] J. Sorva, V. Karavirta and L. Malmi, *A Review of Generic Program Visualization Systems for Introductory Programming Education*, ACM Transactions on Computing Education, 13 (2013).

[26] M. Sprankle and J. Hubbard, *Problem Solving & Programming Concepts*, Pearson Education, 2011.

[27] J. L. Whalley, R. Lister and E. Thompson, *An Australasian Study of Reading and Comprehension Skills in Novice Programmers, using Bloom and SOLO Taxonomies*, *ACE2006*, Hobart, 2006.

Perseverance Measures and Attainment in First Year Computing Science Students

Roger McDermott
School of Computing Science and Digital Media
Robert Gordon University
Scotland, U.K.
+44 1224 262717
roger.mcdermott@rgu.ac.uk

Mats Daniels, Åsa Cajander
Department of Information Technology
Uppsala University
Uppsala, Sweden
+46 18 4713160
mats.daniels @it.uu.se
asa.cajander@it.uu.se

ABSTRACT
We investigate the link between concepts of perseverance such as conscientiousness and grit, and the academic attainment of first year computing students. We review the role that perseverance plays in learning models, as well as describing the trait of conscientiousness in the Five Factor Model of personality. We outline research that links this trait with academic success, before focussing on more recent, narrower conceptualisations of perseverance such as academic tenacity and grit. We describe one of the questionnaire tools that have been used to assess the construct of grit. We give details of an investigation that looked for correlations between student responses to Duckworth's Grit Survey, the Big Five Inventory (BFI) Personality Survey and summative attainment scores in a first year programming course. The results suggest a weak but significant correlation between conscientiousness, grit and programming achievement. We discuss these results as well as the limitations of the method used. Finally, we make some observations about the importance of these concepts in Computer Science education and outline further work in this area.

Categories and Subject Descriptors
K.3.2 [**Computers and Education**]: Computer and Information Science Education – *computer science education, information systems information.*

General Terms
Human Factors

Keywords
Perseverance; grit; conscientiousness; personality traits; programming.

1. INTRODUCTION
From any analysis of computer science education it is clear that different people learn things at different rates and that there are

marked differences in academic achievement among learners. This remains true even when situational variables such as age, sex, previous educational experience and social environment are taken into account. That otherwise similar students on similar courses can perform differently suggests that while the teaching and learning environment is undoubtedly important, the characteristics of the individual student and their response to that environment are also significant factors in academic success [1]. It is natural, therefore, to look for predictors of academic achievement and to try to understand their contribution in the educational process. Cognitive factors such as general intelligence, defined as "*the ability to understand complex ideas, to adapt effectively to the environment, to learn from experience, to engage in various form of reasoning, to overcome obstacles by engaging in thought*" [2] have long been seen as one such predictor [3], and measures of intelligence have been found to correlate with both academic and non-academic achievement [2, 4]. Similar results have been found with non-cognitive factors such as motivation, time-management and self-regulation [5 6, 7].

Within the field of computer science education, considerable effort has been expended looking for predictors of academic success in key areas such as programming. Some of these have focussed on aspects of the teaching and learning environment such as curriculum [8] while others have investigated cognitive abilities such as general intelligence [9], logical reasoning ability, previous academic background [10], a deep approach to learning [11] and the ability to articulate strategy [12]. Alongside this, there has also been research into non-cognitive factors which impact on student achievement. Investigations of such influences on motivation have often considered the contribution that a learner's affective reactions have on remaining in education. These studies have frequently used personality traits as significant variables and research suggests that some students may be predisposed to develop and exercise the kind of self-regulatory skills that promote successful academic performance [13]. Among the personality factors that have been studied in this way, those that link to conscientiousness and determination have been reported to provide strong correlation with academic success [19].

We begin this paper by presenting some reasons why we consider the subject of perseverance to be important, both in a general pedagogical sense and specifically for the discipline of computer science. We then give an overview of two distinct lines of educational research that suggest that concept of perseverance is of fundamental importance for successful learning, and consequently, for genuine academic achievement. The first of these concern pedagogical models that draw on the work of John Carroll [14]. We then discuss research on non-cognitive contributions to academic performance often described in terms of personality traits. We describe work done using the conscientiousness factor in the Five Factor model of personality structure as a predictor for academic success. Following this, we focus on a more specific conception of perseverance subsumed in the conscientiousness trait, namely that of academic tenacity [15] or grit [16]. We give some relevant background research in this field and describe the factors that underlie the main tool used in our investigation. We describe an experiment using a group of first year programming students in which data from Duckworth's "Grit Survey" [16] is correlated with data from a "Big Five Inventory" personality questionnaire. We then reflect upon the results of this investigation. Finally, we discuss further research directions that would be relevant to Computer Science Education.

The main contribution of this paper is to initiate a study of the concept of grit in the context of computer science. While computing research linking personality traits, such as conscientiousness, with achievement has been carried out previously, e.g. [17], we believe that this is the first time any investigation has been performed comparing narrower perseverance measures with programming attainment scores in the context of an initial course unit. The results appear to indicate that it would be profitable to carry out further work of this kind.

2. BACKGROUND

As mentioned above, there are a number of different research strands that suggest that the concept of perseverance is particularly significant when considering contributory factors for academic success. Some of these arise from work on the cognitive (and metacognitive) aspects of learning while others emerge from investigation of affective and other non-cognitive elements. In this section, we look at two important constructs that use perseverance as a principal component in their conceptual structure. The first of these is Carroll's Model of School Learning, while the second is the Five Factor Model of Personality that uses conscientiousness as one high-level trait to characterise an individual's patterns of thoughts and behaviours. Since Carroll's model expresses perseverance as a function of time, and the perseverance facet of conscientiousness involves self-regulation of effort over extended periods of time, the concept of "learning time" appears as an important underlying factor in both these models.

2.1 Carroll's Model of Learning

Academic appreciation of the significance, and complex nature, of time, and its importance as a factor in learning, goes back at least as far as John Carroll's 1963 paper "A Model of School Learning" [14]. When considering time in the learning process, it is necessary to mediate between two extreme positions. On the one hand, it is fairly clear that learning takes time and that lack of access to this resource will mean that learning simply does not take place. However, merely increasing the amount of time available to a student to accomplish some activity does not entail that the student will complete the task or indeed will abstract the relevant lessons from the learning activity itself.

Carroll observed that there are two different time variables involved in any learning task: the time spent on the learning activity and the time actually needed to learn the task. He defined the degree of learning or academic achievement to be an increasing function of the ratio of these two times, i.e.

$$\text{degree of learning} = f\left(\frac{\text{time spent learning a task}}{\text{time needed to learn it}}\right)$$

Learning gains therefore emerge through one of two means: increasing the numerator or decreasing the denominator.

Carroll proposed that three factors influence the denominator, i.e. the time needed for learning: student aptitude, the student's ability to understand instruction, and the quality of the instruction. He defined student aptitude as "*the amount of time a student needs to learn a given task, unit of instruction, or curriculum to an acceptable criterion of mastery under optimal conditions of student motivation*" [18], while the ability to understand instruction was defined as the student's ability to figure out independently what the learning task is, and how to go about learning it [14, 18]. The final factor affecting the denominator is the quality of instruction, which Carroll took to depend on both the content of a learning activity and the way it is communicated. The alternative strategy for increasing learning would be to increase the numerator, i.e. the time spent in learning. Carroll suggested that for this to happen, one of two factors would need to be increase: the time allocated for the learning activity, which he termed "opportunity to learn", or the level of student perseverance, which he quantified as the amount of time that the learner is actually engaged in the learning task [18].

Subsequent work has generally tended to focus on characterising the amount of time that the student is actively engaged on the learning activities, i.e. "time on task" or "engaged time". However, as pointed out by Carroll, while it may be possible to measure the various elapsed time intervals, it is impossible to "*meaningfully measure what goes on in the head of the student during that time, or insure in any way that what goes on in the student's head is addressed to learning. All that we can say with some certainty is that any learning that happens to occur does require time*" [18], One consequence of this is that while time on task may be an important variable in learning, it is difficult to measure, especially when trying to differentiate between the time spent engaged in learning and other types of time. One way to mitigate this is to try to increase the perseverance factor since doing this would enhance the quality of the time that is spent on a learning activity by increasing the proportion in which a student is actively engaged with the problem. This then increases the effective time spent on learning.

While Carroll's work has proved very influential as a pedagogical model, for the purposes of this paper, its importance lies in the identification of perseverance as a significant factor in learning. While the focus of later work was on the further refinement of concepts of educational time (e.g. defining *academic learning time*), Carroll's model nevertheless provides a basis from which the concept of perseverance could be further analysed.

2.2 Academic Achievement and Personality Traits

While it is clear that some measure of cognitive ability plays an important role in determining levels of academic achievement, it does not appear to account for the degree of variation that occurs [19] nor does it appear to be a particularly good predictor of success at higher levels of education [20]. Work on other predictors, such as motivational or non-cognitive factors affecting academic performance, have generally focused on attempting to understand which are the personality traits that have a significant contribution to academic success.

One of the most influential current models of personality structure is the Five-Factor model [21]. This model characterises individual behaviours in terms of a "Big Five" set of personality traits that subsume lower level personality attributes. The highest-level personality traits in the five-factor hierarchy are Extraversion, Neuroticism (or, conversely, Emotional Stability), Openness to Experience, Agreeableness and Conscientiousness. These are considered to be more-or-less independent dimensions of personality and individuals can be characterised by their scores in each category. For example, extraversion is characterised by a tendency to engage with the external word and, as such, subsumes lower level personality facets such as friendliness, gregariousness and assertiveness. Individuals high on the neuroticism scale (or conversely, low on an emotional stability scale) tend to strongly experience emotions such as anxiety and vulnerability. Openness to experience is characterised by intellectual curiosity and imagination. Agreeableness reflects tendencies towards sympathy, altruism and helpfulness. High scores on conscientiousness are associated with self-efficacy, organisation, cautiousness, self-discipline and persistence.

There are also developmental generalisations of these models in which personality traits change over time. For example, in the neo-socioanalytic model [22], personality matures with age, reflected in a rise in the levels of agreeableness, conscientiousness, and emotional stability. This maturity arises as individuals reflect upon their identity and engage in a broader range of social roles. These are very interesting extensions of the theory but we do not engage with them in this paper.

While extensive research has been carried out on attempts to link one or more of the five factor traits with academic achievement, only conscientiousness has consistently been associated with academic success [23]. A meta-analysis investigating the five-factor model and academic performance in university education [24] found that performance correlated significantly with the factors of agreeableness, conscientiousness, and openness. In particular, it reported that correlations between conscientiousness and academic performance were largely independent of measures of intelligence. Indeed, after controlling for academic performance at secondary level, conscientiousness added as much to the prediction of academic performance as did intelligence.

Within the academic computing discipline, investigation of the effect of personality traits on performance can be traced back to the work of Kaiser et al [25], who characterised the personality types of software engineers. More recent reviews, such as [26], detail attempts to use personality measures to better predict performance, while other authors found that Openness, Agreeableness, Conscientiousness, and Extraversion were factors affecting leadership abilities [27]. Another recurring context in which personality measures have been used is the effectiveness of pair programming techniques. Salleh [28], for example, lists twelve studies investigating the effect of different personality factors on the success of pair programming.

Despite this, a recent wide-ranging review of thirteen years worth of research into factors affecting university students' GPA [29] found that the importance of conscientiousness was diminished once the concept of "effort regulation" (that is the persistence and effort needed to engage productively with challenging academic situations) was added to the model, although there was a large correlation observed between these two variables. This may suggest that it is not conscientiousness per se that is important but

rather those aspects that promote self-efficacy and self-regulation. This aligns with work done by Paunonen and Ashton [30] which suggests that academic performance can be better predicted by narrower, more specific facets of personality than by the broader personality traits. It seems sensible then to investigate contributions to academic performance from individual components that the Five Factor Model subsumes into the conscientiousness trait. One such component that has recently received prominent attention is what Dweck [15] calls "Academic Tenacity", or what Duckworth [16] terms "Grit".

2.3 Grit, Academic Tenacity and Perseverance

A wide-ranging study by the U.S. Dept of Education, "*Promoting Grit, Tenacity, and Perseverance: Critical Factors for Success in the 21st Century*" [31], details a number of different terms used by various researchers – resilience, conscientiousness, agency – which cover general conceptions of tenacity, perseverance and the ability to keep going in the face of adversity and setbacks. For example, the US National Research Council report, "*Education for Life and Work: Developing Transferable Knowledge and Skills in the 21-st Century*" [32], places the trait of "Conscientiousness" at the heart of their description of intra-personal competency, as a cluster of skills which includes initiative, self-direction, responsibility, perseverance, productivity, grit, forethought, performance, and self-reflection.

Looking at more focussed constructs related to perseverance, Duckworth defines "Grit" as "*the disposition to pursue long-term goals with sustained interest and effort over time*" [16] and considers it to be distinct from other traditionally measured facets of conscientiousness by its emphasis on stamina. In particular, grit entails the capacity to sustain both effort and interest in projects that take months or years to complete. Writing from a perspective of Self-theory [36], Dweck et al [15] use the related term "Academic Tenacity" to denote "*a mindset that looks beyond short-term concerns to longer-term or higher-order goals, and so withstands challenges and setbacks to persevere toward these goals*". Dweck's emphasis on learner mindsets not only brings together aspects of personal epistemology with identity theory, but also considers the skills that are needed to overcome challenges and setbacks. An associated concept is "Academic Perseverance" [37] which refers to a student's tendency to complete learning tasks in a timely and thorough manner despite distractions and, as such, includes elements of delayed gratification and self-control.

Recent research suggests that the concept of grit can be used as a basis for the explanation of educational phenomena such as variation in lifetime educational attainment [19]. More importantly, while it is one facet or component of the Five Factor personality trait of conscientiousness, Duckworth reports that grit better predicts achievement outcomes than the conscientiousness itself [19]. It is reasonable, therefore, to ask if grit predicts academic success in aspects of computing education.

3. METHOD
Our study used data obtained from a group of sixty first year undergraduate students (48 male, 12 female), in the School of Computing Science and Digital Media at Robert Gordon University, UK. The students in the investigation were aged between 17 and 27 with the majority having entered university directly from secondary school. They were registered on three

computing degrees: the largest group was studying Computer Science, with the remainder studying Computing (Graphics and Animation) and Business Information Technology. However, as these students took identical course units in their first year, no differentiation was made between them for the purposes of this study. The students had completed the first of two major sections of their year long programming course unit when the questionnaires were distributed, about three quarters of the way through their first semester of university. The programming class itself contained seventy-six students but data from sixteen of these were disregarded either because they were absent for one or more of the assessed labs (which would skew the attainment mark) or because they did not fill in the questionnaires due to absence.

3.1 The Questionnaires

The students were asked to complete two questionnaires. The first was the 12-item Grit Survey developed by Duckworth et al [19] and the second was the 44-item Big Five Inventory (BFI) [35]. All respondents completed the questionnaires in class time. Data analysis was done using the Minitab 16 statistical package.

The 12-item Grit Survey consists of twelve questions and tracks two factors, consistency of interests and perseverance of effort, both of which are hypothesised to contribute to the psychological construct "grit". Responses are given on a five-point Likert scale ranging from 1 (disagree strongly) to 5 (agree strongly). The "Consistency of Interests" factor was addressed through responses to statements such as "My interests change from year to year" and "I often set a goal but later choose to pursue a different one" whereas the "Perseverance of Effort" factor was tracked by statements such as "I finish whatever I begin", "Setbacks don't discourage me" and "I am diligent". When validating her Grit survey, Duckworth reported high internal consistency scores for both factors ($\square$ = 0.84 and 0.78 resp.) with neither appearing individually to have a greater correlation with academic success. This was consistent with grit being a compound trait comprising perseverance in areas of interest and effort.

The BFI was selected for use in the survey as it was reported to show high convergent validity with similar questionnaires and with peer ratings of the Big Five personality traits. The BFI items were rated on a 5-point Likert scale ranging from 1 (disagree strongly) to 5 (agree strongly) and took the form of responses to the statements starting with "I am someone who...". For example, items related to the Conscientiousness factor were: "does a thorough job", "can be somewhat careless" (reverse coded), "is a reliable worker", "tends to be disorganized" (reverse coded), "tends to be lazy" (reverse coded), "perseveres until the task is finished", "does things efficiently", "is easily distracted" (reverse coded). These reveal the features of "Big Five" conscientiousness as reflecting perseverance, reliability, persistence and orderliness. Factor scores for each of the Big Five traits were calculated for each student. Responses to specific statements were then averaged to calculate scores for each category.

3.2 The Programming Assessment

The students were studying a first semester introductory procedural programming course unit using Javascript as the coding language. The course unit consisted of a nine-week block with six hours class time each week, made up of two one-hour lectures immediately followed by two two-hour labs. The students were not assumed to have any prior knowledge of either the specific language or of programming in general, although there was a range of previous experience within the group and a minority of students had studied some procedural languages at secondary school. Three lab-based programming assessments, each lasting two hours, were administered. These were held in weeks 3, 6 and 9 and completed under exam conditions. The overall assessment mark was calculated as the average of the individual assessment scores. Each exercise was constructed so that the student had to complete a number of individual steps in order to satisfy the assessment marking criteria. For example, one assessment task involved the generation of a password from personal information such as name and date of birth. To complete this task, the student was required to implement a number of transformations using string or array methods.

4. RESULTS

The internal consistency of responses from the group of students (as measured by the Cronbach $\square$ statistic) showed a somewhat lower measure for the two grit factors ($\square$ = 0.70 for Consistency of Interests and 0.73 for Perseverance and Effort) than that reported in the literature. The grit scores themselves ranged from 2.17 to 4.25 with a mean of 3.33 and standard deviation of 0.45. As expected, the grit scores showed a moderate to high correlation with the Conscientiousness factor from the Big Five Inventory with a correlation coefficient $r = 0.59$ and $p < 0.001$.

Factor analysis of the responses to the BFI showed five large eigenvalues for the correlation matrix indicating five factors, with the largest clearly corresponding to the conscientiousness variable. The next two biggest factors were distinguishable as extraversion and agreeableness. Internal consistency for the five factors was good, with $\square$ ranging from 0.88 down to 0.75.

The programming scores ranged from 22% to 88% with a mean of 66% and a standard deviation of 15.4. Analysis of the grit score with the programming mark showed a weak correlation with $r = 0.24$ and $p = 0.02$. The strength of this correlation is, for example, comparable to that found in Duckworth's study of undergraduate psychology majors at University of Pennsylvania [16, Study 3] in which the grit score was correlated with GPAs with $r = 0.25$ and $p < 0.01$. Correlations were also calculated for each of the Big Five personality traits and the programming score. These were not statistically significant ($p > 0.7$) for both agreeableness and openness, while low negative correlations without statistical significance ($r = -0.16$, $p = 0.2$) existed for extraversion and neuroticism. Interestingly, the score for the conscientiousness trait ($r = 0.30$, $p = 0.01$) actually had a higher correlation with the programming scores than the grit scores.

5. DISCUSSION

These results seem to suggest that there is a weak but statistically significant correlation between the concept of grit, as measured by the 12-item Duckworth Grit survey, and academic attainment in the initial programming class. This generally aligns with the experience that programming is hard and that progress can be slow, requiring perseverance and, in Dweck's terminology [36], a "growth mindset" in which failure is seen as providing an opportunity for further learning rather than an indication of lack of ability [37].

While it was expected, given the close relationship between conscientiousness and grit, that there would be a statistically significant correlation between both the conscientiousness trait and academic success, and the grit scores and academic success, it was not expected that the conscientiousness correlation would be higher than that of grit. While our result may be an artefact of the current experimental set up, it might also suggest that those aspects of conscientiousness which were abstracted out of the big five personality trait to form the grit construct actually play a more important role in specific context of programming than were hitherto thought.

The validity of the results reported here can be challenged on a number of grounds. Although the sample size (N = 60) is relatively small and the correlations themselves are low, the results are nevertheless comparable with those found in in more extensive studies on the subject. However, in order to calculate an attainment mark, students needed to be present for all sub-components of the assessment, since a non-submission in one of these would skew the overall mark considerably. In addition, the respondents had to be present on the day that the questionnaires were handed out. Only that subset of the entire cohort of students that satisfied these criteria was admitted for data analysis. This meant that sixteen students in the cohort, who, for whatever reason, missed one of the assessments were not included in the study. The use of a summative attainment score to measure programming achievement also meant that students who took part in the investigation had to have persisted at least to the end of the course unit which introduces a systematic bias into the data that was not quantified in this study.

A greater concern is the question of whether the surveys do in fact succeed in measuring the concepts on which they are based. In the case of the 12-item Grit survey, the overall score relies on responses to statements such as "I am a hard worker". There are certainly questions of reliability here. Students are not immune from cultural norms that tend to stress hard work as a virtue, and as a result, their responses (though perhaps not their actual behaviour) may be conditioned by societal expectations. Duckworth [38] also acknowledges that respondents may answer positively to some items in anticipation of future success and suggested that longitudinal studies of both a quantitative and qualitative nature would be required to mitigate this phenomenon. Conversely, an additional confounding factor may be the predominance of males (80%) in the assessed group. There is anecdotal evidence that, in some programming classes, there exists a subculture of the (generally male) "hero programmer" in which programming ability is believed to be innate and in which it is deemed inappropriate to acknowledge more than minimal effort in such tasks. While no measures of the personal epistemology of individuals in the group were taken alongside the Grit survey, it is interesting to note that there were four examples where the grit score was in the lower quartile and the attainment mark was in the upper quartile. All of these students were male.

A further objection to the Grit survey may be the lack of specificity of some of the statements used. One example (which is also found in the BFI) is the item "My interests change from year to year". It could certainly be argued that this statement is indeterminate as it is almost certain that some interests will indeed change over time while others remain the same. There would clearly then be some subjective judgement needed about the relative importance of the interests that remained unchanged which may not relate in a meaningful way to the "perseverance in interests" component of the grit score.

6. CONCLUSION

As, we hope, is evident from our discussion of the validity of this study, we do not consider that the results of this present work conclusively establish a correlation (still less a causal link) between concepts of conscientiousness, grit and perseverance, and that of achievement, in an initial programming course. We do, however, believe that the results suggest that further study should be carried out in this area. Such investigation would complement the significant amount of research that continues to be done seeking predictors of academic success in computing courses, especially programing course units [11, 12]. These often focus on either cognitive elements of learning or features of the learning environment rather than the non-cognitive aspects discussed here.

We would also argue that the concept of time is an important factor in learning that deserves greater consideration, although we have not made any attempt to capture this aspect in this initial study. Further work would also benefit from trying to understand how these students actually spend their time. This might shed light on some of the low-grit, high attainment behaviour found in our study. There are, however, issues with trying to measure learning time and to do this, it would be necessary to construct questionnaires that are tailored more to the specific computing context, e.g. programming in this case. Much of our previous work has been on upper level students working in open-ended educational settings ([39] and refs therein) some of which have applied similar data analysis to issues such as personal epistemology [40]. Consideration of the current topic, together with previous work strongly suggests that students may have different levels of perseverance for open-ended problems than for problems in more structured contexts. In our experience, we would say that perseverance is even more necessary in an open-ended problem setting than when dealing with more convergent problems, and as such, would give a stronger prediction of how well a student performs. Further investigation of this context would be useful.

In this current study, no differentiation was made between students registered on different degree courses. It would be interesting to investigate if significant differences characterise the responses from the three different degrees. Other issues, such as identity and gender could also be addressed, although this would require data collection that was more targeted towards computing. Finally, we point out that this work, and similar research, has a clear bearing on the issue of study techniques.

7. REFERENCES

[1]   Hook, J. and Eckerdal, A. 2015. An Analysis of Student Performance Factors. To Appear in the Proc. 2015 Learning and Teaching in Comp. & Eng. Conference, Taipei, Taiwan

[2]   Neisser, U., Boodoo, G., Bouchard Jr, T. J., Boykin, A. W., Brody, N., Ceci, S. J., & Urbina, S. 1996. Intelligence: knowns and unknowns. *American Psychologist*, *51* (2), 77.

[3]   Harris, D. 1940. Factors affecting college grades: a review of the literature, 1930-1937. *Psychological Bulletin*, *37*(3), 125.

[4]   Ackerman, P. L., & Heggestad, E. D. 1997. Intelligence, personality, and interests: evidence for overlapping traits. *Psychological Bulletin*, *121* (2), 219.

[5]   Pintrich, P. R., & Schunk, D. H. 1996. *Motivation in education: Theory, research, and applications*. Englewood.

[6]   Busato, V. V., Prins, F. J., Elshout, J. J., & Hamaker, C. 2000. Intellectual ability, learning style, personality, achievement motivation and academic success of psychology students in higher education. *Personality and Individual differences*, *29* (6), 1057-1068.

[7] Heckman, J., and Rubinstein Y. 2001. The importance of noncognitive skills: Lessons from the GED testing program. *American Economic Review* 2001: 145-149.

[8] Gluga, R., Kay, J., Lister, R., & Kleitman, S. 2013. Mastering cognitive development theory in computer science education. *Computer Science Education*, *23* (1), 24-57.

[9] Mayer, R.E., Dyck, J.L., & Vilberg, W. 1989. Learning to program and learning to think: what's the connection? In Soloway, E., & Sphorer, J.C. (Eds.), Studying the Novice Programmer. Hillsdale, New Jersey: Lawrence Erlbaum.

[10] Boyle, R., Carter, J., & Clark, M. 2002. What Makes Them Succeed? Entry, progression and graduation in Computer Science. Journal of Further and Higher Education, 26(1):

[11] Simon, Fincher, S., Robins, A., Baker, B., Box, I., Cutts, Q., De Raadt, M., & Tutty, J. 2006. Predictors of success in a first programming course. In *Proceedings of the 8th Australasian Conference on Computing Education-Volume 52* (pp. 189-196). Australian Computer Society, Inc.

[12] Simon, Cutts, Q., Fincher, S., Haden, P., Robins, A., Sutton, K., Baker, B., & Tutty, J. 2006. The ability to articulate strategy as a predictor of programming skill. In *Proceedings of the 8th Australasian Conference on Computing Education-Volume 52* (pp. 181-188). Australian Computer Society, Inc.

[13] Chamorro-Premuzic, T., & Furnham, A. 2003. Personality predicts academic performance: Evidence from two longitudinal university samples. *Journal of Research in Personality*, *37* (4), 319-338.

[14] Carroll, J. 1963. A model of school learning. *The Teachers College Record*, *64* (8), 723-723.

[15] Dweck, C., Walton, G. M., & Cohen, G. L. 2011. *Academic tenacity: Mindsets and skills that promote log-term learning.* Paper presented at the Gates Foundation, Seattle, WA.

[16] Duckworth, A. L., Peterson, C., Matthews, M. D., & Kelly, D. R. 2007. Grit: perseverance and passion for long-term goals. *Journal of personality and social psychology*, *92*(6).

[17] Salleh, N., Mendes, E., and Grundy, J. 2012. Investigating the effects of personality traits on pair programming in a higher education setting through a family of experiments, Empirical Software Engineering. ☐

[18] Carroll, J. B. 1989. The Carroll model a 25-year retrospective and prospective view. *Educational Researcher*, *18* (1), 26-31.

[19] Chamorro-Premuzic, T., & Furnham, A. 2008. Personality, intelligence and approaches to learning as predictors of academic performance. *Personality and individual differences*, *44* (7), 1596-1603.

[20] Furnham, A., Chamorro-Premuzic, T., & McDougall, F. 2002. Personality, cognitive ability, and beliefs about intelligence as predictors of academic performance. *Learning and Individual Differences*, *14* (1), 47-64.

[21] McCrae, R. R., & Costa Jr, P. T. 1997. Personality trait structure as a human universal. *American Psychologist*, *52* (5), 509.

[22] Roberts, B. W. & Wood, D. 2006. Personality development in context of the neo-socioanalytic model of personality.

[23] Noftle, E. E., & Robins, R. W. 2007. Personality predictors of academic outcomes: big five correlates of GPA and SAT scores. *Journal of personality and social psychology*, *93*(1)

[24] Poropat, A.E. 2009. A meta-analysis of the five-factor model of personality and academic performance. *Psychological bulletin*, *135* (2), 322.

[25] Kaiser, K. M., and Bostrom, R. P. 1982. Personality Characteristics of MIS Project Teams: An Empirical Study and Action-Research Design," MIS Quarterly (6:4) 1982, 43

[26] Cruz, S. S. J. O., Silva, F. Q. B., Monteiro, C. V. F., Santos, P., and Rossilei, I. 2011. Personality in Software Engineering: preliminary findings from a systematic literature review, Conference on Evaluation & Assessment in Software Engineering, Durham, 2011. 1-10. ☐

[27] Aronson, Z. H., Reilly, R. R., and Lynn, G. S. 2006. The impact of leader personality on new product development teamwork and performance: The moderating role of uncertainty, J. of Eng. and Tech. Man. (23:3), 221-247. ☐

[28] Salleh, N., Mendes, E., Grundy, J., and Burch, G. S. J. 2010. An empirical study of the effects of conscientiousness in pair programming using the five-factor personality model," International Conference on Software Engineering, ACM Press, Cape Town, 2010, 577-577. ☐

[29] Richardson, M., Abraham, C., & Bond, R. 2012. Psychological correlates of university students' academic performance: a systematic review and meta-analysis. *Psychological bulletin*, *138* (2), 353.

[30] Paunonen, S. V., & Ashton, M. C. 2001. Big five factors and facets and the prediction of behavior. *Journal of personality and social psychology*, *81* (3), 524.

[31] Shechtman, N., DeBarger, A., Dornsife, C., Rosier, S., & Yarnall, L. 2013. Promoting grit, tenacity, and perseverance: Critical factors for success in the 21st century. *Washington, DC: US Dept of Education, Dept of Educational Technology*.

[32] Pellegrino, J. W., & Hilton, M. L. (Eds.). 2013. Education for life and work: Developing transferable knowledge and skills in the 21st century. National Academies Press.

[33] Dweck, C. S. 2000. Self-theories: Their role in motivation, personality, and development. Psychology Press.

[34] Farrington, C. A., Roderick, M., Allensworth, E., Nagaoka, J., Keyes, T. S., Johnson, D. W., and Beechum, N. O. 2012. Teaching adolescents to become learners. The role of noncognitive factors in shaping school performance: A critical literature review. Chicago, IL.

[35] John, O. P., & Srivastava, S. 1999. The Big Five trait taxonomy: History, measurement, and theoretical perspectives. *Handbook of personality: Theory and research*, *2* (1999), 102-138.

[36] Dweck, C. 2012. Mindset: how you can fulfil your potential. Robinson; 10th Edition. New York.

[37] Cutts, Q., Cutts, E., Draper, S., O'Donnell, P., & Saffrey, P. 2010. Manipulating mindset to positively influence introductory programming performance. In *Proc. 41st ACM symposium on Computer science education*. 431-435. ACM.

[38] Duckworth, A. L., & Quinn, P. D. 2009. Development and validation of the Short Grit Scale (GRIT–S). *Journal of personality assessment*, *91* (2), 166-174.

[39] M. Daniels, Å. Cajander, A. Pears, and T. Clear, Engineering Education Research in Practice: Evolving Use of Open Ended Group Projects as a Pedagogical Strategy for Developing Skills in Global Collaboration, *Int. Journal of Engineering Education*, **26**, 2010, pp. 795-806.

[40] McDermott, R., Pirie, I., Cajander, Å., Daniels, M., and Laxer, C. 2013. Investigation into the personal epistemology of computer science students. In *Proc. of the 18th ACM conf. on Innovation and technology in computer science education* (pp231-236). ACM

Initiatives to Increase Engagement in First-Year ICT

Matthew Butler
Faculty of Information Technology
Monash University
Caulfield East, VIC, Australia
matthew.butler@monash.edu

Michael Morgan
Faculty of Information Technology
Monash University
Caulfield East, VIC, Australia
michael.morgan@monash.edu

Judy Sheard
Faculty of Information Technology
Monash University
Caulfield East, VIC, Australia
judy.sheard@monash.edu

Simon
School of Design, Communication,
and Information Technology
University of Newcastle
Ourimbah, NSW, Australia
simon@newcastle.edu.au

Katrina Falkner
School of Computer Science
University of Adelaide
Adelaide, Australia 5005
katrina.falkner@adelaide.edu.au

Amali Weerasinghe
School of Computer Science
University of Adelaide
Adelaide, Australia 5005
amali.weerasinghe@adelaide.edu.au

ABSTRACT

There is widespread concern about lack of student engagement in Information and Communication Technology (ICT) courses and the influence of this on learning outcomes, retention, and the student experience overall. Lack of engagement is particularly concerning for first-year students, who are developing their study behaviours for the remainder of their degree programs. This study seeks to report on the myriad of current initiatives in Australian universities to increase ICT student engagement. This is explored for both in-class teaching innovations and the support structures with which students interface academically and administratively. The study draws upon data collected from interviews of 30 academics involved with the design and delivery of the first-year learning experience of ICT students in 25 Australian universities. Analysis of this data has provided a comprehensive overview of current initiatives to address student engagement. These covered a range of academic and non-academic aspects of the student experience. Our findings highlight the unique challenges that our first-year ICT students face and we recommend areas for further investigation.

Categories and Subject Descriptors

K.3.2 [**Computer Science Education**]: Computer and Information Science Education

Keywords

Student engagement; CS

1. INTRODUCTION

The university education landscape is constantly changing, and the past few years have seen a particularly dramatic transformation. Arguably the most noticeable change has been the ways in which students *engage* with their learning. Attendance on campus has fallen. Students are under more pressure to manage competing demands for time, such as work and family commitments. With increased amounts of content placed online, some of which was formerly available only in class (e.g. lecture presentations), the need for students to attend face-to-face classes is diminishing [15]. The use of online learning activities has become extensive and many students use these as a substitute for attending class. The maturation of online learning technologies and ready access to instructor-, community- and peer-developed content have changed the nature of student engagement with the on- and off-campus learning experiences.

Student engagement is defined by Coates [3] as "students' involvement with activities and conditions likely to generate high-quality learning" (p.3). Student engagement relates to many aspects of the student experience within the educational environment and is generally considered to be a multidimensional phenomenon. A number of different constructs have been proposed to define student engagement. Fredricks, Blumfield and Paris [5] conceptualise student engagement with three dimensions: *behavioural* – willingness to participate in academic, social, and extracurricular activities; *cognitive* – investment in effort to learn and master new skills and complex ideas; and *affective* – feelings towards and reactions to teachers, classmates and the educational environment. Coates [2] describes student engagement as a broad construct encompassing five aspects of student academic and non-academic experiences: *active and collaborative learning*; *participation in challenging academic activities*; *formative communication with academic staff*; *involvement in enriching educational experiences*; *feeling legitimated and supported by university learning communities*. These definitions substantially overlap. Both are widely used, providing useful frameworks for investigating student engagement and the basis for instruments to measure student engagement [3,7].

Student engagement is frequently discussed within the ICT academic community. Engaging students in their learning is considered vital for successful learning outcomes and a satisfying learning experience. This is particularly important for first-year students, who are developing their learning behaviours for the remainder of their degree programs. As Kuh [7] proposes, "engagement helps to develop habits of the mind and heart that enlarge their capacity for continuous learning and personal development" (p.5). There is considerable research highlighting

ITiCSE'15, July 04 – 08, 2015, Vilnius, Lithuania.
Copyright 2015 ACM 978-1-4503-3440-2/15/07...$15.00.
http://dx.doi.org/10.1145/2729094.2742629

concerns and discussing techniques and technologies to address student engagement in ICT courses. However, this has given rise to a number of disparate stories of attempts to tackle these issues, with little done to present the work, both published and unpublished, as a cohesive collection. This paper presents a survey of many unpublished initiatives being conducted across Australia, collected through interviews with key ICT academic staff from 25 Australian universities. Using Coates' five aspects [2], the paper identifies current efforts to address student engagement and areas requiring further research.

2. MOTIVATIONS FOR IMPROVING STUDENT ENGAGEMENT

There are a number of imperatives for seeking to improve first-year student engagement within university ICT study. These relate broadly to issues of poor learning outcomes, high attrition rates, and low levels of student satisfaction with ICT courses. Zepke, Butler and Leach [22] argue that student engagement provides useful indicators of quality in higher education.

A key motivation for improving student engagement in ICT courses relates to learning outcomes. Decades of academic literature have reported the inherent difficulties that students face with many aspects of ICT education. The learning of introductory programming has been acknowledged as especially difficult [1]. While a great deal of research has been undertaken to improve learning outcomes in this area, failure rates are still acknowledged as high [17, 20]. A related concern is the issue of high attrition rates among ICT students [21], particularly female students [14]. A large study (n=6,193) by Kuh et al [8] concluded that "student engagement in educationally purposeful activities is positively related to academic outcomes as represented by first-year student grades and by persistence between first and second year of college" (p.555).

A number of key student experience surveys worldwide indicate low levels of student satisfaction with the current manner in which ICT education is delivered. Results obtained in the US National Survey of Student Engagement (NSSE) point to issues within ICT education [12]. All but one of the ten areas rated in the survey scored lower in ICT than the overall average, with the final area scoring just on the average. The lowest scores were for the areas of Reflective and Integrative Learning, Learning Strategy, and Effective Teaching Practice.

In Australia, the University Experience Survey (UES) [6, 19] is administered regularly at all universities across the country and the results reported on the MyUniversity website [11]. Survey results in the area of Computing and Information Systems show that ICT students consistently rate their experiences with Skills Development and Teaching Quality significantly lower than other disciplines [6].

While there can be debate as to the meaning of such results, at the very least they give indications that there are issues relating to the student educational experience that require deeper examination. Given that UES results are made publicly available, there is a self-interest argument for the need to find ways to improve public perception of ICT study programs.

Concerns about poor learning outcomes, retention and student satisfaction have provided impetus for academics and universities to explore ways to improve their students' engagement. Zepke [23] proposes that student engagement is "a partnership to which learners, teachers and institutions contribute to achieve quality learning" (p.4). Therefore academics should endeavour to provide curriculum, activities and resources that actively involve students in their learning, and institutions should provide resources and programs to encourage students to participate in university life.

There are a number of reports of successful efforts to increase student engagement in first-year of ICT courses. These broadly cover the five aspects of student engagement described by Coates [2]. As an example of active and collaborative learning, Simon et al [17] report on an application of peer instruction using clicker technology in an introductory programming class. Providing an example of a challenging learning activity, Lee, Ko and Kwan [10] embedded assessment into an educational computer game designed to teach programming. In another example, Kurkovsky [9] used mobile game development to motivate and enthuse students in an introductory programming course. These studies all report success in increasing students' participation in the learning activities. As an example of formative communication with academic staff, Pears [13] reports on the use of portfolio assessment in an introductory programming course for the purpose of implementing a continuous assessment model. Pears found that students who completed the course produced code of a higher quality than typically found in an introductory programming unit. As an example of involvement in enriching educational experiences, Smet et al [18] describe a peer support scheme in which senior students are used as online peer-tutors to facilitate online collaboration and knowledge construction among first-year students. The study concluded that this approach was valuable for supporting students' personal development. Finally, as an example of a supportive learning community, Doerschuk, Liu and Mann [4] describe a transition program targeted at female computing students with the aim of increasing participation and retention. A study tracking student progress across two cohorts identified a significant increase in course completion rate and retention.

Continual improvement is an important facet of university education, and academics typically strive to make an impact on the overall student experience. Unfortunately, many student engagement initiatives go unrecognised or are disseminated only within restricted academic forums. Even for those that are made widely available through key academic publication outlets, little is done to link the key findings to form a more strategic picture of ways to tackle engagement issues. We aim to provide a more complete picture through a comprehensive study of current initiatives being carried out by academics in universities across Australia.

3. METHODOLOGY

In 2014, a national study was conducted that sought to capture the current state of experiences of first-year students in ICT courses [16]. This was undertaken through a systematic review of recent literature, complemented by interviews with key academic staff from universities across Australia. Thirty academics from 25 of the 39 Australian universities were interviewed. The purpose of the interviews was to collect detailed information about teaching practices and factors impacting the first-year experience of ICT students. In order to gather this information the project targeted academic staff directly involved in the design, coordination and delivery of first-year courses, as these participants were likely to provide the required insights into the first-year experience and to be in a position to highlight recent changes and examples of good practice. All interviews were conducted by telephone between February and March 2014. The interviews were recorded and were typically 45-60 minutes in duration.

The interview questions covered areas of teaching and the educational environment we provide for our first-year ICT students: how, where and what we teach, how we strengthen the learning environment, and how we support our students. Analysis of interview data focused on discussions of student engagement using Coates's five aspects of student engagement as a framework. The key interview question relating to this study was: "Do you take any special measures to try to encourage student engagement?" In addition to answering this question, interviewees often mentioned engagement when responding to other questions about their teaching practice. We did not discuss definitions of engagement with the interviewees.

4. TEACHING PRACTICE TO PROMOTE STUDENT ENGAGEMENT

This section reports on the key teaching initiatives being used to promote student engagement, as described by the interviewees, here coded U*x*. These are presented under the five aspects of the student experience identified by Coates [2] to describe student engagement.

4.1 Active and Collaborative Learning

This aspect of student engagement describes teaching strategies that encourage students to actively construct their knowledge by working individually or in collaboration with others.

Much recent effort to increase student engagement has focused on lectures. A current innovation is the "flipped classroom" [17], in which the traditional home and lecture activities are reversed in order to transform classes from vehicles for dissemination of information to active learning experiences. Flipped classrooms often incorporate peer instruction and clicker technologies, with the aim of getting students to actively engage with the fundamental concepts through a process of discussion and responses in conjunction with their peers. In addition, the electronically submitted responses from the clickers enable the lecturer to better judge the current state of understanding of the class. U15b described the use of clicker technology in a flipped classroom for first-year students:

> Clickers ran in three first-year [courses], with both formal and informal evaluations. Attendance saw a significant improvement; [in the course] evaluations, quantitative numbers did not change much … but the qualitative comments were promising. A handful of students did not like it but a number felt it was really of benefit for them.

A number of interviewees indicated that they had implemented components of the flipped classroom model, but some added that it had proved problematic to motivate students to do the required pre-reading, so the approach was discarded.

Role-playing was used by a couple of lecturers to improve engagement in their lectures. U23 explains:

> I do a lot of role play in lectures to try to reinforce some of the concepts. So I have people acting out variables and loops and things like that. It's a bit of a giggle, but students who struggle initially to try to understand what these concepts are, seem to find that really helps.

A number of interviewees discussed teaching approaches that involve students in collaborative or cooperative learning activities. U10 explains:

> 'We do a lot of student contribution work in first-year. … In first-year it is very much based upon peer assessment and peer

review, peers working together in collaboration. So our curriculum was restructured … about 4 years ago now. We completely rebuilt the first-year curriculum around collaborative learning.

The aim here is to recast learning from being an isolated and solitary activity to being an intensely social activity where the student is engaged and motivated by negotiating shared goals, responsibilities, and cooperative tasks involving their peers. The social nature of this learning experience and the intense engagement is intended to reduce the social isolation of students, which has been shown to be one of the significant risk factors for students dropping out of courses. U10 elaborates:

> In the collaborative workshop sessions students do a lot of very active learning, they have little mini-lectures interjected between collaborative learning activities where the students are often asked to build upon each other's work, to share each other's work and do peer review and peer assessment.

Here the aim is to foster a range of skills related to the ability to plan solutions, negotiate roles, and evaluate progress, rather than just to absorb specific information. These social skills are deemed to be important in the context of future employment in the ICT field and tend to produce a more engaging learning experience.

A number of interviewees were using social media as a collaborative learning space. U15b explained how he used different social media forms: "Twitter more for the instant feedback, instant connection. Facebook is more for building a bit of a community". U24 used Skype for external presentations and web-based clicker systems for in-class polling. He found that the use of social networking can increase peer feedback and facilitates the integration of online and on-campus student cohorts.

Another interviewee, U4, found issues in using social media:

> It is pretty much open slather for Facebook in the course, none of the staff are watching that space. It is difficult to encourage students to use it because they think this is just another burden on what they're required to do. But again it's something that we encourage and point out that it's for their benefit because there are theories that if they interact with each other it will enhance learning.

4.2 Challenging Academic Activities

This aspect of student engagement describes activities and assessments that motivate and challenge students to learn.

Interviewees stressed the importance of providing opportunities to do meaningful and motivating work. Authentic project work is used in some courses to promote engagement. As U6 explained: "The students engage in projects that are fascinating and do authentic tasks of real-world challenges and coming up and creating something new. Not just learning by rote." This is demonstrated by U9:

> We have got peer collaboration within classes and some courses use partnership learning. And there is a student focus of what is going to be taught. There is a course in which students undertake an external challenge of a real world scenario for Engineers without borders.

U9 describes an activity she has designed that focuses on students' interests in order to increase engagement:

> Every single week we have two or three 3-minute oral presentations by students on any topic of interest to them. Other students give feedback, because we're scaffolding their learning about how to present at the end of the semester. And

that's great fun. .... They don't get marked on it; it's formative.

A number of interviewees had designed assessment strategies to address lack of student engagement. U7a explains:

> I have implemented some rules for encouraging student engagement. For example, the tutorial attendance must be no lower than 85% ... students' tutorial attendance is marked and also we have some in-class quizzes.

U20 describes how assessment of study skills is built into the early assessments of the first-year at their university for the purpose of early identification of engagement problems:

> All courses have early assessment tasks ... particularly in the first first-year course, they're the type of thing that will ease people in. We'll graduate the complexity and the way that the early assessments are structured so that the early ones are fairly easy but illustrate the sorts of work practices that they should be doing.

4.3 Communication with Academic Staff

This aspect of student engagement is concerned with the level and nature of students' contact with staff. Several interviewees stressed the importance of assigning first-year courses to teachers who were able to provide a high-quality learning experience. U5 commented: "Concerted effort to ensure that the best staff are allocated to first-year courses, [staff] who have had the best feedback over a number of years." According to U7b:

> We're actually really trying to keep the kids interested and in some instances that is a younger person. ... We have definitely got great engagement, or better engagement. The staff themselves have noticed a great change in the students, particularly at the smaller campuses. They are really starting to get some great interaction with the students.

Interviewee U23 shared his experience of having guest lecturers in his course in order to increase student engagement:

> We have guest lecturers every second week and try to mix them up across different fields so you get very engaging, inspiring people. ... We're very selective about who we approach to do [the lecture] and students love it. Of course we make that examinable so they actually have to come along.

Regular contact with staff was viewed as important for encouraging student engagement. One strategy used to ensure contact was formative assessment. Some universities use portfolios to achieve this purpose. At one university portfolio assessment is embedded into each year level, and students are given training in their first-year to help them understand the expectations of this form of assessment. At another university portfolio assessment has been used for the past five years in an introductory programming course. The portfolio assessment has been designed using Biggs's constructive alignment. U1 described this as a direct effort to encourage student engagement.

Another strategy for ensuring regular contact with staff is in-class assessment. U8 stated "there might be marks associated with practical work to encourage them to come to the classes and engage with that."

Feedback provides another opportunity for student-staff contact. Interviewees indicated that feedback is an important part of their assessment processes. At most institutions feedback is given on all forms of in-semester assessment. Formative feedback on assignments is often given verbally during tutorials or consultation times. Portfolio assessment allows for continuous formative feedback throughout the semester.

A number of interviewees described detailed critiques for summative assessment of assignment work involving comments and scores for individual components. A couple of interviewees stated that they give summative feedback on assignment work as a summary at a lecture. In one case feedback on assignment work is given only in this open forum; however, students are also given the opportunity to discuss their work individually with their lecturer.

Several interviewees described their use of social media in first-year ICT to provide online contact with students and support the formation of learning communities. U24 describes the use of an in-house educational social networking software that is based on Facebook and has a rich tool set of features to promote social connections.

> It is a lot more friendly to use as a tool than the stuff that is packaged in the learning management system. Blackboard [was] built in 1997, so is very old and clunky. The institution insists that we use those sorts of tools but they just don't resonate with students at all.

U9 mentioned how students are encouraged to use LinkedIn to "be professional from the start. So there's collegiality with their lecturers and higher grade students in LinkedIn as well".

4.4 Enriching Educational Experiences

This aspect of student engagement is concerned with participation in broadening academic activities. As the interview cohort consisted of many academics who perform key administrative roles within their departments, valuable insight was obtained into the support initiatives made available to students.

Mentoring programs were recognised as key mechanisms for academic support. Several interviewees described the introduction of peer-assisted study schemes within first-year introductory courses. In the scheme, second- or third-year students facilitate an environment where course concepts can be discussed and problems can be solved, rather than simply repeating the formal course content in a similar manner.

Interviewee U5 described a more formal mentoring program that was not a voluntary academic support session, rather designed to be more holistic in the support offered:

> We have a mentoring system in first-year with groups of 6-8 students supported by a member of academic staff and a 2nd or 3rd year student to try to encourage them to speak about positive or what challenges they have. They are allocated at the beginning of first-year and the groups meet several times a year for discussions.

There were also examples of mentoring from specialised discipline coordinators appointed to support students both academically and administratively.

All the universities in our survey have programs to help support at-risk students, primarily through mentoring, first-year advisors, and drop-in centres that support, and in some cases initiate, contact with first-year students. Students are typically identified as at-risk via analysis of their attendance and/or performance in early assessment opportunities or class activities, although some universities contact all new students. U21 describes a strategy used:

> At-risk students are identified in the first few weeks and they are contacted by email, and if no response a telephone call,

and at the end sending a letter. So we try to identify them: we use a matrix to identify at-risk students – it includes attendance; we put a very low-stakes assessment item in the first three weeks of the course, such as an online quiz at the end of week 2 which is worth 2% of the final grade. We can use that to identify students who are not engaging.

Other academics discuss the use of telephone contact:

We normally ring around after about 4 weeks if they haven't engaged in the course and say "what's happening, do you have a problem?" The university has actually finally decided that it's a university problem and has established a student experience team to look at that problem and do the ringing themselves rather than relying on academics to do it. (U22)

A variety of approaches are used to help first-year students with study skills. Interviewees described programs developed at their institutions to help students with skills including researching material, time management, exam preparation, and communication skills. Many universities offer study skills programs, some of them compulsory, run by the library or by a central learning and teaching unit. When they are not compulsory, lecturers are usually expected to identify students in need and direct them to these programs. At one university an innovative study skills program involves workshops and incorporates peer mentoring. U11b explains how the program works:

the workshops that we run for the on campus students ... go for three hours and we have a ... session for half an hour each week [with] higher-level students who have been trained to deliver information to students on time management, essay writing, and study skills. These are all recorded and put up on the study desk for the external students.

Some interviewees emphasised a need to integrate study skills throughout a degree program. U9 explained: "we scaffold their learning so that [the soft skills] would appear in first-year and there is also something in second year and then there are capstone topics and they are specifically bringing in those soft skills."

There were a number of programs to help first-year students with the process of transition from school to university. These ranged from formal programs at a top level of the university to ad-hoc programs run by departments. At a university level, students were often targeted based on their profile. Some interviewees reported support for specific at-risk groupings, such as maintaining contact lists for at-risk groups, including first-in-family and equity groups within the discipline (e.g. female students within ICT). One interviewee described a transition program in detail, indicating many elements identified in the literature as good practice, such as the activation of direct contact based on indications of poor engagement in online learning systems.

At the university level the main program is the student success project. ... It is interventionist and this is one reason why the uni encourages or dictates that 15% of the assessment must be completed before week 5. I think that is mandated now across the university. (U4)

4.5 Supportive Learning Environment

This aspect of student engagement is concerned with feelings of legitimation within the university community. Social support and community-building activities were present in most universities, both within academic programs and as extra-curricular activities. Interviewees mentioned a number of initiatives being employed to encourage interaction at a social level in their departments.

Several interviewees discussed how an increase in social support can have a positive impact on student engagement. U10 explains:

The whole curriculum restructure that we did was pretty much based around that. What we found is that students tend to be much more engaged when they have the social structures around them to support their learning …We wanted our students to have those social bonds, to have a group and to feel like they were actually contributing and having ownership of what they were doing.

Providing opportunities for extra-curricular social activities was also seen as key to fostering positive student engagement. U12 discussed how extra-curricular activities could be used to build relationships between students and staff:

We encourage them to take part in things such as games nights. In the past we've had things such as pool competitions between staff and students, cricket, social events, to try to make them see that we're not people that aren't approachable. Particularly for students that are struggling, that they can approach us and talk about any issues; talk about the problems that they're experiencing. So it's more about showing them that we're people that can help.

Across the 30 interviews, a number of extra-curricular activities or programs were mentioned. These included staff-student barbecues, pizza lunches, games nights, student IT clubs, and importantly forming clubs to support specific demographics, such as women in IT, or those from low socioeconomic groups. Several interviewees mentioned student social clubs designed to support female students:

We have our group called Women in Engineering and Technology and that's run by our Faculty office. It sets up large social events for women within the Faculty to get together and have a bit of a chat but also they talk about problems they might be having in their courses. As part of that, they also have mentoring and industry events so female students can talk to female industry members. (U12)

Several interviewees reported on their programs to support low-socio-economic status (low-SES) students.

In terms of having something specifically for certain demographics, our funding for [mentoring programs] is based on low-SES students. But it's still voluntary. We don't ask them to put up their hand based on their parent's income or whether they're first in family. We recognise that our cohort has quite a high percentage of first in family and low-SES based on where we are. We do have programs that are based on that but are not restricted to that. (U15)

Few interviewees reported on reviews of their support programs for at-risk students, but one interviewee did provide some evidence for the effectiveness of their programs. This indicates a need to further discuss and share knowledge on such programs.

5. RECOMMENDATIONS AND CONCLUSION

This paper provides a snapshot of current issues regarding first-year ICT student engagement, and offers a number of insights into efforts to address this at both academic and administrative levels. Although we did not discuss a definition of student engagement with interviewees, we found their responses gave information about teaching approaches and institutional programs addressing all five aspects of student engagement identified by Coates [2]. We found there has been a shift away from the traditional lecture activity of one-way delivery of large volumes of content, and the in-class experience is in a period of transition as academics seek ways to involve students in active and collaborative learning experiences. It is interesting, however, to note that most initiatives about student engagement were concerned with on-campus experiences, which seems at odds with the current push from universities to move more online presence for their courses.

Many innovative teaching techniques and tools have been developed to enhance student engagement by encouraging students to attend, participate, actively engage in their learning, and collaborate with others. The success of the initiatives was often deduced from increases in activity; however, in most cases there was no real evidence of the effectiveness of the programs.

This suggests a number of areas that require further study:

- more formal evaluations of the effects of these teaching initiatives;
- collation of examples of good practice for wider dissemination;
- further investigation of how social media can be used effectively to strengthen learning support;
- identification of effective support programs for at-risk students and programs to encourage community building, particularly for female students.

6. ACKNOWLEDGMENTS

This project was undertaken with the support of the Australian Council of Deans of Information and Communication Technology through the ALTA Good Practice Reports Commissioned for 2013–2014 grant scheme (http://www.acdict.edu.au/ALTA.htm). The project team would also like to acknowledge the work of Beth Cook who worked as a research assistant to conduct the interviews and to prepare the detailed interview notes.

7. REFERENCES

[1] Bennedsen, J. and Caspersen, M.E. (2007). Failure rates in introductory programming. ACM SIGCSE Bulletin, 39(2): 32-36.

[2] Coates, H. (2007). A model of online and general campus-based student engagement. Assessment & Evaluation In Higher Education, 32(2): 121-141.

[3] Coates, H. (2009). Engaging students for success – 2008 Australian Survey of Student Engagement. Victoria, Australia: Australian Council for Educational Research.

[4] Doerschuk, P., Liu, J. and Mann, J. (2009). INSPIRED broadening participation: first year experience and lessons learned. ACM SIGCSE Bulletin, 41(3): 238-242.

[5] Fredricks, A.J., Blumenfeld, C.P. and Paris, H.A. (2004). School engagement: Potential of the concept, state of the evidence. Review of Educational Research, 74(1), 59-109.

[6] Graduate Careers Australia and the Social Research Centre. (2014). 2013 University Experience Survey National Report, Accessed 10 Jan 2015, from https://education.gov.au/university-experience-survey

[7] Kuh, G.D. (2009). The National Survey of Student Engagement: Conceptual and Empirical Foundations. New Directions for Empirical Research, 2009: 5-20.

[8] Kuh, G.D., Cruce, T.M., Shoup, R., Kinzie, J. and Gonyea, R.M. (2008). Unmasking the effects of student engagement on first-year college grades and persistence. Journal of Higher Education, 79(5): 540-563.

[9] Kurkovsky, S. (2013). Mobile game development: improving student engagement and motivation in introductory computing courses. Computer Science Education, 23(2), 138-157.

[10] Lee, M.J., Ko, A.J. and Kwan, I. (2013). In-game assessments increase novice programmers' engagement and level completion speed. 9th International Computing Education Research Conference, 153-160.

[11] MyUniversity, Australian Government, myuniversity.gov.au

[12] National Survey of Student Engagement, Accessed 10 Jan 2015, from http://nsse.iub.edu/

[13] Pears, A. (2010). Conveying conceptions of quality through instruction. 7th International Conference on the Quality of Information and Communications Technology, 7-14.

[14] Roberts, M., Tanya J., McGill, T.J. and Hyland, P.N. (2012). Attrition from Australian ICT degrees: why women leave. 14th Australasian Computing Education Conference-Volume 123. Australian Computer Society, Inc.

[15] Sheard, J., Carbone, A. and Hurst, A.J. (2010). Student engagement in first year of an ICT degree: staff and student perceptions. Computer Science Education, 20(1): 1-16.

[16] Sheard, J., Morgan, M., Butler, M., Falkner, K., Weerasinghe, A. and Simon. (2014). Experiences of first-year students in ICT courses: good teaching practices. ALTA Commissioned Report, Australian Council of Deans of ICT (http://www.acdict.edu.au/ALTA.htm).

[17] Simon, B., Esper, S., Porter, L., and Cutts, Q. (2013). Student experience in a student-centered peer instruction classroom. 9th International Computing Education Research Conference, 129-136.

[18] Smet, M. De, Keer, H. Van, Wever, B.De, & Valcke, M. (2010). Cross-age peer tutors in asynchronous discussion groups: Exploring the impact of three types of tutor training on patterns in tutor support and on tutor characteristics. Computers & Education, 54: 1167-1181.

[19] University Experience Survey, Accessed 10 Jan 2015, from http://www.ues.edu.au/

[20] Vihavainen, A., Airaksinen, J. and Watson, C. (2014). A systematic review of approaches for teaching introductory programming and their influence on success. 10th annual conference on International computing education research. ACM, 2014.

[21] Yadin, A. (2011). Reducing the dropout rate in an introductory programming course. ACM Inroads, 2(4): 71-76.

[22] Zepke, N., Butler, P. and Leach, L. (2012). Institutional research and improving the quality of student engagement. Quality in Higher Education. 18(3): 329-347.

[23] Zepke, N. (2013). Threshold concepts and student engagement: Revisiting pedagogical content knowledge. Active Learning in Higher Education. 0(0):1-1

Solving Code-tracing Problems and its Effect on Code-writing Skills Pertaining to Program Semantics

Amruth N. Kumar
Ramapo College of New Jersey
505 Ramapo Valley Road
Mahwah, NJ 07430, USA
1 201 684 7712
amruth@ramapo.edu

ABSTRACT

An earlier study had found that solving code tracing problems helped improve code writing skills of students. But, given the instruments used in the earlier study, the improvement in code writing pertained primarily to language syntax. A follow-up within-subjects controlled study was conducted to investigate whether solving code tracing problems could help improve code writing skills pertaining to the semantics of a program. In the study, students were asked to write code for a control and a test problem both before and after a problem-solving session on code tracing. Increase in the score from pre-quiz to post-quiz was treated as improvement in code writing attributable to code tracing. Repeated measures ANOVA was used to analyze the data collected over four semesters. A statistically significant improvement in code writing skills pertaining to program semantics was observed on the test problems, but not on control concepts in the control problems. The improvement in code-writing skills as they pertain to program semantics accrued to the students who scored 90% or more on code-tracing problems in this study. Finally, the transfer in learning from code-tracing activities to code-writing skills may be near as well as far.

Categories and Subject Descriptors

K.3.2 [**Computer and Information Science Education**]: Computer Science Education

General Terms

Measurement, Performance, Experimentation

Keywords

Code-reading, Code-writing, Code-tracing, Problem-solving

1. INTRODUCTION

Code tracing and code writing are two of the activities used for both learning and assessing programming (e.g., [6]). Code tracing problems (e.g., debugging a program, identifying the output of a program) are attractive in that they can be solved in shorter stints

of time, using formats such as multiple-choice that are easier to grade. In this context, a question of interest to Computer Science researchers has been whether there is a correlation between students' performance on code tracing problems and their ability to write code [13] – if such a correlation exists, assessment in introductory Computer Science courses can be simplified and even automated. One study [10] found a positive correlation between code reading and code writing tasks using SOLO (Structure of the Observed Learning Outcome) taxonomy. Another study [1] found low correlation between code tracing and code writing problems, and yet another found a positive correlation between the two [8], which was later replicated with a follow-up study [12]. Other researchers have reported inability to replicate results establishing a relationship between the two [11]. Based on Piaget's theory of intellectual development, yet others have argued that code-tracing is a legitimate phase in a novice student's development into a programmer [7].

A recent study [5] reported finding a significant improvement in code-writing skills attributable to code-tracing activity. However, due to the topic selected for the study and the design of the instruments used in the study, the improvement found in code writing pertained primarily to language syntax. A follow-up study was conducted to see if code-tracing activity would benefit code-writing skills as they pertain to program semantics rather than language syntax. In this paper, the protocol, data collection and analysis, and results of the study will be discussed. This study is of interest because learning program semantics is harder than learning language syntax; and enabling students to passively learn program semantics by solving code-tracing problems would provide another pedagogic tool to Computer Science educators.

2. METHODOLOGY

In this study, the influence of solving code-tracing problems on the ability to write `for` loops was evaluated. A within-subjects controlled study was conducted – the students were asked to write code for a control problem and a test problem both before (pre-quiz) and after (post-quiz) solving code-tracing problems on `for` loops. The test problem pertained to writing a `for` loop, whereas the control problem pertained to writing a conditional `break` statement, a concept that was not covered in the intervening code-tracing problems. If code-tracing helps improve code-writing skills, significant improvement in code-writing skills should be observed on the test problem, but not the control problem.

2.1 Protocol

The protocol consisted of the following stages administered to the students back-to-back, with no break in between:

Pre-Quiz on code writing: Students were asked to write code for two problems:

1. **Pre-quiz control problem:** "A loop repeatedly reads values into the variable `number` and prints them. Write the code that must be inserted between reading and printing so that the loop is exited if the value of `number` is greater than 100."

2. **Pre-quiz test problem:** "Write a for loop to print all the multiples of 5 from 25 up to and including the value of the integer variable `limit`."

Problem-Solving session on code tracing: Students were presented a series of problems. In each problem, students were presented a program that contained one or more `for` loops, and asked to identify the output of the program – Please see Figure 1 at the end of the paper for a screen shot of a problem-solving session in progress. The problems were designed to test the students' knowledge of the semantics of `for` loops, and their ability to trace programs. The concepts covered by the code-tracing problems included: zero-iteration loops, single iteration loops, dependent and independent nested loops, dependent and independent back-to-back loops, loops with simple and compound statement for body, up-counting and down-counting loops, and loops wherein the loop counter is updated again within the loop body. None of these problems included any other type of control statement (`if`, `while`, `do-while`), `break` or `continue` statements.

Pre-test-practice-post-test protocol was used for the session [4]: all the students initially answered a pre-test consisting of 10 problems, one per concept. If a student answered a pre-test problem incorrectly, the student was presented feedback explaining the correct answer, and was presented additional problems on the concept during the adaptive practice and post-test that followed. If a student solved a problem correctly during pre-test, no additional practice or post-test problems were presented on the concept. In order to stay within the typical attention span of learners, the entire pre-test-practice-post-test protocol was limited to 30 minutes.

Post-Quiz on code writing: Students were again asked to write code for two problems:

1. **Post-quiz control problem:** "A loop repeatedly reads values into the variable `temperature` and prints them. Write the code that must be inserted between reading and printing so that the loop is exited if the value of `temperature` is less than 0."

2. **Post-quiz test problem:** "Write a for loop to print all the multiples of 7 from 21 up to and including the value of the integer variable `finish`."

Note that the post-quiz control problem is isomorphic to pre-quiz control problem, i.e., identical modulo variable names, literal constants and output strings. Similarly, post-quiz test problem is isomorphic to pre-quiz test problem, in order to ensure that the difficulty level of pre- and post- quiz problems are comparable, as required for sound pre-post evaluation design. Control problems covered two constructs that were never included in any intervening code-tracing problem: `if` and `break` statements.

Students were required to answer pre- and post-quiz, although, they were allowed to side-step by entering "Don't know." No time limit was placed on answering pre- and post-quizzes.

The entire protocol was administered online, back-to-back, with no break in between. Students entered the answers to pre-quiz and post-quiz questions in free-form. They answered code-tracing problems using a combination of drop-down menus and free-form input, as shown in Figure 1. Problets (problets.org) were used to administer the protocol, collect data and provide feedback on code-tracing problems.

2.2 Data collection and analysis

The study was conducted over four semesters: fall 2010, spring 2011, fall 2012 and spring 2013. The subjects of the study were 728 students in introductory programming courses who were being taught loops midway through the semester. By then, they had studied `if-else` statements, and may or may not have learned about `break` statements. The students were given completion credit in the course for solving code-tracing problems. Since students had the ability to side-step one or both the quizzes, only those students were considered who had attempted both the quizzes, leaving a total of 312 students in the study.

Grading control problems: The answers to pre- and post-quiz control problems were graded in terms of 7 components, themselves combined into three **subgroups**:

- **Shell**, consisting of 2 components: the reserved word `if`, and parentheses;
- **Condition expression**, consisting of 3 components: the condition variable, relational operator and sentinel value;
- **Break statement**, consisting of 2 components: the reserved word `break` and the semi-colon that follows it.

Note that the 2 components of the shell and the semi-colon in the break statement pertain to language syntax – errors in these components are traditionally detected and reported by the compiler. The condition expression and the reserved word `break` pertain to program semantics – errors in these are likely to change the behavior of the program. Among the two statements never included in any code-tracing problem, `if` is a construct that students would have typically already encountered in their course before loops, and `break` statement is a construct they may or may not have encountered before `for` loops.

The student solutions were manually graded on a 3-point scale for each component as follows: 0 if the component was not used (e.g., no `if`), 1 if it was incorrectly used (e.g., `return` or `exit` used instead of `break`), and 2 if it was completely and correctly used. In addition:

- Condition expression was graded as 1 or 2 if it was part of an `if` statement, or if it was written without any control statement. If the condition expression was written as the condition of some other control statement such as a `while` loop, it was graded as 0.
- Condition expression was graded as a 0 if it was not a relational expression, e.g., `temperature++` was graded as 0.
- Extraneous code such as redundant loops, input and output statements was ignored.

Grading test problems: The answers to pre- and post-quiz test problems were graded along 16 components, themselves combined into five **subgroups**:

- **Shell**, consisting of 3 components: the reserved word `for`, parentheses and the two semi-colons within the parentheses;

- **Initialization expression**, consisting of 3 components: the loop counter, assignment operator and the initialization value;
- **Condition expression**, consisting of 3 components: the loop counter, relational operator and the terminal value;
- **Update expression,** consisting of 3 components: the loop counter, assignment operator and the step value;
- **Loop action**, i.e., the output statement, consisting of 4 components: the output statement (e.g., `cout` in C++, `System.out.println` in Java), output operator (`<<` in C++)/parentheses (in Java), the expression being output, and the statement delimiter semi-colon.

Note that the 3 components of shell and the 3 components of Loop action other than the expression being output all pertain to language syntax. The remaining 10 components – initialization expression, condition expression, update expression and the expression being output in loop action pertain to program semantics.

In order to reduce the time and effort needed for grading, while also maintaining consistency of grading, a Java program was written to automatically grade all 16 components of each student program. The grading program compared each student program against reference solutions, and awarded grade on a 3-point scale for each component as follows: 0 if the component was not used (e.g., no `for`, or no output statement), 1 if it was incorrectly used (e.g., `for` in the wrong case, incorrect output statement), and 2 if it was completely and correctly used. The grading program resolved all the syntax components, but resolved only unambiguously correct semantic components.

Thereafter, all the student solutions were manually graded to resolve components that the grading program could not automatically grade. This was necessary in all the cases where the student's program diverged significantly from the reference solutions built into the grading program. Manual grading was primarily needed for the 10 components pertaining to program semantics. In order to ensure consistent grading, especially of partially correct code, the following principles were followed:

- Partial credit was calculated based on the fewest text changes needed to make a student program completely correct, and not based on the concurrence of its output with that of the correct program, e.g., suppose a student wrote the following program for pre-quiz problem:

```
for( var = 25; var <= limit; var + 5 )
    cout << var;
```

Even though this is an infinite loop, it was penalized only for the assignment operator in the update expression, which should have been += instead of +.

- When grading semantic components, syntax errors were ignored, e.g., consider the following student code for pre-quiz problem:

```
for( var = 5; var <= limit / 5; var++ )
    cout << 5 var;
```

The student was given full credit (2) for the output expression, even though multiplication operator is missing between 5 and `var`.

- Extraneous code such as variable declarations before the loop, declaration of loop counter within the loop header and inclusion of `endl` in C++ output statement was ignored.

- Incorrect use of sentinel variable as loop counter was graded as incorrect at each occurrence, e.g., consider the following student code for post-quiz problem:

```
for( finish=21; finish<=100; finish+=7 )
    System.out.println( finish );
```

Since `finish` holds the sentinel value, its use was graded as incorrect (1) in the initialization expression, condition expression, as well as update expression.

Since the focus of this study was semantics, the total score on pre-quiz and post-quiz was calculated as the sum of the scores on the 10 semantic components – initialization, condition, update and output expressions, for a maximum score of 20 on both pre-quiz and post-quiz problem.

Scoring code-tracing problems: Students also received a score on the code-tracing problems they solved during the pre-test-practice-post-test problem-solving session. On each problem, they received partial credit for all the outputs they correctly identified in a program up to the first incorrect output. Given that practice and post-test were adaptive, pre-test was the only stage attempted by all the students. So, only pre-test stage data was used in this study. Since the problem-solving session was limited to 30 minutes, the number of pre-test problems solved varied among the students. So, for analysis purposes, the score per problem (normalized to a maximum of 1.0) and the time spent per problem (in seconds) were used instead of total score and total time.

3. RESULTS

First, pre-post change in score will be analyzed for test problems, in order to find out whether students could write better code after the problem-solving session on code tracing, and if so, in which component(s) pertaining to program semantics. Next, pre-post change in score will be analyzed for control problems to see if any improvement in the score on test problems may merely be due to Hawthorne effect [3]. Finally, quiz scores will be compared with the scores on the code-tracing session to see how students who knew code-tracing did on code-writing and vice versa.

3.1 Analysis of semantic components

Test problems: Repeated measures ANOVA analysis of the total score yielded significant main effect [$F(1,311) = 7.093$, $p = 0.008$], i.e., in a test with one degree of freedom between subjects (two groups) and 311 degrees of freedom within subjects (312 students), the ratio of the mean squares between-subjects and within-subjects, also called F-ratio, was 7.093. (The F-ratio is a measure of how different the means are relative to the variability within each group - the larger the F-ratio, the greater the likelihood that the difference between the groups is due to more than chance alone.) The significant main effect indicates that the treatment (code-tracing session) indeed had an effect on the pre-post change in scores on test problems. Finally, the result was statistically significant since the probability p was less than 0.05.

Post-hoc tests revealed that students scored higher on the post-quiz than on the pre-quiz as shown in Table 1, and the improvement was statistically significant (means are listed with confidence intervals at 95% confidence level). Since pre-quiz, code-tracing session and post-quiz were administered back-to-back with no break in between, the pre-post improvement in quiz score can be attributed to the intervening problem-solving session on code tracing. However, the effect size was small (0.11), i.e., the test group mean was at 54 percentile of control group.

Table 1. Total score on test problems before and after solving code-tracing problems

Score (out of 20)	Pre-Quiz	Post-Quiz
Mean	17.051 ± 0.419	17.455 ± 0.377
Std. Deviation	3.763	3.384

The maximum score on the test problem was 20. Those who scored 19 or 20 on the pre-quiz had little or no room for pre-post improvement in score. In order to eliminate this ceiling effect, analysis was re-run with only the students who had scored less than 19 points on the pre-quiz, i.e., 154 students. Once again, a significant main effect was found [$F(1,153) = 12.43$, $p = 0.001$]. The F-ratio corresponding to the change in pre-post scores was much larger at 12.43, and the result was once again statistically significant. The improvement in score from pre-quiz to post-quiz was much larger too, as shown in Table 2. The effect size was larger (0.25), considered small to medium.

Table 2. Total score on test problems before and after solving code-tracing problems – after eliminating ceiling effect

Score (out of 20)	Pre-Quiz	Post-Quiz
Mean	14.571 ± 0.357	15.565 ± 0.395
Std. Deviation	4.037	3.799

Post-hoc analysis of the 10 semantic components was conducted to identify the components on which students had shown significant improvement in code writing skills. Once again, ceiling effect was accounted for by eliminating students who had scored 19 or 20 on the pre-quiz test problem. Significant pre-post improvement was found on the following components:

- Initialization operator: [$F(1,153) = 6.43$, $p = 0.012$]: the mean score improved from 1.76 to 1.896 (out of a maximum of 2 points)

- Initialization value: [$F(1,153) = 19.304$, $p < 0.001$]: the mean score improved from 1.247 to 1.474

- Update operator: [$F(1,153) = 9.865$, $p = 0.002$]: the mean score improved from 1.26 to 1.422

- Update value: [$F(1,153) = 7.144$, $p = 0.008$]: the mean score improved from 1.545 to 1.695.

So, the improvement in the ability to write `for` loops occurred in the students' ability to start and step the loop counter. These four components pertain to program semantics rather than language syntax.

Control problems: Control problems covered two constructs that were not included in any code-tracing problem: `if` and `break` statements. `if` shell in the control problems pertains to syntax and `break` statement pertains to semantics.

Repeated measures ANOVA analysis found no significant main effect for `break` statement [$F(1,67) = 0.33$, $p = 0.568$]: among the 68 students who attempted to write `break` statement on pre- and post-quiz, no statistically significant improvement was observed from pre-quiz to post-quiz, as shown in Table 3. Since the maximum score on `break` statement was 2, the lack of improvement cannot be attributed to ceiling effect.

Table 3. Score on `break` statement in control problems before and after solving code-tracing problems

Score (out of 2)	Pre-Quiz	Post-Quiz
Mean	1.574 ± 0.153	1.588 ± 0.158
Std. Deviation	0.076	0.079

Similarly, repeated measures ANOVA analysis found no significant main effect for `if` shell [$F(1,140) = 0.307$, $p = 0.58$]: among the 141 students who attempted to write `if` shell on pre- and post-quiz, no statistically significant change was observed from pre-quiz to post-quiz, as shown in Table 4. Once again, since the maximum score on `if` shell was 4, the lack of improvement cannot be attributed to ceiling effect.

Table 4. Score on `if` shell in control problems before and after solving code-tracing problems

Score (out of 4)	Pre-Quiz	Post-Quiz
Mean	1.972 ± 0.333	1.936 ± 0.332
Std. Deviation	0.168	0.168

So, solving code-tracing problems did *not* help students learn syntactic or semantic constructs that were not included in code-tracing problems. This discredits alternative explanations (e.g., Hawthorne effect – improved performance due to awareness of being observed) for the improvement observed earlier in code-writing due to code-tracing.

Condition expression of an `if` statement is similar in semantics to the condition expression of a `for` loop. This explains why ANOVA analysis of the condition expression yielded significant main effect [$F(1,124) = 9.271$, $p = 0.003$]: a small, but significant increase was observed in the mean score from pre-quiz (5.432 ± 0.134) to post-quiz (5.592 ± 0.115). Post-hoc analysis showed that the significant improvement was only in writing the conditional operator [$F(1,124) = 7.089$, $p = 0.009$]: the mean score increased from pre-quiz (1.6 ± 0.09) to post-quiz (1.704 ± 0.081), and the increase was significant. This indicates that *the transfer in learning from code-tracing activities to code-writing skills may be near as well as far* [9]: near transfer being defined as when original (tracing `for` loops) and transfer (writing `for` loops) contexts are similar, and far transfer being defined as when original (tracing `for` loop condition) and transfer (writing `if` statement condition) contexts are dissimilar. Further studies are needed to evaluate whether the example of far transfer qualifies as non-specific transfer [9].

3.2 Analysis of subjects

Next, the subjects were partitioned into two groups based on their score during the problem-solving session on code tracing: those who scored 90% or more versus those who scored less than 90% (referred to as sub-90%). Mixed factor ANOVA analysis was conducted with quiz scores on test problems as repeated measure and 90%+ versus sub-90% grouping as the between-subjects factor. No significant main effect was found for group [F(1,310) = 0.52, p = 0.471]. But, the quiz scores of both the groups increased from pre-quiz to post-quiz, as shown in Table 5. Ironically, the pre-post improvement was significant for 90%+ group [F(1,197) = 5.561, p = 0.019], but not for sub-90% group [F(1,113) = 1.533, p = 0.218]! *So, the improvement in code-writing skills as they pertain to program semantics accrued to the students who scored 90% or more on code-tracing problems in this study.*

Table 5. Pre and Post-quiz test problem scores: 90% versus sub-90% scorers on problem-solving session

Score (out of 20)	Pre-Quiz	Post-Quiz
90%+ scorers during problem-solving session (N=198)		
Mean	17.111 ± 0.527	17.601 ± 0.473
Std Deviation	3.928	3.261
Sub-90% scorers during problem-solving session (N=114)		
Mean	16.947 ± 0.694	17.202 ± 0.623
Std Deviation	3.471	3.588

Finally, the subjects were partitioned into three groups based on the change in their score on test problem from pre-quiz to post-quiz: negative, zero and positive. Negative change meant code on the post-quiz qualified for fewer points than code on the pre-quiz; positive change meant improvement in coding from pre-quiz to post-quiz.

The mean scored per problem during the problem-solving session on code tracing was analyzed using univariate ANOVA, with the group being the fixed factor. No significant main effect was found for group [F(2,311) = 0.041, p = 0.96], i.e., the code-tracing skills of the three groups are not significantly different. Similarly, analysis of the mean time spent per code-tracing problem did not yield a significant main effect for group [F(2,311) = 0.804, p = 0.449].

4. DISCUSSION

It was surprising to find that the students whose code-writing skills significantly improved, as they pertain to program semantics, were the ones who scored 90% or more on code-tracing problems, presumably, the better-prepared students. One needs a good mental model of programming [2] in order to be able to trace code. We argue that the availability of such a mental model helps these students pick up code-writing skills, particularly as they pertain to program semantics, passively by reading code, whereas, the students who struggle to trace code cannot allocate similar mental resources for passive learning – they are too busy trying to trace the code at hand. Would this mean that code-tracing (knowing how a given piece of code works) is essential for learning code-writing (how to construct the code, bearing the desired semantics in mind), as some have recently argued (e.g., [7])? Or, can a novice learn to write code without learning to trace it first? These questions could benefit from additional studies of the relationship between code-tracing and code-writing.

One of the most challenging aspects of this study was manual grading of student code - it was found that even with the benefit

of codified grading principles, it was quite easy to arrive at two entirely different grades for the same snippet of code, especially when the grader took into account speculations about the student's design and thought process. Given this, there is likely to be some inconsistency in grading, especially when hundreds of students are involved in the study. It is hoped that the large sample size counters any adverse effects of stray inconsistencies in grading.

A three-point scale was used for grading in this study. A more elaborate grading policy might better elicit subtle differences between student populations, and correlations between code tracing and code writing skills. Then again, such a policy would entail larger commitment of resources for grading.

The hypothesis of this study was that tracing code leads to improvement in code-writing skills, not that tracing code is necessary for improving code-writing skills. Therefore, the within-subjects design of the evaluation protocol was adequate: while other activities such as reading about loops may also lead to improvement in code-writing skills, this study establishes that so does code-tracing activity.

The results of this study, combined with that of an earlier study [5], indicate that code-tracing activity helps students learn to write both syntactic and semantic components of code. However, the effect size was found to be small-to-medium in both studies. So, code-tracing can be used as a supplement to rather than a substitute for code-writing exercises.

Our serendipitous discovery of far-transfer of learning from code-tracing to code-writing is promising, and warrants additional studies. Could there be a few key programming concepts (e.g., condition expression evaluation, transfer of control in statements, side-effect tracking), tracing code on which might lead to disproportionate gains in code-writing skills in general? We plan to start by investigating whether evaluating expressions will help students learn to write the correct expression for a given problem.

5. ACKNOWLEDGMENTS

Partial support for this work was provided by the National Science Foundation under grants DUE-0817187 and DUE-1432190.

6. REFERENCES

[1] Denny, P., Luxton-Reilly, A. and Simon, B. 2008. Evaluating a new exam question: Parsons problems. In *Proceedings of the Fourth international Workshop on Computing Education Research* (ICER '08). ACM, New York, NY, USA, 113-124.

[2] Fix, V., Wiedenbeck, S., and Scholtz, J. 1993. Mental representations of programs by novices and experts. In *Proceedings of the INTERACT '93 and CHI '93 Conference on Human Factors in Computing Systems* (CHI '93). ACM, New York, NY, USA, 74-79.

[3] Franke, R.H. and Kaul, J.D.: The Hawthorne experiments: First statistical interpretation, American Sociological Review, 1978, 43, 623-643.

[4] Kumar, A.N. A Model for Deploying Software Tutors. IEEE 6th International Conference on Technology for Education (T4E), Amritapuri, India, December 2014. 3-9.

[5] Kumar, A.N. A study of the influence of code-tracing problems on code-writing skills. Proc. ITiCSE 2013. Canterbury, U.K. July 2013. 183-187.

[6] Lister, R., Clear, T., Simon, B., Bouvier, D.J., Carter, P., Eckerdal, A., Jacková, J., Lopez, M., McCartney, R., Robbins P., Seppälä, O., and Thompson, E. 2010. Naturally occurring data as research instrument: analyzing examination responses to study the novice programmer. *SIGCSE Bull.* 41, 4 (January 2010), 156-173.

[7] Lister, R. Concrete and other neo-Piagetian forms of reasoning in the novice programmer. In *Thirteenth Australasian Computing Education Conference (ACE 2011),* January 2011. *CRPIT* (Vol. 114).

[8] Lopez, M., Whalley, J., Robbins, P., and Lister, R. 2008. Relationships between reading, tracing and writing skills in introductory programming. In *Proceedings of the Fourth international Workshop on Computing Education Research* (ICER '08). ACM, New York, NY, USA, 101-112.

[9] Royer, J.M. Theories of the transfer of learning. *Educational Psychologist.* 14(1), 1979, 53-69.

[10] Sheard, J., Carbone, A., Lister, R., Simon, B., Thompson, E., and Whalley, J. 2008. Going SOLO to assess novice programmers. In *Proceedings of the 13th annual conference on Innovation and technology in computer science education* (ITiCSE '08). ACM, New York, NY, USA, 209-213.

[11] Simon, B., Lopez, M., Sutton, K., and Clear, T. 2009. Surely we must learn to read before we learn to write!. In *Proceedings of the Eleventh Australasian Conference on Computing Education - Volume 95* (ACE '09), Margaret Hamilton and Tony Clear (Eds.), Vol. 95. Australian Computer Society, Inc., Darlinghurst, Australia, Australia, 165-170.

[12] Venables, A., Tan, G. and Lister, R. 2009. A closer look at tracing, explaining and code writing skills in the novice programmer. In *Proceedings of the fifth international workshop on computing education research workshop* (ICER '09). ACM, New York, NY, USA, 117-128.

[13] Whalley, J., and Lister, R. 2009. The BRACElet 2009.1 (Wellington) specification. In *Proceedings of the Eleventh Australasian Conference on Computing Education - Volume 95* (ACE '09), Margaret Hamilton and Tony Clear (Eds.), Vol. 95. Australian Computer Society, Inc., Darlinghurst, Australia, Australia, 9-18.

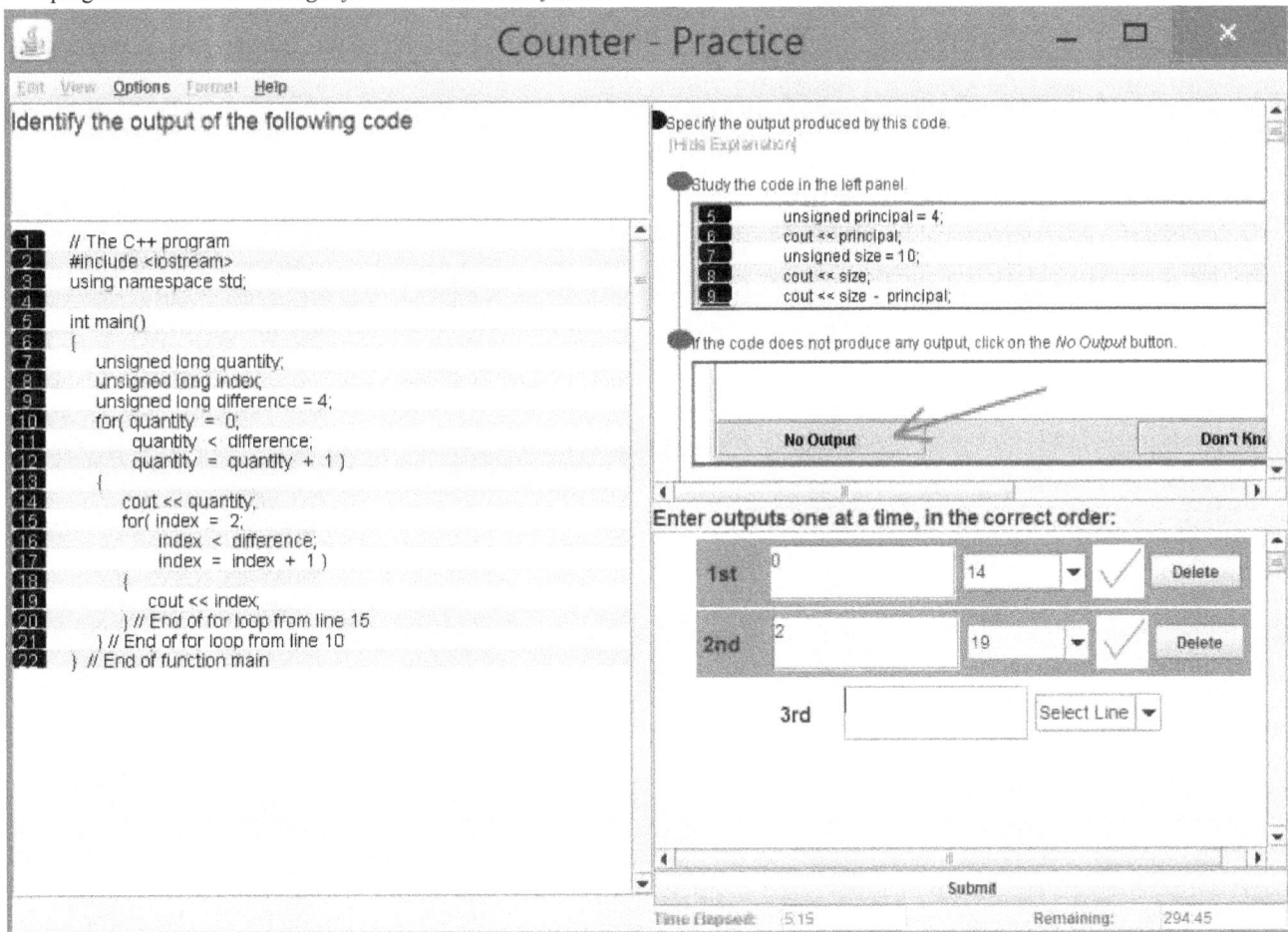

Figure 1 (© Amruth N. Kumar): Screen shot of a problem-solving session on code-tracing: a C++ program involving nested `for` loops is presented in the left panel. The student has entered the first two outputs of the program in the bottom right panel. Each output includes the printed value as well as the line number of the line of code that produces that output. Instructions for entering the answer are shown in the top right panel.

An Incremental Hint System For Automated Programming Assignments

Paolo Antonucci
ETH Zurich
paolanto17@gmail.com

Christian Estler
ETH Zurich
christian.estler@inf.ethz.ch

Đurica Nikolić
ETH Zurich
durica.nikolic@inf.ethz.ch

Marco Piccioni
ETH Zurich
marco.piccioni@inf.ethz.ch

Bertrand Meyer
ETH Zurich
bertrand.meyer@inf.ethz.ch

ABSTRACT

The advent of Massive Open Online Courses makes it essential to develop tools and techniques that automatically support computer science students in solving programming assignments. Complementing existing tools for automatically checking the correctness of students' programs, we have developed and evaluated an *incremental hint system* for programming exercises. The hint system displays, upon request from a student, a series of hints on how to approach a solution. The hints are created in advance from the source code of the exercise's reference solution using our hint generation tool. This tool can run in fully automatic mode, where hints reveal more and more parts of the solution code; in manual mode, where teachers can customize hints by annotating the input source code; and in a combination of the two modes. We evaluated the hint system throughout our Introduction to Programming course which provides a companion online course. The findings suggest that students who needed assistance with an exercise used the hint system and found it helpful to guide them through the process of building a solution.

Categories and Subject Descriptors

K.3.2 [**Computers and Education**]: Computer and Information Science Education—*Computer science education*

Keywords

CS1, MOOC, Pedagogy, SPOC

1. INTRODUCTION

A big hurdle for beginner students attempting to solve a programming exercise is to come up with an initial, albeit not perfect, solution. Once such a initial solution is found, the process of transforming it into a fully correct solution can be tackled with skill and some patience: refining the initial solution through a series of compilation, execution, and testing steps until the desired result is achieved. But what can a student do when unable to find such an initial solution? Asking peers or a teacher is an obvious thing to try, but sometimes this is not possible or practical, as for example in the context of online courses and MOOCs.

In the Autumn semester 2014 we offered a companion online course to our Introduction to Programming residential course, in which we used and evaluated an incremental hint system for programming exercises. The hint system displays, upon request from the student, a series of hints, incrementally unveiling new suggestions and details of the expected solution. The hint system also aims at supporting self-study and minimizing the need to ask for assistance to a teacher or to peers in a forum. A series of hints for each given exercise is created in advance by the teacher, using our tool either in automatic or manual mode (or a combination of both). The automatic mode obeys to some predefined (customizable) rules and generates all the needed files completely automatically. However, teachers can always tweak and personalize the hints for any given exercise by using an ad hoc mini-language embedded in the exercise's code comments. The tool was evaluated by making it available to the students, logging and observing how it was used, and administering a final questionnaire. The results are, in general, encouraging, and show that the students a) used the hint system and b) found it to be helpful.

The rest of this paper is organized as follows: Section 2 provides some background on our residential Introduction to Programming course and its structure; Section 3 describes the infrastructure we used for our online course; Section 4 describes the hint system in detail; Section 5 summarizes the data we collected; Section 6 details related work; and Section 7 concludes with final comments.

2. OUR INTRODUCTION TO PROGRAMMING COURSE

Our Introduction to Programming course is a fourteen week long residential course. It includes four hours of frontal lectures and two hours of exercise sessions each week. The live lectures are of two kinds: traditional (frontal) lectures, and Socratic lectures. There are ten home assignments and two mock exams that simulate the final exam setting. Exercise groups typically include twenty students each and are differentiated by skill level (beginners, intermediate, or advanced) and language (English or German). Differentiating

ITICSE'15, July 04–08, 2015, Vilnius, Lithuania.
Copyright is held by the owner/author(s). Publication rights licensed to ACM.
ACM ACM 978-1-4503-3440-2/15/07 ...$15.00
http://dx.doi.org/10.1145/2729094.2742607.

the exercise groups according to students' self-assessed skill levels proved to be beneficial, as it lead to more homogeneous groups, which helped to keep students of different skill levels interested and motivated.

Throughout the rest of this paper we refer to the Introduction to Programming course we taught in the Autumn semester of 2014. Its students reported, similarly to previous years, the following distribution of preexisting programming experience: 64% of students came with some object-oriented programming experience, 25% had non-object-oriented programming experience, and only 11% had never programmed before. Additionally, 19% of our students attended the residential course while having a part-time job that required some programming.

The programming language of choice for our course was Eiffel [6]. Eiffel makes it easy to express and teach object-oriented concepts and methods, and allows for a gentle introduction to program verification through design by contract [5].

3. OUR ONLINE LEARNING PLATFORM

The residential course described in Section 2 was accompanied by an online course, which provided video lectures, quizzes and programming exercises. The infrastructure we used for the online course consisted of three parts: a Moodle[1] installation, enhanced with a plugin we developed for in-video quizzes, a web-based programming environment, Codeboard[2], for compiling and executing programs in the browser, and our incremental hint system.

The online course sequence is linear and consists of 14 lectures. Every online lecture is divided into one or more segments (of variable duration), one or more quizzes, and zero or more programming exercises. Topics' durations vary between 5 and 40 minutes, with an average of 17 minutes.

To tackle the known issues deriving from reduced attention span [7], we embedded quizzes within longer video lecture segments. The purpose of the quizzes is twofold: to allow attention span recovery by breaking the online lecture flow, and to test short-term topic comprehension. In general, we designed quizzes and exercises to be useful in the short term (after taking an online lecture) and in the long term (for reviewing material for the exam, that in our case takes place 8 months after the course end).

Our web-based programming environment, Codeboard, allows students to write, compile, test, and submit programs from within the browser. Submissions are automatically graded based on a set of unit tests provided by the teacher. Using this web-based tool removes the need to install any ad hoc software for the students and simplifies the distribution and grading of exercises for the teacher. Codeboard integrates seamlessly with Moodle (and other e-learning platforms as well), making it possible to exchange data about students' progress and grades between the two systems.

4. THE INCREMENTAL HINT SYSTEM

When solving in-browser programming exercises students have the option to request hints by clicking "hint" buttons. For each exercise there can be one or more hint buttons. At the beginning only the first button (corresponding to a level 1 hint) is active. Each other button becomes available after pushing the previous one. This section describes the hint system in detail.

4.1 Hint mechanism

AutoTeach [3], our hint generator, provides hints directly from within the source code. Hints are incremental, that is, they are organized in *hint levels*, each level containing more hints than the previous one. In practice, this means that for every exercise to be solved, which in most cases consists of a single class file, there are n versions of the class file that are generated in advance and served to students upon request, with the first file containing just the skeleton of the code (feature declarations, possibly routine contracts, etc.) and the following ones containing incrementally more information.

Hints are of two kinds:

- **Textual hints:** comments in the code manually written by the teacher which become visible from a specific hint level on.

- **Code-revealing hints:** a part of the solution the student is expected to implement. They are generated automatically by AutoTeach according to certain customizable rules.

These two kinds of hints can be combined at will for greater flexibility, allowing teachers, for example, to refer in a textual hint to a part of the code which they know it will become visible on the next hint level.[3]

4.2 Meta-commands and textual hints

Teachers write textual hints directly within the code by taking the solution files, annotating them with special processing directives called **meta-commands**, and passing them to AutoTeach. AutoTeach will then scan the file multiple times, once for each hint level, process the meta-commands, and generate the output files.

Meta-commands have the form of special comments within the code. They can either contain a textual hint, which should be printed to the output, or alter AutoTeach's default behavior in processing the code. In both cases, they may specify a range of hint levels, outside of which they are ignored. As an example:

```
--# [3] HINT: Start by iterating on 'a_numbers'
--# [0-4] HIDE_NEXT if
```

The first meta-command is a textual hint which must be printed to the output at hint level three and higher. The second meta-command shows one of the many supported processing directives, and indicates that between hint levels 0 and 4, the subsequent 'if' instruction should be hidden from the output.

4.3 Code processing

Although until now we have referred to "code-revealing hints", we have in fact developed a multi-level code processing model which determines the visibility of every part of the code. This model fits particularly well our purpose of generating hints based on revealing parts of the code, but nothing prevents it from being used for more general code processing tasks that need to distinguish between the visibility of different sections of the code.

[1] https://moodle.org, accessed April 22, 2015
[2] https://codeboard.io, accessed April 22, 2015
[3] For a code example, see http://goo.gl/YBVQpp, accessed April 22, 2015

The main design goal of this code visibility model and the related code processing system is to be as flexible and powerful as possible, and at the same time simple enough to be used in those cases where no particular customization is required. Ideally, we want our Hint Generator to be able to run on most exercises *without any kind of extra annotation* and yield a satisfactory result, which could be further refined with additional annotations only in cases where a high granularity of hints is important (mostly very short exercises).

4.4 Code blocks

An important choice in designing the code visibility model is the granularity, that is, the elementary units which the Hint Generator should be able to handle. With respect to this, we define a list of supported code syntactic elements which we call "blocks". Blocks are classified as **atomic blocks** and **complex blocks**. The difference between the two is that complex blocks may contain other blocks (either atomic or complex) nested in them, while atomic blocks cannot contain any other kind of block. Examples of *atomic* blocks are instructions (excluding compound statements such as 'if's and loops), assertions in contracts, and conditions within 'if' statements. Examples of *complex* blocks are routine preconditions, 'if' statements, and 'if' branches. Figure 1 shows the decomposition of a code sample into blocks.

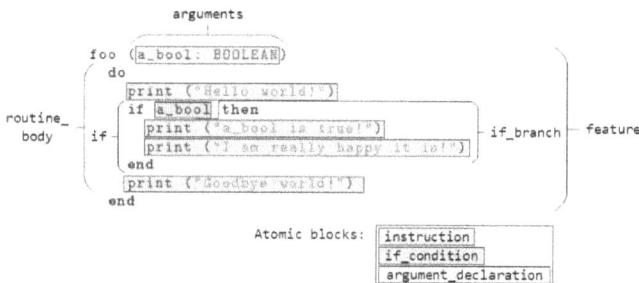

Figure 1: Decomposition of code into blocks.

4.5 Block basic visibility

AutoTeach works by scanning class files sequentially, writing their content to the output files on the fly and replacing the sections of the source code that should be hidden at the selected hint level with a placeholder. As AutoTeach abstracts the input code into blocks, the ultimate question for every occurrence of a code block is for us: "should we print this block or should we hide it?".

The question is answered by a lookup in the **basic visibility table** (see Table 1). The basic visibility table is a table associating block types (rows) with hint levels (columns). Every cell of the table contains a boolean value indicating whether or not the corresponding block type should be visible, and thus be printed to the output, at that level. Cells can also be undefined (allowing for three possible values: *true*, *false*, and *undefined*), but we will ignore this for now.

4.6 Block content visibility

The approach shown in the previous section is very simple and quite flexible, yet not flexible enough. For example,

Table 1: Simplified basic visibility table. Rows correspond to block types, columns to hint levels.

	0	1	2
feature	True	True	True
if	False	True	True
instruction	False	False	True

consider the code in Figure 1. Assume that, on a certain hint level, the teacher wants to show all the instructions appearing directly within the body of a routine, but wants to hide all those inside the body of an *if* statement, having therefore the output shown in Listing 1.

Listing 1: Desired output processing the code of Figure 1.
```
foo (a_bool: BOOLEAN)
   do
      print ("Hello world!")
      if a_bool then

         -- Your code here!

      end
      print ("Goodbye world!")
   end
```

According to what we have said so far, there is no way to achieve this. Working with the visibility of *instruction* blocks will not help, as it will affect both instructions inside and outside the 'if' statement. To make this possible, we need a new paradigm, which we call **content visibility**. This paradigm is orthogonal to and independent from the paradigm of basic visibility.

Every point in the code, where "point" means any place in the text on which we could click and set the cursor for editing, has a **content visibility policy** in force in that place. The content visibility policy is a boolean value which, as an approximate definition, indicates whether or not the code appearing in that region should be visible (i.e. printed to the output). The policy may also be undefined, which effectively allows for three different values for the content visibility policy (*true*, *false*, and *undefined*). In our case, to achieve the desired goal, we need to ensure that the content visibility policy be *false* within the body of the *if* instruction and *true* outside of it.

The distinction between atomic and complex blocks, which we introduced in section 4.4, becomes relevant here, as complex blocks can specify a **content visibility policy**, which is valid within their body. The content visibility policy for complex block types is defined in the **content visibility table**. This table is totally analogous to the basic visibility table: every row represents a complex block type and every column a hint level. The value in every cell (which may be undefined) indicates the content visibility policy for that block type on that hint level. Complex blocks for which the policy is *undefined* inherit the content visibility of the parent block, if any.

We can now be more precise and state that the effective visibility of a code block is affected by the content visibility policy applicable at its position in the following way:

- **Atomic blocks**: their visibility is defined by the content visibility policy in force at their location. If the content visibility policy at their location is *true*, they will be printed to the output, if it is *false* they will be hidden.

- **Complex blocks**: **no effect**. Complex blocks are immune to the content visibility policy in force at their location. This design choice, which might be perplexing, is motivated by the thought that complex blocks build up the "boning" of the structure of the code. Setting the content visibility to *false* indicates the wish of hiding the "flesh" of the code, not the boning.

By now it should be clear that in our example we can obtain the output of Listing 1 by using the content visibility table shown in Table 2.

Table 2: Simplified example of a content visibility table. Rows correspond to block types, columns to hint levels.

	0	1	2
routine_body	False	True	True
if	False	False	True

4.7 Joining the concepts: hint tables

In the previous sections we have introduced the two orthogonal concepts of blocks' **basic visibility** and **content visibility**. In both cases, we left open the question of what happens if the visibility of a block is undefined. We can now join the two concepts and provide the final visibility rules for code blocks, which will answer this question.

- The visibility of **complex blocks** is simply equal to their basic visibility. However, they have the ability of *specifying* a content visibility policy valid within their body.

- The visibility of **atomic blocks** is equal to their basic visibility, *if it is defined*. If it is undefined, then their effective visibility *is equal to the content visibility in force at their location*, which in this case has to be defined (otherwise the table is malformed).

- In addition to the previous rule, no block can be printed if its parent block is not visible. This is in order to avoid having "detached" blocks in the output, which would be confusing to students and possibly break the syntactic validity of the generated output.

Clearly, these rules require the two visibility tables (basic and content) to be harmoniously used together, which is only possible if they are thought from the beginning as the two sides of the same coin. The combination of both tables takes the name of **hint table**.

In addition to these rules, AutoTeach supports overriding the processing policies defined in hint tables through the use of specific meta-commands. These make it possible, for example, to force all argument declarations to be always visible throughout a file, or a specific crucial instruction to remain hidden until a higher hint level than the one defined in the table is reached. The teacher can even decide to load a blank (all *undefined*) hint table and exclusively rely on visibility meta-commands to define how an exercise should be processed. This is thoroughly discussed in [3].

4.8 Flexibility of the mechanism

AutoTeach ships with a default hint table, for which we tried to find good general-purpose values which work well for the majority of exercises without requiring additional intervention. The table starts by only showing the bare feature[4] declarations at level one, and then incrementally revealing routine arguments, contracts, and local variable declarations. The *existence* of complex instructions is then revealed, without their content, so that students get an idea of how the code is structured (for example, how many nested loops are needed). On the following step, some more information about complex instructions is revealed (the condition of 'if' instructions and the termination condition of loops). At this point, basic instructions are not visible yet. Going up one more level will then reveal all the instructions which are not contained in any complex instruction, producing an output similar to Listing 1. At this point the student sees almost everything, but still can't see the instructions within 'if' statements and loops, which are often the core of the solution of many programming tasks. Only at the highest hint level all instructions are eventually shown. For our course we decided to never show the whole solution, to avoid the scenario in which a students just unveils all the hints and then copy-pastes the solution without too much thinking.

In our experience, this table works remarkably well for most medium-sized exercises, providing good results without the need of even touching the source code. It is not unrealistic to imagine of using AutoTeach in a setting where teachers writing the exercises have no knowledge at all of the hint mechanism, and where batches of existing exercises need to be processed in this fully automated way, which would not have been possible if the hint system had only consisted of manual annotations defining the visibility of single instances of blocks.

AutoTeach also comes with the ability of loading alternative custom hint tables. This enables teacher to define a custom processing policy which may be completely different from our approach. The flexibility of the hint table model give teachers ample freedom.

Finally, there are cases where greater accuracy is required and where teachers may want to define the visibility of *single instances* of blocks. This is especially true for very short exercises, where students are only required to write a handful of lines of code and where showing a crucial instruction too early can spoil the solution. For these exercises, and wherever else necessary, teachers can use manual visibility annotations, slightly tweaking or radically redefining the processing policy of AutoTeach.

With AutoTeach, we believe we are providing an extremely flexible code processing tool. Although the basic processing is entirely automatic, teachers can step in at any time and take full control. Besides the AutoTeach tool itself, this code processing model is general enough to be applicable

---

[4]In Eiffel, the term 'feature' indicates routines, functions, and class attributes.

Table 3: Hint system usage: NH is no. of students not using any hints, L_i is usage at hint level i, - indicates non-existent hint levels.

EXERCISE	NH	L_1	L_2	L_3	L_4	L_5	L_6
Object creation	34	40	32	29	-	-	-
Refs and assignment	39	17	17	14	12	11	10
Control structures	28	21	19	-	-	-	-
Palindrome	25	14	12	9	7	6	5
Queue inverter	21	19	18	16	16	15	-
Recursive gcd	25	11	9	8	8	-	-
Decimal to binary converter	16	21	20	19	18	18	-

to any general-purpose programming language with little or no changes, and we are looking forward to seeing alternative implementations of it which will make it available it to a broader audience.

5. DATA ANALYSIS AND RESULTS

We automatically collected usage data from the hint system, and asked students to answer a questionnaire to assess their experience using it. Table 3 shows which and how many hints the students used per programming exercise. These data suggest that a large number of students who submitted a solution did indeed use the hint system.

The ratio of students using hints (columns "L1" to "L6") to those not using them (column "NH") is non-negligible for all exercises. It also noteworthy that certain exercises like the one on object creation, which is perceived as more difficult, have a high hint usage ratio, while others, like the one on references and assignments, have a low hint usage ratio. Such information can be useful when assessing the exercises and possibly updating them for future iterations of the course.

Table 4 shows a more detailed view of the data from Table 3. For every exercise we show how many students submitted correct and incorrect solutions while using or not using the hint system. We observed that students who did not use the hints submitted almost all correct solutions (99.5%). In contrast, there are much fewer correct submissions by students who used the hints (63%). A possible explanation is that students with incorrect solutions (37%) would have needed further assistance. One way of achieving that could be by adding more hint levels and explanations within the hints.

Table 4: Number of correct and incorrect submissions, differentiated by usage or non-usage of the hint system.

EXERCISE	SUBMISSIONS			
	not using hints		using hints	
	correct	incorr.	correct	incorr.
Object creation	33	1	27	13
Refs and assignment	39	0	11	6
Control structures	28	0	11	10
Palindrome	25	0	13	1
Queue inverter	21	0	6	13
Recursive gcd	25	0	9	2
Decimal to binary converter	16	0	13	8
Total	187 (99.5%)	1 (0.5%)	90 (63%)	53 (37%)

During our data collection students did not get penalties for using the hint system. Furthermore, students had unrestricted access to the hints. The only limitation we enforced was that students can access the hints only in sequential order from the least detailed to the most detailed, i.e hint level L_{i+1} only became accessible after accessing hint level L_i. We also controlled the students who solved an exercise more than six hours after using the hint system, as well as for students who solved an exercise without hints but subsequently accessed the hints out of curiosity. In both cases the numbers were negligible.

We had 38 students answering the final questionnaire, among which 16 (42%) actually used the hint system in at least one exercise. Among those, 5 students (33%) found the hint system *too difficult to use*, while for the rest (66%) it was *about right*, or *easy to use*. In general, 73% of the students who tried the hint system found it useful, and 80% stated that the level of granularity of the hints was appropriate. Among the students who answered the questionnaire and did not use the hint system (58%), 68% said they did not need hints while solving the programming exercises, while 32% claimed they did not know they could use a hint system. The latter finding is interesting, as apparently advertising the hint system via email, in the lecture, and in the exercise sessions was not sufficient. Additionally, the minimalistic GUI we designed (just a "hint" button close to the frame in which students are supposed to write the code) might have negatively impacted the ability to notice the tool for some students.

In conclusion, our data indicates that the hint system was used by a large number of students and found to be helpful when solving programming exercises.

6. RELATED WORK

Maximizing learning for students is an obvious goal for educators, both in a frontal and in an online lecture scenario. A programming task can become frustrating when a student does not know where to start.

To the best of our knowledge, this is the first paper introducing an automatic hint system assisting students of an introductory programming online course in solving programming tasks. In recent years researchers in software engineering for education have worked on different critical challenges, such as problem generation [2, 4, 1], intelligent tutoring [8], automatic grading [10, 11], and facilitating human interaction in an online programming course [12].

Tillmann et al. [11] introduced Pex4Fun, an environment for teaching and learning programming. Their basic idea is that, given a task and a sample solution invisible to the student, the latter tries to work towards the solution by iteratively supplying code. At each iteration, Pex4Fun returns some passing and failing test-cases for the submitted code. The test-cases are computed automatically by using symbolic execution and a theorem prover. Students keep submitting new versions of the code until the tool cannot find any more failing test-cases. The failing test-cases can be seen as a kind of automatically provided semantical hints that students use to iteratively construct a solution, ideally semantically equivalent to the hidden one. In contrast, our hints are both syntactic and semantic, they are inferred from the sample implementation or provided by the teacher, and are preprocessed, which means they do not depend on the students' solutions. Our hints guide the students to our master solution, while alternative solutions are anyway evaluated by running them against a series of unit tests.

Singh et al. [10] introduced an error-model language used to model possible errors that students might make while trying to solve a programming assignment. Starting from these error models, from an implementation provided by a student, and from the one provided by a teacher, their approach produces hints suggesting students how to modify their code in order to remove the errors. In contrast our hints, rather than analyzing the student's solutions, guide the students through the construction of the master solution.

CodeSkulptor [12] is a system helping students to learn programming in Python, that also assists them during the construction of an assignment's solution. However, this assistance is not automatic, it is provided by other students via a forum or by a teaching assistant via email. Our hint system is totally automatic and hints are obtained immediately by a simple click.

Peddycord et al. [9] introduce a technique based on BOTS, an educational programming game teaching the basic concepts of programming through block-moving puzzles. The goal of their hints is to help a student solving a puzzle pass from the current state to another one, which is closer to the goal. The hints are generated by using successful solutions of other students who dealt with the same puzzle and who were in the same state. Although the approach is supposed to be used for teaching concepts of programming languages, it does not use any concrete programming language. The idea of hint generation starting from the correct solutions of other students is, however, interesting, and we plan to investigate it in the future as part of our hint generation.

7. CONCLUSIONS

Finding ways to assist introduction to programming students in an automatic fashion is, nowadays, with the advent of MOOCs, becoming even more relevant. We contribute a programming environment in the cloud with an associated hint system, which gradually unveils parts of the desired solution to students that require support to produce a solution. We designed our hint system to provide flexibility in how teachers can generate hints while requiring little to no input when using default settings.

Our hint system was able to effectively process most of our programming exercises without any extra annotation in the source files, yielding satisfactory hints. Wherever needed, teachers could easily step in and redefine the processing policy by defining a custom hint table.

The data we collected using questionnaires and usage logs suggest that the hint system is a beneficial addition to our teaching programming platform in the cloud. We are now running a larger experiment in the edX MOOC "Computing: Art, Magic, Science" in Spring 2015, and we are developing a Java version of our hint system.

Acknowledgments

We would like to thank Andre Macejko for his work on many technical aspects of our online course.

8. REFERENCES

[1] U. Z. Ahmed, S. Gulwani, and A. Karkare. Automatically Generating Problems and Solutions for Natural Deduction. In *IJCAI*, 2013.

[2] E. Andersen, S. Gulwani, and Z. Popovic. A Trace-based Framework for Analyzing and Synthesizing Educational Progressions. In *SIGCHI*, pages 773–782, 2013.

[3] P. Antonucci. Autoteach: incremental hints for programming exercises. Master's thesis, ETH Zurich, sep 2014.

[4] S. Gulwani, V. A. Korthikanti, and A. Tiwari. Synthesizing Geometry Constructions. In *PLDI*, pages 50–61, 2011.

[5] B. Meyer. Applying Design by Contract. *Computer*, 25(10):40–51, 1992.

[6] B. Meyer. *Object-Oriented Software Construction, 2nd edition*. Prentice Hall, 1997.

[7] J. Middendorf and A. Kalish. The "change-up" in lectures. *The National Teaching & Learning Forum*, 5(2), 1996.

[8] T. Murray. Authoring Intelligent Tutoring Systems: an Analysis of the State of the Art. *Intern. Journal of Artificial Intelligence in Education*, (10):98–129, 1999.

[9] B. Peddycord III, A. Hicks, and T. Barnes. Generating hints for programming problems using intermediate output. In *EDM*, pages 92–98, 2014.

[10] R. Singh, S. Gulwani, and A. Solar-Lezama. Automated Feedback Generation for Introductory Programming Assignments. In *PLDI*, pages 15–26, 2013.

[11] N. Tillmann, J. De Halleux, T. Xie, S. Gulwani, and J. Bishop. Teaching and Learning Programming and Software Engineering via Interactive Gaming. In *ICSE*, 2013.

[12] J. Warren, S. Rixner, J. Greiner, and S. Wong. Facilitating Human Interaction in an Online Programming Course. In *SIGCSE*, pages 665–670, 2014.

Global Perspectives on Assessing Educational Performance and Quality

Alison Clear
Auckland, New Zealand
aclear@eit.ac.nz

Janet Carter
Canterbury, United Kingdom
j.e.carter@kent.ac.uk

Amruth Kumar
Mahwah, USA
amruth@ramapo.edu

Cary Laxer
Terre Haute, USA
laxer@rose-hulman.edu

Simon
Newcastle, Australia
simon@newcastle.edu.au

Ernesto Cuadros-Vargas
Arequipa, Peru
ecuadros@spc.org.pe

ABSTRACT
Educational performance indicators are being considered or implemented in different ways by institutions and governments in different countries. What impact is this likely to have on computing education?

Categories and Subject Descriptors
K.3.2 [**Computer and Information Science Education**]: Accreditation

Keywords
Quality Assurance, Educational Performance Indicators.

1. INTRODUCTION
Educational performance indicators (EPIs) are measures of student achievement, including student retention, progression, course completion, and qualification completion, that have some international currency. A comparison of such measures should help to ensure that a degree in Europe is comparable with one in Australasia or the USA. Yet with no clear indication of how different countries measure and compare the results, there is little likelihood that EPIs can do anything to ensure international consistency and standards. EPIs are being used in different ways in different countries. Where they are being externally enforced, this can pose challenges to computing educators in adapting to an EPI-driven regime.

2. COUNTRY PERSPECTIVES

2.1 New Zealand
New Zealand's Government has embarked on a process of progressively raising the expectations of educational performance, asking tertiary institutions to set high EPI targets (eg 85% pass rates in courses) and to increase the targets each year. Failure to meet the targets can lead to courses being defunded.

Institutions are required to submit three-year plans in which they nominate their EPIs for the period in negotiation with the Tertiary

ITiCSE'15, July 04-08, 2015, Vilnius, Lithuania
ACM 978-1-4503-3440-2/15/07.
http://dx.doi.org/10.1145/2729094.2754843

Education Commission, which controls government funding to all tertiary institutions. Institutions then report annually on the EPIs, measuring them either against previous years or against similar institutions in the sector. The measures can thus have a normative effect on institutions.

This application of EPIs intensifies the pressure on institutions, departments, and educators. Arbitrarily nominated EPIs and the subsequent reporting might lead to dubious behavior among senior management. Clear and Clear [5] ask "If an educator reports a 'below target' course completion result and it is changed by the higher levels of institutional management for whatever reason, what sort of impact will that have on the credibility and integrity of that institution?"

A recent study by Watson and Li [4] analysed a large number of published studies and found a mean pass rate of 68% in introductory programming courses. When a course is known world-wide for low pass rates, the external imposition of higher rates is unlikely to help. New Zealand's setting of educational performance indicators without regard to the discipline areas or the students involved appears to be ill advised and ill judged.

2.2 United Kingdom
Between 1995 and 2008 the proportion of young people going to university in the UK doubled from 20% to almost 40%. Attending university has become a mainstream expectation and the standard route to employment. There are now more people obtaining degrees in the UK than completed high school a generation ago.

It is also now expected that 60% of students will attain a 'good' degree, which means that 24% of young people (more than used to attend university) will graduate in one of the two top levels of award – all without a drop in educational standards.

Whilst the proportion of graduates in these two levels is not an enforced target, it is factored into institutional rankings that are widely disseminated, so institutions face pressure to maintain and increase the proportion. At the chalk face this leads to pass rate targets for individual years of study and for their component modules. There is a broad expectation that 95% of students will proceed to the next stage of study and that 85% will pass any particular module.

A national qualifications framework and subject benchmarks [1] provide descriptors and expectations about standards of degrees for credits and levels, and define the abilities, skills and subject-matter competence that can be expected of a graduate. Institutions are required to demonstrate that their qualifications are granted in accordance with these benchmarks, helping to ensure that standards are maintained.

2.3 USA

In the United States, emphasis is being placed on the ability of colleges and universities to help students complete a bachelor's degree in four years. The 'four-year graduation rate' contributes to public rankings of colleges and universities [2]. The federal and state governments use 'graduation rate' as a metric, calculated as the percentage of students who complete their program within 150 percent of the normal time for completion, as required by the 1990 Student Right to Know Act. President Obama has proposed a college score card based on graduation and retention rates [3], and proposes to tie funding of public institutions to their performance on these measures.

As the mean graduation rate for colleges and universities is only 59%, and the costs of higher education have outpaced inflation for more than 20 years, institutions are under pressure to increase graduation rates. This can translate to closer administrative scrutiny of courses in which large numbers of students fail, such as *Computer Science 1*.

Another initiative being deployed by accredited colleges and universities to control costs is to increase student-credit-hours per course (SCH), favouring larger enrolments and bounded only by infrastructure limitations such as classroom capacity. The capacity to increase SCH is typically limited to introductory courses that are subscribed to by majors as well as non-majors. However, the push to drive up SCH in introductory courses can have a negative impact on graduation rates, because those are the courses in which students tend to need more personal attention and assistance.

Following a dramatic increase in Computer Science enrolments, some educators are themselves imposing minimum GPA requirements in pre-requisite courses in order to prevent unprepared students from advancing through the major. This also impacts graduation rates, not to mention SCH in upper-level courses, trading capacity and throughput for quality.

Faculty members generally have the freedom to set their own grading standards, which leads to a variety of approaches. Some grade on a bell-shaped curve, much like the standardised tests in the U.S., where the mean is a C, one standard deviation above the mean is a B, and two standard deviations above is an A. Others use a standard 10-point scale, where 90%+ is an A, 80%+ is a B, 70%+ is a C, etc. Such systems are seldom externally imposed, and in some institutions it is still notionally possible to give everyone in the class an A if they deserve it.

Faculty members' performance is typically appraised through student evaluations, sometimes supplemented by peer observation. There is little evidence of evaluation being linked to pass rates, or of externally imposed pass-rate targets

2.4 Australia

There is no evidence that the Australian government is considering external pass rate targets. However, the government is keen to increase the number of university graduates.

Some Australian universities are clearly trying to improve overall pass rates. With increased student intakes, this might appear to necessitate a lowering of standards, but the universities do not seem to see it this way. They appear to expect the academic staff to teach the same material to students who might be academically less capable, to assess them comparably to the way students have

been assessed in the past, and to ensure that more of them pass. We have not heard any of these universities espousing norm-referenced assessment, but that appears to be the direction in which they are heading.

Many universities look closely at any course in which the pass rates are lower than a specified target. Some offer assistance in improving teaching approaches, while others leave the teaching staff to find their own improvements. At other universities the approach or policy is found at a lower level, such as the faculty, school, or department. A typical practice is to require that the course be reviewed, or to ask the coordinator to explain, if pass rates are below some nominated figure such as 80% or 70%. At the same time, some interesting techniques are employed to artificially inflate the pass rates.

2.5 Peru

The government in Peru has recently approved a new law aimed at improving the quality of undergraduate programs. One goal of the law is to increase the low number of academic staff who have PhDs. Institutions that fail to meet the new targets risk having their programs closed. Accreditation of degrees is not mandatory, but under the new law it will be necessary in order to access public funding.

In the past four decades universities have been free to create any degree program with any name, resulting in a number of similar degrees with different names. Institutions are now working towards a more consistent naming, guided in the computing area by the IEEE-CS/ACM Computing Curricula. This process will help to identify similar programs and measure them by the same rules.

3. CONCLUSION

As described in this paper there is a wide difference in the setting and monitoring of educational performance indicators around the world. If the purpose of education performance indicators or other means of measuring teaching performance is to enhance quality, the measures set must be consistent with the discipline and of value internationally.

There is research showing that despite the best efforts of computing education researchers, success rates in introductory programming average about 68% around the world [4]. It might follow that such success rates are a reasonable expectation in these courses, but there is no evidence that universities or governments are inclined to accept that conclusion.

4. REFERENCES

[1] http://www.qaa.ac.uk/assuring-standards-and-quality/the-quality-code/subject-benchmark-statements

[2] http://colleges.usnews.rankingsandreviews.com/best-colleges/rankings/highest-grad-rate

[3] http://www.whitehouse.gov/issues/education/higher-education/college-score-card

[4] Watson, C., & Li, F. W. B. (2014). Failure rates in introductory programming revisited. ACM Conference on Innovation & Technology in Computer Science Education, 39-44.

[5] Clear, A. & Clear, T. (2014) Introductory programming and educational performance indicators – a mismatch. ITx Conference, 123-128.

Detailed Recordings of Student Programming Sessions

Daniel Toll, Tobias Olsson
Dept. of Computer Science
Linnaeus University
Kalmar, Sweden
daniel.toll|tobias.ohlsson@lnu.se

Morgan Ericsson, Anna Wingkvist
Dept. of Computer Science
Linnaeus University
Växjö, Sweden
morgan.ericsson|anna.wingkvist@lnu.se

ABSTRACT

Observation is important when we teach programming. It can help identify students that struggle, concepts that are not clearly presented during lectures, poor assignments, etc. However, as development tools become more widely available or courses move off-campus and online, we lose our ability to naturally observe students.

Online programming environments provide an opportunity to record how students solve assignments and the data recorded allows for in-depth analysis. For example, file activities, mouse movements, text-selections, and text caret movements provide a lot of information on when a programmer collects information and what task is currently worked on. We developed CSQUIZ to allow us to observe students on our online courses through data analysis. Based on our experience with the tool in a course, we find recorded sessions a sufficient replacement for natural observations.

1. CSQUIZ

CSQUIZ is a browser-based programming and learning environment that present instructions and theory relevant for an assignment. CSQUIZ currently supports only PHP assignments. It includes a multi-file code-editor that can run code and provide feedback from the interpreter and an automated test tool. A programming session is recorded as a collection of timestamped events, such as a source file is changed, the cursor is moved, text is selected, a file is reset (all changes dropped), CSQUIZ is reloaded, the produced code is executed (output and errors are logged), the active file is switched. Each session is stored on the server and the instructor can either replay it, or generate and visualize descriptive statistics for one or several sessions. We can, for example, compare a single student's performance to the class average or determine how and when students work on their assignments.

Figure 1 shows a replay of a single session. The upper grey area shows a timeline with activities (mouse, writing, selections, copy paste, and compilations) in different files

ITiCSE'15, July 04-08, 2015, Vilnius, Lithuania.
ACM 978-1-4503-3440-2/15/07.
http://dx.doi.org/10.1145/2729094.2754859.

Figure 1: Replaying a programming session in CSQUIZ.

and the bottom half shows a playback of the student's mouse cursor and text caret.

2. RUNNING A COURSE WITH CSQUIZ

We used CSQUIZ in a PHP programming class with 66 students fall 2014, and recorded 1028 programming sessions. The students used the tool to solve 17 different assignments. CSQUIZ allowed us to focus teaching resources on problematic assignments. For example, the average time to complete one assignment was much higher than expected and seven students seemed to be stuck on it. Based on this information we could add additional material on some of the concepts covered by the assignment.

After the course, we studied an anonymized sample of students that took the longest to solve an assignment to understand why they struggled. We found that these students had difficulties with both syntax and semantics, they for example placed code inside a class but outside any function and used the string concatenation operator to add integers. Since CSQUIZ was a new tool, we could see that they did not understand how code was executed by it and how automated testing worked. One student inserted the provided example that showed how to use the class inside the constructor of the same class. This resulted in infinite recursion and an "Out of memory" exception. The student did not seem to understand the error message or how code was executed.

Tips and Techniques for MOOC Production

Carlos Delgado Kloos
Universidad Carlos III de Madrid
Av. Universidad, 30
28911 Leganés (Madrid/Spain)
cdk@it.uc3m.es

Carlos Alario-Hoyos
Universidad Carlos III de Madrid
Av. Universidad, 30
28911 Leganés (Madrid/Spain)
calario@it.uc3m.es

Mar Pérez-Sanagustín
Pontif. Universidad Católica de Chile
Av. Vicuña Mackenna 4860
894000 Santiago de Chile (Chile)
mar.perez@ing.puc.cl

ABSTRACT
MOOCs represent a new medium for education. In this paper, we describe some of the best practices identified after having produced and run a MOOC in 2013 for the first run of MiríadaX, having set up a service unit at Univ. Carlos III de Madrid (UC3M) for the production of MOOCs (mainly for edX) and SPOCs for internal use, and continuing to be active in MOOCs and MOOC-related production at both sides of the Atlantic (in Spain and Chile).

Categories and Subject Descriptors
K.3 [**Computers and Education**]: K.3.0 General, K.3.1 Computer Uses in Education: Distance Learning

Keywords
MOOCs, SPOCs, best practices, production, educational content

1. INTRODUCTION
With MOOCs, teaching has transitioned from being volatile and done in a closed space, to becoming an open permanent record accessible to the world. MOOC teaching is closer to written education than to oral education, with the disadvantage that its production is much more complex and time-consuming and requires the participation of many stakeholders. Univ. Carlos III de Madrid (UC3M) has addressed the growing need of specialized support and guidance to faculty producing MOOCs through the creation of a service unit, called UTEID (*Educational Technology and Innovative Teaching Unit*), composed of specialists in instructional design, ICT, video recording and production, social media, and best practices in education and e-learning [1]. This paper collects some tips and techniques from the experience of UC3M and Pontificia Univ. Católica de Chile for the production of MOOCs, and to some extent, for the production of SPOCs [2].

2. TIPS AND TECHNIQUES
Here are some concrete tips and techniques for faculty who want to produce MOOCs (and SPOCs). It is easy to underestimate the difficulty and time needed to design and build a successful MOOC. Therefore, some general project management techniques become necessary:

- Put together a team of professors and assistants with different profiles to distribute the workload and define tasks: making videos, creating activities, defining the facilitator who will lead discussions in social tools, etc.

- Get help from experts in your institution. They will help you to better design your course, tailor existing content, enhance the quality of your audiovisual resources and deploy the course in the corresponding platform.

- Set a schedule from the beginning (and stick to it), with enough time for discussing the design of the course and generating all the materials, but also allowing enough time for testing your course and tuning final details such as the presentation of the materials in the platform and the subtitling of audiovisual contents.

Then, there are other tips specific to the new educational medium:

- Learn the necessary acting skills for talking in front of a camera (smile, intonation, speed, hands, face). At UC3M, we have given an acting course to MOOCers.

- Get familiar with the platform and plan your content to be activity rather than lecture-oriented. MOOC platforms offer many possibilities that have not been exploited in traditional courses, such as a rich range of multimedia exercises and the massive social component. Try to include interactive simulations and animations.

- Make your videos engaging. Find a good narrative. Make the videos very short. It is better to have two of 4 min, than one of 8 min. length. Get to the point.

- Do not forget about maintainability and reuse. It might be of advantage to plan not to always appear on screen. It is not necessary at all, it might even be better from an audiovisual design point of view, but above all it has the advantage that changes are easier to make at any time. Neither it is a good idea to refer to dates nor to past and future videos from your course. Think about version #2!

- Be careful with the images and resources from third parties you might use. Copyright infringements can lead to a course withdrawal. Open third-party images and resources must be recognized appropriately.

3. ACKNOWLEDGMENTS
We acknowledge UNESCO Chair on "Scalable Digital Education for All" at UC3M and eMadrid (Madrid Gov, S2013/ICE-2715) and EEE (Spanish Ministry, TIN2011-28308-C03-01) projects.

4. REFERENCES
[1] Alario-Hoyos, C., Pérez-Sanagustín, M., Delgado Kloos, C. et al. Designing your first MOOC from Scratch: Recommen-dations after teaching "Digital Education of the Future", *eLearning Papers*, Vol. 37, PAU Education 2014, pp. 1-7

[2] Delgado Kloos, C., Muñoz-Merino, P.J., Muñoz-Organero, M. et al. Experiences of Running MOOCs and SPOCs at UC3M, *Proc. IEEE Global Engineering Education Conf., EDUCON 2014*, Istanbul, Turkey, pp. 884-891

Department Programs to Encourage and Support Service Learning and Community Engagement

Douglas Harms
DePauw University
Department of Computer Science
Greencastle, Indiana 46135, USA
+1 765 658 4727
dharms@depauw.edu

ABSTRACT

Service Learning (SL) is an established practice in which course objectives are met by having students engage in activities with individuals and/or organizations within the community in a way that is mutually beneficial to both the student and the community, In this paper the author describes a comprehensive department-wide approach to service learning and community engagement where students have multiple opportunities to learn computer science material by engaging with community members.

Categories and Subject Descriptors

K.3.2 [**Computers and Education**]: Computer and Information Science Education – *computer science education, curriculum.*

General Terms

Human Factors

Keywords

Service Learning, Community Engagement

1. INTRODUCTION

Service Learning (SL) is an established practice in which course objectives are met by having students engage in activities with individuals and/or organizations within the community in a way that is mutually beneficial to both the student and the community [1, 3]. In recent years many CS courses have included service learning components [2, 4–6]. In this paper the author describes a comprehensive department-wide approach to service learning and community engagement where students have multiple opportunities to learn computer science material by engaging with community members.

2. DEPARTMENT SL OPPORTUNITIES

The Computer Science department at DePauw University provides CS students with many opportunities to engage with community members, including:

- **Service Learning courses**, including sections of CS1 where students organize and conduct computer literacy workshops for local residents; a digital divide course where students teach CS material to local middle school students; a web development course where students design web sites for local non profits.

- **CTEP (Community Technology Enrichment Program)** where students refurbish donated computers and distribute them to qualifying local families.

- **Work with at-risk high school students** who are interested in learning about computers. Students work 1-on-1 with a local high school student to refurbish a computer and install/configure software. The student keeps the refurbished system.

- **Work with local middle school teachers** to bring technology into the classroom, including robotics, 3D printing, ad digital art.

- **International Service Trips** where students install computers in schools and/or community internet cafes and teach computer literacy to local school children.

3. REFERENCES

[1] Cooksey, M.A. and Olivares, K.T. eds. 2010. *Quick Hits for Service-Learning: Successful Strategies by Award-Winning Teachers*. Indiana University Press.

[2] Egan, M.A.L. and Johnson, M. 2010. Service learning in introductory computer science. *Proceedings of the fifteenth annual conference on Innovation and technology in computer science education* (Bilkent, Ankara, Turkey, 2010), 8–12.

[3] Jacoby, B. 2009. *Civic Engagement in Higher education : Concepts and Practices*. Jossey-Bass.

[4] Linos, P.K. et al. 2003. A service-learning program for computer science and software engineering. *Proceedings of the 8th annual conference on Innovation and technology in computer science education* (Thessaloniki, Greece, 2003), 30–34.

[5] Rosmaita, B.J. 2007. Making service learning accessible to computer scientists. *Proceedings of the 38th SIGCSE technical symposium on Computer science education* (Covington, Kentucky, USA, 2007), 541–545.

[6] Tan, J. and Phillips, J. 2005. Incorporating service learning into computer science courses. *J. Comput. Sci. Coll.* 20, 4 (2005), 57–62.

ITICSE '15, July 04-08, 2015, Vilnius, Lithuania
ACM 978-1-4503-3440-2/15/07.
http://dx.doi.org/10.1145/2729094.2754865

Tools for Outreach Presentations

Ronald I. Greenberg
Loyola University Dept. of Computer Science
820 N. Michigan Ave.
Chicago, IL 60611-2147
rig@cs.luc.edu

Dale Reed
U. of Illinois at Chicago Dept. of Computer Sci.
851 S. Morgan St. (MC 152)
Chicago, IL 60607-7053
reed@uic.edu

ABSTRACT

We present resources we have constructed and culled from the internet that can be used in computing outreach visits in K–12 classrooms, especially high schools. We have used such tools at about 100 schools, reaching several thousand students, and achieving positive attitudinal responses in surveys of several hundred of these students.

Categories and Subject Descriptors

K.3.0 [**Computers and Education**]: General

Keywords

Computing outreach; computer science outreach

1. INTRODUCTION

Inspired by Carnegie Mellon University's Women@SCS Roadshow, we embarked on an extensive effort (assisted by university students and staff and National Science Foundation funding) to visit high school classrooms in the Chicago area; we reached several thousand students and surveyed over 400. 74% to 88% of survey respondents liked ("good" or "very good") each of our presentation elements. Furthermore, 63% to 70% agreed or strongly agreed that they gained a greater recognition of the diversity of people working in computing-related fields, learned more about the kinds of computing-related work people do, and learned more about the availability of computing-related career opportunities; additionally, over half the respondents indicated increased interest in pursuing a college major in computer science. Our efforts also enhanced our network of high school contacts, contributing to the Chicago CSTA group being one of the largest in the country, and helping to build the community that has led to professional development for the Exploring Computer Science (ECS) curriculum being provided to 140 Chicago Public Schools high school teachers.

We provide here an overview of effective elements from which our presentations sampled. Most can be accessed at

ITiCSE'15, July 6–8, 2015, Vilnius, Lithuania.
ACM 978-1-4503-3440-2/15/07.
http://dx.doi.org/10.1145/2729094.2754866.

http://illinoiscomputes.org/hspresent; they are generally suitable for continued use or provide good examples on which to base an update or adaptation to a different locale.

2. PRESENTATION ELEMENTS

The elements used in our presentations can be broadly characterized as responding to four questions as follows:

Who does computer science?
The main approach to increase appreciation of the diversity of computer scientists was to show many pictures of computer scientists (more than in other outreach presentations), along with a few of other people, and to ask students to identify the people who are *not* computer scientists.

What is computer science about?
Principal items utilized in this area included excerpts from the CMU Roadshow, a slide show by Jeanette Wing on uses of computational thinking in various subject areas, robotics videos, visualization sites such as Name Voyager and Photosynth, and technologies to assist persons with disabilities, such as Dasher and "tongue vision"; these all helped students see some of the kinds of things they could work on as computer scientists. We also created handy online tools to perform "magic" tricks based on computer science concepts.

Are there jobs for computer scientists?
Data and news articles were presented to show that computing is dominant among occupations providing high pay, good working conditions, and strong projected growth in number of jobs. Also often cited was the gap between job openings and university degree production in computing fields.

How can I prepare to be active in computer science?
Presenters generally incorporated pointers about preparing for computing studies and careers in the overall presentation as well as during the question/answer period at the end. Reassurance also was provided for students who may have limited pre-college options to study computing or misconceptions about their own match for the subject. For example, students were told that computing can be studied at the college level without substantial prior experience, but that it is always good to seek out computing-related instruction in high school that goes beyond just using applications such as word processors and spreadsheets. Students were also encouraged to learn about application areas of interest, since computing is so interdisciplinary, and they were reassured that whether they love mathematics or not, there are appropriate areas of computer science. Sometimes, the presenters also pointed out contests for high school students.

Using Personal Robots and Myro/Java in the First Computer Science Course

Douglas Harms
DePauw University
Department of Computer Science
Greencastle, Indiana 46135, USA
+1 765 658 4727
dharms@depauw.edu

ABSTRACT

Myro/Java is an implementation of the Python-based Myro API for controlling personal robots used in introductory Computer Science courses. This paper describes the author's experience using Myro/Java in his Computer Science 1 courses over eight semesters.

Categories and Subject Descriptors

K.3.2 [**Computers and Education**]: Computer and Information Science Education – *computer science education.*

General Terms

Design, Languages

Keywords

Personal Robots, CS1 Curricula, Java, IPRE

1. INTRODUCTION

Many schools are using personal robots (where each student has his or her own robot on which to work, both in and out of class) in their beginning Computer Science course because they are tangible, fun to program, and provide immediate feedback to students [1, 4]. IPRE defined a Python-based API called Myro (for *My Ro*bot) that allows students to write programs that interact with and control a personal robot[3]. The author implemented a Myro API in Java called Myro/Java [2, 5] and has used this API to teach eight sections of Computer Science 1. This paper briefly describes some of his experiences teaching this course using Myro/Java.

2. SCRIBBLER/FLUKE ROBOT

The Scribbler robot and IPRE Fluke add-on board are shown in Figure 1. The Scribbler is a rugged and small (188 x 158.8 x 81 mm) robot with two independently controlled wheels, three light sensors, two IR obstacle sensors, two line sensors, a speaker that can produce simple tones, and several programmable LED lights. The IPRE Fluke add-on board attaches to the Scribbler's serial port; it has a low-resolution (256 x 192) color camera, three IR obstacle sensors, a Bluetooth adapter for wireless communication

ITiCSE '15, July 04-08, 2015, Vilnius, Lithuania
ACM 978-1-4503-3440-2/15/07.
http://dx.doi.org/10.1145/2729094.2754864

with the host computer, and the ability to communicate with other Scribbler/Fluke robots via IR signals. The cost of the Scribbler/Fluke robot is approximately US$220.

Figure 1. The Scribbler Robot with IPRE Fluke Add-on

3. EXPERIENCES

CSC121 is the first CS course most students take, and students are introduced to software development and Java. Most students taking the courses have no prior programming experience. The author has developed a set of twelve closed-lab exercises and several programming projects for Myro/Java. He has found that students enjoy using robots, are motivated to work on assignments, and are well-prepared to take subsequent CS courses that do not utilize robots. He also finds that using robots helps "recruit" students (including many women) to the CS major who had not considered this prior to taking the course.

4. REFERENCES

[1] Blank, D. 2006. Robots Make Computer Science Personal. *Communications of the ACM.* 49, (Dec. 2006), 25–27.

[2] Harms, D.E. 2011. Personal Robots in CS1: Implementing the Myro API in Java. *International Conference on Computer Systems and Technologies* (Vienna, Austria, Jun. 2011), 552–557.

[3] Institute for Personal Robots in Education: *http://www.roboteducation.org/*. Accessed: 2011-03-17.

[4] Markham, S.A. and King, K.N. 2010. Using Personal Robots in CS1: Experiences, Outcomes, and Attitudinal Influences. *Proceedings of the Fifteenth Annual Conference on Innovation and Technology in Computer Science Education - ITiCSE'10* (2010), 204–208.

[5] Myro in Java - IPRE Wiki: *http://wiki.roboteducation.org/Myro_in_Java*. Accessed: 2015-03-16.

A Numpy-First Approach to Teaching CS1 to Natural Science Students

Elizabeth Patitsas
University of Toronto, Toronto, Canada
patitsas@cs.toronto.edu

ABSTRACT

Numpy (Numerical Python) and Scipy (Scientific Python) are Python libraries for doing numerical/scientific work that are popular with research scientists, as they allow for matrix-based computation in Python. I report on my initial experiences teaching a CS1 in Python to natural/social science students using a "numpy-first" approach. Students were taught about numpy arrays and matrix manipulations before learning lists and loops. I found this approach helped this audience appreciate the relevance of CS to their own fields, and possibly better learn topics such as logic and file I/O.

Categories and Subject Descriptors

K.3.2 [**Computers and Information Science Education**]: Pedagogy, non-majors

Keywords

CS1, non-majors, computer science education

1. INTRODUCTION

I will share my initial experience teaching a CS1 for non-majors using a "numpy-first" approach. The course is a 12-week, 100-level course directed at natural/social science students at a large research-intensive university, and covers the basics of Python with a focus on scientific applications. Half of the students are upper-level; most plan to go to grad school. Few students formally take any CS past this course.

The first time I taught the course (spring 2014), I followed the usual sequence of topics: variables and expressions; conditionals and logic; loops, strings and lists; file I/O; numpy/scipy. The students overwhelmingly perceived numpy/scipy as most relevant to their interests.

1.1 Motivation

Reflecting after the term, there were three issues I wanted to address for the next offering of the course:

1. Early in the term, students struggled to see the **immediate relevance of Python** to their lives, instead trusting it would be "useful later".
2. Students struggled with **conditionals and logic**, perhaps since we introduced both topics together.

ITiCSE'15, July 6–8, 2015, Vilnius, Lithuania.
ACM 978-1-4503-3440-2/15/07.
http://dx.doi.org/10.1145/2729094.2754861 .

3. **File I/O**: students had no notion of what a 'file' is from a CS perspective, nor what it meant to 'read' it.

1.2 Changes made

Teaching the class in spring 2015, I decided to move numpy earlier in the curriculum, so that the order was: variables and expressions; functions; numpy/scipy; conditionals and logic; loops, strings and lists; file I/O. My rationale for this was to address the three issues listed in subsection 1.1:

1. The early introduction of numpy/scipy makes the relevance of programming immediately clear to students. Students can promptly perform data analysis and graphing that is immediately usable in their other classes.
2. Numpy introducing array filtering, which means that students work with arrays of booleans before encountering conditionals. This reduces cognitive load.
3. Numpy provides the functions which encapsulate reading csv files to and from arrays. As a result, students can gain comfort with importing and exporting arrays before having to learn the details of `read` and `write`.

2. OBSERVATIONS ON NUMPY-FIRST

The numpy-first approach was well-received by students. It addressed the three issues in subsection 1.1. Students found the early focus on complex data analysis to be motivating for learning how to program.

This group of students has a background in linear algebra, and when they first see arrays/lists, they expect operators like + and * to add/multiple elements together, rather than concatenate/repeat. Introducing arrays before lists meant that the first time students saw a data structure its behaviour was congruent with their expectations.

The approach I took to teaching numpy involved teaching students about many of numpy/scipy's builtin functions. From early on, students got in the habit of looking up builtin functions rather than reinventing functions from scratch.

I needed to spend more time on numerical error and multiple return values than I expected. Both came up in using numpy for data analysis, and were confusing to students.

A downside of the numpy-first approach is that there are few resources for beginning programmers to learn about numpy: most numpy resources assume the audience can program already. There was also nothing in the class textbook on the topic. When numpy was at the end of term, students were better able to handle this.

Interestingly, when I introduced loops, many students expressed a distaste for them, preferring array manipulations.

Overall the numpy-first approach worked well for this science-focused audience, and I plan to use it again.

RAPT: Relational Algebra Parsing Tools

Olessia Karpova, Noel D'Souza, Diane Horton, and Andrew Petersen
Department of Computer Science
University of Toronto
olessia.karpova@utoronto.ca, noel@noeldsouza.com, dianeh@cs.utoronto.ca,
petersen@cs.toronto.edu

ABSTRACT

Many database courses rely on relational algebra (RA) to provide a theoretical foundation for database query languages such as SQL. However, few tools exist to support students in learning RA. To fill this need, we created RAPT. RAPT uses a syntactic and semantic understanding of RA to transform input statements into a variety of outputs, including LaTeX formatted queries, parse tree diagrams, and executable SQL statements. The translation to SQL is particularly important, as it enables the creation of automatically tested exercises and allows students to view the result of executing an RA statement. RAPT-supported exercises have been integrated into PCRS, a system for creating online learning modules, and deployed to a third year databases course with over 350 students.

Categories and Subject Descriptors

K.3.2 [**Computers and Education**]: Computer and Information Science Education—*Computer Science Education*

Keywords

courseware, relational algebra, sql

1. INTRODUCTION

RAPT is one of a few tools that provide support to students learning Relational Algebra (RA) [1, 2, 3, 4]. RAPT's distinguishing feature is its focus on an intermediate representation that it can translate into LaTeX formatted queries, parse tree diagrams, and executable SQL statements. This facilitates creation of interactive RA exercises that provide students with immediate feedback and that can be graded automatically.

2. PARSING RA

RAPT takes as input RA expressions written in a LaTeX-like syntax. It parses them into an intermediate representation using a grammar that defines the flavour of RA being used. Two grammars are provided: a core grammar with the five primitive operators σ, Π, $\times$, $\cup$, and $-$ (set difference), and an extended grammar that adds $\bowtie$, θ, and $\cap$. In addition, RAPT supports renaming of attributes and of relations, and provides an assignment operator. An instructor

ITiCSE'15, July 6–8, 2015, Vilnius, Lithuania.
ACM 978-1-4503-3440-2/15/07.
http://dx.doi.org/10.1145/2729094.2754862.

can easily configure the grammar, operator keywords, and choice of set/bag semantics and is easily extensible to additional operators. This combination of features is not available in other tools.

The intermediate representation, a collection of decorated abstract syntax trees (dASTs), facilitates semantic analysis. Semantic analysis solves a difficult problem: resolving names of relations and attributes. While humans can (usually) resolve ambiguities in RA, a query must be unambiguous to be executed by SQL.

To infer fully specified names, RAPT uses semantic information from a node's children, its operator, and a user-provided database schema. This analysis identifies and reports common errors such as references to non-existent identifiers and, more importantly, identifiers that are invalid within the context of the current subexpression.

3. TEACHING USING RAPT

The traditional pencil-and-paper approach to teaching relational algebra does not allow students to quickly determine if their RA is correct. By translating RA to SQL, RAPT provides a mechanism for issuing immediate, formative feedback to students as they work on RA exercises. Furthermore, with RAPT, grading RA assignments can be fully automated. We have used RAPT with PCRS [5], a system for deploying online learning materials, to provide RA exercises to a third year database class of over 350 students.

Executing RA also enables the creation of debugging aids. Visualization of program execution is a valuable tool, especially for novices, and is widely used in computer science instruction. RAPT was designed to be easily extendable for this purpose: visualization of the intermediate relations within an RA statement can be implemented by traversing the abstract syntax tree and evaluating the partial query at every node.

RAPT is available through GitHub and PyPI. PCRS, which supports Python, C, RA, and SQL exercises, is available by request.

4. REFERENCES

[1] J. Gorman, S. Gsell, and C. Mayfield. Learning relational algebra by snapping blocks. In *Proceedings of the 45th ACM Technical Symposium on Computer Science Education*, 2014.

[2] J. Kessler. relational algebra calculator. http://138.232.66.66/ra/index.htm. Accessed: 2015-04-20.

[3] K. McMaster, S. Sambasivam, and N. Anderson. Relational algebra programming with microsoft access databases. *Interdisciplinary Journal of Information, Knowledge, and Management*, 6:73–83, 2011.

[4] J. Yang. RA: A relational algebra interpreter. http://www.cs.duke.edu/ ~junyang/ra/. Accessed: 2015-04-20.

[5] D. Zingaro, Y. Cherenkova, O. Karpova, and A. Petersen. Facilitating code-writing in PI classes. In *Proceedings of the 44th ACM Technical Symposium on Computer Science Education*, pages 585–590, 2013.

Websheets: A Templated Online Coding Exercise System

David Pritchard
Department of Computer Science
University of Southern California
Los Angeles, CA, USA
david.pritchard@usc.edu

ABSTRACT

Websheets is an online exercise system providing rigorous "fill-in-the-blank" programming exercises. It allows an instructor to quickly create exercises by writing a correct reference solution and indicating the parts to be "blanked out." It is open-source and has been used successfully in Java and C++ by a half-dozen instructors and over 1000 students.

Categories and Subject Descriptors

K.3.2 [**Computers and Education**]: Computer and Information Science Education

General Terms

Design, Human Factors, Languages

Keywords

Automatic Assessment; Java; C++; CS1; Open Source

1. GOALS

Websheets is an online exercise system. It began as a way of trying to automate and formalize a collection of "fill-in-the-blank" programming exercises in a large introductory Java course. Fill-in-the-blank exercises are excellent pedagogically since they allow you to focus attention on the new and interesting parts of the code, rather than the boilerplate.

Those exercises were previously provided as `.java` files with underscores indicating parts to be added. With Websheets, our goals were (1) to provide an online interface which would highlight the editable parts, (2) to make it easy for students to submit their code in the browser and test it, and (3) to rigorously enforce that only the selected parts could be changed. Additionally, we wanted (4) to make it easy for instructors to create new exercises, and (5) to make it open-source so instructors can contribute new exercises or infrastructural improvements. We have implemented the system and provided backends in both Java and C++.

ITiCSE'15, July 6–8, 2015, Vilnius, Lithuania.
ACM 978-1-4503-3440-2/15/07
http://dx.doi.org/10.1145/2729094.2754863.

```
Exercise Description: DigitSum
Write a program that takes an integer command-line argument, and outputs the sum of its digits, by
using while loop.
 1  public class DigitSum {
 2      public static void main(String[] args) {
 3          int n = Integer.parseInt(args[0]);
 4          int total = 0; // running sum
 5
 6          while (        ) {
 7
 8
 9          }
10
11          System.out.println(total);
12      }
13 }
               Submit code
Results will appear below.
```

Figure 1: Students' view of an exercise.

2. INTERFACES

Ease of use is a main goal for the Websheets system, both for the student and the instructor. In Figure 1 we show the students' view of an exercise called DigitSum. The student accesses the exercise and its description in their browser, fills it out, and submits it, receiving instant feedback on multiple test cases. The yellow areas expand horizontally and vertically to accommodate solutions of any length.

To define an exercise, you must create a template, which acts as both a reference solution *and* the scaffolding for the student. It is a normal program augmented by delimiters \[and]\ which represent the start and end of a blank. Here's the template for DigitSum:

```
public static void main(String[] args) {
    int n = Integer.parseInt(args[0]);
    int total = 0; // running sum

    while (\[n > 0]\) {
\[
        total = total + n%10;
        n = n/10;
]\
...
```

The system has received extremely positive feedback from instructors and students. We use it for in-class activities, mandatory homework, and optional practice. Try it out, read the documentation, or obtain the source at:

```
http://cscircles.cemc.uwaterloo.ca/websheets.html
```

Capstone Projects Evolution over a Decade in a Computer Science Engineering Degree

Juan J. Olarte, César Domínguez, Arturo Jaime, Francisco J. García-Izquierdo

Dpto. Matemáticas y Computación. University of La Rioja, 26005 Logroño. Spain

{jjolarte, cesar.dominguez, arturo.jaime, francisco.garcia }@unirioja.es

ABSTRACT

This study describes the capstone projects evolution over the last ten years at our university. During this period, two different degrees have existed: "Technical Engineering in Computer Science" with graduated students from 2005 through 2012, and a "Degree in Computer Science Engineering" from 2013 through 2014. Herein, the evolution of some important features of the Capstone Projects is examined: duration, grade and time devoted by the advisor. This evolution defines some phases in the first degree: beginning, stabilization, maturity, and completion. The change in the degree structure is associated with changes in the performance on projects.

Categories and Subject Descriptors

D.2.9 [**Management of Computing and Information Systems**]: Project and People Management – *Life cycle*, *management technique, systems development.*

General Terms

Management; experimentation.

Keywords

Capstone project; computer science engineering.

1. INTRODUCTION

Computer Science Engineering degrees often culminate in a capstone project, usually consisting of completing a software development project [1]. The capstone project represents a task of considerably larger scope and difficulty than any other work that students have tackled during their academic career. In order to address the project with greater possibilities of success, an advisor who guides the student and supervises his work is assigned [2, 3]. Studies in Computer Science Engineering commenced at our university in 2002 with the "Technical Engineering in Computer Science" degree and changed to the "Degree in Computer Science Engineering" in 2009. This work conducts a longitudinal study over a decade of some significant parameters of capstone projects such as project duration, grade, and time devoted by the advisor.

2. RESULTS AND DISCUSSION

In order to collect projects data, surveys corresponding to 203 projects developed in our university during the last decade were successfully gathered. The manner in which projects have been performed was studied, particularly how the following three parameters evolved: project duration, grade obtained by students, and amount of time devoted by advisors (Figure 1).

ITiCSE'15, July 4–8, 2015, Vilnius, Lithuania.
ACM 978-1-4503-3440-2/15/07.
http://dx.doi.org/10.1145/2729094.2754845

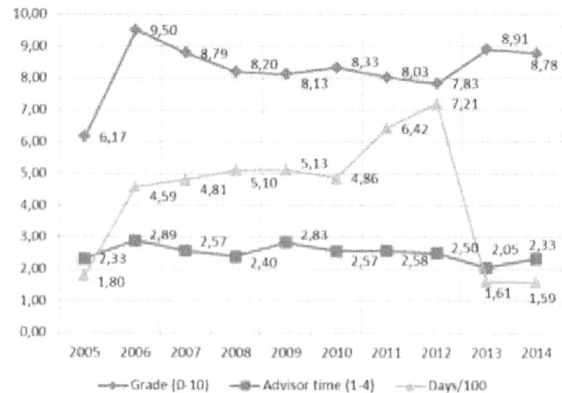

Figure 1. Grade, duration and time devoted by advisors

The evolution of projects is described through these phases below: *Beginning phase (2005-06).* The low grade in the first year can be explained since these students prioritized finishing their degree over creating a quality project. In 2006 an abrupt rise can be observed in the three graphs. The students decided to devote more time to their projects and postpone completion to the following year obtaining better results. *Stabilization phase (2007-08).* A sharp decline in grade and a slight increase in duration were observed. The time spent by the advisor maintained from this moment on with small variations. *Maturity phase (2009-10).* Grade and duration stabilized, and time devoted by advisors also remained stable. *Completion phase (2011-12).* Duration rose sharply since several projects that were long overdue had to be finalized before the end of the current degree program. Grade decreased slightly because several projects were forced to finish for the deadline, thereby compromising quality. *Initial phase of the new degree (2013-14).* A remarkable rise in the grade and a decrease in duration can be observed, as well as a noticeable decrease in advisor time.

The new program has positively affected the performance on projects. The most important changes related to capstone projects include a previous mandatory internship and the company orientation projects in the new degree, usually in the same company where student internships were conducted. A more in-depth invest in the factors which may have influenced this improvement could be necessary, particularly the organizational changes introduced by the new program.

3. REFERENCES

[1] ACM/IEEE-CS, Computer Science Curricula 2013.

[2] Domínguez, C., Jaime, A., García-Izquierdo, F.J., Olarte, J.J. Supervision Typology in Computer Science Engineering Capstone Projects. J. Eng. Educ. 101(4): 679-697, 2012.

[3] Olarte, J. J., Domínguez, C., García-Izquierdo, F. J., & Jaime, A. (2014). Capstone Projects in Computer Science: Evaluated by Stakeholders. ITiCSE'14 (pp. 345-345)

Keystroke Biometrics for Student Authentication: A Case Study

Aythami Morales, Julian Fierrez
Universidad Autonoma de Madrid
Dept. de Tecnología Electronica y de las Comunicaciones, EPS, C\Francisco Tomas y Valiente, 28049 Madrid, Spain
{aythami.morales, julian.fierrez}@uam.es

ABSTRACT

This work presents a case study on the application of biometric systems for student authentication services. We analyze the accuracy of a keystroke dynamics algorithm used to authenticate students during a real online exam of an introductory computer science course.

Categories and Subject Descriptors

D.4.6 [Security and Protection]: *Access controls and Authentication*

Keywords

MOOCs, POOCs, authentication, keystroke dynamics, biometrics.

1. SUMMARY OF THE POSTER

The MOOCs have emerged in recent years as a new way to educate students in the basis of open, free, distributed and participatory courses. The online courses break with the barriers associated to traditional lessons and provide a new widely accessible education over the internet. However there is a discussion among all the academic sectors about the new educational scenario proposed by MOOCs. Among several topics, this controversial discussion includes the challenges related with the "certificates" or "statements of completion" of courses without classroom attendance. How can we certify that the student who is being certified is the one who perform the activities of the course? How can we avoid/detect anomalous users? The widely and accessible nature of the MOOCs increase the vulnerability of the systems and the authentication of the students emerges as a challenging and unsolved task. Researchers and MOOCs instructors are aware of the importance of reliable authentication for the future of online education and they have made efforts to propose and analyze convenient authentication approaches [1]. Among all the proposed approaches, biometric technologies seem to be the most attractive solutions. Biometric recognition technologies allow to authenticate users based on "something that users are" instead of traditional authentication based on "something that users know" such as PIN or passwords. Keystroke dynamic authentication is a well-known technology which has attracted much interest of industry and researchers during the last decade. Keystroke dynamics are interesting for MOOCs authentication because it is: i) transparent (it runs in the background without requiring explicit user interaction), and ii) continuous (authentication can be performed over all the user activity, not only based on an initial access to the platform). Transparent authentication is strongly related with the user experience and usability of the platform. The authentication service must be simple and not affect the normal activity of the MOOC. Continuous authentication is critical because an authentication system based on PIN codes assumes that the user will not provide his/her code to any other user. That assumption is not valid in a scenario in which the user could be interested in providing his/her PIN code to other user to pass an exam.

The experiments reported in this poster are performed over OhKBIC dataset (available at http://biometric-competitions.com/mod/competition/dataset.php?id=7). The database includes the responses of 64 students to five questions directly into the web-platform of the course which logged the keystroke pattern of each of the students (500 keystrokes per user). Therefore we consider here a text independent authentication scenario. The aim of the experiment is to analyze the performance of keystroke dynamics among the different responses. The experimental protocol is summarized as: i) for each user, the database is divided into enrollment (first 300 characters) and test (last 100 characters) not using the 100 characters in between in order to give time separation between enrollment and test data; ii) we search for common digraphs and trigraphs (sequences of two and three characters respectively) between the gallery and test set; iii) a cross-validation protocol is applied to measure the distance between gallery and test using a keystroke classifier based on Normalized Manhattan Distance [2]; iv) the final score is obtained as the mean of the best 40 distances (20 digraphs and 20 trigraphs); v) the performance of the overall experiment is provided according the average accuracy in authenticating each user (100-Equal Error Rate), see Table 1.

Table 1. Student authentication accuracy (100-EER)

Digraph	Trigraph	Combined
90.54%	91.97%	93.93%

The results show a promising performance with a correct student authentication over 90% using only 100 keystrokes. Although there is room for improvements, this work encourages to further explore in authentication services based on keystroke dynamics for online courses.

REFERENCES

[1] Miguel, J., Caballe, S., Prieto, J. 2013. Providing information security to MOOC: Towards effective student ′ authentication. In *Proc. of the Int. Conf. on Intelligent Networking and Collaborative Systems* (Xian, China), IEEE Press, 289–292.

[2] Morales, A., Fierrez, J., Ortega-Garcia, J. 2014. Towards predicting good users for biometric recognition based on keystroke dynamics. *In Proc. of Int. Workshop on Soft Biometrics*, 1-14, Zurich, Switzerland, LNCS 8926, 1-14.

ITiCSE'15, July 6–8, 2015, Vilnius, Lithuania.
ACM 978-1-4503-3440-2/15/07.
http://dx.doi.org/10.1145/2729094.2754847

Learning and Teaching Computing Sustainability

Margaret Hamilton

RMIT University, GPO Box 2476,

Melbourne, 61 3 9925 2939

margaret.hamilton@rmit.edu.au

ABSTRACT

In this paper we present a new course designed around computing sustainability, and aimed at encouraging students to analyse, design, create and maintain more sustainable workplaces which reduce the overall carbon footprint into the future. We explain the curriculum for this course, the concepts of green variables, green clouds, sustainable computing as well as the sensing and gathering of relevant crowdsourced information which can be integrated onto a green virtual platform.

Categories and Subject Descriptors

H. [**Information Systems**]. User/Machine Systems, *Performance evaluation (efficiency and effectiveness);* K.3.2 [**Computer and Information Science Education**]: Computer science education

General Terms

Human Factors; Documentation; Measurement; Performance; Design; Reliability; Management.

Keywords

Sustainability; Professionalism; Green Computing.

1. INTRODUCTION

There are many courses where various different aspects of computing sustainability can be incorporated. We have developed our new course on sustainability with many small modules, typical of learning objects and have gathered as many different resources as we can to enable them to be incorporated into many different university courses.

Our university has a strategic plan to be global, urban and connected, and our students are now using computing resources consolidated in the cloud, which enables improved global connectivity while reducing power consumption. Virtual classrooms can enable more education about sustainability by providing access to resources around the clock, and encouraging cross-disciplinary approaches to learning and research.

We aim to encourage our students to consider computing sustainability and actively seek opportunities where sustainable choices can be implemented.

2. CURRICULUM

We are adapting an existing course on professionalism in computing to incorporate more of these sustainability modules, such as: green mobile cloud computing systems; integration of

green clouds and the internet of things; energy saving solutions and trade-offs; sensors and monitoring software tools for evaluating energy use, among other topics.

Our aim is for this integrated data to be visualised for engagement and monitoring by future students, who will be encouraged to reduce their carbon footprint through accumulating green rewards. Also, the gathering of resources and posting on the cloud can encourage further collaboration and development of sustainable computing.

Authentic learning and assessment activities are important for course design [1]. We have invited guest speakers and we are recording lectures, seminars, workshops and discussions about green education, about gathering data which monitors and measures green variables, and about designing for green environments. Students using arduino boards are coding them to gather data to measure power usage for lighting and computers, air quality, actual paper usage and discussing their results. Green variables which can be identified, recorded, measured, monitored are being described and evaluated. Problems with data accuracy are being identified and ways of cleansing the data will be evaluated and implemented.

By providing green lectures, seminars, workshops in the virtual classroom in the cloud, learning and teaching resources can be shared and renewed. Some green lectures have been delivered, along with a seminar for students of an advanced professional development course, as well as assessments based on the sustainability topics covered. The students undertook the research and data gathering with much enthusiasm, developing interesting resources. However, this is the beginning only and much more remains to be done with the organisation of videos, both existing and from YouTube as well as newly commissioned ones. We are encouraging other courses such as capstone projects and introduction to IT courses to access the resources.

As well as the many green initiatives being undertaken by architects, our students are encouraged to become engaged and actively promote the gathering of data about the buildings which will include sensor data, images and statistics. They are taking measurements and monitoring their own environments and to design a rewards system for carbon credits gained by taking greener initiatives, such as walking or cycling to university, as opposed to catching public transport, or driving, to encourage a smaller global carbon footprint.

3. ACKNOWLEDGMENTS

This work is supported by a **Sustainable Urban Precincts Program (SUPP) Learning and Teaching Project** grant from Siemens and RMIT University

4. REFERENCES

[1] Margaret Hamilton and Joan Richardson "An Academic Approach to Learning and Assessment Design", Journal of Learning Design, 2007, ISSN : 1832-8342, Vol 2(1), p37-51.

Delegate, Decorate, State, and Illustrate in the OOP Course

Mark A. Boshart and
Martha J. Kosa
Department of Computer Science
Tennessee Technological University
Cookeville, Tennessee, USA
+1(931)372-3579
{mboshart,mjkosa}@tntech.edu

ABSTRACT

We regularly teach a required OOP course which serves as the bridge between the introductory CS1/CS2 sequence and the senior software engineering sequence. We stress the fundamental concepts of polymorphism, inheritance, and encapsulation. The students transition from writing small programs to larger programs with multiple classes and hierarchical structures. They learn and apply several of the original Gang of Four (GoF) design patterns [1]. We share practical and fun examples of applying the decorator, state, and model-view-controller (MVC) design patterns, along with the critical OOP concept of delegation, that we have used in the classroom and our weekly labs and programming assignments.

Categories and Subject Descriptors

D.2.2 [**Software Engineering**]: Design Tools and Techniques – *object-oriented design methods.*

General Terms

Design

Keywords

Design patterns, Object-oriented programming

1. DELEGATE

Delegation exploits the crucial OOP "has a" relationship. It appears in multiple contexts. Students first see traditional delegation, where an object is asked to perform a method. Later, they see delegation within a collection, where an object from a collection is selected based on its key, and then is asked to perform a method. In addition, they see delegation over a full collection, using both loops and iterators. The most powerful form of delegation allows for dynamic changeability. If the declared type of an object reference is an interface type, program behavior can be changed at runtime by changing the object to which it refers. Traditional delegation is ubiquitous in our course. We explore collection delegation via stock portfolios in the classroom and managers of concerts, parties, student tutors, CDs/MP3s, and conferences in programming assignments so far. We apply dynamic changeability in lab for a Master Mind game with a dynamically changeable computer strategy.

ITICSE '15, July 04-08, 2015, Vilnius, Lithuania
ACM 978-1-4503-3440-2/15/07
http://dx.doi.org/10.1145/2729094.2754853

2. DECORATE

The decorator design pattern is relevant to any situation in which an arbitrary number of miscellaneous items can be grouped together to create a customized unit. It is especially interesting if the items are related in a class hierarchy where polymorphism can be exploited. The students explore the pattern in a programming assignment. This pattern is relevant to numerous real-world situations. We have applied it to ordering ice cream cones, sandwiches, pizzas, burritos, cars, and cruise vacations so far. The complexity of decoration also gives a context for introducing the builder design pattern, which is useful in building robust software.

3. STATE

The state design pattern is an application of a two-way "has a" relationship. One class is the manager, which has a polymorphic reference to the current state. All states implement a common interface, and have a reference back to the manager. When certain conditions are met, individual states direct the manager to update its current state at runtime, changing program behavior to match the current state. In the classroom, we have applied the pattern to the craps dice game, and we have redone some of our decorator examples (burritos and cars) using the state design pattern. In lab, students implement the logic for the triangle peg solitaire game. They implement an XML validity checker in a programming assignment where the state changes based on the current XML tag type.

4. ILLUSTRATE

The students build a graphical user interface (GUI) as a culminating application of OOP concepts and an exposure to the MVC and observer design patterns. In their final programming assignment, they build a GUI, such as a graphical MP3 player or a GUI driver for their delegation-based manager from a previous assignment. Before building GUIs, students are exposed to GUIs in the lab assignments and in the classroom. The GUIs delegate to their classes, the model in MVC. Students implement the logic for a GUI maze solver, a GUI blackjack game, a GUI Master Mind game, and a triangle peg solitaire game. In the last lab assignment, students complete the implementation of a GUI which uses drag and drop to select various toppings for a pizza.

5. REFERENCES

[1] Gamma, Erich, et al. 1994. *Design patterns: elements of reusable object-oriented software.* Pearson Education.

Automatic Categorization of Introductory Programming Students using Cluster Analysis

Miguel A. Rubio
Computer Science Department
University of Granada - Spain
marubio@ugr.es

ABSTRACT

We present the preliminary results of an ongoing study on using clustering techniques to automatically categorize the learning stage of students at the end of an introductory programming course.

We have obtained some success in inferring some learning stages but work remains to be done to classify students at the intermediate levels.

Categories and Subject Descriptors

K.3. [**Computers & Education**]: Computer & Information Science Education – *Computer Science Education*

Keywords

Programming, novice programmers, cluster analysis, machine learning.

1. INTRODUCTION

Learning to program can be very difficult for the students involved. Students must master language syntax, programming theory and problem solving techniques in a short period of time. Not all students progress at the same pace. As a consequence students usually present different learning stages at the end of the semester.

The aim of our study is to explore the feasibility of using reading and writing programming questions in combination with cluster analysis to automatically assess the learning stage of the novice programmer at the end of an introductory programming course.

2. METHODS

The data used in this study was obtained in an introductory programming course in a Biology degree. Students in this course learn basic computing skills and devote ten weeks to learn to program using MATLAB.

We used the final exam to assess the students' learning outcomes. The exam contained questions asking to read and write code. We analyzed students' reading and writing code grades using clustering techniques: a class of computational methods that has been shown to be effective in modeling novice programmers' code [2].

3. RESULTS

Cluster analysis grouped students in five different clusters. The location of these clusters along the writing-reading dimensions is shown in Figure 1.

We have tentatively identified the different clusters following a classification proposed by Lahtinen [1]. Clusters corresponding to competent and unprepared students are easily identifiable: they occupy the upper-right and lower-left corners of the graph. The identification of the other clusters is less clear.

One noticeable fact is the absence of students with high writing scores and low reading scores. This makes sense as it would be hard for a student to be able to write meaningful code without the ability to read it.

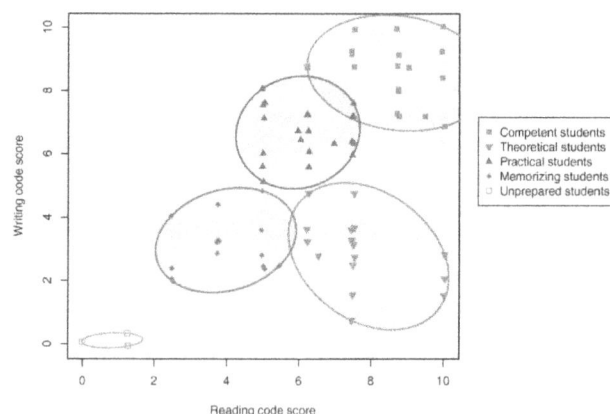

Figure 1. Clustering of students' reading and writing scores.

4. CONCLUSSIONS

In this study we have categorized introductory programming students analyzing their final exam results using cluster techniques.

We have successfully inferred the learning stage of some students but work remains to be done to classify students at the intermediate stages. In a future work we will study whether using exam questions based on the Neo-Piagetian theory of cognitive development improves our results.

5. REFERENCES

[1] Lahtinen, E. 2007. A categorization of Novice Programmers: a cluster analysis study. *Proceedings of the 19th annual Workshop of the Psychology of Programming Interest Group, Joensuu, Finnland*, 32–41.

[2] Piech, C. et al. 2012. Modeling how students learn to program. *Proceedings of the 43rd ACM technical symposium on Computer Science Education*, 153–160.

"Computer Science, Academia and Industry" as Pedagogical Model to Enhance Computational Thinking

Orni Meerbaum-Salant
Davidson Institute
of Science Education
Weizmann Institute of Science
Rehovot 76100, Israel
Orni.Meerbaum-
salant@weizmann.ac.il

Bruria Haberman
Computer Science Department,
Holon Institute of Technology,
Holon, Israel, and Davidson
Institute of Science Education,
Weizmann Institute of Science,
Rehovot 76100, Israel
bruria.haberman@weizmann.ac.il

Sarah Pollack
Davidson Institute
of Science Education
Weizmann Institute of Science
Rehovot 76100, Israel
Sarah.pollack@weizmann.ac.il

ABSTRACT
The Computer Science, Academia and Industry extra-curricular program has been operated for Israeli high school students majoring in computer science. A case study was conducted aimed to identify computational thinking in students' project development processes.

Categories and Subject Descriptors
K.3.2 [**Computer and Information Science Education**]: Computer Science Education

Keywords
K-12; computational thinking

1. CSAI- A PEDAGOGICAL MODEL TO ENHANCE COMPUTATIONAL THINKING

The term "computational thinking" (CT) has been recently recognized as a fundamental competency of youngsters in various domains, specifically in the fields of science, technology, engineering, math (STEM) and computer science (CS). Important characteristics of CT refer, for example, to: (a) using abstraction and decomposition when solving large complex tasks; (b) using mathematical thinking to develop solutions; and (c) the capacity to focus on ideas rather than on the artifacts functionality [1,2,3].

In the poster we introduce the "Computer Science, Academia and Industry" (CSAI) extra-curricular program designed for high-school students majoring in computer science. The program has been running at the Davidson Institute of Science Education for the last ten years [4]. In the first stage, experts from academia and hi-tech industry expose students to state-of-the-art research and development in various computing domains. Special effort is made to emphasize relevance of computing to the everyday life as well as the limitation of computers. In the second stage students develop projects guided and monitored by mentors from academia and hi-tech industry fields. Students are required to learn independently new topics/domains, as well as new programming languages, methods and development tools. Students are required to submit 3 reports regarding their progress.

We believe that the characteristics and pedagogy of the CSAI program which focuses on the uniqueness and challenges of contemporary computing problems, emphasizes different aspects of computational thinking.

2. CASE-STUDY
We analyzed 50 students' midterm reports. Our goal was to identify elements of computational thinking that were expressed by the students in their reports. We choose to demonstrate identified CT elements using one student's report. Alan chose to develop a racecourse game which integrates Artificial Intelligence principles. Alan defined the main goal of his project as "building an intelligent agent who will drive the car efficiently and will finish the racecourse in the shortest time. The agent has to take into consideration different difficulty levels and may earn bonuses to improve its drive." The CT elements that we identified in his report were:

Different abstraction levels: to model the physical winding's racecourse, Alan used two dimensional matrix data structure, realizing that is good enough proximity representation.

Identified ideas that characterize the problem rather than focusing in its functionality. Alan described the "big idea" (i.e., the computational concepts and algorithms) which will help him to obtain eventually a good artifact. His main challenge was to identify the rational position of the car in the winding's racecourse and to drive it gradually and efficiently toward the endpoint. He decided to put many static targets throughout the racecourse and to compute the distance between static targets and the car position.

Integrating mathematical, science and engineering knowledge: In his project, Alan referred to physics' Newton's laws of motion and mathematical matrix computations.

3. REFERENCES
[1] Wing, J. M. (2006). Computational thinking. *Communications of the ACM,49*(3), 33-35.

[2] Denning, P. J. 2009. The profession of IT Beyond computational thinking. *Communications of the ACM*, 52(6), 28-30.

[3] Grover, S., & Pea, R. (2013). Computational Thinking in K-12: A Review of the State of the Field. Educational Researcher, 42(1), 38–43.

[4] Yehezkel, C., and Haberman, B. 2006. Bridging the gap between school computing and the "real world". *Lecture Notes in Computer Science*, 4226, 38-47.

ITiCSE'15, July 6–8, 2015, Vilnius, Lithuania.
ACM 978-1-4503-3440-2/15/07
http://dx.doi.org/10.1145/2729094.2754857

TOPT: A Tree-based Online Presentation Tool [*]

Yufeng Cheng, Jiayu Sun, Junfeng Hu [†]
School of Electronics Engineering and Computer Science,
Peking University, Beijing, P.R.China
{chengyf,jiayusun,hujf}@pku.edu.cn

ABSTRACT

This poster presents a tree-based online presentation strategy and its implementation. In this strategy, instructors and students can interactively add sub-branches on the Web-based presentations, either for extending a sub-topic or to raise questions under a specific slide. A hierarchical visualisation method is provided to support the recursive interactions of branch expanding and tree browsing.

Categories and Subject Descriptors

K.3.1 [**Computers and Education**]: Computer Uses in Education—*computer-assisted instruction (CAI), collaborative learning*

Keywords

Online Presentation, Tree Structure, Collaboration, HTML

1. INTRODUCTION

Many instructors tend to have online teaching material for their courses. Most of them merely put a copy of presentation used in class on their course websites. A more advanced form of online material is HTML-based presentations like those created by Impress.js.[1] HTML-based presentations can be viewed more easily by students but need much additional effort to create, that is why they are less used in course websites behind a real class. We have created an online presentation tool named TOPT, which allow instructors to reuse their presentation documents for class by directly uploading them. TOPT can automatically convert these documents into HTML format with the help of applications like Microsoft PowerPoint.[2]

Traditional presentation documents have linear structures. Slides in those documents are displayed one after another.

---

[*]This work is supported by the National Natural Science Foundation of China (grant 61472017).

[†]To whom all correspondence should be addressed.

[1]http://bartaz.github.com/impress.js
[2]http://products.office.com/en-us/powerpoint

ITiCSE'15, July 6–8, 2015, Vilnius, Lithuania.
ACM 978-1-4503-3440-2/15/07.
http://dx.doi.org/10.1145/2729094.2754851.

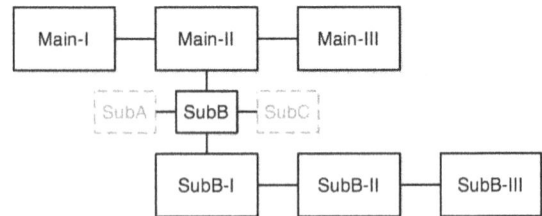

Figure 1: A main presentation with three subdocuments

This is good for class presentation in which the progress of teaching is fully controlled by instructors. But in online presentations, the learning pace is controlled by students themselves, so linear structure is a limit of the learning efficiency. TOPT organizes documents in tree-structures. A document in TOPT can have many subdocuments, which are attached below the slides in the document. Subdocuments can also have its own subdocuments, thus produce a tree-structure. With TOPT, instructor can give students a better understanding of the knowledge presenting by organizing their courseware in a hierarchical way.

Collaborative learning helps students understand things better. The author of slides2wiki gave a way for students to collaboratively create lecture notes by maintaining a wiki page together. [1] TOPT provides more than a wiki page. When a student is faced to a confusion of the material, he can post a comment to the corresponding slide. Comments on a slide are gathered into a special subdocument below the slide. Or if he has more material related to share with others, he can make a presentation himself just like instructors do, and attach it to the original presentation as a subdocument. As many students do so, the knowledge in the lecture material will expand beyond what the instructor originally taught, so students who view this material later can benefit from both the instructor and their classmates.

2. CONTENT OF POSTER

This poster discusses difficulties in online courseware management at present and how our new tool TOPT solves them. A live demonstration is available at `topt.lencomputer.com`.

3. REFERENCES

[1] M. E. O'Neill. Automated use of a wiki for collaborative lecture notes. *ACM SIGCSE Bulletin*, 37(1):267–271, 2005.

Thonny, a Python IDE for Learning Programming

Aivar Annamaaa
Institute of Computer Science
University of Tartu
aivar.annamaa@ut.ee

ABSTRACT

Thonny is a new Python IDE for learning and teaching programming that can make program visualization a natural part of the beginners' workflow. Among its prominent features are different ways of stepping through the code, step-by-step expression evaluation, intuitive visualization of the call stack and a mode for explaining the concepts of references and heap. It is free to use and open for extension.

Categories and Subject Descriptors

K.3.2 [**Computers & Education**]: Computer & Information Science Education—*Computer Science Education*; D.2.3 [**Software Engineering**]: Coding Tools and Techniques

Keywords

Computing education, CS1, Programming, IDE, Python, Program animation, Program visualization

1. INTRODUCTION

Thonny is a new beginner-friendly Python IDE, developed in University of Tartu, meant to help students who struggle in beginners' programming courses. It has comprehensive support for *program animation* as defined by Sorva et al [2]. More specifically, it has features to illustrate the concepts of variables, control flow, expression evaluation, function calls, recursion, references and heap, objects (including classes and functions as values), composite data (lists, dictionaries and sets) and file IO. It can log user actions in detail sufficient for replaying the programming process.

It has been successfully tested for one semester in the context of a CS1 course at our university. The majority of the students using Thonny during a midterm said it helped them with debugging. It is free to use, open source, and developed with the goal of supporting extensions written by third parties. The source code is available under GPLv3 license at [1].

ITiCSE '15 Vilnius, Lithuania
ACM 978-1-4503-3440-2/15/07.
http://dx.doi.org/10.1145/2729094.2754849 .

2. PROGRAM ANIMATION FEATURES

Programs written by the user can be easily executed in stepping mode, where the execution is paused before executing each statement and evaluating each (sub)expression. The updates to global and local variables appear automatically in corresponding table widgets.

When the stepping command is issued on an expression, Thonny opens a small box hovering above the original expression, showing the copy of the expression. Each step in this box evaluates the (sub)expression in focus and replaces it with its value. When the whole expression gets evaluated, the control goes back to the statement level and the next step hides the expression evaluation box.

After evaluating the last argument in a function call, the whole call expression gets focused again. If the user now chooses to step into, Thonny opens a small window titled by the call expression with evaluated arguments, containing the source code of the function and a table with local variables, including parameter values already filled in.

Stepping through the function body works just like on program's top level. If another function call is stepped into, a new window is created on top of current window and execution is continued there. After executing the return statement or last statement of the function, the window is destroyed and original call expression gets replaced by the return value. We believe this helps user understand correct semantics of function call, which is especially important when learning recursion.

For explaining the concept of references and heap, Thonny offers separate mode of visualizing memory, where textual value representations in variable tables get replaced by the addresses or ID-s of corresponding objects and another table titled "Heap" appears, which maps ID-s to value representations. This makes it easy to demonstrate that `y = x` only copies the ID given in `x` to `y`.

3. REFERENCES

[1] A. Annamaa. Thonny home page. http://thonny.cs.ut.ee.

[2] J. Sorva, V. Karavirta, and L. Malmi. A review of generic program visualization systems for introductory programming education. *Trans. Comput. Educ.*, 13(4):15:1–15:64, Nov. 2013.

Student Projects with Real-time Sensor Data

Stan Kurkovsky, Melissa Mulcahy
Central Connecticut State University
kurkovsky@ccsu.edu

ABSTRACT

Applications of mobile computing in education go far beyond being a motivating and engaging tool, introducing fundamental programming concepts, or teaching basic mobile application development. Mobile devices also provide an excellent platform for a broad class of advanced student projects leveraging the real-time data streamed from embedded hardware sensors.

Categories and Subject Descriptors

K.3.2 **[Computers & Education]**: Computer and Information Science Education - *Computer Science Education.*

General Terms

Algorithms, Experimentation, Human Factors.

Keywords

Sensors; accelerometer; mobile computing; student projects.

1. INTRODUCTION

Smartphones, tablets, and, most recently, smart watches, have been embraced by many computer science educators on three fronts: as a tool to engage entry-level students, to introduce computer science concepts to students with little or no computing background, and to teach mobile application development to upper-level students. Regardless of their education level, many mobile applications developed by students rarely extend beyond creating a mobile interface and leveraging the basic capabilities of built-in hardware, such as capturing images with the camera, identifying the current location with the GPS sensor, or reacting to the device being shaken as registered by the accelerometer.

A distinct fourth type of using mobile computing in the educational setting includes advanced and/or research projects that leverage real-time data streamed from a hardware sensor, e.g. accelerometer. This could include applications using the device as a 3D joystick, real-time hand gesture detection, voice activated control, studying collision detection between a wirelessly controlled robot and obstacles, and many others. Student work on such projects is typically partitioned into three phases (applied by us over several years and recently described in [2]): sensor data collection and visualization, prototyping and verification, and mobile app development and validation. We believe that this type of educational use of mobile computing deserves further attention of the computing education community.

2. SAMPLE PROJECT: FALL DETECTION

The objective of the project was to design and implement a wearable system for automatic fall detection and notification of

the appropriate personnel implemented using a smartphone or a similar device. A fall event can be detected by separately detecting the following three stages of the event: 1) changes in the person's gait immediately preceding a fall; 2) free fall phase; and 3) impact of the person's body against the floor.

A triaxial accelerometer found on most iOS and Android devices can be used to collect real-time data that would enable a reliable detection of all three stages of the fall event. Using digital signal processing algorithms, changes in real-time accelerometer readouts can be detected and interpreted as indicators of the three separate stages of the fall [1,3]: 1) gait changes can be viewed as a distinct change in device orientation; 2) free fall results in zero acceleration on all axes; and 3) impact against the floor produces a sharp spike in the acceleration vector. An immediate succession of the accelerometer events corresponding to the above stages would indicate that a fall event has occurred.

For non-clinical applications of fall detection where the primary objective is to make a prompt notification of the fall event, a fall detection system must conform to a number of requirements: the system must provide continuous monitoring; it must be unobtrusive for the user; all fall events must be detected; normal daily activities should not generate false alarms; and no special operating procedures or frequent maintenance should be required.

This project began by implementing a basic application to collect real-time accelerometer data from an Android device for later analysis. Once implemented, data collection began in a safe environment where different test subjects fell, jumped, walked, ran, and dropped the phone. The collected data was transferred from a mobile device to a desktop computer for pre-processing, analysis, and visualization. An algorithm was devised for determining if a fall has occurred. It utilized the three stages of a fall as the basic conditions. This algorithm was tested on the previously recorded real-time accelerometer data reflecting falls and other activities in order to improve the robustness of the algorithms and minimize the number of false positives. The application that collected real-time accelerometer data was modified in order to utilize the algorithm during runtime. With the algorithm in place, a series of additional tests were performed to tweak the specific parameters of the algorithm.

3. REFERENCES

[1] Bouten, C., Koekkoek, K., Verduin, M., Kodde, R., and Janssen, J., A triaxial accelerometer and portable data processing unit for the assessment of daily physical activity, *IEEE Trans. Biomed. Engr.*, 44(3), 136-147, Mar. 1997.

[2] Chen, H. and Damevski, K., A teaching model for development of sensor-driven mobile applications. *2014 Conference on Innovation & technology in computer science education.* 147-152, June 2014.

[3] Srinivasan, S., Han, J., Lal, and D. Gacic, A., Towards automatic detection of falls using wireless sensors, *Engr. in Medicine and Biology*, 2007, 1379-138

Towards a Competency Model for Object-Oriented Programming

Torsten Brinda, Matthias Kramer
Didactics of Informatics
University of Duisburg-Essen
Essen, Germany
firstname.lastname@uni-due.de

Peter Hubwieser, Alexander Ruf
Didactics of Informatics
TUM School of Education
Munich, Germany
firstname.lastname@tum.de

ABSTRACT

The German educational system is shifting towards the competences of learners since the publication of the national results of the OECD PISA studies with the goals to improve the overall learning outcomes, better individualize learning and teaching processes and also to promote the comparability of federal educational systems. Many disciplines have already developed empirically founded competency models and associated instruments to measure, compare, and interpret learner performance . Computer science education research is still in its infancy in this regard. It is therefore the aim of this project to develop such a model for the basics of object-oriented programming.

Categories and Subject Descriptors

K.3.2 [**Computers and Education**]: Computer and Information Science Education—*Computer science education*

General Terms

Human factors, languages, measurement

Keywords

Competency model; OOP; K-12; secondary education

1. INTRODUCTION

Competency models describe, in which dimensions subject-specific competence can be structured and how the performance of a learner population can be interpreted. They have become the theoretical basis for national and international student assessment programs. In computer science education (CSE) only few such models have been described (e.g. in the fields of "Informatics systems and object-oriented modelling" [2] and "didactic skills of computer science teachers" [1]) and tested empirically yet. It is therefore the authors' aim to develop and test such a competency model for object-oriented programming (OOP), another important CSE field.

ITiCSE '15 Vilnius, Lithuania
ACM 978-1-4503-3440-2/15/07.
http://dx.doi.org/10.1145/2729094.2754848.

2. METHOD AND FIRST RESULTS

Competent behaviour can be observed in requirement situations, e.g. when working on tasks and especially in problem solving. The mastering of typical subject-specific requirements is a prerequisite for being able to solve problems. To develop a model, tasks and their solutions in the field of introductory OOP are analysed using qualitative content analysis according to Mayring. Such requirements each combine a knowledge element (e.g. method) with a cognitive operator. After analysis of more than 110 tasks (coding is continuing), 113 knowledge elements and 70 operators have been identified by two coders. The spectrum ranges from codings of the type "specify attribute" over "explain object" "implement class" up to "test program". Analysis of the attribute variation in the task material reveals further dimension candidates such as source code complexity (in terms of software metrics) and the source code representation (e.g. diagram, pseudo code, source code). This could indicate - in consistence with models of other disciplines - at least a technical dimension, a dimension of cognitive processes, a dimension of complexity and a representation dimension to be considered in the model, which has to be enhanced by literature studies. Additionally interviews with beginners in programming will be conducted to discover, at which point of the learning process difficulties arise. Interviews with subject matter experts will be conducted to ensure the completeness of the model. The result is expected to represent a normative competency structure model for OOP. By collaborating with research fellows of psychology and psychometrics, the resulting normative model will then be transferred into a psychometric measuring model and used as a basis for developing, enhancing, piloting test items, which will finally be tested on a representative cohort.

3. REFERENCES

[1] P. Hubwieser, J. Magenheim, A. Mühling, and A. Ruf. Towards a conceptualization of pedagogical content knowledge for computer science. In *Proc. of the 9th Ann. Int. ACM Conf. on International Computing Education Research*, ICER '13, pages 1–8, New York, NY, USA, 2013. ACM.

[2] J. Neugebauer, P. Hubwieser, J. Magenheim, L. Ohrndorf, N. Schaper, and S. Schubert. Measuring student competences in german upper secondary computer science education. In Y. Gülbahar and E. Karataş, editors, *Informatics in Schools. Teaching and Learning Perspectives*, volume 8730 of *LNCS*, pages 100–111. Springer International Publishing, 2014.

Reliability in the Assessment of Program Quality by Teaching Assistants During Code Reviews

Michael James Scott
Department of Computer Science
Brunel University London
United Kingdom
michael.scott@brunel.ac.uk

Gheorghita Ghinea
Department of Computer Science
Brunel University London
United Kingdom
george.ghinea@brunel.ac.uk

ABSTRACT

It is of paramount importance that formative feedback is meaningful in order to drive student learning. Achieving this, however, relies upon a clear and constructively aligned model of quality being applied consistently across submissions. This poster presentation raises concerns about the inter-rater reliability of code reviews conducted by teaching assistants in the absence of such a model. Five teaching assistants each reviewed 12 purposely selected programs submitted by introductory programming students. An analysis of their reliability revealed that while teaching assistants were self-consistent, they each assessed code quality in different ways. This suggests a need for standard models of program quality, alongside supporting rubrics and other tools, to be used during code reviews to improve the reliability of formative feedback.

Categories and Subject Descriptors

K.3.2 [**Computers and Education**]: Computer and Information Science Education

Keywords

Programming, Code Review, Code Inspection, Grading, Quality, Assessment, Reliability, Agreement, Consistency.

1. INTRODUCTION

Guidance is important when first learning computer programming to help students develop an appreciation for quality. This often consists of feedback provided during code reviews. However, for such feedback to be meaningful, it should be clear, reliable and constructively align with relevant learning objectives (c.f. [2, 4]). This is because conflicting feedback from different teaching assistants could cause confusion. Previous work suggests that reviews by experienced faculty tend to be correlated, but different reasoning is sometimes applied [1]. However, it remains unclear whether those done by teaching assistants are as

Table 1: Reliability of Assessment ($E(\alpha) \geq .667$)

Measure	Krippendorff's α
Self-Consistency	.841
Agreement Between Teaching Assistants	.607
Agreement with Faculty Assessments	.522

consistent. Of particular concern is that the reviews may reflect more on the reviewer than on the student (see [3] for detail on the idiosyncratic rater effect).

2. FINDINGS

Five experienced teaching assistants ($> 1yr$) reviewed 12 programs selected from first-year undergraduate computing submissions and made holistic assessments of their quality using a 3-point scale (pass, merit, distinction). Minimal instruction was provided to reflect a less formal context. After two weeks, they re-reviewed the programs. On each occasion the programs were presented in a random order and some elements (e.g., identifiers) were transformed. The data were analysed using Krippendorff's alpha.

The results, shown in Table 1, reveal that while the assessments were adequately self-consistent, there was low inter-rater reliability and there was considerable disagreement with ratings provided by a team of faculty. This finding suggests that teaching assistants apply different standards of program quality when conducting code reviews and therefore require support to improve reliability. As such, this study provides a foundation for future work on the development and evaluation of code review processes, models of program quality, as well as rubrics and other tools.

3. REFERENCES

[1] S. Fitzgerald, B. Hanks, R. Lister, R. McCauley, and L. Murphy. What are we thinking when we grade programs? In *SIGCSE '13*, pages 471–476. ACM, 2013.

[2] A. Pears, J. Harland, M. Hamilton, and R. Hadgraft. Four feed-forward principles enhance students' perception of feedback as meaningful. In *LaTiCE '14*, pages 272–277. IEEE, 2014.

[3] S. E. Scullen, M. K. Mount, and M. Goff. Understanding the latent structure of job performance ratings. *Journal of Applied Psychology*, 85(6):956, 2000.

[4] M. Stegeman, E. Barendsen, and S. Smetsers. Towards an empirically validated model for assessment of code quality. In *Koli Calling '14*, pages 99–108. ACM, 2014.

PCRS-C: Helping Students Learn C

Daniel Marchena Parreira
University of Toronto
daniel.marchenaparreira
@utoronto.ca

Andrew Petersen
University of Toronto
Mississauga
petersen@cs.toronto.edu

Michelle Craig
University of Toronto
mcraig@cs.toronto.edu

ABSTRACT

The C programming language is an important piece of many undergraduate CS programs, as it provides an environment for interacting directly with memory and exploring systems-programming concepts. However, while many common introductory languages have rich tools that support instruction, C has received relatively little attention [2, 1]. To provide students with rapid feedback and tools for understanding C, we have extended PCRS, a web-based platform for deploying programming exercises and content such as videos. Students submit C code to solve programming exercises and receive immediate feedback generated by running the submission against a set of instructor-defined testcases. Students also have access to graphical traces of execution, so they can explore how their code manipulates memory. The system has been deployed to two second-year systems-programming courses with a total enrollment over 600, and a set of modules, consisting of videos and exercises, is being developed for use by the community.

Categories and Subject Descriptors

K.3.2 [**Computers and Education**]: Computer and Information Science Education—*Computer Science Education*

Keywords

introductory programming, C, courseware

1. INTRODUCTION

PCRS-C, based on the Programming Course Resource System [3], is a web-based platform for deploying content modules. It allows instructors to build online learning objects including containing videos, text, and multiple forms of exercises, including automatically-tested C programming problems. The original system had been used to deploy materials for a full introductory programming course in Python with over 4000 users. Extending the system to support the C language posed a number of interesting challenges.

2. FEATURES

To provide support for C, a compiled and directly-executed language with significant "boilerplate" required to execute a program,

we identified mechanisms for focusing student attention on relatively small slices of execution, and we resolved issues with scaling and security.

Early C exercises emphasize small code elements, rather than whole programs. To reduce the cognitive load on students, instructors must be able to restrict what a student sees. We introduced mechanisms for hiding sections of the starter code and "freezing" other sections so that students can see but not modify them. This requires interpreting the error messages presented to the user, since errors in submission code may be revealed within hidden sections.

Testing code elements requires access to internal state. Submitted code must be fully instrumented so instructors are able to specify test cases that evaluate internal state. We introduced facilities for extracting information from internal variables for testing.

Providing a graphical representation of execution traces requires a full representation of the environment at each step. C is often used as a platform for learning how code and memory interact, so the system must be able to expose pointers and actual addresses. The same facilities used to test the code are used to extract full traces. We also developed a graphical model to help students understand control structures, interactions between variables and values, and the relationship between pointers and memory.

Compiling and generating C traces is computationally intensive. To scale to hundreds of student users, the work was distributed across multiple servers. The system can be hosted on a cloud service (such as Amazon web services), and servers can be added and removed as necessary.

Executing untrusted code requires a sandboxed environment. Our solution builds on existing programming-contest jury systems.

3. ONGOING DEVELOPMENT

PCRS-C is also the platform for a set of content modules to support an introductory C or systems-programming course. Each module contains videos, comprehension questions, and programming exercises. The full module set will be released to the community in fall 2015, with active development through summer 2015.

4. REFERENCES

[1] S. H. Edwards and M. A. Perez-Quinones. Web-CAT: Automatically grading programming assignments. *SIGCSE Bull.*, 40(3):328–328, June 2008.

[2] D. Hovemeyer and J. Spacco. CloudCoder: A web-based programming exercise system. *J. Comput. Sci. Coll.*, 28(3):30, Jan. 2013.

[3] D. Zingaro, Y. Cherenkova, O. Karpova, and A. Petersen. Facilitating code-writing in PI classes. In *Proceeding of the 44th ACM Technical Symposium on Computer Science Education*, pages 585–590, 2013.

Virtual Learning Laboratory about Query Optimization against XML Data

Liviana Nicoleta Tudor
Petroleum-Gas University of Ploiesti
Bd. Bucuresti Nr. 39, Ploiesti,100680 Romania, Tel. 040244573171
Tudor.Liviana@gmail.com

ABSTRACT

This paper describes the development of a virtual learning laboratory; the system is intented to be used by undergraduate students which learn about query optimization against XML data. The virtual lab is based on Open Source data collections that contain teaching materials about Databases and it is characterized by the safety and transparent control offered by the environments used in the connected learning.

Categories and Subject Descriptors

K.3.2 [**Computing Milieux**]: Computer and Information Science Education – *Computer science education.*

General Terms

Algorithms, Performance, Experimentation, Human Factors.

Keywords

Open and Collaborative Learning Model, Databases, XML data, Algorithm, Optimization

1. INTRODUCTION

Our proposal is based on the use of learning management platform (such as Moodle) and Open Source data collections that contain teaching materials for Oracle Databases (SQL Language, PL/SQL Language, Semantic technologies, XML data, and Query optimization) [1]. Moodle platform supports open standards, and is interoperable to enable integration of external applications. Proposed laboratory encourages the connection with mentors for learning heuristic methods to optimization queries on XML data.

2. DESIGN OF VIRTUAL LEARNING LABORATORY

In our university there has been identified the necessity to building an online platform for open and collaborative learning, by promoting some basic Web principles such as respect and data protection. The site for implementing this proposal is hosted at http://www.programare.biz/E/indexE.html. The virtual lab offers the Web community Open Source data collections in relational databases as well as a Moodle platform for teaching, learning, collaboration and evaluation activities. Open source data

ITICSE '15, July 04-08, 2015, Vilnius, Lithuania
ACM 978-1-4503-3440-2/15/07.
http://dx.doi.org/10.1145/2729094.2764861

collections for relational databases are stored at http://www.programare.biz/BD/ORACLE/ora.html and the educational Moodle software is hosted at http://programare.biz/moodle/login/index.php.

3. QUERY OPTIMIZATION AGAINST XML DATA

To optimize XML data queries from Oracle databases, we can use a semantic cache for XPath views. Heuristic algorithms can select XPath views from cache to quickly process an XPath query. For each view selected by the heuristic algorithm, a compensation query can be found, to which it is composed to supply the results of a data query [2]. XML benchmark sets of data offer the possibility of performing standard tests for the scientific papers registered in the SIGMOD database.

4. EXPERIMENTAL STUDY

A traffic analysis has been done and an analysis of the log events for the Open Source data collections with Oracle Databases and Moodle platform (Table 1). To assess students' opinion on the usefulness and completeness of virtual learning laboratory, was used five-point Likert scale. Frequency analysis of students' responses is based on descriptive statistics such as mean and standard deviation.

5. CONCLUSIONS

Virtual lab's goal is to be fully accessible and usable for all users who want to learn about Query Optimization against XML Data. Statistical analysis shows that virtual learning lab is used and appreciated by students and has a large impact on learning.

6. REFERENCES

[1] Tudor, L., Moise, A. 2015. Open and Collaborative Learning Model Based on Metacognitive Strategies, *Studies in Informatics and Control*, 24, 1 (March. 2015), 71-78.

[2] Mandhani, B., Suciu, D. 2005. *Query Caching and View Selection for XML Databases*, Proceedings of the 31st VLDB Conference, Trondheim, Norway.

Table 1. Virtual learning laboratory accessing statistics.

Access mode	Unique IP	Number of visitors
Open source data collections	696	1321
Users in 2015	**Accesses**	**Bytes**
Login with users on Moodle platform	102	11 GB

Motivation and Grade Gap Related to Gender in a Programming Course

Virginia Grande
Uppsala University
Department of Information Technology
Polacksbacken (Lägerhyddsvägen 2)
+46(0)765653744
virginia.grande@it.uu.se

Joachim Parrow
Uppsala University
Department of Information Technology
Polacksbacken (Lägerhyddsvägen 2)
+46184715704
joachim.parrow@it.uu.se

ABSTRACT
In a programming course at Uppsala University, Sweden, there has been a significant difference between the average grade of female students and that of their male counterparts. This work in progress presents some results and potential solutions related to this problem, and makes them explicit.

Categories and Subject Descriptors
K.3.2 [**Computers and Education**]: Computer and Information Science Education – *Computer science education, Information systems.*

Keywords
Motivation, grade gap, gender and computing.

1. MOTIVATION AND BACKGROUND
Women experience unconscious bias [1,2], applied by people they interact with or by themselves, which affects their performance at work. Women apply for jobs only when they meet 100% of the requirements, whereas men may do so at just a 60% of the requirements [3]. Clearly, there are differences in how women and men experience their professional life.

At Uppsala University, the grades for the required Programming course in the System i Teknik och Samhälle program can be 3, 4, and 5. In order to get a grade higher than 3, students must submit additional work, the completed amount of which qualifies them for a 4 or a 5. The last two instances of the course (autumn 2013 and 2014) showed a significant difference in average grade: while men had a 4.3 (2013 and 2014), women reached a 3.4 (2013) and 3.7 (2014). The gender distribution regarding enrolment is balanced.

The main question addressed in this study is: what caused this difference in the results?

2. METHOD
Data has been gathered at teacher's meetings (from the instructors, i.e. course coordinator and assistants), course evaluations and semi structured interviews (from the students), as well as observations during the lab sessions, of the instance of the course run in the autumn 2014. The majority of the data has been analysed, and interviews will be conducted and analysed during this spring semester.

ITICSE '15, July 04-08, 2015, Vilnius, Lithuania
ACM 978-1-4503-3440-2/15/07.

http://dx.doi.org/10.1145/2729094.2754858

3. RESULTS
The middle and end of the course evaluations showed that women were less motivated than men to follow the course. Students also expressed their belief in the need of prior programming experience (more common among men) in order to obtain a higher grade. However, the course grades show that this is not true.

The instructors did not seem to perceive any difference in their interactions with male and female students. However, several mentioned that they paid special attention to women because they *"wanted them to succeed"*.

During the lab sessions, some students asked the grading assistant to assess their incomplete work, arguing that, even though it did not meet 100% of the requirements, it was good enough for the higher grade. This fact may imply that students who were not so proactive or confident in their possibilities of achieving the higher grade (according to [3], more common among women) did not receive more than a 3, even though their work may have been similar to the one by the more confident students.

4. DISCUSSION
Motivation is an important success factor in all learning, and it connects closely to grit and perseverance. One important implication of this study is to provide a learning environment that strengthens the motivation of the female students.

Future work involves compiling similar data from future instances of the course. This way, data related to different instances of the course can be collected and triangulated.

Based on our results, some questions raised so far are: Are female students less likely to ask for a higher grade based on incomplete work? Do women feel more pressured to perform well in all parallel courses (regardless of the actual results or grades)? Do male students receive more scaffolding than female students (e.g. they have more friends who have programmed before)?

Future instances of the course will "debunk the myths" pointed out in the course evaluations (e.g. need of prior experience) and instructors' training will include awareness of unconscious biases.

The interviews will allow us to ask the students whether they perceived any bias in the assistance and assessment by the instructors, among other related topics of interest.

5. REFERENCES
[1] Banaji, M. R., & Greenwald, A. G. (2013). *Blind Spot: Hidden Biases of Good People.* Random House LLC.

[2] Kermarrec, Anne-Marie. "Computer Science: Too Young to Fall into the Gender Gap." *IEEE Internet Computing* 18.3 (2014): 4-6

[3] Sandberg, S. (2014). *Lean in.* Random House.

Author Index

www.ingramcontent.com/pod-product-compliance
Lightning Source LLC
Chambersburg PA
CBHW080713220326
41598CB00033B/5399

* 9 7 8 1 4 5 0 3 3 8 8 0 6 *